From Modernism to Postmodernism:

An Anthology

Lawrence E. Cahoone

BLACKWELL PHILOSOPHY ANTHOLOGIES

Each volume in this outstanding new series provides a comprehensive and authoritative collection of the essential primary readings from philosophy's main fields of study. Designed to complement the *Blackwell Companions to Philosophy* series, each volume represents an unparalleled resource in its own right, and will provide the ideal platform for course use.

Forthcoming

For my son,
Harrison Baeten Cahoone

The right of Lawrence Cahoone to be identified as author of this work has been asserted in accordance with the Copyright, Designs and Patents Act 1988.

First published 1996
Reprinted 1996 (twice)

Blackwell Publishers Inc.
238 Main Street
Cambridge, Massachusetts 02142, USA

Blackwell Publishers Ltd
108 Cowley Road
Oxford OX4 1JF, UK

Library of Congress Cataloging in Publication Data
From modernism to postmodernism: an anthology/[compiled by] Lawrence E. Cahoone.
p. cm.
Includes bibliographical references and index.
ISBN 1-55786-602-3 — ISBN 1-55786-603-1 (Pbk)
1. Postmodernism.   I. Cahoone, Lawrence E., 1954–.
B831.2.P.677   1995   95–11583
149-dc.20   CIP

British Library Cataloguing in Publication Data
A CIP catalogue record for this book is available from the British Library.

Typeset in 10.5 on 12.5 pt Photina
by Pure Tech India Ltd, Pondicherry
Printed and bound in Great Britain by Hartnolls Limited, Bodmin, Cornwall.

This book is printed on acid-free paper.

Contents

Contents

Part II Modernity Realized

Part III Postmodernism and the Revaluation of Modernity

Contents

Preface

The problem with introducing students to any discussion of postmodernism is not merely the notorious difficulties of the meaning of the term. It is that most students do not adequately understand what is "modern," what it is whose obsolescence the term "postmodern" presumably announces. Any discussion of postmodernism assumes a great deal of knowledge about modernism, or modernity, or the modern world, and how it has been interpreted. It is senseless to try to teach students about the sophisticated methods of contemporary postmodernists without first teaching them the tradition from which these methods are a departure. Yet current anthologies of postmodernism generally ignore history and collect only contemporary essays; indeed, usually essays representing only a narrow range of philosophical perspectives. The purpose of the present volume is to examine both modernism and postmodernism by presenting prominent philosophical components of, and sociological theories about, modernity as background for the various writers involved in the debate over postmodernism. Its aim is, in short, to put postmodernism in context. Certainly this is a task to which no anthology can be adequate, yet some attempt in that direction is, I believe, better than none.

In making the selections I have tried to balance a number of preferences for: writers who formulate positions, rather than comment on them; substantive, rather than minimal, selections; selections that are historically connected to each other; and pieces that engender a deeper understanding of the philosophical basis for postmodernism, rather than those that are more superficially relevant to postmodern themes. The last of these has led me to omit some well-known essays that explicitly express or comment on postmodernism, but remain inscrutable unless the reader already has a deeper familiarity with the author's perspective, a familiarity I hope my selections will better provide. So the volume aims at philosophical understanding rather than a hit parade of recent cultural politics. The selections are arranged chronologically.

Every step has been taken to make the volume user-friendly. Author's notes appear at the end of each selection. Editor's annotations to historical

references and technical terms appear at the foot of the page. Headnotes
introduce each selected author. References to the selected works on the first
page of each selection indicate whether the relevant textual subdivision
(book, essay, chapter, section) appears whole or in part. A select bibliography is included.

This volume would not exist but for the vision and encouragement of
Stephan Chambers of Blackwell. Steven Smith of Blackwell has ushered the
book admirably into print. Judy Marshall's careful copy-editing has saved
me from numerous embarrassments. A semester sabbatical from Boston
University gave me the time to turn a skeletal list of selections into a flesh
and blood book. Margaret Rose was helpful and encouraging in my search
for early uses of the term "postmodern." The staff of the Department of
Philosophy at Boston University, Carolyn Evans and Sara Martin, have
helped to make my professional life these past years not only more
productive, but more human. During the planning and composition of the
volume, Jeffrey Jampel and especially Deborah Hirschland have been of
invaluable help to me.

Acknowledgments

The editor and the publisher wish to acknowledge with thanks the permission to reprint from the following previously published material:

René Descartes, *Meditations on First Philosophy*, trans. Elizabeth Haldane and G.R.T. Ross, in *The Philosophical Works of Descartes*, vol. I (Cambridge: Cambridge University Press, 1975), Meditations One and Two, pp. 144–57. Reprinted with the permission of Cambridge University Press.

Jean-Jacques Rousseau, *Discourse on the Sciences and the Arts*, Part One, in *The Basic Political Writings of Jean-Jacques Rousseau*, trans. Donald Cress (Indianapolis: Hackett, 1987) pp. 3–10. Reprinted by permission of Hackett Publishing Company.

Immanuel Kant, "An Answer to the Question: What is Enlightenment?" in *Kant's Political Writings*, trans. H.B. Nisbet, ed. Hans Reiss (Cambridge: Cambridge University Press, 1970), pp. 54–60. © Cambridge University Press 1970. Reprinted with the permission of Cambridge University Press and the editor.

Edmund Burke, *Reflections on the Revolution in France*, ed. J.G.A. Pocock (Indianapolis: Hackett, 1987), pp. 12–19, 25–6, 29–31, 51–2, 76–7, 216–18. Reprinted by permission of Hackett Publishing Company.

Marie Jean Antoine Nicolas Caritat, marquis de Condorcet, *Sketch for an Historical Picture of the Progress of the Human Mind*, trans. June Barraclough (New York: Hyperion, rpt. of 1955 Noonday Press edition), "The Ninth Stage: From Descartes to the Foundation of the French Republic," pp. 124–37. Reprinted with acknowledgment to Hyperion Press.

Georg Wilhelm Friedrich Hegel, *Phenomenology of Spirit*, trans. A.V. Miller (Oxford: Oxford University Press, 1977), pp. 355–63, paragraphs 582–95. © Oxford University Press 1977. Reprinted by permission of Oxford University Press.

Karl Marx with Friedrich Engels, "Bourgeois and Proletarians," Section One of *Manifesto of the Communist Party*, trans. Samuel Moore, in Robert Tucker,

Acknowledgments

The Marx–Engels Reader (New York: Norton, 1978), pp. 473–83. Reprinted with acknowledgment to W.W. Norton & Company.

Friedrich Nietzsche, *The Gay Science*, Part Three, Sec. 125, trans. with commentary by Walter Kaufmann (New York: Random House, 1974), pp. 181–2. Copyright © 1974 by Random House, Inc. *Beyond Good and Evil*, trans. with commentary by Walter Kaufmann (New York: Random House, 1989), Part Five: "The Natural History of Morals," Sec.186–203, pp. 97–118. Copyright © 1966 by Random House, Inc. *The Genealogy of Morals*, trans. by Walter Kaufmann and R.J. Hollingdale (New York: Random House, 1989), Sec.24–28, pp.148–63. Copyright © 1967 by Random House, Inc. *The Will to Power*, ed. Walter Kaufmann, trans. Walter Kaufmann and R. J. Hollingdale (New York: Random House, 1967), para. 1067, pp. 449–50. Copyright © 1967 by Random House, Inc. All four selections reprinted by permission of Random House, Inc.

Charles Baudelaire, "The Painter of Modern Life," trans. Jonathan Mayne, copyright ©, in *The Painter of Modern Life and Other Essays* (London: Phaidon, 1964), sec. 3–4, pp. 5–15. Reprinted by permission of Phaidon Press Ltd, in accordance with the information given on the imprint page of the book.

Charles S. Peirce, "How to Make Our Ideas Clear," *Collected Papers of Charles Sanders Peirce*, ed. Charles Hartshorne and Paul Weiss (Cambridge: Harvard University Press, 1965), vol. v, para. 394–402, pp. 252–60, and para. 405–10, pp. 265–71. Copyright © 1934, 1935 by the President and Fellows of Harvard College. Reprinted by permission of Harvard University Press.

Max Weber, "Author's Introduction" to *The Protestant Ethic and the Spirit of Capitalism*, trans. Talcott Parsons (New York: Scribner, 1958), pp. 13–31. Copyright © 1958 Charles Scribner's Sons. Introduction copyright © 1976 George Allen & Unwin (Publishers) Ltd. Reprinted with permission of Simon and Schuster from the Macmillan College text. "Science as a Vocation," in *From Max Weber: Essays in Sociology*, trans. and ed. H.H. Gerth and C. Wright Mills (New York: Oxford University Press, 1946), pp. 138–40, 143–9, 155–6. Copyright © Oxford University Press 1946. Reprinted by permission of Oxford University Press.

Ferdinand de Saussure, *Course in General Linguistics*, trans. Wade Baskin (New York: McGraw-Hill, 1966), Part One, chapter 1, pp. 65–70, and Part Two, chapter 4, pp. 120–2. Reprinted by permission of McGraw-Hill, Inc.

Filippo Tommaso Marinetti, "The Founding and Manifesto of Futurism," trans. R.W. Flint and Arthur W. Coppotelli, in *Marinetti: Selected Writings*, ed. R.W. Flint (New York: Farrar, Straus, Giroux, 1972). Copyright ©

1971, 1972 by Farrar, Straus & Giroux, Inc. Reprinted by permission of Farrar, Straus & Giroux, Inc.

Ludwig Wittgenstein, "Lecture on Ethics," *The Philosophical Review*, 74, no. 1, January 1965, pp.3–12. Reprinted with acknowledgment to *The Philosophical Review*. *Tractatus Logico-Philosophicus*, trans. D.F. Pears and B.F. McGuinness (London: Routledge and Kegan Paul, 1961) para. 6.53–6.57, pp. 73–4. Copyright © Routledge & Kegan Paul Ltd, 1961. Reprinted by permission of Routledge.

Le Corbusier, *Towards a New Architecture*, trans. Frederick Etchells (New York: Dover, 1986), pp. 1–8, 29–31, 47–64. Reprinted with acknowledgment to Dover Publications.

Sigmund Freud, *Civilization and its Discontents*, trans. from the German by James Strachey (New York: Norton, 1961), chapters 6 and 7, pp. 64–80. Copyright © 1961 by James Strachey, renewed 1989 by Alix Strachey. Reprinted by permission of W.W. Norton & Company, Inc.

Jose Ortega y Gasset, "The Crowd Phenomenon," chapter 1, *The Revolt of the Masses*, trans. from the Spanish by Anthony Kerrigan, ed. Kenneth Moore (Notre Dame, Ind.: University of Notre Dame Press, 1985), pp. 3–10. Copyright © 1985 W.W. Norton & Company, Inc. Reprinted by permission of W.W. Norton & Company, Inc.

Edmund Husserl, *The Crisis of European Sciences and Transcendental Phenomenology*, trans. David Carr (Evanston: Northwestern University Press, 1970), Part One, sec. 3–5, pp.7–14 and Part Two, sec. 9h–91, pp. 48–59. Copyright © by Northwestern University Press. Reprinted by permission of Northwestern University Press.

Max Horkheimer and Theodor Adorno, *Dialectic of Enlightenment*, trans. John Cumming (New York: Seabury, 1972), pp. 23–9, and pp. 81–93. Copyright © 1993 The Continuum Publishing Company. Reprinted by permission of The Continuum Publishing Company.

Jean-Paul Sartre, "Existentialism," trans. Bernard Frechtman in *Existentialism and Human Emotions* (New York: Citadel, 1985), pp. 15–24, and pp. 46–51. Copyright © 1957, 1985 by Philosophical Library, Inc. Published by arrangement with Carol Publishing Group.

Martin Heidegger, "Letter on Humanism," from David Farrell Krell (ed.), *Martin Heidegger: Basic Writings*, trans. Frank A. Capuzzi, with J. Glenn Gray and David Farrell Krell (New York: Harper and Row, 1977), pp. 193–242. English translation copyright © 1977 by Harper & Row, Publishers, Inc. General Introductions and Introductions to each selection copyright © 1977 by David Farrell Krell. Reprinted by permission of HarperCollins Publishers, Inc.

Acknowledgments

Thomas Kuhn, *The Structure of Scientific Revolutions* (Chicago: University of Chicago Press, 1962), chapter IX, "The Nature and Necessity of Scientific Revolutions," pp. 92–110. Copyright © 1962, 1970 the University of Chicago. Reprinted by permission of University of Chicago Press.

Robert Venturi, *Complexity and Contradiction in Architecture* (New York: Museum of Modern Art, 1966) pp. 16–17, 23–5, 38–41, 88, and 102–4. Copyright © The Museum of Modern Art, 1966, 1977. Reprinted by permission of The Museum of Modern Art.

Jacques Derrida, "The End of the Book and the Beginning of Writing," chapter 1, *Of Grammatology*, trans. Gayatri Chakravorty Spivak (Baltimore: Johns Hopkins University Press, 1974), pp. 6–26. Reprinted by permission of Johns Hopkins University Press.

Michel Foucault, "Nietzsche, Genealogy, History," trans. from the French by Donald Bouchard and Sherry Simon, in *Language, Counter-Memory, Practise: Selected Essays and Interviews*, ed. Donald Bouchard (Ithaca, NY: Cornell University Press, 1977), pp. 139–64. Copyright © 1977 by Cornell University. Used by permission of the publisher, Cornell University Press. "Truth and Power," trans. Colin Gordon, in *Power/Knowledge: Selected Interviews and Other Writings 1972–77*, ed. Colin Gordon (New York: Pantheon, 1972), pp. 131–3. Text copyright © 1972, 1975, 1976, 1977 by Michel Foucault. Collection copyright © 1980 by The Harvester Press. Reprinted by permission of Pantheon Books, a division of Random House, Inc.

Ihab Hassan, "POSTmodernISM: A Paracritical Bibliography," in *Paracriticisms: Seven Speculations of the Times* (Urbana: University of Illinois Press, 1975), pp. 39–59. Copyright © 1975 by the Board of Trustees of the University of Illinois. Used with permission of the author and the University of Illinois Press.

Gilles Deleuze and Félix Guattari, *Anti-Oedipus: Capitalism and Schizophrenia* trans. Helen Lane, Mark Seem, and Robert Hurley (New York: Viking Penguin, 1977), chapter 1: Introduction, pp. 1–8 and 22–35. Translation copyright © 1977 by Viking Penguin, a division of Penguin Books USA Inc., English language translation. Used by permission of Viking Penguin, a division of Penguin Books USA Inc., and by permission of Athlone Press of London.

Daniel Bell, *The Coming of Post-Industrial Society* (New York: Basic Books, 1976), "Foreword: 1976," pp. ix–xxii. Reprinted by permission of Basic Books. Copyright © 1973 by Daniel Bell. Foreword copyright © 1976 by Daniel Bell. Reprinted by permission of BasicBooks, a division of HarperCollins Publishers, Inc.

Jean Baudrillard, *Symbolic Exchange and Death*, trans. Iain H. Grant (London: Sage, 1993), chapter 1, pp. 6–12; from chapter 2, pp. 50, 55–61,

70–6. English translation copyright © Sage Publications 1993. Introduction and Bibliography copyright © Mike Gane 1993. Originally published as *L'échange symbolique et la mort*, copyright © Editions Gallimard, Paris, 1976. Reprinted by permission of Sage Publications Ltd.

Luce Irigaray, "The Sex Which is Not One", trans. Claudia Reeder, in *New French Feminisms*, ed. Elaine Marks and Isabelle de Courtivron (New York: Schoken, 1981), pp. 99–106. Copyright © 1980 by the University of Massachusetts Press. Reprinted by permission of University of Massachusetts Press.

Charles Jencks, *The Language of Post-Modern Architecture* (New York: Rizzoli, 1984), Part One, "The Death of Modern Architecture," pp. 9–10. Reprinted by permission of Rizzoli of New York. *What Is Post-Modernism?* (London: Academy Editions, 1986), chapter 2, pp. 14–20, and chapter 7, pp. 57–9. Reprinted by permission of Academy Group Ltd.

Jean-François Lyotard, *The Postmodern Condition: A Report on Knowledge*, trans. Geoff Bennington and Brian Massumi (Minneapolis: University of Minnesota Press, 1984), Introduction and Sections 9 to 11, and 14, pp. xxiii–xxv, 31–47, 64–7. Originally published in France as *La condition postmodern: rapport sur le savoir*, copyright © 1979 by Les Editions de Minuit, Paris. English translation and foreword copyright © 1984 by the University of Minnesota. Reprinted by permission of the University of Minnesota, and by the kind permission of Manchester University Press.

Mark Taylor, *Erring: A Postmodern A/theology* (Chicago: University of Chicago Press, 1984), pp. 6–13, 103–7, 115–20. Copyright © 1984 by the University of Chicago. Reprinted by permission of University of Chicago Press.

Alisdair MacIntyre, "The Virtues, the Unity of a Human Life and the Concept of a Tradition," chapter 15 of *After Virtue* (Notre Dame: University of Notre Dame Press, 1984), pp. 204–25. Copyright © 1984 (Revised Edition) by the University of Notre Dame Press. Reprinted by permission of the publisher and the author.

Fredric Jameson, "Postmodernism, Or, The Cultural Logic of Late Capitalism," chapter 1 of *Postmodernism, Or, The Cultural Logic of Late Capitalism* (Durham: Duke University Press, 1991), pp. 1–6, 32–8, 45–51 and 54. Reprinted by permission of Duke University Press.

Richard Rorty, "Solidarity or Objectivity" in John Rajchman and Cornel West, *Post-Analytic Philosophy* (New York: Columbia University Press, 1985). Copyright © 1985 Columbia University Press. Reprinted by permission of Columbia University Press, Cambridge University Press, and the author.

Jürgen Habermas, *Philosophical Discourse of Modernity*, trans. Frederick Lawrence (Cambridge: MIT Press, 1987), chapter 11, pp. 294–326. Trans-

Acknowledgments

lation copyright © 1987 by the Massachusetts Institute of Technology. Original publication copyright © 1985 Suhrkamp Verlag, Frankfurt am Main, Federal Republic of Germany. Reprinted by permission of MIT Press and the author.

Sandra Harding, "From Feminist Empiricism to Feminist Standpoint Epistemologies," chapter 6 of her *The Science Question in Feminism* (Ithaca, NY: Cornell University Press, 1986), pp. 141–61. Copyright © 1986 by Cornell University. Published in England by Open University Press of London in 1986. Reprinted by permission of Cornell University Press, Open University Press, and the author.

Susan Bordo, "The Cartesian Masculinization of Thought," chapter 6 of *The Flight to Objectivity: Essays on Cartesianism and Culture* (Albany: State University of New York Press, 1987), pp. 97–118. Copyright © 1987 State University of New York. Reprinted by permission of State University of New York Press and the author.

David Ray Griffin, "Introduction: The Reenchantment of Science," in his edited volume, *The Reenchantment of Science* (Albany: State University of New York Press, 1988), Sections One and Three, pp. 2–8 and 22–30. Copyright © 1988 State University of New York. Reprinted by permission of State University of New York Press.

Henry A. Giroux, "Towards a Postmodern Pedagogy," section of the Introduction to *Postmodernism, Feminism, and Cultural Politics* (Albany: State University of New York Press, 1991), pp. 45–55. Copyright © 1991 State University of New York. Reprinted by permission of State University of New York Press.

David Hall, "Modern China and the Postmodern West," in *Culture and Modernity: East-West Philosophic Perspectives*, edited by Eliot Deutsch (Honolulu: University of Hawaii, Press 1991), pp. 57–67. Copyright © the University of Hawaii 1991. Reprinted by permission of University of Hawaii Press and the author.

The publishers apologize for any errors or omissions in the above list and would be grateful to be notified of any corrections that should be incorporated in the next edition or reprint of this book.

Introduction

The term "postmodern" has in the last decade become an increasingly popular label for something about the end of the twentieth century. It also refers to a contemporary intellectual movement, or rather, a not very happy family of intellectual movements. But as it often happens, dysfunctional families are the most interesting ones. The members of the postmodern family not only express conflicting views, but are interested in barely overlapping subject matters: art, communications media, history, economics, politics, ethics, cosmology, theology, methodology, literature, education. Some of the most important members of the family refuse to be called by the family name. And there are distant relations who deny that they are related at all.

Philosophical opinion regarding the postmodern family is deeply divided. For some, postmodernism connotes the final escape from the stultifying legacy of modern European theology, metaphysics, authoritarianism, colonialism, racism, and domination. To others it represents the attempt by disgruntled left-wing intellectuals to destroy Western civilization. To yet others it labels a goofy collection of hermetically obscure writers who are really talking about nothing at all.

All three reactions are misguided. Certainly the term "postmodern," like any slogan widely used, has been attached to so many different kinds of intellectual, social, and artistic phenomena that it can be subjected to easy ridicule as hopelessly ambiguous or empty. This shows only that it is a mistake to seek a single, essential meaning applicable to all the term's instances. As one of the inspirers of postmodernism would say, the members of the postmodern clan resemble each other in the overlapping way that family members do; two members may share the same eye color, one of these may have the same ears as a third, the third may have the same hair color as a fourth, and so on. More important than discovering an essential commonality is recognizing that there are some important new developments in the world that deserve examination, that "postmodern" labels some of them, and that there are some very important works, raising deep questions, written by people labelled "postmodernists." Neither

1

members of the family, nor their critics, ought to be too concerned with the label. Theoretical labels are nothing to be feared, they have a purpose as long as they are thought's servant, rather than its master. Postmodernism deserves careful, sober scrutiny, devoid of trendy enthusiasm, indignant condemnation, or reactionary fear. Its appearance is unlikely either to save the Western world or destroy it.

When most philosophers use the word "postmodernism" they mean to refer to a movement that developed in France in the 1960s, more precisely called "poststructuralism," along with subsequent and related developments. They have in mind that this movement denies the possibility of objective knowledge of the real world, "univocal" (single or primary) meaning of words and texts, the unity of the human self, the cogency of the distinctions between rational inquiry and political action, literal and metaphorical meaning, science and art, and even the possibility of truth itself. Simply put, they regard it as rejecting most of the fundamental intellectual pillars of modern Western civilization. They may further associate this rejection with political movements like multiculturalism and feminism, which sometimes regard the rejected notions as the ideology of a privileged sexual, ethnic and economic group, and aim to undermine established educational and political authorities and transfer their power to the previously disenfranchised.

This view is neither entirely right nor entirely wrong. There certainly are writers who make the philosophical denials listed above, and there is a connection between some of them and the political aims of feminists and multiculturalists. But not everyone who engages in the postmodern critique of truth or meaning can be politically characterized; and not all feminists or multiculturalists could accept all that goes under the name of postmodernism. Postmodernism, multiculturalism, and feminism represent overlapping but different intellectual tendencies.

At a minimum, postmodernism regards certain important principles, methods, or ideas characteristic of modern Western culture as obsolete or illegitimate. In this sense, postmodernism is the latest wave in the critique of the Enlightenment, the critique of the cultural principles characteristic of modern society that trace their legacy to the eighteenth century, a critique that has been going on since that time. Modernity has been criticizing itself all its life. Some postmodernists explicitly make the historical claim that modernity is or ought to be at an end. Others never speak of "the modern" or "modernism" at all, but instead criticize certain principles that most philosophers would regard as essential to the modern world. Some call for the rejection of modernity, while some only question it, problematize it, without implying that there is any alternative.

Facing all this diversity, the sincere observer of the debate may be understandably confused. The present volume will try to lift some of the confusion by putting philosophical postmodernism in context, or rather in several contexts. The aim is to arm the reader with most of the background that is necessary to participate in the current debate over postmodernism among philosophers. That means knowing something about: modernism, or the characteristic doctrines of modern philosophy that postmodernism is criticizing; the wide variety of criticisms of modern thought that are current today, of which postmodernism is only one; and postmodernism as it is expressed in a number of fields – architecture, literature, sociology – not just philosophy. The effect of this contextualization will be to render postmodernism less mysterious and less frightening, which may also make it less exciting. Whether the last effect is for good or ill will be up to the reader.

1   The History of Postmodernism

The term "postmodern," understood as distinguishing the contemporary scene from the modern, seems first to have been used in 1917 by the German philosopher Rudolf Pannwitz to describe the "nihilism" of twentieth-century Western culture, a theme he took from Friedrich Nietzsche.[1] It appeared again in the work of the Spanish literary critic Federico de Onis in 1934 to refer to the backlash against literary modernism.[2] It was taken up in two very different ways in English in 1939: by the theologian Bernard Iddings Bell, to mean the recognition of the failure of secular modernism and a return to religion;[3] and by the historian Arnold Toynbee to mean the post-World War I rise of mass society, in which the working class surpasses the capitalist class in importance.[4] It then most prominently appeared in literary criticism in the 1950s and 1960s, referring to the reaction against aesthetic modernism, and in the 1970s was pressed into the same use in architecture. In philosophy it came in the 1980s to refer primarily to French poststructuralist philosophy, and secondarily to a general reaction against modern rationalism, utopianism, and what came to be called "foundationalism," the attempt to establish the foundations of knowledge and judgment, an attempt that had been a preoccupation of philosophy since René Descartes in the seventeenth century (although arguably since Plato). At the same time, the term was adopted in the social sciences to indicate a new approach to methodology, and even served this purpose, although more controversially, in the natural sciences.[5] It became linked to the concept of "post-industrialism," the notion that advanced industrial societies were in the post-World War II period radically changing their earlier industrial character. Eventually, the word burst into popular attention through journalists who have used it for everything from rock

3

videos to the demographics of Los Angeles to the whole cultural style and mood of the 1990s.

Despite the divergence among these usages of "postmodern" one could find some commonality centering on: a recognition of pluralism and indeterminacy in the world that modern or modernist thought had evidently sought to disavow, hence a renunciation of intellectual hopes for simplicity, completeness, and certainty; a new focus on representation or images or information or cultural signs as occupying a dominant position in social life; and an acceptance of play and fictionalization in cultural fields that had earlier sought a serious, realist truth. This is a vague commonality, to be sure. In order to gain some finer resolution in our picture, let us focus on the development of the most famous strain of postmodernism in philosophy. For this we must travel to France.

In the 1960s philosophy in France underwent a major change. A new group of young intellectuals emerged who were not only deeply critical of the French academic and political establishment – a rebelliousness not new in French intellectual circles – but also critical of the very forms of radical philosophy that had given the establishment headaches in the past, primarily, Marxism and existentialism, and to some extent phenomenology and psychoanalysis as well.[6]

Marxism, existentialism and phenomenology had been, perhaps awkwardly, combined by the great French philosophers of the middle of the century, especially Jean-Paul Sartre and Maurice Merleau-Ponty, along with a dash of Freudian psychoanalysis. These intellectual movements had pictured the individual human subject or consciousness as alienated in contemporary society, estranged from his or her authentic modes of experience and being – whether the source of that estrangement was capitalism (for Marxism), the scientific naturalism pervading modern Western culture (for phenomenology), excessively repressive social mores (for Freud), bureaucratically organized social life and mass culture (for existentialism), or religion (for all of them). Methodologically, they rejected the belief that the study of humanity could be modeled on or reduced to the physical sciences, hence they avoided behaviorism and naturalism. Unlike physics, chemistry, or biology the human sciences must understand the experience, the first person point of view, of their objects of study: they are concerned not merely with facts but with the *meaning* of facts for human subjects.[7] To diagnose contemporary alienation they produced an historical analysis of how human society and the human self develop over time, in order to see how and why modern civilization had gone wrong. What was needed, it seemed, was a return to the true, or authentic, or free, or integrated human self as the center of lived experience. This meant not an abandonment of modern industry, technology, and secularism, but some reconstruction of society (for Marx), or of moral culture (for Freud), or of

4

our openness to the vicissitudes of our own authentic experience (for phenomenology and existentialism).

Now, Marxism, existentialism, phenomenology, and psychoanalysis never ruled the academic roost in France or anywhere else. They represented the major theoretical opposition to the status quo in the first half of the century. Young intellectuals dissatisfied with the neo-Scholastic, rationalistic, theologically or scientifically oriented forms of thought dominant in the academy – forms of thought which seemed well-suited to endorsing current institutional and political authority – tended to see these movements as the main alternatives. In the post-World War II period they constituted a major intellectual subculture in Europe, gradually influencing American thought as well.

The new French philosophers of the 1960s – the most influential of whom were Gilles Deleuze, Jacques Derrida, Michel Foucault, and Jean-François Lyotard – also wanted to fight the political and academic establishment. But their approach was different from that of Sartre and Merleau-Ponty. They had been schooled by another theoretical movement, structuralism, developed earlier by the linguist Ferdinand de Saussure and championed after the war by the anthropologist Claude Lévi-Strauss. Structuralism rejected the focus on the self and its historical development that had characterized Marxism, existentialism, phenomenology, and psychoanalysis. The social or human sciences, like anthropology, linguistics, and philosophy, needed to focus instead on the super-individual structures of language, ritual, and kinship which make the individual what he or she is. Simply put, it is not the self that creates culture, but culture that creates the self. The study of abstract relations within systems or "codes" of cultural signs (words, family relations, etc.) is the key to understanding human existence. Structuralism seemed to offer the student of humanity a way of avoiding reduction to the natural sciences, while yet retaining objective, scientific methods, unlike the apparently subjective orientation of phenomenology, existentialism, and psychoanalysis. At the same time, it also implied that nothing is "authentic," that there is no fundamental, originary nature of the human self against which we could judge a culture.

The new philosophers of the 1960s accepted structuralism's refusal to worship at the altar of the self. But they rejected its scientific pretensions. They saw deep self-reflexive philosophical problems in the attempt by human beings to be "objective" about themselves. They applied the structural-cultural analysis of human phenomena to the human sciences themselves, which are, after all, human cultural constructions. Hence they are best named "poststructuralists." The import of their work appeared radical indeed. They seemed to announce the end of rational inquiry into truth, the illusory nature of any unified self, the impossibility of clear and unequivocal meaning, the illegitimacy of Western civilization, and the oppressive nature of all modern institutions. They appeared critically to undermine any and all positive philosophical and political positions, to exhibit hidden paradoxes and modes of social domination operating within all products of reason. Whether they were really as radical as they appeared is less clear, as we shall see. In the 1960s and 1970s, however, their critique had a patently political meaning. It served to undermine the claims to legitimacy by academic authorities and the State, and was connected to the critique of Western imperialism and racism, especially during American involvement in Indochina, and eventually to the feminist critique of male power.

Simultaneously, in British and American philosophy, where phenomenology, existentialism, Marxism and psychoanalysis had been far less influential, a related albeit quieter change was taking place.

Logical empiricism, also called positivism, which had by mid-century swept aside the indigenous American pragmatist philosophical tradition (of Charles Sanders Peirce, William James, George Herbert Mead, Josiah Royce, and John Dewey) as well as English idealism and empiricism (e.g. of F.H. Bradley and John Stuart Mill, respectively), believed that a systematization of human knowledge was possible based in the certainties of modern logic combined with a scientific explanation of "sense data." Philosophy had traditionally been hoodwinked by a failure to employ a perfectly clear, logical, "ideal language," which the new advances in logic – rooted in Gottlob Frege's *Begriffsschrift* (or "concept notation," 1879) and Bertrand Russell's and Alfred North Whitehead's attempt to reduce mathematics to logic in their *Principia Mathematica* (1910–13) – had made possible. Ludwig Wittgenstein's attempt to undercut traditional philosophy by distinguishing all that could be said clearly from what is "nonsense" in his *Tractatus Logico-Philosophicus* (1921) had a powerful effect. Philosophy was to shed its metaphysical musings and ethical pretensions and concern itself with logic, the clarification of science's method and results, and the dismissal of traditional philosophical questions through a careful analysis of linguistic errors. Positivism was only one of a wide variety of philosophical movements of the first half of the twentieth century that attacked the very possibility of philosophical inquiry into the ultimate nature of reality, the existence of God, the meaning of existence.

But subsequent philosophers of language, logic, and science had begun to cast doubt on the adequacy of the positivist picture. A complete and consistent logic complex enough to include arithmetic was shown by Kurt Gödel to be impossible, rendering the greatest hopes of an ideal language philosophy unfulfillable. The distinction between analytic or logical statements and synthetic or empirical statements, and the distinction between statements of observed sense data and statements of theoretical explanations of those data – distinctions crucial to positivism – appeared more and more to be porous: there seemed no way to say what we sense without already using some yet unverified theoretical language in order to say it. But this implies that verification in a strict sense is impossible, since any statement of "fact" (sense experience) must presuppose the theoretical perspective it might seem to verify. Wittgenstein's own later philosophy (in his *Philosophical Investigations*, 1953) suggested that the very attempt to discover the foundations of knowledge was as senseless as that of speculative metaphysics. Even science itself, the model of knowledge for so many British and American philosophers, came to be seen as partly non-systematic, hence perhaps partly non-rational, in its development. By no means did most English and American philosophers feel kinship with the French poststructuralists, but by the 1960s they were becoming equally dubious about the canonical aims of modern philosophy and the ultimate hopes of rational inquiry. This led to a widespread attempt to pursue philosophical aims without recourse to foundations (what I call "nonfoundationalism"). On both sides of the Atlantic the study of language and, in effect, *culture*, was superseding the study of the previously alleged *source* of culture in logic, in nature, or in the self.[8]

Meanwhile, outside of philosophy, new tendencies in art, literature, music, and especially architecture were critically superseding movements that had earlier been considered radical. Through the first half of the century a new art and literature that would eventually be called "modernist" had seemed to critique the bourgeois, capitalist social order that carried the economic load of modernity. Dissonant and atonal music, impressionism, surrealism, and expressionism in painting, literary realism, the stream of consciousness novel, to name only a few developments, seemed to open the imagination to a subjective world of experience ignored by the official cultures of societies that were in a schizophrenic rush to modernize technologically and economically, to absorb the natural scientific view of the world, while yet trying to hold onto traditional religious imagery and morality. Often in league with the philosophies of alienated subjectivity (phenomenology, existentialism, Marxism, psychoanalysis), they became identified with an "oppositionist," "avant-garde" subculture. This may seem odd in the case of architecture, since modernist architecture embraced the new technologies of construction and eventually became the official architecture of the advanced industrial world. Nevertheless, its radically "truthful," de-ornamented style – for which, in Mies van der Rohe's famous slogan, "Less is more" – had been intended to counter what it regarded as the official culture's refusal to recognize the reality of modern industrial life, and was supported by utopian, egalitarian social theory. (Ironically, its official adoption was to be echoed by apparently more oppositionist forms of modernist art; modernist painting and sculpture eventually came to grace the lobbies of corporate headquarters and the plazas of government institutions.)

By the time of the 1960s, a new generation of writers, painters, and architects began to react against modernism. The "end" of modernism in literature was recognized as early as the 1950s by Irving Howe and in the 1960s by Leslie Fiedler.[9] Literary irony and camp seemed to capture the sensibility of the time more than the seriousness of the modernist search for the alienated soul and the essence of reality. This period saw the development of art which seemingly renounced unity of style for pastiche – and which in some cases threatened to break down the very notion of art – writing that embraced eclecticism and laughed at (or with?) alienation rather than complaining of it, and music that eschewed emotional themes and celebrated chaos and discontinuity (e.g. in the work of John Cage). The idea of an avant-garde, of art as the most serious and truthful of cultural occupations, was increasingly abandoned, most famously by Pop Art in the work of Andy Warhol. The heroic distinction between high and low, fine and commercial art, the truth-seeking modern avant-garde and the superficial, hedonistic marketplace was being abandoned in an anti-heroic embrace of pop culture.

It was in the most socially consequential of arts, architecture, that postmodernism had its most widespread influence in the 1960s and 1970s. The groundwork had been laid in 1961 by Jane Jacobs's devastating book, *The Death and Life of Great American Cities*.[10] Jacobs lashed out at the orthodox urban reform movement of the day, in which modernism had been joined with welfare state policy to create vast "single use" housing complexes for the poor. She exposed the virtually anti-urban, anti-human impulses of this alleged humanitarian policy, whose abstract grids undercut the social mechanisms by which urban neighborhoods had traditionally maintained themselves as viable communities. Then in 1966 in his *Complexity and Contradiction in Architecture* Robert Venturi insisted that architectural communication requires not simplicity but complexity and even contradiction. To the modernist slogan, "Less is more," Venturi replied: "Less is a bore." In the decade to come both the modernist style and the idea of social reform through uniform, technocratic, top-down solutions increasingly fell out of favor.

Not to mention that society was undergoing other radical changes: the end of the last vestiges of European colonialism after World War II, the development of mass communications and a media culture in the advanced industrial countries, the rapid modernization of much of the non-Western world, and the shrinking of the globe by international marketing, telecommunications, and intercontinental missiles. In many Western nations there was a significant delegitimation of authority. Social theorists claimed that some of these changes were indicative of a transition to a new "post-industrial" society, in which the production and control of information, rather than materials, would be the hallmark of economic life. Most famously formulated by Daniel Bell, this thesis implied that the forms of social, political, and cultural order characteristic of the late nineteenth and early twentieth centuries, the era in which industrialism triumphantly reconstructed life for most Western human beings, would no longer hold.[11]

There was then the political explosion of students virutally around the world, culminating in 1968: in the USA, Paris, Prague, and China (towards different ends, to be sure). The revolt against authority among the young educated, or about-to-be-educated, classes was profound. It was in this highly charged university setting, within an increasingly complex social context, that postmodernism in the strictest sense was born in France among some younger professors. The attack of Parisian students on the French government, on the university that was literally one of its branches, on capitalism, and on the American war in South East Asia, all seemed to resonate with the poststructuralist critique of Reason and Authority.

But the moment passed: the war ended, the universities placated the students, and the real world of money, power and geo-politics continued much as before. For a decade or more after 1968 poststructuralism's influence outside of France remained limited to comparative literature departments and philosophical circles already devoted to European philosophy.

The term "postmodern" gradually came into expanded use in the 1970s. Ihab Hassan, who would become one of postmodernism's most well-known spokesmen, connected literary, philosophical, and social trends under the term in 1971.[12] Charles Jencks applied it to architecture in 1975.[13] Postmodernism as a cultural phenomenon was attacked by Daniel Bell in 1976.[14] In the late 1970s, three books galvanized postmodernism as a movement: Jencks's *The Language of Post-Modern Architecture* (1977); Jean-François Lyotard's *La Condition postmoderne: rapport sur le savoir* (1979; English translation: *The Postmodern Condition: A Report on Knowledge*, 1984); and Richard Rorty's *Philosophy and the Mirror of Nature* (1979). The last, while not discussing postmodernism per se, argued that the developments of post-Heideggerian European philosophy and post-Wittgensteinian analytic philosophy were converging on a kind of pragmatic antifoundationalism. Rorty thereby became an American representative of postmodernism, albeit in pragmatic garb. It was partly through Rorty's influence that in the 1980s postmodernism came to have a meaning for most American philosophers, and not just architectural and literary critics. Simultaneously the term came into general use as a label for the current era, our own *fin de siècle* (end of century) mood.

Of course, postmodernism is not the only philosophical *ism* to rebel against the status quo since the 1960s. More prominent in Western society as a whole has been the desire to turn back the clock, to respond to the problems of modern society and culture with a partial return to or reincorporation of earlier, traditional cultural forms. This "premodernism"

9

can be seen in the widespread political conservatism of the 1980s, the call for moral regeneration, for a return to community and religion, and in an extreme form, in religious fundamentalism (most famously, Islamic and Christian). In political theory, communitarianism and other forms of "neo-liberalism" have accused modern liberal individualism of undermining the fabric of society. At the same time, other intellectuals have sought to defend the modern legacy of rationalism and liberal individualism through reinterpreting it. Usually limiting the traditional philosophical search for ultimate certainty, these (using my own term) "promodernists" have tried to reinvigorate the modern tradition, rather than either returning to the premodern past or leaping into the postmodern future.

One other factor in the development of postmodernism since the early 1970s deserves special mention: the decline of Marxism. The new left of the 1960s, and some of the new French philosophers, reinterpreted their Marxism through Freud and Ferdinand de Saussure, and so had already begun to shake off Marxist-Leninist orthodoxy. But a deeper disenchantment can be traced to the 1973 publication of the first volume of Alexander Solzhenitsyn's *The Gulag Archipelago*, a monumental recounting of Stalinist atrocities in the Soviet Union. After this, it was no longer possible for people of the left to look to the Soviet Union as a free society in any sense. The Western European and North American professoriate became increasingly unsympathetic with Marxism and to some extent with socialism over the next decade. This coincided with the popular turn to the right in many Western societies during the 1980s.

The result of this change was profound, and not limited to yet another swing in the pendulum of popular opinion between the demand for a freer market and the demand for greater government control over the market. Marxism had provided a philosophy of history that served for a sizable segment of the secularized Western intelligentsia as a worldly religion, a particularly potent fulfillment of that great modern hope in progress, what Christopher Lasch called the "One and Only Heaven."[15] For many irreligious intellectuals, the hope for a utopian socialist future gave badly needed significance to a life lived after the "death of god." The loss of this hope struck a sizable portion of this group much as the loss of religion had already struck traditional society: lacking a historical *telos* or goal, it seemed that the world had become centerless and pointless once again. Postmodernism, a wayward stepchild of Marxism, is in this sense a generation's realization that it is orphaned.

Thus ends our brief lesson in recent history. But, as postmodernists would insist, how postmodernism developed and what it *means* are two separate questions. In order to examine the meaning of postmodernism, we must first understand what it is whose decline postmodernism announces. We must gain some understanding of what is meant by *modernity*.

2 What is Modern?

The term "modern," derived from the Latin *modo*, simply means "of today" or what is current, as distinguished from earlier times. It has been used in various periods and places to distinguish contemporary from traditional ways, and in principle can refer to any sphere of life. It is still used in this local, contextually determined way; hence when someone speaks of "modern English" or of "modern dance" it does not imply that the historical period of "modern English" and "modern dance" are the same. They are, in effect, two totally different "moderns"; the use of the term modern merely distinguishes recent English from Middle and Old English, or a twentieth-century dance style from ballet.

"Modernity" on the other hand, has a relatively fixed reference in contemporary intellectual discussion. It refers to the new civilization developed in Europe and North America over the last several centuries and fully evident by the early twentieth century. "Modernity" implies that this civilization is modern in the strong sense that it is unique in human history. Exactly what makes this civilization unique is to some extent uncontroversial. Everyone admits that Europe and North America developed a new, powerful technique for the study of nature, as well as new machine technologies and modes of industrial production that have led to an unprecedented rise in material living standards. It is this form of "modernity" that is today described as "modernization" or simply "development" in the non-Western world. This modern Western civilization is generally characterized as well by other traits, such as capitalism, a largely secular culture, liberal democracy, individualism, rationalism, humanism. However, whether *these* traits are unique in human history is controversial. Many historical societies have had relatively free markets, have respected individuality, engaged in rational planning and rational inquiry, regarded at least part of social life as largely secular or profane, and so on. As a package, the modern Western combination of science, technology, industry, free market, liberal democracy, etc., certainly is unique in human history, but whether each of the elements separately considered is unique is less clear. This makes the more precise definition of modernity – beyond science, technology, industry, and high living standards – rather difficult.

One may be tempted to say, "Who cares about the non-technological components of modernity? What makes modernity modern is machines, industrialization, advanced living standards; the rest is unimportant." But here the American sociologist Peter Berger asks the right question: are we simply ancient Egyptians in airplanes? That is, is the sole important shift in modernity a difference in the tools that human beings use, rather than a difference in the human beings themselves, their worldview, their sense of self? If only the tools matter, then the sole significant difference between a contemporary corporate executive riding in a Boeing 747 and an astrologer in the Pharoah's court is the 747. This would imply that the modernization of undeveloped countries is a purely technical affair, having nothing to do with culture and psychology. But, as the complex cultural and social problems arising from modernization have shown, this is not the case. The difference between executive and astrologer lies not only in the airplane, but in the human mind, or in what might be the same thing, human culture. But because minds and cultures are harder to understand and specify than airplanes, this recognition makes the specification of what makes modernity modern endlessly controversial.

The positive self-image modern Western culture has often given to itself, a picture born in the eighteenth-century Enlightenment, is of a civilization founded on scientific knowledge of the world and rational knowledge of value, which places the highest premium on individual human life and freedom, and believes that such freedom and rationality will lead to social progress through virtuous, self-controlled work, creating a better material, political, and intellectual life for all. This combination of science, reason, individuality, freedom, truth, and social progress has, however, been questioned and criticized by many. Some critics see modernity instead as a movement of ethnic and class domination, European imperialism, anthropocentrism, the destruction of nature, the dissolution of community and tradition, the rise of alienation, the death of individuality in bureaucracy. More benign critics have argued skeptically that modernity cannot achieve what it hopes, e.g. that objective truth or freedom is unavailable, or that modernity's gains are balanced by losses, and that there is no alternative either to modernity or to its discontents. This is not the place to debate the relative truth of these claims; nevertheless, it can at least be said that while there is some truth in each of them, the whole truth is more complex. More than any other topic, the evaluation of modernity brings to mind the story of the elephant and the blind men, each of whom grasped one part of the elephant – trunk, side, tail, leg, ear, tusk – leading to an interminable argument about their utterly dissimilar, fantastic conclusions regarding the beast – "It's a snake," "No, a wall," "No, a rope," "No, a tree," "No, a fan," "No, a spear." Contemporary theorists often take one part of modernity to be the whole.

The debate is complicated by the question of the historical parameters of modernity. The reason is that the location of the historical starting point of modernity depends on what one regards as modernity's essential feature. Did modernity in the West begin in the sixteenth century with the Protestant reformation, the rejection of the universal power of the Roman Catholic Church, and the development of a humanistic skepticism epitomized by Erasmus and Montaigne? Or was it in the seventeenth century with the scientific revolution of Galileo, Harvey, Hobbes, Descartes, Boyle, Leibniz, and Newton? Or with the republican political theories and revolutions of the United States and France in the eighteenth century? What about the industrial revolution of the nineteenth century? Very interesting theories have argued for each of these theses, and for yet others, and much can be learned about the pieces of the puzzle from them. There is no way to resolve this issue, but fortunately, also no need to resolve it. The primary question for a philosopher is not, When did modernity begin? but: What is the nature, the destiny, and the validity of this new way of life? It is enough to know that some new form of human society evolved in Europe and North America, fully evident by, say, 1914, whose various pieces had fallen into place gradually over several centuries. If our primary interest lies in diagnosing the illnesses of the present, the onset of the disease is relegated to secondary significance.

The term "modernism" is used in a famously ambiguous way. It can refer to the philosophy or culture of the modern period as a whole, as in the title of the present volume. It can also refer to a much more historically circumscribed movement in the arts during the period 1850 to 1950. As mentioned above, this period saw unprecedented experimentation in the arts: in painting, from the realism of Gustave Courbet and the impressionism of Claude Monet to the abstract expression of Jackson Pollack; in literature, the abandonment of objective narrative in Virginia Woolf and James Joyce, and of idealized treatment of subject matter in Ernest Hemingway; in music, Arnold Schönberg's and Alban Berg's atonality, and Igor Stravinsky's dissonance and non-thematic structure, to name but a few examples. In architecture, the modernism of Le Corbusier, Ludwig Mies van der Rohe, and Walter Gropius has played a particularly important role. At any rate, one way of understanding the relation of the terms "modern," "modernity," and "modernism" is that aesthetic modernism is a form of art characteristic of high or actualized or late modernity, that is, of that period in which social, economic, and cultural life in the widest sense were revolutionized by modernity. By no means does this imply that modernist art endorses modernization, or simply expresses the aims of modernity. But it does mean that modernist art is scarcely thinkable outside the context of the modernized society of the late nineteenth and twentieth centuries. Social modernity is the home of modernist art, even where that art rebels against it.

3   What Postmodernism Means

It is difficult – some would say, impossible – to summarize what postmodernism means, not only because there is much disagreement among writers labelled postmodern, but also because some postmodernists would deny having any doctrines or theories at all. Perhaps the very idea of a summary is antithetical to postmodernism. Still, understanding must begin somewhere, and there is no good alternative to listing: first, the most famous themes or ideas that appear in most postmodernist work; second, the different kinds of claims that postmodernists make; and last, some of the issues that divide postmodernists.

Five prominent postmodern themes can be distinguished; four are objects of its criticism, and one constitutes its positive method. Postmodernism typically criticizes: *presence* or presentation (versus representation and construction), *origin* (versus phenomena), *unity* (versus plurality), and *transcendence* of norms (versus their immanence). It typically offers an analysis of phenomena through *constitutive otherness*.

Presence refers to the quality of immediate experience and to the objects thereby immediately "presented." What is directly, immediately given in experience has traditionally been contrasted both with representation, the sphere of linguistic signs and concepts, and construction, the products of human invention, hence whatever is mediated by the human factor. So, for example, perception or sensation or sense data have been considered, at various times, as immediate conduits for reality, more reliable or certain than mental contents subsequently modified, represented, and altered by thought or language. Postmodernism questions and sometimes rejects this distinction. It denies that anything is "immediately present," hence independent of signs, language, interpretation, disagreement, etc. In some cases, it argues that presentation actually presupposes representation. Thus Derrida literally denies that there is such a thing as "perception," that is, an immediate, transparent reception of the given.

The denial of presence occasionally leads postmodernists to substitute the analysis of *representations of* a thing for discussion of *the thing*. For example, in a debate over whether to use intelligence tests in a local school system, a postmodernist might produce a long analysis of how the term "intelligence" has been used by the test's proponents, implying that the object or referent of the term "intelligence" is never present to us, so it is the history of those representations and their political use which is really at issue. The critique of presence is sometimes expressed by saying that, "There is nothing outside the text." This need not mean that there is no real world, but that we only encounter real referents through texts, representations, mediation. We can never say what is independent of all saying.

Origin is the notion of the source of whatever is under consideration, a return to which is often considered the aim of rational inquiry. Inquiry into origins is an attempt to see behind or beyond phenomena to their ultimate foundation. For modern philosophies of the self (e.g. existenialism, psychoanalysis, phenomenology, even Marxism), the attempt to discover the

14

origin of the self is the road to authenticity. Postmodernism in the strict sense denies any such possibility.[16] It denies the possibility of returning to, recapturing, or even representing the origin, source, or any deeper reality behind phenomena, and casts doubt on or even denies its existence. In a sense, postmodernism is intentionally superficial, not through eschewing rigorous analysis, but by regarding the surface of things, the phenomena, as not requiring a reference to anything deeper or more fundamental. Nietzsche's claim that the ancient Greeks were superficial "out of profundity" could be a postmodern slogan. The saying, "Every author is a dead author," is an example of the denial of origin, because it denies that the meaning of a text can be "authoritatively" revealed through reference to authorial intentions. An author's intentions are no more relevant to understanding the text than any other set of considerations; they are not the "origin" of the text and so have no "privilege" over other factors.

Virtually in every kind of intellectual endeavor, postmodernism tries to show that what others have regarded as a *unity*, a single, integral existence or concept, is plural. This is to some extent a reflection of structuralism, which understood cultural elements – words, meanings, experiences, human selves, societies – as constituted by relations to other elements. Since such relations are inevitably plural, the individual in question is plural as well. Everything is constituted by relations to other things, hence nothing is simple, immediate, or totally present, and no analysis of anything can be complete or final. For example, a text can be read in an indefinitely large number of ways, none of which provides the complete or true meaning. The human self is not a simple unity, hierarchically composed, solid, self-controlled; rather it is a multiplicity of forces or elements. It would be more true to say that I have *selves*, than *a self*.

The denial of the *transcendence* of norms is crucial to postmodernism. Norms such as truth, goodness, beauty, rationality, are no longer regarded as independent of the processes they serve to govern or judge, but are rather products of and immanent in those processes. For example, where most philosophers might use the idea of justice to judge a social order, postmodernism regards that idea as itself the product of the social relations that it serves to judge; that is, the idea was created at a certain time and place, to serve certain interests, and is dependent on a certain intellectual and social context, etc. This greatly complicates any claims about the justice of social relations. It is in effect the rejection of idealism, and of any dualism which asserts that some things (e.g. norms) are independent of nature or semiosis (sign-production) or experience or social interests. The concept "good" and the act of calling something good are not independent of the things we want to call "good." This leads postmodernists to respond to the normative claims of others by displaying the processes of thought, writing, negotiation, and power which produced those very normative

15

claims. It does not mean that postmodernists fail to make their own normative claims, but that they unleash a form of critical analysis which makes all normative claims problematic, including their own.

Lastly, there is a characteristic strategy of many forms of postmodernism, which is the complex application of the four themes just mentioned. The strategy is to use the idea of *constitutive otherness* in analyzing any cultural entity. What appear to be cultural units – human beings, words, meanings, ideas, philosophical systems, social organizations – are maintained in their apparent unity only through an active process of exclusion, opposition, and hierarchization. Other phenomena or units must be represented as foreign or "other" through representing a hierarchical dualism in which the unit is "privileged" or favored, and the other is devalued in some way. For example, in examining social systems characterized by class or ethnic division, postmodernists will discover that the privileged groups must actively produce and maintain their position by representing or picturing themselves – in thought, in literature, in law, in art – as not having the properties ascribed to the under-privileged groups, and must represent those groups as lacking the properties of the privileged groups. In a human psyche, the self may feel compelled to represent itself as excluding sexual or aggressive feelings, which, however, cannot simply be obliterated, and so must be ascribed to chance situations, to idiosyncratic events (e.g. "I was not myself that day"), etc. In a philosophical system, a dualism like that between "reality" and "appearance" involves the construction of a kind of waste basket into which phenomena that the system does not want to sanctify with the privileged term "real" can be tossed (mere "appearances"). Only in this way can the pristine integrity of the idealized or privileged term be maintained.[17]

Metaphorically, this can be expressed by saying that it is the *margins that constitute the text*. Apparent unities are constituted by repressing their dependency on and relations to others. Consequently, the informed analyst will attend to the apparently excluded or "marginalized" elements of any system or text. Postmodernists, especially in literary studies, turn their attention away from the well-known, openly announced themes in a text toward the seldom mentioned, the virtually absent, the implicitly or explicitly devalued. For presence is constituted by absence, the real is constituted by appearance, the ideal by the mundane. This applies not only to the stated message or theme of a text, but to its style as well. Linguistic tropes, such as metaphors, which other readers may take as secondary or peripheral to the meaning of a text, are read by postmodernists as crucial to the constitution of the text's privileged theme.

Sometimes implicit and sometimes explicit in this kind of analysis through constitutive otherness is the claim that the process of exclusion or repression is false, unstable, and/or immoral: false in that it is mendacious, a lie; unstable in that the repression must sooner or later be admitted, forcing an acceptance of the excluded factors into the representation of the privileged unit; immoral when it takes the form of social oppression. Every text is built on some kind of exclusion or repression, hence it belies itself and, when read carefully, undermines its own message. Once we become aware of the constitutive otherness in the text, we see that the text itself, despite its own intentions, alerts us to the dependence of the privileged theme on the marginalized element. The repressed eventually returns to haunt us. Social disenfranchisement, marginalization of sexual and racial groups, is the moral and political case of this pattern. Some postmodernists wish to remove such repression, while others, seeing in that wish a longing for an impossible authenticity, admit that there is no escape from repression and hope only to render repressive forces more diverse and fluid, so that none becomes monopolistic and hence excessively onerous.

Regarding the types of postmodernism, while no categorization can be adequate to capture the diversity among postmodernists, a three-part classification can make most of this material easier to digest. The categories are not mutually exclusive, they are intentionally overlapping. They merely indicate the kinds of aims that can be embodied by writing called postmodern.

Historical postmodernism argues that the social and/or political and/or cultural organization of modernity has changed fundamentally, so that we now face a novel world. This is simply the basic historical claim of postmodernism, or better, it is postmodernism *as* an historical claim. Modernity is at an end, or is undergoing a deep transformation. This claim can be applied to any kind of subject matter, social, cultural, artistic, or theoretical. It need not make any normative claims, that is, it need not say that modernity was wrong.

Methodological postmodernism rejects the possibility of establishing the foundations, hence the ultimate reliability, of knowledge understood as valid in a realist sense, that is, knowledge claimed to represent the true, independent "real" nature of its objects. It shows that traditional philosophical distinctions between real and ideal, objective and subjective, reality and appearance, fact and theory, are problematic. It does this on the basis of criticizing either traditional theories of knowledge and linguistic meaning, or the human interests evident in the construction of these distinctions. Methodological postmodernism is antirealist – claiming that knowledge is made valid not by its relation to its objects, but by its relation to our pragmatic interests, our communal perspectives, our needs, our rhetoric, and so on – and/or antifoundationalist – undercutting the philosophical attempt to justify realism. Some forms of methodological postmodernism appear to undermine the very possibility of rational inquiry, by subjecting the very notions of "truth," "rationality," and "meaning" to critique. Methodological postmodernism is purely negative, that is, it claims or shows the inadequacy or problematic nature of other forms of writing and talking and theorizing, but does not explicitly offer an alternative.

Positive postmodernism is a positive reinterpretation of any phenomenon on the basis of the foregoing methodological critique. It may reconceive the self, or God, or nature, or knowledge, or society, or art, or anything, given the critique of unity, origin, presence, etc. This category refers to writing that applies general postmodern themes to particular subject matters in order to offer a new vision or understanding of them. It offers an alternative.

There are several important issues that divide writers associated with postmodernism. First, implicit in the categorization above, one must recognize whether any alleged postmodernist is: (a) merely making the historical claim that modern ideas and methods are being superseded or abandoned in the present age; (b) questioning the validity of modern methods without making any explicit claims about their falsity or suggesting that they be abandoned; or (c) claiming the inadequacy of the modern methods and inviting us to abandon them in favor of something else. Some of the thinkers labelled postmodern are wrongly accused of rejecting modern philosophy and society, when in fact they are only questioning them, albeit radically, or only reporting their obsolescence, without suggesting that modernity be exchanged for some alternative. For example, while Jacques Derrida has been interpreted as undermining all of Western thought, Derrida specifically states that there is no alternative to "logocentrism," or the traditional foundationalism of the West: it cannot be abandoned. If this is true, then Derrida's critique, and other forms of methodological postmodernism, begin to look similar to various forms of skepticism familiar within the Western tradition (e.g. of the ancient Greek Sextus Empiricus and the eighteenth-century Scotsman David Hume).

As a result there is a tension between methodological postmodernism and various positive applications of postmodernism. The most extreme case is that some self-labelled postmodernists are speculative metaphysicians who use elements of the postmodern critique to reformulate fundamental conceptions of God and the universe. This task is in principle anathema to poststructuralism and antifoundationalism, and hence to much of what goes under the name "postmodernism." But the speculators have as much right to the name as anyone, and they clearly do base their work on some notions shared with other postmodernists. Still, they avoid those elements of methodological postmodernism which effectively undermine any speculative project.

Second, while postmodernism may seem antithetical to any attempt to recapture the past, this is not always true. For example, while most postmodernists in philosophy or social theory would have nothing in common with those who wish to reincorporate elements of tradition, such

18

a return is precisely what architectural postmodernism means. The postmodern architect often incorporates ornamentation that modernism had banished into an otherwise modernist setting. But notice that this is not premodernism pure and simple; rather it is a kind of pluralism. Architectural postmodernism uses premodern elements within a whole that is anything but traditional. Synthesizing, juxtaposing, and ironically commenting on traditions is *not* traditional. To be a traditionalist or premodernist is to be faithful to *one* tradition, not all traditions. To respect and sample from all traditions is precisely to be modern and cosmopolitan, not traditional. Traditionalism is no more compatible with a plurality of traditions than monogamy is compatible with a plurality of sexual partners. Nevertheless, postmodernism may often exhibit similarities to premodernism, since they share the same enemy.

Third, there is the question of the political implications of postmodernism. Its most well-known political manifestation is the attempt to make contemporary culture acknowledge and respond to "difference," or "otherness," under the names of *feminism*, a vastly influential intellectual movement, and *multiculturalism*, which as a program has been primarily a phenomenon in the field of education. Both of these movements overlap with postmodernism, so that some feminists and some multiculturalists are postmodernists while others are not. Most poststructuralists, feminists, and multiculturalists are associated with the left. But others are not, like Richard Rorty, who has labelled himself a "postmodernist bourgeois liberal." Indeed, some critics from the left have criticized postmodernism for just this, that it opens the way to reactionary forces or to an acquiescence in the status quo, by undermining the modernist justifications for leftist political reform. Hence Jürgen Habermas once called the French poststructuralists the "Young Conservatives."[18] There is nothing confusing about this diversity; it is arguable that postmodernism by itself need not lead in any particular political direction. Its political usefulness lies in criticizing any established authority.

4 Putting Postmodernism in Context

This volume is structured chronologically around three phases in the development of the modern West's philosophical evaluation of itself.

Part I presents the reader with a very small selection of some of the most influential statements of modernity from the seventeenth through the nineteenth centuries, as well as some of the most famous criticisms of that evolving culture. Throughout these centuries most human beings in Europe and North America continued to live and think as they had for the thousand years preceding: in small towns and agricultural communities, imagining the world in more or less religious terms, uninfluenced by the scientific and secular ideas emerging in educated circles in the great cities. It was not until the republican political revolutions of the eighteenth century that modern ideas had widespread concrete effect. But even then, daily life for most people continued relatively unchanged until almost the twentieth century. Each new element of modern thought was opposed by cultural inertia, political and religious leaders, and by various intellectuals, several of whom are included here. It is crucial to understand that what we have called modernity was always under attack. Postmodernism is only the newest wave of such criticism. The final reading of this section is from Friedrich Nietzsche, the pre-twentieth-century philosopher who is the most influential for postmodernism.[19]

Part II presents the critical analysis of modern art, society, and philosophy that came with the triumph of modernity, the full establishment of a society unique in human history. It is in this period, roughly from 1860 to 1950, that Western modernity ceases to be a primarily intellectual and political phenomenon and dramatically remakes the everyday socio-economic world in which average people live. It is also the period in which Western modernity becomes the dominant geo-political force in the world. This actualization of modernity provoked a new reaction from intellectuals and artists, instigating a debate over bourgeois values and mass culture, and provoking an unprecedented period of aesthetic and intellectual experimentation. The artistic modernism that resulted is both a critique of bourgeois modernity and an expression of it. A number of writers in this period are crucial for the latter development of postmodernism.

The selections in Part III are from the post-World War II period. They include: the most prominent writers identified with postmodernism since the 1960s; some of their important immediate predecessors; a number of critics of modernity who share some postmodern themes but are not postmodernists; and several influential critics of postmodernism. The section thus brings together many of the prominent voices in the contemporary debate over postmodernism, both pro and con.

The volume's selections are ordered chronologically. Editor's notes, referenced by lower case roman numerals, are at the bottom of the page; all author's notes, referenced by Arabic numerals, appear as endnotes. My additions to the author's endnotes are in square brackets; any other additions to the text in square brackets, unless otherwise noted, are the translators', or in rare cases a former editor's. The reference at the foot of the first page of each selection makes it clear what works of the author's have been selected, the word 'from' there indicating that only a part of the relevant subdivision (book, essay, chapter, section) has been selected. Omitted material is indicated in the text by ellipses.

It may be well to conclude this introduction with a general comment about the validity of postmodernism. Some philosophers dismiss postmodernism for using intentionally elusive rhetoric, in part to avoid self-contradiction. If, they say, postmodernists literally and explicitly undermine truth, objectivity, and the univocal meanings of words, then this would undermine their own writing as well. That is, postmodern texts would undercut their own possibility of having a cogent meaning and of being true. Postmodernists would then be in the position of denying the validity of their own denials. To avoid this self-contradiction, the critics continue, postmodernists write in a coy or ironic fashion, unwilling to make explicit methodological or philosophical claims. Hence they dodge criticism by a subterfuge unbefitting an inquirer.

Rhetorical flourishes on both sides notwithstanding, postmodernism raises crucial questions to which philosophy is bound by its own commitments to respond. The charge of self-contradiction is an important one; nevertheless, it is a purely negative argument that does nothing to blunt the criticisms postmodernism makes of traditional inquiry. The sometimes obscure rhetorical strategies of postmodernism make sense if one accepts its critique of such inquiry. To say then that the postmodern critique is invalid because the kind of theory it produces does not meet the standards of traditional or normal inquiry is a rather weak counter-attack. It says in effect that whatever critique does not advance the interests of traditional inquiry is invalid. The same charge was made against the very patron saint of philosophy, Socrates, whose infernal questioning, it was said, led to nothing positive and practical, undermined socially important beliefs, and could not justify itself except for his eccentric claim to be on a mission from God (in Plato's *Apology*). So, while the threat of self-contradiction does raise a serious problem for postmodernism, one that would prevent postmodernism from regarding itself as valid in the way traditional philosophies hope to be, that fact does nothing to show that normal inquiry is immune to its critique. Postmodernism raises a serious challenge which cannot be so easily dismissed. Whether it is *right*, is, of course, another matter, and one that is up to the reader to decide.

Notes

1   See Rudolf Pannwitz, *Die Krisis der Europaeischen Kultur* (Nuernberg: Hans Carl, 1917), p. 64. It has been suggested that the term was used even earlier by the British painter John Watkins Chapman in the 1870s; however, my efforts to verify this have been inconclusive. Also, in the present discussion I shall ignore the difference between the employment of "postmodern" and "post-modern."

2 See Federico de Onis, *Antologia de la Poesia española e hispanoamericana: 1882–1932* (Madrid, 1934), pp. xviii–xix. For the best historical discussion of the term, and the best bibliographical account of postmodernism in general, see Margaret Rose's *The Post-Modern and the Post-Industrial: A Critical Analysis* (Cambridge: Cambridge University Press, 1991).

3 Bernard Iddings Bell, *Religion For Living: A Book for Postmodernists* (London: The Religious Book Club, 1939). I thank Margaret Rose for bringing this reference to my attention.

4 Arnold Toynbee, *A Study of History* (London: Oxford University Press, 1939), vol. V, p. 43. Toynbee referred to postmodernism again in vol. VIII, published 1954, p. 338.

5 See for example, Pauline Marie Rosenau's *Post-Modernism and the Social Sciences: Insights, Inroads, and Intrusions* (Princeton, NJ: Princeton University Press, 1992), and David Griffin's *The Reenchantment of Science* (Albany: State University Press of New York, 1988).

6 While the term "phenomenology" has been used by several philosophers (e.g. Hegel and Peirce), here it refers to the study of how the world we know is constituted within and through the sheer lived experience of human consciousness prior to any scientific or cultural learning. Created by the German Edmund Husserl (1859–1938), it became extremely influential in France. For the story of the French reception of phenomenology, and the rise of postmodernism in France, see Vincent Descombes, *Modern French Philosophy*, trans. L. Schott-Fox and J.M.Harding (New York: Cambridge University Press, 1980).

7 Marxism, under some interpretations, is an exception to this trend. Some, emphasizing Marx's historical determinism, have aspired to the model of the sciences, while others, more concerned with individualism and alienation (sometimes called "Western Marxists"), have rejected pretensions to scientific methodology.

8 Not that these aims disappeared entirely. Indeed, the search for a naturalistic basis for language and thought through the use of advances in the study of artificial intelligence and linguistics has become an increasingly powerful philosophical program in recent years, under the name of "cognitive science." But here too, the direction of movement is away from the self of phenomenology, existentialism, and psychoanalysis, and toward super-individual structures. For cognitive science, as opposed to structuralism and poststructuralism, those structures are neural and/or logical rather than cultural.

9 See Irving Howe, "Mass Society and Postmodern Fiction," in *The Decline of the New* (New York: Harcourt, Brace and World, 1970), pp. 190–207, and Leslie Fiedler, "The New Mutants," in *The Collected Essays of Leslie Fiedler*, vol. II (New York: Stein and Day, 1971), pp. 379–99.

10 Jane Jacobs, *The Death and Life of Great American Cities* (New York: Vintage, 1961).

11 See Daniel Bell, *The Coming of Post-Industrial Society: A Venture in Social Forecasting* (New York: Basic Books, 1973). His book was immediately preceded by Alan Touraine's rather different *The Post-Industrial Society*, trans. Leonard F.X. Mayhew (New York: Random House, 1971; original, 1969). The

concept of post-industrial society is, however, at least as old as 1914 and Arthur J. Penty's and Ananda K. Coomaraswamy's *Essays in Post-Industrialism: A Symposium of Prophecy Concerning the Future of Society* (London: 1914). Penty attributed the invention of the term to Coomaraswamy. Their book is now virtually unavailable, but according to Roger Lipsey's account in his *Coomaraswamy: His Life and Work* (Princeton, NJ: Princeton University Press, 1977), Coomaraswamy's post-industrialism was a straightforward premodernism, in which he hoped for and foresaw the end of industrialism and a return to village life.

12 See Ihab Hassan, *The Dismemberment of Orpheus: Toward a Postmodern Literature* (Madison: University of Wisconsin Press, 1971).

13 The term had already been used by Joseph Hudnut in the 1940s to mean extreme- or *ultra*-modern architecture. See his "The Post-Modern House," *Architectural Record*, 97 (May 1945), pp. 70–5. Charles Jencks was the first to use the word to mean the end or transformation of modernism.

14 See Daniel Bell, *The Cultural Contradictions of Capitalism* (New York: Basic Books, 1976), especially pp. 51–5.

15 See Christopher Lasch, *The True and Only Heaven: Progress and its Critics* (New York: Norton, 1991). I must add here my posthumous appreciation for Professor Lasch's having many years ago taken seriously the work of a graduate student that he had never met, and responding sensitively and intelligently.

16 I use the qualification ("in the strict sense") because some thinkers associated with postmodernism do call for such a return, and this call usually serves a political purpose. But it is not clear how such a call is compatible with other postmodern themes.

17 This postmodern strategy is, as alluded to above, not entirely new; it was implicit in the dialectical method of the great German philosopher G.W.F. Hegel (1770–1831).

18 See Jürgen Habermas, "Modernity versus Postmodernity," *New German Critique* (Winter 1981), No. 22, p. 10.

19 I have placed Nietzsche in this first period rather than the second for thematic reasons. The world Nietzsche critically analyzed is not the recent world of mass culture and modern industry, but the Western tradition of idealism, Christianity, and Romanticism, all of which predate the period of what I am calling the realization of modernity.

Part I

Modern Civilization and its Critics

It is impossible to recount the dramatic changes that stimulated European modernity; certainly the voyages of discovery of the fifteenth century, the Protestant Reformation of the sixteenth century, and the scientific revolution of the seventeenth, to name but a few, had a profound effect on the European mind. In the seventeenth and eighteenth centuries momentum began to gather behind a new *view* of the world, which would eventually create a new *world*, the modern world of industry and business and cities and cosmopolitanism and republicanism, where the rhythm of life was to be increasingly dictated by machines rather than by nature, where the Rights of Man would replace the Divine Right of Kings, where the merchant would displace the landed aristocrat, where cities would become home to pragmatic strangers who had left their local communities, where beliefs were increasingly to be generated from the printing press, the laboratory, and the street, rather than from parents, princes or pulpit. It meant the beginning of an accelerating process of change whereby modes of living that had altered little in over a thousand years would eventually be turned upside down.

Philosophically, the novelty of the age centered on the idea of reason. The seventeenth and eighteenth centuries in the West are often referred to as the "Age of Reason," with the latter century called the "Enlightenment." Enlightened intellectuals believed above all that humans more or less universally possess a faculty called "reason," less a body of truths than a capacity and a method for grasping them, perhaps endowed us by God as the essence of humanity; that reason, independent of the dictates of tradition and authority, is the ultimate and legitimate earthly judge of truth, beauty, moral goodness and political order; that this reason is at war with ignorance and superstition; that its exercise by the individual is to be encouraged; and that the meaning of human existence is in some measure to be fulfilled by using reason to grasp a larger share of truth and to reconstruct human society, materially and politically – all this is largely a product of certain great minds of the seventeenth century, and first suffused throughout larger segments of society in the political changes of the eighteenth century. This is the legacy of the Enlightenment, the simple, profound, unquestioned conviction that Reason, Freedom, and Progress naturally imply one another, a conviction which we have ever since imbibed as if with our mother's milk.

This is so even if we have come to find the milk sour, and demanded a more varied diet, as some European intellectuals did almost from the start. European modernity was never without critics from within its own house. The impression that a universal naïve acceptance of Enlightenment rationalism dominated early modernity, to be upset only by the sophistication of the twentieth century, is the result of historical ignorance. It was always plain to anyone with eyes and mind that modernity meant the exchange of one kind of life for another, hence a very real loss: community, tradition, religion, familiar political authority, customs and manners were all at the very least to be transformed, if not utterly displaced. This sense of loss was reflected by some of the greatest thinkers of the eighteenth and nineteenth centuries.

In our brief selection, just as Descartes, Condorcet, and Kant are formulating and celebrating the new rationality, Rousseau and Burke are warning against it. Then in the nineteenth century, some of the most powerful criticisms of modern life will be made by Hegel, Marx, and Nietzsche. But however much they criticize modernity in some respects, they are entangled in it in others. Such is forever the fate of the critics of modernity, who oppose a force so encompassing that even its enemies must borrow its power to fight against it.

chapter one

Meditations on First Philosophy
René Descartes

Frenchman René Descartes (1596–1650) is often considered the father of modern philosophy. Scientist, mathematician, and philosopher, he recognized the problems raised for traditional Christian thought by the scientific revolution of his century. Spending much of his productive life in Holland, he sought an absolutely certain foundation from which he could prove the existence of God, the proper method of science, and the existence of the material world, thereby harmonizing theology and the new science. His aptly named *Meditations on First Philosophy* (1641) is virtually a personal diary tracing his journey from the despair of doubt to the peace of certainty. In the following selection, he begins his *Meditations* by attempting to doubt all his beliefs in order to discover whether any are indubitable. He famously found his indubitable starting point in consciousness, the individual human mind's certainty of its own existence in absolute distinction from matter and from all other minds. The effect was to shift subjectivity to the center of philosophy.

Meditation I

Of the things which may be brought within the sphere of the doubtful.
It is now some years since I detected how many were the false beliefs that I had from my earliest youth admitted as true, and how doubtful was everything I had since constructed on this basis; and from that time I was convinced that I must once for all seriously undertake to rid myself of all the opinions which I had formerly accepted, and commence to build anew from the foundation, if I wanted to establish any firm and permanent structure in the sciences. But as this enterprise appeared to be a very great one, I waited until I had attained an age so mature that I could not hope that at any later date I should be better fitted to execute my design. This reason caused me to delay so long that I should feel that I was doing wrong

René Descartes, *Meditations on First Philosophy* (1641), trans. Elizabeth Haldane and G.R.T.Ross, in *The Philosophical Works of Descartes*, vol. I (Cambridge: Cambridge University Press, 1975), Meditations One and Two, pp. 144–57.

were I to occupy in deliberation the time that yet remains to me for action. To-day, then, since very opportunely for the plan I have in view I have delivered my mind from every care [and am happily agitated by no passions][i] and since I have procured for myself an assured leisure in a peaceable retirement, I shall at last seriously and freely address myself to the general upheaval of all my former opinions.

Now for this object it is not necessary that I should show that all of these are false – I shall perhaps never arrive at this end. But inasmuch as reason already persuades me that I ought no less carefully to withhold my assent from matters which are not entirely certain and indubitable than from those which appear to me manifestly to be false, if I am able to find in each one some reason to doubt, this will suffice to justify my rejecting the whole. And for that end it will not be requisite that I should examine each in particular, which would be an endless undertaking; for owing to the fact that the destruction of the foundations of necessity brings with it the downfall of the rest of the edifice, I shall only in the first place attack those principles upon which all my former opinions rested.

All that up to the present time I have accepted as most true and certain I have learned either from the senses or through the senses; but it is sometimes proved to me that these senses are deceptive, and it is wiser not to trust entirely to any thing by which we have once been deceived.

But it may be that although the senses sometimes deceive us concerning things which are hardly perceptible, or very far away, there are yet many others to be met with as to which we cannot reasonably have any doubt, although we recognise them by their means. For example, there is the fact that I am here, seated by the fire, attired in a dressing gown, having this paper in my hands and other similar matters. And how could I deny that these hands and this body are mine, were it not perhaps that I compare myself to certain persons, devoid of sense, whose cerebella are so troubled and clouded by the violent vapours of black bile, that they constantly assure us that they think they are kings when they are really quite poor, or that they are clothed in purple when they are really without covering, or who imagine that they have an earthenware head or are nothing but pumpkins or are made of glass. But they are mad, and I should not be any the less insane were I to follow examples so extravagant.

At the same time I must remember that I am a man, and that consequently I am in the habit of sleeping, and in my dreams representing to myself the same things or sometimes even less probable things, than do those who are insane in their waking moments. How often has it happened

---

[i] Passages in square brackets are from a French translation of the *Meditations* which Descartes himself corrected, and which the translators from the Latin text have included for the sake of their greater clarity.

to me that in the night I dreamt that I found myself in this particular place, that I was dressed and seated near the fire, whilst in reality I was lying undressed in bed! At this moment it does indeed seem to me that it is with eyes awake that I am looking at this paper; that this head which I move is not asleep, that it is deliberately and of set purpose that I extend my hand and perceive it; what happens in sleep does not appear so clear nor so distinct as does all this. But in thinking over this I remind myself that on many occasions I have in sleep been deceived by similar illusions, and in dwelling carefully on this reflection I see so manifestly that there are no certain indications by which we may clearly distinguish wakefulness from sleep that I am lost in astonishment. And my astonishment is such that it is almost capable of persuading me that I now dream.

Now let us assume that we are asleep and that all these particulars, e.g. that we open our eyes, shake our head, extend our hands, and so on, are but false delusions; and let us reflect that possibly neither our hands nor our whole body are such as they appear to us to be. At the same time we must at least confess that the things which are represented to us in sleep are like painted representations which can only have been formed as the counterparts of something real and true, and that in this way those general things at least, i.e. eyes, a head, hands, and a whole body, are not imaginary things, but things really existent. For, as a matter of fact, painters, even when they study with the greatest skill to represent sirens and satyrs by forms the most strange and extraordinary cannot give them natures which are entirely new, but merely make a certain medley of the members of different animals; or if their imagination is extravagant enough to invent something so novel that nothing similar has ever before been seen, and that then their work represents a thing purely fictitious and absolutely false, it is certain all the same that the colours of which this is composed are necessarily real. And for the same reason, although these general things, to wit, [a body], eyes, a head, hands, and such like, may be imaginary, we are bound at the same time to confess that there are at least some other objects yet more simple and more universal, which are real and true; and of these just in the same way as with certain real colours, all these images of things which dwell in our thoughts, whether true and real or false and fantastic, are formed.

To such a class of things pertains corporeal nature in general, and its extension,[ii] the figure of extended things, their quantity or magnitude and number, as also the place in which they are, the time which measures their duration, and so on.

That is possibly why our reasoning is not unjust when we conclude from this that Physics, Astronomy, Medicine and all other sciences which have

---

[ii] "Extension" means the space the thing takes up, i.e. its size or volume.

as their end the consideration of composite things, are very dubious and uncertain; but that Arithmetic, Geometry and other sciences of that kind which only treat of things that are very simple and very general, without taking great trouble to ascertain whether they are actually existent or not, contain some measure of certainty and an element of the indubitable. For whether I am awake or asleep, two and three together always form five, and the square can never have more than four sides, and it does not seem possible that truths so clear and apparent can be suspected of any falsity [or uncertainty].

Nevertheless I have long had fixed in my mind the belief that an all-powerful God existed by whom I have been created such as I am. But how do I know that He has not brought it to pass that there is no earth, no heaven, no extended body, no magnitude, no place, and that nevertheless [I possess the perceptions of all these things and that] they seem to me to exist just exactly as I now see them? And, besides, as I sometimes imagine that others deceive themselves in the things which they think they know best, how do I know that I am not deceived every time that I add two and three, or count the sides of a square, or judge of things yet simpler, if anything simpler can be imagined? But possibly God has not desired that I should be thus deceived, for He is said to be supremely good. If, however, it is contrary to His goodness to have made me such that I constantly deceive myself, it would also appear to be contrary to His goodness to permit me to be sometimes deceived, and nevertheless I cannot doubt that He does permit this.

There may indeed be those who would prefer to deny the existence of a God so powerful, rather than believe that all other things are uncertain. But let us not oppose them for the present, and grant that all that is here said of a God is a fable; nevertheless in whatever way they suppose that I have arrived at the state of being that I have reached – whether they attribute it to fate or to accident, or make out that it is by a continual succession of antecedents, or by some other method – since to err and deceive oneself is a defect, it is clear that the greater will be the probability of my being so imperfect as to deceive myself ever, as is the Author to whom they assign my origin the less powerful. To these reasons I have certainly nothing to reply, but at the end I feel constrained to confess that there is nothing in all that I formerly believed to be true, of which I cannot in some measure doubt, and that not merely through want of thought or through levity, but for reasons which are very powerful and maturely considered so that henceforth I ought not the less carefully to refrain from giving credence to these opinions than to that which is manifestly false, if I desire to arrive at any certainty [in the sciences].

But it is not sufficient to have made these remarks, we must also be careful to keep them in mind. For these ancient and commonly held opinions still revert frequently to my mind, long and familiar custom having given them the right to occupy my mind against my inclination and rendered them almost masters of my belief; nor will I ever lose the habit of deferring to them or of placing my confidence in them, so long as I consider them as they really are, i.e. opinions in some measure doubtful, as I have just shown, and at the same time highly probable, so that there is much more reason to believe in than to deny them. That is why I consider that I shall not be acting amiss, if, taking of set purpose a contrary belief, I allow myself to be deceived, and for a certain time pretend that all these opinions are entirely false and imaginary, until at last, having thus balanced my former prejudices with my latter [so that they cannot divert my opinions more to one side than to the other], my judgment will no longer be dominated by bad usage or turned away from the right knowledge of the truth. For I am assured that there can be neither peril nor error in this course, and that I cannot at present yield too much to distrust, since I am not considering the question of action, but only of knowledge.

I shall then suppose, not that God who is supremely good and the fountain of truth, but some evil genius not less powerful than deceitful, has employed his whole energies in deceiving me; I shall consider that the heavens, the earth, colours, figures, sound, and all other external things are nought but the illusions and dreams of which this genius has availed himself in order to lay traps for my credulity; I shall consider myself as having no hands, no eyes, no flesh, no blood, nor any senses, yet falsely believing myself to possess all these things; I shall remain obstinately attached to this idea, and if by this means it is not in my power to arrive at the knowledge of any truth, I may at least do what is in my power [i.e. suspend my judgment], and with firm purpose avoid giving credence to any false thing, or being imposed upon by this arch deceiver, however powerful and deceptive he may be. But this task is a laborious one, and insensibly a certain lassitude leads me into the course of my ordinary life. And just as a captive who in sleep enjoys an imaginary liberty, when he begins to suspect that his liberty is but a dream, fears to awaken, and conspires with these agreeable illusions that the deception may be prolonged, so insensibly of my own accord I fall back into my former opinions, and I dread awakening from this slumber, lest the laborious wakefulness which would follow the tranquillity of this repose should have to be spent not in daylight, but in the excessive darkness of the difficulties which have just been discussed.

Meditation II

Of the Nature of the Human Mind; and that it is more easily known than the Body.

33

The Meditation of yesterday filled my mind with so many doubts that it is no longer in my power to forget them. And yet I do not see in what manner I can resolve them; and, just as if I had all of a sudden fallen into very deep water, I am so disconcerted that I can neither make certain of setting my feet on the bottom, nor can I swim and so support myself on the surface. I shall nevertheless make an effort and follow anew the same path as that on which I yesterday entered, i.e. I shall proceed by setting aside all that in which the least doubt could be supposed to exist, just as if I had discovered that it was absolutely false; and I shall ever follow in this road until I have met with something which is certain, or at least, if I can do nothing else, until I have learned for certain that there is nothing in the world that is certain. Archimedes, in order that he might draw the terrestrial globe out of its place, and transport it elsewhere, demanded only that one point should be fixed and immoveable; in the same way I shall have the right to conceive high hopes if I am happy enough to discover one thing only which is certain and indubitable.[iii]

I suppose, then, that all the things that I see are false; I persuade myself that nothing has ever existed of all that my fallacious memory represents to me. I consider that I possess no senses; I imagine that body, figure, extension, movement and place are but the fictions of my mind. What, then, can be esteemed as true? Perhaps nothing at all, unless that there is nothing in the world that is certain.

But how can I know there is not something different from those things that I have just considered, of which one cannot have the slightest doubt? Is there not some God, or some other being by whatever name we call it, who puts these reflections into my mind? That is not necessary, for is it not possible that I am capable of producing them myself? I myself, am I not at least something? But I have already denied that I had senses and body. Yet I hesitate, for what follows from that? Am I so dependent on body and senses that I cannot exist without these? But I was persuaded that there was nothing in all the world, that there was no heaven, no earth, that there were no minds, nor any bodies: was I not then likewise persuaded that I did not exist? Not at all; of a surety I myself did exist since I persuaded myself of something [or merely because I thought of something]. But there is some deceiver or other, very powerful and very cunning, who ever employs his ingenuity in deceiving me. Then without doubt I exist also if he deceives me, and let him deceive me as much as he will, he can never cause me to be nothing so long as I think that I am something. So that after having reflected well and carefully examined

iii Greek mathematician Archimedes (287–212 BC) boasted that with a lever long enough and the right place to stand, he could move the Earth.

all things, we must come to the definite conclusion that this proposition: I am, I exist, is necessarily true each time that I pronounce it, or that I mentally conceive it.

But I do not yet know clearly enough what I am, I who am certain that I am; and hence I must be careful to see that I do not imprudently take some other object in place of myself, and thus that I do not go astray in respect of this knowledge that I hold to be the most certain and most evident of all that I have formerly learned. That is why I shall now consider anew what I believed myself to be before I embarked upon these last reflections; and of my former opinions I shall withdraw all that might even in a small degree be invalidated by the reasons which I have just brought forward, in order that there may be nothing at all left beyond what is absolutely certain and indubitable.

What then did I formerly believe myself to be? Undoubtedly I believed myself to be a man. But what is a man? Shall I say a reasonable animal? Certainly not; for then I should have to inquire what an animal is, and what is reasonable; and thus from a single question I should insensibly fall into an infinitude of others more difficult; and I should not wish to waste the little time and leisure remaining to me in trying to unravel subtleties like these. But I shall rather stop here to consider the thoughts which of themselves spring up in my mind, and which were not inspired by anything beyond my own nature alone when I applied myself to the consideration of my being. In the first place, then, I considered myself as having a face, hands, arms, and all that system of members composed of bones and flesh as seen in a corpse which I designated by the name of body. In addition to this I considered that I was nourished, that I walked, that I felt, and that I thought, and I referred all these actions to the soul: but I did not stop to consider what the soul was, or if I did stop, I imagined that it was something extremely rare and subtle like a wind, a flame, or an ether, which was spread throughout my grosser parts. As to body I had no manner of doubt about its nature, but thought I had a very clear knowledge of it; and if I had desired to explain it according to the notions that I had then formed of it, I should have described it thus: By the body I understand all that which can be defined by a certain figure: something which can be confined in a certain place, and which can fill a given space in such a way that every other body will be excluded from it; which can be perceived either by touch, or by sight, or by hearing, or by taste, or by smell: which can be moved in many ways not, in truth, by itself, but by something which is foreign to it, by which it is touched [and from which it receives impressions]: for to have the power of self-movement, as also of feeling or of thinking, I did not consider to appertain to the nature of body: on the contrary, I was rather astonished to find that faculties similar to them existed in some bodies.

35

But what am I, now that I suppose that there is a certain genius which is extremely powerful, and, if I may say so, malicious, who employs all his powers in deceiving me? Can I affirm that I possess the least of all those things which I have just said pertain to the nature of body? I pause to consider, I revolve all these things in my mind, and I find none of which I can say that it pertains to me. It would be tedious to stop to enumerate them. Let us pass to the attributes of soul and see if there is any one which is in me? What of nutrition or walking [the first mentioned]? But if it is so that I have no body it is also true that I can neither walk nor take nourishment. Another attribute is sensation. But one cannot feel without body, and besides I have thought I perceived many things during sleep that I recognised in my waking moments as not having been experienced at all. What of thinking? I find here that thought is an attribute that belongs to me; it alone cannot be separated from me. I am, I exist, that is certain. But how often? Just when I think; for it might possibly be the case if I ceased entirely to think, that I should likewise cease altogether to exist. I do not now admit anything which is not necessarily true: to speak accurately I am not more than a thing which thinks, that is to say a mind or a soul, or an understanding, or a reason, which are terms whose significance was formerly unknown to me. I am, however, a real thing and really exist; but what thing? I have answered: a thing which thinks.

And what more? I shall exercise my imagination [in order to see if I am not something more]. I am not a collection of members which we call the human body: I am not a subtle air distributed through these members, I am not a wind, a fire, a vapour, a breath, nor anything at all which I can imagine or conceive; because I have assumed that all these were nothing. Without changing that supposition I find that I only leave myself certain of the fact that I am somewhat. But perhaps it is true that these same things which I supposed were non-existent because they are unknown to me, are really not different from the self which I know. I am not sure about this, I shall not dispute about it now; I can only give judgment on things that are known to me. I know that I exist, and I inquire what I am, I whom I know to exist. But it is very certain that the knowledge of my existence taken in its precise significance does not depend on things whose existence is not yet known to me; consequently it does not depend on those which I can feign in imagination. And indeed the very term *feign* in imagination proves to me my error, for I really do this if I image myself a something, since to imagine is nothing else than to contemplate the figure or image of a corporeal thing. But I already know for certain that I am, and that it may be that all these images, and, speaking generally, all things that relate to the nature of body are nothing but dreams [and chimeras]. For this reason I see clearly that I have as little reason to say, 'I shall stimulate my imagination in order to know more distinctly what I am,' than if I were to say, 'I am now awake, and I perceive somewhat that is real and true: but because I do not yet perceive it distinctly enough, I shall go to sleep of express purpose, so that my dreams may represent the perception with greatest truth and evidence.' And, thus, I know for certain that nothing of all that I can understand by means of my imagination belongs to this knowledge which I have of myself, and that it is necessary to recall the mind from this mode of thought with the utmost diligence in order that it may be able to know its own nature with perfect distinctness.

But what then am I? A thing which thinks. What is a thing which thinks? It is a thing which doubts, understands, conceives, affirms, denies, wills refuses, which also imagines and feels.

Certainly it is no small matter if all these things pertain to my nature. But why should they not so pertain? Am I not that being who now doubts nearly everything, who nevertheless understands certain things, who affirms that one only is true, who denies all the others, who desires to know more, is averse from being deceived, who imagines many things, sometimes indeed despite his will, and who perceives many likewise, as by the intervention of the bodily organs? Is there nothing in all this which is as true as it is certain that I exist, even though I should always sleep and though he who has given me being employed all his ingenuity in deceiving me? Is there likewise any one of these attributes which can be distinguished from my thought, or which might be said to be separated from myself? For it is so evident of itself that it is I who doubts, who understands, and who desires, that there is no reason here to add anything to explain it. And I have certainly the power of imagining likewise; for although it may happen (as I formerly supposed) that none of the things which I imagine are true, nevertheless this power of imagining does not cease to be really in use, and it forms part of my thought. Finally, I am the same who feels, that is to say, who perceives certain things, as by the organs of sense, since in truth I see light, I hear noise, I feel heat. But it will be said that these phenomena are false and that I am dreaming. Let it be so; still it is at least quite certain that it seems to me that I see light, that I hear noise and that I feel heat. That cannot be false; properly speaking it is what is in me called feeling; and used in this precise sense that is no other thing than thinking.

From this time I begin to know what I am with a little more clearness and distinction than before; but nevertheless it still seems to me, and I cannot prevent myself from thinking, that corporeal things, whose images are framed by thought, which are tested by the senses, are much more distinctly known than that obscure part of me which does not come under the imagination. Although really it is very strange to say that I know and understand more distinctly these things whose existence seems to me dubious, which are unknown to me, and which do not belong to me, than others of the truth of which I am convinced, which are known to me and which pertain to my real nature, in a word, than myself. But I see clearly how the case stands: my mind loves to wander, and cannot yet suffer itself to be retained within the just limits of truth. Very good, let us once more give it the freest rein, so that, when afterwards we seize the proper occasion for pulling up, it may the more easily be regulated and controlled.

Let us begin by considering the commonest matters, those which we believe to be the most distinctly comprehended, to wit, the bodies which we touch and see; not indeed bodies in general, for these general ideas are usually a little more confused, but let us consider one body in particular. Let us take, for example, this piece of wax: it has been taken quite freshly from the hive, and it has not yet lost the sweetness of the honey which it contains; it still retains somewhat of the odour of the flowers from which it has been culled; its colour, its figure, its size are apparent; it is hard, cold, easily handled, and if you strike it with the finger, it will emit a sound. Finally all the things which are requisite to cause us distinctly to recognise a body, are met with in it. But notice that while I speak and approach the fire what remained of the taste is exhaled, the smell evaporates, the colour alters, the figure is destroyed, the size increases, it becomes liquid, it heats, scarcely can one handle it, and when one strikes it, no sound is emitted. Does the same wax remain after this change? We must confess that it remains, none would judge otherwise. What then did I know so distinctly in this piece of wax? It could certainly be nothing of all that the senses brought to my notice, since all these things which fall under taste, smell, sight, touch, and hearing, are found to be changed, and yet the same wax remains.

Perhaps it was what I now think, viz. that this wax was not that sweetness of honey, nor that agreeable scent of flowers, nor that particular whiteness, nor that figure, nor that sound, but simply a body which a little while before appeared to me as perceptible under these forms, and which is now perceptible under others. But what, precisely, is it that I imagine when I form such conceptions? Let us attentively consider this, and, abstracting from all that does not belong to the wax, let us see what remains. Certainly nothing remains excepting a certain extended thing which is flexible and movable. But what is the meaning of flexible and movable? Is it not that I imagine that this piece of wax being round is capable of becoming square and of passing from a square to a triangular figure? No, certainly it is not that, since I imagine it admits of an infinitude of similar changes, and I nevertheless do not know how to compass the infinitude by my imagination, and consequently this conception which I have of the wax is not brought about by the faculty of imagination. What now is this extension? Is it not also unknown? For it becomes greater when the wax is melted, greater when it is boiled, and greater still when the heat increases; and I should not conceive [clearly] according to truth what wax is, if I did not think that even this piece that we are considering is capable of receiving more variations in extension than I have ever imagined. We must then grant that I could not even understand through the imagination what this piece of wax is, and that it is my mind alone which perceives it. I say this piece of wax in particular, for as to wax in general it is yet clearer. But what is this piece of wax which cannot be understood excepting by the [understanding or] mind? It is certainly the same that I see, touch, imagine, and finally it is the same which I have always believed it to be from the beginning. But what must particularly be observed is that its perception is neither an act of vision, nor of touch, nor of imagination, and has never been such although it may have appeared formerly to be so, but only an intuition of the mind, which may be imperfect and confused as it was formerly, or clear and distinct as it is at present, according as my attention is more or less directed to the elements which are found in it, and of which it is composed.

Yet in the meantime I am greatly astonished when I consider [the great feebleness of mind] and its proneness to fall [insensibly] into error; for although without giving expression to my thoughts I consider all this in my own mind, words often impede me and I am almost deceived by the terms of ordinary language. For we say that we see the same wax, if it is present, and not that we simply judge that it is the same from its having the same colour and figure. From this I should conclude that I knew the wax by means of vision and not simply by the intuition of the mind; unless by chance I remember that, when looking from a window and saying I see men who pass in the street, I really do not see them, but infer that what I see is men, just as I say that I see wax. And yet what do I see from the window but hats and coats which may cover automatic machines? Yet I judge these to be men. And similarly solely by the faculty of judgment which rests in my mind, I comprehend that which I believed I saw with my eyes.

A man who makes it his aim to raise his knowledge above the common should be ashamed to derive the occasion for doubting from the forms of speech invented by the vulgar; I prefer to pass on and consider whether I had a more evident and perfect conception of what the wax was when I first perceived it, and when I believed I knew it by means of the external senses or at least by the common sense as it is called, that is to say by the imaginative faculty, or whether my present conception is clearer now that I have most carefully examined what it is, and in what way it can be known. It would certainly be absurd to doubt as to this. For what was there in this first perception which was distinct? What was there which might not as well have been perceived by any of the animals? But when I distinguish the wax from its external forms, and when, just as if I had taken from it its vestments, I consider it quite naked, it is certain that although some error may still be found in my judgment, I can nevertheless not perceive it thus without a human mind.

But finally what shall I say of this mind, that is, of myself, for up to this point I do not admit in myself anything but mind? What then, I who seem to perceive this piece of wax so distinctly, do I not know myself, not only with much more truth and certainty, but also with much more distinctness and clearness? For if I judge that the wax is or exists from the fact that I see it, it certainly follows much more clearly that I am or that I exist myself from the fact that I see it. For it may be that what I see is not really wax, it may also be that I do not possess eyes with which to see anything; but it cannot be that when I see, or (for I no longer take account of the distinction) when I think I see, that I myself who think am nought. So if I judge that the wax exists from the fact that I touch it, the same thing will follow, to wit, that I am; and if I judge that my imagination, or some other cause, whatever it is, persuades me that the wax exists, I shall still conclude the same. And what I have here remarked of wax may be applied to all other things which are external to me [and which are met with outside of me]. And further, if the [notion or] perception of wax has seemed to me clearer and more distinct, not only after the sight or the touch, but also after many other causes have rendered it quite manifest to me, with how much more [evidence] and distinctness must it be said that I now know myself, since all the reasons which contribute to the knowledge of wax, or any other body whatever, are yet better proofs of the nature of my mind! And there are so many other things in the mind itself which may contribute to the elucidation of its nature, that those which depend on body such as these just mentioned, hardly merit being taken into account.

But finally here I am, having insensibly reverted to the point I desired, for, since it is now manifest to me that even bodies are not properly speaking known by the senses or by the faculty of imagination, but by the understanding only, and since they are not known from the fact that they are seen or touched, but only because they are understood, I see clearly that there is nothing which is easier for me to know than my mind. But because it is difficult to rid oneself so promptly of an opinion to which one was accustomed for so long, it will be well that I should halt a little at this point, so that by the length of my meditation I may more deeply imprint on my memory this new knowledge.

chapter two

"Discourse on the Sciences and the Arts"

Jean-Jacques Rousseau

Jean-Jacques Rousseau (1712–78) was virtually alone among eighteenth-century intellectuals, the first great critic of the new Enlightenment faith in science and progress. A native of his beloved Geneva, he led an emotionally complex and troubled life. Rousseau felt uncomfortable in the emerging cosmopolitan world, which he believed made genuine selfhood impossible. He established his reputation in 1750 by arguing in the essay excerpted here that modern learning does not improve, but on the contrary harms, human morals. In a later work, his *Discourse on the Origins of Inequality among Men* (1754), he revealed his concern for social equality, foreshadowing the views of Marx, and roundly condemned modern culture. He was chastised by the great Voltaire, who wrote to Rousseau: "no one has ever been so witty as you are in trying to turn us into brutes: to read your book makes one long to go on all fours. Since, however, it is now some sixty years since I gave up the practice, I feel that it is unfortunately impossible for me to resume it." Voltaire's wit to the contrary notwithstanding, Rousseau never argued for an actual return to primitive existence; rather, he sought a new egalitarian way of life that would be just as authentic in the modern context as was primitive existence in its context.

We are deceived by the appearance of right.[i]

Has the restoration of the sciences and the arts contributed to the purification of mores, or to their corruption? That is what is to be examined. Which side should I take in this question? The one, gentlemen, that is appropriate to an honest man who knows nothing and who thinks no less of himself for it.

Jean-Jacques Rousseau, Part One of *Discourse on the Sciences and the Arts*, in *The Basic Political Writings of Jean-Jacques Rousseau*, trans. Donald Cress (Indianapolis: Hackett, 1987, pp. 3–10.
[i] Horace, *On the Art of Poetry*, v. 25.

It will be difficult, I feel, to adapt what I have to say to the tribunal before which I appear. How can I dare to blame the sciences before one of Europe's most learned societies, praise ignorance in a famous Academy, and reconcile contempt for study with respect for the truly learned? I have seen these points of conflict, and they have not daunted me. I am not abusing science, I told myself; I am defending virtue before virtuous men. Integrity is even dearer to good men than erudition is to the studious. What then have I to fear? The enlightenment of the assembly that listens to me? I admit it; but this is owing to the composition of the discourse and not to the sentiment of the speaker. Fair-minded sovereigns have never hesitated to pass judgments against themselves in disputes whose outcomes are uncertain; and the position most advantageous for a just cause is to have to defend oneself against an upright and enlightened opponent who is judge in his own case.

To this motive which heartens me is joined another which determines me, namely that, having upheld, according to my natural light, the side of truth, whatever my success, there is a prize which I cannot fail to receive; I will find it within the depths of my heart.

It is a grand and beautiful sight to see man emerge somehow from nothing by his own efforts; dissipate, by the light of his reason, the shadows in which nature had enveloped him; rise above himself; soar by means of his mind into the heavenly regions; traverse, like the sun, the vast expanse of the universe with giant steps; and, what is even grander and more difficult, return to himself in order to study man and know his nature, his duties, and his end. All of these marvels have been revived in the past few generations.

Europe had relapsed into the barbarism of the first ages. A few centuries ago the peoples of that part of the world, who today live such enlightened lives, lived in a state worse than ignorance. Some nondescript scientific jargon, even more contemptible than ignorance, had usurped the name of knowledge, and posed a nearly invincible obstacle to its return. A revolution was needed to bring men back to common sense; it finally came from the least expected quarter. It was the stupid Moslem, the eternal scourge of letters, who caused them to be reborn among us. The fall of the throne of Constantinople[ii] brought into Italy the debris of ancient Greece. France in turn was enriched by these precious spoils. Soon the sciences followed letters. To the art of writing was joined the art of thinking – a sequence of events that may seem strange, but which perhaps is only too natural. And

[ii] The capital of the Byzantine (formerly the Eastern Roman) Empire fell to the Turks in 1453.

the chief advantage of commerce with the Muses began to be felt, namely, that of making men more sociable by inspiring in them the desire to please one another with works worthy of their mutual approval.

The mind has its needs, as does the body. The needs of the latter are the foundations of society; the needs of the former make it pleasant. While the government and the laws see to the safety and well-being of assembled men, the sciences, letters and the arts, less despotic and perhaps more powerful, spread garlands of flowers over the iron chains with which they are burdened, stifle in them the sense of that original liberty for which they seem to have been born, make them love their slavery, and turn them into what is called civilized peoples. Need raised up thrones; the sciences and the arts have strengthened them. Earthly powers, love talents and protect those who cultivate them![1] Civilized peoples, cultivate them! Happy slaves, you owe them that delicate and refined taste on which you pride yourselves; that sweetness of character and that urbanity in mores which make relationships among you so cordial and easy; in a word, the appearances of all the virtues without having any.

By this sort of civility, all the more agreeable as it puts on fewer airs, Athens and Rome once distinguished themselves in the much vaunted days of their magnificence and splendor. By it our century and our nation will doubtlessly surpass all times and all peoples. A philosophic tone without pedantry, manners natural yet engaging, equally removed from Teutonic rusticity as from Italian pantomine. These are the fruits of the taste acquired by good schooling and perfected in social interaction.

How sweet it would be to live among us, if outer appearances were always the likeness of the heart's dispositions, if decency were virtue, if our maxims served as our rules, if true philosophy were inseparable from the title of philosopher! But so many qualities are all too rarely found in combination, and virtue seldom goes forth in such great pomp. Expensive finery can betoken a wealthy man, and elegance a man of taste. The healthy and robust man is recognized by other signs. It is in the rustic clothing of the fieldworker and not underneath the gilding of the courtier that one will find bodily strength and vigor. Finery is no less alien to virtue, which is the strength and vigor of the soul. The good man is an athlete who enjoys competing in the nude. He is contemptuous of all those vile ornaments which would impair the use of his strength, most of which were invented merely to conceal some deformity.

Before art had fashioned our manners and taught our passions to speak an affected language, our mores were rustic but natural, and, differences in behavior heralded, at first glance, differences of character. At base, human nature was no better, but men found their safety in the ease with which they saw through each other, and that advantage, which we no longer value, spared them many vices.

43

Today, when more subtle inquiries and a more refined taste have reduced the art of pleasing to established rules, a vile and deceitful uniformity reigns in our mores, and all minds seem to have been cast in the same mold. Without ceasing, politeness makes demands, propriety gives orders; without ceasing, common customs are followed, never one's own lights. One no longer dares to seem what one really is; and in this perpetual constraint, the men who make up this herd we call society will, if placed in the same circumstances, do all the same things unless stronger motives deter them. Thus no one will ever really know those with whom he is dealing. Hence in order to know one's friend, it would be necessary to wait for critical occasions, that is, to wait until it is too late, since it is for these very occasions that it would have been essential to know him.

What a retinue of vices must attend this incertitude! No more sincere friendships, no more real esteem, no more well-founded confidence. Suspicions, offenses, fears, coldness, reserve, hatred, betrayal will unceasingly hide under that uniform and deceitful veil of politeness, under that much vaunted urbanity that we owe to the enlightenment of our century. The name of the master of the universe will no longer be profaned with oaths; rather it will be insulted with blasphemies without our scrupulous ears being offended by them. No one will boast of his own merit, but will disparage that of others. No one will crudely wrong his enemy, but will skillfully slander him. National hatreds will die out, but so will love of country. Scorned ignorance will be replaced by a dangerous Pyrrhonism.[iii] Some excesses will be forbidden, some vices held in dishonor, but others will be adorned with the name of virtues. One must either have them or affect them. Let those who wish extoll the sobriety of the wise men of the present. For my part, I see in it merely a refinement of intemperance as unworthy of my praise as their artful simplicity.[2]

Such is the purity that our mores have acquired. Thus have we become decent men. It is for letters, the sciences, and the arts to claim their part in so wholesome an achievement. I will add but one thought: an inhabitant of some distant lands who sought to form an idea of European mores on the basis of the state of the sciences among us, the perfection of our arts, the seemliness of our theatrical performances, the civilized quality of our manners, the affability of our speech, our perpetual displays of goodwill, and that tumultuous competition of men of every age and circumstance who, from morning to night, seem intent on being obliging to one another; that foreigner, I say, would guess our mores to be exactly the opposite of what they are.

Where there is no effect, there is no cause to seek out. But here the effect is certain, the depravation real, and our souls have become corrupted in

---

[iii] An ancient school of skeptical philosophers.

proportion as our sciences and our arts have advanced toward perfection. Will it be said that this is a misfortune peculiar to our age? No, gentlemen, the evils caused by our vain curiosity are as old as the world. The daily rise and fall of the ocean's waters have not been more unvaryingly subjected to the star which provides us with light during the night, than has the fate of mores and integrity been to the progress of the sciences and the arts. Virtue has been seen taking flight in proportion as their light rose on our horizon, and the same phenomenon has been observed in all times and in all places.

Consider Egypt, that first school of the universe, that climate so fertile beneath a brazen sky, that famous country from which Sesostris[iv] departed long ago to conquer the world. She became the mother of philosophy and the fine arts, and soon thereafter was conquered by Cambyses,[v] then by Greeks, Romans, Arabs, and finally Turks.

Consider Greece, formerly populated by heroes who twice conquered Asia, once at Troy and once on their own home ground. Nascent letters had not yet brought corruption into the hearts of her inhabitants; but the progress of the arts, the dissolution of mores and the Macedonian's yoke followed closely upon one another; and Greece, ever learned, ever voluptuous, and ever the slave, experienced nothing in her revolutions but changes of masters. All the eloquence of Demosthenes could never revive a body which luxury and the arts had enervated.

It is at the time of the likes of Ennius and Terence[vi] that Rome, founded by a shepherd and made famous by fieldworkers, began to degenerate. But after the likes of Ovid, Catullus, Martial,[vii] and that crowd of obscene writers whose names alone offend modesty, Rome, formerly the temple of virtue, became the theater of crime, the disgrace of nations, and the plaything of barbarians. Finally, that capital of the world falls under the yoke which she had imposed on so many peoples, and the day of her fall was the eve of the day when one of her citizens was given the title of Arbiter of Good Taste.[viii]

What shall I say about that capital of the Eastern Empire, which, by virtue of its location, seemed destined to be the capital of the entire world, that refuge of the sciences and the arts banished from the rest of Europe – more perhaps out of wisdom than barbarism. All that is most shameful about debauchery and corruption; blackest in betrayals, assassinations, and

---

iv A legendary pharoah.

v King of Persia in 6th century BC.

vi Quintus Ennius (239–c. 170 BC) was the father of Roman poetry, and Publius Terentius Afer (c. 190–c. 159 BC) was a Roman playwright.

vii Publius Ovidus Naso (93 BC–18AD) was one of the greatest Roman writers. Caius Valerius Catullus (c. 84–c. 54 BC) was a famous Roman lyric poet. Marcus Valerius Martialis (c. 40–c. 104 AD) was a Roman satirist.

viii Tacitus claims that the Roman Emperor Nero made the idler Petronius (d. 66 AD) "Arbiter of Good Taste."

45

poisons; most atrocious in the coexistence of every sort of crime: that is what constitutes the fabric of the history of Constantinople. That is the pure source whence radiates to us the enlightenment on which our century prides itself.

But why seek in remote times proofs of a truth for which we have existing evidence before our eyes? In Asia there is an immense country where acknowledgement in the field of letters leads to the highest offices of the state. If the sciences purified mores, if they taught men to shed their blood for their country, if they enlivened their courage, the peoples of China should be wise, free and invincible. But if there is not a single vice that does not have mastery over them; not a single crime that is unfamiliar to them; if neither the enlightenment of the ministers, nor the alleged wisdom of the laws, nor the multitude of the inhabitants of that vast empire have been able to shield her from the yoke of the ignorant and coarse Tartar, what purpose has all her learned men served? What benefit has been derived from the honors bestowed upon them? Could it be to be peopled by slaves and wicked men?

Contrast these scenes with that of the mores of the small number of peoples who, protected against this contagion of vain knowledge, have by their virtues brought about their own happiness and the model for other nations. Such were the first Persians, a singular nation in which virtue was learned just as science is among us, which subjugated Asia so easily, and which alone has enjoyed the distinction of having the history of its institutions taken for a philosophical novel.[ix] Such were the Scythians, about whom we have been left such magnificent praises. Such were the Germans, whose simplicity, innocence, and virtues a pen – weary of tracing the crimes and atrocities of an educated, opulent and voluptuous people – found relief in depicting. Such had been Rome herself in the times of her poverty and ignorance. Such, finally, has that rustic nation shown herself to this day – so vaunted for her courage which adversity could not overthrow, and for her faithfulness which example could not corrupt.[3]

It is not out of stupidity that these people have preferred other forms of exercise to those of the mind. They were not unaware of the fact that in other lands idle men spent their lives debating about the sovereign good, about vice and about virtue; and that arrogant reasoners, bestowing on themselves the highest praises, grouped other peoples under the contemptuous name of barbarians. However, they considered their mores and learned to disdain their teaching.[4]

Could I forget that it was in the very bosom of Greece that there was seen to arise that city as famous for her happy ignorance as for the wisdom of her laws, that republic of demi-gods rather than men, so superior to

---

[ix] Probably Xenophon's (430–354 BC) *Education of Cyrus*.

humanity did their virtues seem? O Sparta! Eternal shame to a vain doctrine! While the vices, led by the fine arts, intruded themselves together into Athens, while a tyrant there gathered so carefully the works of the prince of poets,[x] you drove out from your walls the arts and artists, the sciences and scientists.

The event confirmed this difference. Athens became the abode of civility and good taste, the country of orators and philosophy. The elegance of her buildings paralleled that of the language. Marble and canvas, animated by the hands of the most capable masters, were to be seen everywhere. From Athens came those astonishing works that will serve as models in every corrupt age. The picture of Lacedaemon is less brilliant. "There," said the other peoples, "men are born virtuous, and the very air of the country seems to inspire virtue." Nothing of her inhabitants is left to us except the memory of their heroic actions. Are such monuments worth less to us than the curious marbles that Athens has left us?

Some wise men, it is true, had resisted the general torrent and protected themselves from vice in the abode of the Muses. But listen to the judgment that the first and unhappiest of them made of the learned men and artists of his time.

"I have," he says, "examined the poets, and I view them as people whose talent makes an impression on them and on others who claim to be wise, who are taken to be such, and who are nothing of the sort.

"From poets," continues Socrates, "I moved on to artists. No one knew less about the arts than I; no one was more convinced that artists possessed some especially fine secrets. Still, I perceived that their condition is no better than that of the poets, and that they are both laboring under the same prejudice. Because the most skillful among them excel in their specialty, they view themselves as the wisest of men. To my way of thinking, this presumption has completely tarnished their knowledge. From this it follows that, as I put myself in the place of the oracle and ask myself whether I would prefer to be what I am or what they are, to know what they have learned or to know that I know nothing, I answered myself and God: I want to remain what I am.

"We do not know – neither the sophists, nor the poets, nor the orators, nor the artists, nor I – what is the true, the good, and the beautiful. But there is this difference between us: that although these people know nothing, they all believe they know something. I, however, if I know nothing, at least am not in doubt about it. Thus all that superiority in wisdom accorded me by the oracle, reduces to being convinced that I am ignorant of what I do not know."

---

[x] Pisistratus (c. 605–527 BC) allegedly directed the collection of Homer's works.

Here then is the wisest of men in the judgment of the gods, and the most learned of Athenians in the opinion of all Greece, Socrates, speaking in praise of ignorance! Does anyone believe that, were he to be reborn among us, our learned men and our artists would make him change his mind? No, gentlemen, this just man would continue to hold our vain sciences in contempt. He would not aid in the enlargement of that mass of books which inundate us from every quarter, and the only precept he would leave is the one left to his disciples and to our descendants: the example and the memory of his virtue. Thus is it noble to teach men!

Socrates had begun in Athens, Cato[xi] the Elder continued in Rome to rail against those artful and subtle Greeks who seduced the virtue and enervated the courage of his fellow citizens. But the sciences, the arts, and dialectic prevailed once again. Rome was filled with philosophers and orators; military discipline was neglected, agriculture scorned, sects embraced, and the homeland forgotten. The sacred names of liberty, disinterestedness, obedience to the laws were replaced by the names of Epicurus, Zeno, Arcesilaus.[xii] "Ever since learned men have begun to appear in our midst," their own philosophers said, "good men have vanished." Until then the Romans had been content to practice virtue; all was lost when they began to study it.

O Fabricius![xiii] What would your great soul have thought, if, had it been your misfortune to be returned to life, you had seen the pompous countenance of that Rome saved by your arm and honored more by your good name than by all her conquests? "Gods!" you would have said, "what has become of those thatched roofs and those rustic hearths where moderation and virtue once dwelt? What fatal splendor has followed upon Roman simplicity? What is this strange speech? What are these effeminate mores? What is the meaning of these statues, these paintings, these buildings? Fools, what have you done? You, the masters of nations, have you made yourselves the slaves of the frivolous men you conquered? Do rhetoricians govern you? Was it to enrich architects, painters, sculptors, and actors that you soaked Greece and Asia with your blood? Are the spoils of Carthage the prey of a flute player? Romans make haste to tear down these amphitheaters; shatter these marbles; burn these paintings; drive out these slaves who subjugate you and whose fatal arts corrupt you. Let others achieve notoriety by vain talents; the only talent worthy of Rome is that of conquering the world and making virtue reign in it. When Cineas[xiv] took

---

[xi] Marcus Porcius Cato "the Elder" (243–149 BC) was a highly respected Roman general and statesman, famous for simplicity of virtue.

[xii] Epicurus (341–270 BC), founder of Epicureanism; Zeno of Citium (336–264 BC), founder of Stoicism; and Arcesilaus (316–241 BC), a famous Skeptic.

[xiii] Caius Fabricius Luscinus (d. 250 BC) was a great Roman general.

[xiv] An ambassador of the Thessalian king Pyrrhus.

our Senate for an assembly of kings, he was dazzled neither by vain pomp nor by studied elegance. There he did not hear that frivolous eloquence, the focus of study and delight of futile men. What then did Cineas see that was so majestic? O citizens! He saw a sight which neither your riches nor all your arts could ever display; the most beautiful sight ever to have appeared under the heavens, the assembly of two hundred virtuous men, worthy of commanding in Rome and of governing the earth."

But let us leap over the distance of place and time and see what has happened in our countries and before our eyes; or rather, let us set aside odious pictures that offend our delicate sensibilities, and spare ourselves the trouble of repeating the same things under different names. It was not in vain that I summoned the shade of Fabricius; and what did I make that great man say that I could not have placed in the mouth of Louis XII or Henry IV? Among us, it is true, Socrates would not have drunk the hemlock; but he would have drunk from a cup more bitter still: the insulting ridicule and scorn that are a hundred times worse than death.

That is how luxury, dissolution and slavery have at all times been the punishment for the arrogant efforts that we have made to leave the happy ignorance where eternal wisdom had placed us. The heavy veil with which she had covered all her operations seemed to give us sufficient warning that she had not destined us for vain inquiries. But is there even one of her lessons from which we have learned to profit, or which we have neglected with impunity? Peoples, know then once and for all that nature wanted to protect you from science just as a mother wrests a dangerous weapon from the hands of her child; that all the secrets she hides from you are so many evils from which she is protecting you, and that the difficulty you find in teaching yourselves is not the least of her kindnesses. Men are perverse; they would be even worse if they had had the misfortune of being born learned.

How humiliating are these reflections for humanity! How mortified our pride must be! What! Could probity be the daughter of ignorance? Science and virtue incompatible? What consequences might not be drawn from these prejudices? But to reconcile these apparent points of conflict, one need merely examine at close range the vanity and the emptiness of those proud titles which overpower us and which we so gratuitously bestow upon human knowledge. Let us then consider the sciences and the arts in themselves. Let us see what must result from their progress; and let us no longer hesitate to be in agreement on all the points where our reasoning will be found to be in accord with historical inductions.

49

Notes

1 Princes always view with pleasure the spread, among their subjects, of the taste for pleasant arts and luxuries not resulting in the exporting of money. For, in addition to nurturing in them that pettiness of soul so appropriate to servitude, they know very well that all the needs the populace imposes on itself are so many chains which burden it. Alexander, wishing to keep the Ichthyophagi in a state of dependency, forced them to renounce fishing and to eat foods common to other peoples. And the savages of America who go totally naked and who live off the fruit of their hunting have never been tamed. Indeed, what yoke could be imposed upon men who need nothing?

2 "I love," says Montaigne, "to debate and discuss, but only with a few men and for my own sake. For I find it an especially unworthy profession for a man of honor to serve as a spectacle to the great and shamelessly parade one's mind and one's prattling." It is the profession of all our wits, save one.

3 I dare not speak of those happy nations which do not know even by name the vices that we have so much trouble repressing, those savages in America whose simple and natural polity Montaigne unhesitatingly prefers not only to Plato's *Laws* but even to everything philosophy could ever imagine as most perfect for the government of peoples. He cites a number of examples that are striking for someone who would know how to admire them. "What!" he says, "why they don't wear pants!" Montaigne, "Of Cannibals," *Essays*, Book I, chapter 31.

4 Will someone honestly tell me what opinion the Athenians themselves must have held regarding eloquence, when they were so fastidious about banning it from that upright tribunal whose judgments the gods themselves did not appeal? What did the Romans think of medicine, when they banished it from their republic? And when a remnant of humanity led the Spanish to forbid their lawyers to enter America, what idea must they have had of jurisprudence? Could it not be said that they believed that by this single act they had made reparation for all the evils they had brought upon those unfortunate Indians?

chapter three

"An Answer to the Question: What is Enlightenment?"

Immanuel Kant

> Immanuel Kant (1724–1804), perhaps the greatest modern philosopher, was deeply inspired by Rousseau. What Kant took from Rousseau was not the latter's critique of modernity, but his notion of freedom as autonomy or self-legislation, the belief that human dignity requires humans to make the laws that they themselves must obey. Kant made reason the center of his conception of human being, and reason's self-legislation the basis for his philosophy. Characteristic of the German Enlightenment (the *Aufklärung*), he recognized the threat that the modern scientific view of the world posed to morality and religion. But this led him to reformulate and limit science in a profound way, not reject it. In the famous 1784 essay that follows he defines the meaning of the Enlightenment with the Horatian motto, *Sapere Aude*, "Think for yourself."

Enlightenment is man's emergence from his self-incurred immaturity. Immaturity is the inability to use one's own understanding without the guidance of another. This immaturity is *self-incurred* if its cause is not lack of understanding, but lack of resolution and courage to use it without the guidance of another. The motto of enlightenment is therefore: *Sapere aude!*[i] Have courage to use your *own* understanding!

Laziness and cowardice are the reasons why such a large proportion of men, even when nature has long emancipated them from alien guidance (*naturaliter maiorennes*),[ii] nevertheless gladly remain immature for life. For the same reasons, it is all too easy for others to set themselves up as their guardians. It is so convenient to be immature! If I have a book to have

---

Immanuel Kant, "An Answer to the Question: What is Enlightenment?" in *Kant's Political Writings*, trans. H. B. Nisbet, ed. Hans Reiss (Cambridge: Cambridge University Press 1970), pp. 54–60.

[i] From Horace, literally, "Dare to be wise."
[ii] "Those who have come of age by virtue of nature."

understanding in place of me, a spiritual adviser to have a conscience for me, a doctor to judge my diet for me, and so on, I need not make any efforts at all. I need not think, so long as I can pay; others will soon enough take the tiresome job over for me. The guardians who have kindly taken upon themselves the work of supervision will soon see to it that by far the largest part of mankind (including the entire fair sex) should consider the step forward to maturity not only as difficult but also as highly dangerous. Having first infatuated their domesticated animals, and carefully prevented the docile creatures from daring to take a single step without the leading-strings to which they are tied, they next show them the danger which threatens them if they try to walk unaided. Now this danger is not in fact so very great, for they would certainly learn to walk eventually after a few falls. But an example of this kind is intimidating, and usually frightens them off from further attempts.

Thus it is difficult for each separate individual to work his way out of the immaturity which has become almost second nature to him. He has even grown fond of it and is really incapable for the time being of using his own understanding, because he was never allowed to make the attempt. Dogmas and formulas, those mechanical instruments for rational use (or rather misuse) of his natural endowments, are the ball and chain of his permanent immaturity. And if anyone did throw them off, he would still be uncertain about jumping over even the narrowest of trenches, for he would be unaccustomed to free movement of this kind. Thus only a few, by cultivating their own minds, have succeeded in freeing themselves from immaturity and in continuing boldly on their way.

There is more chance of an entire public enlightening itself. This is indeed almost inevitable, if only the public concerned is left in freedom. For there will always be a few who think for themselves, even among those appointed as guardians of the common mass. Such guardians, once they have themselves thrown off the yoke of immaturity, will disseminate the spirit of rational respect for personal value and for the duty of all men to think for themselves. The remarkable thing about this is that if the public, which was previously put under this yoke by the guardians, is suitably stirred up by some of the latter who are incapable of enlighten-ment, it may subsequently compel the guardians themselves to remain under the yoke. For it is very harmful to propagate prejudices, because they finally avenge themselves on the very people who first encouraged them (or whose predecessors did so). Thus a public can only achieve enlightenment slowly. A revolution may well put an end to autocratic despotism and to rapacious or power-seeking oppression, but it will never produce a true reform in ways of thinking. Instead, new prejudices, like the ones they replaced, will serve as a leash to control the great unthinking mass.

52

For enlightenment of this kind, all that is needed is *freedom*. And the freedom in question is the most innocuous form of all–freedom to make *public use* of one's reason in all matters. But I hear on all sides the cry: *Don't argue!* The officer says: Don't argue, get on parade! The tax-official: Don't argue, pay! The clergyman: Don't argue, believe! (Only one ruler in the world says: *Argue* as much as you like and about whatever you like, *but obey!*)[iii] All this means restrictions on freedom everywhere. But which sort of restriction prevents enlightenment, and which, instead of hindering it, can actually promote it? I reply: The *public* use of man's reason must always be free, and it alone can bring about enlightenment among men; the *private use* of reason may quite often be very narrowly restricted, however, without undue hindrance to the progress of enlightenment. But by the public use of one's own reason I mean that use which anyone may make of it *as a man of learning* addressing the entire *reading public*. What I term the private use of reason is that which a person may make of it in a particular *civil* post or office with which he is entrusted.

Now in some affairs which affect the interests of the commonwealth, we require a certain mechanism whereby some members of the commonwealth must behave purely passively, so that they may, by an artificial common agreement, be employed by the government for public ends (or at least deterred from vitiating them). It is, of course, impermissible to argue in such cases; obedience is imperative. But in so far as this or that individual who acts as part of the machine also considers himself as a member of a complete commonwealth or even of cosmopolitan society, and thence as a man of learning who may through his writings address a public in the truest sense of the word, he may indeed argue without harming the affairs in which he is employed for some of the time in a passive capacity. Thus it would be very harmful if an officer receiving an order from his superiors were to quibble openly, while on duty, about the appropriateness or usefulness of the order in question. He must simply obey. But he cannot reasonably be banned from making observations as a man of learning on the errors in the military service, and from submitting these to his public for judgement. The citizen cannot refuse to pay the taxes imposed upon him; presumptuous criticisms of such taxes, where someone is called upon to pay them, may be punished as an outrage which could lead to general insubordination. Nonetheless, the same citizen does not contravene his civil obligations if, as a learned individual, he publicly voices his thoughts on the impropriety or even injustice of such fiscal measures. In the same way, a clergyman is bound to instruct his pupils and his congregation in accordance with the doctrines of the church he serves, for he was employed by it on that condition. But as a scholar, he is completely free as well as

[iii] Frederick II, also called "the Great" (1712–86), King of Prussia from 1740 to 1786.

obliged to impart to the public all his carefully considered, well-intentioned thoughts on the mistaken aspects of those doctrines, and to offer suggestions for a better arrangement of religious and ecclesiastical affairs. And there is nothing in this which need trouble the conscience. For what he teaches in pursuit of his duties as an active servant of the church is presented by him as something which he is not empowered to teach at his own discretion, but which he is employed to expound in a prescribed manner and in someone else's name. He will say: Our church teaches this or that, and these are the arguments it uses. He then extracts as much practical value as possible for his congregation from precepts to which he would not himself subscribe with full conviction, but which he can nevertheless undertake to expound, since it is not in fact wholly impossible that they may contain truth. At all events, nothing opposed to the essence of religion is present in such doctrines. For if the clergyman thought he could find anything of this sort in them, he would not be able to carry out his official duties in good conscience, and would have to resign. Thus the use which someone employed as a teacher makes of his reason in the presence of his congregation is purely *private*, since a congregation, however large it is, is never any more than a domestic gathering. In view of this, he is not and cannot be free as a priest, since he is acting on a commission imposed from outside. Conversely, as a scholar addressing the real public (i.e. the world at large) through his writings, the clergyman making *public use* of his reason enjoys unlimited freedom to use his own reason and to speak in his own person. For to maintain that the guardians of the people in spiritual matters should themselves be immature, is an absurdity which amounts to making absurdities permanent.

But should not a society of clergymen, for example an ecclesiastical synod or a venerable presbytery (as the Dutch call it), be entitled to commit itself by oath to a certain unalterable set of doctrines, in order to secure for all time a constant guardianship over each of its members, and through them over the people? I reply that this is quite impossible. A contract of this kind, concluded with a view to preventing all further enlightenment of mankind for ever, is absolutely null and void, even if it is ratified by the supreme power, by Imperial Diets[iv] and the most solemn peace treaties. One age cannot enter into an alliance on oath to put the next age in a position where it would be impossible for it to extend and correct its knowledge, particularly on such important matters, or to make any progress whatsoever in enlightenment. This would be a crime against human nature, whose original destiny lies precisely in such progress. Later generations are thus perfectly entitled to dismiss these agreements as unauthorised and criminal. To test whether any particular measure can be agreed upon as a

---

[iv] A diet is a legislative assembly.

law for a people, we need only ask whether a people could well impose such a law upon itself. This might well be possible for a specified short period as a means of introducing a certain order, pending, as it were, a better solution. This would also mean that each citizen, particularly the clergyman, would be given a free hand as a scholar to comment publicly, i.e. in his writings, on the inadequacies of current institutions. Meanwhile, the newly established order would continue to exist, until public insight into the nature of such matters had progressed and proved itself to the point where, by general consent (if not unanimously), a proposal could be submitted to the crown. This would seek to protect the congregations who had, for instance, agreed to alter their religious establishment in accordance with their own notions of what higher insight is, but it would not try to obstruct those who wanted to let things remain as before. But it is absolutely impermissible to agree, even for a single lifetime, to a permanent religious constitution which no-one might publicly question. For this would virtually nullify a phase in man's upward progress, thus making it fruitless and even detrimental to subsequent generations. A man may for his own person, and even then only for a limited period, postpone enlightening himself in matters he ought to know about. But to renounce such enlightenment completely, whether for his own person or even more so for later generations, means violating and trampling underfoot the sacred rights of mankind. But something which a people may not even impose upon itself can still less be imposed on it by a monarch; for his legislative authority depends precisely upon his uniting the collective will of the people in his own. So long as he sees to it that all true or imagined improvements are compatible with the civil order, he can otherwise leave his subjects to do whatever they find necessary for this salvation, which is none of his business. But it is his business to stop anyone forcibly hindering others from working as best they can to define and promote their salvation. It indeed detracts from his majesty if he interferes in these affairs by subjecting the writings in which his subjects attempt to clarify their religious ideas to governmental supervision. This applies if he does so acting upon his own exalted opinions – in which case he exposes himself to the reproach: *Caesar non est supra Grammaticos*[v] – but much more so if he demeans his high authority so far as to support the spiritual despotism of a few tyrants within his state against the rest of his subjects.

If it is now asked whether we at present live in an *enlightened* age, the answer is: No, but we do live in an age of *enlightenment*. As things are at present, we still have a long way to go before men as a whole can be in a position (or can even be put into a position) of using their own understanding confidently and well in religious matters, without outside

[v] "Caesar is not above the grammarians."

guidance. But we do have distinct indications that the way is now being cleared for them to work freely in this direction, and that the obstacles to universal enlightenment, to man's emergence from his self-incurred immaturity, are gradually becoming fewer. In this respect our age is the age of enlightenment, the century, of *Frederick*.[vi]

A prince who does not regard it as beneath him to say that he considers it his duty, in religious matters, not to prescribe anything to his people, but to allow them complete freedom, a prince who thus even declines to accept the presumptuous title of *tolerant*, is himself enlightened. He deserves to be praised by a grateful present and posterity as the man who first liberated mankind from immaturity (as far as government is concerned), and who left all men free to use their own reason in all matters of conscience. Under his rule, ecclesiastical dignitaries, notwithstanding their official duties, may in their capacity as scholars freely and publicly submit to the judgement of the world their verdicts and opinions, even if these deviate here and there from orthodox doctrine. This applies even more to all others who are not restricted by any official duties. This spirit of freedom is also spreading abroad, even where it has to struggle with outward obstacles imposed by governments which misunderstand their own function. For such governments can now witness a shining example of how freedom may exist without in the least jeopardising public concord and the unity of the commonwealth. Men will of their own accord gradually work their way out of barbarism so long as artificial measures are not deliberately adopted to keep them in it.

I have portrayed *matters of religion* as the focal point of enlightenment, i.e. of man's emergence from his self-incurred immaturity. This is firstly because our rulers have no interest in assuming the role of guardians over their subjects so far as the arts and sciences are concerned, and secondly, because religious immaturity is the most pernicious and dishonourable variety of all. But the attitude of mind of a head of state who favours freedom in the arts and sciences extends even further, for he realises that there is no danger even to his *legislation* if he allows his subjects to make *public* use of their own reason and to put before the public their thoughts on better ways of drawing up laws, even if this entails forthright criticism of the current legislation. We have before us a brilliant example of this kind, in which no monarch has yet surpassed the one to whom we now pay tribute.

But only a ruler who is himself enlightened and has no fear of phantoms, yet who likewise has at hand a well-disciplined and numerous army to guarantee public security, may say what no republic would dare to say: *Argue as much as you like and about whatever you like, but obey!* This reveals

---

[vi] Again, Frederick the Great.

to us a strange and unexpected pattern in human affairs (such as we shall always find if we consider them in the widest sense, in which nearly everything is paradoxical). A high degree of civil freedom seems advantageous to a people's *intellectual* freedom, yet it also sets up insuperable barriers to it. Conversely, a lesser degree of civil freedom gives intellectual freedom enough room to expand to its fullest extent. Thus once the germ on which nature has lavished most care – man's inclination and vocation to *think freely* – has developed within this hard shell, it gradually reacts upon the mentality of the people, who thus gradually become increasingly able to *act freely*. Eventually, it even influences the principles of governments, which find that they can themselves profit by treating man, who is *more than a machine*, in a manner appropriate to his dignity.[1]

Notes

1   I read today on the 30th September in Büsching's *Wöchentliche Nachrichten* of 13th September a notice concerning this month's *Berlinische Monatsschrift*. The notice mentions Mendelssohn's answer to the same question as that which I have answered. I have not yet seen this journal, otherwise I should have held back the above reflections. I let them stand only as a means of finding out by comparison how far the thoughts of two individuals may coincide by chance. [Moses Mendelssohn (1729–86) published an essay, "*über die Frage: was heisst Aufklärung?*" ("On the Question: What is Enlightenment"), in 1784.]

chapter four

Reflections on the Revolution in France

Edmund Burke

The French Revolution seemed to many to embody the new ideals of modern, Enlightened culture, while to others it threatened a new barbarism. Edmund Burke (1729–97), Irish by birth and a member of the English Parliament, provides us with the most famous critique of revolutionary modernity. His *Reflections on the Revolution in France* (1790), a letter to a French correspondent, was inspired by several events: the arrest of the royal family of France by a mob on October 6, 1789; the seizure of all Church property by the French republic; and closer to home, a sermon by an Englishman, Dr Richard Price of the Revolution Society, endorsing the principles of the French Revolution for England. (All of this was years before the worst revolutionary violence in France, the "Terror.") Critical of the modern attempt to replace traditional social arrangements with abstract principles like equality and individual rights, Burke's work remains the classical source of true conservatism. But his traditionalism is no simple authoritarianism; Burke supported Irish and American independence from Great Britain because he felt that the Crown had abused the traditionally recognized rights of Ireland and the American colonies. He approved the 1688 revolution of the English Parliament against James II as a conservative revolution aimed at restoring the traditional distribution of power which the King had disturbed.

But I may say of our preacher "*utinam nugis tota illa dedisset tempora saevitiae*".[i] – All things in this his fulminating bull are not of so innoxious a tendency. His doctrines affect our constitution in its vital parts. He tells the Revolution Society in this political sermon that this Majesty "is almost the *only* lawful king in the world because the *only* one who owes his crown

---

From Edmund Burke, *Reflections on the Revolution in France*, ed. J. G. A. Pocock (Indianapolis: Hackett, 1987). A selection of unmarked sections, in each case separated by space in the text: pp. 12–19, 25–6, 29–31, 51–2, 76–7, 216–18.

[i] "Would that he had devoted to trifles all the time he spent in violence." Juvenal, *Satires*, IV, 150–1. The preacher is Dr Richard Price.

to the *choice of his people"*. As to the kings of *the world*, all of whom (except one) this archpontiff of the *rights of men*, with all the plenitude and with more than the boldness of the papal deposing power in its meridian fervor of the twelfth century, puts into one sweeping clause of ban and anathema and proclaims usurpers by circles of longitude and latitude, over the whole globe, it behooves them to consider how they admit into their territories these apostolic missionaries who are to tell their subjects they are not lawful kings. That is their concern. It is ours, as a domestic interest of some moment, seriously to consider the solidity of the *only* principle upon which these gentlemen acknowledge a king of Great Britain to be entitled to their allegiance.

This doctrine, as applied to the prince now on the British throne, either is nonsense and therefore neither true nor false, or it affirms a most unfounded, dangerous, illegal, and unconstitutional position. According to this spiritual doctor of politics, if his Majesty does not owe his crown to the choice of his people, he is no *lawful king*. Now nothing can be more untrue than that the crown of this kingdom is so held by his Majesty. Therefore, if you follow their rule, the king of Great Britain, who most certainly does not owe his high office to any form of popular election, is in no respect better than the rest of the gang of usurpers who reign, or rather rob, all over the face of this our miserable world without any sort of right or title to the allegiance of their people. The policy of this general doctrine, so qualified, is evident enough. The propagators of this political gospel are in hopes that their abstract principle (their principle that a popular choice is necessary to the legal existence of the sovereign magistracy) would be overlooked, whilst the king of Great Britain was not affected by it. In the meantime the ears of their congregations would be gradually habituated to it, as if it were a first principle admitted without dispute. For the present it would only operate as a theory, pickled in the preserving juices of pulpit eloquence, and laid by for future use. *Condo et compono quae mox depromere possim.*[ii] By this policy, whilst our government is soothed with a reservation in its favor, to which it has no claim, the security which it has in common with all governments, so far as opinion is security, is taken away.

Thus these politicians proceed whilst little notice is taken of their doctrines; but when they come to be examined upon the plain meaning of their words and the direct tendency of their doctrines, then equivocations and slippery constructions come into play. When they say the king owes his crown to the choice of his people and is therefore the only lawful sovereign in the world, they will perhaps tell us they mean to say no more than that some of the king's predecessors have been called to the throne by

[ii] "I concoct and compound what soon I may bring forth." Horace, *Epistles,* I, 1, 12.

some sort of choice, and therefore he owes his crown to the choice of his people. Thus, by a miserable subterfuge, they hope to render their proposition safe by rendering it nugatory. They are welcome to the asylum they seek for their offense, since they take refuge in their folly. For if you admit this interpretation, how does their idea of election differ from our idea of inheritance?

And how does the settlement of the crown in the Brunswick line derived from James the First come to legalize our monarchy rather than that of any of the neighboring countries? At some time or other, to be sure, all the beginners of dynasties were chosen by those who called them to govern. There is ground enough for the opinion that all the kingdoms of Europe were, at a remote period, elective, with more or fewer limitations in the objects of choice. But whatever kings might have been here or elsewhere a thousand years ago, or in whatever manner the ruling dynasties of England or France may have begun, the king of Great Britain is, at this day, king by a fixed rule of succession according to the laws of his country; and whilst the legal conditions of the compact of sovereignty are performed by him (as they are performed), he holds his crown in contempt of the choice of the Revolution Society, who have not a single vote for a king amongst them, either individually or collectively, though I make no doubt they would soon erect themselves into an electoral college if things were ripe to give effect to their claim. His Majesty's heirs and successors, each in his time and order, will come to the crown with the same contempt of their choice with which his Majesty has succeeded to that he wears.

Whatever may be the success of evasion in explaining away the gross error of *fact*, which supposes that his Majesty (though he holds it in concurrence with the wishes) owes his crown to the choice of his people, yet nothing can evade their full explicit declaration concerning the principle of a right in the people to choose; which right is directly maintained and tenaciously adhered to. All the oblique insinuations concerning election bottom in this proposition and are referable to it. Lest the foundation of the king's exclusive legal title should pass for a mere rant of adulatory freedom, the political divine[iii] proceeds dogmatically to assert that, by the principles of the Revolution, the people of England have acquired three fundamental rights, all which, with him, compose one system and lie together in one short sentence, namely, that we have acquired a right:

1 to choose our own governors.
2 to cashier them for misconduct.
3 to frame a government for ourselves.

iii Dr Price.

This new and hitherto unheard-of bill of rights, though made in the name of the whole people, belongs to those gentlemen and their faction only. The body of the people of England have no share in it. They utterly disclaim it. They will resist the practical assertion of it with their lives and fortunes. They are bound to do so by the laws of their country made at the time of that very Revolution which is appealed to in favor of the fictitious rights claimed by the Society which abuses its name.

These gentlemen of the Old Jewry, in all their reasonings on the Revolution of 1688,[iv] have a revolution which happened in England about forty years before and the late French revolution, so much before their eyes and in their hearts that they are constantly confounding all the three together. It is necessary that we should separate what they confound. We must recall their erring fancies to the *acts* of the Revolution which we revere, for the discovery of its true *principles*. If the *principles* of the Revolution of 1688 are anywhere to be found, it is in the statute called the *Declaration of Right*. In that most wise, sober, and considerate declaration, drawn up by great lawyers and great statesmen, and not by warm and inexperienced enthusiasts, not one word is said, nor one suggestion made, of a general right "to choose our own *governors*, to cashier them for misconduct, and to *form* a government for *ourselves*."

This Declaration of Right (the act of the 1st of William and Mary, sess. 2, ch. 2) is the cornerstone of our constitution as reinforced, explained, improved, and in its fundamental principles for ever settled. It is called, "An Act for declaring the rights and liberties of the subject, and for *settling* the *succession* of the crown." You will observe that these rights and this succession are declared in one body and bound indissolubly together.

A few years after this period, a second opportunity offered for asserting a right of election to the crown. On the prospect of a total failure of issue from King William, and from the Princess, afterwards Queen Anne, the consideration of the settlement of the crown and of a further security for the liberties of the people again came before the legislature. Did they this second time make any provision for legalizing the crown on the spurious revolution principles of the Old Jewry? No. They followed the principles which prevailed in the Declaration of Right, indicating with more precision the persons who were to inherit in the Protestant line. This act also incorporated, by the same policy, our liberties and an hereditary succession in the same act. Instead of a right to choose our own governors, they

---

[iv] Dr Price's lecture was delivered in the Old Jewry, a district of London. In the "Glorious Revolution" of 1688, Parliament successfully ousted Catholic James II and installed William III. Burke approved this revolution as having reinstated the traditional rights of Parliament which James had threatened.

declared that the *succession* in that line (the Protestant line drawn from James the First), was absolutely necessary "for the peace, quiet, and security of the realm," and that it was equally urgent on them "to maintain a *certainty in the succession* thereof, to which the subjects may safely have recourse for their protection." Both these acts, in which are heard the unerring, unambiguous oracles of revolution policy, instead of countenancing the delusive, gipsy predictions of a "right to choose our governors," prove to a demonstration how totally adverse the wisdom of the nation was from turning a case of necessity into a rule of law.

Unquestionably, there was at the Revolution, in the person of King William, a small and a temporary deviation from the strict order of a regular hereditary succession; but it is against all genuine principles of jurisprudence to draw a principle from a law made in a special case and regarding an individual person. *Privilegium non transit in exemplum.*[v] If ever there was a time favorable for establishing the principle that a king of popular choice was the only legal king, without all doubt it was at the Revolution. Its not being done at that time is a proof that the nation was of opinion it ought not to be done at any time. There is no person so completely ignorant of our history as not to know that the majority in parliament of both parties were so little disposed to anything resembling that principle that at first they were determined to place the vacant crown, not on the head of the Prince of Orange, but on that of his wife Mary, daughter of King James, the eldest born of the issue of that king, which they acknowledged as undoubtedly his. It would be to repeat a very trite story, to recall to your memory all those circumstances which demonstrated that their accepting King William was not properly a *choice*; but to all those who did not wish, in effect, to recall King James or to deluge their country in blood and again to bring their religion, laws, and liberties into the peril they had just escaped, it was an act of *necessity*, in the strictest moral sense in which necessity can be taken.

In the very act in which for a time, and in a single case, parliament departed from the strict order of inheritance in favor of a prince who, though not next, was, however, very near in the line of succession, it is curious to observe how Lord Somers, who drew the bill called the Declaration of Right, has comported himself on that delicate occasion. It is curious to observe with what address this temporary solution of continuity is kept from the eye, whilst all that could be found in this act of necessity to countenance the idea of an hereditary succession is brought forward, and fostered, and made the most of, by this great man and by the legislature who followed him. Quitting the dry, imperative style of an act of parliament, he makes the Lords and Commons fall to a pious, legislative

[v] "A privilege does not become a precedent."

ejaculation and declare that they consider it "as a marvellous providence and merciful goodness of God to this nation to preserve their said Majesties' *royal* persons most happily to reign over us *on the throne of their ancestors,* for which, from the bottom of their hearts, they return their humblest thanks and praises." – The legislature plainly had in view the act of recognition of the first of Queen Elizabeth, chap. 3rd, and of that of James the First, chap. 1st, both acts strongly declaratory of the inheritable nature of the crown; and in many parts they follow, with a nearly literal precision, the words and even the form of thanksgiving which is found in these old declaratory statutes.

The two Houses, in the act of King William, did not thank God that they had found a fair opportunity to assert a right to choose their own governors, much less to make an election the *only lawful* title to the crown. Their having been in a condition to avoid the very appearance of it, as much as possible, was by them considered as a providential escape. They threw a politic, well-wrought veil over every circumstance tending to weaken the rights which in the meliorated order of succession they meant to perpetuate, or which might furnish a precedent for any future departure from what they had then settled forever. Accordingly, that they might not relax the nerves of their monarchy, and that they might preserve a close conformity to the practice of their ancestors, as it appeared in the declaratory statutes of Queen Mary and Queen Elizabeth, in the next clause they vest, by recognition, in their Majesties *all* the legal prerogatives of the crown, declaring "that in them they are most *fully*, rightfully, and *entirely* invested, incorporated, united, and annexed." In the clause which follows, for preventing questions by reason of any pretended titles to the crown, they declare (observing also in this the traditionary language, along with the traditionary policy of the nation, and repeating as from a rubric the language of the preceding acts of Elizabeth and James,) that on the preserving "a *certainty* in the SUCCESSION thereof, the unity, peace, and tranquillity of this nation doth, under God, wholly depend."

They knew that a doubtful title of succession would but too much resemble an election, and that an election would be utterly destructive of the "unity, peace, and tranquillity of this nation," which they thought to be considerations of some moment. To provide for these objects and, therefore, to exclude for ever the Old Jewry doctrine of "a right to choose our own governors," they follow with a clause containing a most solemn pledge, taken from the preceding act of Queen Elizabeth, as solemn a pledge as ever was or can be given in favor of an hereditary succession, and as solemn a renunciation as could be made of the principles by this Society imputed to them: The Lords spiritual and temporal, and Commons, do, in the name of all the people aforesaid, most humbly and faithfully submit *themselves, their heirs and posterities for ever*; and do faithfully promise that they will stand to maintain, and defend their said Majesties, and also the *limitation of the crown*, herein specified and contained, to the utmost of their powers, etc. etc.

So far is it from being true that we acquired a right by the Revolution to elect our kings that, if we had possessed it before, the English nation did at that time most solemnly renounce and abdicate it, for themselves and for all their posterity forever. These gentlemen may value themselves as much as they please on their whig[vi] principles, but I never desire to be thought a better whig than Lord Somers, or to understand the principles of the Revolution better than those by whom it was brought about, or to read in the Declaration of Right any mysteries unknown to those whose penetrating style has engraved in our ordinances, and in our hearts, the words and spirit of that immortal law.

It is true that, aided with the powers derived from force and opportunity, the nation was at that time, in some sense, free to take what course it pleased for filling the throne, but only free to do so upon the same grounds on which they might have wholly abolished their monarchy and every other part of their constitution. However, they did not think such bold changes within their commission. It is indeed difficult, perhaps impossible, to give limits to the mere *abstract* competence of the supreme power, such as was exercised by parliament at that time, but the limits of a *moral* competence subjecting, even in powers more indisputably sovereign, occasional will to permanent reason and to the steady maxims of faith, justice, and fixed fundamental policy, are perfectly intelligible and perfectly binding upon those who exercise any authority, under any name or under any title, in the state. The House of Lords, for instance, is not morally competent to dissolve the House of Commons, no, nor even to dissolve itself, nor to abdicate, if it would, its portion in the legislature of the kingdom. Though a king may abdicate for his own person, he cannot abdicate for the monarchy. By as strong, or by a stronger reason, the House of Commons cannot renounce its share of authority. The engagement and pact of society, which generally goes by the name of the constitution, forbids such invasion and such surrender. The constituent parts of a state are obliged to hold their public faith with each other and with all those who derive any serious interest under their engagements, as much as the whole state is bound to keep its faith with separate communities. Otherwise competence and power would soon be confounded and no law be left but the will of a prevailing force. On this principle the succession of the crown has always been what it now is, an hereditary succession by law; in the old line it was a succession by the common law; in the new, by the statute law operating

---

[vi] The Whigs were the party that advocated the removal of James II from the English throne in 1688. They were opposed by the Tories.

on the principles of the common law, not changing the substance, but regulating the mode and describing the persons. Both these descriptions of law are of the same force and are derived from an equal authority emanating from the common agreement and original compact of the state, *communi sponsione reipublicae,*[vii] and as such are equally binding on king and people, too, as long as the terms are observed and they continue the same body politic.

I should have considered all this as no more than a sort of flippant, vain discourse, in which, as in an unsavory fume, several persons suffer the spirit of liberty to evaporate, if it were not plainly in support of the idea and a part of the scheme of "cashiering kings for misconduct." In that light it is worth some observation.

Kings, in one sense, are undoubtedly the servants of the people because their power has no other rational end than that of the general advantage; but it is not true that they are, in the ordinary sense (by our constitution, at least), anything like servants; the essence of whose situation is to obey the commands of some other and to be removable at pleasure. But the king of Great Britain obeys no other person; all other persons are individually, and collectively too, under him and owe to him a legal obedience. The law, which knows neither to flatter nor to insult, calls this high magistrate not our servant, as this humble divine calls him, but *"our sovereign Lord the king"*; and we, on our parts, have learned to speak only the primitive language of the law, and not the confused jargon of their Babylonian pulpits.[viii]

As he is not to obey us, but as we are to obey the law in him, our constitution has made no sort of provision toward rendering him, as a servant, in any degree responsible. Our constitution knows nothing of a magistrate like the *Justicia* of Aragon,[ix] nor of any court legally appointed, nor of any process legally settled, for submitting the king to the responsibility belonging to all servants. In this he is not distinguished from the Commons and the Lords, who, in their several public capacities, can never be called to an account for their conduct, although the Revolution Society chooses to assert, in direct opposition to one of the wisest and most beautiful parts of our constitution, that "a king is no more than the first servant of the public, created by it, *and responsible to it.*"

Ill would our ancestors at the Revolution have deserved their fame for wisdom if they had found no security for their freedom but in rendering their government feeble in its operations, and precarious in its tenure; if

---

[vii] "By the common volition of the Commonwealth."
[viii] Perhaps a reference to the confusion of tongues preceding the fall of the Tower of Babel in the Hebrew Bible.
[ix] Chief magistrate of Aragón, an historical autonomous region of Spain.

they had been able to contrive no better remedy against arbitrary power than civil confusion. Let these gentlemen state who that *representative* public is to whom they will affirm the king, as a servant, to be responsible. It will then be time enough for me to produce to them the positive statute law which affirms that he is not.

You will observe that from Magna Charta to the Declaration of Right it has been the uniform policy of our constitution to claim and assert our liberties as an *entailed inheritance* derived to us from our forefathers, and to be transmitted to our posterity – as an estate specially belonging to the people of this kingdom, without any reference whatever to any other more general or prior right. By this means our constitution preserves a unity in so great a diversity of its parts. We have an inheritable crown, an inheritable peerage, and a House of Commons and a people inheriting privileges, franchises, and liberties from a long line of ancestors.

This policy appears to me to be the result of profound reflection, or rather the happy effect of following nature, which is wisdom without reflection, and above it. A spirit of innovation is generally the result of a selfish temper and confined views. People will not look forward to posterity, who never look backward to their ancestors. Besides, the people of England well know that the idea of inheritance furnishes a sure principle of conservation and a sure principle of transmission, without at all excluding a principle of improvement. It leaves acquisition free, but it secures what it acquires. Whatever advantages are obtained by a state proceeding on these maxims are locked fast as in a sort of family settlement, grasped as in a kind of mortmain[x] forever. By a constitutional policy, working after the pattern of nature, we receive, we hold, we transmit our government and our privileges in the same manner in which we enjoy and transmit our property and our lives. The institutions of policy, the goods of fortune, the gifts of providence are handed down to us, and from us, in the same course and order. Our political system is placed in a just correspondence and symmetry with the order of the world and with the mode of existence decreed to a permanent body composed of transitory parts, wherein, by the disposition of a stupendous wisdom, molding together the great mysterious incorporation of the human race, the whole, at one time, is never old or middle-aged or young, but, in a condition of unchangeable constancy, moves on through the varied tenor of perpetual decay, fall, renovation, and progression. Thus, by preserving the method of nature in the conduct of the state, in what we improve we are never wholly new; in what we retain we are never wholly obsolete. By adhering in this manner and on those principles to our forefathers, we are guided not by the superstition of antiquarians,

[x] Literally "deadhand," a legal means making possession perpetual in a corporation.

but by the spirit of philosophic analogy. In this choice of inheritance we have given to our frame of polity the image of a relation in blood, binding up the constitution of our country with our dearest domestic ties, adopting our fundamental laws into the bosom of our family affections, keeping inseparable and cherishing with the warmth of all their combined and mutually reflected charities our state, our hearths, our sepulchres, and our altars.

Through the same plan of a conformity to nature in our artificial institutions, and by calling in the aid of her unerring and powerful instincts to fortify the fallible and feeble contrivances of our reason, we have derived several other, and those no small, benefits from considering our liberties in the light of an inheritance. Always acting as if in the presence of canonized forefathers, the spirit of freedom, leading in itself to misrule and excess, is tempered with an awful gravity. This idea of a liberal descent inspires us with a sense of habitual native dignity which prevents that upstart insolence almost inevitably adhering to and disgracing those who are the first acquirers of any distinction. By this means our liberty becomes a noble freedom. It carries an imposing and majestic aspect. It has a pedigree and illustrating ancestors. It has its bearings and its ensigns armorial. It has its gallery of portraits, its monumental inscriptions, its records, evidences, and titles. We procure reverence to our civil institutions on the principle upon which nature teaches us to revere individual men: on account of their age and on account of those from whom they are descended. All your sophisters cannot produce anything better adapted to preserve a rational and manly freedom than the course that we have pursued, who have chosen our nature rather than our speculations, our breats rather than our inventions, for the great conservatories and magazines of our rights and privileges.

Far am I from denying in theory, full as far is my heart from withholding in practice (if I were of power to give or to withhold) the real rights of men. In denying their false claims of right, I do not mean to injure those which are real, and are such as their pretended rights would totally destroy. If civil society be made for the advantage of man, all the advantages for which it is made become his right. It is an institution of beneficence; and law itself is only beneficence acting by a rule. Men have a right to live by that rule; they have a right to do justice, as between their fellows, whether their fellows are in public function or in ordinary occupation. They have a right to the fruits of their industry and to the means of making their industry fruitful. They have a right to the acquisitions of their parents, to the nourishment and improvement of their offspring, to instruction in life, and to consolation in death. Whatever each man can separately do, without trespassing upon others, he has a right to do for himself; and he has a right to a fair portion of all which society, with all its combinations

67

of skill and force, can do in his favor. In this partnership all men have equal rights, but not to equal things. He that has but five shillings in the partnership has as good a right to it as he that has five hundred pounds has to his larger proportion. But he has not a right to an equal dividend in the product of the joint stock; and as to the share of power, authority, and direction which each individual ought to have in the management of the state, that I must deny to be amongst the direct original rights of man in civil society; for I have in my contemplation the civil social man, and no other. It is a thing to be settled by convention.

If civil society be the offspring of convention, that convention must be its law. That convention must limit and modify all the descriptions of constitution which are formed under it. Every sort of legislative, judicial, or executory power are its creatures. They can have no being in any other state of things; *and how can any man claim under the conventions of civil society rights which do not so much as suppose its existence – rights which are absolutely repugnant to it?* One of the first motives to civil society, and which becomes one of its fundamental rules, is *that no man should be judge in his own cause.* By this each person has at once divested himself of the first fundamental right of unconvenanted man, that is, to judge for himself and to assert his own cause. He abdicates all right to be his own governor. He inclusively, in a great measure, abandons the right of self-defense, the first law of nature. Men cannot enjoy the rights of an uncivil and of a civil state together. That he may obtain justice, he gives up his right of determining what it is in points the most essential to him. That he may secure some liberty, he makes a surrender in trust of the whole of it.

You see, Sir, that in this enlightened age I am bold enough to confess that we are generally men of untaught feelings, that, instead of casting away all our old prejudices, we cherish them to a very considerable degree, and, to take more shame to ourselves, we cherish them because they are prejudices; and the longer they have lasted and the more generally they have prevailed, the more we cherish them. We are afraid to put men to live and trade each on his own private stock of reason, because we suspect that this stock in each man is small, and that the individuals would do better to avail themselves of the general bank and capital of nations and of ages. Many of our men of speculation, instead of exploding general prejudices, employ their sagacity to discover the latent wisdom which prevails in them. If they find what they seek, and they seldom fail, they think it more wise to continue the prejudice, with the reason involved, than to cast away the coat of prejudice and to leave nothing but the naked reason; because prejudice, with its reason, has a motive to give action to that reason, and an affection which will give it permanence. Prejudice is of ready application in the emergency; it previously engages the mind in a steady course of wisdom and virtue and does not leave the man hesitating in the moment of decision skeptical, puzzled, and unresolved. Prejudice renders a man's virtue his habit, and not a series of unconnected acts. Through just prejudice, his duty becomes a part of his nature.

The effects of the incapacity shown by the popular leaders in all the great members of the commonwealth are to be covered with the "all-atoning name" of liberty. In some people I see great liberty indeed; in many, if not in the most, an oppressive, degrading servitude. But what is liberty without wisdom and without virtue? It is the greatest of all possible evils; for it is folly, vice, and madness, without tuition or restraint. Those who know what virtuous liberty is cannot bear to see it disgraced by incapable heads on account of their having high-sounding words in their mouths. Grand, swelling sentiments of liberty I am sure I do not despise. They warm the heart; they enlarge and liberalize our minds; they animate our courage in a time of conflict. Old as I am, I read the fine raptures of Lucan and Corneille with pleasure.[xi] Neither do I wholly condemn the little arts and devices of popularity. They facilitate the carrying of many points of moment; they keep the people together; they refresh the mind in its exertions; and they diffuse occasional gaiety over the severe brow of moral freedom. Every politician ought to sacrifice to the graces, and to join compliance with reason. But in such an undertaking as that in France, all these subsidiary sentiments and artifices are of little avail. To make a government requires no great prudence. Settle the seat of power, teach obedience, and the work is done. To give freedom is still more easy. It is not necessary to guide; it only requires to let go the rein. But to form a *free government*, that is, to temper together these opposite elements of liberty and restraint in one consistent work, requires much thought, deep reflection, a sagacious, powerful, and combining mind. This I do not find in those who take the lead in the National Assembly. Perhaps they are not so miserably deficient as they appear. I rather believe it. It would put them below the common level of human understanding. But when the leaders choose to make themselves bidders at an auction of popularity, their talents, in the construction of the state, will be of no service. They will become flatterers instead of legislators, the instruments, not the guides, of the people. If any of them should happen to propose a scheme of liberty, soberly limited and defined with proper qualifications, he will be immediately outbid by his competitors who will produce something more splendidly popular. Suspicions will be raised of his fidelity to his cause. Moderation will be stigmatized as the virtue of cowards, and compromise as the

[xi] Marcus Annaeus Lucanus (AD 39–65), a Roman who wrote a famous historical epic poem, and Pierre Corneille (1606–84), father of French classical tragic drama.

prudence of traitors, until, in hopes of preserving the credit which may enable him to temper and moderate, on some occasions, the popular leader is obliged to become active in propagating doctrines and establishing powers that will afterwards defeat any sober purpose at which he ultimately might have aimed.

But am I so unreasonable as to see nothing at all that deserves commendation in the indefatigable labors of this Assembly? I do not deny that, among an infinite number of acts of violence and folly, some good may have been done. They who destroy everything certainly will remove some grievance. They who make everything new have a chance that they may establish something beneficial. To give them credit for what they have done in virtue of the authority they have usurped, or which can excuse them in the crimes by which that authority has been acquired, it must appear that the same things could not have been accomplished without producing such a revolution. Most assuredly they might, because almost every one of the regulations made by them which is not very equivocal was either in the cession of the king, voluntarily made at the meeting of the states, or in the concurrent instructions to the orders. Some usages have been abolished on just grounds, but they were such that if they had stood as they were to all eternity, they would little detract from the happiness and prosperity of any state. The improvements of the National Assembly are superficial, their errors fundamental.

Whatever they are, I wish my countrymen rather to recommend to our neighbours the example of the British constitution than to take models from them for the improvement of our own. In the former, they have got an invaluable treasure. They are not, I think, without some causes of apprehension and complaint, but these they do not owe to their constitution but to their own conduct. I think our happy situation owing to our constitution, but owing to the whole of it, and not to any part singly, owing in a great measure to what we have left standing in our several reviews and reformations as well as to what we have altered or superadded. Our people will find employment enough for a truly patriotic, free, and independent spirit in guarding what they possess from violation. I would not exclude alteration neither, but even when I changed, it should be to preserve. I should be led to my remedy by a great grievance. In what I did, I should follow the example of our ancestors. I would make the reparation as nearly as possible in the style of the building. A politic caution, a guarded circumspection, a moral rather than a complexional timidity were among the ruling principles of our forefathers in their most decided conduct. Not being illuminated with the light of which the gentlemen of France tell us they have got so abundant a share, they acted under a strong impression of the ignorance and fallibility of mankind. He that had made them thus fallible rewarded them for having in their conduct attended to their nature. Let us imitate their caution if we wish to deserve their fortune or to retain their bequests. Let us add, if we please, but let us preserve what they have left; and, standing on the firm ground of the British constitution, let us be satisfied to admire rather than attempt to follow in their desperate flights the aeronauts of France.

I have told you candidly my sentiments. I think they are not likely to alter yours. I do not know that they ought. You are young; you cannot guide but must follow the fortune of your country. But hereafter they may be of some use to you, in some future form which your commonwealth may take. In the present it can hardly remain; but before its final settlement it may be obliged to pass, as one of our poets says, "through great varieties of untried being",[xii] and in all its transmigrations to be purified by fire and blood.

I have little to recommend my opinions but long observation and much impartiality. They come from one who has been no tool of power, no flatterer of greatness; and who in his last acts does not wish to belie the tenor of his life. They come from one almost the whole of whose public exertion has been a struggle for the liberty of others; from one in whose breast no anger, durable or vehement, has ever been kindled but by what he considered as tyranny; and who snatches from his share in the endeavors which are used by good men to discredit opulent oppression the hours he has employed on your affairs; and who in so doing persuades himself he has not departed from his usual office; they come from one who desires honors, distinctions, and emoluments but little, and who expects them not at all; who has no contempt for fame, and no fear of obloquy; who shuns contention, though he will hazard an opinion; from one who wishes to preserve consistency, but who would preserve consistency by varying his means to secure the unity of his end, and, when the equipoise of the vessel in which he sails may be endangered by overloading it upon one side, is desirous of carrying the small weight of his reasons to that which may preserve its equipoise.

[xii] Addison, *Cato*, Act V, scene i.

chapter five

Sketch for an Historical Picture of the Progress of the Human Mind

Marquis de Condorcet

Marie Jean Antoine Nicolas Caritat, the marquis de Condorcet (1743–94), was one of *les philosophes*, philosophers who led the French Enlightenment. He was associated with that characteristic Enlightenment project, the composition of the *Encyclopédie* of all knowledge. A journalist and supporter of the initial phase of the French Revolution, he became a member of the Legislative Assembly during its radical phase, but his constitutional and non-violent views led him publicly to attack the 1793 Jacobin Constitution. He was forced into hiding for nine months, during which he wrote his *Sketch*. Subsequently arrested, he died in his cell, presumably a suicide. Condorcet distills in his book what would become the canonical self-interpretation of the modern European world, in which rational inquiry spurs progress not only in science, but in society and politics. He foresaw a coming era of "reason, tolerance, humanity."

We have watched man's reason being slowly formed by the natural progress of civilization; we have watched superstition seize upon it and corrupt it, and tyranny degrade and deaden the minds of men under the burden of misery and fear.

One nation alone escapes the two-fold influence of tyranny and superstition. From that happy land where freedom had only recently kindled the torch of genius, the mind of man, released from the leading-strings of its infancy, advances with firm steps towards the truth.[i] But this triumph soon encourages tyranny to return, followed by its faithful companion superstition, and the whole of mankind is plunged once more into darkness, which

---

Marie Jean Antoine Nicolas Caritat, marquis de Condorcet, *Sketch for an Historical Picture of the Progress of the Human Mind*, trans. June Barraclough (New York; Hyperion, rpt of 1955 Noonday Press edn), from "The Ninth Stage: From Descartes to the Foundation of the French Republic, " pp. 124–37.

[i] "That happy land" is presumably France.

72

seems as if it must last for ever. Yet, little by little, day breaks again; eyes long condemned to darkness catch a glimpse of the light and close again, then slowly become accustomed to it, and at last gaze on it without flinching; once again genius dares to walk abroad on the earth, from which fanaticism and barbarism had exiled it.

We have already seen reason lift her chains, shake herself free from some of them, and, all the time regaining strength, prepare for and advance the moment of her liberation. It remains for us to study the stage in which she finally succeeds in breaking these chains, and when, still compelled to drag their vestiges behind her, she frees herself from them one by one; when at last she can go forward unhindered, and the only obstacles in her path are those that are inevitably renewed at every fresh advance because they are the necessary consequence of the very constitution of our understanding – of the connection, that is, between our means of discovering the truth and the resistance that it offers to our efforts.

Religious intolerance had forced seven of the Belgian provinces to throw off the yoke of Spain and form a federal republic. Religious intolerance alone had aroused the spirit of English liberty, which, exhausted by a protracted and bloody civil war, was finally embodied in a constitution that was for long the admiration of philosophers, but owes its preservation merely to the superstition of the English nation and the hypocrisy of their politicians. And, finally, it was also through priestly persecution that the Swedish nation found courage to reclaim a portion of their rights.

However, in the midst of all these advances, which owed their origin to theological disputes, France, Spain, Hungary and Bohemia saw their feeble liberties extinguished, or so at least it seemed.

It would be vain to look, in those countries which we call free, for that liberty which infringes none of the natural rights of man; a liberty which not only allows man to possess these rights but allows him to exercise them. For the liberty we find there is based on a system of positive rights, unequally distributed among men, and grants them different privileges according to the town in which they live, the class into which they have been born, the means of which they can dispose, and the profession that they follow. A comparative sketch of the curious inequalities to be found in different countries is the best retort that we can make to those who still uphold their virtue or necessity.

But in these same countries the law guarantees individual and civil liberty, so that if man has not there reached a state of perfection, his natural dignity is not degraded; some at least of his rights are recognized; he can no longer be said to be a slave though he can be said to be not truly free.

In those nations where at this time there was, to a greater or less extent, a genuine loss of liberty, the political rights enjoyed by the great mass of the people had been confined within such narrow limits that the destruction of the virtually arbitrary power of the aristocracy under which man had groaned, seems to have more than compensated for their loss. Man lost the title of citizen, which inequality had rendered little more than a name, but the quality of man was accorded greater respect; royal despotism saved him from feudal oppression, and relieved him from a state of humiliation all the more painful because the awareness of his condition was constantly kept alive in him by the number and actual presence of his tyrants. The system of laws tended to improve, both in those states whose constitution was partly free, and in those ruled by despots: in the former because the interests of those who exercised the real power did not invariably conflict with the interests of the people; in the latter because the interests of the despot were often indistinguishable from those of public prosperity, or because the despot's endeavours to destroy the vestiges of feudal or clerical power had imparted to the law a spirit of equality, whose inspiration may have been the desire to establish equality in slavery, but whose effects were often salutary.

We shall give a detailed exposition of the causes that have produced in Europe a kind of despotism for which there is no precedent in earlier ages or in other parts of the world, a despotism in which an all but arbitrary authority, restrained by public opinion, controlled by enlightenment, tempered by self-interest, has often contributed to the progress of wealth, industry, and education, and sometimes even to that of liberty.

Manners have become less violent through the weakening of the prejudices that had maintained their savagery, through the influence of the spirit of industry and commerce which is inimical to unrest and violence as the natural enemies of wealth, through the sense of horror inspired by the none too distant picture of the barbarism of the preceding stage, through a wider diffusion of the philosophical ideas of equality and humanity, and, finally, through the influence, slow but sure, of the general progress of enlightenment.

Religious intolerance remains, but more as an instrument of human prudence, as a tribute to popular prejudice, or as a precaution against popular unrest. Its fury abates; the fires at the stake are seldom lit, and have been replaced by a form of oppression that, if it is often more arbitrary, is less barbarous; and of recent years the persecutions have become much rarer, and the result rather of complacency or habit. Everywhere, and in every respect, governmental practice has slowly and regretfully followed the progress of public opinion and even of philosophy.

Indeed, if in the moral and political sciences there is always a large interval between the point to which philosophers have carried the progress of enlightenment and the degree of enlightenment attained by the average man of education (and it is the body of beliefs held in common by such men

74

that constitutes the generally accepted creed known as public opinion), those who direct public affairs and who immediately influence the fate of the common people, under whatever constitution they may hold their powers, are very far from rising to the level of public opinion; they follow its advance, without ever overtaking it and are always many years behind it and therefore always ignorant of many of the truths that it has learned.

This sketch of the progress of philosophy and of the dissemination of enlightenment, whose more general and more evident effects we have already examined, brings us up to the stage when the influence of progress upon public opinion, of public opinion upon nations or their leaders, suddenly ceases to be a slow, imperceptible affair, and produces a revolution in the whole order of several nations, a certain earnest of the revolution that must one day include in its scope the whole of the human race.

After long periods of error, after being led astray by vague or incomplete theories, publicists have at last discovered the true rights of man and how they can all be deduced from the single truth, that *man is a sentient being, capable of reasoning and of acquiring moral ideas.*

They have seen that the maintenance of these rights was the sole object of men's coming together in political societies, and that the social art is the art of guaranteeing the preservation of these rights and their distribution in the most equal fashion over the largest area. It was felt that in every society the means of assuring the rights of the individual should be submitted to certain common rules, but that the authority to choose these means and to determine these rules could belong only to the majority of the members of the society itself; for in making this choice the individual cannot follow his own reason without subjecting others to it, and the will of the majority is the only mark of truth that can be accepted by all without loss of equality.

Each man can in fact genuinely bind himself in advance to the will of the majority which then becomes unanimous; but he can bind only himself; and he cannot engage even himself towards this majority when it fails to respect the rights of the individual, after having once recognized them.

Here we see at once the rights of the majority over society or its members, and the limits of these rights. Here we see the origin of that unanimity which allows the decisions taken by the majority alone to impose an obligation upon all; an obligation which ceases to be legitimate when, with a change in the individuals constituting the majority, the sanction of unanimity no longer exists. Doubtless there are issues on which the decision of the majority is likely to be in favour of error and against the interests of all; but it is still this majority that must decide which issues are not to be subjected to its own direct decision; it is the majority that must appoint those persons whose judgment it considers to be more reliable than its own; it is the majority that must lay down the procedure that it considers most likely to conduct them to the truth; and it may not abdicate its authority to decide whether the decisions they take on its behalf do or do not infringe the rights that are common to all.

So, in the face of such simple principles, we see the disappearance of the belief in the existence of a contract between the people and their lawgivers, which can be annulled only by mutual consent or by the defection of one of the parties; and along with it there disappeared the less servile but no less absurd opinion according to which a nation was for ever chained to its constitution once this constitution had been established – as though the right to change it were not the guarantee of every other right, and as though human institutions, which are necessarily defective and capable of perfection as men become more enlightened, could be condemned to remain for ever in their infancy. Man was thus compelled to abandon that astute and false policy, which, forgetful of the truth that all men possess equal rights by nature, would seek to apportion those rights unequally between countries, according to the character or prosperity of a country, the conditions of its industry and commerce, and unequally between men, according to a man's birth, fortune, or profession, and which then calls into being conflicting interests and opposing forces to restore the balance, measures which would have been unnecessary without this policy and which are in any event impotent to control its more dangerous tendencies.

Nor did men any longer dare to divide humanity into two races, the one fated to rule, the other to obey, the one to deceive, the other to be deceived. They had to recognize that all men have an equal right to be informed on all that concerns them, and that none of the authorities established by men over themselves has the right to hide from them one single truth.

These principles, which the noble Sydney paid for with his blood and on which Locke set the authority of his name, were later developed by Rousseau with greater precision,[ii] breadth and energy, and he deserves renown for having established them among the truths that it is no longer permissible to forget or to combat. Man has certain needs and also certain faculties with which to satisfy them; from these faculties and from their products, modified and distributed in different ways, there results an accumulation of wealth out of which must be met the common needs of mankind. But what are the laws according to which this wealth is produced or distributed, accumulated or consumed, increased or dissipated? What, too, are the laws governing that general tendency towards an

[ii] Three republican political writers: the English philosopher John Locke (1632–1704); Jean-Jacques Rousseau; and presumably Algernon Sidney (1622–89), a Whig martyr who was exiled during the Restoration of the English monarchy in 1660, eventually returned to England, and was executed.

equilibrium between supply and demand from which it follows that, with any increase in wealth, life becomes easier and men are happier, until a point is reached when no further increase is possible; or that, again, with any decrease in wealth, life becomes harder, suffering increases, until the consequent fall in population restores the balance? How, with all the astonishing multifariousness of labour and production, supply and demand, with all the frightening complexity of conflicting interests that link the survival and well-being of one individual to the general organization of societies, that make his well-being dependent on every accident of nature and every political event, his pain and pleasure on what is happening in the remotest corner of the globe, how, with all this seeming chaos, is it that, by a universal moral law, the efforts made by each individual on his own behalf minister to the welfare of all, and that the interests of society demand that everyone should understand where his own interests lie, and should be able to follow them without hindrance?

Men, therefore, should be able to use their faculties, dispose of their wealth and provide for their needs in complete freedom. The common interest of any society, far from demanding that they should restrain such activity, on the contrary, forbids any interference with it; and as far as this aspect of public order is concerned, the guaranteeing to each man his natural rights is at once the whole of social utility, the sole duty of the social power, the only right that the general will can legitimately exercise over the individual.

But it is not enough merely that this principle should be acknowledged by society; the public authority has specific duties to fulfil. It must establish by law recognized measures for the determination of the weight, volume, size and length of all articles of trade; it must create a coinage to serve as a common measure of value and so to facilitate comparison between the value of one article of trade and that of another, so that having a value itself, it can be exchanged against anything else that can be given one; for without this common measure trade must remain confined to barter, and can acquire very little activity or scope.

The wealth produced each year provides a portion for disposal which is not required to pay for either the labour that has produced it or the labour required to ensure its replacement by an equal or greater production of wealth. The owner of this disposable portion does not owe it directly to his work; he possesses it independently of the use to which he puts his faculties in order to provide for his needs. Hence it is out of this available portion of the annual wealth that the public authority, without violating anyone's rights, can establish the funds required for the security of the State, the preservation of peace within its borders, the protection of individual rights, the exercise of those powers established for the formation or execution of the law, and, finally, the maintenance of public prosperity.

There are certain undertakings and institutions which are beneficial to society in general, and which it therefore ought to initiate, control and supervise; these provide services which the wishes and interests of individuals cannot provide by themselves, and which advance the progress of agriculture, industry or trade or the prevention or alleviation of inevitable natural hardships or unforeseen accidents.

Up to the stage of which we speak and even for a long time afterwards, these various undertakings were left to chance, to the greed of governments, to the skill of charlatans or to the prejudices or self-interest of powerful sections of the community. A disciple of Descartes, however, the famous and ill-starred John de Witt,[iii] felt that political economy ought like every other science to submit itself to the principles of philosophy and the rigour of calculation.

Political economy made little progress until the Peace of Utrecht[iv] gave Europe the promise of lasting peace. From then onwards one notices an increasing intellectual interest taken in this hitherto neglected subject; and the new science was advanced by Stewart, Smith[v] and more particularly the French economists, at least as far as precision and the purity of its principles are involved, to a point that one could hardly have hoped to reach so soon after such a long period of indifference.

But this progress in politics and political economy was caused primarily by the progress in general philosophy and metaphysics, if we take the latter word in its broadest sense.

Descartes had brought philosophy back to reason; for he had understood that it must be derived entirely from those primary and evident truths which we can discover by observing the operations of the human mind. Soon, however, his impatient imagination snatched it from the path that he had traced for it, and for a time it seemed that philosophy had regained her independence only to be led astray by new errors.

At last, Locke grasped the thread by which philosophy should be guided; he showed that an exact and precise analysis of ideas, which reduces them step by step to other ideas of more immediate origin or of simpler composition, is the only way to avoid being lost in that chaos of incomplete, incoherent and indeterminate notions which chance presents to us at hazard and we unthinkingly accept.

By this same analysis he proved that all ideas are the result of the operations of our minds upon sensations we have received, or, to put it more exactly, that they are the combinations of these sensations presented to us simultaneously by the faculty of memory in such a way that our

---

[iii] Presumably Johan de Witt (1625–72), Dutch statesman.
[iv] Of 1713, which ended the War of the Spanish Succession.
[v] The Scottish philosophers Dugald Stewart (1753–1828) and Adam Smith (1723–90).

attention is arrested and our perception is thereby limited to no more than a part of such compound sensations.

He showed that if we attach a word to each idea after analysing it and circumscribing it, we shall succeed in remembering the idea ever afterwards in a uniform fashion; that is to say, the idea will always be formed of the same simple ideas, it will always be enclosed within the same limits, and it can in consequence be used in a chain of reasoning without any risk of confusion. On the other hand, if a word is used in such a way that it does not correspond to a determinate idea, it can at different times arouse different ideas in the same person's mind, and this is the most fecund source of error in reasoning.

Locke, finally, was the first man who dared to set a limit to the human understanding, or rather to determine the nature of the truths that it can come to know and of the objects it can comprehend.

This method was soon adopted by all philosophers and, by applying it to moral science, to politics and to social economy, they were able to make almost as sure progress in these sciences as they had in the natural sciences. They were able to admit only proven truths, to separate these truths from whatever as yet remained doubtful and uncertain, and to ignore whatever is and always will be impossible to know.

Similarly the analysis of our feelings, leads to our finding, in the development of our capacity to feel pleasure and pain, the origin of our moral ideas, the foundation of those general truths which, resulting from these ideas, determine the necessary and immutable laws of justice and injustice, and, finally, the motives that we have for conforming to them, motives which spring from the very nature of our sensibility, from what might be called our moral constitution.

This metaphysical method became virtually a universal instrument. Men learnt to use it in order to perfect the methods of the physical sciences, to throw light on their principles and to examine the validity of their proofs; and it was extended to the examination of facts and to the rules of taste.

Thus it was applied to all the various undertakings of the human understanding, and by means of it the operations of the mind in every branch of knowledge were subjected to analysis, and the nature of the truths and the kind of certainty we can expect to find from each of these branches of knowledge was thereby revealed. It is this new step in philosophy that has for ever imposed a barrier between mankind and the errors of its infancy, a barrier that should save it from relapsing into its former errors under the influence of new prejudices, just as it should assure the eventual eradication of those that still survive unrecognized, and should make it certain that any that may take their place will exercise only a faint influence and enjoy only an ephemeral existence.

In Germany, however, a man of vast and profound genius laid the foundations of a new doctrine.[vi] His ardent and passionate imagination could not rest satisfied with a modest philosophy and leave unsolved those great questions about the spirituality or the survival of the human soul, about man's freedom or the freedom of God, about the existence of pain and evil in a universe governed by an all-powerful intelligence whose wisdom, justice and loving-kindness ought, it would seem, to exclude the possibility of their existence. He cut the knot which the most skilful analysis would never have been able to untie and constructed the universe from simple, indestructible, entities equal by their very nature. The relations of each of these entities with all the others, which with it form part of the system of the universe, determine those qualities of it whereby it differs from every other. The human soul and the least atom of a block of stone are, each of them, one of these monads, and they differ only in the different place assigned to them in the universal order. Out of all the possible combinations of these beings an infinite intelligence has preferred one, and could have preferred one only, the most perfect of all. If that which exists offends us by the misery and crime that we see in it, it is still true that any other combination would have had more painful results.

We shall explain this system which, being adopted, or at least upheld, by Leibniz's compatriots, has retarded the progress of philosophy amongst them. One entire school of English philosophers enthusiastically embraced and eloquently defended the doctrine of optimism, but they were less subtle and less profound than Leibniz, for whereas he based his doctrine on the belief that an all-powerful intelligence, by the very necessity of its nature, could choose only the best of all possible worlds, the English philosophers sought to prove their doctrine by appealing to observation of the particular world in which we live and, thereby sacrificing all the advantages possessed by this system so long as it remains abstract and general; they lost themselves in details, which were too often either revolting or ridiculous.

In Scotland, however, other philosophers finding that the analysis of the development of our actual faculties led to no principle that could provide a sufficiently pure or solid basis for the morality of our actions, thought to attribute a new faculty to the human soul,[vii] distinct from but associated with those of feeling or thinking, a faculty whose existence they proved only by showing that they could not do without it. We shall recount the history of these opinions and shall show how, if they have retarded the progress of philosophy, they have advanced the dissemination of philosophical ideas.

[vi] German philosopher and mathematician G. W. Leibniz (1646–1716).
[vii] Presumably the faculty of "commonsense".

Up till now we have shown the progress of philosophy only in the men who have cultivated, deepened and perfected it. It remains for us to show what have been its effects on public opinion; how reason, while it learnt to safeguard itself against the errors into which the imagination and respect for authority had so often led it, at last found a sure method of discovering and recognizing truth; and how at the same time it destroyed the prejudices of the masses which had for so long afflicted and corrupted the human race.

At last man could proclaim aloud his right, which for so long had been ignored, to submit all opinions to his own reason and to use in the search for truth the only instrument for its recognition that he has been given. Every man learnt with a sort of pride that nature had not for ever condemned him to base his beliefs on the opinions of others; the superstitions of antiquity and the abasement of reason before the transports of supernatural religion disappeared from society as from philosophy.

Soon there was formed in Europe a class of men who were concerned less with the discovery or development of the truth than with its propagation, men who whilst devoting themselves to the tracking down of prejudices in the hiding places where the priests, the schools, the governments and all long-established institutions had gathered and protected them, made it their life-work to destroy popular errors rather than to drive back the frontiers of human knowledge – an indirect way of aiding its progress which was not less fraught with peril, nor less useful.

In England Collins and Bolingbroke, in France Bayle, Fontenelle, Voltaire, Montesquieu and the schools founded by these famous men,[viii] fought on the side of truth, using in turn all the weapons with which learning, philosophy, wit and literary talent can furnish reason; using every mood from humour to pathos, every literary form from the vast erudite encyclopædia to the novel or the broadsheet of the day; covering truth with a veil that spared weaker eyes and excited one to guess what lay beyond it; skilfully flattering prejudices so as to attack them the better; seldom threatening them, and then always either only one in its entirety or several partially; sometimes conciliating the enemies of reason by seeming to wish only for a half-tolerance in religious matters, only for a half-freedom in politics; sparing despotism when tilting against the absurdities of religion, and religion when abusing tyranny; yet always attacking the principles of these two scourges even when they seemed to be against only their more revolting or ridiculous abuses, and laying their axes to the very roots of

---

[viii] Philosopher Arthur Collins (1680–1732), statesman Henry Bolingbroke (1678–1751), philosopher Pierre Bayle (1647–1706), writer Bernard de Fontenelle (1657–1757), influential Enlightenment intellectual François de Voltaire (1694–1778), and political philosopher Charles de Secondat, Baron de Montesquieu (1689–1755).

these sinister trees when they appeared to be lopping off a few stray branches; sometimes teaching the friends of liberty that superstition is the invincible shield behind which despotism shelters and should therefore be the first victim to be sacrificed, the first chain to be broken, and sometimes denouncing it to the despots as the real enemy of their power, and frightening them with stories of its secret machinations and its bloody persecutions; never ceasing to demand the independence of reason and the freedom of the press as the right and the salvation of mankind; protesting with indefatigable energy against all the crimes of fanaticism and tyranny; pursuing, in all matters of religion, administration, morals and law, anything that bore the marks of tyranny, harshness or barbarism; invoking the name of nature to bid kings, captains, magistrates and priests to show respect for human life; laying to their charge, with vehemence and severity, the blood their policy or their indifference still spilled on the battlefield or on the scaffold; and finally, taking for their battle cry – *reason, tolerance, humanity.* . . .

chapter six

"Absolute Freedom and Terror"
G. W. F. Hegel

The most influential European philosopher of the first half of the nineteenth century was the German thinker Georg Wilhelm Friedrich Hegel (1770–1831). His idealistic system saw all reality as *Geist* or Spirit developing through a dialectical process of self-opposition and higher incorporation, a process embodied in the actual stages and events of human history. He endorsed Enlightenment ideals – the idea of consciousness as individual freedom, and of the objects of consciousness as value-neutral objects of potential utility – as a necessary but incomplete stage through which the human spirit must pass in its journey to complete self-understanding. In this excerpt from his most beautiful work, *Phenomenology of Spirit* (1807), Hegel characterizes what is wrong with the Enlightened consciousness: it is one-sided and unbalanced, the freedom of a solipsistic, empty individual who sees others as mere objects for use. Hence it led to the worst violence of the French Revolution, the Terror of 1793–4, during which the French ruling "Committee of Public Safety" executed about 40,000 alleged enemies of the fledgling republic. For true freedom, Spirit must await its further development, when it discovers that real, concrete freedom can only be achieved in the context of membership in a moral community under the institutions of the State.

Consciousness has found its Notion in Utility.[i] But it is partly still an *object*, and partly, for that very reason, still an *End* to be attained, which consciousness does not find itself to possess immediately. Utility is still a predicate of the object, not itself a subject or the immediate and sole *actuality* of the object. It is the same thing that appeared before, when being-for-self had not yet shown itself to be the substance[ii] of the other moments, a demonstration which would have meant that the Useful was directly nothing else but the self of consciousness and that this latter was

Georg Wilhelm Friedrich Hegel, *Phenomenology of Spirit*, trans. A. V. Miller (Oxford: Oxford University Press, 1977), "Absolute Freedom and Terror," paras 582–95, pp. 355–63.

[i] "Notion" refers to the pure, comprehensive understanding of a thing. Hegel is claiming that the Enlightenment regards the essence of reality as mere utility.

thereby in possession of it. This withdrawal from the form of objectivity of the Useful has, however, already taken place in principle and from this inner revolution there emerges the actual revolution of the actual world, the new shape of consciousness, *absolute freedom*.

In fact, what we have here is no more than an empty show of objectivity separating self-consciousness from possession. For, partly, all existence and validity of the specific members of the organization of the actual world and the world of faith[iii] have, in general, returned into this simple determination as into their ground and spiritual principle; partly, however, this simple determination no longer possesses anything of its own, it is rather pure metaphysic, pure Notion, or a pure knowing by self-consciousness. That is to say, of the *being-in-and-for-itself* of the Useful *qua* object, consciousness recognizes that its *being-in-itself*, is essentially a *being-for-an-other*; being-in-itself, as *devoid of self*, is in truth a passive self, or that which is a self for another self.[iv] The object, however, exists for consciousness in this abstract form of pure being-in-itself, for consciousness is pure *insight* whose distinctions are in the pure form of Notions. But the *being-for-self* into which being-for-an-other returns, i.e. the self, is not a self belonging exclusively to what is called object and distinct from the "I"; for consciousness, *qua* pure insight, is not a *single* self which could be confronted by the object as equally having a self of its own, but is pure Notion, the gazing of the self into the self, the absolute seeing of *itself* doubled; the certainty of itself is the universal Subject, and its conscious Notion is the essence of all actuality. If, then, the Useful was merely the alternation of the moments, an alternation which did not return into its own *unity*, and hence was still an object for knowing, it now ceases to be this. For knowing is itself the movement of those abstract moments, it is the universal self, the self of itself as well as of the object and, as universal, is the self-returning unity of this movement.

Spirit thus comes before us as *absolute freedom*. It is self-consciousness which grasps the fact that its certainty of itself is the essence of all the spiritual 'masses', or spheres, of the real as well as of the supersensible world, or conversely, that essence and actuality are consciousness's knowledge of *itself*. It is conscious of its pure personality and therein of all spiritual reality, and all reality is solely spiritual; the world is for it simply its own will, and this is a general will.[v] And what is more, this will is not the empty thought of will which consists in silent assent, or assent by a

---

[ii] "Substance" refers to the underlying reality, the true being, of a thing.

[iii] The world beyond the actual world, as pictured by religious faith.

[iv] Being "in-itself" simply is; being "for-another" is an object for consciousness; being "in-and-for-itself" both is and is an object for itself, as in a self-aware human being.

[v] A reference to Rousseau's concept of the general will of a free society, which was influential during the French Revolution.

representative, but a real general will, the will of all *individuals* as such. For will is in itself the consciousness of personality, or of each, and it is as this genuine actual will that it ought to be, as the *self-conscious* essence of each and every personality, so that each, undivided from the whole, always does everything, and what appears as done by the whole is the direct and conscious deed of each.

This undivided Substance of absolute freedom ascends the throne of the world without any power being able to resist it. For since, in truth, consciousness alone is the element in which the spiritual beings or powers have their substance, their entire system which is organized and maintained by division into 'masses' or spheres has collapsed, now that the individual consciousness conceives the object as having no other essence than self-consciousness itself, or as being absolutely Notion. What made the Notion into an existent *object* was its diremption into separate *subsistent* spheres, but when the object becomes a Notion, there is no longer anything in it with a continuing existence; negativity has permeated all its moments. It comes into existence in such a way that each individual consciousness raises itself out of its allotted sphere, no longer finds its essence and its work in this particular sphere, but grasps itself as the *Notion* of will, grasps all spheres as the essence of this will, and therefore can only realize itself in a work which is a work of the whole. In this absolute freedom, therefore, all social groups or classes which are the spiritual spheres into which the whole is articulated are abolished; the individual consciousness that belonged to any such sphere, and willed and fulfilled itself in it, has put aside its limitation; its purpose is the general purpose, its language universal law, its work the universal work.

The object and the [moment of] *difference* have here lost the meaning of *utility*, which was the predicate of all real being; consciousness does not begin its movement in the object as if this were something *alien* from which it first had to return into itself; on the contrary, the object is for it consciousness itself. The antithesis, consists, therefore, solely in the difference between the *individual* and the *universal* consciousness; but the individual consciousness itself is directly in its own eyes that which had only the *semblance* of an antithesis; it is universal consciousness and will. The *beyond* of this its actual existence hovers over the corpse of the vanished independence of real being, or the being of faith, merely as the exhalation of a stale gas, of the vacuous *Être suprême*.[vi]

After the various spiritual spheres and the restricted life of the individual have been done away with, as well as his two worlds, all that remains, therefore, is the immanent movement of universal self-consciousness as a reciprocity of self-consciousness in the form of *universality* and of *personal*

[vi] Supreme Being.

consciousness: the universal will goes *into itself* and is a *single, individual* will to which universal law and work stand opposed. But this *individual* consciousness is no less directly conscious of itself as universal will; it is aware that its object is a law given by that will and a work accomplished by it; therefore, in passing over into action and in creating objectivity, it is doing nothing individual, but carrying out the laws and functions of the state.

This movement is thus the interaction of consciousness with itself in which it lets nothing break loose to become a *free object* standing over against it. It follows from this that it cannot achieve anything positive, either universal works of language or of reality, either of laws and general institutions of *conscious* freedom, or of deeds and works of a freedom that *wills* them. The work which *conscious* freedom might accomplish would consist in that freedom, *qua universal* substance, making itself into an *object* and into an *enduring being*. This otherness would be the moment of difference in it whereby it divided itself into stable spiritual 'masses' or spheres and into the members of various powers. These spheres would be partly the 'thought-things' of a *power* that is separated into legislative, judicial, and executive powers; but partly, they would be the *real essences* we found in the real world of culture, and, looking more closely at the content of universal action, they would be the particular spheres of labour which would be further distinguished as more specific 'estates' or classes. Universal freedom, which would have separated itself in this way into its constituent parts and by the very fact of doing so would have made itself into an *existent* Substance, would thereby be free from *particular* individuality, and would apportion the *plurality* of individuals to its various constituent parts. This, however, would restrict the activity and the being of the personality to a branch of the whole, to one kind of activity and being; when placed in the element of *being*, personality would have the significance of a specific personality; it would cease to be in truth universal self-consciousness. Neither by the mere idea of obedience to *self-given* laws which would assign to it only a part of the whole, nor by its being *represented* in law-making and universal action, does self-consciousness let itself be cheated out of *reality*, the reality of *itself* making the law and accomplishing, not a particular work, but the universal work itself. For where the self is merely *represented* and is present only as an idea, there it is not *actual*; where it is represented by proxy, it *is not*.

Just as the individual self-consciousness does not find itself in this *universal work* of absolute freedom *qua* existent Substance, so little does it find itself in the *deeds* proper and *individual* actions of the will of this freedom. Before the universal can perform a deed it must concentrate itself into the One of individuality and put at the head an individual self-consciousness; for the universal will is only an *actual* will in a self, which is a

One. But thereby all other individuals are excluded from the entirety of this deed and have only a limited share in it, so that the deed would not be a deed of the *actual universal* self-consciousness. Universal freedom, therefore, can produce neither a positive work nor a deed; there is left for it only *negative* action; it is merely the *fury* of destruction.

But the supreme reality and the reality which stands in the greatest antithesis to universal freedom, or rather the sole object that will still exist for that freedom, is the freedom and individuality of actual self-consciousness itself. For that universality which does not let itself advance to the reality of an organic articulation, and whose aim is to maintain itself in an unbroken continuity, at the same time creates a distinction within itself, because it is movement or consciousness in general. And, moreover, by virtue of its own abstraction, it divides itself into extremes equally abstract, into a simple, inflexible cold universality, and into the discrete, absolute hard rigidity and self-willed atomism of actual self-consciousness. Now that it has completed the destruction of the actual organization of the world, and exists now just for itself, this is its sole object, an object that no longer has any content, possession, existence, or outer extension, but is merely this knowledge of itself as an absolutely pure and free individual self. All that remains of the object by which it can be laid hold of is solely its *abstract* existence as such. The relation, then, of these two, since each exists indivisibly and absolutely for itself, and thus cannot dispose of a middle term which would link them together, is one of wholly *unmediated* pure negation, a negation, moreover, of the individual as a being *existing* in the universal. The sole work and deed of universal freedom is therefore *death*, a death too which has no inner significance or filling, for what is negated is the empty point of the absolutely free self. It is thus the coldest and meanest of all deaths, with no more significance than cutting off a head of cabbage or swallowing a mouthful of water.[vii]

In this flat, commonplace monosyllable is contained the wisdom of the government, the abstract intelligence of the universal will, in the fulfilling of itself. The government is itself nothing else but the self-established focus, or the individuality, of the universal will. The government, which wills and executes its will from a single point, at the same time wills and executes a specific order and action. On the one hand, it excludes all other individuals from its act, and on the other hand, it thereby constitutes itself a government that is a specific will, and so stands opposed to the universal will; consequently, it is absolutely impossible for it to exhibit itself as anything else but a *faction*. What is called government is merely the *victorious* faction, and in the very fact of its being a faction lies the direct

---

[vii] During the Terror thousands died on the guillotine, and thousands more on boats that were floated into the Loire river, then sunk. I thank James Schmidt for the latter reference.

necessity of its overthrow; and its being government makes it, conversely, into a faction, and [so] guilty. When the universal will maintains that what the government has actually done is a crime committed against it, the government, for its part, has nothing specific and outwardly apparent by which the guilt of the will opposed to it could be demonstrated; for what stands opposed to it as the *actual* universal will is only an unreal pure will, *intention. Being suspected*, therefore, takes the place, or has the significance and effect, of *being guilty*; and the external reaction against this reality that lies in the simple inwardness of intention, consists in the cold, matter-of-fact annihilation of this existent self, from which nothing else can be taken away but its mere being.

In this its characteristic *work*, absolute freedom becomes explicitly objective to itself, and self-consciousness learns what absolute freedom in effect is. *In itself*, it is just this *abstract self-consciousness*, which effaces all distinction and all continuance of distinction within it. It is as such that it is objective to itself; the *terror* of death is the vision of this negative nature of itself. But absolutely free self-consciousness finds this its reality quite different from what its own Notion of itself was, viz. that the universal will is merely the *positive* essence of personality, and that this latter knows itself in it only positively, or as preserved therein. Here, however, this self-consciousness which, as pure insight, completely separates its positive and its negative nature – completely separates the predicateless Absolute as pure *Thought* and as pure *Matter* – is confronted with the absolute *transition* of the one into the other as a present reality. The universal will, *qua* absolutely *positive*, actual self-consciousness, because it is this self-conscious reality heightened to the level of *pure* thought or of *abstract* matter, changes round into its negative nature and shows itself to be equally that which *puts an end to the thinking of oneself*, or to self-consciousness.

Absolute freedom as *pure* self-identity of the universal will thus has within it *negation*; but this means that it contains *difference* in general, and this again it develops as an *actual* difference. For pure *negativity* has in the self-identical universal will the element of subsistence, or the *Substance* in which its moments are realized; it has the matter which it can utilize in accordance with its own determinateness; and in so far as this Substance has shown itself to be the negative element for the individual consciousness, the organization of spiritual 'masses' or spheres to which the plurality of individual consciousnesses are assigned thus takes shape once more. These individuals who have felt the fear of death, of their absolute master, again submit to negation and distinctions, arrange themselves in the various spheres, and return to an apportioned and limited task, but thereby to their substantial reality.

Out of this tumult, Spirit would be thrown back to its starting-point, to the ethical and real world of culture, which would have been merely refreshed and rejuvenated by the fear of the lord and master which has again entered men's hearts. Spirit would have to traverse anew and continually repeat this cycle of necessity if the result were only the complete interpenetration of self-consciousness and Substance – an interpenetration in which self-consciousness, which has experienced the negative power of its universal essence acting on it, would desire to know and find itself, not as this particular individual, but only as a universal, and therefore, too, would be able to endure the objective reality of universal Spirit, a reality excluding self-consciousness *qua* particular. But in absolute freedom there was no reciprocal action between a consciousness that is immersed in the complexities of existence, or that sets itself specific aims and thoughts, and a valid *external* world, whether of reality or thought; instead, the world was absolutely in the form of consciousness as a universal will, and equally self-consciousness was drawn together out of the whole expanse of existence or manifested aims and judgements, and concentrated into the simple self. The culture to which it attains in interaction with that essence is, therefore, the grandest and the last, is that of seeing its pure, simple reality immediately vanish and pass away into empty nothingness. In the world of culture itself it does not get as far as to behold its negation or alienation in this form of pure abstraction; on the contrary, its negation is filled with a content, either honour or wealth, which it gains in place of the self that it has alienated from itself; or the language of Spirit and insight which the disrupted consciousness acquires; or it is the heaven of faith, or the Utility of the Enlightenment. All these determinations have vanished in the loss suffered by the self in absolute freedom; its negation is the death that is without meaning, the sheer terror of the negative that contains nothing positive, nothing that fills it with a content. At the same time, however, this negation in its real existence is not something alien; it is neither the universal inaccessible *necessity* in which the ethical world perishes, nor the particular accident of private possession, nor the whim of the owner on which the disrupted consciousness sees itself dependent; on the contrary, it is the *universal will* which in this its ultimate abstraction has nothing positive and therefore can give nothing in return for the sacrifice. But for that very reason it is immediately one with self-consciousness, or it is the pure positive, because it is the pure negative; and the meaningless death, the unfilled negativity of the self, changes round in its inner Notion into absolute positivity. For consciousness, the immediate unity of itself with the universal will, its demand to know itself as this specific point in the universal will, is changed round into the absolutely opposite experience. What vanishes for it in that experience is abstract *being* or the immediacy of that insubstantial point, and this vanished immediacy is the universal will itself which it now knows itself to be in so far as it is a pure knowing or pure will. Consequently, it knows that will to be itself, and knows itself to be essential being; but not essential being as an *immediate existence*, not will as revolutionary government or anarchy striving to establish anarchy, nor itself as the centre of this faction or the opposite faction; on the contrary, the *universal will* is its *pure knowing and willing* and *it* is the universal will *qua* this pure knowing and willing. It does not lose *itself* in that will, for pure knowing and willing is much more *it* than is that atomic point of consciousness. It is thus the interaction of pure knowing with itself; pure *knowing qua essential being* is the universal will; but this essential being is abolutely nothing else but pure knowing. Self-consciousness is, therefore, the pure knowing of essential being *qua* pure knowing. Further, as an *individual self*, it is only the form of the subject or of real action, a form which is known by it as *form*. Similarly, *objective* reality, *being*, is for it simply a selfless form; for that reality would be something that is not known. This knowing, however, knows knowing to be essential being.

Absolute freedom has thus removed the antithesis between the universal and the individual will. The self-alienated Spirit, driven to the extreme of its antithesis in which pure willing and the agent of that pure willing are still distinct, reduces the antithesis to a transparent form and therein finds itself. Just as the realm of the real world passes over into the realm of faith and insight, so does absolute freedom leave its self-destroying reality and pass over into another land of self-conscious Spirit where, in this unreal world, freedom has the value of truth. In the thought of this truth Spirit refreshes itself, in so far as *it is* and remains *thought*, and knows this being which is enclosed within self-consciousness to be essential being in its perfection and completeness. There has arisen the new shape of Spirit, that of the *moral* Spirit.

chapter seven

"Bourgeois and Proletarians"
Karl Marx and Friedrich Engels

Marxism is the most important criticism of the dominant Western form of economic modernity, capitalism. Among the various forms of socialism and anti-industrialism common in the nineteenth century, the German thinkers Karl Marx (1818–83) and his collaborator Friedrich Engels (1820–95) uniquely devised what they regarded as a "scientific" socialism. Borrowing Hegel's notion of dialectical development, they formulated a comprehensive theory of human history in which capitalism is a necessary but temporary stage whose industrial development would prepare the way for the eventual communist abolition of private property. They did not object to modern industry, science, technology, and secularism, but only to the restriction of ownership and benefits to the capitalist or "bourgeois" class. The following excerpt from their famous pamphlet, *Manifesto of the Communist Party* (1848), represents one of the most moving and prescient depictions of modern society. Capitalism is itself an ongoing economic revolution that continually builds and demolishes society, in the process demystifying all non-monetary forms of authority, thereby making class struggle naked and shameless. However abhorrent this capitalism is to the authors, it is hard not to hear in their words a hostile awe at the monumental changes it was working on the human condition.

The history of all hitherto existing society is the history of class struggles.[i]

Freeman and slave, patrician and plebeian, lord and serf, guild-master and journeyman, in a word, oppressor and oppressed, stood in constant opposition to one another, carried on an uninterrupted, now hidden, now open fight, a fight that each time ended, either in a revolutionary re-constitution of society at large, or in the common ruin of the contending classes.

Karl Marx and Friedrich Engels, "Bourgeois and Proletarians," Section One of *Manifesto of the Communist Party*, trans. Samuel Moore, in Robert Tucker, *The Marx–Engels Reader* (New York: Norton, 1978), pp. 473–83.

[i] In capitalism, the most important classes are the bourgeoisie, that is, the owners of modern industry, and the proletariat, the class of industrial workers.

In the earlier epochs of history, we find almost everywhere a complicated arrangement of society into various orders, a manifold gradation of social rank. In ancient Rome we have patricians, knights, plebeians, slaves; in the Middle Ages, feudal lords, vassals, guild-masters, journeymen, apprentices, serfs; in almost all of these classes, again, subordinate gradations.

The modern bourgeois society that has sprouted from the ruins of feudal society has not done away with class antagonisms. It has but established new classes, new conditions of oppression, new forms of struggle in place of the old ones.

Our epoch, the epoch of the bourgeoisie, possesses, however, this distinctive feature: it has simplified the class antagonisms: Society as a whole is more and more splitting up into two great hostile camps, into two great classes directly facing each other: Bourgeoisie and Proletariat.

From the serfs of the Middle Ages sprang the chartered burghers of the earliest towns.[ii] From these burgesses the first elements of the bourgeoisie were developed.

The discovery of America, the rounding of the Cape, opened up fresh ground for the rising bourgeoisie. The East-Indian and Chinese markets, the colonisation of America, trade with the colonies, the increase in the means of exchange and in commodities generally, gave to commerce, to navigation, to industry, an impulse never before known, and thereby, to the revolutionary element in the tottering feudal society, a rapid development.

The feudal system of industry, under which industrial production was monopolised by closed guilds, now no longer sufficed for the growing wants of the new markets. The manufacturing system took its place. The guild-masters were pushed on one side by the manufacturing middle class; division of labour between the different corporate guilds vanished in the face of division of labour in each single workshop.[iii]

Meantime the markets kept ever growing, the demand ever rising. Even manufacture no longer sufficed. Thereupon, steam and machinery revolutionised industrial production. The place of manufacture was taken by the giant, Modern Industry, the place of the industrial middle class, by industrial millionaires, the leaders of whole industrial armies, the modern bourgeois.

Modern industry has established the world-market, for which the discovery of America paved the way. This market has given an immense development to commerce, to navigation, to communication by land. This development has, in its turn, reacted on the extension of industry; and in

---

[ii] Burghers were the residents of legally independent towns, whose lands (borough) had been freed from the control of the rural, feudal lords, ultimately by a royal charter granting their freedoms. Later, charters would primarily grant trading and commercial rights.

[iii] Guilds were trade associations of medieval craftsmen.

proportion as industry, commerce, navigation, railways extended, in the same proportion the bourgeoisie developed, increased its capital, and pushed into the background every class handed down from the Middle Ages.

We see, therefore, how the modern bourgeoisie is itself the product of a long course of development, of a series of revolutions in the modes of production and of exchange.

Each step in the development of the bourgeoisie was accompanied by a corresponding political advance of that class. An oppressed class under the sway of the feudal nobility, an armed and self-governing association in the mediaeval commune,[iv] here independent urban republic (as in Italy and Germany), there taxable "third estate" of the monarchy (as in France), afterwards, in the period of manufacture proper, serving either the semi-feudal or the absolute monarchy as a counterpoise against the nobility, and, in fact, corner-stone of the great monarchies in general, the bourgeoisie has at last, since the establishment of Modern Industry and of the world-market, conquered for itself, in the modern representative State, exclusive political sway. The executive of the modern State is but a committee for managing the common affairs of the whole bourgeoisie.

The bourgeoisie, historically, has played a most revolutionary part.

The bourgeoisie, wherever it has got the upper hand, has put an end to all feudal, patriarchal, idyllic relations. It has pitilessly torn asunder the motley feudal ties that bound man to his "natural superiors," and has left remaining no other nexus between man and man than naked self-interest, than callous "cash payment." It has drowned the most heavenly ecstasies of religious fervour, of chivalrous enthusiasm, of philistine sentimentalism, in the icy water of egotistical calculation. It has resolved personal worth into exchange value, and in place of the numberless indefeasible chartered freedoms, has set up that single, unconscionable freedom – Free Trade. In one word, for exploitation, veiled by religious and political illusions, it has substituted naked, shameless, direct, brutal exploitation.

The bourgeoisie has stripped of its halo every occupation hitherto honoured and looked up to with reverent awe. It has converted the physician, the lawyer, the priest, the poet, the man of science, into its paid wage-labourers.

The bourgeoisie has torn away from the family its sentimental veil, and has reduced the family relation to a mere money relation.

The bourgeoisie has disclosed how it came to pass that the brutal display of vigour in the Middle Ages, which Reactionists so much admire, found its fitting complement in the most slothful indolence. It has been the first to show what man's activity can bring about. It has accomplished wonders

---

[iv] "Commune" was an early term for the independent town.

far surpassing Egyptian pyramids, Roman aqueducts, and Gothic cathedrals; it has conducted expeditions that put in the shade all former Exoduses of nations and crusades.

The bourgeoisie cannot exist without constantly revolutionising the instruments of production, and thereby the relations of production, and with them the whole relations of society. Conservation of the old modes of production in unaltered form, was, on the contrary, the first condition of existence for all earlier industrial classes. Constant revolutionising of production, uninterrupted disturbance of all social conditions, everlasting uncertainty and agitation distinguish the bourgeois epoch from all earlier ones. All fixed, fast-frozen relations, with their train of ancient and venerable prejudices and opinions, are swept away, all new-formed ones become antiquated before they can ossify. All that is solid melts into air, all that is holy is profaned, and man is at last compelled to face with sober senses, his real conditions of life, and his relations with his kind.

The need of a constantly expanding market for its products chases the bourgeoisie over the whole surface of the globe. It must nestle everywhere, settle everywhere, establish connexions everywhere.

The bourgeoisie has through its exploitation of the world-market given a cosmopolitan character to production and consumption in every country. To the great chagrin of Reactionists, it has drawn from under the feet of industry the national ground on which it stood. All old-established national industries have been destroyed or are daily being destroyed. They are dislodged by new industries, whose introduction becomes a life and death question for all civilised nations, by industries that no longer work up indigenous raw material, but raw material drawn from the remotest zones; industries whose products are consumed, not only at home, but in every quarter of the globe. In place of the old wants, satisfied by the productions of the country, we find new wants, requiring for their satisfaction the products of distant lands and climes. In place of the old local and national seclusion and self-sufficiency, we have intercourse in every direction, universal inter-dependence of nations. And as in material, so also in intellectual production. The intellectual creations of individual nations become common property. National one-sidedness and narrow-mindedness become more and more impossible, and from the numerous national and local literatures, there arises a world literature.

The bourgeoisie, by the rapid improvement of all instruments of production, by the immensely facilitated means of communication, draws all, even the most barbarian, nations into civilisation. The cheap prices of its commodities are the heavy artillery with which it batters down all Chinese walls, with which it forces the barbarians' intensely obstinate hatred of foreigners to capitulate. It compels all nations, on pain of extinction, to adopt the bourgeois mode of production; it compels them to introduce what it calls civilisation into their midst, *i.e.*, to become bourgeois themselves. In one word, it creates a world after its own image.

The bourgeoisie has subjected the country to the rule of the towns. It has created enormous cities, has greatly increased the urban population as compared with the rural, and has thus rescued a considerable part of the population from the idiocy of rural life. Just as it has made the country dependent on the towns, so it has made barbarian and semi-barbarian countries dependent on the civilised ones, nations of peasants on nations of bourgeois, the East on the West.

The bourgeoisie keeps more and more doing away with the scattered state of the population, of the means of production, and of property. It has agglomerated population, centralised means of production, and has concentrated property in a few hands. The necessary consequence of this was political centralisation. Independent, or but loosely connected provinces, with separate interests, laws, governments and systems of taxation, became lumped together into one nation, with one government, one code of laws, one national class-interest, one frontier and one customs-tariff.

The bourgeoisie, during its rule of scarce one hundred years, has created more massive and more colossal productive forces than have all preceding generations together. Subjection of Nature's forces to man, machinery, application of chemistry to industry and agriculture, steam-navigation, railways, electric telegraphs, clearing of whole continents for cultivation, canalisation of rivers, whole populations conjured out of the ground – what earlier century had even a presentiment that such productive forces slumbered in the lap of social labour?

We see then: the means of production and of exchange, on whose foundation the bourgeoisie built itself up, were generated in feudal society. At a certain stage in the development of these means of production and of exchange, the conditions under which feudal society produced and exchanged, the feudal organisation of agriculture and manufacturing industry, in one word, the feudal relations of property became no longer compatible with the already developed productive forces; they became so many fetters. They had to be burst asunder; they were burst asunder.

Into their place stepped free competition, accompanied by a social and political constitution adapted to it, and by the economical and political sway of the bourgeois class.

A similar movement is going on before our own eyes. Modern bourgeois society with its relations of production, of exchange and of property, a society that has conjured up such gigantic means of production and of exchange, is like the sorcerer, who is no longer able to control the powers of the nether world whom he has called up by his spells. For many a decade past the history of industry and commerce is but the history of the revolt of modern productive forces against modern conditions of production, against the property relations that are the conditions for the existence of the bourgeoisie and of its rule. It is enough to mention the commercial crises that by their periodical return put on its trial, each time more threateningly, the existence of the entire bourgeois society. In these crises a great part not only of the existing products, but also of the previously created productive forces, are periodically destroyed. In these crises there breaks out an epidemic that, in all earlier epochs, would have seemed an absurdity – the epidemic of over-production. Society suddenly finds itself put back into a state of momentary barbarism; it appears as if a famine, a universal war of devastation had cut off the supply of every means of subsistence; industry and commerce seem to be destroyed; and why? Because there is too much civilisation, too much means of subsistence, too much industry, too much commerce. The productive forces at the disposal of society no longer tend to further the development of the conditions of bourgeois property; on the contrary, they have become too powerful for these conditions, by which they are fettered, and so soon as they overcome these fetters, they bring disorder into the whole of bourgeois society, endanger the existence of bourgeois property. The conditions of bourgeois society are too narrow to comprise the wealth created by them. And how does the bourgeoisie get over these crises? On the one hand by enforced destruction of a mass of productive forces; on the other, by the conquest of new markets, and by the more thorough exploitation of the old ones. That is to say, by paving the way for more extensive and more destructive crises, and by diminishing the means whereby crises are prevented.

The weapons with which the bourgeoisie felled feudalism to the ground are now turned against the bourgeoisie itself.

But not only has the bourgeoisie forged the weapons that bring death to itself; it has also called into existence the men who are to wield those weapons – the modern working class – the proletarians.

In proportion as the bourgeoisie, *i.e.*, capital, is developed, in the same proportion is the proletariat, the modern working class, developed – a class of labourers, who live only so long as they find work, and who find work only so long as their labour increases capital. These labourers, who must sell themselves piece-meal, are a commodity, like every other article of commerce, and are consequently exposed to all the vicissitudes of competition, to all the fluctuations of the market.

Owing to the extensive use of machinery and to division of labour, the work of the proletarians has lost all individual character, and consequently, all charm for the workman. He becomes an appendage of the machine, and it is only the most simple, most monotonous, and most easily acquired knack, that is required of him. Hence, the cost of production of a workman is restricted, almost entirely, to the means of subsistence that he requires for his maintenance, and for the propagation of his race. But the price of a commodity, and therefore also of labour, is equal to its cost of production. In proportion, therefore, as the repulsiveness of the work increases, the wage decreases. Nay more, in proportion as the use of machinery and division of labour increases, in the same proportion the burden of toil also increases, whether by prolongation of the working hours, by increase of the work exacted in a given time or by increased speed of the machinery, etc.

Modern industry has converted the little workshop of the patriarchal master into the great factory of the industrial capitalist. Masses of labourers, crowded into the factory, are organised like soldiers. As privates of the industrial army they are placed under the command of a perfect hierarchy of officers and sergeants. Not only are they slaves of the bourgeois class, and of the bourgeois State; they are daily and hourly enslaved by the machine, by the over-looker, and, above all, by the individual bourgeois manufacturer himself. The more openly this despotism proclaims gain to be its end and aim, the more petty, the more hateful and the more embittering it is.

The less the skill and exertion of strength implied in manual labour, in other words, the more modern industry becomes developed, the more is the labour of men superseded by that of women. Differences of age and sex have no longer any distinctive social validity for the working class. All are instruments of labour, more or less expensive to use, according to their age and sex.

No sooner is the exploitation of the labourer by the manufacturer, so far, at an end, that he receives his wages in cash, than he is set upon by the other portions of the bourgeoisie, the landlord, the shopkeeper, the pawn-broker, etc.

The lower strata of the middle class – the small tradespeople, shop-keepers, and retired tradesmen generally, the handicraftsmen and peasants – all these sink gradually into the proletariat, partly because their diminutive capital does not suffice for the scale on which Modern Industry is carried on, and is swamped in the competition with the large capitalists, partly because their specialised skill is rendered worthless by new methods of production. Thus the proletariat is recruited from all classes of the population.

The proletariat goes through various stages of development. With its birth begins its struggle with the bourgeoisie. At first the contest is carried on by individual labourers, then by the workpeople of a factory, then by the operatives of one trade, in one locality, against the individual bourgeois who directly exploits them. They direct their attacks not against the bourgeois conditions of production, but against the instruments of production themselves; they destroy imported wares that compete with their labour, they smash to pieces machinery, they set factories ablaze, they seek to restore by force the vanished status of the workman of the Middle Ages.

At this stage the labourers still form an incoherent mass scattered over the whole country, and broken up by their mutual competition. If anywhere they unite to form more compact bodies, this is not yet the consequence of their own active union, but of the union of the bourgeoisie, which class, in order to attain its own political ends, is compelled to set the whole proletariat in motion, and is moreover yet, for a time, able to do so. At this stage, therefore, the proletarians do not fight their enemies, but the enemies of their enemies, the remnants of absolute monarchy, the landowners, the non-industrial bourgeois, the petty bourgeoisie. Thus the whole historical movement is concentrated in the hands of the bourgeoisie; every victory so obtained is a victory for the bourgeoisie.

But with the development of industry the proletariat not only increases in number; it becomes concentrated in greater masses, its strength grows, and it feels that strength more. The various interests and conditions of life within the ranks of the proletariat are more and more equalised, in proportion as machinery obliterates all distinctions of labour, and nearly everywhere reduces wages to the same low level. The growing competition among the bourgeois, and the resulting commercial crises, make the wages of the workers ever more fluctuating. The unceasing improvement of machinery, ever more rapidly developing, makes their livelihood more and more precarious; the collisions between individual workmen and individual bourgeois take more and more the character of collisions between two classes. Thereupon the workers begin to form combinations (Trades Unions) against the bourgeois; they club together in order to keep up the rate of wages; they found permanent associations in order to make provision beforehand for these occasional revolts. Here and there the contest breaks out into riots.

Now and then the workers are victorious, but only for a time. The real fruit of their battles lies, not in the immediate result, but in the ever-expanding union of the workers. This union is helped on by the improved means of communication that are created by modern industry and that place the workers of different localities in contact with one another. It was just this contact that was needed to centralise the numerous local struggles, all of the same character, into one national struggle between classes. But every class struggle is a political struggle. And that union, to attain which the burghers of the Middle Ages, with their miserable highways, required centuries, the modern proletarians, thanks to railways, achieve in a few years.

This organisation of the proletarians into a class, and consequently into a political party, is continually being upset again by the competition between the workers themselves. But it ever rises up again, stronger, firmer, mightier. It compels legislative recognition of particular interests of the workers, by taking advantage of the divisions among the bourgeoisie itself. Thus the ten-hours' bill in England was carried.[v]

Altogether collisions between the classes of the old society further, in many ways, the course of development of the proletariat. The bourgeoisie finds itself involved in a constant battle. At first with the aristocracy; later on, with those portions of the bourgeoisie itself, whose interests have become antagonistic to the progress of industry; at all times, with the bourgeoisie of foreign countries. In all these battles it sees itself compelled to appeal to the proletariat, to ask for its help, and thus, to drag it into the political arena. The bourgeoisie itself, therefore, supplies the proletariat with its own elements of political and general education, in other words, it furnishes the proletariat with weapons for fighting the bourgeoisie.

Further, as we have already seen, entire sections of the ruling classes are, by the advance of industry, precipitated into the proletariat, or are at least threatened in their conditions of existence. These also supply the proletariat with fresh elements of enlightenment and progress.

Finally, in times when the class struggle nears the decisive hour, the process of dissolution going on within the ruling class, in fact within the whole range of society, assumes such a violent, glaring character, that a small section of the ruling class cuts itself adrift, and joins the revolutionary class, the class that holds the future in its hands. Just as, therefore, at an earlier period, a section of the nobility went over to the bourgeoisie, so now a portion of the bourgeoisie goes over to the proletariat, and in particular, a portion of the bourgeois ideologists, who have raised themselves to the level of comprehending theoretically the historical movement as a whole.

Of all the classes that stand face to face with the bourgeoisie today, the proletariat alone is a really revolutionary class. The other classes decay and finally disappear in the face of Modern Industry; the proletariat is its special and essential product.

The lower middle class, the small manufacturer, the shopkeeper, the artisan, the peasant, all these fight against the bourgeoisie, to save from extinction their existence as fractions of the middle class. They are therefore not revolutionary, but conservative. Nay more, they are reactionary, for they try to roll back the wheel of history. If by chance they are revolutionary, they are so only in view of their impending transfer into the proletariat, they thus defend not their present, but their future interests, they desert their own standpoint to place themselves at that of the proletariat.

The "dangerous class," the social scum, that passively rotting mass thrown off by the lowest layers of old society, may, here and there, be swept

---

[v] Passed in 1847, the bill limited the work day to ten hours, but only for women and children.

into the movement by a proletarian revolution; its conditions of life, however, prepare it far more for the part of a bribed tool of reactionary intrigue.

In the conditions of the proletariat, those of old society at large are already virtually swamped. The proletarian is without property; his relation to his wife and children has no longer anything in common with the bourgeois family-relations; modern industrial labour, modern subjection to capital, the same in England as in France, in America as in Germany, has stripped him of every trace of national character. Law, morality, religion, are to him so many bourgeois prejudices, behind which lurk in ambush just as many bourgeois interests.

All the preceding classes that got the upper hand, sought to fortify their already acquired status by subjecting society at large to their conditions of appropriation. The proletarians cannot become masters of the productive forces of society, except by abolishing their own previous mode of appropriation, and thereby also every other previous mode of appropriation. They have nothing of their own to secure and to fortify; their mission is to destroy all previous securities for, and insurances of, individual property.

All previous historical movements were movements of minorities, or in the interests of minorities. The proletarian movement is the self-conscious, independent movement of the immense majority, in the interests of the immense majority. The proletariat, the lowest stratum of our present society, cannot stir, cannot raise itself up, without the whole superincumbent strata of official society being sprung into the air.

Though not in substance, yet in form, the struggle of the proletariat with the bourgeoisie is at first a national struggle. The proletariat of each country must, of course, first of all settle matters with its own bourgeoisie.

In depicting the most general phases of the development of the proletariat, we traced the more or less veiled civil war, raging within existing society, up to the point where that war breaks out into open revolution, and where the violent overthrow of the bourgeoisie lays the foundation for the sway of the proletariat.

Hitherto, every form of society has been based, as we have already seen, on the antagonism of oppressing and oppressed classes. But in order to oppress a class, certain conditions must be assured to it under which it can, at least, continue its slavish existence. The serf, in the period of serfdom, raised himself to membership in the commune, just as the petty bourgeois, under the yoke of feudal absolutism, managed to develop into a bourgeois. The modern labourer, on the contrary, instead of rising with the progress of industry, sinks deeper and deeper below the conditions of existence of his own class. He becomes a pauper, and pauperism develops more rapidly than population and wealth. And here it becomes evident, that the bourgeoisie is unfit any longer to be the ruling class in society, and to impose its conditions of existence upon society as an over-riding law. It is unfit to rule because it is incompetent to assure an existence to its slave within his slavery, because it cannot help letting him sink into such a state, that it has to feed him, instead of being fed by him. Society can no longer live under this bourgeoisie, in other words, its existence is no longer compatible with society.

The essential condition for the existence, and for the sway of the bourgeois class, is the formation and augmentation of capital; the condition for capital is wage-labour. Wage-labour rests exclusively on competition between the labourers. The advance of industry, whose involuntary promoter is the bourgeoisie, replaces the isolation of the labourers, due to competition, by their revolutionary combination, due to association. The development of Modern Industry, therefore, cuts from under its feet the very foundation on which the bourgeoisie produces and appropriates products. What the bourgeoisie, therefore, produces, above all, is its own grave-diggers. Its fall and the victory of the proletariat are equally inevitable.

chapter eight

"The Madman"
"The Natural History of Morals"
The Genealogy of Morals
The Will to Power

Friedrich Nietzsche

A student of ancient languages by trade and a philosopher by predilection, Friedrich Nietzsche (1844–1900) was a unique and misunderstood genius. Retiring in ill health from his only university post at age 34, he wrote feverishly in relative isolation until becoming insane at the age of 44. Nietzsche's concern was nothing less than the conditions of health, greatness, and sickness in human cultures. He was deeply critical of Judaism and Christianity, which he saw as destroying the health of Western humanity by undermining human instincts through a slavish, nihilistic belief in the unreality of this world and the promise of happiness in the next. Nietzsche was one of the first to foresee the waning of Christianity in an increasingly secular Europe, and famously coined the phrase, "God is dead." He asked what values would replace Christian values as the guide for Western culture. His notion of an "overman," the authentic individual of the post-Christian era, was, like his critique of Judaism and morality, later taken by some National Socialists as justification of their policies (although nothing could be more foreign to Nietzsche than a mass, collectivist movement). Nietzsche's radical critique of metaphysics, the unity of the self, even of truth itself, and his conception of all reality and all values as expressing the "will to power," make him the grandfather of postmodernism.

Friedrich Nietzsche, *The Gay Science*, trans. and ed. Walter Kaufmann (New York: Vintage, 1974), Part Three, Sec. 125 ("The Madman"), pp. 181–2; *Beyond Good and Evil*, trans. Walter Kaufmann (New York: Vintage, 1989), Part Five: "The Natural History of Morals," Sec. 186–203, pp. 97–118; *The Genealogy of Morals*, trans. by Walter Kaufmann and R. J. Hollingdale (New York: Vintage, 1989), from the Third Essay, Sec. 24–8, pp. 148–63; and from *The Will to Power*, ed. Walter Kaufmann, trans. Walter Kaufmann and R. J. Hollingdale (New York: Random House, 1967), para. 1067, pp. 449–50.

"The Madman"

Have you not heard of that madman who lit a lantern in the bright morning hours, ran to the market place, and cried incessantly: "I seek God! I seek God!" – As many of those who did not believe in God were standing around just then, he provoked much laughter. Has he got lost? asked one. Did he lose his way like a child? asked another. Or is he hiding? Is he afraid of us? Has he gone on a voyage? emigrated? – Thus they yelled and laughed.

The madman jumped into their midst and pierced them with his eyes. "Whither is God?" he cried; "I will tell you. *We have killed him* – you and I. All of us are his murderers. But how did we do this? How could we drink up the sea? Who gave us the sponge to wipe away the entire horizon? What were we doing when we unchained this earth from its sun? Whither is it moving now? Whither are we moving? Away from all suns? Are we not plunging continually? Backward, sideward, forward, in all directions? Is there still any up or down? Are we not straying as through an infinite nothing? Do we not feel the breath of empty space? Has it not become colder? Is not night continually closing in on us? Do we not need to light lanterns in the morning? Do we hear nothing as yet of the noise of the gravediggers who are burying God? Do we smell nothing as yet of the divine decomposition? Gods, too, decompose. God is dead. God remains dead. And we have killed him.

"How shall we comfort ourselves, the murderers of all murderers? What was holiest and mightiest of all that the world has yet owned has bled to death under our knives: who will wipe this blood off us? What water is there for us to clean ourselves? What festivals of atonement, what sacred games shall we have to invent? Is not the greatness of this deed too great for us? Must we ourselves not become gods simply to appear worthy of it? There has never been a greater deed; and whoever is born after us – for the sake of this deed he will belong to a higher history than all history hitherto."

Here the madman fell silent and looked again at his listeners; and they, too, were silent and stared at him in astonishment. At last he threw his lantern on the ground, and it broke into pieces and went out. "I have come too early," he said then; "my time is not yet. This tremendous event is still on its way, still wandering; it has not yet reached the ears of men. Lightning and thunder require time; the light of the stars requires time; deeds, though done, still require time to be seen and heard. This deed is still more distant from them than the most distant stars – *and yet they have done it themselves.*"

It has been related further that on the same day the madman forced his way into several churches and there struck up his *requiem aeternam deo*[i]. Led out and called to account, he is said always to have replied nothing but: "What after all are these churches now if they are not the tombs and sepulchers of God?"

"The Natural History of Morals"

186

The moral sentiment in Europe today is as refined, old, diverse, irritable, and subtle, as the "science of morals" that accompanies it is still young, raw, clumsy, and butterfingered – an attractive contrast that occasionally even becomes visible and incarnate in the person of a moralist. Even the term "science of morals" is much too arrogant considering what it designates, and offends *good* taste – which always prefers more modest terms.

One should own up in all strictness to what is still necessary here for a long time to come, to what alone is justified so far: to collect material, to conceptualize and arrange a vast realm of subtle feelings of value and differences of value which are alive, grow, beget, and perish – and perhaps attempts to present vividly some of the more frequent and recurring forms of such living crystallizations – all to prepare a *typology* of morals.

To be sure, so far one has not been so modest. With a stiff seriousness that inspires laughter, all our philosophers demanded something far more exalted, presumptuous, and solemn from themselves as soon as they approached the study of morality: they wanted to supply a *rational foundation* for morality – and every philosopher so far has believed that he has provided such a foundation. Morality itself, however, was accepted as "given." How remote from their clumsy pride was that task which they considered insignificant and left in dust and must – the task of description – although the subtlest fingers and senses can scarcely be subtle enough for it.

Just because our moral philosophers knew the facts of morality only very approximately in arbitrary extracts or in accidental epitomes – for example, as the morality of their environment, their class, their church, the spirit of their time, their climate and part of the world – just because they were poorly informed and not even very curious about different peoples, times, and past ages – they never laid eyes on the real problems of morality; for these emerge only when we compare *many* moralities. In all "science of morals" so far one thing was *lacking*, strange as it may sound: the problem of morality itself; what was lacking was any suspicion that there was

---

[i] A "requiem" is a Latin prayer for the dead, in which eternal rest (*requiem aeternam*) is asked for the deceased. Here it is being asked for God (*deo*).

something problematic here. What the philosophers called "a rational foundation for morality" and tried to supply was, seen in the right light, merely a scholarly variation of the common *faith* in the prevalent morality; a new means of *expression* for this faith; and thus just another fact within a particular morality; indeed, in the last analysis a kind of denial that this morality might ever be considered problematic – certainly the very opposite of an examination, analysis, questioning, and vivisection of this very faith.

Listen, for example, with what almost venerable innocence Schopenhauer still described his task, and then draw your conclusions about the scientific standing of a "science" whose ultimate masters still talk like children and little old women: "The principle," he says (p. 136 of *Grundprobleme der Moral*), "the fundamental proposition on whose contents all moral philosophers are *really* agreed – *neminem laede, immo omnes, quantum potes, juva*ii – that is *really* the proposition for which all moralists endeavor to find the rational foundation . . . the *real* basis of ethics for which one has been looking for thousands of years as for the philosopher's stone."

The difficulty of providing a rational foundation for the principle cited may indeed be great – as is well known, Schopenhauer did not succeed either – and whoever has once felt deeply how insipidly false and sentimental this principle is in a world whose essence is will to power, may allow himself to be reminded that Schopenhauer, though a pessimist, *really* – played the flute. Every day, after dinner: one should read his biography on that. And incidentally: a pessimist, one who denies God and the world but *comes to a stop* before morality – who affirms morality and plays the flute – the *laede neminem* morality – what? is that really – a pessimist?

187

Even apart from the value of such claims as "there is a categorical imperative in us," one can still always ask: what does such a claim tell us about the man who makes it? There are moralities which are meant to justify their creator before others. Other moralities are meant to calm him and lead him to be satisfied with himself. With yet others he wants to crucify himself and humiliate himself. With others he wants to wreak revenge, with others conceal himself, with others transfigure himself and place himself way up, at a distance. This morality is used by its creator to forget, that one to have others forget him or something about him. Some moralists want to vent their power and creative whims on humanity; some others, perhaps including Kant, suggest with their morality: "What deserves respect in me is that I can obey – and you *ought* not to be different from me." – In short, moralities are also merely a *sign language of the affects.*

ii "Hurt no one; rather, help all as much as you can."

105

188

Every morality is, as opposed to *laisser aller*,[iii] a bit of tyranny against "nature"; also against "reason"; but this in itself is no objection, as long as we do not have some other morality which permits us to decree that every kind of tyranny and unreason is impermissible. What is essential and inestimable in every morality is that it constitutes a long compulsion: to understand Stoicism or Port-Royal[iv] or Puritanism, one should recall the compulsion under which every language so far has achieved strength and freedom – the metrical compulsion of rhyme and rhythm.

How much trouble the poets and orators of all peoples have taken – not excepting a few prose writers today in whose ear there dwells an inexorable conscience – "for the sake of some foolishness," as utilitarian dolts say, feeling smart – "submitting abjectly to capricious laws," as anarchists say, feeling "free," even "free-spirited." But the curious fact is that all there is or has been on earth of freedom, subtlety, boldness, dance, and masterly sureness, whether in thought itself or in government, or in rhetoric and persuasion, in the arts just as in ethics, has developed only owing to the "tyranny of such capricious laws"; and in all seriousness, the probability is by no means small that precisely this is "nature" and "natural" – and *not* that *laisser aller*.

Every artist knows how far from any feeling of letting himself go his "most natural" state is – the free ordering, placing, disposing, giving form in the moment of "inspiration" – and how strictly and subtly he obeys thousandfold laws precisely then, laws that precisely on account of their hardness and determination defy all formulation through concepts (even the firmest concept is, compared with them, not free of fluctuation, multiplicity, and ambiguity).

What is essential "in heaven and on earth" seems to be, to say it once more, that there should be *obedience* over a long period of time and in a *single* direction: given that, something always develops, and has developed, for whose sake it is worth while to live on earth; for example, virtue, art, music, dance, reason, spirituality – something transfiguring, subtle, mad, and divine. The long unfreedom of the spirit, the mistrustful constraint in the communicability of thoughts, the discipline thinkers imposed on themselves to think within the directions laid down by a church or court, or under Aristotelian presuppositions, the long spiritual will to interpret all events under a Christian schema and to rediscover and justify the Christian

---

iii "Letting go," or letting things happen as they naturally would.

iv A system of logic and grammar composed by Antoine Arnauld (1612–94) and Pierre Nicole (1625–95), named after a Jansenist French abbey.

god in every accident – all this, however forced, capricious, hard, grue-some, and anti-rational, has shown itself to be the means through which the European spirit has been trained to strength, ruthless curiosity, and subtle mobility, though admittedly in the process an irreplaceable amount of strength and spirit had to be crushed, stifled, and ruined (for here, as everywhere, "nature" manifests herself as she is, in all her prodigal and indifferent magnificence which is outrageous but noble).

That for thousands of years European thinkers thought merely in order to prove something – today, conversely, we suspect every thinker who "wants to prove something" – that the conclusions that *ought* to be the result of their most rigorous reflection were always settled from the start, just as it used to be with Asiatic astrology, and still is today with the innocuous Christian-moral interpretation of our most intimate personal experiences "for the glory of God" and "for the salvation of the soul" – this tyranny, this caprice, this rigorous and grandiose stupidity has *educated* the spirit. Slavery is, as it seems, both in the cruder and in the more subtle sense, the indispensable means of spiritual discipline and cultivation, too. Consider any morality with this in mind: what there is in it of "nature" teaches hatred of the *laisser aller*, of any all-too-great freedom, and implants the need for limited horizons and the nearest tasks – teaching the *narrowing of our perspective*, and thus in a certain sense stupidity, as a condition of life and growth.

"You shall obey – someone and for a long time: *else* you will perish and lose the last respect for yourself" – this appears to me to be the moral imperative of nature which, to be sure, is neither "categorical" as the old Kant would have it (hence the "else") nor addressed to the individual (what do individuals matter to her?), but to peoples, races, ages, classes – but above all to the whole human animal, to *man*.

189

Industrious races find it very troublesome to endure leisure: it was a masterpiece of *English* instinct to make the Sabbath so holy and so boring that the English begin unconsciously to lust again for their work-and week-day. It is a kind of cleverly invented, cleverly inserted *fast*, the like of which is also encountered frequently in the ancient world (although, in fairness to southern peoples, not exactly in regard to work). There have to be fasts of many kinds; and wherever powerful drives and habits prevail, legislators have to see to it that intercalary days are inserted on which such a drive is chained and learns again to hunger. Viewed from a higher vantage point, whole generations and ages that make their appearance, infected with some moral fanaticism, seem to be such times of constraint and fasting during which a drive learns to stoop and submit, but also to *purify* and *sharpen* itself. A few philosophical sects, too, permit such an interpretation (for example, the Stoa in the midst of Hellenistic culture with its lascivious atmosphere, over-charged with aphrodisiac odors).

This is also a hint for an explanation of the paradox: why it was precisely during the most Christian period of Europe and altogether only under the pressure of Christian value judgments that the sex drive sublimated[v] itself into love (*amour-passion*).

190

There is something in the morality of Plato that does not really belong to Plato but is merely encountered in his philosophy – one might say, in spite of Plato: namely, the Socratism for which he was really too noble. "Nobody wants to do harm to himself, therefore all that is bad is done involuntarily. For the bad do harm to themselves: this they would not do if they knew that the bad is bad. Hence the bad are bad only because of an error; if one removes the error, one necessarily makes them – good."

This type of inference smells of the *rabble* that sees nothing in bad actions but the unpleasant consequences and really judges, "it is *stupid* to do what is bad," while "good" is taken without further ado to be identical with "useful and agreeable." In the case of every moral utilitarianism one may immediately infer the same origin and follow one's nose: one will rarely go astray.

Plato did everything he could in order to read something refined and noble into the proposition of his teacher – above all, himself. He was the most audacious of all interpreters and took the whole Socrates only the way one picks a popular tune and folk song from the streets in order to vary it into the infinite and impossible – namely, into all of his own masks and multiplicities. In a jest, Homeric at that: what is the Platonic Socrates after all if not *prosthe Platōn opithen te Platōn messē te Chimaira*.[vi]

191

The ancient theological problem of "faith" and "knowledge" – or, more clearly, of instinct and reason – in other words, the question whether regarding the valuation of things instinct deserves more authority than rationality, which wants us to evaluate and act in accordance with

---

[v] Sublimation is one of a number of Nietzsche's ideas that anticipate Freud.
[vi] "Plato in front and Plato behind, in the middle Chimaera." Chimaera was a monster in Greek mythology.

reasons, with a "why?" – in other words, in accordance with expedience and utility – this is still the ancient moral problem that first emerged in the person of Socrates and divided thinking people long before Christianity. Socrates himself, to be sure, with the taste of his talent – that of a superior dialectician – had initially sided with reason; and in fact, what did he do his life long but laugh at the awkward incapacity of noble Athenians who, like all noble men, were men of instinct and never could give sufficient information about the reasons for their actions? In the end, however, privately and secretly, he laughed at himself, too: in himself he found, before his subtle conscience and self-examination, the same difficulty and incapacity. But is that any reason, he encouraged himself, for giving up the instincts? One has to see to it that they as well as reason receive their due – one must follow the instincts but persuade reason to assist them with good reasons. This was the real *falseness* of that great ironic, so rich in secrets; he got his conscience to be satisfied with a kind of self-trickery: at bottom, he had seen through the irrational element in moral judgments.

Plato, more innocent in such matters and lacking the craftiness of the plebeian, wanted to employ all his strength – the greatest strength any philosopher so far has had at his disposal – to prove to himself that reason and instinct of themselves tend toward one goal, the good, "God." And since Plato, all theologians and philosophers are on the same track – that is, in moral matters it has so far been instinct, or what the Christians call "faith," or "the herd," as I put it, that has triumphed. Perhaps Descartes should be excepted, as the father of rationalism (and hence the grandfather of the Revolution) who conceded authority to reason alone: but reason is merely an instrument, and Descartes was superficial.

192

Whoever has traced the history of an individual science finds a clue in its development for understanding the most ancient and common processes of all "knowledge and cognition." There as here it is the rash hypotheses, the fictions, the good dumb will to "believe," the lack of mistrust and patience that are developed first; our senses learn only late, and never learn entirely, to be subtle, faithful, and cautious organs of cognition. Our eye finds it more comfortable to respond to a given stimulus by reproducing once more an image that it has produced many times before, instead of registering what is different and new in an impression. The latter would require more strength, more "morality." Hearing something new is embarrassing and difficult for the ear; foreign music we do not hear well. When we hear another language we try involuntarily to form the sounds we hear into words that sound more familiar and more like home to us: thus the

German, for example, transformed *arcubalista*, when he heard that, into *Armbrust*.[vii] What is new finds our senses, too, hostile and reluctant; and even in the "simplest" processes of sensation the affects dominate, such as fear, love, hatred, including the passive affects of laziness.

Just as little as a reader today reads all of the individual words (let alone syllables) on a page – rather he picks about five words at random out of twenty and "guesses" at the meaning that probably belongs to these five words – just as little do we see a tree exactly and completely with reference to leaves, twigs, color, and form; it is so very much easier for us simply to improvise some approximation of a tree. Even in the midst of the strangest experiences we still do the same: we make up the major part of the experience and can scarcely be forced *not* to contemplate some event as its "inventors." All this means: basically and from time immemorial we are – *accustomed to lying*. Or to put it more virtuously and hypocritically, in short, more pleasantly: one is much more of an artist than one knows.

In an animated conversation I often see the face of the person with whom I am talking so clearly and so subtly determined in accordance with the thought he expresses, or that I believe has been produced in him, that this degree of clarity far surpasses my powers of vision: so the subtle shades of the play of the muscles and the expression of the eyes *must* have been made up by me. Probably the person made an altogether different face, or none at all.

193

Quidquid luce fuit, tenebris agit:[viii] but the other way around, too. What we experience in dreams – assuming that we experience it often – belongs in the end just as much to the over-all economy of our soul as anything experienced "actually": we are richer or poorer on account of it, have one need more or less, and finally are led a little by the habits of our dreams even in broad daylight and in the most cheerful moments of our wide-awake spirit.

Suppose someone has flown often in his dreams and finally, as soon as he dreams, he is conscious of his power and art of flight as if it were his privilege, also his characteristic and enviable happiness. He believes himself capable of realizing every kind of arc and angle simply with the lightest impulse; he knows the feeling of a certain divine frivolity, an "upward" without tension and constraint, a "downward" without condescension and humiliation – without *gravity*! How could a human being who had had such dream experiences and dream habits fail to find that the word "happiness" had a different color and definition in his waking life, too? How

---

[vii] Both italicized words refer to the crossbow.
[viii] "What occurred in the light, goes on in the dark."

could he fail to – desire happiness differently? "Rising" as described by poets must seem to him, compared with this "flying," too earthbound, muscle-bound, forced, too "grave."

194

The difference among men becomes manifest not only in the difference between their tablets of goods – in the fact that they consider different goods worth striving for and also disagree about what is more and less valuable, about the order of rank of the goods they recognize in common – it becomes manifest even more in what they take for really *having* and *possessing* something good.

Regarding a woman, for example, those men who are more modest consider the mere use of the body and sexual gratification a sufficient and satisfying sign of "having," of possession. Another type, with a more suspicious and demanding thirst for possession, sees the "question mark," the illusory quality of such "having" and wants subtler tests, above all in order to know whether the woman does not only give herself to him but also gives up for his sake what she has or would like to have: only then does she seem to him "possessed." A third type, however, does not reach the end of his mistrust and desire for having even so: he asks himself whether the woman, when she gives up everything for him, does not possibly do this for a phantom of him. He wants to be known deep down, abysmally deep down, before he is capable of being loved at all; he dares to let himself be fathomed. He feels that his beloved is fully in his possession only when she no longer deceives herself about him, when she loves him just as much for his devilry and hidden insatiability as for his graciousness, patience, and spirituality.

One type wants to possess a people – and all the higher arts of a Cagliostro and Catiline suit him to that purpose.[ix] Someone else, with a more subtle thirst for possession, says to himself: "One may not deceive where one wants to possess." The idea that a mask of him might command the heart of the people irritates him and makes him impatient: "So I must *let* myself be known, and first must know myself."

Among helpful and charitable people one almost regularly encounters that clumsy ruse which first doctors the person to be helped – as if, for example, he "deserved" help, required just *their* help, and would prove to be profoundly grateful for all help, faithful and submissive. With these fancies they dispose of the needy as of possessions, being charitable and helpful people from a desire for possessions. One finds them jealous if one crosses or anticipates them when they want to help.

[ix] Alessandro Cagliostro (1743–95), Sicilian alchemist; Lucius Sergius Catiline (d. 62 BC), Roman conspirator.

Involuntarily, parents turn children into something similar to themselves – they call that "education." Deep in her heart, no mother doubts that the child she has borne is her property; no father contests his own right to subject it to *his* concepts and valuations. Indeed, formerly it seemed fair for fathers (among the ancient Germans, for example) to decide on the life or death of the new born as they saw fit. And like the father, teachers, classes, priests, and princes still see, even today, in every new human being an unproblematic opportunity for another possession. So it follows—

195

The Jews – a people "born for slavery," as Tacitus and the whole ancient world say; "the chosen people among the peoples," as they themselves say and believe – the Jews have brought off that miraculous feat of an inversion of values, thanks to which life on earth has acquired a novel and dangerous attraction for a couple of millennia: their prophets have fused "rich," "godless," "evil," "violent," and "sensual" into one and were the first to use the word "world" as an opprobrium. This inversion of values (which includes using the word "poor" as synonymous with "holy" and "friend") constitutes the significance of the Jewish people: they mark the beginning of the slave rebellion in morals.[x]

196

Countless dark bodies are to be *inferred* beside the sun – and we shall never see them. Among ourselves, this is a parable; and a psychologist of morals reads the whole writing of the stars only as a parable-and sign-language which can be used to bury much in silence.

197

We misunderstand the beast of prey and the man of prey (for example, Cesare Borgia)[xi] thoroughly, we misunderstand "nature," as long as we still look for something "pathological" at the bottom of these healthiest of all tropical monsters and growths, or even for some "hell" that is supposed to

---

[x] In the *Genealogy of Morals* Nietzsche argues that all Judeo-Christian morality results from the resentful attempt by slaves to achieve an imaginary revenge on their betters, i.e. God will punish their evil masters.

[xi] Cesare Borgia (1475–1507), ruthless political figure of Renaissance Italy, and Niccolò Machiavelli's (1469–1527) model for *The Prince*.

be innate in them; yet this is what almost all moralists so far have done. Could it be that moralists harbor a hatred of the primeval forest and the tropics? And that the "tropical man" must be discredited at any price, whether as sickness and degeneration of man or as his own hell and self-torture? Why? In favor of the "temperate zones"? In favor of temperate men? Of those who are "moral"? Who are mediocre? – This for the chapter "Morality as Timidity."

<h1 style="text-align:center">198</h1>

All these moralities that address themselves to the individual, for the sake of his "happiness," as one says – what are they but counsels for behavior in relation to the degree of *dangerousness* in which the individual lives with himself; recipes against his passions, his good and bad inclinations insofar as they have the will to power and want to play the master; little and great prudences and artifices that exude the nook odor of old nostrums and of the wisdom of old women; all of them baroque and unreasonable in form – because they address themselves to "all," because they generalize where one must not generalize. All of them speak unconditionally, take themselves for unconditional, all of them flavored with more than one grain of salt and tolerable only – at times even seductive – when they begin to smell over-spiced and dangerous, especially "of the other world." All of it is, measured intellectually, worth very little and not by a long shot "science," much less "wisdom," but rather, to say it once more, three times more, prudence, prudence, prudence, mixed with stupidity, stupidity, stupidity – whether it be that indifference and statue coldness against the hot-headed folly of the affects which the Stoics advised and administered; or that laughing-no-more and weeping-no-more of Spinoza, his so naïvely advocated destruction of the affects through their analysis and vivisection; or that tuning down of the affects to a harmless mean according to which they may be satisfied, the Aristotelianism of morals; even morality as enjoyment of the affects in a deliberate thinness and spiritualization by means of the symbolism of art, say, as music, or as love of God and of man for God's sake – for in religion the passions enjoy the rights of citizens again, assuming that—; finally even that accommodating and playful surrender to the affects, as Hafiz and Goethe taught it, that bold dropping of the reins, that spiritual-physical *licentia morum*[xii] in the exceptional case of wise old owls and sots for whom it "no longer holds much danger." This, too, for the chapter "Morality as Timidity."

[xii] "Moral license." Mohammed Hāfiz (1325–89), Persian lyric poet; Johann Wolfgang von Goethe (1749–1832), great German dramatist and writer.

199

Inasmuch as at all times, as long as there have been human beings, there have also been herds of men (clans, communities, tribes, peoples, states, churches) and always a great many people who obeyed, compared with the small number of those commanding – considering, then, that nothing has been exercised and cultivated better and longer among men so far than obedience – it may fairly be assumed that the need for it is now innate in the average man, as a kind of *formal conscience* that commands: "thou shalt unconditionally do something, unconditionally not do something else," in short, "thou shalt." This need seeks to satisfy itself and to fill its form with some content. According to its strength, impatience, and tension, it seizes upon things as a rude appetite, rather indiscriminately, and accepts whatever is shouted into its ears by someone who issues commands – parents, teachers, laws, class prejudices, public opinions.

The strange limits of human development, the way it hesitates, takes so long, often turns back, and moves in circles, is due to the fact that the herd instinct of obedience is inherited best, and at the expense of the art of commanding. If we imagine this instinct progressing for once to its ultimate excesses, then those who command and are independent would eventually be lacking altogether; or they would secretly suffer from a bad conscience and would find it necessary to deceive themselves before they could command – as if they, too, merely obeyed. This state is actually encountered in Europe today: I call it the moral hypocrisy of those commanding. They know no other way to protect themselves against their bad conscience than to pose as the executors of more ancient or higher commands (of ancestors, the constitution, of right, the laws, or even of God). Or they even borrow herd maxims from the herd's way of thinking, such as "first servants of their people" or "instruments of the common weal."

On the other side, the herd man in Europe today gives himself the appearance of being the only permissible kind of man, and glorifies his attributes, which make him tame, easy to get along with, and useful to the herd, as if they were the truly human virtues: namely, public spirit, benevolence, consideration, industriousness, moderation, modesty, indulgence, and pity. In those cases, however, where one considers leaders and bellwethers indispensable, people today make one attempt after another to add together clever herd men by way of replacing commanders: all parliamentary constitutions, for example, have this origin. Nevertheless, the appearance of one who commands unconditionally strikes these herd-animal Europeans as an immense comfort and salvation from a gradually intolerable pressure, as was last attested in a major way by the effect of Napoleon's appearance. The history of Napoleon's reception is almost the history of the higher happiness attained by this whole century in its most valuable human beings and moments.

200

In an age of disintegration that mixes races indiscriminately, human beings have in their bodies the heritage of multiple origins, that is, opposite, and often not merely opposite, drives and value standards that fight each other and rarely permit each other any rest. Such human beings of late cultures and refracted lights will on the average be weaker human beings: their most profound desire is that the war they *are* should come to an end. Happiness appears to them, in agreement with a tranquilizing (for example, Epicurean or Christian) medicine and way of thought, pre-eminently as the happiness of resting, of not being disturbed, of satiety, of finally attained unity, as a "sabbath of sabbaths," to speak with the holy rhetorician Augustine who was himself such a human being.

But when the opposition and war in such a nature have the effect of one more charm and incentive of life – and if, moreover, in addition to his powerful and irreconcilable drives, a real mastery and subtlety in waging war against oneself, in other words, self-control, self-outwitting, has been inherited or cultivated, too – then those magical, incomprehensible, and unfathomable ones arise, those enigmatic men predestined for victory and seduction, whose most beautiful expression is found in Alcibiades and Caesar (to whose company I should like to add that *first* European after my taste, the Hohenstaufen Frederick II),[xiii] and among artists perhaps Leonardo da Vinci. They appear in precisely the same ages when that weaker type with its desire for rest comes to the fore: both types belong together and owe their origin to the same causes.

201

As long as the utility reigning in moral value judgments is solely the utility of the herd, as long as one considers only the preservation of the community, and immorality is sought exactly and exclusively in what seems dangerous to the survival of the community – there can be no morality of "neighbor love." Supposing that even then there was a constant little exercise of consideration, pity, fairness, mildness, reciprocity of assistance; supposing that even in that state of society all those drives are active that later receive the honorary designation of "virtues" and eventually almost

---

[xiii] Alcibiades (450–404 BC), Athenian general. Frederick II, of the Hohenstaufen dynasty, Holy Roman Emperor during 1220–50.

coincide with the concept of "morality" – in that period they do not yet at all belong in the realm of moral valuations; they are still *extra-moral*. An act of pity, for example, was not considered either good or bad, moral or immoral, in the best period of the Romans; and even when it was praised, such praise was perfectly compatible with a kind of disgruntled disdain as soon as it was juxtaposed with an action that served the welfare of the whole, of the *res publica*.[xiv]

In the last analysis, "love of the neighbor" is always something secondary, partly conventional and arbitrary-illusory in relation to *fear of the neighbor*. After the structure of society is fixed on the whole and seems secure against external dangers, it is this fear of the neighbor that again creates new perspectives of moral valuation. Certain strong and dangerous drives, like an enterprising spirit, foolhardiness, vengefulness, craftiness, rapacity, and the lust to rule, which had so far not merely been honored insofar as they were socially useful – under different names, to be sure, from those chosen here – but had to be trained and cultivated to make them great (because one constantly needed them in view of the dangers to the whole community, against the enemies of the community), are now experienced as doubly dangerous, since the channels to divert them are lacking, and, step upon step, they are branded as immoral and abandoned to slander.

Now the opposite drives and inclinations receive moral honors; step upon step, the herd instinct draws its conclusions. How much or how little is dangerous to the community, dangerous to equality, in an opinion, in a state or affect, in a will, in a talent – that now constitutes the moral perspective: here, too, fear is again the mother of morals.

The highest and strongest drives, when they break out passionately and drive the individual far above the average and the flats of the herd conscience, wreck the self-confidence of the community, its faith in itself, and it is as if its spine snapped. Hence just these drives are branded and slandered most. High and independent spirituality, the will to stand alone, even a powerful reason are experienced as dangers; everything that elevates an individual above the herd and intimidates the neighbor is henceforth called *evil*; and the fair, modest, submissive, conforming mentality, the *mediocrity* of desires attains moral designations and honors. Eventually, under very peaceful conditions, the opportunity and necessity for educating one's feelings to severity and hardness is lacking more and more; and every severity, even in justice, begins to disturb the conscience; any high and hard nobility and self-reliance is almost felt to be an insult and arouses mistrust; the "lamb," even more the "sheep," gains in respect.

[xiv] Literally, "public substance" or "public entity," usually translated as "republic" or "commonwealth".

There is a point in the history of society when it becomes so pathologi-cally soft and tender that among other things it sides even with those who harm it, criminals, and does this quite seriously and honestly. Punishing somehow seems unfair to it, and it is certain that imagining "punishment" and "being supposed to punish" hurts it, arouses fear in it. "Is it not enough to render him *undangerous?* Why still punish? Punishing itself is terrible." With this question, herd morality, the morality of timidity, draws its ultimate consequence. Supposing that one could altogether abolish danger, the reason for fear, this morality would be abolished, too, *eo ipso:* it would no longer be needed, it would no longer *consider itself* necessary.

Whoever examines the conscience of the European today will have to pull the same imperative out of a thousand moral folds and hideouts – the imperative of herd timidity: "we want that some day there should be *nothing any more to be afraid of!*" Some day – throughout Europe, the will and way to this day is now called "progress."

202

Let us immediately say once more what we have already said a hundred times, for today's ears resist such truths – *our* truths. We know well enough how insulting it sounds when anybody counts man, unadorned and without metaphor, among the animals; but it will be charged against us as almost a *guilt* that precisely for the men of "modern ideas" we constantly employ such expressions as "herd," "herd instincts," and so forth. What can be done about it? We cannot do anything else; for here exactly lies our novel insight. We have found that in all major moral judgments Europe is now of one mind, including even the countries dominated by the influence of Europe: plainly, one now *knows* in Europe what Socrates thought he did not know and what that famous old serpent once promised to teach – today one "knows" what is good and evil.

Now it must sound harsh and cannot be heard easily when we keep insisting: that which here believes it knows, that which here glorifies itself with its praises and reproaches, calling itself good, that is the instinct of the herd animal, man, which has scored a breakthrough and attained pre-valence and predominance over other instincts – and this development is continuing in accordance with the growing physiological approximation and assimilation of which it is the symptom. *Morality in Europe today is herd animal morality* – in other words, as we understand it, merely *one* type of human morality beside which, before which, and after which many other types, above all *higher* moralities, are, or ought to be, possible. But this morality resists such a "possibility," such an "ought" with all its power: it says stubbornly and inexorably, "I am morality itself, and nothing besides is morality." Indeed, with the help of a religion which indulged and flattered the most sublime herd-animal desires, we have reached the point where we find even in political and social institutions an ever more visible expression of this morality: the *democratic* movement is the heir of the Christian movement.

But there are indications that its tempo is still much too slow and sleepy for the more impatient, for the sick, the sufferers of the instinct mentioned: witness the ever madder howling of the anarchist dogs who are baring their fangs more and more obviously and roam through the alleys of European culture. They seem opposites of the peacefully industrious democrats and ideologists of revolution, and even more so of the doltish philosophasters and brotherhood enthusiasts who call themselves socialists and want a "free society"; but in fact they are at one with the lot in their thorough and instinctive hostility to every other form of society except that of the *autonomous* herd (even to the point of repudiating the very concepts of "master" and "servant" – *ni dieu ni maître*[xv] runs a socialist formula). They are at one in their tough resistance to every special claim, every special right and privilege (which means in the last analysis, *every* right: for once all are equal nobody needs "rights" any more). They are at one in their mistrust of punitive justice (as if it were a violation of those who are weaker, a wrong against the *necessary* consequence of all previous society). But they are also at one in the religion of pity, in feeling with all who feel, live, and suffer (down to the animal, up to "God" – the excess of a "pity with God" belongs in a democratic age). They are at one, the lot of them, in the cry and the impatience of pity, in their deadly hatred of suffering generally, in their almost feminine inability to remain spectators, to *let* someone suffer. They are at one in their involuntary plunge into gloom and unmanly tenderness under whose spell Europe seems threatened by a new Buddhism. They are at one in their faith in the morality of *shared* pity, as if that were morality in itself, being the height, the *attained* height of man, the sole hope of the future, the consolation of present man, the great absolution from all former guilt. They are at one, the lot of them, in their faith in the community as the *savior*, in short, in the herd, in "themselves" –

203

We have a different faith; to us the democratic movement is not only a form of the decay of political organization but a form of the decay, namely the

---

[xv] Neither god nor master.

diminution, of man, making him mediocre and lowering his value. Where, then, must *we* reach with our hopes?

Toward *new philosophers;* there is no choice; toward spirits strong and original enough to provide the stimuli for opposite valuations and to revalue and invert "eternal values"; toward forerunners, toward men of the future who in the present tie the knot and constraint that forces the will of millennia upon *new* tracks. To teach man the future of man as his *will*, as dependent on a human will, and to prepare great ventures and over-all attempts of discipline and cultivation by way of putting an end to that gruesome dominion of nonsense and accident that has so far been called "history" – the nonsense of the "greatest number" is merely its ultimate form: at some time new types of philosophers and commanders will be necessary for that, and whatever has existed on earth of concealed, terrible, and benevolent spirits, will look pale and dwarfed by comparison. It is the image of such leaders that *we* envisage: may I say this out loud, you free spirits? The conditions that one would have partly to create and partly to exploit for their genesis; the probable ways and tests that would enable a soul to grow to such a height and force that it would feel the *compulsion* for such tasks; a revaluation of values under whose new pressure and hammer a conscience would be steeled, a heart turned to bronze, in order to endure the weight of such responsibility; on the other hand, the necessity of such leaders, the frightening danger that they might fail to appear or that they might turn out badly or degenerate – these are *our* real worries and gloom – do you know that, you free spirits? – these are the heavy distant thoughts and storms that pass over the sky of *our* life.

There are few pains as sore as once having seen, guessed, felt how an extraordinary human being strayed from his path and degenerated. But anyone who has the rare eye for the over-all danger that "man" himself *degenerates;* anyone who, like us, has recognized the monstrous fortuity that has so far had its way and play regarding the future of man – a game in which no hand, and not even a finger, of God took part as a player; anyone who fathoms the calamity that lies concealed in the absurd guilelessness and blind confidence of "modern ideas" and even more in the whole Christian-European morality – suffers from an anxiety that is past all comparisons. With a single glance he sees what, given a favorable accumulation and increase of forces and tasks, might yet *be made of man;* he knows with all the knowledge of his conscience how man is still unexhausted for the greatest possibilities and how often the type "man" has already confronted enigmatic decisions and new paths – he knows still better from his most painful memories what wretched things have so far usually broken a being of the highest rank that was in the process of becoming, so that it broke, sank, and became contemptible.

119

The *over-all degeneration of man* down to what today appears to the socialist dolts and flatheads as their "man of the future" – as their ideal – this degeneration and diminution of man into the perfect herd animal (or, as they say, to the man of the "free society"), this animalization of man into the dwarf animal of equal rights and claims, is *possible*, there is no doubt of it. Anyone who has once thought through this possibility to the end knows one kind of nausea that other men don't know – but perhaps also a new *task!* –

The Genealogy of Morals

24

And now look, on the other hand, at those rarer cases of which I spoke, the last idealists left among philosophers and scholars: are they perhaps the desired *opponents* of the ascetic ideal, the *counteridealists?* Indeed, they *believe* they are, these "unbelievers" (for that is what they are, one and all); they are so serious on this point, so passionate about it in word and gesture, that the faith that they are opponents of this ideal seems to be the last ramnant of faith they have left – but does this mean that their faith is *true?*

We "men of knowledge" have gradually come to mistrust believers of all kinds; our mistrust has gradually brought us to make inferences the reverse of those of former days: wherever the strength of a faith is very prominently displayed, we infer a certain weakness of demonstrability, even the *improbability* of what is believed. We, too, do not deny that faith "makes blessed": that is precisely *why* we deny that faith *proves* anything – a strong faith that makes blessed raises suspicion against that which is believed; it does not establish "truth," it establishes a certain probability – of *deception*. What is the situation in the present case?

These Nay-sayers and outsiders of today who are unconditional on one point – their insistence on intellectual cleanliness; these hard, severe, abstinent, heroic spirits who constitute the honor of our age; all these pale atheists, anti-Christians, immoralists, nihilists; these skeptics, ephectics,[xvi] *hectics* of the spirit (they are all hectics in some sense or other); these last idealists of knowledge in whom alone the intellectual conscience dwells and is incarnate today – they certainly believe they are as completely liberated

---

[xvi] "Ephectic" refers to those who suspend judgement, "hectic" to those suffering from tuberculosis.

from the ascetic ideal as possible, these "free, *very* free spirits"; and yet, to disclose to them what they themselves cannot see – for they are too close to themselves: this ideal is precisely *their* ideal, too; they themselves embody it today and perhaps they alone; they themselves are its most spiritualized product, its most advanced front-line troops and scouts, its most captious, tender, intangible form of seduction – if I have guessed any riddles, I wish that *this* proposition might show it! – They are far from being *free* spirits: *for they still have faith in truth.*

When the Christian crusaders in the Orient encountered the invincible order of Assassins,[xvii] that order of free spirits *par excellence,* whose lowest ranks followed a rule of obedience the like of which no order of monks ever attained, they obtained in some way or other a hint concerning that symbol and watchword reserved for the highest ranks alone as their *secretum:* "Nothing is true, everything is permitted." – Very well, *that* was *freedom* of spirit; in *that* way the faith in truth itself was *abrogated.*

Has any European, any Christian free spirit ever strayed into this proposition and into its labyrinthine consequences? has one of them ever known the Minotaur of this cave *from experience?* – I doubt it; more, I know better: nothing is more foreign to these men who are unconditional about *one* thing, these *so-called* "free spirits," than freedom and liberation in this sense; in no respect are they more rigidly bound; it is precisely in their faith in truth that they are more rigid and unconditional than anyone. I know all this from too close up perhaps: that venerable philosopher's abstinence to which such a faith commits one; that intellectual stoicism which ultimately refuses not only to affirm but also to deny; that *desire* to halt before the factual, the *factum brutum;* that fatalism of *"petits faits" (ce petit faitalisme,*[xviii] as I call it) through which French scholarship nowadays tries to establish a sort of moral superiority over German scholarship; that general renunciation of all interpretation (of forcing, adjusting, abbreviating, omitting, padding, inventing, falsifying, and whatever else is of the *essence* of interpreting) – all this expresses, broadly speaking, as much ascetic virtue as any denial of sensuality (it is at bottom only a particular mode of this denial). That which *constrains* these men, however, this unconditional will to truth, is *faith in the ascetic ideal itself,* even if as an unconscious imperative – don't be deceived about that – it is the faith in a *metaphysical* value, the absolute value of *truth,* sanctioned and guaranteed by this ideal alone (it stands or falls with this ideal).

Strictly speaking, there is no such thing as science "without any presuppositions"; this thought does not bear thinking though it is paralogical: a

---

[xvii] A medieval Islamic Shiite sect.

[xviii] *"Factum brutum"* means brute facts; *"petits faits,"* little facts; and *"ce petit faitalisme"* is Nietzsche's pun, meaning "little fact-alism," but sounding like the French word *"fatalisme."*

philosophy, a "faith," must always be there first of all, so that science can acquire from it a direction, a meaning, a limit, a method, a *right* to exist. (Whoever has the opposite notion, whoever tries, for example, to place philosophy "on a strictly scientific basis," first needs to stand not only philosophy but truth itself *on its head* – the grossest violation of decency possible in relation to two such venerable females!) There is no doubt of it – and here I cite the fifth book of my *Gay Science* (section 344):

"The truthful man, in the audacious and ultimate sense presupposed by the faith in science, *thereby affirms another world* than that of life, nature, and history; and insofar as he affirms this 'other world,' does this not mean that he has to deny its antithesis, this world, *our* world? . . . It is still a *metaphysical faith* that underlies our faith in science – and we men of knowledge of today, we godless men and anti-metaphysicians, we, too, still derive *our* flame from the fire ignited by a faith millennia old, the Christian faith, which was also Plato's, that God is truth, that truth is *divine*. – But what if this belief is becoming more and more unbelievable, if nothing turns out to be divine any longer unless it be error, blindness, lies – if God himself turns out to be our *longest lie?*"

At this point it is necessary to pause and take careful stock. Science itself henceforth *requires* justification (which is not to say that there is any such justification). Consider on this question both the earliest and most recent philosophers: they are all oblivious of how much the will to truth itself first requires justification; here there is a lacuna in every philosophy – how did this come about? Because the ascetic ideal has hitherto *dominated* all philosophy, because truth was posited as being, as God, as the highest court of appeal – because truth was not *permitted* to be a problem at all. Is this "permitted" understood? – From the moment faith in the God of the ascetic ideal is denied, a *new problem arises:* that of the *value* of truth.

The will to truth requires a critique – let us thus define our own task – the value of truth must for once be experimentally *called into question.*

(Whoever feels that this has been stated too briefly should read the section of the *Gay Science* entitled "To What Extent We, Too, Are Still Pious" (section 344), or preferably the entire fifth book of that work, as well as the Preface to *The Dawn.*)

25

No! Don't come to me with science when I ask for the natural antagonist of the ascetic ideal, when I demand: "where is the opposing will expressing the *opposing ideal?*" Science is not nearly self-reliant enough to be that; it first requires in every respect an ideal of value, a value-creating power, in the *service* of which it could *believe* in itself – it never creates values. Its relation to the ascetic ideal is by no means essentially antagonistic; it might even be said to represent the driving force in the latter's inner development. It opposes and fights, on closer inspection, not the ideal itself but only its exteriors, its guise and masquerade, its temporary dogmatic hardening and stiffening, and by denying what is exoteric in this ideal, it liberates what life is in it. This pair, science and the ascetic ideal, both rest on the same foundation – I have already indicated it: on the same overestimation of truth (more exactly: on the same belief that truth is inestimable and cannot be criticized). Therefore they are *necessarily* allies, so that if they are to be fought they can only be fought and called in question together. A depreciation of the ascetic ideal unavoidably involves a depreciation of science: one must keep one's eyes and ears open to this fact!

(*Art* – to say it in advance, for I shall some day return to this subject at greater length – art, in which precisely the *lie* is sanctified and the *will to deception* has a good conscience, is much more fundamentally opposed to the ascetic ideal than is science: this was instinctively sensed by Plato, the greatest enemy of art Europe has yet produced. Plato versus Homer: that is the complete, the genuine antagonism – there the sincerest advocate of the "beyond," the great slanderer of life; here the instinctive deifier, the *golden* nature. To place himself in the service of the ascetic ideal is therefore the most distinctive *corruption* of an artist that is at all possible; unhappily, also one of the most common forms of corruption, for nothing is more easily corrupted than an artist.)

Physiologically, too, science rests on the same foundation as the ascetic ideal: a certain *impoverishment of life* is a presupposition of both of them – the affects grown cool, the tempo of life slowed down, dialectics in place of instinct, seriousness imprinted on faces and gestures (seriousness, the most unmistakable sign of a labored metabolism, of struggling, laborious life). Observe the ages in the history of people when the scholar steps into the foreground: they are ages of exhaustion, often of evening and decline; overflowing energy, certainty of life and of the *future*, are things of the past. A predominance of mandarins always means something is wrong; so do the advent of democracy, international courts in place of war, equal rights for women, the religion of pity, and whatever other symptoms of declining life there are. (Science posed as a problem; what is the meaning of science? – cf. the Preface to *The Birth of Tragedy*.)

No! this "modern science" – let us face this fact! – is the *best* ally the ascetic ideal has at present, and precisely because it is the most unconscious, involuntary, hidden, and subterranean ally! They have played the same game up to now, the "poor in spirit" and the scientific opponents of this ideal (one should not think, by the way, that they are their opposites, the *rich* in spirit perhaps – they are *not;* I have called them the hectics of the spirit). As for the famous *victories* of the latter, they undoubtedly are victories – but over what? The ascetic ideal has decidedly not been conquered: if anything, it became stronger, which is to say, more elusive, more spiritual, more captious, as science remorselessly detached and broke off wall upon wall, external additions that had coarsened its appearance. Does anyone really believe that the defeat of theological astronomy represented a defeat for that ideal?

Has man perhaps become *less desirous* of a transcendent solution to the riddle of his existence, now that this existence appears more arbitrary, beggarly, and dispensable in the *visible* order of things? Has the self-belittlement of man, his *will* to self-belittlement, not progressed irresistibly since Copernicus?[xix] Alas, the faith in the dignity and uniqueness of man, in his irreplaceability in the great chain of being, is a thing of the past – he has become an *animal,* literally and without reservation or qualification, he who was, according to his old faith, almost God ("child of God," "God-man").

Since Copernicus, man seems to have got himself on an inclined plane – now he is slipping faster and faster away from the center into – what? into nothingness? into a *"penetrating* sense of his nothingness"?[xvii] Very well! hasn't this been the straightest route to – the *old* ideal?

All science (and by no means only astronomy, on the humiliating and degrading effect of which Kant made the noteworthy confession: "it destroys my importance" . . .), all science, natural as well as *unnatural* – which is what I call the self-critique of knowledge – has at present the object of dissuading man from his former respect for himself, as if this had been nothing but a piece of bizarre conceit. One might even say that its own pride, its own austere form of stoical ataraxy, consists in sustaining this hard-won *self-contempt* of man as his ultimate and most serious claim to self-respect (and quite rightly, indeed: for he that despises is always one who "has not forgotten how to respect" . . .) Is this really to *work against* the ascetic ideal? Does one still seriously believe (as theologians imagined for a while) that Kant's *victory* over the dogmatic concepts of theology ("God," "soul," "freedom," "immortality") damaged that ideal? – it being no concern of ours for the present whether Kant ever had any intention of doing such a thing. What is certain is that, since Kant, transcendentalists of every kind have once more won the day – they have been emancipated from the theologians: what joy! – Kant showed them a secret path by which they may, on their own initiative and with all scientific respectability, from now on follow their "heart's desire."

[xix] Nicholaus Copernicus (1473–1543), Polish astronomer, formulated the modern heliocentric model of the solar system.

[xx] Nietzsche is quoting himself.

In the same vein: who could hold it against the agnostics if, as votaries of the unknown and mysterious as such, they now worship the *question mark itself* as God? (Xaver Doudan once spoke of the *ravages* worked by *"l'habitude d'admirer l'inintelligible au lieu de rester tout simplement dans l'inconnu"*;[xxi] he thought the ancients had avoided this.) Presuming that everything man "knows" does not merely fail to satisfy his desires but rather contradicts them and produces a sense of horror, what a divine way out to have the right to seek the responsibility for this not in "desire" but in "knowledge"!

"There is no knowledge: *consequently* – there is a God": what a new *elegantia syllogismi!*[xxii] what a *triumph* for the ascetic ideal! –

26

Or does modern historiography perhaps display an attitude more assured of life and ideals? Its noblest claim nowadays is that it is a mirror; it rejects all teleology; it no longer wishes to "prove" anything; it disdains to play the judge and considers this a sign of good taste – it affirms as little as it denies; it ascertains, it "describes" . . . All this is to a high degree ascetic; but at the same time it is to an even higher degree *nihilistic*, let us not deceive ourselves about that! One observes a sad, stern, but resolute glance – an eye that looks far, the way a lonely Arctic explorer looks far (so as not to look within, perhaps? so as not to look back? . . .) Here is snow; here life has grown silent; the last crows whose cries are audible here are called "wherefore?," "in vain!," "*nada!*" – here nothing will grow or prosper any longer, or at the most Petersburg metapolitics and Tolstoian "pity."

As for that other type of historian, an even more "modern" type perhaps, a hedonist and voluptuary who flirts both with life and with the ascetic ideal, who employs the word "artist" as a glove and has today taken sole lease of the praise of contemplation: oh how these sweetish and clever fellows make one long even for ascetics and winter landscapes! No! the devil take this type of "contemplative"! I would even prefer to wander through the gloomy, gray, cold fog with those historical nihilists! Indeed, if I *had* to choose I might even opt for some completely unhistorical, anti-historical person (such as Dühring, whose voice today intoxicates in Germany a hitherto shy and unavowed species of "beautiful soul," the *species anarchistica* within the educated proletariat).[xxiii]

[xxi] "The habit of admiring the unintelligible instead of staying quite simply in the unknown." Xaver Doudan (1800–72) was a French writer.   [xxii] Elegant syllogism.

[xxiii] Karl Eugen Dühring (1833–1921), German socialist philosopher, avowed an "ethics of sympathy," which Nietzsche says appealed to the "anarchistic type."

The "contemplatives" are a hundred times worse: I know of nothing that excites such disgust as this kind of "objective" armchair scholar, this kind of scented voluptuary of history, half parson, half satyr, perfume by Renan,[xxiv] who betrays immediately with the high falsetto of his applause what he lacks, *where* he lacks it, *where* in this case the Fates have applied their cruel shears with, alas, such surgical skill! This offends my taste; also my patience: let him have patience with such sights who has nothing to lose by them – such a sight arouses my ire, such "spectators" dispose me against the "spectacle" more than the spectacle itself (the spectacle of history, you understand); I fall unawares into an Anacreontic mood. Nature, which gave the bull his horns and the lion his *chasm odonton*,[xxv] why did nature give me my foot? . . . To kick, Holy Anacreon! and not only for running away; for kicking to pieces these rotten armchairs, this cowardly contemplativeness, this lascivious historical eunuchism, this flirting with ascetic ideals, this justice-tartuffery of impotence!

All honor to the ascetic ideal *insofar as it is honest!* so long as it believes in itself and does not play tricks on us! But I do not like all these coquettish bedbugs with their insatiable ambition to smell out the infinite, until at last the infinite smells of bedbugs; I do not like these whited sepulchers who impersonate life; I do not like these weary and played-out people who wrap themselves in wisdom and look "objective"; I do not like these agitators dressed up as heroes who wear the magic cap of ideals on their straw heads; I do not like these ambitious artists who like to pose as ascetics and priests but who are at bottom only tragic buffoons; and I also do not like these latest speculators in idealism, the anti-Semites, who today roll their eyes in a Christian-Aryan-bourgeois manner and exhaust one's patience by trying to rouse up all the horned-beast elements in the people by a brazen abuse of the cheapest of all agitator's tricks, moral attitudinizing (that *no* kind of swindle fails to succeed in Germany today is connected with the undeniable and palpable stagnation of the German spirit; and the cause of that I seek in a too exclusive diet of newspapers, politics, beer, and Wagnerian music, together with the presuppositions of such a diet: first, national constriction and vanity, the strong but narrow principle "*Deutschland, Deutschland über alles*," and then the *paralysis agitans* of "modern ideas").[xxvi]

Europe is rich and inventive today above all in means of excitation; it seems to need nothing as much as it needs stimulants and brandy: hence also the tremendous amount of forgery in ideals, this most potent brandy of the spirit; hence also the repulsive, ill-smelling, mendacious, pseudo-

---

[xxiv] Ernest Renan (1823–92), French author of *Life of Jesus* (1863).

[xxv] "Chasm of teeth," from Anacreon's, "Nature gave . . . the lion a chasm of teeth."

[xxvi] Richard Wagner (1813–83), German Romantic composer and nationalist, admired and later despised by Nietzsche. *Paralysis agitans*, "shaking paralysis," is Parkinson's disease.

alcoholic air everywhere. I should like to know how many shiploads of sham idealism, heroic trappings and grand-word-rattles, how many tons of sugared sympathy-spirits (distillers: *la religion de la souffrance*[xxvii]), how many "noble-indignation" stilts for the aid of the spiritually flatfooted, how many *comedians* of the Christian-moral ideal would have to be exported from Europe today before its air would begin to smell fresh again.

With this overproduction there is obviously a new opening for *trade* here; there is obviously a "business" to be made out of little ideal-idols and the "idealists" who go with them: don't let this opportunity slip! Who has the courage for it? – we have in our *hands* the means to "idealize" the whole earth!

But why am I speaking of courage: only one thing is needed here, the hand, an uninhibited, a very uninhibited hand. –

27

Enough! Enough! Let us leave these curiosities and complexities of the most modern spirit, which provoke as much laughter as chagrin: *our* problem, the problem of the *meaning* of the ascetic ideal, can dispense with them: what has this problem to do with yesterday or today! I shall probe these things more thoroughly and severely in another connection (under the title "On the History of European Nihilism"; it will be contained in a work in progress: *The Will to Power: Attempt at a Revaluation of All Values*). All I have been concerned to indicate here is this: in the most spiritual sphere, too, the ascetic ideal has at present only *one* kind of real enemy capable of *harming* it: the comedians of this ideal – for they arouse mistrust of it. Everywhere else that the spirit is strong, mighty, and at work without counterfeit today, it does without ideals of any kind – the popular expression for this abstinence is "atheism" – *except for its will to truth.* But this will, this *remnant* of an ideal, is, if you will believe me, this ideal itself in its strictest, most spiritual formulation, esoteric through and through, with all external additions abolished, and thus not so much its remnant as its *kernel.* Unconditional honest atheism (and *its* is the only air we breathe, we more spiritual men of this age!) is therefore *not* the antithesis of that ideal, as it appears to be; it is rather only one of the latest phases of its evolution, one of its terminal forms and inner consequences – it is the awe-inspiring *catastrophe* of two thousand years of training in truthfulness that finally forbids itself the *lie involved in belief in God.*

[xxvii] The religion of suffering.

(The same evolutionary course in India, completely independent of ours, should prove something: the same ideal leads to the same conclusion; the decisive point is reached five centuries before the beginning of the European calendar, with Buddha; more exactly, with the Sankhya philosophy, subsequently popularized by Buddha and made into a religion.)

What, in all strictness, has really *conquered* the Christian God? The answer may be found in my *Gay Science* (section 357): "Christian morality itself, the concept of truthfulness taken more and more strictly, the confessional subtlety of the Christian conscience translated and sublimated into the scientific conscience, into intellectual cleanliness at any price. To view nature as if it were a proof of the goodness and providence of a God; to interpret history to the glory of a divine reason, as the perpetual witness to a moral world order and moral intentions; to interpret one's own experiences, as pious men long interpreted them, as if everything were preordained, everything a sign, everything sent for the salvation of the soul – that now belongs to the *past*, that has the conscience *against* it, that seems to every more sensitive conscience indecent, dishonest, mendacious, feminism, weakness, cowardice: it is this rigor if anything that makes us *good Europeans* and the heirs of Europe's longest and bravest self-overcoming."

All great things bring about their own destruction through an act of self-overcoming: thus the law of life will have it, the law of the necessity of "self-overcoming" in the nature of life – the law giver himself eventually receives the call: "*patere legem, quam ipse tulisti.*"[xxviii] In this way Christianity *as a dogma* was destroyed by its own morality; in the same way Christianity *as morality* must now perish, too: we stand on the threshold of *this* event. After Christian truthfulness has drawn one inference after another, it must end by drawing its *most striking inference*, its inference *against* itself; this will happen, however, when it poses the question "*what is the meaning of all will to truth?*"

And here I again touch on my problem, on our problem, my *unknown* friends (for as yet I *know* of no friend): what meaning would *our* whole being possess if it were not this, that in us the will to truth becomes conscious of itself as a *problem?*

As the will to truth thus gains self-consciousness – there can be no doubt of that – morality will gradually *perish* now: this is the great spectacle in a hundred acts reserved for the next two centuries in Europe – the most terrible, most questionable, and perhaps also the most hopeful of all spectacles. –

[xxviii] Submit to the law you yourself proposed.

28

Apart from the ascetic ideal, man, the human *animal*, had no meaning so far. His existence on earth contained no goal; "why man at all?" – was a question without an answer; the *will* for man and earth was lacking; behind every great human destiny there sounded as a refrain a yet greater "in vain!" *This* is precisely what the ascetic ideal means: that something was *lacking*, that man was surrounded by a fearful *void* – he did not know how to justify, to account for, to affirm himself; he *suffered* from the problem of his meaning. He also suffered otherwise, he was in the main a sickly animal: but his problem was *not* suffering itself, but that there was no answer to the crying question, "*why* do I suffer?"

Man, the bravest of animals and the one most accustomed to suffering, does *not* repudiate suffering as such; he *desires* it, he even seeks it out, provided he is shown a *meaning* for it, a *purpose* of suffering. The meaninglessness of suffering, *not* suffering itself, was the curse that lay over mankind so far – *and the ascetic ideal offered man meaning!* It was the only meaning offered so far; any meaning is better than none at all; the ascetic ideal was in every sense the "*faute de mieux*" *par excellence*xxix so far. In it, suffering was *interpreted*; the tremendous void seemed to have been filled; the door was closed to any kind of suicidal nihilism. This interpretation – there is no doubt of it – brought fresh suffering with it, deeper, more inward, more poisonous, more life-destructive suffering: it placed all suffering under the perspective of *guilt*.

But all this notwithstanding – man was *saved* thereby, he possessed a meaning, he was henceforth no longer like a leaf in the wind, a plaything of nonsense – the "sense-less" – he could now *will* something; no matter at first to what end, why, with what he willed: *the will itself was saved.*

We can no longer conceal from ourselves *what* is expressed by all that willing which has taken its direction from the ascetic ideal: this hatred of the human, and even more of the animal, and more still of the material, this horror of the senses, of reason itself, this fear of happiness and beauty, this longing to get away from all appearance, change, becoming, death, wishing, from longing itself – all this means – let us dare to grasp it – *a will to nothingness*, an aversion to life, a rebellion against the most fundamental presuppositions of life; but it is and remains a *will!* . . . And, to repeat in conclusion what I said at the beginning: man would rather will *nothingness* than *not* will. –

---

xxix *"Faute de mieux"* means "for want of something better." So the italicized phrase means something like, "the pre-eminent next-best-thing."

Friedrich Nietzsche

The Will to Power

And do you know what "the world" is to me? Shall I show it to you in my mirror? This world: a monster of energy, without beginning, without end; a firm, iron magnitude of force that does not grow bigger or smaller, that does not expend itself but only transforms itself; as a whole, of unalterable size, a household without expenses or losses, but likewise without increase or income; enclosed by "nothingness" as by a boundary; not something blurry or wasted, not something endlessly extended, but set in a definite space as a definite force, and not a space that might be "empty" here or there, but rather as force throughout, as a play of forces and waves of forces, at the same time one and many, increasing here and at the same time decreasing there; a sea of forces flowing and rushing together, eternally changing, eternally flooding back, with tremendous years of recurrence, with an ebb and a flood of its forms; out of the simplest forms striving toward the most complex, out of the stillest, most rigid, coldest forms toward the hottest, most turbulent, most self-contradictory, and then again returning home to the simple out of this abundance, out of the play of contradictions back to the joy of concord, still affirming itself in this uniformity of its courses and its years, blessing itself as that which must return eternally,[xxx] as a becoming that knows no satiety, no disgust, no weariness: this, my *Dionysian* world of the eternally self-creating, the eternally self-destroying, this mystery world of the twofold voluptuous delight, my "beyond good and evil," without goal, unless the joy of the circle is itself a goal; without will, unless a ring feels good-will toward itself – do you want a *name* for this world? A *solution* for all its riddles? A *light* for you, too, you best-concealed, strongest, most intrepid, most midnightly men? – *This world is the will to power – and nothing besides*! And you yourselves are also this will to power – and nothing besides!

[xxx] A reference to Nietzsche's idea of the "eternal recurrence," that in our finite material universe all events must be endlessly repeated. "Dionysian" below refers to Dionysus, the Greek god of intoxication and sexuality.

Part II

Modernity Realized

The century from 1860 to 1950 brought the the triumph of modernity, and simultaneously its greatest crises, both intellectual and social. It is in this period that the industrial revolution, which had begun earlier, actually changed the lives of most human beings living in Europe, North America, and indirectly, much of the world. Peoples bound to a local agrarian lifestyle were thrown, either by choice or necessity, into the cities and into a new industrial world market. A second wave of scientific revolution, in cosmology, physics, geology, chemistry, and biology deeply altered our view of the world, and unleashed new technologies of unprecedented power. The conditions of life changed, and the mere fact of change seemed to make traditional wisdom and religion less relevant to everyday life. Two world wars, using new communications and military technologies, devastated Europe and much of the developed world. Liberal democracy became widespread, then was challenged by fascism and communism, both of which can be regarded as reactions against features of modernity. And there was a cultural reaction to the new conditions of life, in which some artists and thinkers embraced the new, fluid, non-traditional environment, and others were revolted by it.

Western philosophy reflected this transformation by regarding itself as in crisis. Many of the most important philosophers of the period claimed that earlier philosophy had suffered from some deep flaw requiring radical revision, a break with the past. The most prominent movements of the late nineteenth and early twentieth centuries – analytical and logical philosophy, phenomenology and existentialism, pragmatism, Marxism – rejected what they regarded as the speculative, metaphysical, and quasi-theological tendencies of earlier modern philosophy. In their radical criticism of the philosophical tradition, these movements also diverged from each other, leaving Western philosophy in the mid-twentieth century fragmented into divergent styles or subcultures which sometimes ceased to regard each other as legitimate philosophy at all. Other philosophers remained faithful to the tradition, to be sure; but it was the new methods that defined the era.

It is in this period that the dominant forms of philosophy in the Western world in the twentieth century were formulated: pragmatism, by Charles Sanders Peirce, George Herbert Mead, William James, Josiah Royce, and

133

John Dewey; existentialism, by Friedrich Nietzsche, Søren Kierkegaard, Paul Tillich, Jean-Paul Sartre, Simone de Beauvoir; phenomenology, by Edmund Husserl, Martin Heidegger, and Maurice Merleau-Ponty; logic and analytic philosophy, by Gottlob Frege, G.E. Moore, Bertrand Russell, Ludwig Wittgenstein, Rudolf Carnap, and J.L. Austin; process philosophy, by Henri Bergson and Alfred North Whitehead. To a very large degree we philosophers are in the 1990s still looking back to the creativity of the late nineteenth and early twentieth centuries for inspiration.

Art, politics, and science were simultaneously revolutionized. Artistic modernism belongs to this period. Too complex to summarize here, in painting it at times took the form of a new realism that renounced the idealization of subject matter, but more prominently it was the age of abstraction, of the non-realistic imaginations of Impressionism, Cubism, Expressionism, Futurism, Surrealism, Symbolism, Dada, and ultimately Abstract Expressionism. In other arts as well it was a period of explosive waves of experimentation: the poetry of Ezra Pound and T.S.Eliot, the stream of consciousness novels of James Joyce and Virginia Woolf, the existential realism of Hemingway; the atonal music of Arnold Schönberg and Alban Berg, the non-thematic dissonance of Igor Stravinsky; and the architectural modernism of Le Corbusier, Ludwig Mies van der Rohe, Walter Gropius, and the Bauhaus school. Simultaneously new forms of social radicalism developed in response to the coming of mass, industrial society: socialism, bolshevism, futurism, syndicalism, fascism, anarchism. Discontents and intellectuals sought new alternatives to the juggernaut of modernization and mass culture. Scientifically, this period is unparalleled in its novelty. Charles Darwin and Sigmund Freud recast our model of human being, while in physics the greatest revolution in our model of the universe since the seventeenth century was led by Neils Bohr, Max Planck, Albert Einstein, Erwin Schrödinger, Werner Heisenberg, and Paul Dirac. Particularly important for understanding modernity, the field of sociology established itself in this period as an independent discipline, largely through providing theories of modernization. Besides Marx and Weber, the work of Emile Durkheim, Georg Simmel, Ferdinand Tönnies, Walter Benjamin, Talcott Parsons and Arnold Gehlen, to name but a few, are crucial to further study of modernity.[1]

Several writers from this era influenced postmodernism. Peirce is the inventor of pragmatism, and pragmatism forms the basis for Richard Rorty's version of postmodernism, as well as an important resource for more moderate "nonfoundationalist" critics of the philosophical tradition. Edmund Husserl's phenomenology is the background from which Martin Heidegger and later Jacques Derrida sprang. Wittgenstein's critique of the traditional aims of philosophy has been enormously influential for the current debate, and has especially impacted Rorty and Jean-François

134

Lyotard. Ferdinand de Saussure's structuralist linguistics serves as the background for poststructuralism, hence for the French postmodernists.

The selections are as follows. Baudelaire is the first to use the term "*modernité*." Marinetti and Le Corbusier extol new forms of literature and architecture, respectively, that reflect the utopian social theories characteristic of the time. Freud and Weber are perhaps the most influential theorists of the new modern society (with Marx). Ortega expresses a prominent negative reaction to the development of mass society. Wittgenstein's radical critique of philosophical hopes is well expressed by his "Lecture on Ethics." Husserl diagnoses the "crisis" of modernity with his new philosophy of phenomenology. Peirce's pragmatism and de Saussure's structuralism are crucial for later developments. Adorno's and Horkheimer's classic *Dialectic of Enlightenment* has been central to the debate over the fate of modernity (and, with Weber, forms the basis for Jürgen Habermas' work). Sartre's existentialism was an important mid-century response to the problem of modern alienation, and a prime target for Heidegger.

Note

1 Also, the study of development, or modernization outside the Western world, has blossomed since World War II. More recent sociologists of modernity and modernization would include David Reisman, Anthony Giddens, Marion Levy Jr, and Peter Berger.

chapter nine

"The Painter of Modern Life"
Charles Baudelaire

Charles Baudelaire (1821–67), controversial Parisian poet and critic of the arts, was the first to use the term "modernity" (*modernité*). For Baudelaire modernity is the attitude or sensibility of the *flâneur*, idler or "dandy," the non-productive aesthete who embodies the sensibility of the outdoor café, that vantage point from which the passing carnival of city life can be observed. Most famous for the collection of poems, *The Flowers of Evil*, for which he was legally charged with offending public morality, Baudelaire revolutionized French poetry with his realistic attention to the disorder and depravity of urban life, in which he nevertheless saw a characteristically modern beauty. The essay, "The Painter of Modern Life" (1863), was inspired by his observations of the French artist Constantine Guys.

The Artist, Man of the World, Man of the Crowd, and Child

Today I want to discourse to the public about a strange man, a man of so powerful and so decided an originality that it is sufficient unto itself and does not even seek approval. Not a single one of his drawings is signed, if by signature you mean that string of easily forgeable characters which spell a name and which so many other artists affix ostentatiously at the foot of their least important trifles. Yet all his works are signed – with his dazzling *soul*; and art-lovers who have seen and appreciated them will readily recognize them from the description that I am about to give.

A passionate lover of crowds and incognitos, Monsieur C. G.[i] carries originality to the point of shyness. Mr Thackeray, who, as is well known, is deeply interested in matters of art, and who himself executes the illustrations to his novels, spoke one day of Monsieur G. in the columns of

---

Charles Baudelaire, "The Painter of Modern Life," trans. Jonathan Mayne, in *The Painter of Modern Life and Other Essays* (London: Phaidon, 1964), sec. 3–4, pp. 5–15.

[i] Constantin Guys (1802–92), Parisian painter and journalist.

a London review. The latter was furious, as though at an outrage to his virtue. Recently again, when he learnt that I had it in mind to write an appreciation of his mind and his talent, be begged me – very imperiously, I must admit – to suppress his name, and if I must speak of his works, to speak of them as if they were those of an anonymous artist. I will humbly comply with this singular request. The reader and I will preserve the fiction that Monsieur G. does not exist, and we shall concern ourselves with his drawings and his watercolours (for which he professes a partician scorn) as though we were scholars who had to pronounce upon precious historical documents, thrown up by chance, whose author must remain eternally unknown. And finally, to give complete reassurance to my conscience, it must be supposed that all that I have to say of his strangely and mysteriously brilliant nature is more or less justly suggested by the works in question – pure poetic hypothesis, conjecture, a labour of the imagination.

Monsieur G. is an old man. Jean-Jacques[ii] is said to have reached the age of forty-two before he started writing. It was perhaps at about the same age that Monsieur G., obsessed by the throng of pictures which teemed in his brain, was first emboldened to throw ink and colours on to a white sheet of paper. Truth to tell, he drew like a barbarian, or a child, impatient at the clumsiness of his fingers and the disobedience of his pen. I have seen a large number of these primitive scribbles, and I must own that the majority of those who are, or claim to be, connoisseurs in this matter, might well have been pardoned for failing to discern the latent genius which abode in such murky daubs. Today, after discovering by himself all the little tricks of his trade and accomplishing, without advice, his own education, Monsieur G. has become a powerful master in his own way, and of his early artlessness he has retained no more than what was needed to add an unexpected seasoning to his rich gifts. When he comes across one of those early efforts of his, he tears it up or burns it with a most comical show of bashfulness and indignation.

For ten years I had wanted to get to know Monsieur G., who is by nature a great traveller and cosmopolitan. I knew that for some time he had been on the staff of an English illustrated journal, and that engravings after his travel-sketches, made in Spain, Turkey and the Crimea, had been published there. Since then I have seen a considerable quantity of those drawings, hastily sketched on the spot, and thus I have been able to *read*, so to speak, a detailed account of the Crimean campaign which is much preferable to any other that I know. The same paper had also published, always without signature, a great number of his illustrations of new ballets and operas. When at last I ran him to earth, I saw at once that it was not precisely an

---

[ii] Rousseau.

artist, but rather a *man of the world* with whom I had to do. I ask you to understand the word *artist* in a very restricted sense, and *man of the world* in a very broad one. By the second I mean a man of the whole world, a man who understands the world and the mysterious and lawful reasons for all its uses; by the first, a specialist, a man wedded to his palette like the serf to the soil. Monsieur G. does not like to be called an artist. Is he not perhaps a little right? His interest is the whole world; he wants to know, understand and appreciate everything that happens on the surface of our globe. The artist lives very little, if at all, in the world of morals and politics. If he lives in the Bréda district, he will be unaware of what is going on in the Faubourg Saint-Germain. Apart from one or two exceptions whom I need not name, it must be admitted that the majority of artists are no more than highly skilled animals, pure artisans, village intellects, cottage brains. Their conversation, which is necessarily limited to the narrowest of circles, becomes very quickly unbearable to the *man of the world*, to the spiritual citizen of the universe.

And so, as a first step towards an understanding of Monsieur G., I would ask you to note at once that the mainspring of his genius is *curiosity*.

Do you remember a picture (it really is a picture!), painted – or rather written – by the most powerful pen of our age, and entitled *The Man of the Crowd?*[iii] In the window of a coffee-house there sits a convalescent, pleasurably absorbed in gazing at the crowd, and mingling, through the medium of thought, in the turmoil of thought that surrounds him. But lately returned from the valley of the shadow of death, he is rapturously breathing in all the odours and essences of life; as he has been on the brink of total oblivion, he remembers, and fervently desires to remember, everything. Finally he hurls himself headlong into the midst of the throng, in pursuit of an unknown, half-glimpsed countenance that has, on an instant, bewitched him. Curiosity has become a fatal, irresistible passion!

Imagine an artist who was always, spiritually, in the condition of that convalescent, and you will have the key to the nature of Monsieur G.

Now convalescence is like a return towards childhood. The convalescent, like the child, is possessed in the highest degree of the faculty of keenly interesting himself in things, be they apparently of the most trivial. Let us go back, if we can, by a retrospective effort of the imagination, towards our most youthful, our earliest, impressions, and we will recognize that they had a strange kinship with those brightly coloured impressions which we were later to receive in the aftermath of a physical illness, always provided that that illness had left our spiritual capacities pure and unharmed. The child sees everything in a state of newness; he is always *drunk*. Nothing more resembles what we call inspiration than the delight with which a

---

[iii] By Edgar Allan Poe, in his *Tales* (1845), translated into French by Baudelaire.

child absorbs form and colour. I am prepared to go even further and assert that inspiration has something in common with a convulsion, and that every sublime thought is accompanied by a more or less violent nervous shock which has its repercussion in the very core of the brain. The man of genius has sound nerves, while those of the child are weak. With the one, Reason has taken up a considerable position; with the other, Sensibility is almost the whole being. But genius is nothing more nor less than *childhood recovered* at will – a childhood now equipped for self-expression with manhood's capacities and a power of analysis which enables it to order the mass of raw material which it has involuntarily accumulated. It is by this deep and joyful curiosity that we may explain the fixed and animally ecstatic gaze of a child confronted with something new, whatever it be, whether a face or a landscape, gilding, colours, shimmering stuffs, or the magic of physical beauty assisted by the cosmetic art. A friend of mine once told me that when he was quite a small child, he used to be present when his father dressed in the mornings, and that it was with a mixture of amazement and delight that he used to study the muscles of his arms, the gradual transitions of pink and yellow in his skin, and the bluish network of his veins. The picture of external life was already filling him with awe and taking hold of his brain. He was already being obsessed and possessed by form. Predestination was already showing the tip of its nose. His sentence was sealed. Need I add that today that child is a well-known painter?

I asked you a moment ago to think of Monsieur G. as an eternal convalescent. To complete your idea, consider him also as a man-child, as a man who is never for a moment without the genius of childhood – a genius for which no aspect of life has become *stale*.

I have told you that I was reluctant to describe him as an artist pure and simple, and indeed that he declined this title with a modesty touched with aristocratic reserve. I might perhaps call him a dandy, and I should have several good reasons for that; for the word 'dandy' implies a quintessence of character and a subtle understanding of the entire moral mechanism of this world; with another part of his nature, however, the dandy aspires to insensitivity, and it is in this that Monsieur G., dominated as he is by an insatiable passion – for seeing and feeling – parts company decisively with dandyism. '*Amabam amare*,' said St Augustine. 'I am passionately in love with passion,' Monsieur G. might well echo. The dandy is blasé, or pretends to be so, for reasons of policy and caste. Monsieur G. has a horror of blasé people. He is a master of that only too difficult art – sensitive spirits will understand me – of being sincere without being absurd. I would bestow upon him the title of philosopher, to which he has more than one right, if his excessive love of visible, tangible things, condensed to their plastic state, did not arouse in him a certain repugnance for the things that form the impalpable kingdom of the metaphysician. Let us be content therefore to consider him as a pure pictorial moralist, like La Bruyère.[iv]

The crowd is his element, as the air is that of birds and water of fishes. His passion and his profession are to become one flesh with the crowd. For the perfect *flâneur*, for the passionate spectator, it is an immense joy to set up house in the heart of the multitude, amid the ebb and flow of movement, in the midst of the fugitive and the infinite. To be away from home and yet to feel oneself everywhere at home; to see the world, to be at the centre of the world, and yet to remain hidden from the world – such are a few of the slightest pleasures of those independent, passionate, impartial natures which the tongue can but clumsily define. The spectator is a *prince* who everywhere rejoices in his incognito. The lover of life makes the whole world his family, just like the lover of the fair sex who builds up his family from all the beautiful women that he has ever found, or that are – or are not – to be found; or the lover of pictures who lives in a magical society of dreams painted on canvas. Thus the lover of universal life enters into the crowd as though it were an immense reservoir of electrical energy. Or we might liken him to a mirror as vast as the crowd itself; or to a kaleidoscope gifted with consciousness, responding to each one of its movements and reproducing the multiplicity of life and the flickering grace of all the elements of life. He is an 'I' with an insatiable appetite for the 'non-I', at every instant rendering and explaining it in pictures more living than life itself, which is always unstable and fugitive. 'Any man,' he said one day, in the course of one of those conversations which he illumines with burning glance and evocative gesture, 'any man who is not crushed by one of those griefs whose nature is too real not to monopolize all his capacities, and who can yet be *bored in the heart of the multitude*, is a blockhead! a blockhead! and I despise him!'

When Monsieur G. wakes up and opens his eyes to see the boisterous sun beating a tattoo upon his window-pane, he reproaches himself remorsefully and regretfully: 'What a peremptory order! what a bugle-blast of life! Already several hours of light – everywhere – lost by my sleep! How many *illuminated* things might I have seen and have missed seeing!' So out he goes and watches the river of life flow past him in all its splendour and majesty. He marvels at the eternal beauty and the amazing harmony of life in the capital cities, a harmony so providentially maintained amid the turmoil of human freedom. He gazes upon the landscapes of the great city – landscapes of stone, caressed by the mist or buffeted by the sun. He delights in fine carriages and proud horses, the dazzling smartness of the grooms, the expertness of the footmen, the sinuous gait of the women, the beauty of the children, happy to be alive and nicely dressed – in a word, he delights

[iv] Jean La Bruyère (1645–96), French moralist.

in universal life. If a fashion or the cut of a garment has been slightly modified, if bows and curls have been supplanted by cockades, if *bavolets* have been enlarged and *chignons* have dropped a fraction towards the nape of the neck, if waists have been raised and skirts have become fuller, be very sure that his eagle eye will already have spotted it from however great a distance. A regiment passes, on its way, as it may be, to the ends of the earth, tossing into the air of the boulevards its trumpet-calls as winged and stirring as hope; and in an instant Monsieur G. will already have seen, examined and analysed the bearing and external aspect of that company. Glittering equipment, music, bold determined glances, heavy, solemn moustaches – he absorbs it all pell-mell; and in a few moments the resulting 'poem' will be virtually composed. See how his soul lives with the soul of that regiment, marching like a single animal, a proud image of joy in obedience!

But now it is evening. It is that strange, equivocal hour when the curtains of heaven are drawn and cities light up. The gas-light makes a stain upon the crimson of the sunset. Honest men and rogues, sane men and mad, are all saying to themselves, 'The end of another day!' The thoughts of all, whether good men or knaves, turn to pleasure, and each one hastens to the place of his choice to drink the cup of oblivion. Monsieur G. will be the last to linger wherever there can be a glow of light, an echo of poetry, a quiver of life or a chord of music; wherever a passion can *pose* before him, wherever natural man and conventional man display themselves in a strange beauty, wherever the sun lights up the swift joys of the *depraved animal!*[v] 'A fine way to fill one's day, to be sure,' remarks a certain reader whom we all know so well. 'Which one of us has not every bit enough genius to fill it in the same way?' But no! Few men are gifted with the capacity of seeing; there are fewer still who possess the power of expression. So now, at a time when others are asleep, Monsieur G. is bending over his table, darting on to a sheet of paper the same glance that a moment ago he was directing towards external things, skirmishing with his pencil, his pen, his brush, splashing his glass of water up to the ceiling, wiping his pen on his shirt, in a ferment of violent activity, as though afraid that the image might escape him, cantankerous though alone, elbowing himself on. And the external world is reborn upon his paper, natural and more than natural, beautiful and more than beautiful, strange and endowed with an impulsive life like the soul of its creator. The phantasmagoria has been distilled from nature. All the raw materials with which the memory has loaded itself are put in order, ranged and harmonized, and undergo that forced idealization which is the result of a childlike percep-

[v] Rousseau's phrase: "The man who meditates is a depraved animal." From his *Discourse on the Origin and Foundations of Inequality Among Men*, Part One.

tiveness – that is to say, a perceptiveness acute and magical by reason of its innocence!

Modernity

And so away he goes, hurrying, searching. But searching for what? Be very sure that this man, such as I have depicted him – this solitary, gifted with an active imagination, ceaselessly journeying across the great human desert – has an aim loftier than that of a mere *flâneur*, an aim more general, something other than the fugitive pleasure of circumstance. He is looking for that quality which you must allow me to call 'modernity'; for I know of no better word to express the idea I have in mind. He makes it his business to extract from fashion whatever element it may contain of poetry within history, to distil the eternal from the transitory. Casting an eye over our exhibitions of modern pictures, we are struck by a general tendency among artists to dress all their subjects in the garments of the past. Almost all of them make use of the costumes and furnishings of the Renaissance, just as David employed the costumes and furnishings of Rome.[vi] There is however this difference, that David, by choosing subjects which were specifically Greek or Roman, had no alternative but to dress them in antique garb, whereas the painters of today, though choosing subjects of a general nature and applicable to all ages, nevertheless persist in rigging them out in the costumes of the Middle Ages, the Renaissance or the Orient. This is clearly symptomatic of a great degree of laziness; for it is much easier to decide outright that everything about the garb of an age is absolutely ugly than to devote oneself to the task of distilling from it the mysterious element of beauty that it may contain, however slight or minimal that element may be. By 'modernity' I mean the ephemeral, the fugitive, the contingent, the half of art whose other half is the eternal and the immutable. Every old master has had his own modernity; the great majority of fine portraits that have come down to us from former generations are clothed in the costume of their own period. They are perfectly harmonious, because everything – from costume and coiffure down to gesture, glance and smile (for each age has a deportment, a glance and a smile of its own) – everything, I say, combines to form a completely viable whole. This transitory, fugitive element, whose metamorphoses are so rapid, must on no account be despised or dispensed with. By neglecting it, you cannot fail to tumble into the abyss of an abstract and indeterminate beauty, like that of the first woman before the fall of man. If for the necessary and inevitable costume of the age you substitute another, you will be guilty of a mistranslation

[vi] Jacques Louis David (1748–1825), French neo-classical painter.

only to be excused in the case of a masquerade prescribed by fashion. (Thus, the goddesses, nymphs and sultanas of the eighteenth century are still convincing portraits, *morally* speaking.)

It is doubtless an excellent thing to study the old masters in order to learn how to paint; but it can be no more than a waste of labour if your aim is to understand the special nature of present-day beauty. The draperies of Rubens or Veronese will in no way teach you how to depict *moire antique, satin à la reine* or any other fabric of modern manufacture, which we see supported and hung over crinoline or starched muslin petticoat. In texture and weave these are quite different from the fabrics of ancient Venice or those worn at the court of Catherine.[vii] Furthermore the cut of skirt and bodice is by no means similar; the pleats are arranged according to a new system. Finally the gesture and the bearing of the woman of today give to her dress a life and a special character which are not those of the woman of the past. In short, for any 'modernity' to be worthy of one day taking its place as 'antiquity', it is necessary for the mysterious beauty which human life accidentally puts into it to be distilled from it. And it is to this task that Monsieur G. particularly addresses himself.

I have remarked that every age had its own gait, glance and gesture. The easiest way to verify this proposition would be to betake oneself to some vast portrait-gallery, such as the one at Versailles. But it has an even wider application. Within that unity which we call a Nation, the various professions and classes and the passing centuries all introduce variety, not only in manners and gesture, but even in the actual form of the face. Certain types of nose, mouth and brow will be found to dominate the scene for a period whose extent I have no intention of attempting to determine here, but which could certainly be subjected to a form of calculation. Considerations of this kind are not sufficiently familiar to our portrait-painters; the great failing of M. Ingres, in particular, is that he seeks to impose upon every type of sitter a more or less complete, by which I mean a more or less despotic, form of perfection, borrowed from the repertory of classical ideas.

In a matter of this kind it would be easy, and indeed legitimate, to argue *a priori*. The perpetual correlation between what is called the 'soul' and what is called the 'body' explains quite clearly how everything that is 'material', or in other words an emanation of the 'spiritual', mirrors, and will always mirror, the spiritual reality from which it derives. If a painstaking, scrupulous, but feebly imaginative artist has to paint a courtesan of today and takes his 'inspiration' (that is the accepted word) from a courtesan by Titian or Raphael, it is only too likely that he will produce a work which is false, ambiguous and obscure. From the study of a masterpiece of that time and type he will learn nothing of the bearing, the glance,

---

[vii] Russian Empress, Catherine the Great (1684–1727).

the smile or the living 'style' of one of those creatures whom the dictionary of fashion has successively classified under the coarse or playful titles of 'doxies', 'kept women', *lorettes*, or *biches*.

The same criticism may be strictly applied to the study of the military man and the dandy, and even to that of animals, whether horses or dogs; in short, of everything that goes to make up the external life of this age. Woe to him who studies the antique for anything else but pure art, logic and general method! By steeping himself too thoroughly in it, he will lose all memory of the present; he will renounce the rights and privileges offered by circumstance – for almost all our originality comes from the seal which Time imprints on our sensations. I need hardly tell you that I could easily support my assertions with reference to many objects other than women. What would you say, for example, of a marine-painter (I am deliberately going to extremes) who, having to depict the sober and elegant beauty of a modern vessel, were to tire out his eyes by studying the overcharged, involved forms and the monumental poop of a galleon, or the complicated rigging of the sixteenth century? Again, what would you think if you had commissioned an artist to paint the portrait of a thoroughbred, famed in the annals of the turf, and he then proceeded to confine his researches to the Museums and contented himself with a study of the horse in the galleries of the past, in Van Dyck, Borgognone or Van der Meulen?[viii]

Under the direction of nature and the tyranny of circumstance, Monsieur G. has pursued an altogether different path. He began by being an observer of life, and only later set himself the task of acquiring the means of expressing it. This has resulted in a thrilling originality in which any remaining vestiges of barbarousness or *naïveté* appear only as new proofs of his faithfulness to the impression received, or as a flattering compliment paid to truth. For most of us, and particularly for men of affairs, for whom nature has no existence save by reference to utility, the fantastic reality of life has become singularly diluted. Monsieur G. never ceases to drink it in; his eyes and his memory are full of it.

[viii] Seventeenth-century Flemish painters Anthony Van Dyck and Adam Van der Meulen, and their French contemporary Jacques Courtois (known as "Il Borgognone").

chapter ten

"How to Make Our Ideas Clear"
Charles S. Peirce

America's most original philosophic genius, Charles S. Peirce (1839–1914), is the inventor of pragmatism, America's most famous contribution to world philosophy. His career was marked by brilliance in a variety of mathematical, scientific and philosophical pursuits, and by the tragedy of unfulfilled promise. He was fired from Johns Hopkins University at the age of 45, never held another regular academic appointment, and lived his later life in abject poverty. In its critique of metaphysics pragmatism is consonant with much of twentieth-century philosophy – like logical positivism and phenomenology – but it has more recently served the radical purposes of antifoundationalism and postmodernism. Peirce, however, regarded pragmatism as perfectly compatible with metaphysics and cosmology; his was a truly systematic philosophy. In "How to Make Our Ideas Clear" (1878) Peirce explains pragmatism for the first time, although he does not use the term, which would not appear in print until William James introduced it in 1898. In fact, in order to distinguish his views from those that James and others were promoting as pragmatism, Peirce later changed the name of his doctrine to "pragmaticism," which, he said, was "ugly enough to be safe from kidnappers."

The principles set forth in the first part of this essay[i] lead, at once, to a method of reaching a clearness of thought of higher grade than the "distinctness" of the logicians. It was there noticed that the action of thought is excited by the irritation of doubt, and ceases when belief is attained; so that the production of belief is the sole function of thought. All these words, however, are too strong for my purpose. It is as if I had described the phenomena as they appear under a mental microscope. Doubt and Belief, as the words are commonly employed, relate to religious or other grave discussions. But here I use them to designate the starting of

---

Charles S. Peirce, "How to Make Our Ideas Clear," *Collected Papers of Charles Sanders Peirce*, ed. Charles Hartshorne and Paul Weiss (Cambridge, MA: Harvard University Press, 1965), vol. V, para. 394–402, pp. 252–60, and para. 405–10, pp. 265–71.

[i] In which Peirce argues that while traditional logic and philosophy have claimed to prize clarity, they have never been clear about what clarity involves.

any question, no matter how small or how great, and the resolution of it. If, for instance, in a horse-car, I pull out my purse and find a five-cent nickel and five coppers, I decide, while my hand is going to the purse, in which way I will pay my fare. To call such a question Doubt, and my decision Belief, is certainly to use words very disproportionate to the occasion. To speak of such a doubt as causing an irritation which needs to be appeased, suggests a temper which is uncomfortable to the verge of insanity. Yet, looking at the matter minutely, it must be admitted that, if there is the least hesitation as to whether I shall pay the five coppers or the nickel (as there will be sure to be, unless I act from some previously contracted habit in the matter), though irritation is too strong a word, yet I am excited to such small mental activity as may be necessary to deciding how I shall act. Most frequently doubts arise from some indecision, however momentary, in our action. Sometimes it is not so. I have, for example, to wait in a railway-station, and to pass the time I read the advertisements on the walls. I compare the advantages of different trains and different routes which I never expect to take, merely fancying myself to be in a state of hesitancy, because I am bored with having nothing to trouble me. Feigned hesitancy, whether feigned for mere amusement or with a lofty purpose, plays a great part in the production of scientific inquiry. However the doubt may originate, it stimulates the mind to an activity which may be slight or energetic, calm or turbulent. Images pass rapidly through consciousness, one incessantly melting into another, until at last, when all is over – it may be in a fraction of a second, in an hour, or after long years – we find ourselves decided as to how we should act under such circumstances as those which occasioned our hesitation. In other words, we have attained belief.

In this process we observe two sorts of elements of consciousness, the distinction between which may best be made clear by means of an illustration. In a piece of music there are the separate notes, and there is the air. A single tone may be prolonged for an hour or a day, and it exists as perfectly in each second of that time as in the whole taken together; so that, as long as it is sounding, it might be present to a sense from which everything in the past was as completely absent as the future itself. But it is different with the air, the performance of which occupies a certain time, during the portions of which only portions of it are played. It consists in an orderliness in the succession of sounds which strike the ear at different times; and to perceive it there must be some continuity of consciousness which makes the events of a lapse of time present to us. We certainly only perceive the air by hearing the separate notes; yet we cannot be said to directly hear it, for we hear only what is present at the instant, and an orderliness of succession cannot exist in an instant. These two sorts of objects, what we are *immediately* conscious of and what we are *mediately* conscious of, are found in all consciousness. Some elements (the sensations) are completely present at every instant so long as they last, while others (like thought) are actions having beginning, middle, and end, and consist in a congruence in the succession of sensations which flow through the mind. They cannot be immediately present to us, but must cover some portion of the past or future. Thought is a thread of melody running through the succession of our sensations.

We may add that just as a piece of music may be written in parts, each part having its own air,[ii] so various systems of relationship of succession subsist together between the same sensations. These different systems are distinguished by having different motives, ideas, or functions. Thought is only one such system, for its sole motive, idea, and function is to produce belief, and whatever does not concern that purpose belongs to some other system of relations. The action of thinking may incidentally have other results; it may serve to amuse us, for example, and among *dilettanti* it is not rare to find those who have so perverted thought to the purposes of pleasure that it seems to vex them to think that the questions upon which they delight to exercise it may ever get finally settled; and a positive discovery which takes a favorite subject out of the arena of literary debate is met with ill-concealed dislike. This disposition is the very debauchery of thought. But the soul and meaning of thought, abstracted from the other elements which accompany it, though it may be voluntarily thwarted, can never be made to direct itself toward anything but the production of belief. Thought in action has for its only possible motive the attainment of thought at rest; and whatever does not refer to belief is no part of the thought itself.

And what, then, is belief? It is the demi-cadence which closes a musical phrase in the symphony of our intellectual life. We have seen that it has just three properties: First, it is something that we are aware of; second, it appeases the irritation of doubt; and, third, it involves the establishment in our nature of a rule of action, or, say for short, a *habit*. As it appeases the irritation of doubt, which is the motive for thinking, thought relaxes, and comes to rest for a moment when belief is reached. But, since belief is a rule for action, the application of which involves further doubt and further thought, at the same time that it is a stopping-place, it is also a new starting-place for thought. That is why I have permitted myself to call it thought at rest, although thought is essentially an action. The *final* upshot of thinking is the exercise of volition, and of this thought no longer forms a part; but belief is only a stadium of mental action, an effect upon our nature due to thought, which will influence future thinking.

[ii] Melody

147

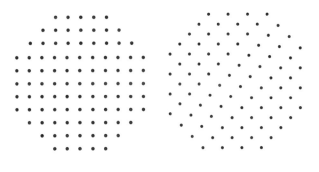

Fig. 1   Fig. 2

The essence of belief is the establishment of a habit; and different beliefs are distinguished by the different modes of action to which they give rise. If beliefs do not differ in this respect, if they appease the same doubt by producing the same rule of action, then no mere differences in the manner of consciousness of them can make them different beliefs, any more than playing a tune in different keys is playing different tunes. Imaginary distinctions are often drawn between beliefs which differ only in their mode of expression; – the wrangling which ensues is real enough, however. To believe that any objects are arranged among themselves as in Fig. 1, and to believe that they are arranged [as] in Fig. 2, are one and the same belief; yet it is conceivable that a man should assert one proposition and deny the other. Such false distinctions do as much harm as the confusion of beliefs really different, and are among the pitfalls of which we ought constantly to beware, especially when we are upon metaphysical ground. One singular deception of this sort, which often occurs, is to mistake the sensation produced by our own unclearness of thought for a character of the object we are thinking. Instead of perceiving that the obscurity is purely subjective, we fancy that we contemplate a quality of the object which is essentially mysterious; and if our conception be afterward presented to us in a clear form we do not recognize it as the same, owing to the absence of the feeling of unintelligibility. So long as this deception lasts, it obviously puts an impassable barrier in the way of perspicuous thinking; so that it equally interests the opponents of rational thought to perpetuate it, and its adherents to guard against it.

Another such deception is to mistake a mere difference in the grammatical construction of two words for a distinction between the ideas they express. In this pedantic age, when the general mob of writers attend so much more to words than to things, this error is common enough. When I just said that thought is an *action*, and that it consists in a *relation*,

148

although a person performs an action but not a relation, which can only be the result of an action, yet there was no inconsistency in what I said, but only a grammatical vagueness.

From all these sophisms we shall be perfectly safe so long as we reflect that the whole function of thought is to produce habits of action; and that whatever there is connected with a thought, but irrelevant to its purpose, is an accretion to it, but no part of it. If there be a unity among our sensations which has no reference to how we shall act on a given occasion, as when we listen to a piece of music, why we do not call that thinking. To develop its meaning, we have, therefore, simply to determine what habits it produces, for what a thing means is simply what habits it involves. Now, the identity of a habit depends on how it might lead us to act, not merely under such circumstances as are likely to arise, but under such as might possibly occur, no matter how improbable they may be. What the habit is depends on *when* and *how* it causes us to act. As for the *when*, every stimulus to action is derived from perception; as for the *how*, every purpose of action is to produce some sensible result. Thus, we come down to what is tangible and conceivably practical, as the root of every real distinction of thought, no matter how subtle it may be; and there is no distinction of meaning so fine as to consist in anything but a possible difference of practice.

To see what this principle leads to, consider in the light of it such a doctrine as that of transubstantiation. The Protestant churches generally hold that the elements of the sacrament are flesh and blood only in a tropical sense; they nourish our souls as meat and the juice of it would our bodies. But the Catholics maintain that they are literally just meat and blood; although they possess all the sensible qualities of wafer-cakes and diluted wine. But we can have no conception of wine except what may enter into a belief, either –

1   That this, that, or the other, is wine; or,
2   That wine possesses certain properties.

Such beliefs are nothing but self-notifications that we should, upon occasion, act in regard to such things as we believe to be wine according to the qualities which we believe wine to possess. The occasion of such action would be some sensible perception, the motive of it to produce some sensible result. Thus our action has exclusive reference to what affects the senses, our habit has the same bearing as our action, our belief the same as our habit, our conception the same as our belief; and we can consequently mean nothing by wine but what has certain effects, direct or indirect, upon our senses; and to talk of something as having all the sensible characters of wine, yet being in reality blood, is senseless jargon. Now, it is not my object to pursue the theological question; and having used it as a logical example I drop it, without caring to anticipate the

149

theologian's reply. I only desire to point out how impossible it is that we should have an idea in our minds which relates to anything but conceived sensible effects of things. Our idea of anything *is* our idea of its sensible effects; and if we fancy that we have any other we deceive ourselves, and mistake a mere sensation accompanying the thought for a part of the thought itself. It is absurd to say that thought has any meaning unrelated to its only function. It is foolish for Catholics and Protestants to fancy themselves in disagreement about the elements of the sacrament, if they agree in regard to all their sensible effects, here and hereafter.

It appears, then, that the rule for attaining the third grade of clearness of apprehension is as follows: Consider what effects, that might conceivably have practical bearings, we conceive the object of our conception to have. Then, our conception of these effects is the whole of our conception of the object. . . .[1]

Let us now approach the subject of logic, and consider a conception which particularly concerns it, that of *reality*. Taking clearness in the sense of familiarity, no idea could be clearer than this. Every child uses it with perfect confidence, never dreaming that he does not understand it. As for clearness in its second grade, however, it would probably puzzle most men, even among those of a reflective turn of mind, to give an abstract definition of the real. Yet such a definition may perhaps be reached by considering the points of difference between reality and its opposite, fiction. A figment is a product of somebody's imagination; it has such characters as his thought impresses upon it. That those characters are independent of how you or I think is an external reality. There are, however, phenomena within our own minds, dependent upon our thought, which are at the same time real in the sense that we really think them. But though their characters depend on how we think, they do not depend on what we think those characters to be. Thus, a dream has a real existence as a mental phenomenon, if somebody has really dreamt it; that he dreamt so and so, does not depend on what anybody thinks was dreamt, but is completely independent of all opinion on the subject. On the other hand, considering, not the fact of dreaming, but the thing dreamt, it retains its peculiarities by virtue of no other fact than that it was dreamt to possess them. Thus we may define the real as that whose characters are independent of what anybody may think them to be.

But, however satisfactory such a definition may be found, it would be a great mistake to suppose that it makes the idea of reality perfectly clear. Here, then, let us apply our rules. According to them, reality, like every other quality, consists in the peculiar sensible effects which things partaking of it produce. The only effect which real things have is to cause belief, for all the sensations which they excite emerge into consciousness in the form of beliefs. The question therefore is, how is true belief (or belief in the real) distinguished from false belief (or belief in fiction). Now, as we have seen in the former paper, the ideas of truth and falsehood, in their full development, appertain exclusively to the experiential method of settling opinion. A person who arbitrarily chooses the propositions which he will adopt can use the word truth only to emphasize the expression of his determination to hold on to his choice. Of course, the method of tenacity never prevailed exclusively; reason is too natural to men for that. But in the literature of the dark ages we find some fine examples of it. When Scotus Erigena is commenting upon a poetical passage in which hellebore is spoken of as having caused the death of Socrates, he does not hesitate to inform the inquiring reader that Helleborus and Socrates were two eminent Greek philosophers, and that the latter, having been overcome in argument by the former, took the matter to heart and died of it![iii] What sort of an idea of truth could a man have who could adopt and teach, without the qualification of a perhaps, an opinion taken so entirely at random? The real spirit of Socrates, who I hope would have been delighted to have been "overcome in argument," because he would have learned something by it, is in curious contrast with the naïve idea of the glossist, for whom (as for "the born missionary" of today) discussion would seem to have been simply a struggle. When philosophy began to awake from its long slumber, and before theology completely dominated it, the practice seems to have been for each professor to seize upon any philosophical position he found unoccupied and which seemed a strong one, to intrench himself in it, and to sally forth from time to time to give battle to the others. Thus, even the scanty records we possess of those disputes enable us to make out a dozen or more opinions held by different teachers at one time concerning the question of nominalism and realism. Read the opening part of the *Historia Calamitatum* of Abelard, who was certainly as philosophical as any of his contemporaries, and see the spirit of combat which it breathes.[iv] For him, the truth is simply his particular stronghold. When the method of authority prevailed, the truth meant little more than the Catholic faith. All the efforts of the scholastic doctors are directed toward harmonizing their faith in Aristotle and their faith in the Church, and one may search their ponderous folios through without finding an argument which goes any further. It is noticeable that where different faiths flourish side by side, renegades are looked upon with contempt even by the party whose belief they adopt; so completely has the idea of loyalty replaced that of truth-seeking. Since the time of Descartes, the defect in the conception of truth has been

---

iii "Hellebore" refers to a plant of the lily family; Socrates actually died from drinking a potion made from hemlock, a different plant. John Scotus Erigena (b. 810) was a medieval philosopher.

iv Peter Abelard (1079–1142), medieval theologian and logician.

less apparent. Still, it will sometimes strike a scientific man that the philosophers have been less intent on finding out what the facts are, than on inquiring what belief is most in harmony with their system. It is hard to convince a follower of the *a priori* method by adducing facts; but show him that an opinion he is defending is inconsistent with what he has laid down elsewhere, and he will be very apt to retract it. These minds do not seem to believe that disputation is ever to cease; they seem to think that the opinion which is natural for one man is not so for another, and that belief will, consequently, never be settled. In contenting themselves with fixing their own opinions by a method which would lead another man to a different result, they betray their feeble hold of the conception of what truth is.

On the other hand, all the followers of science are animated by a cheerful hope that the processes of investigation, if only pushed far enough, will give one certain solution to each question to which they apply it. One man may investigate the velocity of light by studying the transits of Venus and the aberration of the stars; another by the oppositions of Mars and the eclipses of Jupiter's satellites; a third by the method of Fizeau; a fourth by that of Foucault;[v] a fifth by the motions of the curves of Lissajoux; a sixth, a seventh, an eighth, and a ninth, may follow the different methods of comparing the measures of statical and dynamical electricity. They may at first obtain different results, but, as each perfects his method and his processes, the results are found to move steadily together toward a destined centre. So with all scientific research. Different minds may set out with the most antagonistic views, but the progress of investigation carries them by a force outside of themselves to one and the same conclusion. This activity of thought by which we are carried, not where we wish, but to a fore-ordained goal, is like the operation of destiny. No modification of the point of view taken, no selection of other facts for study, no natural bent of mind even, can enable a man to escape the predestinate opinion. This great hope is embodied in the conception of truth and reality. The opinion which is fated[2] to be ultimately agreed to by all who investigate, is what we mean by the truth, and the object represented in this opinion is the real. That is the way I would explain reality.

But it may be said that this view is directly opposed to the abstract definition which we have given of reality, inasmuch as it makes the characters of the real depend on what is ultimately thought about them. But the answer to this is that, on the one hand, reality is independent, not necessarily of thought in general, but only of what you or I or any finite number of men may think about it; and that, on the other hand, though

---

[v] Armand-Hippolyte-Louis Fizeau (1819–96) and Jean-Bernard-Léon Foucault (1819–68) were French physicists; Jules-Antoine Lissajoux (1822–80) was a French mathematician.

the object of the final opinion depends on what that opinion is, yet what that opinion is does not depend on what you or I or any man thinks. Our perversity and that of others may indefinitely postpone the settlement of opinion; it might even conceivably cause an arbitrary proposition to be universally accepted as long as the human race should last. Yet even that would not change the nature of the belief, which alone could be the result of investigation carried sufficiently far; and if, after the extinction of our race, another should arise with faculties and disposition for investigation, that true opinion must be the one which they would ultimately come to. "Truth crushed to earth shall rise again," and the opinion which would finally result from investigation does not depend on how anybody may actually think. But the reality of that which is real does depend on the real fact that investigation is destined to lead, at last, if continued long enough, to a belief in it.

But I may be asked what I have to say to all the minute facts of history, forgotten never to be recovered, to the lost books of the ancients, to the buried secrets.

> "Full many a gem of purest ray serene
>   The dark, unfathomed caves of ocean bear;
> Full many a flower is born to blush unseen,
>   And waste its sweetness on the desert air."[vi]

Do these things not really exist because they are hopelessly beyond the reach of our knowledge? And then, after the universe is dead (according to the prediction of some scientists), and all life has ceased forever, will not the shock of atoms continue though there will be no mind to know it? To this I reply that, though in no possible state of knowledge can any number be great enough to express the relation between the amount of what rests unknown to the amount of the known, yet it is unphilosophical to suppose that, with regard to any given question (which has any clear meaning), investigation would not bring forth a solution of it, if it were carried far enough. Who would have said, a few years ago, that we could ever know of what substances stars are made whose light may have been longer in reaching us than the human race has existed? Who can be sure of what we shall not know in a few hundred years? Who can guess what would be the result of continuing the pursuit of science for ten thousand years, with the activity of the last hundred? And if it were to go on for a million, or a billion, or any number of years you please, how is it possible to say that there is any question which might not ultimately be solved?

But it may be objected, "Why make so much of these remote considerations, especially when it is your principle that only practical distinctions

---

[vi] Thomas Grey (1716–71), *Elegy Written in a Country Churchyard*, ll. 53–6.

have a meaning?" Well, I must confess that it makes very little difference whether we say that a stone on the bottom of the ocean, in complete darkness, is brilliant or not – that is to say, that it *probably* makes no difference, remembering always that that stone *may* be fished up tomorrow. But that there are gems at the bottom of the sea, flowers in the untraveled desert, etc., are propositions which, like that about a diamond being hard when it is not pressed, concern much more the arrangement of our language than they do the meaning of our ideas.

It seems to me, however, that we have, by the application of our rule, reached so clear an apprehension of what we mean by reality, and of the fact which the idea rests on, that we should not, perhaps, be making a pretension so presumptuous as it would be singular, if we were to offer a metaphysical theory of existence for universal acceptance among those who employ the scientific method of fixing belief. However, as metaphysics is a subject much more curious than useful, the knowledge of which, like that of a sunken reef, serves chiefly to enable us to keep clear of it, I will not trouble the reader with any more Ontology at this moment. I have already been led much further into that path than I should have desired; and I have given the reader such a dose of mathematics, psychology, and all that is most abstruse, that I fear he may already have left me, and that what I am now writing is for the compositor and proof-reader exclusively. I trusted to the importance of the subject. There is no royal road to logic, and really valuable ideas can only be had at the price of close attention. But I know that in the matter of ideas the public prefer the cheap and nasty; and in my next paper[vii] I am going to return to the easily intelligible, and not wander from it again. The reader who has been at the pains of wading through this paper, shall be rewarded in the next one by seeing how beautifully what has been developed in this tedious way can be applied to the ascertainment of the rules of scientific reasoning.

We have, hitherto, not crossed the threshold of scientific logic. It is certainly important to know how to make our ideas clear, but they may be ever so clear without being true. How to make them so, we have next to study. How to give birth to those vital and procreative ideas which multiply into a thousand forms and diffuse themselves everywhere, advancing civilization and making the dignity of man, is an art not yet reduced to rules, but of the secret of which the history of science affords some hints.

[vii] "The Fixation of Belief" (1877).

Notes

1   [The editors of Peirce's *Collected Papers* report that Peirce added a note here in
    1903, "Long addition refuting what comes next," which apparently refers to
    the following unpublished passage written in 1893.] Before we undertake
    to apply this rule, let us reflect a little upon what it implies. It has been said
    to be a sceptical and materialistic principle. But it is only an application of
    the sole principle of logic which was recommended by Jesus; "Ye may know
    them by their fruits," and it is very intimately allied with the ideas of the
    gospel. We must certainly guard ourselves against understanding this rule
    in too individualistic a sense. To say that man accomplishes nothing but that
    to which his endeavors are directed would be a cruel condemnation of the
    great bulk of mankind, who never have leisure to labor for anything but
    the necessities of life for themselves and their families. But, without directly
    striving for it, far less comprehending it, they perform all that civilization
    requires, and bring forth another generation to advance history another
    step. Their fruit is, therefore, collective; it is the achievement of the whole
    people. What is it, then, that the whole people is about, what is this
    civilization that is the outcome of history, but is never completed? We
    cannot expect to attain a complete conception of it; but we can see that it is
    a gradual process, that it involves a realization of ideas in man's conscious-
    ness and in his works, and that it takes place by virtue of man's capacity
    for learning, and by experience continually pouring upon him ideas he has
    not yet acquired. We may say that it is the process whereby man, with all his
    miserable littlenesses, becomes gradually more and more imbued with the
    Spirit of God, in which Nature and History are rife. We are also told to believe
    in a world to come; but the idea is itself too vague to contribute much to
    the perspicuity of ordinary ideas. It is a common observation that those who
    dwell continually upon their expectations are apt to become oblivious to
    the requirements of their actual station. The great principle of logic is self-
    surrender, which does not mean that self is to lay low for the sake of an
    ultimate triumph. It may turn out so; but that must not be the governing
    purpose.
        When we come to study the great principle of continuity and see how all is
    fluid and every point directly partakes the being of every other, it will appear
    that individualism and falsity are one and the same. Meantime, we know that
    man is not whole as long as he is single, that he is essentially a possible
    member of society. Especially, one man's experience is nothing, if it stands
    alone. If he sees what others cannot, we call it hallucination. It is not "my"
    experience, but "our" experience that has to be thought of; and this "us" has
    indefinite possibilities.
        Neither must we understand the practical in any low and sordid sense.
    Individual action is a means and not our end. Individual pleasure is not our
    end; we are all putting our shoulders to the wheel for an end that none of us
    can catch more than a glimpse at – that which the generations are working

out. But we can see that the development of embodied ideas is what it will consist in.

2 Fate means merely that which is sure to come true, and can nohow be avoided. It is a superstition to suppose that a certain sort of events are ever fated, and it is another to suppose that the word fate can never be freed from its superstitious taint. We are all fated to die.

chapter eleven

The Protestant Ethic and the Spirit of Capitalism "Science as a Vocation"

Max Weber

Max Weber (1864–1920), German thinker and one of the founders of sociology, stands with Freud and Marx as one of the great theorists of modern society. A supporter of liberal republicanism in imperialist, quasi-feudal Germany, Weber famously opposed the politicization of science, arguing for the need for dispassionate objectivity, a stance directly connected to his view of modernity. In the following Introduction to his most famous book, *The Protestant Ethic and the Spirit of Capitalism* (1904–5), he presents the essence of modernization as an expanding "rationalism," by which he meant an increasing subjection of spheres of life to instrumental rationality (*Zweckrationalität*), the analysis, planning, and manipulation of means in order to serve worldly goals. He soberly viewed modernity as progress bought at a high price. It bought individual liberty, rational thought, and progress in material well-being, but in exchange for a "disenchantment of the world," a permanent state of dissatisfaction, and an "iron cage" of bureaucratic alienation. There is no way around this bargain, Weber argues in his marvelous 1918 lecture "Science as a Vocation," our second selection. He concludes that one must either "bear the fate of the times like a man," or sacrifice rational intelligence and "return [to] the arms of the old churches . . ." There is no third option.

The Protestant Ethic and the Spirit of Capitalism

A product of modern European civilization, studying any problem of universal history, is bound to ask himself to what combination of circum-

Max Weber, "Author's Introduction" to *The Protestant Ethic and the Spirit of Capitalism*, trans. Talcott Parsons (New York: Scribner, 1958), pp. 13–31; and from "Science as a Vocation," in *From Max Weber: Essays in Sociology*, trans. and ed. H.H. Gerth and C. Wright Mills (New York: Oxford University Press, 1946), pp. 138–40, 143–9, 155–6.

stances the fact should be attributed that in Western civilization, and in Western civilization only, cultural phenomena have appeared which (as we like to think) lie in a line of development having *universal* significance and value.

Only in the West does science exist at a stage of development which we recognize to-day as valid. Empirical knowledge, reflection on problems of the cosmos and of life, philosophical and theological wisdom of the most profound sort, are not confined to it, though in the case of the last the full development of a systematic theology must be credited to Christianity under the influence of Hellenism, since there were only fragments in Islam and in a few Indian sects. In short, knowledge and observation of great refinement have existed elsewhere, above all in India, China, Babylonia, Egypt. But in Babylonia and elsewhere astronomy lacked – which makes its development all the more astounding – the mathematical foundation which it first received from the Greeks. The Indian geometry had no rational proof; that was another product of the Greek intellect, also the creator of mechanics and physics. The Indian natural sciences, though well developed in observation, lacked the method of experiment, which was, apart from beginnings in antiquity, essentially a product of the Renaissance, as was the modern laboratory. Hence medicine, especially in India, though highly developed in empirical technique, lacked a biological and particularly a biochemical foundation. A rational chemistry has been absent from all areas of culture except the West.

The highly developed historical scholarship of China did not have the method of Thucydides.[i] Machiavelli, it is true, had predecessors in India; but all Indian political thought was lacking in a systematic method comparable to that of Aristotle, and, indeed, in the possession of rational concepts. Not all the anticipations in India (School of Mimamsa), nor the extensive codification especially in the Near East, nor all the Indian and other books of law, had the strictly systematic forms of thought, so essential to a rational jurisprudence, of the Roman law and of the Western law under its influence. A structure like the canon law is known only to the West.

A similar statement is true of art. The musical ear of other peoples has probably been even more sensitively developed than our own, certainly not less so. Polyphonic music of various kinds has been widely distributed over the earth. The co-operation of a number of instruments and also

---

[i] Ancient Greek historian.

point and harmony, formation of the tone material on the basis of three triads with the harmonic third; our chromatics and enharmonics, not interpreted in terms of space, but, since the Renaissance, of harmony; our orchestra, with its string quartet as a nucleus, and the organization of ensembles of wind instruments; our bass accompaniment; our system of notation, which has made possible the composition and production of modern musical works, and thus their very survival; our sonatas, symphonies, operas; and finally, as means to all these, our fundamental instruments, the organ, piano, violin, etc.; all these things are known only in the Occident, although programme music, tone poetry, alteration of tones and chromatics, have existed in various musical traditions as means of expression.

In architecture, pointed arches have been used elsewhere as a means of decoration, in antiquity and in Asia; presumably the combination of pointed arch and cross-arched vault was not unknown in the Orient. But the rational use of the Gothic vault as a means of distributing pressure and of roofing spaces of all forms, and above all as the constructive principle of great monumental buildings and the foundation of a *style* extending to sculpture and painting, such as that created by our Middle Ages, does not occur elsewhere. The technical basis of our architecture came from the Orient. But the Orient lacked that solution of the problem of the dome and that type of classic rationalization of all art – in painting by the rational utilization of lines and spatial perspective – which the Renaissance created for us. There was printing in China. But a printed literature, designed *only* for print and only possible through it, and, above all, the Press and periodicals, have appeared only in the Occident. Institutions of higher education of all possible types, even some superficially similar to our universities, or at least academies, have existed (China, Islam). But a rational, systematic, and specialized pursuit of science, with trained and specialized personnel, has only existed in the West in a sense at all approaching its present dominant place in our culture. Above all is this true of the trained official, the pillar of both the modern State and of the economic life of the West. He forms a type of which there have heretofore only been suggestions, which have never remotely approached its present importance for the social order. Of course the official, even the specialized official, is a very old constituent of the most various societies. But no country and no age has ever experienced, in the same sense as the modern Occident, the absolute and complete dependence of its whole existence, of the political, technical, and economic conditions of its life, on a specially trained *organization* of officials. The most important functions of the everyday life of society have come to be in the hands of technically, commercially, and above all legally trained government officials.

159

of technically, commercially, and above all legally trained government officials.

Organization of political and social groups in feudal classes has been common. But even the feudal state of *rex et regnum*[ii] in the Western sense has only been known to our culture. Even more are parliaments of periodically elected representatives, with government by demagogues and party leaders as ministers responsible to the parliaments, peculiar to us, although there have, of course, been parties, in the sense of organizations for exerting influence and gaining control of political power, all over the world. In fact, the State itself, in the sense of a political association with a rational, written constitution, rationally ordained law, and an administration bound to rational rules or laws, administered by trained officials, is known, in this combination of characteristics, only in the Occident, despite all other approaches to it.

And the same is true of the most fateful force in our modern life, capitalism. The impulse to acquisition, pursuit of gain, of money, of the greatest possible amount of money, has in itself nothing to do with capitalism. This impulse exists and has existed among waiters, physicians, coachmen, artists, prostitutes, dishonest officials, soldiers, nobles, crusaders, gamblers, and beggars. One may say that it has been common to all sorts and conditions of men at all times and in all countries of the earth, wherever the objective possibility of it is or has been given. It should be taught in the kindergarten of cultural history that this naïve idea of capitalism must be given up once and for all. Unlimited greed for gain is not in the least identical with capitalism, and is still less its spirit. Capitalism *may* even be identical with the restraint, or at least a rational tempering, of this irrational impulse. But capitalism is identical with the pursuit of profit, and forever *renewed* profit, by means of continuous, rational, capitalistic enterprise. For it must be so: in a wholly capitalistic order of society, an individual capitalistic enterprise which did not take advantage of its opportunities for profit-making would be doomed to extinction.

Let us now define our terms somewhat more carefully than is generally done. We will define a capitalistic economic action as one which rests on the expectation of profit by the utilization of opportunities for exchange, that is on (formally) peaceful chances of profit. Acquisition by force (formally and actually) follows its own particular laws, and it is not expedient, however little one can forbid this, to place it in the same category with action which is, in the last analysis, oriented to profits from exchange.[1] Where capitalistic acquisition is rationally pursued, the corresponding action is adjusted to calculations in terms of capital. This means

[ii] King and kingdom.

that the action is adapted to a systematic utilization of goods or personal services as means of acquisition in such a way that, at the close of a business period, the balance of the enterprise in money assets (or, in the case of a continuous enterprise, the periodically estimated money value of assets) exceeds the capital, i.e. the estimated value of the material means of production used for acquisition in exchange. It makes no difference whether it involves a quantity of goods entrusted *in natura* to a travelling merchant, the proceeds of which may consist in other goods *in natura* acquired by trade, or whether it involves a manufacturing enterprise, the assets of which consist of buildings, machinery, cash, raw materials, partly and wholly manufactured goods, which are balanced against liabilities. The important fact is always that a calculation of capital in terms of money is made, whether by modern book-keeping methods or in any other way, however primitive and crude. Everything is done in terms of balances: at the beginning of the enterprise an initial balance, before every individual decision a calculation to ascertain its probable profitableness, and at the end a final balance to ascertain how much profit has been made. For instance, the initial balance of a *commenda*[iii] transaction would determine an agreed money value of the assets put into it (so far as they were not in money form already), and a final balance would form the estimate on which to base the distribution of profit and loss at the end. So far as the transactions are rational, calculation underlies every single action of the partners. That a really accurate calculation or estimate may not exist, that the procedure is pure guess-work, or simply traditional and conventional, happens even to-day in every form of capitalistic enterprise where the circumstances do not demand strict accuracy. But these are points affecting only the *degree* of rationality of capitalistic acquisition.

For the purpose of this conception all that matters is that an actual adaptation of economic action to a comparison of money income with money expenses takes place, no matter how primitive the form. Now in this sense capitalism and capitalistic enterprises, even with a considerable rationalization of capitalistic calculation, have existed in all civilized countries of the earth, so far as economic documents permit us to judge. In China, India, Babylon, Egypt, Mediterranean antiquity, and the Middle Ages, as well as in modern times. These were not merely isolated ventures, but economic enterprises which were entirely dependent on the continual renewal of capitalistic undertakings, and even continuous operations. However, trade especially was for a long time not continuous like our own, but consisted essentially in a series of individual undertakings. Only gradually did the activities of even the large merchants acquire an inner cohesion (with branch organizations, etc.). In any case, the capitalistic

---

[iii] A medieval contractual association of producers and shippers.

161

enterprise and the capitalistic entrepreneur, not only as occasional but as regular entrepreneurs, are very old and were very widespread.

Now, however, the Occident has developed capitalism both to a quantitative extent, and (carrying this quantitative development) in types, forms, and directions which have never existed elsewhere. All over the world there have been merchants, wholesale and retail, local and engaged in foreign trade. Loans of all kinds have been made, and there have been banks with the most various functions, at least comparable to ours of, say, the sixteenth century. Sea loans, *commenda*, and transactions and associations similar to the *Kommanditgesellschaft*,[iv] have all been widespread, even as continuous businesses. Whenever money finances of public bodies have existed, money-lenders have appeared, as in Babylon, Hellas, India, China, Rome. They have financed wars and piracy, contracts and building operations of all sorts. In overseas policy they have functioned as colonial entrepreneurs, as planters with slaves, or directly or indirectly forced labour, and have farmed domains, offices, and, above all, taxes. They have financed party leaders in elections and *condottieri*[v] in civil wars. And, finally, they have been speculators in chances for pecuniary gain of all kinds. This kind of entrepreneur, the capitalistic adventurer, has existed everywhere. With the exception of trade and credit and banking transactions, their activities were predominantly of an irrational and speculative character, or directed to acquisition by force, above all the acquisition of booty, whether directly in war or in the form of continuous fiscal booty by exploitation of subjects.

The capitalism of promoters, large-scale speculators, concession hunters, and much modern financial capitalism even in peace time, but, above all, the capitalism especially concerned with exploiting wars, bears this stamp even in modern Western countries, and some, but only some, parts of large-scale international trade are closely related to it, to-day as always.

But in modern times the Occident has developed, in addition to this, a very different form of capitalism which has appeared nowhere else: the rational capitalistic organization of (formally) free labour. Only suggestions of it are found elsewhere. Even the organization of unfree labour reached a considerable degree of rationality only on plantations and to a very limited extent in the *Ergasteria*[vi] of antiquity. In the manors, manorial workshops, and domestic industries on estates with serf labour it was probably somewhat less developed. Even real domestic industries with free labour have definitely been proved to have existed in only a few isolated cases outside the Occident. The frequent use of day labourers led in a very few cases – especially State monopolies, which are, however, very different from

---

[iv] A corporation in which one partner has unlimited, and the others limited, liability.
[v] Military adventurers.   [vi] Workshops.

modern industrial organization – to manufacturing organizations, but never to a rational organization of apprenticeship in the handicrafts like that of our Middle Ages.

Rational industrial organization, attuned to a regular market, and neither to political nor irrationally speculative opportunities for profit, is not, however, the only peculiarity of Western capitalism. The modern rational organization of the capitalistic enterprise would not have been possible without two other important factors in its development: the separation of business from the household, which completely dominates modern economic life, and closely connected with it, rational book-keeping. A spatial separation of places of work from those of residence exists elsewhere, as in the Oriental bazaar and in the *ergasteria* of other cultures. The development of capitalistic associations with their own accounts is also found in the Far East, the Near East, and in antiquity. But compared to the modern independence of business enterprises, those are only small beginnings. The reason for this was particularly that the indispensable requisites for this independence, our rational business book-keeping and our legal separation of corporate from personal property, were entirely lacking, or had only begun to develop.[2] The tendency everywhere else was for acquisitive enterprises to arise as parts of a royal or manorial *household* (of the *oikos*), which is, as Rodbertus has perceived, with all its superficial similarity, a fundamentally different, even opposite, development.[vii]

However, all these peculiarities of Western capitalism have derived their significance in the last analysis only from their association with the capitalistic organization of labour. Even what is generally called commercialization, the development of negotiable securities and the rationalization of speculation, the exchanges, etc., is connected with it. For without the rational capitalistic organization of labour, all this, so far as it was possible at all, would have nothing like the same significance, above all for the social structure and all the specific problems of the modern Occident connected with it. Exact calculation – the basis of everything else – is only possible on a basis of free labour.[viii]

And just as, or rather because, the world has known no rational organization of labour outside the modern Occident, it has known no rational socialism. Of course, there has been civic economy, a civic food-supply policy, mercantilism and welfare policies of princes, rationing, regulation of economic life, protectionism, and *laissez-faire* theories (as in China). The world has also known socialistic and communistic experiments of various sorts: family, religious, or military communism, State socialism (in Egypt),

---

[vii] Oikos, ancient Greek for "household" is the root of the English word "economy"; German sociologist Karl Rodbertus (1805–75).

[viii] Free labor refers to the emancipation of peasants from the feudal condition of serfdom.

monopolistic cartels, and consumers' organizations. But although there have everywhere been civic market privileges, companies, guilds, and all sorts of legal differences between town and country, the concept of the citizen has not existed outside the Occident, and that of the bourgeoisie outside the modern Occident. Similarly, the proletariat as a class could not exist, because there was no rational organization of free labour under regular discipline. Class struggles between creditor and debtor classes; landowners and the landless, serfs, or tenants; trading interests and consumers or landlords, have existed everywhere in various combinations. But even the Western mediæval struggles between putters-out and their workers exist elsewhere only in beginnings. The modern conflict of the large-scale industrial entrepreneur and free-wage labourers was entirely lacking. And thus there could be no such problems as those of socialism.

Hence in a universal history of culture the central problem for us is not, in the last analysis, even from a purely economic view-point, the development of capitalistic activity as such, differing in different cultures only in form: the adventurer type, or capitalism in trade, war, politics, or administration as sources of gain. It is rather the origin of this sober bourgeois capitalism with its rational organization of free labour. Or in terms of cultural history, the problem is that of the origin of the Western bourgeois class and of its peculiarities, a problem which is certainly closely connected with that of the origin of the capitalistic organization of labour, but is not quite the same thing. For the bourgeois as a class existed prior to the development of the peculiar modern form of capitalism, though, it is true, only in the Western hemisphere.

Now the peculiar modern Western form of capitalism has been, at first sight, strongly influenced by the development of technical possibilities. Its rationality is to-day essentially dependent on the calculability of the most important technical factors. But this means fundamentally that it is dependent on the peculiarities of modern science, especially the natural sciences based on mathematics and exact and rational experiment. On the other hand, the development of these sciences and of the technique resting upon them now receives important stimulation from these capitalistic interests in its practical economic application. It is true that the origin of Western science cannot be attributed to such interests. Calculation, even with decimals, and algebra have been carried on in India, where the decimal system was invented. But it was only made use of by developing capitalism in the West, while in India it led to no modern arithmetic or book-keeping. Neither was the origin of mathematics and mechanics determined by capitalistic interests. But the *technical* utilization of scientific knowledge, so important for the living conditions of the mass of people, was certainly encouraged by economic considerations, which were extremely favourable to it in the Occident. But this encouragement was derived from the peculiarities of the social structure of the Occident. We must hence ask, from *what* parts of that structure was it derived, since not all of them have been of equal importance?

Among those of undoubted importance are the rational structures of law and of administration. For modern rational capitalism has need, not only of the technical means of production, but of a calculable legal system and of administration in terms of formal rules. Without it adventurous and speculative trading capitalism and all sorts of politically determined capitalisms are possible, but no rational enterprise under individual initiative, with fixed capital and certainty of calculations. Such a legal system and such administration have been available for economic activity in a comparative state of legal and formalistic perfection only in the Occident. We must hence inquire where that law came from. Among other circumstances, capitalistic interests have in turn undoubtedly also helped, but by no means alone nor even principally, to prepare the way for the predominance in law and administration of a class of jurists specially trained in rational law. But these interests did not themselves create that law. Quite different forces were at work in this development. And why did not the capitalistic interests do the same in China or India? Why did not the scientific, the artistic, the political, or the economic development there enter upon that path of rationalization which is peculiar to the Occident?

For in all the above cases it is a question of the specific and peculiar rationalism of Western culture. Now by this term very different things may be understood, as the following discussion will repeatedly show. There is, for example, rationalization of mystical contemplation, that is of an attitude which, viewed from other departments of life, is specifically irrational, just as much as there are rationalizations of economic life, of technique, of scientific research, of military training, of law and administration. Furthermore, each one of these fields may be rationalized in terms of very different ultimate values and ends, and what is rational from one point of view may well be irrational from another. Hence rationalizations of the most varied character have existed in various departments of life and in all areas of culture. To characterize their differences from the view-point of cultural history it is necessary to know what departments are rationalized, and in what direction. It is hence our first concern to work out and to explain genetically the special peculiarity of Occidental rationalism and within this field that of the modern Occidental form. Every such attempt at explanation must, recognizing the fundamental importance of the economic factor, above all take account of the economic conditions. But at the same time the opposite correlation must not be left out of consideration. For though the development of economic rationalism is partly dependent on rational technique and law, it is at the same time determined by the ability and disposition of men to adopt certain types of practical rational conduct.

165

When these types have been obstructed by spiritual obstacles, the development of rational economic conduct has also met serious inner resistance. The magical and religious forces, and the ethical ideas of duty based upon them, have in the past always been among the most important formative influences on conduct. In the studies collected here we shall be concerned with these forces.[ix]

Two older essays have been placed at the beginning which attempt, at one important point, to approach the side of the problem which is generally most difficult to grasp: the influence of certain religious ideas on the development of an economic spirit, or the ethos of an economic system. In this case we are dealing with the connection of the spirit of modern economic life with the rational ethics of ascetic Protestantism. Thus we treat here only one side of the causal chain. The later studies on the Economic Ethics of the World Religions attempt, in the form of a survey of the relations of the most important religions to economic life and to the social stratification of their environment, to follow out both causal relationships, so far as it is necessary in order to find points of comparison with the Occidental development. For only in this way is it possible to attempt a causal evaluation of those elements of the economic ethics of the Western religions which differentiate them from others, with a hope of attaining even a tolerable degree of approximation. Hence these studies do not claim to be complete analyses of cultures, however brief. On the contrary, in every culture they quite deliberately emphasize the elements in which it differs from Western civilization. They are, hence, definitely oriented to the problems which seem important for the understanding of Western culture from *this* view-point. With our object in view, any other procedure did not seem possible. But to avoid misunderstanding we must here lay special emphasis on the limitation of our purpose.

In another respect the uninitiated at least must be warned against exaggerating the importance of these investigations. The Sinologist, the Indologist, the Semitist, or the Egyptologist, will of course find no facts unknown to him. We only hope that he will find nothing definitely wrong in points that are essential. How far it has been possible to come as near this ideal as a non-specialist is able to do, the author cannot know. It is quite evident that anyone who is forced to rely on translations, and furthermore on the use and evaluation of monumental, documentary, or literary sources, has to rely himself on a specialist literature which is often highly controversial, and the merits of which he is unable to judge accurately. Such a writer must make modest claims for the value of his work. All the more so since the number of available translations of real

---

[ix] *The Protestant Ethic and the Spirit of Capitalism* is part of a series of Weber's works on the sociology of religion.

sources (that is, inscriptions and documents) is, especially for China, still very small in comparison with what exists and is important. From all this follows the definitely provisional character of these, studies, and especially of the parts dealing with Asia.[3] Only the specialist is entitled to a final judgment. And, naturally, it is only because expert studies with this special purpose and from this particular view-point have not hitherto been made, that the present ones have been written at all. They are destined to be superseded in a much more important sense than this can be said, as it can be, of all scientific work. But however objectionable it may be, such trespassing on other special fields cannot be avoided in comparative work. But one must take the consequences by resigning oneself to considerable doubts regarding the degree of one's success.

Fashion and the zeal of the *literati* would have us think that the specialist can to-day be spared, or degraded to a position subordinate to that of the seer. Almost all sciences owe something to dilettantes, often very valuable view-points. But dilettantism as a leading principle would be the end of science. He who yearns for seeing should go to the cinema, though it will be offered to him copiously to-day in literary form in the present field of investigation also.[4] Nothing is farther from the intent of these thoroughly serious studies than such an attitude. And, I might add, whoever wants a sermon should go to a conventicle. The question of the relative value of the cultures which are compared here will not receive a single word. It is true that the path of human destiny cannot but appall him who surveys a section of it. But he will do well to keep his small personal commentaries to himself, as one does at the sight of the sea or of majestic mountains, unless he knows himself to be called and gifted to give them expression in artistic or prophetic form. In most other cases the voluminous talk about intuition does nothing but conceal a lack of perspective toward the object, which merits the same judgment as a similar lack of perspective toward men.

Some justification is needed for the fact that ethnographical material has not been utilized to anything like the extent which the value of its contributions naturally demands in any really thorough investigation, especially of Asiatic religions. This limitation has not only been imposed because human powers of work are restricted. This omission has also seemed to be permissible because we are here necessarily dealing with the religious ethics of the classes which were the culture-bearers of their respective countries. We are concerned with the influence which *their* conduct has had. Now it is quite true that this can only be completely known in all its details when the facts from ethnography and folk-lore have been compared with it. Hence we must expressly admit and emphasize that this is a gap to which the ethnographer will legitimately object. I hope to contribute something to the closing of this gap in a systematic study of the Sociology of Religion. But such an undertaking would have transcended the limits of this investigation with its closely circumscribed purpose. It has been necessary to be content with bringing out the points of comparison with our Occidental religions as well as possible.

Finally, we may make a reference to the *anthropological* side of the problem. When we find again and again that, even in departments of life apparently mutually independent, certain types of rationalization have developed in the Occident, and only there, it would be natural to suspect that the most important reason lay in differences of heredity. The author admits that he is inclined to think the importance of biological heredity very great. But in spite of the notable achievements of anthropological research, I see up to the present no way of exactly or even approximately measuring either the extent or, above all, the form of its influence on the development investigated here. It must be one of the tasks of sociological and historical investigation first to analyse all the influences and causal relationships which can satisfactorily be explained in terms of reactions to environmental conditions. Only then, and when comparative racial neurology and psychology shall have progressed beyond their present and in many ways very promising beginnings, can we hope for even the probability of a satisfactory answer to that problem.[5] In the meantime that condition seems to me not to exist, and an appeal to heredity would therefore involve a premature renunciation of the possibility of knowledge attainable now, and would shift the problem to factors (at present) still unknown.

Notes

1 Here, as on some other points, I differ from our honoured master, Lujo Brentano (in his work to be cited later). Chiefly in regard to terminology, but also on questions of fact. It does not seem to me expedient to bring such different things as acquisition of booty and acquisition by management of a factory together under the same category; still less to designate every tendency to the acquisition of money as the spirit of capitalism as against other types of acquisition. The second sacrifices all precision of concepts, and the first the possibility of clarifying the specific difference between Occidental capitalism and other forms. Also in Simmel's *Philosophie des Geldes* [*The Philosophy of Money*] money economy and capitalism are too closely identified, to the detriment of his concrete analysis. In the writings of Werner Sombart, above all in the second edition of his most important work, *Der moderne Kapitalismus* [*Modern Capitalism*], the *differentia specifica* [what differentiates the species] of Occidental capitalism – at least from the view-point of my problem – the rational organization of labour, is strongly overshadowed by genetic factors which have been operative everywhere in the world.

2 Naturally the difference cannot be conceived in absolute terms. The politically oriented capitalism (above all tax-farming) of Mediterranean and Oriental

antiquity, and even of China and India, gave rise to rational, continuous enterprises whose book-keeping – though known to us only in pitiful fragments – probably had a rational character. Furthermore, the politically oriented adventurers' capitalism has been closely associated with rational bourgeois capitalism in the development of modern banks, which, including the Bank of England, have for the most part originated in transactions of a political nature, often connected with war. The difference between the characters of Paterson, for instance – a typical promoter – and of the members of the directorate of the Bank who gave the keynote to its permanent policy, and very soon came to be known as the "Puritan usurers of Grocers' Hall", is characteristic of it. Similarly, we have the aberration of the policy of this most solid bank at the time of the South Sea Bubble. Thus the two naturally shade off into each other. But the difference is there. The great promoters and financiers have no more created the rational organization of labour than – again in general and with individual exceptions – those other typical representatives of financial and political capitalism, the Jews. That was done, typically, by quite a different set of people.

3   The remains of my knowledge of Hebrew are also quite inadequate.

4   I need hardly point out that this does not apply to attempts like that of Karl Jasper's (in his book *Psychologie der Weltanschauungen* [*Psychology of world views*], 1919), nor to Klages's *Charakterologie*, and similar studies which differ from our own in their point of departure. There is no space here for a criticism of them.

5   Some years ago an eminent psychiatrist expressed the same opinion to me.

"Science as a Vocation"

Scientific progress is a fraction, the most important fraction, of the process of intellectualization which we have been undergoing for thousands of years and which nowadays is usually judged in such an extremely negative way. Let us first clarify what this intellectualist rationalization, created by science and by scientifically oriented technology, means practically.

Does it mean that we, today, for instance, everyone sitting in this hall, have a greater knowledge of the conditions of life under which we exist than has an American Indian or a Hottentot?[x] Hardly. Unless he is a physicist, one who rides on the streetcar has no idea how the car happened to get into motion. And he does not need to know. He is satisfied that he may 'count' on the behaviour of the streetcar, and he orients his conduct according to this expectation; but he knows nothing about what it takes to produce such a car so that it can move. The savage knows incomparably

[x]   A southern African people.

more about his tools. When we spend money today I bet that even if there are colleagues of political economy here in the hall, almost every one of them will hold a different answer in readiness to the question: How does it happen that one can buy something for money – sometimes more and sometimes less? The savage knows what he does in order to get his daily food and which institutions serve him in this pursuit. The increasing intellectualization and rationalization do *not*, therefore, indicate an increased and general knowledge of the conditions under which one lives.

It means something else, namely, the knowledge or belief that if one but wished one *could* learn it at any time. Hence, it means that principally there are no mysterious incalculable forces that come into play, but rather that one can, in principle, master all things by calculation. This means that the world is disenchanted. One need no longer have recourse to magical means in order to master or implore the spirits, as did the savage, for whom such mysterious powers existed. Technical means and calculations perform the service. This above all is what intellectualization means.

Now, this process of disenchantment, which has continued to exist in Occidental culture for millennia, and, in general, this "progress," to which science belongs as a link and motive force, do they have any meanings that go beyond the purely practical and technical? You will find this question raised in the most principled form in the works of Leo Tolstoi.[xi] He came to raise the question in a peculiar way. All his broodings increasingly revolved around the problem of whether or not death is a meaningful phenomenon. And his answer was: for civilized man death has no meaning. It has none because the individual life of civilized man, placed into an infinite 'progress,' according to its own imminent meaning should never come to an end; for there is always a further step ahead of one who stands in the march of progress. And no man who comes to die stands upon the peak which lies in infinity. Abraham, or some peasant of the past, died "old and satiated with life" because he stood in the organic cycle of life; because his life, in terms of its meaning and on the eve of his days, had given to him what life had to offer; because for him there remained no puzzles he might wish to solve; and therefore he could have had "enough" of life. Whereas civilized man, placed in the midst of the continuous enrichment of culture by ideas, knowledge, and problems, may become "tired of life" but not "satiated with life." He catches only the most minute part of what the life of the spirit brings forth ever anew, and what he seizes is always something provisional and not definitive, and therefore death for him is a meaningless occurrence. And because death is meaningless, civilized life as such is meaningless; by its very "progressiveness" it gives death the imprint of

[xi] A great Russian writer (1828–1910).

meaninglessness. Throughout his late novels one meets with this thought as the keynote of the Tolstoyan art.

What stand should one take? Has "progress" as such a recognizable meaning that goes beyond the technical, so that to serve it is a meaningful vocation? The question must be raised. But this is no longer merely the question of man's calling *for* science, hence, the problem of what science as a vocation means to its devoted disciples. To raise this question is to ask for the vocation of science within the total life of humanity. What is the value of science? . . .

Today one usually speaks of science as "free from presuppositions." Is there such a thing? It depends upon what one understands thereby. All scientific work presupposes that the rules of logic and method are valid; these are the general foundations of our orientation in the world; and, at least for our special question, these presuppositions are the least problematic aspect of science. Science further presupposes that what is yielded by scientific work is important in the sense that it is "worth being known." In this, obviously, are contained all our problems. For this presupposition cannot be proved by scientific means. It can only be *interpreted* with reference to its ultimate meaning, which we must reject or accept according to our ultimate position towards life.

Furthermore, the nature of the relationship of scientific work and its presuppositions varies widely according to their structure. The natural sciences, for instance, physics, chemistry, and astronomy, presuppose as self-evident that it is worth while to know the ultimate laws of cosmic events as far as science can construe them. This is the case not only because with such knowledge one can attain technical results but for its own sake, if the quest for such knowledge is to be a "vocation." Yet this presupposition can by no means be proved. And still less can it be proved that the existence of the world which these sciences describe is worth while, that it has any "meaning," or that it makes sense to live in such a world. Science does not ask for the answers to such questions.

Consider modern medicine, a practical technology which is highly developed scientifically. The general "presupposition" of the medical enterprise is stated trivially in the assertion that medical science has the task of maintaining life as such and of diminishing suffering as such to the greatest possible degree. Yet this is problematical. By his means the medical man preserves the life of the mortally ill man, even if the patient implores us to relieve him of life, even if his relatives, to whom his life is worthless and to whom the costs of maintaining his worthless life grow unbearable, grant his redemption from suffering. Perhaps a poor lunatic is involved, whose relatives, whether they admit it or not, wish and must wish for his death. Yet the presuppositions of medicine, and the penal code, prevent the

171

physician from relinquishing his therapeutic efforts. Whether life is worth while living and when – this question is not asked by medicine. Natural science gives us an answer to the question of what we must do if we wish to master life technically. It leaves quite aside, or assumes for its purposes, whether we should and do wish to master life technically and whether it ultimately makes sense to do so.

Consider a discipline such as aesthetics. The fact that there are works of art is given for aesthetics. It seeks to find out under what conditions this fact exists, but it does not raise the question whether or not the realm of art is perhaps a realm of diabolical grandeur, a realm of this world, and therefore, in its core, hostile to God and, in its innermost and aristocratic spirit, hostile to the brotherhood of man. Hence, aesthetics does not ask whether there *should* be works of art.

Consider jurisprudence. It establishes what is valid according to the rules of juristic thought, which is partly bound by logically compelling and partly by conventionally given schemata. Juridical thought holds when certain legal rules and certain methods of interpretations are recognized as binding. Whether there should be law and whether one should establish just these rules – such questions jurisprudence does not answer. It can only state: If one wishes this result, according to the norms of our legal thought, this legal rule is the appropriate means of attaining it.

Consider the historical and cultural sciences. They teach us how to understand and interpret political, artistic, literary, and social phenomena in terms of their origins. But they give us no answer to the question, whether the existence of these cultural phenomena have been and are *worth while*. And they do not answer the further question, whether it is worth the effort required to know them. They presuppose that there is an interest in partaking, through this procedure, of the community of "civilized men." But they cannot prove "scientifically" that this is the case; and that they presuppose this interest by no means proves that it goes without saying. In fact it is not at all self-evident.

Finally, let us consider the disciplines close to me: sociology, history, economics, political science, and those types of cultural philosophy that make it their task to interpret these sciences. It is said, and I agree, that politics is out of place in the lecture-room. It does not belong there on the part of the students. If, for instance, in the lecture-room of my former colleague Dietrich Schäfer in Berlin, pacifist students were to surround his desk and make an uproar, I should deplore it just as much as I should deplore the uproar which anti-pacifist students are said to have made against Professor Förster, whose views in many ways are as remote as could be from mine. Neither does politics, however, belong in the lecture-room on the part of the docents, and when the docent is scientifically concerned with politics, it belongs there least of all.

To take a practical political stand is one thing, and to analyze political structures and party positions is another. When speaking in a political meeting about democracy, one does not hide one's personal standpoint; indeed, to come out clearly and take a stand is one's damned duty. The words one uses in such a meeting are not means of scientific analysis but means of canvassing votes and winning over others. They are not plow-shares to loosen the soil of contemplative thought; they are swords against the enemies: such words are weapons. It would be an outrage, however, to use words in this fashion in a lecture or in the lecture-room. If, for instance, 'democracy' is under discussion, one considers its various forms, analyzes them in the way they function, determines what results for the conditions of life the one form has as compared with the other. Then one confronts the forms of democracy with non-democratic forms of political order and endeavors to come to a position where the student may find the point from which, in terms of his ultimate ideals, he can take a stand. But the true teacher will beware of imposing from the platform any political position upon the student, whether it is expressed or suggested. "To let the facts speak for themselves" is the most unfair way of putting over a political position to the student.

Why should we abstain from doing this? I state in advance that some highly esteemed colleagues are of the opinion that it is not possible to carry through this self-restraint and that, even if it were possible, it would be a whim to avoid declaring oneself. Now one cannot demonstrate scientifically what the duty of an academic teacher is. One can only demand of the teacher that he have the intellectual integrity to see that it is one thing to state facts, to determine mathematical or logical relations or the internal structure of cultural values, while it is another thing to answer questions of the *value* of culture and its individual contents and the question of how one should act in the cultural community and in political associations. These are quite heterogeneous problems. If he asks further why he should not deal with both types of problems in the lecture-room, the answer is: because the prophet and the demagogue do not belong on the academic platform. . . .

Thus far I have spoken only of practical reasons for avoiding the imposition of a personal point of view. But these are not the only reasons. The impossibility of "scientifically" pleading for practical and interested stands – except in discussing the means for a firmly given and presupposed end – rests upon reasons that lie far deeper.

"Scientific" pleading is meaningless in principle because the various value spheres of the world stand in irreconcilable conflict with each other. The elder Mill,[xii] whose philosophy I will not praise otherwise, was on this

---

[xii] Scottish utilitarian philosopher James Mill (1773–1836), father of philosopher John Stuart Mill.

point right when he said: If one proceeds from pure experience, one arrives at polytheism. This is shallow in formulation and sounds paradoxical, and yet there is truth in it. If anything we realize again today that something can be sacred not only in spite of its not being beautiful, but rather because and in so far as it is not beautiful. You will find this documented in the fifty-third chapter of the book of Isaiah and in the twenty-first Psalm. And, since Nietzsche, we realize that something can be beautiful, not only in spite of the aspect in which it is not good, but rather in that very aspect. You will find this expressed earlier in the *Fleurs du mal*, as Baudelaire named his volume of poems.[xiii] It is commonplace to observe that something may be true although it is not beautiful and not holy and not good. Indeed it may be true in precisely those aspects. But all these are only the most elementary cases of the struggle that the gods of the various orders and values are engaged in. I do not know how one might wish to decide "scientifically" the value of French and German culture; for here, too, different gods struggle with one another, now and for all times to come.

We live as did the ancients when their world was not yet disenchanted of its gods and demons, only we live in a different sense. As Hellenic man at times sacrificed to Aphrodite and at other times to Apollo, and, above all, as everybody sacrificed to the gods of his city, so do we still nowadays, only the bearing of man has been disenchanted and denuded of its mystical but inwardly genuine plasticity. Fate, and certainly not "science," holds sway over these gods and their struggles. One can only understand what the godhead is for the one order or for the other, or better, what godhead is in the one or in the other order. With this understanding, however, the matter has reached its limit so far as it can be discussed in a lecture-room and by a professor. Yet the great and vital problem that is contained therein is, of course, very far from being concluded. But forces other than university chairs have their say in this matter.

What man will take upon himself the attempt to "refute scientifically" the ethic of the Sermon on the Mount? For instance, the sentence, "resist no evil," or the image of turning the other cheek? And yet it is clear, in mundane perspective, that this is an ethic of undignified conduct; one has to choose between the religious dignity which this ethic confers and the dignity of manly conduct which preaches something quite different; "resist evil – lest you be co-responsible for an overpowering evil." According to our ultimate standpoint, the one is the devil and the other the God, and the individual has to decide which is God for him and which is the devil. And so it goes throughout all the orders of life.

[xiii] "Flowers of Evil," by Charles Baudelaire (1821–67). See the editor's headnote to the Baudelaire selection in the present volume (Chapter 9).

The grandiose rationalism of an ethical and methodical conduct of life which flows from every religious prophecy has dethroned this polytheism in favor of the "one thing that is needful." Faced with the realities of outer and inner life, Christianity has deemed it necessary to make those compromises and relative judgments, which we all know from its history. Today the routines of everyday life challenge religion. Many old gods ascend from their graves; they are disenchanted and hence take the form of impersonal forces. They strive to gain power over our lives and again they resume their eternal struggle with one another. What is hard for modern man, and especially for the younger generation, is to measure up to *workaday* existence. The ubiquitous chase for "experience" stems from this weakness; for it is weakness not to be able to be countenance the stern seriousness of our fateful times. . . .

The fate of our times is characterized by rationalization and intellectualization and, above all, by the "disenchantment of the world." Precisely the ultimate and most sublime values have retreated from public life either into the transcendental realm of mystic life or into the brotherliness of direct and personal human relations. It is not accidental that our greatest art is intimate and not monumental, nor is it accidental that today only within the smallest and intimate circles, in personal human situations, in *pianissimo*,[xiv] that something is pulsating that corresponds to the prophetic *pneuma*,[xv] which in former times swept through the great communities like a firebrand, welding them together. If we attempt to force and to "invent" a monumental style in art, such miserable monstrosities are produced as the many monuments of the last twenty years. If one tries intellectually to construe new religions without a new and genuine prophecy, then, in an inner sense, something similar will result, but with still worse effects. And academic prophecy, finally, will create only fanatical sects but never a genuine community.

To the person who cannot bear the fate of the times like a man, one must say: may he rather return silently, without the usual publicity build-up of renegades, but simply and plainly. The arms of the old churches are opened widely and compassionately for him. After all, they do not make it hard for him. One way or another he has to bring his "intellectual sacrifice" – that is inevitable. If he can really do it, we shall not rebuke him. For such an intellectual sacrifice in favor of an unconditional religious devotion is ethically quite a different matter than the evasion of the plain duty of intellectual integrity, which sets in if one lacks the courage to clarify one's own ultimate standpoint and rather facilitates this duty by feeble relative judgments. In my eyes, such religious return stands higher than the

[xiv] Very softly or quietly.
[xv] Spirit.

175

academic prophecy, which does not clearly realize that in the lecture-rooms of the university no other virtue holds but plain intellectual integrity. Integrity, however, compels us to state that for the many who today tarry for new prophets and saviors, the situation is the same as resounds in the beautiful Edomite watchman's song of the period of exile that has been included among Isaiah's oracles:[xvi]

> He calleth to me out of Seir, Watchman, what of the night? The watchman said, The morning cometh, and also the night: if ye will enquire, enquire ye: return, come.

The people to whom this was said has enquired and tarried for more than two millennia, and we are shaken when we realize its fate. From this we want to draw the lesson that nothing is gained by yearning and tarrying alone, and we shall act differently. We shall set to work and meet the "demands of the day," in human relations as well as in our vocation. This, however, is plain and simple, if each finds and obeys the demon who holds the fibers of his very life.

[xvi] The Edomites were the descendants of Esau, Jacob's brother, who lived in the land of Edom. In the following Oracle from Isaiah 21: 11–12 "Seir" is another name for Edom and its people.

chapter twelve

Course in General Linguistics
Ferdinand de Saussure

Genevan linguist Ferdinand de Saussure (1857–1913) presented a new approach to the study of language, and hence implicitly to all cultural phenomena, which not only revolutionized linguistics but had a great impact on structuralism and the poststructuralism that succeeded it. His influence lay not in a published work, but in his *Course in General Linguistics* (1906–11), a reconstruction of his lectures from the notes of students. Of particular importance was his attempt to analyze language (or *langue*, rather than *parole*, or speech) as a system in which each element is dependent on relations to other elements. For Saussure the meaning of a word is determined, not by any natural or pre-conventional relation of word to object, but by the word's relation to other words. Meaning rests on the differences among words in a linguistic system. This is summarized in his famous phrase: "in language there are only differences."

Sign, Signified, Signifier

Some people regard language, when reduced to its elements, as a naming-process only – a list of words, each corresponding to the thing that it names. For example [see figure 1].

This conception is open to criticism at several points. It assumes that ready-made ideas exist before words; it does not tell us whether a name is vocal or psychological in nature (*arbor*, for instance, can be considered from either viewpoint); finally, it lets us assume that the linking of a name and a thing is a very simple operation – an assumption that is anything but true. But this rather naïve approach can bring us near the truth by showing us that the linguistic unit is a double entity, one formed by the associating of two terms.

Ferdinand de Saussure, *Course in General Linguistics*, trans. Wade Baskin (New York: McGraw-Hill, 1966), Part One, chapter 1, pp. 65–70, and Part Two, chapter 4, section 4, pp. 120–2.

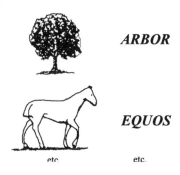

ARBOR

EQUOS

etc.   etc.

Figure 1

We have seen in considering the speaking-circuit that both terms involved in the linguistic sign are psychological and are united in the brain by an associative bond. This point must be emphasized.

The linguistic sign unites, not a thing and a name, but a concept and a sound-image. The latter is not the material sound, a purely physical thing, but the psychological imprint of the sound, the impression that it makes on our senses. The sound-image is sensory, and if I happen to call it "material," it is only in that sense, and by way of opposing it to the other term of the association, the concept, which is generally more abstract.

The psychological character of our sound-images becomes apparent when we observe our own speech. Without moving our lips or tongue, we can talk to ourselves or recite mentally a selection of verse. Because we regard the words of our language as sound-images, we must avoid speaking of the "phonemes" that make up the words. This term, which suggests vocal activity, is applicable to the spoken word only, to the realization of the inner image in discourse. We can avoid that misunderstanding by speaking of the *sounds* and *syllables* of a word provided we remember that the names refer to the sound-image.

The linguistic sign is then a two-sided psychological entity that can be represented by the drawing [in figure 2].

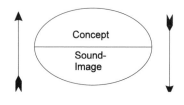

Figure 2

The two elements are intimately united, and each recalls the other. Whether we try to find the meaning of the Latin word *arbor* or the word that Latin uses to designate the concept "tree," it is clear that only the associations sanctioned by that language appear to us to conform to reality, and we disregard whatever others might be imagined.

Our definition of the linguistic sign poses an important question of terminology. I call the combination of a concept and a sound-image a *sign*, but in current usage the term generally designates only a sound-image, a word, for example (*arbor*, etc.). One tends to forget that *arbor* is called a sign only because it carries the concept "tree," with the result that the idea of the sensory part implies the idea of the whole [figure 3].

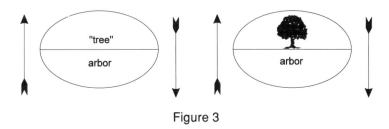

Figure 3

Ambiguity would disappear if the three notions involved here were designated by three names, each suggesting and opposing the others. I propose to retain the word *sign* [*signe*] to designate the whole and to replace *concept* and *sound-image* respectively by *signified* and *signifier*;[i] the last two terms have the advantage of indicating the opposition that separates them from each other and from the whole of which they are parts. As regards *sign*, if I am satisfied with it, this is simply because I do not know of any word to replace it, the ordinary language suggesting no other.

The linguistic sign, as defined, has two primordial characteristics. In enunciating them I am also positing the basic principles of any study of this type.

Principle I: The Arbitrary Nature of the Sign

The bond between the signifier and the signified is arbitrary. Since I mean by sign the whole that results from the associating of the signifier with the signified, I can simply say: *the linguistic sign is arbitrary*.

The idea of "sister" is not linked by any inner relationship to the succession of sounds *s-ö-r* which serves as its signifier in French; that it could be represented equally by just any other sequence is proved by differences among languages and by the very existence of different

---

[i] The French terms are *signifié* (signified) and *signifiant* (signifier).

languages: the signified "ox" has as its signifier *b-ö-f* on one side of the border and *O-k-s* (*Ochs*) on the other.

No one disputes the principle of the arbitrary nature of the sign, but it is often easier to discover a truth than to assign to it its proper place. Principle I dominates all the linguistics of language; its consequences are numberless. It is true that not all of them are equally obvious at first glance; only after many detours does one discover them, and with them the primordial importance of the principle.

One remark in passing: when semiology becomes organized as a science, the question will arise whether or not it properly includes modes of expression based on completely natural signs, such as pantomime. Supposing that the new science welcomes them, its main concern will still be the whole group of systems grounded on the arbitrariness of the sign. In fact, every means of expression used in society is based, in principle, on collective behavior or – what amounts to the same thing – on convention. Polite formulas, for instance, though often imbued with a certain natural expressiveness (as in the case of a Chinese who greets his emperor by bowing down to the ground nine times), are nonetheless fixed by rule; it is this rule and not the intrinsic value of the gestures that obliges one to use them. Signs that are wholly arbitrary realize better than the others the ideal of the semiological process; that is why language, the most complex and universal of all systems of expression, is also the most characteristic; in this sense linguistics can become the master-pattern for all branches of semiology although language is only one particular semiological system.

The word *symbol* has been used to designate the linguistic sign, or more specifically, what is here called the signifier. Principle I in particular weighs against the use of this term. One characteristic of the symbol is that it is never wholly arbitrary; it is not empty, for there is the rudiment of a natural bond between the signifier and the signified. The symbol of justice, a pair of scales, could not be replaced by just any other symbol, such as a chariot.

The word *arbitrary* also calls for comment. The term should not imply that the choice of the signifier is left entirely to the speaker (we shall see below that the individual does not have the power to change a sign in any way once it has become established in the linguistic community); I mean that it is unmotivated, i.e. arbitrary in that it actually has no natural connection with the signified.

In concluding let us consider two objections that might be raised to the establishment of Principle I:

(1) *Onomatopoeia*[ii] might be used to prove that the choice of the signifier

---

[ii] Words that, when spoken, make the sound they refer to (e.g. "buzz" to describe the activity of a bee).

180

is not always arbitrary. But onomatopoeic formations are never organic elements of a linguistic system. Besides, their number is much smaller than is generally supposed. Words like French *fouet* "whip" or *glas* "knell" may strike certain ears with suggestive sonority, but to see that they have not always had this property we need only examine their Latin forms (*fouet* is derived from *fāgus* "beech-tree," *glas* from *classicum* "sound of a trumpet"). The quality of their present sounds, or rather the quality that is attributed to them, is a fortuitous result of phonetic evolution.

As for authentic onomatopoeic words (e.g. *glug-glug, tick-tock*, etc.), not only are they limited in number, but also they are chosen somewhat arbitrarily, for they are only approximate and more or less conventional imitations of certain sounds (cf. English *bow-wow* and French *ouaoua*). In addition, once these words have been introduced into the language, they are to a certain extent subjected to the same evolution – phonetic, morphological, etc – that other words undergo (cf. *pigeon*, ultimately from Vulgar Latin *pīpiō*, derived in turn from an onomatopoeic formation): obvious proof that they lose something of their original character in order to assume that of the linguistic sign in general, which is unmotivated.

(2) *Interjections*, closely related to onomatopoeia, can be attacked on the same grounds and come no closer to refuting our thesis. One is tempted to see in them spontaneous expressions of reality dictated, so to speak, by natural forces. But for most interjections we can show that there is no fixed bond between their signified and their signifier. We need only compare two languages on this point to see how much such expressions differ from one language to the next (e.g. the English equivalent of French *aïe!* is *ouch!*). We know, moreover, that many interjections were once words with specific meanings (cf. French *diable!* 'darn!' *mordieu!* 'golly!' from *mort Dieu* 'God's death,' etc.).

Onomatopoeic formations and interjections are of secondary importance, and their symbolic origin is in part open to dispute.

Principle II: The Linear Nature of the Signifier

The signifier, being auditory, is unfolded solely in time from which it gets the following characteristics: (a) it represents a span, and (b) the span is measurable in a single dimension; it is a line.

While Principle II is obvious, apparently linguists have always neglected to state it, doubtless because they found it too simple; nevertheless, it is fundamental, and its consequences are incalculable. Its importance equals that of Principle I; the whole mechanism of language depends upon it. In contrast to visual signifiers (nautical signals, etc.) which can offer simultaneous groupings in several dimensions, auditory signifiers have at their command only the dimension of time. Their elements are presented in succession; they form a chain. This feature becomes readily apparent when they are represented in writing and the spatial line of graphic marks is substituted for succession in time.

Sometimes the linear nature of the signifier is not obvious. When I accent a syllable, for instance, it seems that I am concentrating more than one significant element on the same point. But this is an illusion; the syllable and its accent constitute only one phonational act. There is no duality within the act but only different oppositions to what precedes and what follows.

The Sign Considered in Its Totality

Everything that has been said up to this point boils down to this: in language there are only differences. Even more important: a difference generally implies positive terms between which the difference is set up; but in language there are only differences *without positive terms*. Whether we take the signified or the signifier, language has neither ideas nor sounds that existed before the linguistic system but only conceptual and phonic differences that have issued from the system. The idea or phonic substance that a sign contains is of less importance than the other signs that surround it. Proof of this is that the value of a term may be modified without either its meaning or its sound being affected, solely because a neighboring term has been modified.

But the statement that everything in language is negative is true only if the signified and the signifier are considered separately; when we consider the sign in its totality, we have something that is positive in its own class. A linguistic system is a series of differences of sound combined with a series of differences of ideas; but the pairing of a certain number of acoustical signs with as many cuts made from the mass of thought engenders a system of values; and this system serves as the effective link between the phonic and psychological elements within each sign. Although both the signified and the signifier are purely differential and negative when considered separately, their combination is a positive fact; it is even the sole type of facts that language has, for maintaining the parallelism between the two classes of differences is the distinctive function of the linguistic institution.

Certain diachronic facts are typical in this respect. Take the countless instances where alteration of the signifier occasions a conceptual change and where it is obvious that the sum of the ideas distinguished corresponds

182

in principle to the sum of the distinctive signs. When two words are confused through phonetic alteration (e.g. French *décrépit* from *dēcrepitus* and *décrépi* from *crispus*), the ideas that they express will also tend to become confused if only they have something in common. Or a word may have different forms (cf. *chaise* 'chair' and *chaire* 'desk'). Any nascent difference will tend invariably to become significant but without always succeeding or being successful on the first trial. Conversely, any conceptual difference perceived by the mind seeks to find expression through a distinct signifier, and two ideas that are no longer distinct in the mind tend to merge into the same signifier.

When we compare signs – positive terms – with each other, we can no longer speak of difference; the expression would not be fitting, for it applies only to the comparing of two sound-images, e.g. *father* and *mother*, or two ideas, e.g. the idea "father" and the idea "mother"; two signs, each having a signified and signifier, are not different but only distinct. Between them there is only *opposition*. The entire mechanism of language, with which we shall be concerned later, is based on oppositions of this kind and on the phonic and conceptual differences that they imply.

What is true of value is true also of the unit. A unit is a segment of the spoken chain that corresponds to a certain concept; both are by nature purely differential.

Applied to units, the principle of differentiation can be stated in this way: the characteristics of the unit blend with the unit itself. In language, as in any semiological system, whatever distinguishes one sign from the others constitutes it. Difference makes character just as it makes value and the unit.

Another rather paradoxical consequence of the same principle is this: in the last analysis what is commonly referred to as a "grammatical fact" fits the definition of the unit, for it always expresses an opposition of terms; it differs only in that the opposition is particularly significant (e.g. the formation of German plurals of the type *Nacht: Nächte*). Each term present in the grammatical fact (the singular without umlaut or final *e* in opposition to the plural with umlaut and *e*) consists of the interplay of a number of oppositions within the system. When isolated, neither *Nacht* nor *Nächte* is anything: thus everything is opposition. Putting it another way, the *Nacht: Nächte* relation can be expressed by an algebraic formula a/b in which a and b are not simple terms but result from a set of relations. Language, in a manner of speaking, is a type of algebra consisting solely of complex terms. Some of its oppositions are more significant than others; but units and grammatical facts are only different names for designating diverse aspects of the same general fact: the functioning of linguistic oppositions. This statement is so true that we might very well approach the problem of units by starting from grammatical facts. Taking an opposition like *Nacht: Nächte*, we might ask what are the units involved in it. Are they only the two words, the whole series of similar words, *a* and *ä*, or all singulars and plurals, etc.?

Units and grammatical facts would not be confused if linguistic signs were made up of something besides differences. But language being what it is, we shall find nothing simple in it regardless of our approach; everywhere and always there is the same complex equilibrium of terms that mutually condition each other. Putting it another way, *language is a form and not a substance*. This truth could not be overstressed, for all the mistakes in our terminology, all our incorrect ways of naming things that pertain to language, stem from the involuntary supposition that the linguistic phenomenon must have substance.

chapter thirteen

"The Founding and Manifesto of Futurism"

Filippo Tommaso Marinetti

The cosmopolitan writer Filippo Tommaso Marinetti (1876–1944), who wrote for a French and Italian magazine, founded the movement of Futurism in 1909 by publishing "The Manifesto of Futurism" in a Paris newspaper. Marinetti's Futurism is a prime example of the artistic and social movements that exploded in the period between the world wars. Utopian, modern, intense, Marinetti wants an art that can re-make the world by recognizing the novel possibilities of industrial, mass society. This is not a purely aesthetic view, nor is it benign in its implications. Marinetti urged Italian involvement in World War I and later became an enthusiastic supporter of Benito Mussolini, arguing that fascisim was an expression of Futurism. Like Mussolini, Marinetti regarded war as an heroic intensification of life.

We had stayed up all night, my friends and I, under hanging mosque lamps with domes of filigreed brass, domes starred like our spirits, shining like them with the prisoned radiance of electric hearts. For hours we had trampled our atavistic ennui into rich oriental rugs, arguing up to the last confines of logic and blackening many reams of paper with our frenzied scribbling.

An immense pride was buoying us up, because we felt ourselves alone at that hour, alone, awake, and on our feet, like proud beacons or forward sentries against an army of hostile stars glaring down at us from their celestial encampments. Alone with stokers feeding the hellish fires of great ships, alone with the black specters who grope in the red-hot bellies of locomotives launched down their crazy courses, alone with drunkards reeling like wounded birds along the city walls.

Suddenly we jumped, hearing the mighty noise of the huge double-decker trams that rumbled by outside, ablaze with colored lights, like villages on

---

Filippo Tommaso Marinetti, "The Founding and Marifesto of Futurism," trans. R. W. Flint and Arthur W. Coppotelli, in *Marinetti: Selected Writings*, ed. R. W. Flint (New York: Farrar, Straus, Giroux, 1972), pp. 39–44.

holiday suddenly struck and uprooted by the flooding Po and dragged over falls and through gorges to the sea.

Then the silence deepened. But, as we listened to the old canal muttering its feeble prayers and the creaking bones of sickly palaces above their damp green beards, under the windows we suddenly heard the famished roar of automobiles.

"Let's go!" I said. "Friends, away! Let's go! Mythology and the Mystic Ideal are defeated at last. We're about to see the Centaur's birth and, soon after, the first flight of Angels! . . . We must shake the gates of life, test the bolts and hinges. Let's go! Look there, on the earth, the very first dawn! There's nothing to match the splendor of the sun's red sword, slashing for the first time through our millennial gloom!"

We went up to the three snorting beasts, to lay amorous hands on their torrid breasts. I stretched out on my car like a corpse on its bier, but revived at once under the steering wheel, a guillotine blade that threatened my stomach.

The raging broom of madness swept us out of ourselves and drove us through streets as rough and deep as the beds of torrents. Here and there, sick lamplight through window glass taught us to distrust the deceitful mathematics of our perishing eyes.

I cried, "The scent, the scent alone is enough for our beasts."

And like young lions we ran after Death, its dark pelt blotched with pale crosses as it escaped down the vast violet living and throbbing sky.

But we had no ideal Mistress raising her divine form to the clouds, nor any cruel Queen to whom to offer our bodies, twisted like Byzantine rings! There was nothing to make us wish for death, unless the wish to be free at last from the weight of our courage!

And on we raced, hurling watchdogs against doorsteps, curling them under our burning tires like collars under a flatiron. Death, domesticated, met me at every turn, gracefully holding out a paw, or once in a while hunkering down, making velvety caressing eyes at me from every puddle.

"Let's break out of the horrible shell of wisdom and throw ourselves like pride-ripened fruit into the wide, contorted mouth of the wind! Let's give ourselves utterly to the Unknown, not in desperation but only to replenish the deep wells of the Absurd!!"

The words were scarcely out of my mouth when I spun my car around with the frenzy of a dog trying to bite its tail, and there, suddenly, were two cyclists coming toward me, shaking their fists, wobbling like two equally convincing but nevertheless contradictory arguments. Their stupid dilemma was blocking my way – damn! Ouch! . . . I stopped short and to my disgust rolled over into a ditch with my wheels in the air. . . .

Oh! Maternal ditch, almost full of muddy water! Fair factory drain! I gulped down your nourishing sludge; and I remembered the blessed black breast of my Sudanese nurse. . . . When I came up – torn, filthy, and stinking – from under the capsized car, I felt the white-hot iron of joy deliciously pass through my heart!

A crowd of fishermen with handlines and gouty naturalists were already swarming around the prodigy. With patient, loving care those people rigged a tall derrick and iron grapnels to fish out my car, like a big beached shark. Up it came from the ditch, slowly, leaving in the bottom like scales its heavy framework of good sense and its soft upholstery of comfort.

They thought it was dead, my beautiful shark, but a caress from me was enough to revive it; and there it was, alive again, running on its powerful fins!

And so, faces smeared with good factory muck – plastered with metallic waste, with senseless sweat, with celestial soot – we, bruised, our arms in slings, but unafraid, declared our high intentions to all the *living* of the earth:

MANIFESTO OF FUTURISM

1 We intend to sing the love of danger, the habit of energy and fearlessness.

2 Courage, audacity, and revolt will be essential elements of our poetry.

3 Up to now literature has exalted a pensive immobility, ecstasy, and sleep. We intend to exalt aggressive action, a feverish insomnia, the racer's stride, the mortal leap, the punch and the slap.

4 We say that the world's magnificence has been enriched by a new beauty; the beauty of speed. A racing car whose hood is adorned with great pipes, like serpents of explosive breath – a roaring car that seems to ride on grapeshot – is more beautiful than the *Victory of Samothrace*.[i]

5 We want to hymn the man at the wheel, who hurls the lance of his spirit across the Earth, along the circle of its orbit.

6 The poet must spend himself with ardor, splendor, and generosity, to swell the enthusiastic fervor of the primordial elements.

7 Except in struggle, there is no more beauty. No work without an aggressive character can be a masterpiece. Poetry must be conceived as a violent attack on unknown forces, to reduce and prostrate them before man.

8 We stand on the last promontory of the centuries! . . . Why should we look back, when what we want is to break down the mysterious doors of the Impossible? Time and Space died yesterday. We already live in the absolute, because we have created eternal, omnipresent speed.

9 We will glorify war – the world's only hygiene – militarism, patriotism, the destructive gesture of freedom-bringers, beautiful ideas worth dying for, and scorn for woman.

[i] A second century BC Greek sculpture.

10 We will destroy the museums, libraries, academies of every kind, will fight moralism, feminism, every opportunistic or utilitarian cowardice.

11 We will sing of great crowds excited by work, by pleasure, and by riot; we will sing of the multicolored, polyphonic tides of revolution in the modern capitals; we will sing of the vibrant nightly fervor of arsenals and shipyards blazing with violent electric moons; greedy railway stations that devour smoke-plumed serpents; factories hung on clouds by the crooked lines of their smoke; bridges that stride the rivers like giant gymnasts, flashing in the sun with a glitter of knives; adventurous steamers that sniff the horizon; deep-chested locomotives whose wheels paw the tracks like the hooves of enormous steel horses bridled by tubing; and the sleek flight of planes whose propellers chatter in the wind like banners and seem to cheer like an enthusiastic crowd.

It is from Italy that we launch through the world this violently upsetting, incendiary manifesto of ours. With it, today, we establish *Futurism* because we want to free this land from its smelly gangrene of professors, archaeologists, ciceroni, and antiquarians.[ii] For too long has Italy been a dealer in second hand clothes. We mean to free her from the numberless museums that cover her like so many graveyards.

Museums: cemeteries! . . . Identical, surely, in the sinister promiscuity of so many bodies unknown to one another. Museums: public dormitories where one lies forever beside hated or unknown beings. Museums; absurd abattoirs of painters and sculptors ferociously macerating each other with color-blows and line-blows, the length of the fought-over walls!

That one should make an annual pilgrimage, just as one goes to the graveyard on All Souls' Day – that I grant. That once a year one should leave a floral tribute beneath the *Gioconda*,[iii] I grant you that. . . . But I don't admit that our sorrows, our fragile courage, our morbid restlessness should be given a daily conducted tour through the museums. Why poison ourselves? Why rot?

And what is there to see in an old picture except the laborious contortions of an artist throwing himself against the barriers that thwart his desire to express his dream completely? . . . Admiring an old picture is the same as pouring our sensibility into a funerary urn instead of hurling it far off, in violent spasms of action and creation.

Do you, then, wish to waste all your best powers in this eternal and futile worship of the past, from which you emerge fatally exhausted, shrunken, beaten down?

In truth I tell you that daily visits to museums, libraries, and academies

[ii] Ciceroni are guides who explain antiquities to tourists.
[iii] Leonardo da Vinci's painting *Mona Lisa*.

(cemeteries of empty exertion, calvaries of crucified dreams, registries of aborted beginnings!) is, for artists, as damaging as the prolonged supervision by parents of certain young people drunk with their talent and their ambitious wills. When the future is barred to them, the admirable past may be a solace for the ills of the moribund, the sickly, the prisoner. . . . But we want no part of it, the past, we the young and strong *Futurists*!

So let them come, the gay incendiaries with charred fingers! Here they are! Here they are! . . . Come on! set fire to the library shelves! Turn aside the canals to flood the museums! . . . Oh, the joy of seeing the glorious old canvases bobbing adrift on those waters, discolored and shredded! . . . Take up your pickaxes, your axes and hammers, and wreck, wreck the venerable cities, pitilessly!

The oldest of us is thirty: so we have at least a decade for finishing our work. When we are forty, other younger and stronger men will probably throw us in the wastebasket like useless manuscripts – we want it to happen!

They will come against us, our successors, will come from far away, from every quarter, dancing to the winged cadence of their first songs, flexing the hooked claws of predators, sniffing doglike at the academy doors the strong odor of our decaying minds, which already will have been promised to the literary catacombs.

But we won't be there. . . . At last they'll find us – one winter's night – in open country, beneath a sad roof drummed by a monotonous rain. They'll see us crouched beside our trembling airplanes in the act of warming our hands at the poor little blaze that our books of today will give out when they take fire from the flight of our images.

They'll storm around us, panting with scorn and anguish, and all of them, exasperated by our proud daring, will hurtle to kill us, driven by hatred: the more implacable it is, the more their hearts will be drunk with love and admiration for us.

Injustice, strong and sane, will break out radiantly in their eyes.

Art, in fact, can be nothing but violence, cruelty, and injustice.

The oldest of us is thirty: even so we have already scattered treasures, a thousand treasures of force, love, courage, astuteness, and raw will power; have thrown them impatiently away, with fury, carelessly, unhesitatingly, breathless and unresting. . . . Look at us! We are still untired! Our hearts know no weariness because they are fed with fire, hatred, and speed! . . . Does that amaze you? It should, because you can never remember having lived! Erect on the summit of the world, once again we hurl our defiance at the stars!

You have objections? – Enough! Enough! We know them . . . we've understood! . . . Our fine deceitful intelligence tells us that we are the revival and extension of our ancestors – perhaps! . . . If only it were so! – But who cares? We don't want to understand! . . . Woe to anyone who says those infamous words to us again!

Lift up your heads!

Erect on the summit of the world, once again we hurl defiance to the stars!

chapter fourteen

"Lecture on Ethics"
Tractatus Logico-Philosophicus
Ludwig Wittgenstein

Austrian philosopher Ludwig Wittgenstein (1889–1953), student of Bertrand Russell, is perhaps the most influential Western philosopher of the twentieth century. Brilliant and unhappy, Wittgenstein struggled all his life against the "bewitchment" of his mind by philosophical questions. After his early work on fundamental issues in the philosophy of mathematics, logic, and the nature of philosophy (which gave major impetus to logical positivism), Wittgenstein declared that he had put all philosophical questions to rest and left academia. Years later, after a major change in outlook, he returned to philosophy and his later work gave rise to "ordinary language" philosophy, which was highly influential in Britain and the United States after World War II. Most of the following excerpt is his lesser known "Lecture on Ethics" (1929), in which he explains the limits of human inquiry. Following this is the famous conclusion to his first book, *Tractatus Logico-Philosophicus* (1921), in which Wittgenstein announces the end of traditional philosophical reflection.

"Lecture on Ethics"

Before I begin to speak about my subject proper let me make a few introductory remarks. I feel I shall have great difficulties in communicating my thoughts to you and I think some of them may be diminished by mentioning them to you beforehand. The first one, which almost I need not mention, is that English is not my native tongue and my expression therefore often lacks that precision and subtlety which would be desirable if one talks about a difficult subject. All I can do is to ask you to make my task easier by trying to get at my meaning in spite of the faults which I will

Ludwig Wittgenstein, "Lecture on Ethics," *The Philosophical Review*, 74, no.1 (January 1965), pp.3–12; and, from *Tractatus Logico-Philosophicus* (1921), trans. D.F. Pears and B.F.McGuinness (London: Routledge and Kegan Paul, 1961), para. 6.53–6.57, pp.73–4.

constantly be committing against the English grammar. The second difficulty I will mention is this, that probably many of you come up to this lecture of mine with slightly wrong expectations. And to set you right in this point I will say a few words about the reason for choosing the subject I have chosen: When your former secretary honoured me by asking me to read a paper to your society, my first thought was that I would certainly do it and my second thought was that if I was to have the opportunity to speak to you I should speak about something which I am keen on communicating to you and that I should not misuse this opportunity to give you a lecture about, say, logic. I call this a misuse, for to explain a scientific matter to you it would need a course of lectures and not an hour's paper. Another alternative would have been to give you what's called a popular-scientific lecture, that is a lecture intended to make you believe that you understand a thing which actually you don't understand, and to gratify what I believe to be one of the lowest desires of modern people, namely the superficial curiosity about the latest discoveries of science. I rejected these alternatives and decided to talk to you about a subject which seems to me to be of general importance, hoping that it may help to clear up your thoughts about this subject (even if you should entirely disagree with what I will say about it). My third and last difficulty is one which, in fact, adheres to most lengthy philosophical lectures and it is this, that the hearer is incapable of seeing both the road he is led and the goal which it leads to. That is to say: he either thinks: "I understand all he says, but what on earth is he driving at" or else he thinks "I see what he's driving at, but how on earth is he going to get there." All I can do is again to ask you to be patient and to hope that in the end you may see both the way and where it leads to.

I will now begin. My subject, as you know, is Ethics and I will adopt the explanation of that term which Professor Moore has given in his book *Principia Ethica*. He says: "Ethics is the general enquiry into what is good." Now I am going to use the term Ethics in a slightly wider sense, in a sense in fact which includes what I believe to be the most essential part of what is generally called Aesthetics. And to make you see as clearly as possible what I take to be the subject matter of Ethics I will put before you a number of more or less synonymous expressions each of which could be substituted for the above definition, and by enumerating them I want to produce the same sort of effect which Galton produced when he took a number of photos of different faces on the same photographic plate in order to get the picture of the typical features they all had in common. And as by showing to you such a collective photo I could make you see what is the typical – say – Chinese face; so if you look through the row of synonyms which I will put before you, you will, I hope, be able to see the characteristic features they all have in common and these are the characteristic features of Ethics. Now instead of saying "Ethics is the enquiry into what is good" I could have said Ethics is the enquiry into what is valuable, or, into what is really important, or I could have said Ethics is the enquiry into the meaning of life, or into what makes life worth living, or into the right way of living. I believe if you look at all these phrases you will get a rough idea as to what it is that Ethics is concerned with. Now the first thing that strikes one about all these expressions is that each of them is actually used in two very different senses. I will call them the trivial or relative sense on the one hand and the ethical or absolute sense on the other. If for instance I say that this is a *good* chair this means that the chair serves a certain predetermined purpose and the word good here has only meaning so far as this purpose has been previously fixed upon. In fact the word good in the relative sense simply means coming up to a certain predetermined standard. Thus when we say that this man is a good pianist we mean that he can play pieces of a certain degree of difficulty with a certain degree of dexterity. And similarly if I say that it is *important* for me not to catch cold I mean that catching a cold produces certain describable disturbances in my life and if I say that this is the *right* road I mean that it's the right road relative to a certain goal. Used in this way these expressions don't present any difficult or deep problems. But this is not how Ethics uses them. Supposing that I could play tennis and one of you saw me playing and said "Well, you play pretty badly" and suppose I answered "I know, I'm playing badly but I don't want to play any better," all the other man could say would be "Ah then that's all right." But suppose I had told one of you a preposterous lie and he came up to me and said "You're behaving like a beast" and then I were to say "I know I behave badly, but then I don't want to behave any better," could he then say "Ah, then that's all right"? Certainly not; he would say "Well, you *ought* to want to behave better." Here you have an absolute judgment of value, whereas the first instance was one of a relative judgment. The essence of this difference seems to be obviously this: Every judgment of relative value is a mere statement of facts and can therefore be put in such a form that it loses all the appearance of a judgment of value: Instead of saying "This is the right way to Granchester," I could equally well have said, "This is the right way you have to go if you want to get to Granchester in the shortest time"; "This man is a good runner" simply means that he runs a certain number of miles in a certain number of minutes, etc. Now what I wish to contend is that, although all judgments of relative value can be shown to be mere statements of facts, no statement of fact can ever be, or imply, a judgment of absolute value. Let me explain this: Suppose one of you were an omniscient person and therefore knew all the movements of all the bodies in the world dead or alive and that he also knew all the states of mind of all human beings that ever lived, and suppose this man wrote all he knew in a big book, then this book would contain the whole description of the world; and what I want to say is, that this book would contain nothing that we would call an *ethical* judgment or anything that would logically imply such a judgment. It would of course contain all relative judgments of value and all true scientific propositions and in fact all true propositions that can be made. But all the facts described would, as it were, stand on the same level and in the same way all propositions stand on the same level. There are no propositions which, in any absolute sense, are sublime, important, or trivial. Now perhaps some of you will agree to that and be reminded of Hamlet's words: "Nothing is either good or bad, but thinking makes it so." But this again could lead to a misunderstanding. What Hamlet says seems to imply that good and bad, though not qualities of the world outside us, are attributes to our states of mind. But what I mean is that a state of mind, so far as we mean by that a fact which we can describe, is in no ethical sense good or bad. If for instance in our world-book we read the description of a murder with all its details physical and psychological, the mere description of these facts will contain nothing which we could call an *ethical* proposition. The murder will be on exactly the same level as any other event, for instance the falling of a stone. Certainly the reading of this description might cause us pain or rage or any other emotion, or we might read about the pain or rage caused by this murder in other people when they heard of it, but there will simply be facts, facts, and facts but no Ethics. And now I must say that if I contemplate what Ethics really would have to be if there were such a science, this result seems to me quite obvious. It seems to me obvious that nothing we could ever think or say should be *the* thing. That we cannot write a scientific book, the subject matter of which could be intrinsically sublime and above all other subject matters. I can only describe my feeling by the metaphor, that, if a man could write a book on Ethics which really was a book on Ethics, this book would, with an explosion, destroy all the other books in the world. Our words used as we use them in science, are vessels capable only of containing and conveying meaning and sense, *natural* meaning and sense. Ethics, if it is anything, is supernatural and our words will only express facts; as a teacup will only hold a teacup full of water and if I were to pour out a gallon over it. I said that so far as facts and propositions are concerned there is only relative value and relative good, right, etc. And let me, before I go on, illustrate this by a rather obvious example. The right road is the road which leads to an arbitrarily predetermined end and it is quite clear to us all that there is no sense in talking about the right road apart from such a predetermined goal. Now let us see what we could possibly mean by the expression, "*the* absolutely right road." I think it would be the road which *everybody* on seeing it would, *with logical necessity*, have to go, or be ashamed for not going. And similarly the *absolute good*, if it is a describable state of affairs,

194

would be one which everybody, independent of his tastes and inclinations, would *necessarily* bring about or feel guilty for not bringing about. And I want to say that such a state of affairs is a chimera. No state of affairs has, in itself, what I would like to call the coercive power of an absolute judge. Then what have all of us who, like myself, are still tempted to use such expressions as "absolute good," "absolute value," etc., what have we in mind and what do we try to express? Now whenever I try to make this clear to myself it is natural that I should recall cases in which I would certainly use these expressions and I am then in the situation in which you would be if, for instance, I were to give you a lecture on the psychology of pleasure. What you would do then would be to try and recall some typical situation in which you always felt pleasure. For, bearing this situation in mind, all I should say to you would become concrete and, as it were, controllable. One man would perhaps choose as his stock example the sensation when taking a walk on a fine summer's day. Now in this situation I am, if I want to fix my mind on what I mean by absolute or ethical value. And there, in my case, it always happens that the idea of one particular experience presents itself to me which therefore is, in a sense, my experience *par excellence* and this is the reason why, in talking to you now, I will use this experience as my first and foremost example. (As I have said before, this is an entirely personal matter and others would find other examples more striking.) I will describe this experience in order, if possible, to make you recall the same or similar experiences, so that we may have a common ground for our investigation. I believe the best way of describing it is to say that when I have it *I wonder at the existence of the world*. And I am then inclined to use such phrases as "how extraordinary that anything should exist" or "how extraordinary that the world should exist." I will mention another experience straight away which I also know and which others of you might be acquainted with: it is, what one might call, the experience of feeling *absolutely* safe. I mean the state of mind in which one is inclined to say "I am safe, nothing can injure me whatever happens." Now let me consider these experiences, for, I believe, they exhibit the very characteristics we try to get clear about. And there the first thing I have to say is, that the verbal expression which we give to these experiences is nonsense! If I say "I wonder at the existence of the world" I am misusing language. Let me explain this: It has a perfectly good and clear sense to say that I wonder at something being the case, we all understand what it means to say that I wonder at the size of a dog which is bigger than anyone I have ever seen before or at any thing which, in the common sense of the word, is extraordinary. In every such case I wonder at something being the case which I *could* conceive *not* to be the case. I wonder at the size of this dog because I could conceive of a dog of another, namely the ordinary size, at which I should not wonder. To say "I wonder at such and such being

195

the case" has only sense if I can imagine it not to be the case. In this sense one can wonder at the existence of, say, a house when one sees it and has not visited it for a long time and has imagined that it had been pulled down in the meantime. But it is nonsense to say that I wonder at the existence of the world, because I cannot imagine it not existing. I could of course wonder at the world round me being as it is. If for instance I had this experience while looking into the blue sky, I could wonder at the sky being blue as opposed to the case when it's clouded. But that's not what I mean. I am wondering at the sky being *whatever it is*. One might be tempted to say that what I am wondering at is a tautology, namely at the sky being blue or not blue. But then it's just nonsense to say that one is wondering at a tautology. Now the same applies to the other experience which I have mentioned, the experience of absolute safety. We all know what it means in ordinary life to be safe. I am safe in my room, when I cannot be run over by an omnibus. I am safe if I have had whooping cough and cannot therefore get it again. To be safe essentially means that it is physically impossible that certain things should happen to me and therefore it's nonsense to say that I am safe *whatever* happens. Again this is a misuse of the word "safe" as the other example was of a misuse of the word "existence" or "wondering." Now I want to impress on you that a certain characteristic misuse of our language runs through *all* ethical and religious expressions. All these expressions *seem*, prima facie, to be just *similes*. Thus it seems that when we are using the word *right* in an ethical sense, although, what we mean, is not right in its trivial sense, it's something similar, and when we say "This is a good fellow," although the word good here doesn't mean what it means in the sentence "This is a good football player" there seems to be some similarity. And when we say "This man's life was valuable" we don't mean it in the same sense in which we would speak of some valuable jewelry but there seems to be some sort of analogy. Now all religious terms seem in this sense to be used as similes or allegorically. For when we speak of God and that he sees everything and when we kneel and pray to him all our terms and actions seem to be parts of a great and elaborate allegory which represents him as a human being of great power whose grace we try to win, etc., etc. But this allegory also describes the experience which I have just referred to. For the first of them is, I believe, exactly what people were referring to when they said that God had created the world; and the experience of absolute safety has been described by saying that we feel safe in the hands of God. A third experience of the same kind is that of feeling guilty and again this was described by the phrase that God disapproves of our conduct. Thus in ethical and religious language we seem constantly to be using similes. But a simile must be the simile for *something*. And if I can describe a fact by means of a simile I must also be able to drop the simile and to describe the facts without it. Now in our case as soon as we try to drop the simile and simply to state the facts which stand behind it, we find that there are no such facts. And so, what at first appeared to be a simile now seems to be mere nonsense. Now the three experiences which I have mentioned to you (and I could have added others) seem to those who have experienced them, for instance to me, to have in some sense an intrinsic, absolute value. But when I say they are experiences, surely, they are facts; they have taken place then and there, lasted a certain definite time and consequently are describable. And so from what I have said some minutes ago I must admit it is nonsense to say that they have absolute value. And I will make my point still more acute by saying "It is the paradox that an experience, a fact, should seem to have supernatural value." Now there is a way in which I would be tempted to meet this paradox. Let me first consider, again, our first experience of wondering at the existence of the world and let me describe it in a slightly different way; we all know what in ordinary life would be called a miracle. It obviously is simply an event the like of which we have never yet seen. Now suppose such an event happened. Take the case that one of you suddenly grew a lion's head and began to roar. Certainly that would be as extraordinary a thing as I can imagine. Now whenever we should have recovered from our surprise, what I would suggest would be to fetch a doctor and have the case scientifically investigated and if it were not for hurting him I would have him vivisected. And where would the miracle have got to? For it is clear that when we look at it in this way everything miraculous has disappeared; unless what we mean by this term is merely that a fact has not yet been explained by science which again means that we have hitherto failed to group this fact with others in a scientific system. This shows that it is absurd to say "Science has proved that there are no miracles." The truth is that the scientific way of looking at a fact is not the way to look at it as a miracle. For imagine whatever fact you may, it is not in itself miraculous in the absolute sense of that term. For we see now that we have been using the word "miracle" in a relative and an absolute sense. And I will now describe the experience of wondering at the existence of the world by saying: it is the experience of seeing the world as a miracle. Now I am tempted to say that the right expression in language for the miracle of the existence of the world, though it is not any proposition *in* language, is the existence of language itself. But what then does it mean to be aware of this miracle at some times and not at other times? For all I have said by shifting the expression of the miraculous from an expression *by means of* language to the expression *by the existence* of language, all I have said is again that we cannot express what we want to express and that all we *say* about the absolute miraculous remains nonsense. Now the answer to all this will seem perfectly clear to many of you. You will say: Well, if certain

197

experiences constantly tempt us to attribute a quality to them which we call absolute or ethical value and importance, this simply shows that by these words we *don't* mean nonsense, that after all what we mean by saying that an experience has absolute value *is just a fact like other facts* and that all it comes to is that we have not yet succeeded in finding the correct logical analysis of what we mean by our ethical and religious expressions. Now when this is urged against me I at once see clearly, as it were in a flash of light, not only that no description that I can think of would do to describe what I mean by absolute value, but that I would reject every significant description that anybody could possibly suggest, *ab initio*, on the ground of its significance. That is to say: I see now that these nonsensical expressions were not nonsensical because I had not yet found the correct expressions, but that their nonsensicality was their very essence. For all I wanted to do with them was just *to go beyond* the world and that is to say beyond significant language. My whole tendency and I believe the tendency of all men who ever tried to write or talk Ethics or Religion was to run against the boundaries of language. This running against the walls of our cage is perfectly, absolutely hopeless. Ethics so far as it springs from the desire to say something about the ultimate meaning of life, the absolute good, the absolute valuable, can be no science. What it says does not add to our knowledge in any sense. But it is a document of a tendency in the human mind which I personally cannot help respecting deeply and I would not for my life ridicule it.

Tractatus Logico-Philosophicus

6.53   The correct method in philosophy would really be the following: to say nothing except what can be said, i.e. propositions of natural science – i.e. something that has nothing to do with philosophy – and then, whenever someone else wanted to say something metaphysical, to demonstrate to him that he had failed to give a meaning to certain signs in his propositions. Although it would not be satisfying to the other person – he would not have the feeling that we were teaching him philosophy – *this* method would be the only strictly correct one.

6.54   My propositions serve as elucidations in the following way: anyone who understands me eventually recognizes them as nonsensical, when he has used them – as steps – to climb up beyond them. (He must, so to speak, throw away the ladder after he has climbed up it.)

He must transcend these propositions, and then he will see the world aright.

7   What we cannot speak about we must pass over in silence.

chapter fifteen

Towards a New Architecture

Le Corbusier

Charles-Édouard Jeanneret, a.k.a. Le Corbusier (1887–1965), was a Swiss architect whose 1923 collection of magazine articles *Vers une Architecture* (translated as *Towards a New Architecture*) is perhaps the most important architectural book of this century. Le Corbusier took it as his generation's task fundamentally to rethink architecture's meaning for a new technological and socially egalitarian age. De-ornamentation and geometrical simplicity are not only functional and egalitarian, but they reveal the truth of a building, naked and essential. When his innovative design for the first League of Nations center in Geneva in 1927 was disqualified (because it had not been drawn using India ink!), the International Congresses of Modern Architecture (CIAM) was formed, largely to defend his kind of avant-garde work. His architectural style was based on a vision of a future society that would be true to its own industrial nature.

The Engineer's Æsthetic and Architecture

The Engineer's Æsthetic, and Architecture, are two things that march together and follow one from the other: the one being now at its full height, the other in an unhappy state of retrogression.

The Engineer, inspired by the law of Economy and governed by mathematical calculation, puts us in accord with universal law. He achieves harmony.

The Architect, by his arrangement of forms, realizes an order which is a pure creation of his spirit; by forms and shapes he affects our senses to an acute degree and provokes plastic emotions; by the relationships which he creates he wakes profound echoes in us, he gives us the measure of an

---

Le Corbusier, *Towards a New Architecture*, trans. Frederick Etchells (New York: Dover, 1986): "Argument," pp. 1–8; "First Reminder: Mass," pp. 29–31; "Third Reminder: The Plan," pp. 47–64.

order which we feel to be in accordance with that of our world, he determines the various movements of our heart and of our understanding; it is then that we experience the sense of beauty.

Three Reminders to Architects

MASS

Our eyes are constructed to enable us to see forms in light.

Primary forms are beautiful forms because they can be clearly appreciated.

Architects to-day no longer achieve these simple forms.

Working by calculation, engineers employ geometrical forms, satisfying our eyes by their geometry and our understanding by their mathematics; their work is on the direct line of good art.

SURFACE

A mass is enveloped in its surface, a surface which is divided up according to the directing and generating lines of the mass; and this gives the mass its individuality.

Architects to-day are afraid of the geometrical constituents of surfaces.

The great problems of modern construction must have a geometrical solution.

Forced to work in accordance with the strict needs of exactly determined conditions, engineers make use of generating and accusing lines in relation to forms. They create limpid and moving plastic facts.

PLAN

The Plan is the generator.

Without a plan, you have lack of order, and wilfulness.

The Plan holds in itself the essence of sensation.

The great problems of to-morrow, dictated by collective necessities, put the question of "plan" in a new form.

Modern life demands, and is waiting for, a new kind of plan, both for the house and for the city.

Regulating Lines

An inevitable element of Architecture.

The necessity for order. The regulating line is a guarantee against wilfulness. It brings satisfaction to the understanding.

The regulating line is a means to an end; it is not a recipe. Its choice and the modalities of expression given to it are an integral part of architectural creation.

Eyes Which Do Not See

LINERS[i]

A great epoch has begun.

There exists a new spirit.

There exists a mass of work conceived in the new spirit; it is to be met with particularly in industrial production.

Architecture is stifled by custom.

The "styles" are a lie.

Style is a unity of principle animating all the work of an epoch, the result of a state of mind which has its own special character.

Our own epoch is determining, day by day, its own style.

Our eyes, unhappily, are unable yet to discern it.

AIRPLANES

The airplane is the product of close selection.

The lesson of the airplane lies in the logic which governed the statement of the problem and its realization.

The problem of the house has not yet been stated.

Nevertheless there do exist standards for the dwelling house.

Machinery contains in itself the factor of economy, which makes for selection.

The house is a machine for living in.

AUTOMOBILES

We must aim at the fixing of standards in order to face the problem of perfection.

[i] Ocean liners.

The Parthenon is a product of selection applied to a standard.

Architecture operates in accordance with standards.

Standards are a matter of logic, analysis and minute study; they are based on a problem which has been well "stated." A standard is definitely established by experiment.

Architecture

THE LESSON OF ROME

The business of Architecture is to establish emotional relationships by means of raw materials.

Architecture goes beyond utilitarian needs.

Architecture is a plastic thing.

The spirit of order, a unity of intention.

The sense of relationships; architecture deals with quantities.

Passion can create drama out of inert stone.

THE ILLUSION OF PLANS

The Plan proceeds from within to without; the exterior is the result of an interior.

The elements of architecture are light and shade, walls and space.

Arrangement is the gradation of aims, the classification of intentions.

Man looks at the creation of architecture with his eyes, which are 5 feet 6 inches from the ground. One can only deal with aims which the eye can appreciate, and intentions which take into account architectural elements. If there come into play intentions which do not speak the language of architecture, you arrive at the illusion of plans, you transgress the rules of the Plan through an error in conception, or through a leaning towards empty show.

PURE CREATION OF THE MIND

Contour and profile are the touchstone of the architect.

Here he reveals himself as artist or mere engineer.

Contour is free of all constraint.

There is here no longer any question of custom, nor of tradition, nor of construction nor of adaptation to utilitarian needs.

Contour and profile are a pure creation of the mind; they call for the plastic artist.

203

Mass-production Houses

A great epoch has begun.

There exists a new spirit.

Industry, overwhelming us like a flood which rolls on towards its destined ends, has furnished us with new tools adapted to this new epoch, animated by the new spirit.

Economic law inevitably governs our acts and our thoughts.

The problem of the house is a problem of the epoch. The equilibrium of society to-day depends upon it. Architecture has for its first duty, in this period of renewal, that of brining about a revision of values, a revision of the constituent elements of the house.

Mass-production is based on analysis and experiment.

Industry on the grand scale must occupy itself with building and establish the elements of the house on a mass-production basis.

We must create the mass-production spirit.

The spirit of constructing mass-production houses.

The spirit of living in mass-production houses.

The spirit of conceiving mass-production houses.

If we eliminate from our hearts and minds all dead concepts in regard to the house, and look at the question from a critical and objective point of view, we shall arrive at the "House-Machine," the mass-production house, healthy (and morally so too) and beautiful in the same way that the working tools and instruments which accompany our existence are beautiful.

Beautiful also with all the animation that the artist's sensibility can add to severe and pure functioning elements.

Architecture or Revolution

In every field of industry, new problems have presented themselves and new tools have been created capable of resolving them. If this new fact be set against the past, then you have revolution.

In building and construction, mass-production has already been begun; in face of new economic needs, mass-production units have been created both in mass and detail; and definite results have been achieved both in detail and in mass. If this fact be set against the past, then you have revolution, both in the method employed and in the large scale on which it has been carried out.

The history of Architecture unfolds itself slowly across the centuries as a modification of structure and ornament, but in the last fifty years steel and concrete have brought new conquests, which are the index of a greater capacity for construction, and of an architecture in which the old codes have been overturned. If we challenge the past, we shall learn that "styles" no longer exist for us, that a style belonging to our own period has come about; and there has been a Revolution.

Our minds have consciously or unconsciously apprehended these events and new needs have arisen, consciously or unconsciously.

The machinery of Society, profoundly *out of gear*, oscillates between an amelioration, of historical importance, and a catastrophe.

The primordial instinct of every human being is to assure himself of a shelter. The various classes of workers in society to-day *no longer have dwellings adapted to their needs; neither the artizan nor the intellectual.*

It is a question of building which is at the root of the social unrest of to-day: architecture or revolution.

First Reminder: Mass

Architecture is the masterly, correct and magnificent play of masses brought together in light. Our eyes are made to see forms in light; light and shade reveal these forms; cubes, cones, spheres, cylinders or pyramids are the great primary forms which light reveals to advantage; the image of these is distinct and tangible within us and without ambiguity. It is for that reason that these are *beautiful forms, the most beautiful forms*. Everybody is agreed as to that, the child, the savage and the metaphysician. It is of the very nature of the plastic arts.

Egyptian, Greek or Roman architecture is an architecture of prisms, cubes and cylinders, pyramids or spheres: the Pyramids, the Temple of Luxor, the Parthenon, the Coliseum, Hadrian's Villa.

Gothic architecture is not, fundamentally, based on spheres, cones and cylinders. Only the nave is an expression of a simple form, but of a complex geometry of the second order (intersecting arches). It is for that reason that a cathedral is not very beautiful and that we search in it for compensations of a subjective kind outside plastic art. A cathedral interests us as the ingenious solution of a difficult problem, but a problem of which the postulates have been badly stated because they do not proceed from the great primary forms. *The cathedral is not a plastic work; it is a drama; a fight against the force of gravity, which is a sensation of a sentimental nature.*

The Pyramids, the Towers of Babylon, the Gates of Samarkand, the Parthenon, the Coliseum, the Pantheon, the Pont du Gard, Santa Sophia, the Mosques of Stamboul, the Tower of Pisa, the Cupolas of Brunelleschi and of Michael Angelo, the Pont-Royal, the Invalides – all these belong to Architecture.

The Gare du Quai d'Orsay, the Grand Palais do not belong to Architecture.[ii]

The *architects* of to-day, lost in the sterile backwaters of their plans, their foliage, their pilasters and their lead roofs, have never acquired the conception of primary masses. They were never taught that at the Schools.

Not in pursuit of an architectural idea, but simply guided by the results of calculation (derived from the principles which govern our universe) and the conception of A LIVING ORGANISM, *the* ENGINEERS *of to-day make use of the primary elements and, by co-ordinating them in accordance with the rules, provoke in us architectural emotions and thus make the work of man ring in unison with universal order.*

Thus we have the American grain elevators and factories, the magnificent FIRST-FRUITS *of the new age.* THE AMERICAN ENGINEERS OVERWHELM WITH THEIR CALCULATIONS OUR EXPIRING ARCHITECTURE.

Third Reminder: The Plan

The plan is the generator.

The eye of the spectator finds itself looking at a site composed of streets and houses. It receives the impact of the masses which rise up around it. If these masses are of a formal kind and have not been spoilt by unseemly variations, if the disposition of their grouping expresses a clean rhythm and not an incoherent agglomeration, if the relationship of mass to space is in just proportion, the eye transmits to the brain co-ordinated sensations and the mind derives from these satisfactions of a high order: this is architecture.

The eye observes, in a large interior, the multiple surfaces of walls and vaults; the cupolas determine the large spaces; the vaults display their own surfaces; the pillars and the walls adjust themselves in accordance with comprehensible reasons. The whole structure rises from its base and is developed in accordance with a rule which is written on the ground in the plan: noble forms, variety of form, unity of the geometric principle. A profound projection of harmony: this is architecture.

[ii] In the preceding two paragraphs Le Corbusier is contrasting mammoth, geometrical, and relatively non-ornamented buildings, most of them built for religious or practical purposes (e.g. the Parisian hospital, *Les Invalides*; the *Santa Sophia*, a Greek Christian cathedral in Istanbul), with the neo-classically ornamented style to which he denies even the title "Architecture."

The plan is at its basis. Without plan there can be neither grandeur of aim and expression, nor rhythm, nor mass, nor coherence. Without plan we have the sensation, so insupportable to man, of shapelessness, of poverty, of disorder, of wilfulness.

A plan calls for the most active imagination. It calls for the most severe discipline also. The plan is what determines everything; it is the decisive moment. A plan is not a pretty thing to be drawn, like a Madonna face; it is an austere abstraction; it is nothing more than an algebrization and a dry-looking thing. The work of the mathematician remains none the less one of the highest activities of the human spirit.

Arrangement is an appreciable rhythm which reacts on every human being in the same way.

The plan bears within itself a primary and pre-determined rhythm: the work is developed in extent and in height following the prescriptions of the plan, with results which can range from the simplest to the most complex, all coming within the same law. Unity of law is the law of a good plan: a simple law capable of infinite modulation.

Rhythm is a state of equilibrium which proceeds either from symmetries, simple or complex, or from delicate balancings. Rhythm is an equation; Equalization (symmetry, repetition) (*Egyptian and Hindoo temples*); compensation (movement of contrary parts) (*the Acropolis at Athens*); modulation (the development of an original plastic invention) (*Santa Sophia*). So many reactions, differing in the main for every individual, in spite of the unity of aim which gives the rhythm, and the state of equilibrium. So we get the astonishing diversity found in great epochs, a diversity which is the result of architectural principle and not of the play of decoration.

The plan carries in itself the very essence of sensation.

But the sense of the plan has been lost for the last hundred years. The great problems of to-morrow, dictated by collective necessities, based upon statistics and realized by mathematical calculation, once more revive the problem of the plan. When once the indispensable breadth of vision, which must be brought to town planning, has been realized, we shall enter upon a period that no epoch has yet known. Towns must be conceived and planned throughout their entire extent in the same way as were planned the temples of the East and as the Invalides or the Versailles of Louis XIV were laid out.

The technical equipment of this epoch – the technique of finance and the technique of construction – is ready to carry out this task.

Tony Garnier, backed by Herriot at Lyons, planned his "industrial quarter" (*Cité*).[iii] It is an attempt at an ordered scheme and a fusion of

---

[iii] French architect Tony Garnier (1869–1948) devised a plan ("*Cité Industrielle*") for an "ideal" industrial city of 35,000 people, first exhibited in Paris in 1904.

207

utilitarian and plastic solutions. One fixed rule governing the units employed gives, in every quarter of the town, the same choice of essential masses and determines the intervening spaces in accordance with practical necessities and the biddings of a poetical sense peculiar to the architect. Though we may reserve our judgment as to the relationship of the various zones of this industrial city, one experiences here the beneficent results of order. Where order reigns, well-being begins. By the happy creation of a system of arrangement of the various plots, even the residential quarters for artisans take on a high architectural significance. Such is the result of a plan.

In the present state of marking time (for modern town planning is not yet born), the most noble quarters of our towns are inevitably the manufacturing ones where the basis of grandeur and style – namely, geometry – results from the problem itself. The plan has been a weak feature, and is still so to-day. True, an admirable order reigns in the interior of markets and workshops, has dictated the structure of machines and governs their movements, and conditions each gesture of a gang of workmen; but dirt infects their surroundings, and incoherence ran riot when the rule and square dictated the placing of the buildings, spreading them about in a crazy, costly and dangerous way.

It would have been enough if there had been a plan. And one day we shall have a plan for our needs. The extent of the evil will bring us to this.

One day Auguste Perret created the phrase: "The City of Towers."[iv] A glittering epithet which aroused the poet in us. A word which struck the note of the moment because the fact itself is imminent! Almost unknown to us, the "great city" is engendering its plan. This plan may well be a gigantic affair, since the great city is a rising tide. It is time that we should repudiate the existing lay-out of our towns, in which the congestion of buildings grows greater, interlaced by narrow streets full of noise, petrol fumes and dust; and where on each storey the windows open wide on to this foul confusion. The great towns have become too dense for the security of their inhabitants and yet they are not sufficiently dense to meet the new needs of "modern business."

If we take as our basis the vital constructional event which the American sky-scraper has proved to be, it will be sufficient to bring together at certain points (relatively distant) the great density of our modern populations and to build at these points enormous constructions of 60 storeys high. Reinforced concrete and steel allow of this audacity and lend themselves in particular to a certain development of the façade by means of which all the

[iv] French architect Auguste Perret (1874–1934) was a pioneer in the use of modern reinforced-concrete materials and techniques.

windows have an uninterrupted view: in this way, in the future, inside courts and "wells" will no longer exist. Starting from the fourteenth storey you have absolute calm and the purest air.

In these towers which will shelter the worker, till now stifled in densely packed quarters and congested streets, all the necessary services, following the admirable practice in America, will be assembled, bringing efficiency and economy of time and effort, and as a natural result the peace of mind which is so necessary. These towers, rising up at great distances from one another, will give by reason of their height the same accommodation that has up till now been spread out over the superficial area; they will leave open enormous spaces in which would run, well away from them, the noisy arterial roads, full of a traffic which becomes increasingly rapid. At the foot of the towers would stretch the parks: trees covering the whole town. The setting out of the towers would form imposing avenues; there indeed is an architecture worthy of our time.

Auguste Perret set forth the principle of the City of Towers; but he has not produced any designs. On the other hand he allowed himself to be interviewed by a reporter of the "Intransigeant" and to be so far carried away as to swell out his conception beyond reasonable limits. In this way he threw a veil of dangerous futurism over what was a sound idea. The reporter noted that enormous bridges would link each tower to the next; for what purpose? The arteries for traffic would be placed far away from the houses; and the inhabitants, free to disport themselves in the parks among trees planted in ordered patterns, or on the grass or in the places of amusement, would never have the slightest desire to take their exercise on giddy bridges, with nothing at all to do when they got there! The reporter would have it also that the town would be raised on innumerable piles of reinforced concrete carrying the streets at a height of 65 feet (6 storeys if you please!) and linking the towers one to another. These piles would leave an immense space underneath the town in which would be placed the gas and water mains and the sewers, the viscera of the city. Perret had never set out his plan, and the idea could not be carried further without a plan.

I had myself put forward this idea of using piles a long time before Auguste Perret, and it was a conception of a much less grandiose character; but it was capable of meeting a genuine need. I applied it to the existing type of town such as the Paris of to-day. Instead of forming foundations by excavating and constructing thick foundation walls, instead of digging up and digging up again the roadways in order to bury in them (a labour of Sisyphus) the gas and water mains, the sewers and the Tubes,[v] with

---

[v] The Greek mythological character Sisyphus was condemned by the Gods repeatedly to roll a boulder up a hill, only to see it roll back down, for eternity; "Tubes" refers to subways.

constant repairs to execute, it would be agreed that any new districts should be constructed at ground level, the foundations being replaced by the necessary number of concrete piles; these would have carried the ground floor of the houses and, by a system of corbelling, the pavements and the roadways.

Within this space so gained, of a height of from 12 to 18 feet, would run heavy lorries, and the Tubes replacing the encumbrance of tramways, and so on, with a direct service to points immediately below the buildings. This complete network of traffic, working independently of that reserved for pedestrians and quick-moving vehicles, would be a pure gain and would have its own geography independent of any obstruction due to the houses: an ordered forest of pillars in the midst of which the town would exchange its merchandise, bring in its food supplies, and perform all the slow and clumsy tasks which to-day impede the speed of traffic.

Cafes and places for recreation would no longer be that fungus which eats up the pavements of Paris: they would be transferred to the flat roofs, as would be all commerce of a luxury kind (for is it not really illogical that one entire superficies of a town should be unused and reserved for a flirtation between the tiles and the stars?). Short passage-ways in the shape of bridges above the ordinary streets would enable foot traffic to get about among these newly gained quarters consecrated to leisure amidst flowers and foliage.

The result of this conception would be nothing less than a triplication of the traffic area of a town; it was capable of realization *since it corresponded to a need, was less costly and more rational than the aberrations of to-day*. It was a reasonable notion, given the old framework of our towns, just as the conception of the City of Towers will prove a reasonable idea, as regards the towns of to-morrow.

Here, then, we have a lay-out of streets which would bring about an entirely new system of town planning and would provide a radical reform in the tenanted house or apartment; this imminent reform, necessitated by the transformation of domestic economy, demands a new type of plan for dwelling-houses, and an entirely new organization of services corresponding to modern life in a great city. Here again the plan is the generator; without it poverty, disorder, wilfulness reign supreme.

Instead of our towns being laid out in massive quadrangles, with the streets in narrow trenches walled in by seven-storeyed buildings set perpendicular on the pavement and enclosing unhealthy courtyards, airless and sunless wells, our new layout, employing the same area and housing the same number of people, would show great blocks of houses with successive set-backs, stretching along arterial avenues. No more courtyards, but flats opening on every side to air and light, and looking, not on the puny trees of our boulevards of to-day, but upon green sward, sports grounds and abundant plantations of trees.

The jutting prows of these great blocks would break up the long avenues at regular intervals. The various set-backs would promote the play of light and shade, so necessary to architectural expression.

Reinforced concrete has brought about a revolution in the æsthetics of construction. By suppressing the roof and replacing it by terraces, reinforced concrete is leading us to a new æsthetic of the plan, hitherto unknown. These set-backs and recessions are quite possible and will, in the future, lead to a play of half-lights and of heavy shade with the accent running not from top to bottom, but horizontally from left to right.

This is a modification of the first importance in the æsthetic of the plan; it has not yet been realized; but we shall be wise to bear this in our minds, in considering projects for the extension of our towns.

* * *

We are living in a period of reconstruction and of adaptation to new social and economic conditions. In rounding this Cape Horn the new horizons before us will only recover the grand line of tradition by a complete revision of the methods in vogue and by the fixing of a new basis of construction established in logic.

In architecture the old bases of construction are dead. We shall not rediscover the truths of architecture until new bases have established a logical ground for every architectural manifestation. A period of 20 years is beginning which will be occupied in creating these bases. A period of great problems, a period of analysis, of experiment, a period also of great æsthetic confusion, a period in which a new æsthetic will be elaborated.

We must study the *plan*, the key of this evolution.

chapter sixteen

Civilization and its Discontents
Sigmund Freud

Sigmund Freud (1856–1939), Moravian-born Austrian neurologist and founder of psychoanalysis, is the most influential psychological theorist of the twentieth century, despite the continuing reaction against his work. He saw unconscious instincts of sexuality and aggression behind all human life and culture, including the behavior of infants. In a later speculative work, *Civilization and its Discontents* (1930), he used psychoanalytic theory to explore the inherent discomfort human instinctual nature must always feel in the confines of a civilized society. Freud concluded that the more well organized society becomes, the more discomfort or guilt its members must feel, even if they obey its strictures. Freud is, however, no utopian; he does not want to unshackle human instincts. Human beings are innately aggressive, and this aggression must be controlled. His account is poignant in its historical context, written as it was during the rise of Nazism, and preceding a period of violence that perhaps even he could not have imagined. Forced as a Jew into emigration by Hitler's annexation of Austria in 1938, he died in London in exile. The Nazis burned his books as a prime representative of "Jewish science."

The assumption of the existence of an instinct of death or destruction has met with resistance even in analytic circles; I am aware that there is a frequent inclination rather to ascribe whatever is dangerous and hostile in love to an original bipolarity in its own nature. To begin with it was only tentatively that I put forward the views I have developed here, but in the course of time they have gained such a hold upon me that I can no longer think in any other way. To my mind, they are far more serviceable from a theoretical standpoint than any other possible ones; they provide that simplification, without either ignoring or doing violence to the facts, for which we strive in scientific work. I know that in sadism and masochism we have always seen before us manifestations of the destructive instinct

From Sigmund Freud, *Civilization and its Discontents*, trans. James Strachey (New York: Norton, 1961), chapters 6 and 7, pp. 64–80.

(directed outwards and inwards), strongly alloyed with erotism; but I can no longer understand how we can have overlooked the ubiquity of non-erotic aggressivity and destructiveness and can have failed to give it its due place in our interpretation of life. (The desire for destruction when it is directed *inwards* mostly eludes our perception, of course, unless it is tinged with erotism.) I remember my own defensive attitude when the idea of an instinct of destruction first emerged in psycho-analytic literature, and how long it took before I became receptive to it. That others should have shown, and still show, the same attitude of rejection surprises me less. For 'little children do not like it'[i] when there is talk of the inborn human inclination to 'badness', to aggressiveness and destructiveness, and so to cruelty as well. God has made them in the image of His own perfection; nobody wants to be reminded how hard it is to reconcile the undeniable existence of evil – despite the protestations of Christian Science – with His all-powerfulness or His all-goodness. The Devil would be the best way out as an excuse for God; in that way he would be playing the same part as an agent of economic discharge as the Jew does in the world of the Aryan ideal. But even so, one can hold God responsible for the existence of the Devil just as well as for the existence of the wickedness which the Devil embodies. In view of these difficulties, each of us will be well advised, on some suitable occasion, to make a low bow to the deeply moral nature of mankind; it will help us to be generally popular and much will be forgiven us for it.[1]

The name 'libido'[ii] can once more be used to denote the manifestations of the power of Eros in order to distinguish them from the energy of the death instinct.[2] It must be confessed that we have much greater difficulty in grasping that instinct; we can only suspect it, as it were, as something in the background behind Eros, and it escapes detection unless its presence is betrayed by its being alloyed with Eros. It is in sadism, where the death instinct twists the erotic aim in its own sense and yet at the same time fully satisfies the erotic urge, that we succeed in obtaining the clearest insight into its nature and its relation to Eros. But even where it emerges without any sexual purpose, in the blindest fury of destructiveness, we cannot fail to recognize that the satisfaction of the instinct is accompanied by an extraordinarily high degree of narcissistic enjoyment, owing to its presenting the ego with a fulfilment of the latter's old wishes for omnipotence. The instinct of destruction, moderated and tamed, and, as it were, inhibited in its aim, must, when it is directed towards objects, provide the ego with

---

[i] A quotation from a poem of Goethe's.

[ii] "Libido" refers more simply and narrowly to the sexual instinct which Freud is here interpreting broadly as "Eros".

the satisfaction of its vital needs and with control over nature. Since the assumption of the existence of the instinct is mainly based on theoretical grounds, we must also admit that it is not entirely proof against theoretical objections. But this is how things appear to us now, in the present state of our knowledge; future research and reflection will no doubt bring further light which will decide the matter.

In all that follows I adopt the standpoint, therefore, that the inclination to aggression is an original, self-subsisting instinctual disposition in man, and I return to my view that it constitutes the greatest impediment to civilization. At one point in the course of this enquiry I was led to the idea that civilization was a special process which mankind undergoes, and I am still under the influence of that idea. I may now add that civilization is a process in the service of Eros, whose purpose is to combine single human individuals, and after that families, then races, peoples and nations, into one great unity, the unity of mankind. Why this has to happen, we do not know; the work of Eros is precisely this. These collections of men are to be libidinally bound to one another. Necessity alone, the advantages of work in common, will not hold them together. But man's natural aggressive instinct, the hostility of each against all and of all against each, opposes this programme of civilization. This aggressive instinct is the derivative and the main representative of the death instinct which we have found alongside of Eros and which shares world-dominion with it. And now, I think, the meaning of the evolution of civilization is no longer obscure to us. It must present the struggle between Eros and Death, between the instinct of life and the instinct of destruction, as it works itself out in the human species. This struggle is what all life essentially consists of, and the evolution of civilization may therefore be simply described as the struggle for life of the human species. And it is this battle of the giants that our nurse-maids try to appease with their lullaby about Heaven. . . .

Another question concerns us more nearly. What means does civilization employ in order to inhibit the aggressiveness which opposes it, to make it harmless, to get rid of it, perhaps? We have already become acquainted with a few of these methods, but not yet with the one that appears to be the most important. This we can study in the history of the development of the individual. What happens in him to render his desire for aggression innocuous? Something very remarkable, which we should never have guessed and which is nevertheless quite obvious. His aggressiveness is introjected, internalized; it is, in point of fact, sent back to where it came from – that is, it is directed towards his own ego. There it is taken over by a portion of the ego, which sets itself over against the rest of the ego as super-ego, which now, in the form of 'conscience', is ready to put into action against the ego the same harsh aggressiveness that the ego would have liked to satisfy upon other, extraneous individuals. The tension between the harsh super-ego and the ego that is subjected to it, is called by us the sense of guilt; it expresses itself as a need for punishment. Civilization, therefore, obtains mastery over the individual's dangerous desire for aggression by weakening and disarming it and by setting up an agency within him to watch over it, like a garrison in a conquered city. . . .

Thus we know of two origins of the sense of guilt: one arising from fear of an authority, and the other, later on, arising from fear of the super-ego. The first insists upon a renunciation of instinctual satisfactions; the second, as well as doing this, presses for punishment, since the continuance of the forbidden wishes cannot be concealed from the super-ego. We have also learned how the severity of the super-ego – the demands of conscience – is to be understood. It is simply a continuation of the severity of the external authority, to which it has succeeded and which it has in part replaced. We now see in what relationship the renunciation of instinct stands to the sense of guilt. Originally, renunciation of instinct was the result of fear of an external authority: one renounced one's satisfactions in order not to lose its love. If one has carried out this renunciation, one is, as it were, quits with the authority and no sense of guilt should remain. But with fear of the super-ego the case is different. Here, instinctual renunciation is not enough, for the wish persists and cannot be concealed from the super-ego. Thus, in spite of the renunciation that has been made, a sense of guilt comes about. This constitutes a great economic disadvantage in the erection of a super-ego, or, as we may put it, in the formation of a conscience. Instinctual renunciation now no longer has a completely liberating effect; virtuous continence is no longer rewarded with the assurance of love. A threatened external unhappiness – loss of love and punishment on the part of the external authority – has been exchanged for a permanent internal unhappiness, for the tension of the sense of guilt. . . .

It can also be asserted that when a child reacts to his first great instinctual frustrations with excessively strong aggressiveness and with a correspondingly severe super-ego, he is following a phylogenetic model and is going beyond the response that would be currently justified; for the father of prehistoric times was undoubtedly terrible, and an extreme amount of aggressiveness may be attributed to him. Thus, if one shifts over from individual to phylogenetic development, the differences between the two theories of the genesis of conscience are still further diminished. On the other hand, a new and important difference makes its appearance between these two developmental processes. We cannot get away from the assumption that man's sense of guilt springs from the Oedipus complex and was acquired at the killing of the father by the brothers banded together.[iii] On that occasion an act of aggression was not suppressed but carried out; but it was the same act of aggression whose suppression in the child is supposed to be the source of his sense of guilt. At this point I should not be surprised if the reader were to exclaim angrily: 'So it makes no difference whether one kills one's father or not – one gets a feeling of guilt in either case! We may take leave to raise a few doubts here. Either it is not true that the sense of guilt comes from suppressed aggressiveness, or else the whole story of the killing of the father is a fiction and the children of primaeval man did not kill their fathers any more often than children do nowadays. Besides, if it is not fiction but a plausible piece of history, it would be a case of something happening which everyone expects to happen – namely, of a person feeling guilty because he really has done something which cannot be justified. And of this event, which is after all an everyday occurrence, psycho-analysis has not yet given any explanation.'

That is true, and we must make good the omission. Nor is there any great secret about the matter. When one has a sense of guilt after having committed a misdeed, and because of it, the feeling should more properly be called *remorse*. It relates only to a deed that has been done, and, of course, it presupposes that a *conscience* – the readiness to feel guilty – was already in existence before the deed took place. Remorse of this sort can, therefore, never help us to discover the origin of conscience and of the sense of guilt in general. What happens in these everyday cases is usually this: an instinctual need acquires the strength to achieve satisfaction in spite of the conscience, which is, after all, limited in its strength; and with the natural weakening of the need owing to its having been satisfied, the former balance of power is restored. Psycho-analysis is thus justified in excluding from the present discussion the case of a sense of guilt due to remorse, however frequently such cases occur and however great their practical importance.

But if the human sense of guilt goes back to the killing of the primal father, that was after all a case of 'remorse'. Are we to assume that [at that time] a conscience and a sense of guilt were not, as we have presupposed, in existence before the deed? If not, where, in this case, did the remorse come from? There is no doubt that this case should explain the secret of the sense of guilt to us and put an end to our difficulties. And I believe it does. This remorse was the result of the primordial ambivalence of feeling

[iii] In the Oedipus complex, cornerstone of Freud's theory of child development, the normal child develops a sexual attachment to the opposite-gender parent, and competitive anger and fear toward the same-gender parent. The conflict is normally resolved through renunciation of the desire and an identification with the same-gender parent. Strictly, the Oedipal complex refers only to the development of boys, the analogous phase (and the analogy is notoriously tortured) for girls being the Electra complex.

towards the father. His sons hated him, but they loved him, too. After their hatred had been satisfied by their act of aggression, their love came to the fore in their remorse for the deed. It set up the super-ego by identification with the father; it gave that agency the father's power, as though as a punishment for the deed of aggression they had carried out against him, and it created the restrictions which were intended to prevent a repetition of the deed. And since the inclination to aggressiveness against the father was repeated in the following generations, the sense of guilt, too, persisted, and it was reinforced once more by every piece of aggressiveness that was suppressed and carried over to the super-ego. Now, I think, we can at last grasp two things perfectly clearly: the part played by love in the origin of conscience and the fatal inevitability of the sense of guilt. Whether one has killed one's father or has abstained from doing so is not really the decisive thing. One is bound to feel guilty in either case, for the sense of guilt is an expression of the conflict due to ambivalence, of the eternal struggle between Eros and the instinct of destruction or death. This conflict is set going as soon as men are faced with the task of living together. So long as the community assumes no other form than that of the family, the conflict is bound to express itself in the Oedipus complex, to establish the conscience and to create the first sense of guilt. When an attempt is made to widen the community, the same conflict is continued in forms which are dependent on the past; and it is strengthened and results in a further intensification of the sense of guilt. Since civilization obeys an internal erotic impulsion which causes human beings to unite in a closely-knit group, it can only achieve this aim through an ever-increasing reinforcement of the sense of guilt. What began in relation to the father is completed in relation to the group. If civilization is a necessary course of development from the family to humanity as a whole, then – as a result of the inborn conflict arising from ambivalence, of the eternal struggle between the trends of love and death – there is inextricably bound up with it an increase of the sense of guilt, which will perhaps reach heights that the individual finds hard to tolerate. One is reminded of the great poet's moving arraignment of the 'Heavenly Powers':

> Ihr führt in's Leben uns hinein.
> Ihr lasst den Armen schuldig werden,
> Dann überlasst Ihr ihn den Pein,
> Denn jede Schuld rächt sich auf Erden.[iv]

[iv] From Goethe's *Wilhelm Meister*, Carlyle's translation (Boston: Houghton Mifflin, 1890).

> To earth, this weary earth, ye bring us
> To guilt ye let us heedless go,
> Then leave repentance fierce to wring us:
> A moment's guilt, an age of woe!

217

Sigmund Freud

And we may well heave a sigh of relief at the thought that it is nevertheless vouchsafed to a few to salvage without effort from the whirlpool of their own feelings the deepest truths, towards which the rest of us have to find our way through tormenting uncertainty and with restless groping.

Notes

1   In Goethe's Mephistopheles we have a quite exceptionally convincing identification of the principle of evil with the destructive instinct:

> Denn alles, was entsteht,
> Ist wert, dass es zu Grunde geht . . .
> So ist dann alles, was Ihr Sünde,
> Zerstörung, kurz das Böse nennt,
> Mein eigentliches Element.

> [For all things, from the Void
> Called forth, deserve to be destroyed . . .
> Thus, all which you as Sin have rated –
> Destruction, – aught with Evil blent, –
> That is my proper element.]

The Devil himself names as his adversary, not what is holy and good, but Nature's power to create, to multiply life – that is, Eros:

> Der Luft, dem Wasser, wie der Erden
> Entwinden tausend Keime sich,
> Im Trocknen, Feuchten, Warmen, Kalten!
> Hätt' ich mir nicht die Flamme vorbehalten,
> Ich hätte nichts Aparts für mich.

> [From Water, Earth, and Air unfolding,
> A thousand germs break forth and grow,
> In dry, and wet, and warm, and chilly:
> And had I not the Flame reserved, why, really,
> There's nothing special of my own to show.

Both passages are from Goethe's *Faust*, Part I, Scene 3, trans. Bayard Taylor. (New York: Collier, 1962). Ed.]

2   Our present point of view can be roughly expressed in the statement that libido has a share in every instinctual manifestation, but that not everything in that manifestation is libido.

chapter seventeen

"The Crowd Phenomenon"

Jose Ortega y Gasset

Spain's greatest twentieth-century philosopher, Jose Ortega y Gasset (1883–1955) wrote on modern society and art. He became an expatriate at the outset of the Spanish civil war (1936), but returned to Spain in 1945. Influenced by Nietzsche, in *The Revolt of the Masses* (1929) Ortega raised an issue that has concerned traditional thinkers throughout this century, namely, the loss of cultural hierarchy in a mass democratic society, and the rise of a new human type, the "mass-man." For Ortega, as for Burke and all the way back to Plato, democratic egalitarianism leads to an indignant assertion of the rights of the mediocre against any form of superiority. This denies authority not only to the great and the talented, but to the virtuous as well. The mass-man says, "No one is better than me, and I am fine just the way I am. It is wrong of anyone to expect me to be better." Consequently, no one is in need of moral or intellectual improvement. For Ortega, this undercuts any possible meaning or value in human life.

The most important fact in the public life of the West[1] in modern times, for good or ill, is the appearance of the masses in the seats of highest social power. Since the masses, by definition, neither can nor should direct their own existence, let alone that of society as a whole, this new development means that we are now undergoing the most profound crisis which can afflict peoples, nations, or cultures. Such a crisis has occurred more than once in history. Its physiognomy, its outline and profile, and its consequences are known, and the development can be given a name: the rebellion of the masses.

In order to understand this truly formidable phenomenon, we had best avoid the exclusively or primarily political meanings of the words "rebellion," "masses," and "social power." For public life is not only political, but is equally, and even more so, economic, moral, intellectual,

---

Jose Ortega y Gasset, "The Crowd Phenomenon," chapter 1, *The Revolt of the Masses*, trans. Anthony Kerrigan, ed. Kenneth Moore (Notre Dame, Ind.: Notre Dame University Press, 1985), pp. 3–10.

219

and religious. It includes all our collective habits, even our fashions in dress and modes of amusement.

Perhaps the best way of approaching this historical phenomenon is to rely on our visual experience: we can simply look at this aspect of our epoch as it stands plainly before our eyes.

Most simple to enunciate, and not so easy to analyze: I shall call it the phenomenon of agglomeration, of crowding, of the sign which says "Full." The cities are full of people. The houses are full of tenants. The hotels are full of guests. Public transport is full of passengers. The cafes and restaurants are full of customers. The sidewalks are full of pedestrians. The waiting-rooms of famous doctors are full of patients. Public spectacles, unless they be extemporaneous, and public entertainment halls, unless they be minoritarian and experimental, are full of spectators. The beaches are crowded, full. What previously was not a problem, is now an everyday matter: the search – to find room, to find a place, to find space.

Is there any fact simpler, more obvious, more constant in life today? Let us penetrate beneath this superficial observation. We will then be surprised to see how, unexpectedly, a veritable fountain will spout forth, and in it, in this jet, we will see how, in the white light of day, of this very day, it will break down into its rich spectrum of inner colors.

What do we actually see, and in seeing are surprised? We see the multitude as such in possession of the locales and appurtenances created by civilization. Further reflection will make us surprised at our surprise. Is not this plenitude ideal? A theater's seats are made to be occupied by spectators: it should be full. And the same for public transport and hotel rooms. No doubt about it. But the point is that previously none of these establishments and vehicles were full – and now they are overflowing, with people left outside eager to occupy them all. Though this development is natural and even logical, we know this was not the case before. A change, therefore, has taken place. Something new has been added, and this innovation does, at least initially, justify our surprise.

To be surprised, to wonder, is to begin to understand. It is the sport and special pleasure of intellectual man. The specific trade-mark of his guild is to gaze at the world with the wide-open eyes of wonder. The world is always strange and wonderful for wide-open eyes. This faculty of wide-eyed wonder is a delight unavailable to your ordinary football or soccer fan. The man who lives by his intellect goes about the world in the perpetual intoxication of a visionary. His particular attribute: the eyes of wonder, of amazement. Thus the ancients assigned to Minerva an owl, bird of wide open ever-dazzled eyes.[i]

---

[i] Minerva, the goddess of wisdom in ancient Greece, had an owl as her emblem.

Crowding was not a common feature of the past. Everything was not always full. Why is it now?

The members of this ubiquitous mass have not come from out of the blue. The number of people was constant for a good while; moreover, after any war one would expect the number to decrease. But here we come up against the first important modern factor. The individuals who make up the present mass already existed before – but not as a mass, not as "masses." Scattered about the world in small groups, or even alone, they lived in diverse ways, dissociated and distant from one another. Each group, even each individual, occupied a space, each his own space so to say, in the fields, in a village, a town, or even in some quarter of a big city.

Now, suddenly, they appear on the scene as a mass. Wherever we look we see a concentration, masses. *Wherever?* No; more exactly in the places most in demand, the places created by the relatively sophisticated taste of modern culture, places previously reserved for small groups, for select minorities.

The masses, suddenly, have made themselves visible, and have installed themselves in the preferred places of society. In the past, the mass, where it existed, went unnoticed. It was a background to the social scene, to the stage of society. Now it has advanced to the footlights, and plays the part of the leading character. There are no longer protagonists as such: there is only the chorus.

The concept of the masses is quantitative – and visual. Let us translate it, without alteration, into sociological terms. We then encounter the concept of the social mass. Society is always a dynamic unity composed of two factors: masses and minorities. The latter are comprised of especially qualified individuals and groups. The masses are made up of persons not especially qualified. By masses, we do not therefore mean, either simply or even principally, the "working class," the working masses as a whole. The mass is the "average man." Thus, the merely quantitative – the multitude, the mass – becomes a qualitative determinant: it is the common quality, the social animal as stray, man in the measure in which he is undifferentiated from other men, man repeating in himself a generic type. What gain is there in this conversion of quantity into quality? Simply this: by means of quality, we can understand the genesis of quantity. It is as obvious as a platitude that the normal formation of a mass, a multitude, is based on a coincidence of desires, of ideas, of manners among the individuals who compose it. It may be pointed out that precisely the same happens in regard to any social group, however select it may claim to be. True enough: but an essential difference exists.

In those groups which are neither mass nor multitude, the effective cohesion of the members is based on some desire, idea, or ideal, which in itself alone excludes the majority of people. In order to form a minority –

221

of whatever kind it may be – it is first of all necessary that each member separate himself from the multitude for some *special*, relatively personal, reason. His agreement with the others who form the minority is, therefore, secondary, posterior to having adopted an individual attitude, having made himself *singular*; therefore, there is an agreement not to agree with others, a coincidence in not coinciding. A vivid example of this singularity is to be found in the case of the English Nonconformists: they concurred with each other only on their disconformity with the infinite multitude of others.[ii] This formation of a minority precisely in order to separate itself from the majority is a basic impulse. The poet Mallarmé, apropos of the select audience at a recital by a distinguished musician, wittily remarked that by the scarcity of its presence the audience was emphasizing the absence of the multitude.

In all truth, the masses, any mass, can make its presence felt as a psychological fact without the need for individuals to appear in agglomeration. We can tell a mass-man when we see one: one person can represent a mass phenomenon. The mass-man is anyone who does not value himself, for good or ill, by any particular criterion, and who says instead that he is "just like everybody else." Despite this ridiculous claim, he will not feel any disquiet, but rather feel reassured, smugly at ease, to be considered identical with all others. A truly humble man who attempts to evaluate his specific worth, and tries to find if he possesses any talent, or excels in any way, may discover in the end that he is endowed with no remarkable qualities, and may conclude that he is ungifted and depressingly ordinary. But he may still consider that he is not part of the mass, not in his own self a mass-man.

In speaking of "select minorities," universal misunderstanding holds sway and manages as usual to distort the meaning, and to ignore the fact that the select individual is not the petulant snob who thinks he is superior to others, but is, rather, the person who demands more from himself than do others, even when these demands are unattainable. For undoubtedly the most radical division to be made of humanity is between two types: those who demand much of themselves and assign themselves great tasks and duties and those who demand nothing in particular of themselves, for whom living is to be at all times what they already are, without any effort at perfection – buoys floating on the waves.

I am here reminded that orthodox Buddhism is composed of two distinct religions: one, more strict and difficult, the other more lax and easy: the Mahayana, the "great vehicle" or "great way," and the Hinayana, the "lesser vehicle," or "lesser way." The decisive difference lies in choosing one

[ii] Noncomformists were English Protestants who did not belong to the Church of England.

or the other vehicle, in making a maximum of demands on oneself or a minimum.

The division of society into masses and select minorities is not, then, a division into social classes, but into two kinds of men, and it does not depend on hierarchically superior or inferior classes, on upper classes or lower classes. Of course it is plain enough that among the superior classes, when they genuinely achieve this status and maintain it, there is more likelihood of finding men who choose the "great vehicle," while the inferior are those who normally are not concerned with quality. Strictly speaking, there are "masses" and minorities at all levels of society – within every social class. A characteristic of our times is the predominance, even in those groups who were traditionally selective, of mass and popular vulgarity. Even in intellectual life, which by its very essence assumes and requires certain qualifications, we see the progressive triumph of pseudo-intellectuals – unqualified, unqualifiable, and, in their own context, disqualified. The same holds true for the remnants of the nobility, whether male or female. On the other hand, it is not unusual to find among workers, who formerly might have served as the best example of the "mass," outstandingly disciplined minds and souls.

Then there are activities in society which by their very nature call for qualifications: activities and functions of the most diverse order which are special and cannot be carried out without special talent. Thus: artistic and aesthetic enterprises; the functioning of government; political judgment on public matters. Previously these special activities were in the hands of qualified minorities, or those alleged to be qualified. The masses did not try or aspire to intervene: they reckoned that if they did, they must acquire those special graces, and must cease being part of the mass. They knew their role well enough in a dynamic and functioning social order.

If we now revert to the assumptions made at the beginning, the facts will appear as clearly heralding a changed mass attitude. Everything indicates that the "public," that is, the mass, along with wielding power, has decided to occupy the foreground of social life, as well as the front-row seats, and to avail themselves of the pleasures formerly reserved for the few. It is obvious that those seats were never intended for the masses, for they are limited in number; so now there is crowding, making clear to the eye, with visible language, that a new phenomenon exists: the mass, without ceasing to be mass, supplants the minorities.

No one, I believe, begrudges the public's enjoying themselves in greater number and measure than before, since they now have the desire and the means to do so. The only resultant wrong is that the determination of the masses to usurp the place of the minority does not and cannot confine itself to the arena of pleasure alone, but is a generalized practice of the times.

223

And thus (to anticipate what we shall see later), it seems to me that recent political innovations signify nothing less than the political reign of the masses. Western democracy was formerly tempered by a large dash of liberalism and by a ritual trust in the law. In serving these principled ideas the individual bound himself to maintain some discipline in himself. Minorities could take refuge and find support in liberal principles and the judicial norm. Democracy and law (life in common under the law) were synonymous. Today we witness the triumph of hyperdemocracy in which the mass takes direct action oblivious of the law, imposing its own desires and tastes by material pressure. It is false to say that the masses have grown weary of politics and have handed over its operation to selected people. Exactly the opposite is true.

That is what used to happen: that was liberal democracy. The masses took it for granted that, after all, and despite the defects and faults of the select minorities, these minorities understood something more of political problems than they themselves did. Nowadays the mass believes it has the right to impose and lend force to notions deriving from its own platitudes. I doubt that any previous epoch of history has seen such direct government by the multitude as is current in our time. Thus I speak of hyperdemocracy.

The same happens in other orders of life, particularly in the intellectual order. I may be mistaken, but it seems that the writer nowadays, whenever he assumes the task of saying anything on any subject to which he has given thought, must bear in mind that the average reader, who has never pondered the matter – and always assuming that he reads the writer at all – does not read in order to learn anything, but rather reads him in order to pronounce judgment on whether or not the writer's ideas coincide with the pedestrian and commonplace notions the reader already carries in his head. If the individuals who make up the mass thought of themselves as specially qualified, we would have on our hands merely a case of personal error, not a matter of sociological subversion. *The characteristic note of our time is the dire truth that the mediocre soul, the commonplace mind, knowing itself to be mediocre, has the gall to assert its right to mediocrity, and goes on to impose itself wherever it can.* In the United States it is considered indecent to be different. The mass crushes everything different, everything outstanding, excellent, individual, select, and choice. Everybody who is not like everybody else, who does not think like everybody else, runs the risk of being eliminated. Of course "everybody else" is not *everybody*. In normal times, "everybody" was the complex union of mass with special, divergent minorities. Today, "everybody" means the mass, the masses – and only the masses.

Notes

1 I have also dealt with the theme that this essay develops in my book *España invertebrada*, published in 1921, in an article in *El Sol*, entitled "Masas" (1926), and in two lectures before the Association of the Friends of Art in Buenos Aires (in 1928). My purpose now is to review and complete what I have already said so that the result will be an organic doctrine on the most crucial fact of our time.

chapter eighteen

The Crisis of European Sciences and Transcendental Phenomenology

Edmund Husserl

Moravian-born German philosopher Edmund Husserl (1859–1938) is the inventor of twentieth-century phenomenology, perhaps the most important European philosophical reaction against an excessively scientific view of the world. Husserl regards phenomenology's demand that we return to concrete human experience as the proper fulfillment of modernity and as the antidote to the antihumanistic scientific naturalism that has perverted modernity. Husserl was not opposed to modern science, rationalism or foundationalism. He believed that phenomenology alone could provide the foundation for science and reason; it is the philosophical recapture of the source of all meaning and evidence in primary experience. Phenomenology was later taken by Heidegger in an explicitly antiscientific and antifoundationalist direction. Prevented by the Nazis from teaching because he was a Jew, Husserl delivered an invited lecture in Vienna in 1935 on "Philosophy in the Crisis of European Mankind" which became the basis for his last and unfinished book, *The Crisis of the European Sciences and Transcendental Phenomenology*. In the following selection from that book, he sees in the modern mathematical interpretation of nature, epitomized by the great seventeenth-century physicist and astronomer Galileo, the failed promise of modern thought.

Edmund Husserl, *The Crisis of European Sciences and Transcendental Phenomenology*, trans. David Carr (Evanston: Northwestern University Press, 1970), Part One, sec. 3–5, pp. 7–14 and Part Two, sec. 9h–9l, pp. 48–59.

The founding of the autonomy of European humanity through the new formulation of the idea of philosophy in the Renaissance

It was not always the case that science understood its demand for rigorously grounded truth in the sense of that *sort* of objectivity which dominates our positive sciences in respect to method and which, having its effect far beyond the sciences themselves, is the basis for the support and widespread acceptance of a philosophical and ideological positivism. The specifically human questions were not always banned from the realm of science; their intrinsic relationship to all the sciences – even to those of which man is not the subject matter, such as the natural sciences – was not left unconsidered. As long as this had not yet happened, science could claim significance – indeed, as we know, the major role – in the completely new shaping of European humanity which began with the Renaissance. Why science lost this leadership, why there occurred an essential change, a positivistic restriction of the idea of science – to understand this, according to its *deeper motives*, is of great importance for the purpose of these lectures.

In the Renaissance, as is well known, European humanity brings about a revolutionary change. It turns against its previous way of existing – the medieval – and disowns it, seeking to shape itself anew in freedom. Its admired model is ancient humanity. This mode of existence is what it wishes to reproduce in itself.

What does it hold to be essential to ancient man? After some hesitation, nothing less than the "philosophical" form of existence: freely giving oneself, one's whole life, its rule through pure reason or through philosophy. Theoretical philosophy is primary. A superior survey of the world must be launched, unfettered by myth and the whole tradition: universal knowledge, absolutely free from prejudice, of the world and man, ultimately recognizing in the world its inherent reason and teleology and its highest principle, God. Philosophy as theory frees not only the theorist but any philosophically educated person. And theoretical autonomy is followed by practical autonomy. According to the guiding ideal of the Renaissance, ancient man forms himself with insight through free reason. For this renewed "Platonism" this means not only that man should be changed ethically [but that] the whole human surrounding world, the political and social existence of mankind, must be fashioned anew through free reason, through the insights of a universal philosophy.

In accordance with this ancient model, recognized at first only by individuals and small groups, a theoretical philosophy should again be

227

developed which was not to be taken over blindly from the tradition but must grow out of independent inquiry and criticism.

It must be emphasized here that the idea of philosophy handed down from the ancients is not the concept of present-day schoolbooks, merely comprising a group of disciplines; in the first centuries of the modern period – even though it changes not insignificantly as soon as it is taken up – it retains the formal meaning of the one all-encompassing science, the science of the totality of what is. Sciences in the plural, all those sciences ever to be established or already under construction, are but dependent branches of the One Philosophy. In a bold, even extravagant, elevation of the meaning of universality, begun by Descartes, this new philosophy seeks nothing less than to encompass, in the unity of a theoretical system, all meaningful questions in a rigorous scientific manner, with an apodictically intelligible methodology, in an unending but rationally ordered progress of inquiry. Growing from generation to generation and forever, this one edifice of definitive, theoretically interrelated truths was to solve all conceivable problems – problems of fact and of reason, problems of temporality and eternity.

Thus the positivistic concept of science in our time is, historically speaking, a *residual concept*. It has dropped all the questions which had been considered under the now narrower, now broader concepts of metaphysics, including all questions vaguely termed "ultimate and highest." Examined closely, these and all the excluded questions have their inseparable unity in the fact that they contain, whether expressly or as implied in their meaning, the *problems of reason* – reason in all its particular forms. Reason is the explicit theme in the disciplines concerning knowledge (i.e. of true and genuine, rational knowledge), of true and genuine valuation (genuine values as values of reason), of ethical action (truly good acting, acting from practical reason); here reason is a title for "absolute," "eternal," "supertemporal," "unconditionally" valid ideas and ideals. If man becomes a "metaphysical" or specifically philosophical problem, then he is in question as a rational being; if his history is in question, it is a matter of the "meaning" or reason in history. The problem of God clearly contains the problem of "absolute" reason as the teleological source of all reason in the world – of the "meaning" of the world. Obviously even the question of immortality is a question of reason, as is the question of freedom. All these "metaphysical" questions, taken broadly – commonly called specifically philosophical questions – surpass the world understood as the universe of mere facts. They surpass it precisely as being questions with the idea of reason in mind. And they all claim a higher dignity than questions of fact, which are subordinated to them even in the order of inquiry. Positivism, in a manner of speaking, decapitates philosophy. Even the ancient idea of philosophy, as unified in the indivisible unity of all being, implied a meaningful order of being and thus of problems of being. Accordingly, metaphysics, the science of the ultimate and highest questions, was honored as the queen of the sciences; its spirit decided on the ultimate meaning of all knowledge supplied by the other sciences. This, too, was taken over by the reviving philosophy [of the Renaissance]; indeed, it even believed it had discovered the true, universal method through which such a systematic philosophy, culminating in metaphysics, could be constructed as a serious *philosophia perennis*.

In light of this we can understand the energy which animated all scientific undertakings, even the merely factual sciences of the lower level; in the eighteenth century (which called itself the philosophical century) it filled ever widening circles with enthusiasm for philosophy and for all the special sciences as its branches. Hence the ardent desire for learning, the zeal for a philosophical reform of education and of all of humanity's social and political forms of existence, which makes that much-abused Age of Enlightenment so admirable. We possess an undying testimony to this spirit in the glorious "Hymn to Joy" of Schiller and Beethoven. It is only with painful feelings that we can understand this hymn today. A greater contrast with our present situation is unthinkable.

The failure of the new science after its initial success; the unclarified motive for this failure

Now if the new humanity, animated and blessed with such an exalted spirit, did not hold its own, it must have been because it lost the inspiring belief in its ideal of a universal philosophy and in the scope of the new method. And such, indeed, was the case. It turned out that this method could bring unquestionable successes only in the positive sciences. But it was otherwise in metaphysics, i.e. in problems considered philosophical in the special sense – though hopeful, apparently successful beginnings were not lacking even here. Universal philosophy, in which these problems were related – unclearly – to the factual sciences, took the form of system-philosophies, which were impressive but unfortunately were not unified, indeed were mutually exclusive. If the eighteenth century still held the conviction of proceeding toward unity, of arriving at a critically unassailable edifice which grew theoretically from generation to generation, as was undisputedly the case in the universally admired positive sciences – this conviction could not survive for long. The belief in the ideal of philosophy and method, the guideline of all movements since the beginning of the modern era, began to waver; this happened not merely for the external motive that the contrast became monstrous between the repeated failures of metaphysics and the uninterrupted and ever increasing wave of theoretical and practical successes in the positive sciences. This much had its effect on outsiders as well as scientists, who, in the specialized business of the positive sciences, were fast becoming unphilosophical experts. But even among those theorists who were filled with the philosophical spirit, and thus were interested precisely in the highest metaphysical questions, a growing feeling of failure set in – and in their case because the most profound, yet quite *unclarified*, motives protested ever more loudly against the deeply rooted assumptions of the reigning ideal. There begins a long period, extending from Hume and Kant to our own time, of passionate struggle for a clear, reflective understanding of the true reasons for this centuries-old failure; it was a struggle, of course, only on the part of the few called and chosen ones; the mass of others quickly found and still find formulas with which to console themselves and their readers.

The ideal of universal philosophy and the process of its inner dissolution

The necessary consequence was a peculiar change in the whole way of thinking. Philosophy became a problem for itself, at first, understandably, in the form of the [problem of the] possibility of a metaphysics; and, following what we said earlier, this concerned implicitly the meaning and possibility of the whole problematics of reason. As for the positive sciences, at first they were untouchable. Yet the problem of a possible metaphysics also encompassed *eo ipso* that of the possibility of the factual sciences, since these had their relational meaning – that of truths merely for areas of what is – in the indivisible unity of philosophy. *Can reason and that-which-is be separated, where reason, as knowing, determines what is?* This question suffices to make clear in advance that the whole historical process has a remarkable form, one which becomes visible only through an interpretation of its hidden, innermost motivation. Its form is not that of a smooth development, not that of a continual growth of lasting spiritual acquisitions or of a transformation of spiritual configurations – concepts, theories, systems – which can be explained by means of the accidental historical situations. A definite ideal of a universal philosophy and its method forms the beginning; this is, so to speak, the primal establishment of the philosophical modern age and all its lines of development. But instead of being able to work itself out in fact, this ideal suffers an inner dissolution. As against attempts to carry out and newly fortify the ideal, this dissolution gives rise to revolutionary, more or less radical innovations. Thus the problem of the genuine ideal of universal philosophy and its genuine method now actually becomes the innermost driving force of all historical philosophical movements. But this is to say that, ultimately, all modern sciences drifted into a peculiar, increasingly puzzling crisis with regard to the meaning of their original founding as branches of philosophy, a meaning which they continued to bear within themselves. This is a crisis which does not encroach upon the theoretical and practical successes of the special sciences; yet it shakes to the foundations the whole meaning of their truth. This is not just a matter of a special form of culture – "science" or "philosophy" – as one among others belonging to European mankind. For the primal establishment of the new philosophy is, according to what was said earlier, the primal establishment of modern European humanity itself – humanity which seeks to renew itself radically, as against the foregoing medieval and ancient age, precisely and only through its new philosophy. Thus the crisis of philosophy implies the crisis of all modern sciences as members of the philosophical universe: at first a latent, then a more and more prominent crisis of European humanity itself in respect to the total meaningfulness of its cultural life, its total "*Existenz.*"[i]

Skepticism about the possibility of metaphysics, the collapse of the belief in a universal philosophy as the guide for the new man, actually represents a collapse of the belief in "reason," understood as the ancients opposed *epistēmē* to *doxa*.[ii] It is reason which ultimately gives meaning to everything that is thought to be, all things, values, and ends – their meaning understood as their normative relatedness to what, since the beginnings of philosophy, is meant by the word "truth" – truth in itself – and correlatively the term "what is" – ὄντως ὄν. Along with this falls the faith in "absolute" reason, through which the world has its meaning, the faith in the meaning of history, of humanity, the faith in man's freedom, that is, his capacity to secure rational meaning for his individual and common human existence.

If man loses this faith, it means nothing less than the loss of faith "in himself," in his own true being. This true being is not something he always already has, with the self-evidence of the "I am," but something he only has and can have in the form of the struggle for his truth, the struggle to make himself true. True being is *everywhere* an ideal goal, a task of *epistēmē* or "reason," as opposed to being which through *doxa* is merely thought to be, unquestioned and "obvious." Basically every person is acquainted with this difference – one related to his true and genuine humanity – just as truth as a goal or task is not unknown to him even in everyday life – though here it is merely isolated and relative. But this prefiguration is surpassed by philosophy: in its first, original establishment, ancient philos-

---

[i] Literally, "existence," but the term connotes the existential philosophies of Martin Heidegger and Karl Jaspers.
[ii] In Greek, knowledge and opinion, respectively.

231

ophy, it conceives of and takes as its task the exalted idea of universal knowledge concerning the totality of what is. Yet in the very attempt to fulfill it, the naïve obviousness of this task is increasingly transformed – as one feels already in the opposition of the ancient systems – into unintelligibility. More and more the history of philisophy, seen from within, takes on the character of a struggle for existence, i.e. a struggle between the philosophy which lives in the straightforward pursuit of its task – the philosophy of naïve faith in reason – and the skepticism which negates or repudiates it in empiricist fashion. Unremittingly, skepticism insists on the validity of the factually experienced world, that of actual experience, and finds in it nothing of reason or its ideas. Reason itself and its [object,] "that which is," become more and more enigmatic – reason as giving, of itself, meaning to the existing world and, correlatively, the world as existing through reason – until finally the *consciously* recognized world-problem of the deepest essential interrelation between reason and what is in general, the *enigma of all enigmas*, has to become the actual theme of inquiry.

Our interest is confined here to the philosophical modern age. But this is not merely a fragment of the greater historical phenomenon we have just described, that is, humanity struggling to understand itself (for this phrase expresses the whole phenomenon). Rather – as the reestablishment of philosophy with a new universal task and at the same time with the sense of a renaissance of ancient philosophy – it is at once a repetition and a universal transformation of meaning. In this it feels called to initiate a new age, completely sure of its idea of philosophy and its true method, and also certain of having overcome all previous naïvetés, and thus all skepticism, through the radicalism of its new beginning. But it is the fate of the philosophical modern age, laden with its own unnoticed naïvetés, that it has first to seek out, in the course of a gradual self-disclosure motivated by new struggles, the definitive idea of philosophy, its true subject matter and its true method; it has first to discover the genuine world-enigmas and steer them in the direction of a solution.

As men of the present, having grown up in this development, we find ourselves in the greatest danger of drowning in the skeptical deluge and thereby losing our hold on our own truth. As we reflect in this plight, we gaze backward into the history of our present humanity. We can gain self-understanding, and thus inner support, only by elucidating the unitary meaning which is inborn in this history from its origin through the newly established task [of the Renaissance], the driving force of all [modern] philosophical attempts.

The life-world as the forgotten
meaning-fundament of natural science

But now we must note something of the highest importance that occurred
even as early as Galileo: the surreptitious substitution of the mathematically substructed world of idealities for the only real world the one that is
actually given through perception, that is ever experienced and experienceable – our everyday life-world. This substitution was promptly passed on
to his successors, the physicists of all the succeeding centuries.

Galileo was himself an heir in respect to pure geometry. The inherited
geometry, the inherited manner of "intuitive" conceptualizing, proving,
constructing, was no longer original geometry: in this sort of "intuitive-
ness" it was already empty of meaning. Even ancient geometry was, in its
way, τέχνη,[iii] removed from the sources of truly immediate intuition and
originally intuitive thinking, sources from which the so-called geometrical
intuition, i.e. that which operates with idealities, has at first derived its
meaning. The geometry of idealities was preceded by the practical art of
surveying, which knew nothing of idealities. Yet such a pregeometrical
achievement was a meaning- fundament for geometry, a fundament for the
great invention of idealization; the latter encompassed the invention of the
ideal world of geometry, or rather the methodology of the objectifying
determination of idealit'es through the constructions which create "mathematical existence." It was a fateful omission that Galileo did not inquire
back into the original meaning-giving achievement which, as idealization
practiced on the original ground of all theoretical and practical life – the
immediately intuited world (and here especially the empirically intuited
world of bodies) – resulted in the geometrical ideal constructions. He did
not reflect closely on all this: on how the free, imaginative variation of this
world and its shapes results only in possible empirically intuitable shapes
and not in exact shapes; on what sort of motivation and what new
achievement was required for genuinely geometric idealization. For in the
case of inherited geometrical method, these functions were no longer being
vitally practiced; much less were they reflectively brought to theoretical
consciousness as methods which realize the meaning of exactness from the
inside. Thus it could appear that geometry, with its own immediately
evident a priori "intuition" and the thinking which operates with it,
produces a self-sufficient, absolute truth which, as such – "obviously" –
could be applied without further ado. That this obviousness was an illusion

---

[iii] The Greek term *technē* referring to productive art or skill (including fine art, crafts,
engineering, etc.).

– as we have pointed out above in general terms, thinking for ourselves in the course of our exposition of Galileo's thoughts – that even the meaning of the application of geometry has complicated sources: this remained hidden for Galileo and the ensuing period. Immediately with Galileo, then, begins the surreptitious substitution of idealized nature for prescientifically intuited nature.

Thus all the occasional (even "philosophical") reflections which go from technical [scientific] work back to its true meaning always stop at idealized nature; they do not carry out the reflection radically, going back to the ultimate purpose which the new science, together with the geometry which is inseparable from it, growing out of prescientific life and its surrounding world, was from the beginning supposed to serve: a purpose which necessarily lay *in* this prescientific life and was related to its life-world. Man (including the natural scientist), living in this world, could put all his practical and theoretical questions only to *it* – could refer in his theories only to it, in its open, endless horizons of things unknown. All knowledge of laws could be knowledge only of predictions, grasped as lawful, about occurrences of actual or possible experiential phenomena, predictions which are indicated when experience is broadened through observations and experiments penetrating systematically into unknown horizons, and which are verified in the manner of inductions. To be sure, everyday induction grew into induction according to scientific method, but that changes nothing of the essential meaning of the pregiven world as the horizon of all meaningful induction. It is this world that we find to be the world of all known and unknown realities. To it, the world of actually experiencing intuition, belongs the form of space-time together with all the bodily shapes incorporated in it; it is in this world that we ourselves live, in accord with our bodily, personal way of being. But here we find nothing of geometrical idealities, no geometrical space or mathematical time with all their shapes.

This is an important remark, even though it is so trivial. Yet this triviality has been buried precisely by exact science, indeed since the days of ancient geometry, through that substitution of a methodically idealized achievement for what is given immediately as actuality presupposed in all idealization, given by a [type of] verification which is, in its own way, unsurpassable. This actually intuited, actually experienced and experienceable world, in which practically our whole life takes place, remains unchanged as what it is, in its own essential structure and its own concrete causal style, whatever we may do with or without techniques. Thus it is also not changed by the fact that we invent a particular technique, the geometrical and Galilean technique which is called physics. What do we actually accomplish through this technique? Nothing but *prediction* extended to infinity. All life rests upon prediction or, as we can say, upon induction. In the most primitive way, even the ontic certainty of any straightforward experience is inductive. Things "seen" are always more than what we "really and actually" see of them. Seeing, perceiving, is essentially having-something-itself and at the same time having-something-in-advance, meaning-something-in-advance. All praxis, with its projects, involves inductions; it is just that ordinary inductive knowledge (predictions), even if expressly formulated and "verified," is "artless" compared to the artful "methodical" inductions which can be carried to infinity through the method of Galilean physics with its great productivity.

In geometrical and natural-scientific mathematization, in the open infinity of possible experiences, we measure the life-world – the world constantly given to us as actual in our concrete world-life – for a well-fitting *garb of ideas*, that of the so-called objectively scientific truths. That is, through a method which (as we hope) can be really carried out in every particular and constantly verified, we first construct numerical indices for the actual and possible sensible plena of the concretely intuited shapes of the life-world, and in this way we obtain possibilities of predicting concrete occurrences in the intuitively given life-world, occurrences which are not yet or no longer actually given. And this kind of prediction infinitely surpasses the accomplishment of everyday prediction.

Mathematics and mathematical science, as a garb of ideas, or the garb of symbols of the symbolic mathematical theories, encompasses everything which, for scientists and the educated generally, *represents* the life-world, *dresses it up* as "objectively actual and true" nature. It is through the garb of ideas that we take for *true being* what is actually a *method* – a method which is designed for the purpose of progressively improving, *in infinitum*, through "scientific" predictions, those rough predictions which are the only ones originally possible within the sphere of what is actually experienced and experienceable in the life-world. It is because of the disguise of ideas that the true meaning of the method, the formulae, the "theories," remained unintelligible and, in the naïve formation of the method, was *never* understood.

Thus no one was ever made conscious of the radical problem of *how* this sort of naïveté actually became possible and is still possible as a living historical fact; how a method which is actually directed toward a goal, the systematic solution of an endless scientific task, and which continually achieves undoubted results, could ever grow up and be able to function usefully through the centuries when no one possessed a real understanding of the actual meaning and the internal necessity of such accomplishments. What was lacking, and what is still lacking, is the actual self-evidence through which he who knows and accomplishes can give himself an account, not only of what he does that is new and what he works with, but also of the implications of meaning which are closed off through

235

sedimentation or traditionalization, i.e. of the constant presuppositions of his [own] constructions, concepts, propositions, theories. Are science and its method not like a machine, reliable in accomplishing obviously very useful things, a machine everyone can learn to operate correctly without in the least understanding the inner possibility and necessity of this sort of accomplishment? But was geometry, was science, capable of being designed in advance, like a machine, without an understanding which was, in a similar sense, complete – scientific? Does this not lead to a *regressus in infinitum?*

Finally, does this problem not link up with the problem of the instincts in the usual sense? Is it not the problem of *hidden reason*, which knows itself as reason only when it has become manifest?

Galileo, the discoverer – or, in order to do justice to his precursors, the consummating discoverer – of physics, or physical nature, is at once a discovering and a concealing genius. He discovers mathematical nature, the methodical idea, he blazes the trail for the infinite number of physical discoveries and discoverers. By contrast to the universal causality of the intuitively given world (as its invariant form), he discovers what has since been called simply the law of causality, the "a priori form" of the "true" (idealized and mathematized) world, the "law of exact lawfulness" according to which every occurrence in "nature" – idealized nature – must come under exact laws. All this is discovery-concealment, and to the present day we accept it as straightforward truth. In principle nothing is changed by the supposedly philosophically revolutionary critique of the "classical law of causality" made by recent atomic physics. For in spite of all that is new, what is essential in principle, it seems to me, remains: namely, nature, which is in itself mathematical; it is given in formulae, and it can be interpreted only in terms of the formulae.

I am of course quite serious in placing and continuing to place Galileo at the top of the list of the greatest discoverers of modern times. Naturally I also admire quite seriously the great discoverers of classical and postclassical physics and their intellectual accomplishment, which, far from being merely mechanical, was in fact astounding in the highest sense. This accomplishment is not at all disparaged by the above elucidation of it as τέχνη or by the critique in terms of principle, which shows that the true meaning of these theories – the meaning which is genuine in terms of their origins – remained and had to remain hidden from the physicists, including the great and the greatest. It is not a question of a meaning which has been slipped in through metaphysical mystification or speculation; it is, rather, with the most compelling self-evidence, the true, the only real meaning of these theories, as opposed to the meaning of being a *method*, which has its own comprehensibility in operating with the formulae and their practical application, technique.

How what we have said up to now is still one-sided, and what horizons of problems, leading into new dimensions, have not been dealt with adequately – horizons which can be opened up only through a reflection on this life-world and man as its subject – can be shown only when we are much further advanced in the elucidation of the historical development according to its innermost moving forces.

Portentous misunderstandings resulting from lack of clarity about the meaning of mathematization

With Galileo's mathematizing reinterpretation of nature, false consequences established themselves even beyond the realm of nature which were so intimately connected with this reinterpretation that they could dominate all further developments of views about the world up to the present day. I mean Galileo's famous doctrine of the merely subjective character of the specific sense-qualities, which soon afterward was consistently formulated by Hobbes as the doctrine of the subjectivity of all concrete phenomena of sensibly intuitive nature and world in general. The phenomena are only in the subjects; they are there only as causal results of events taking place in true nature, which events exist only with mathematical properties. If the intuited world of our life is merely subjective, then all the truths of pre- and extrascientific life which have to do with its factual being are deprived of value. They have meaning only insofar as they, while themselves false, vaguely indicate an in-itself which lies behind this world of possible experience and is transcendent in respect to it.

In connection with this we arrive at a further consequence of the new formation of meaning, a self-interpretation of the physicists which grows out of this new formation of meaning as "obvious" and which was dominant until recently:

Nature is, in its "true being-in-itself," mathematical. The *pure* mathematics of space-time procures knowledge, with apodictic self-evidence, of a set of laws of this "in-itself" which are unconditionally, universally valid. This knowledge is immediate in the case of the axiomatic elementary laws of the a priori constructions and comes to be through infinite mediations in the case of the other laws. In respect to the space-time form of nature we possess the "innate" faculty (as it is later called) of knowing with definiteness true being-in-itself as mathematically ideal being (before all actual experience). Thus implicitly the space-time form is itself innate in us.

It is otherwise with the more concrete universal lawfulness of nature, although it, too, is mathematical through and through. It is inductively accessible a posteriori through factual experiential data. In a supposedly fully intelligible way, the a priori mathematics of spatiotemporal shapes is sharply distinguished from natural science which, though it applies pure mathematics, is inductive. Or, one can also say: the purely mathematic relationship of ground and consequent is sharply distinguished from that of real ground and real consequent, i.e. that of natural causality.

And yet an uneasy feeling of obscurity gradually asserts itself concerning the relation between the mathematics of nature and the mathematics of spatiotemporal form, which, after all, belongs to the former, between the latter "innate" and the former "non-innate" mathematics. Compared to the absolute knowledge we ascribe to God the creator, one says to oneself, our knowledge in pure mathematics has only one lack, i.e. that, while it is always absolutely self-evident, it requires a systematic process in order to bring to realization as knowing, i.e. as explicit mathematics, all the shapes that "exist" in the spatiotemporal form. In respect to what exists concretely in nature, by contrast, we have no a priori self-evidence at all. The whole mathematics of nature, beyond the spatiotemporal form, we must arrive at inductively through facts of experience. But is nature in itself not thoroughly mathematical? Must it not also be thought of as a coherent mathematical system? Must it not be capable of being represented in a coherent mathematics of nature, precisely the one that natural science is always merely seeking, as encompassed by a system of laws which is "axiomatic" in respect of form, the axioms of which are always only hypotheses and thus never really attainable? Why is it, actually, that they are not? Why is it that we have no prospect of discovering nature's own axiomatic system as one whose axioms are apodictically self-evident? Is it because the appropriate innate faculty is lacking in us in a factual sense?

In the superficialized, more or less already technized meaning-pattern of physics and its methods, the difference in question was "completely clear": it is the difference between "pure" (a priori) and "applied" mathematics, between "mathematical existence" (in the sense of pure mathematics) and the existence of the mathematically formed real (i.e. that of which mathematical shape is a component in the sense of a real property). And yet even such an outstanding genius as Leibniz struggled for a long time with the problem of grasping the correct meaning of the two kinds of existence – i.e. universally the existence of the spatiotemporal form as purely geometrical and the existence of universal mathematical nature with its factual, real form – and of understanding the correct relation of each to the other.

The significance of these obscurities for the Kantian problem of synthetic judgments a priori and for his division between the synthetic judgments of pure mathematics and those of natural science will concern us in detail later.[iv]

The obscurity was strengthened and transformed still later with the development and constant methodical application of pure formal mathematics. "Space" and the purely *formally* defined "Euclidean manifold" were confused; the *true axiom* (i.e. in the old, customary sense of the term), as an ideal norm with unconditional validity, grasped with self-evidence in pure geometric thought or in arithmetical, purely logical thought, was confused with the *inauthentic* "axiom" – a word which in the theory of manifolds signifies not judgments ("propositions") but forms of propositions as components of the definition of a "manifold" to be constructed formally without internal contradiction.

Fundamental significance of the problem of the origin of mathematical natural science

Like all the obscurities exhibited earlier, [the preceding] follow from the transformation of a formation of meaning which was originally vital, or rather of the originally vital consciousness of the task which gives rise to the methods, each with its special sense. The developed method, the progressive fulfillment of the task, is, as method, an art ($\tau\acute{\epsilon}\chi\nu\eta$) which is handed down; but its true meaning is not necessarily handed down with it. And it is precisely for this reason that a theoretical task and achievement like that of a natural science (or any science of the world) – which can master the infinity of its subject matter only through infinities of method and can master the latter infinities only by means of a technical thought and activity which are empty of meaning – can only be and remain meaningful in a true and original sense *if* the scientist has developed in himself the ability to *inquire back* into the *original meaning* of all his meaning-structures and methods, i.e. into the *historical meaning of their primal establishment*, and especially into the meaning of all the *inherited meanings* taken over unnoticed in this primal establishment, as well as those taken over later on.

But the mathematician, the natural scientist, at best a highly brilliant technician of the method – to which he owes the discoveries which are his only aim – is normally not at all able to carry out such reflections. In his actual sphere of inquiry and discovery he does not know at all that

---

[iv] Kant argued that mathematical and scientific knowledge is grounded in judgments universally true, independent of experience (a priori) yet not merely by definition ("synthetic," not "analytic").

Edmund Husserl

everything these reflections must clarify is even in *need* of clarification, and this for the sake of that interest which is decisive for a philosophy or a science, i.e. the interest in true knowledge of the *world itself, nature itself*. And this is precisely what has been lost through a science which is given as a tradition and which has become a τέχνη, insofar as this interest played a determining role at all in its primal establishment. Every attempt to lead the scientist to such reflections, if it comes from a nonmathematical, non-scientific circle of scholars, is rejected as "metaphysical." The professional who has dedicated his life to these sciences must, after all – it seems so obvious to him – know best what he is attempting and accomplishing in his work. The philosophical needs ("philosophicomathematical," "philosoph-icoscientific" needs), aroused even in these scholars by historical motives to be elucidated later, are satisfied by themselves in a way that is sufficient for them – but of course in such a way that the whole dimension which must be inquired into is not seen at all and thus not at all dealt with.

Characterization of the method of our exposition

In conclusion let us say a word about the *method* we have followed in the very intricate considerations of this section, in the service of our over-all aim. The historical reflections we embarked upon, in order to arrive at the self-understanding which is so necessary in our philosophical situation, demanded clarity concerning the *origin of the modern spirit* and, together with that – because of the significance, which cannot be overestimated, of mathematics and mathematical natural science – clarity concerning the origin of these sciences. That is to say: clarity concerning the original motivation and movement of thought which led to the conceiving of their idea of nature, and from there to the movement of its realization in the actual development of natural science itself. With Galileo the idea in question appears for the first time, so to speak, as full-blown; thus I have linked all our considerations to his name, in a certain sense simplifying and idealizing the matter; a more exact historical analysis would have to take account of how much of his thought he owed to his "predecessors." (I shall continue, incidentally, and for good reasons, in a similar fashion.) In respect to the situation as he found it and to the way in which it had to motivate him and did motivate him according to his known pronounce-ments, much can be established immediately, so that we understand the beginning of the whole bestowal of meaning upon natural science. But in this very process we come upon the shifts and concealments of meaning of later and most recent times. For we ourselves, who are carrying out these reflections (and, as I may assume, my readers), stand under the *spell* of

240

these times. Being caught up in them, we at first have no inkling of these shifts of meaning – we who all think we know so well what mathematics and natural science "are" and do. For who today has not learned this in school? But the first elucidation of the original meaning of the new natural science and of its novel methodical style makes felt something of the later shifts in meaning. And clearly they influence, or at least make more difficult, the analysis of the motivation [of science].

Thus we find ourselves in a sort of circle. The understanding of the beginning is to be gained fully only by starting with science as given in its present-day form, looking back at its development. But in the absence of an understanding of the *beginnings* the development is mute as a *development of meaning*. Thus we have no other choice than to proceed forward and backward in a zigzag pattern; the one must help the other in an interplay. Relative clarification on one side brings some elucidation on the other, which in turn casts light back on the former. In this sort of historical consideration and historical critique, then, which begins with Galileo (and immediately afterward with Descartes) and must follow the temporal order, we nevertheless have constantly to make *historical leaps* which are thus not digressions but necessities. They are necessities if we take upon ourselves, as we have said, the task of self-reflection which grows out of the "breakdown" situation of our time, with its "breakdown of science" itself. Of first importance for this task, however, is the reflection on the original meaning of the new sciences, above all that of the exact science of nature; for the latter was and still is, through all its shifts of meaning and misplaced self-interpretations, of decisive significance (in a manner to be pursued further) for the becoming and being of the modern positive sciences, of modern philosophy, and indeed of the spirit of modern European humanity in general.

The following also belongs to the method: readers, especially those in the natural sciences, may have become irritated by the fact – it may appear to them almost as dilettantism – that no use has been made of the natural-scientific way of speaking. It has been consciously avoided. In the kind of thinking which everywhere tries to bring "original intuition" to the fore – that is, the pre-and extrascientific life-world, which contains within itself all actual life, including the scientific life of thought, and nourishes it as the source of all technical constructions of meaning – in this kind of thinking one of the greatest difficulties is that one must choose the naïve way of speaking of [everyday] life, but must also use it in a way which is appropriate for rendering evident what is shown.

It will gradually become clearer, and finally be completely clear, that the proper return to the naïveté of life – but in a reflection which rises above this naïveté – is the only possible way to overcome the philosophical naïveté which lies in the [supposedly] "scientific" character of traditional

241

objectivistic philosophy. This will open the gates to the new dimension we have repeatedly referred to in advance.

We must add here that, properly understood, all our expositions are supposed to aid understanding only from the relative [perspective of our] position and that our expression of doubts, given in the criticisms [of Galileo, etc.] (doubts which we, living in the present, now carrying out our reflections, do not conceal), has the methodical function of preparing ideas and methods which will gradually take shape in us as results of our reflection and will serve to liberate us. All reflection undertaken for "existential" reasons is naturally *critical*. But we shall not fail to bring to a reflective form of knowledge, later on, the basic meaning of the course of our reflections and our particular kind of critique.

chapter nineteen

Dialectic of Enlightenment
Max Horkheimer and Theodor Adorno

Max Horkheimer (1895–1973) and Theodor Adorno (1903–70) were members of
the *Institut für Sozialforschung* (Institute for Social Research) at Frankfurt, Germany.
Their work combined the perspectives of Hegel, Marx, and Freud in an analysis of
social and cultural phenomena. Forced to flee in 1934, they eventually settled in
California, where they composed their classic *Dialectic of Enlightenment* (1944). It is
devoted to answering that most poignant question for any mid-century German
intellectual: how at the apparent height of Enlightened culture in the twentieth
century could the most barbaric of social movements, National Socialism, emerge?
They argue that the Enlightenment's own tendencies are self-negating ("dialectical"). Skeptical, Enlightened reason empties itself of all religious and metaphysical
sources of value, leaving only power and self-interest as its goals. They see this
dialectic prophesied in the literary work of the Marquis de Sade, and actualized in
mass culture and in the new political barbarism of the twentieth century. Their
stunning and frightening conclusion is that Enlightenment is the only road to
social freedom *and* it inevitably leads to totalitarianism. Modernity leaves us, then,
in an impossible situation.

As a nominalist movement,[i] the Enlightenment calls a halt before the
nomen, the exclusive, precise concept, the proper name. Whether – as some
assert[1] – proper names were originally species names as well, can no longer
be ascertained, yet the former have not shared the fate of the latter. The
substantial ego refuted by Hume and Mach is not synonymous with the
name. In Jewish religion, in which the idea of the patriarchate culminates
in the destruction of myth, the bond between name and being is still
recognized in the ban on pronouncing the name of God. The disenchanted

Max Horkheimer and Theodor Adorno, *Dialectic of Enlightenment*, trans. John Cumming (New
York: Seabury, 1972): from "The Concept of Enlightenment," pp.23–9; and from "Juliette,
or Enlightenment and Morality," pp.81–93.

[i] Nominalism claims that only particular things exist, so that general terms (e.g. "horse")
do not refer to a real universal (e.g. horse-ness) but only serve as a sign for any and all
particulars (e.g. particular horses).

world of Judaism conciliates magic by negating it in the idea of God. Jewish religion allows no word that would alleviate the despair of all that is mortal. It associates hope only with the prohibition against calling on what is false as God, against invoking the finite as the infinite, lies as truth. The guarantee of salvation lies in the rejection of any belief that would replace it: it is knowledge obtained in the denunciation of illusion. Admittedly, the negation is not abstract. The contesting of every positive without distinction, the stereotype formula of vanity, as used by Buddhism, sets itself above the prohibition against naming the Absolute with names: just as far above as its contrary, pantheism; or its caricature, bourgeois skepticism. Explanations of the world as all or nothing are mythologies, and guaranteed roads to redemption are sublimated magic practices. The self-satisfaction of knowing in advance and the transfiguration of negativity into redemption are untrue forms of resistance against deception. The justness of the image is preserved in the faithful pursuit of its prohibition. This pursuit, "determinate negativity"[2] does not receive from the sovereignty of the abstract concept any immunity against corrupting intuition, as does skepticism, to which both true and false are equally vain. Determinate negation rejects the defective ideas of the absolute, the idols, differently than does rigorism, which confronts them with the Idea that they cannot match up to. Dialectic, on the contrary, interprets every image as writing. It shows how the admission of its falsity is to be read in the lines of its features – a confession that deprives it of its power and appropriates it for truth. With the notion of determinate negativity, Hegel revealed an element that distinguishes the Enlightenment from the positivist degeneracy to which he attributes it. By ultimately making the conscious result of the whole process of negation – totality in system and in history – into an absolute, he of course contravened the prohibition and himself lapsed into mythology.

This did not happen merely to his philosophy as the apotheosis of progressive thought, but to the Enlightenment itself, as the sobriety which it thought distinguished it from Hegel and from metaphysics. For enlightenment is as totalitarian as any system. Its untruth does not consist in what its romantic enemies have always reproached it for: analytical method, return to elements, dissolution through reflective thought; but instead in the fact that for enlightenment the process is always decided from the start. When in mathematical procedure the unknown becomes the unknown quantity of an equation, this marks it as the well-known even before any value is inserted. Nature, before and after the quantum theory, is that which is to be comprehended mathematically; even what cannot be made to agree, indissolubility and irrationality, is converted by means of mathematical theorems. In the anticipatory indentification of the wholly conceived and mathematized world with truth, enlightenment intends to

244

secure itself against the return of the mythic. It confounds thought and mathematics. In this way the latter is, so to speak, released and made into an absolute instance. "An infinite world, in this case a world of idealities, is conceived as one whose objects do not accede singly, imperfectly, and as if by chance to our cognition, but are attained by a rational, systematically unified method – in a process of infinite progression – so that each object is ultimately apparent according to its full inherent being . . . In the Galilean mathematization of the world, however, *this selfness* is idealized under the guidance of the new mathematics: in modern terms, it becomes itself a mathematical multiplicity."[3] Thinking objectifies itself to become an automatic, self-activating process; an impersonation of the machine that it produces itself so that ultimately the machine can replace it. Enlightenment[4] has put aside the classic requirement of thinking about thought – Fichte is its extreme manifestation – because it wants to avoid the precept of dictating practice that Fichte himself wished to obey.[ii] Mathematical procedure became, so to speak, the ritual of thinking. In spite of the axiomatic self-restriction, it establishes itself as necessary and objective: it turns thought into a thing, an instrument – which is its own term for it. But this kind of mimesis, in which universal thought is equalized, so turns the actual into the unique, that even atheism itself is subjected to the ban on metaphysics. For positivism, which represents the court of judgment of enlightened reason, to digress into intelligible worlds is no longer merely forbidden, but meaningless prattle. It does not need – fortunately – to be atheistic, because objectified thinking cannot even raise the problem. The positivist censor lets the established cult escape as willingly as art – as a cognition-free special area of social activity; but he will never permit that denial of it which itself claims to be knowledge. For the scientific mind, the separation of thought from business for the purpose of adjusting actuality, departure from the privileged area of real existence, is as insane and self-destructive as the primitive magician would consider stepping out of the magic circle he has prepared for his invocation; in both cases the offense against the taboo will actually result in the malefactor's ruin. The mastery of nature draws the circle into which the criticism of pure reason banished thought. Kant joined the theory of its unceasingly laborious advance into infinity with an insistence on its deficiency and everlasting limitation. His judgment is an oracle. There is no form of being in the world that science could not penetrate, but what can be penetrated by science is not being. According to Kant, philosophic judgment aims at the new; and yet it recognizes nothing new, since it always merely recalls what reason has always deposited in the object. But there is a reckoning for this form of thinking that considers itself secure in the various departments of science

[ii] German philosopher, Johann Gottlieb Fichte (1762–1814).

245

– secure from the dreams of a ghost-seer: world domination over nature turns against the thinking subject himself; nothing is left of him but that eternally same *I think* that must accompany all my ideas. Subject and object are both rendered ineffectual. The abstract self, which justifies record-making and systematization, has nothing set over against it but the abstract material which possesses no other quality than to be a substrate of such possession. The equation of spirit and world arises eventually, but only with a mutual restriction of both sides. The reduction of thought to a mathematical apparatus conceals the sanction of the world as its own yardstick. What appears to be the triumph of subjective rationality, the subjection of all reality to logical formalism, is paid for by the obedient subjection of reason to what is directly given. What is abandoned is the whole claim and approach of knowledge: to comprehend the given as such; not merely to determine the abstract spatiotemporal relations of the facts which allow them just to be grasped, but on the contrary to conceive them as the superficies, as mediated conceptual moments which come to fulfillment only in the development of their social, historical, and human significance. The task of cognition does not consist in mere apprehension, classification, and calculation, but in the determinate negation of each immediacy. Mathematical formalism, however, whose medium is number, the most abstract form of the immediate, instead holds thinking firmly to mere immediacy. Factuality wins the day; cognition is restricted to its repetition; and thought becomes mere tautology. The more the machinery of thought subjects existence to itself, the more blind its resignation in reproducing existence. Hence enlightenment returns to mythology, which it never really knew how to elude. For in its figures mythology had the essence of the *status quo:* cycle, fate, and domination of the world reflected as the truth and deprived of hope. In both the pregnancy of the mythical image and the clarity of the scientific formula, the everlastingness of the factual is confirmed and mere existence pure and simple expressed as the meaning which it forbids. The world as a gigantic analytic judgment, the only one left over from all the dreams of science, is of the same mold as the cosmic myth which associated the cycle of spring and autumn with the kidnapping of Persephone. The uniqueness of the mythic process, which tends to legitimize factuality, is deception. Originally the carrying off of the goddess was directly synonymous with the dying of nature. It repeated itself every autumn, and even the repetition was not the result of the buried one but the same every time. With the rigidification of the consciousness of time, the process was fixed in the past as a unique one, and in each new cycle of the seasons an attempt was made ritually to appease fear of death by recourse to what was long past. But the separation is ineffective. Through the establishment of a unique past, the cycle takes on the character of inevitability, and dread radiates from the age-old occurrence to make every event its mere repetition. The absorption of factuality, whether into legendary prehistory or into mathematical formalism, the symbolical relation of the contemporary to the mythic process in the rite or to the abstract category in science, makes the new appear as the predetermined, which is accordingly the old. Not existence but knowledge is without hope, for in the pictorical or mathematical symbol it appropriates and perpetuates existence as a schema.

In the enlightened world, mythology has entered into the profane. In its blank purity, the reality which has been cleansed of demons and their conceptual descendants assumes the numinous character which the ancient world attributed to demons. Under the title of brute facts, the social injustice from which they proceed is now as assuredly sacred a preserve as the medicine man was sacrosanct by reason of the protection of his gods. It is not merely that domination is paid for by the alienation of men from the objects dominated: with the objectification of spirit, the very relations of men – even those of the individual to himself – were bewitched. The individual is reduced to the nodal point of the conventional responses and modes of operation expected of him. Animism spiritualized the object, whereas industrialism objectifies the spirits of men. Automatically, the economic apparatus, even before total planning, equips commodities with the values which decide human behavior. Since, with the end of free exchange, commodities lost all their economic qualities except for fetishism, the latter has extended its arthritic influence over all aspects of social life. Through the countless agencies of mass production and its culture the conventionalized modes of behavior are impressed on the individual as the only natural, respectable, and rational ones. He defines himself only as a thing, as a static element, as success or failure. His yardstick is self-preservation, successful or unsuccessful approximation to the objectivity of his function and the models established for it. Everything else, idea and crime, suffers the force of the collective, which monitors it from the classroom to the trade union. But even the threatening collective belongs only to the deceptive surface, beneath which are concealed the powers which manipulate it as the instrument of power. Its brutality, which keeps the individual up to scratch, represents the true quality of men as little as value represents the things which he consumes. The demonically distorted form which things and men have assumed in the light of unprejudiced cognition, indicates domination, the principle which effected the specification of *mana* in spirits and gods[iii] and occurred in the jugglery of magicians and medicine men. The fatality by means of which prehistory sanctioned the incomprehensibility of death is transferred to wholly comprehensible real

---

[iii] "*Mana*", divine or magical force believed to permeate the world in animistic religion.

existence. The noontide panic fear in which men suddenly became aware of nature as totality has found its like in the panic which nowadays is ready to break out at every moment: men expect that the world, which is without any issue, will be set on fire by a totality which they themselves are and over which they have no control. . . .

Enlightenment, according to Kant, is " . . . man's emergence from his self-incurred immaturity. Immaturity is the inability to use one's understanding without the guidance of another person."[5] "Understanding without the guidance of another person" is understanding guided by reason. This means no more than that, by virtue of its own consistency, it organizes the individual data of cognition into a system. "Reason has . . . for its object only the understanding and its purposive employment."[6] It makes "a certain collective unity the aim of the operations of the understanding,"[7] and this unity is the system. Its rules are the indications for a hierarchical construction of concepts. For Kant, as for Leibniz and Descartes, rationality consists of "completing the systematical connection, both in ascending to higher genera, and in descending to lower species."[8] The "systematizing" of knowledge is "its coherence according to one principle."[9] In the Enlightenment's interpretation, thinking is the creation of unified, scientific order and the derivation of factual knowledge from principles, whether the latter are elucidated as arbitrarily postulated axioms, innate ideas, or higher abstractions. Logical laws produce the most general relations within the arrangement, and define them. Unity resides in agreement. The resolution of contradiction is the system *in nuce*.[iv] Knowledge consists of subsumption under principles. Any other than systematically directed thinking is unoriented or authoritarian. Reason contributes only the idea of systematic unity, the formal elements of fixed conceptual coherence. Every substantial goal which men might adduce as an alleged rational insight is, in the strict Enlightenment sense, delusion, lies or "rationalization," even though individual philosophers try to advance from this conclusion toward the postulate of philanthropic emotion. Reason is the "faculty . . . of deducing the particular from the general."[10] According to Kant, the homogeneity of the general and the particular is guaranteed by the "schematism of pure understanding," or the unconscious operation of the intellectual mechanism which structures perception in accordance with the understanding. The understanding impresses the intelligibility of the matter (which subjective judgment discovers there) on it as an objective quality, before it enters into the ego. Without such a schematism – in short,

---

[iv] In a nut shell.

without intellectual perception – no impression would harmonize with a concept, and no category with an example; and the unity of thought (let alone of system) toward which everything is directed would not prevail. To produce this unity is the conscious task of science. If "all empirical laws . . . are only special determinations of the pure laws of the understanding,"[11] research must always ensure that the principles are always properly linked with factual judgments. "This concurrence of nature with our cognitive faculty is an *a priori* assumption . . . of judgment."[12] It is the "guideline"[13] for organized experience.

The system must be kept in harmony with nature; just as the facts are predicted from the system, so they must confirm it Facts, however, belong to practice; they always characterize the individual's contact with nature as a social object: experience is always real action and suffering. In physics, of course, perception – by means of which a theory may be proved – is usually reduced to the electric sparks visible in the experimental apparatus. Its absence is as a rule without practical consequence, for it destroys no more than a theory – or possibly the career of the assistant responsible for setting up the experiment. But laboratory conditions constitute the exception. Thinking that does not make system and perception accord conflicts with more than isolated visual impressions; it conflicts with practice. The expected event fails to occur, yes, but the unexpected event does occur: the bridge collapses, the crops wither, or the drug kills. The spark which most surely indicates the lack of systematic thinking, the violation of logic, is no transient percept, but sudden death. The system the Enlightenment has in mind is the form of knowledge which copes most proficiently with the facts and supports the individual most effectively in the mastery of nature. Its principles are the principles of self-preservation. Immaturity is then the inability to survive. The burgher, in the successive forms of slaveowner, free entrepreneur, and administrator, is the logical subject of the Enlightenment.

The difficulties in the concept of reason caused by the fact that its subjects, the possessors of that very reason, contradict one another, are concealed by the apparent clarity of the judgments of the Western Enlightenment. In the *Critique of Pure Reason*, however, they are expressed in the unclear relation of the transcendental to the empirical ego, and in the other unresolved contradictions. Kant's concepts are ambiguous. As the transcendental, supraindividual self, reason comprises the idea of a free, human social life in which men organize themselves as the universal subject and overcome the conflict between pure and empirical reason in the conscious solidarity of the whole. This represents the idea of true universality: utopia. At the same time, however, reason constitutes the court of judgment of calculation, which adjusts the world for the ends of self-preservation and recognizes no function other than the preparation of the object from mere sensory material in order to make it the material of subjugation. The true nature of schematism, of the general and the particular, of concept and individual case reconciled from without, is ultimately revealed in contemporary science as the interest of industrial society. Being is apprehended under the aspect of manufacture and administration. Everything – even the human individual, not to speak of the animal – is converted into the repeatable, replaceable process, into a mere example for the conceptual models of the system. Conflict between administrative, reifying science, between the public mind and the experience of the individual, is precluded by circumstances. The conceptual apparatus determines the senses, even before perception occurs; *a priori*, the citizen sees the world as the matter from which he himself manufactures it. Intuitively, Kant foretold what Hollywood consciously put into practice: in the very process of production, images are pre-censored according to the norm of the understanding which will later govern their apprehension. Even before its occurrence, the perception which serves to confirm the public judgment is adjusted by that judgment. Even if the secret utopia in the concept of reason pointed, despite fortuitous distinctions between individuals, to their common interest, reason – functioning, in compliance with ends, as a mere systematic science – serves to level down that same identical interest. It allows no determination other than the classifications of the societal process to operate. No one is other than what he has come to be: a useful, successful, or frustrated member of vocational and national groups. He is one among many representatives of his geographical, psychological and sociological type. Logic is democratic; in this respect the great have no advantage over the insignificant. The great are classed as the important, and the insignificant as prospective objects for social relief. Science in general relates to nature and man only as the insurance company in particular relates to life and death. Whoever dies is unimportant: it is a question of ratio between accidents and the company's liabilities. Not the individuality but the law of the majority recurs in the formula. The concurrence of the general and the particular is no longer hidden in the one intellect which perceives the particular only as one case of the general, and the general only as the aspect of the particular by which it can be grasped and manipulated. Science itself is not conscious of itself; it is only a tool. Enlightenment, however, is the philosophy which equates the truth with scientific systematization. The attempt to establish this identity, which Kant was still able to undertake with a philosophic intention, led to concepts which have no meaning in a scientific sense, because they are not mere indications for manipulation according to the rules of the game. The notion of the self-understanding of science contradicts the notion of science itself. Kant's work transcends experience as mere operation, and for that reason – in accordance with its own principles – is now condemned by the Enlightenment as dogmatic.

With Kant's consequent, full confirmation of the scientific system as the form of truth, thought seals its own nullity, for science is technical practice, as far removed from reflective consideration of its own goal as are other forms of labor under the pressure of the system.

The moral teachings of the Enlightenment bear witness to a hopeless attempt to replace enfeebled religion with some reason for persisting in society when interest is absent. As genuine burghers, the philosophers come to terms with the powers who, in theory, are to be condemned. The theories are firm and consistent, whereas the moral doctrines are propagandist and sentimental (even when they seem rigorous), or else they are mere *coups de main*[v] by reason of the consciousness that morality itself is underivable – as in the case of Kant's recourse to ethical forces as a fact. His attempt (even though more careful than Western philosophy as a whole) to derive the duty of mutual respect from a law of reason finds no support in the *Critique*. It is the conventional attempt of bourgeois thought to ground respect, without which civilization cannot exist, upon something other than material interest and force; it is more sublime and paradoxical than, yet as ephemeral as, any previous attempt. The citizen who would forego profit only on the Kantian motive of respect for the mere form of law would not be enlightened, but superstitious – a fool. The root of Kantian optimism, according to which moral behavior is rational even if the mean and wretched would prevail, is actually an expression of horror at the thought of reversion to barbarism. If (so Kant wrote to Haller) one of these great moral forces of mutual love and respect were to founder, ". . . then nothingness [immorality] would open wide its maw and swallow the whole realm of [moral] virtue as if it were a drop of water."[14] But, according to Kant, in the face of scientific reason moral forces are no less neutral impulses and modes of behavior than the immoral forces into which they suddenly change when directed not to that hidden possibility but to reconciliation with power. Enlightenment expels the distinction from the theory. It treats emotions "*ac si quaestio de lineis, planis aut de corporibus esset.*"[15] The totalitarian order has carried this out with all seriousness. Liberated from the control of the same class which tied the nineteenth-century businessman to Kantian respect and mutual love, Fascism (which by its iron discipline saves its subject peoples the trouble of moral feelings) no longer needs to uphold any disciplines. In contradistinction to the categorical imperative and all the more in accordance with pure reason, it treats men as things – as the loci of modes of behavior. The rulers were anxious to protect the bourgeois world against the ocean of open force (which has now really broken into Europe), only so long as the economic concentration had made inadequate progress. Previously, only the poor and savages

[v] Surprise attacks.

251

were exposed to the fury of the capitalist elements. But the totalitarian order gives full rein to calculation and abides by science as such. Its canon is its own brutal efficiency. It was the hand of philosophy that wrote it on the wall – from Kant's *Critique* to Nietzsche's *Genealogy of Morals;* but one man made out the detailed account. The work of the Marquis de Sade portrays "understanding without the guidance of another person": that is, the bourgeois individual freed from tutelage.[vi]

Self-preservation is the constitutive principle of science, the soul of the table of categories,[vii] even when it is to be deduced idealistically, as with Kant. Even the ego, the synthetic unit of apperception, the instance which Kant calls the highest point, on which the possibility of the logical form of all knowledge necessarily depends,[16] is in fact the product of, as well as the condition for, material existence. Individuals, who have to look after themselves, develop the ego as the instance of the reflective preliminary and general view; it is extended and contracted as the prospects of economic self-sufficiency and productive ownership extend and contract from generation to generation. Finally it passes from the dispossessed bourgeoisie to the totalitarian cartel-lords, whose science has become the inclusive concept of the methods of reproduction of the subjugated mass society. Sade erected an early monument to their sense of planning. The conspiracy of the powerholders against the people by means of undeviating organization is as close as the bourgeois republic to the unenlightened spirit since Machiavelli and Hobbes. It is inimical to authority only when authority does not have power enough to compel obedience – the force which is no fact. So long as the identity of the user of reason is disregarded, the affinity of reason is as much to force as the mediation; according to the individual or group situation, it permits peace or war, tolerance or repression. Since it exposes substantial goals as the power of nature over mind, as the erosion of its self-legislation, reason is – by virtue, too, of its very formality – at the service of any natural interest. Thinking becomes an organic medium pure and simple, and reverts to nature. But for the rulers, men become material, just as nature as a whole is material for society. After the short intermezzo of liberalism, in which the bourgeois kept one another in check, domination appears as archaic terror in a fascistically rationalized form. As Francavilla says at the court of King Ferdinand of Naples: "Religious chimeras must be replaced by the most extreme forms of terror. If the people are freed from fear of a future hell, as soon as it has vanished they will abandon themselves to anything. But if this chimerical fear is

---

[vi] The Marquis de Sade (1740–1814), controversial French author of erotic, violent philosophical works, from whose name English gets "sadism."

[vii] Kant's table of categories through which the human mind constitutes experience (from *The Critique of Pure Reason*).

replaced by utterly relentless penal laws, which of course apply only to the people, then they alone will provoke unrest in the State; the discontented will be born only into the lowest class. What does the idea of a curb which they never experience themselves mean to the rich, if with this empty semblance they are able to preserve a justice that allows them to crush all those who live under their yoke? You will find no one in that class who would not submit to the worst tyranny so long as all others must suffer it."[17] Reason is the organ of calculation, of planning; it is neutral in regard to ends; its element is coordination. What Kant grounded transcendentally, the affinity of knowledge and planning, which impressed the stamp of inescapable expediency on every aspect of a bourgeois existence that was wholly rationalized, even in every breathing-space, Sade realized empirically more than a century before sport was conceived. The teams of modern sport, whose interaction is so precisely regulated that no member has any doubt about his role, and which provide a reserve for every player, have their exact counterpart in the sexual teams of *Juliette*, which employ every moment usefully, neglect no human orifice, and carry out every function. Intensive, purposeful activity prevails in spirit as in all branches of mass culture, while the inadequately initiated spectator cannot divine the difference in the combinations, or the meaning of variations, by the arbitrarily determined rules. The architectonic structure of the Kantian system, like the gymnastic pyramids of Sade's orgies and the schematized principles of the early bourgeois freemasonry – which has its cynical mirror-image in the strict regimentation of the libertine society of the *120 Journées*[viii] – reveals an organization of life as a whole which is deprived of any substantial goal. These arrangements amount not so much to pleasure as to its regimented pursuit – organization – just as in other demythologized epochs (Imperial Rome and the Renaissance, as well as the Baroque) the schema of an activity was more important than its content. In the modern era, enlightenment separated the notions of harmony and fulfillment from their hypostatization in the religious Beyond, and, in the form of systematization, transferred them as criteria to human aspiration. When utopia, which provided the French Revolution with its content of hope, entered German music and philosophy (effectively and ineffectively), the established civil order wholly functionalized reason, which became a purposeless purposiveness which might thus be attached to all ends. In this sense, reason is planning considered solely as planning. The totalitarian State manipulates the people. Or, as Sade's Francavilla puts it: "The government must control the population, and must possess all the means necessary to exterminate them when afraid of them, or to increase their numbers when that seems desirable. There should never be any counterweight to the

---

[viii] *One Hundred and Twenty Days of Sodom*, a book by de Sade.

justice of government other than that of the interests or passions of those who govern, together with the passions and interests of those who, as we have said, have received from it only so much power as is requisite to reproduce their own."[18] Francavilla indicates the road that imperialism, the most terrible form of the *ratio*, has always taken: "Take its god from the people that you wish to subjugate, and then demoralize it; so long as it worships no other god than you, and has no other morals than your morals, you will always be its master ... allow it in return the most extreme criminal license; punish it only when it turns upon you."[19]

Since reason posits no substantial goals, all affects are equally removed from its governance, and are purely natural. The principle by which reason is merely set over against all that is unreasonable, is the basis of the true antithesis of enlightenment and mythology. Mythology recognizes spirit only as immersed in nature, as natural power. Like the powers without, inward impulses appear as living powers of divine or demonic origin. Enlightenment, on the other hand, puts back coherence, meaning and life into subjectivity, which is properly constituted only in this process. For subjectivity, reason is the chemical agent which absorbs the individual substance of things and volatilizes them in the mere autonomy of reason. In order to escape the superstitious fear of nature, it wholly transformed objective effective entities and forms into the mere veils of a chaotic matter, and anathematized their influence on humanity as slavery, until the ideal form of the subject was no more than unique, unrestricted, though vacuous authority.

All the power of nature was reduced to mere indiscriminate resistance to the abstract power of the subject. The particular mythology which the Western Enlightenment, even in the form of Calvinism, had to get rid of was the Catholic doctrine of the *ordo*[ix] and the popular pagan religion which still flourished under it. The goal of bourgeois philosophy was to liberate men from all this. But the liberation went further than its humane progenitors had conceived. The unleashed market economy was both the actual form of reason and the power which destroyed reason. The Romantic reactionaries only expressed what the bourgeois themselves experienced: that in their world freedom tended toward organized anarchy. The Catholic counterrevolution proved itself right as against the Enlightenment, just as the Enlightenment had shown itself to be right in regard to Catholicism. The Enlightenment committed itself to liberalism. If all affects are of equal value, then survival – which anyway governs the form of the system – seems also to be the most probable source of maxims for human conduct. Self-preservation, in fact, was given full rein in the free market economy.

[ix] Presumably the *ordo salutus*, the order of salvation, which for Catholicism sprang from the sacraments and for Protestant reformers from God's decree.

Those somber writers of the bourgeois dawn – Machiavelli, Hobbes, Mandeville, and so on – who decried the egotism of the self, acknowledged in so doing that society was the destructive principle, and denounced harmony before it was elevated as the official doctrine by the serene and classical authors. The latter boosted the totality of the bourgeois order as the misery that finally fused both general and particular, society and self, into one. With the development of the economic system in which control of the economic apparatus by private groups divides men, survival as affirmed by reason – the reified drive of the individual bourgeois – was revealed as destructive natural power, no longer to be distinguished from self-destruction. The two were now indissolubly blended. Pure reason became unreason, a faultless and insubstantial mode of procedure. But the utopia which proclaimed reconciliation between nature and the individual emerged together with the revolutionary avant-garde from its concealment in German philosophy, simultaneously irrational and rational, as the idea of the combination of free men, and called down on itself all the wrath of the *ratio*.[x] In society as it is, despite all the wretched moralistic attempts to propagate humanity as the most rational of means, survival remains free from utopia, which is denounced as myth. Among the rulers, cunning self-preservation takes the form of struggle for Fascist power; among individuals, it is expressed as adaptation to injustice at any price. Enlightened reason is as little capable of finding a standard by which to measure any drive in itself, and in comparison with all other drives, as of arranging the universe in spheres. It established natural hierarchy as a reflex of medieval society, and later enterprises are branded as lies in order to indicate a new, objective value ranking. Irrationalism, as it appears in such empty reconstructions, is far from being able to withstand the *ratio*. With Leibniz and Hegel, mainstream philosophy – even in those subjective and objective assertions which only approximate to thought – discovered the claim to truth in emotions, institutions, and works of art, but irrationalism (close in this as in other respects to modern positivism, that last remnant of the Enlightenment) demarcates emotion, like religion and art, from everything deserving of the title of knowledge or cognition. It limits cold reason in favor of immediate living, yet makes this no more than a principle inimical to thought. Under the cover of this enmity, emotion and finally all human expression, even culture as a whole, are withdrawn from thought; thereby, however, they are transformed into a neutralized element of the comprehensive *ratio* of the economic system – itself irrationalized long ago. From the start, it was unable to rely on its own pull, which it enhanced with the cult of feeling. But wherever it has recourse to the emotions, it militates against their very medium, thought, which was always suspicious

[x] Rationality.

of this self-alienated reason. The exuberantly tender affection of the lover in the movie strikes a blow against the unmoved theory – a blow continued in that sentimental polemic against thought which presents itself as an attack upon injustice. Though feelings are raised in this way to the level of an ideology, they continue to be despised in reality. When set against the firmament to which ideology transfers them, they still seem rather too vulgar; the effect is to exile them all the more. As a natural impulse, self-preservation has, like all other impulses, a bad conscience; but efficiency and the institutions which meant to serve it – that is, independent mediation, the apparatus, the organization, systematization – like to appear reasonable, both in theory and in practice; and the emotions are made to share in this apparent rationality.

The Enlightenment of modern times advanced from the very beginning under the banner of radicalism; this distinguishes it from any of the earlier stages of demythologization. When a new mode of social life allowed room for a new religion and a new way of thinking, the overthrow of the old classes, tribes, and nations was usually accompanied by that of the old gods. But especially where a nation (the Jews, for example) was brought by its own destiny to change to a new form of social life, the time-honored customs, sacred activities, and objects of worship were magically transformed into heinous crimes and phantoms. Present-day fears and idiosyncrasies, derided and execrated character traits, may be deciphered as the marks of the violent onset of this or that stage of progress in human development. From the reflex of disgust at excrement or human flesh to the suspicion of fanaticism, laziness, and poverty, whether intellectual or material, there is a long line of modes of behavior which were metamorphosed from the adequate and necessary into abominations. This is the line both of destruction and of civilization. Each step forward on it represents some progress, a stage of enlightenment. But whereas all earlier changes, from pre-animism to magic, from the matriarchal to a patriarchal culture, from the polytheism of the slaveowners to the Catholic hierarchy, replaced the older mythologies with new – though enlightened – ones, and substituted the god of legions for the Great Mother, the adoration of the Lamb for that of the totem, the brilliance of enlightened reason banished as mythological any form of devotion which claimed to be objective, and grounded in actuality. All previous obligations therefore succumbed to the verdict which pronounced them taboo – not excluding those which were necessary for the existence of the bourgeois order itself. The instrument by means of which the bourgeoisie came to power, the liberation of forces, universal freedom, self- determination – in short, the Enlightenment, itself turned against the bourgeoisie once, as a system of domination, it had recourse to suppression. In accordance with its principle, enlightenment does not stop at the minimum of belief, without which the bourgeois world cannot exist. It does not give domination the reliable service which the old ideologies always allowed it. Its antiauthoritarian tendency, which (though of course only in a subterranean form) still relates to the utopia in the concept of reason, ultimately makes it as inimical to the bourgeoisie as it was to the aristocracy – with which the bourgeoisie is then very soon allied. Finally, the antiauthoritarian principle has to change into its very antithesis – into opposition to reason; the abrogation of everything inherently binding, which it brings about, allows domination to ordain as sovereign and to manipulate whatever bonds and obligations prove appropriate to it. After civil virtue and love of humanity (for which it already had no adequate grounds), philosophy proceeded to proclaim authority and hierarchy as virtues, when the Enlightenment had long posited them as lies. But the Enlightenment possesses no argument against even such a perversion of its proper nature, for the plain truth had no advantage over distortion, and rationalization none over the *ratio*, if they could prove no practical benefit in themselves. With the formalization of reason, to the extent that its preferred function is that of a symbol for neutral procedures theory itself becomes an incomprehensible concept, and thought appears meaningful only when meaning has been discarded. Once it is harnessed to the dominant mode of production, the Enlightenment – which strives to undermine any order which has become repressive – abrogates itself. This was obvious even in the early attacks of the contemporary Enlightenment on Kant, the universal reducer. Just as Kant's moral philosophy restricted his enlightened critique, in order to preserve the possibility of reason, so – conversely – unreflective enlightened thinking based on the notion of survival always tends to convert into skepticism, in order to make enough room for the existing order. . . .

Notes

1 See [Ferdinand] Tönnies, *"Philosophische Terminologie,"* in *Psychologisch-Sozio-logische Ansicht* (Leipzig, 1908), p. 31.
2 *Phänomenologie des Geistes*, p. 65.
3 Edmund Husserl, *"Die Krisis der europäischen Wissenschaften und die transzend-entale Phänomenologie,"* in *Philosophia* (Belgrade, 1936), pp. 95 ff.
4 Cf. Schophenhauer, *Parerga und Paralipomena*, vol. II, S. 356; *Werke*, ed. Deussen, vol. V, p. 671.
5 Kant, *"Beantwortung der Frage: Was ist Aufklärung?"* ["An Answer to the Question: What is Enlightenment?"] *Kants Werke* (Akademie-Ausgabe), vol. VIII, p. 35.
6 *Kritik der reinen Vernunft* [*Critique of Pure Reason*], vol. III (2nd edn), p. 427.
7 Ibid., p. 427.
8 Ibid., pp. 435 f.

9   Ibid., p. 428.
10 Ibid., p. 429.
11 *Kritik der reinen Vernunft*, vol. IV (1st edn), p. 93.
12 *Kritik der Urteilskraft* [*Critique of Judgment*], vol. V, p. 185.
13 Ibid., p. 185.
14 *Metaphysische Anfänge der Tugendlehre*, vol. VI, p. 449.
15 Spinoza, *Ethica*, Pars III. Praefatio ["as if investigating lines, planes, or solids"].
16 *Kritik der reinen Vernunft*, vol. III (2nd edn), p. 109.
17 *Histoire de Juliette* (Holland, 1797), vol. V, pp. 319f.
18 Ibid., pp. 322 f.
19 Ibid., p. 324.

chapter twenty

"Existentialism"

Jean-Paul Sartre

Jean-Paul Sartre (1905–80) was one of the founders of the French Existentialist movement, and perhaps the most famous intellectual in the world for a generation after World War II. A close associate of Maurice Merleau-Ponty, Simone de Beauvoir, and Albert Camus, from 1941 to 1945 he wrote for the French resistance against the German occupation. During the Cold War he became a harsh critic of capitalism and the United States, even associating himself with Maoism in the 1960s, but was critical of communist totalitarianism when he allowed himself to see it (e.g. he condemned the Soviets for their 1956 invasion of Hungary). Only months after the liberation of Paris from the Germans, in October 1945, he gave a famous public lecture (excerpted below) which served to galvanize public interest in the new philosophy. Sartre endorsed the absolute freedom and responsibility of the individual subject to create itself in a world without guidance from God or nature. This heroic subjectivism is characteristic of French existentialism, and precisely what Heidegger and postmodernism would later reject.

Man is nothing else but what he makes of himself. Such is the first principle of existentialism. It is also what is called subjectivity, the name we are labeled with when charges are brought against us. But what do we mean by this, if not that man has a greater dignity than a stone or table? For we mean that man first exists, that is, that man first of all is the being who hurls himself toward a future and who is conscious of imagining himself as being in the future. Man is at the start a plan which is aware of itself, rather than a patch of moss, a piece of garbage, or a cauliflower; nothing exists prior to this plan; there is nothing in heaven; man will be what he will have planned to be. Not what he will want to be. Because by the word "will" we generally mean a conscious decision, which is subsequent to what we have already made of ourselves. I may want to belong to a political party, write a book, get married; but all that is only a manifestation of an earlier, more spontaneous choice that is called "will." But if existence

From Jean-Paul Sartre, "Existentialism," trans. Bernard Frechtman in *Existentialism and Human Emotions* (New York: Citadel, 1985), pp.15–24, and pp. 46–51.

really does precede essence, man is responsible for what he is. Thus, existentialism's first move is to make every man aware of what he is and to make the full responsibility of his existence rest on him. And when we say that a man is responsible for himself, we do not only mean that he is responsible for his own individuality, but that he is responsible for all men.

The word subjectivism has two meanings, and our opponents play on the two. Subjectivism means, on the one hand, that an individual chooses and makes himself; and, on the other, that it is impossible for man to transcend human subjectivity. The second of these is the essential meaning of existentialism. When we say that man chooses his own self, we mean that every one of us does likewise; but we also mean by that that in making this choice he also chooses all men. In fact, in creating the man that we want to be, there is not a single one of our acts which does not at the same time create an image of man as we think he ought to be. To choose to be this or that is to affirm at the same time the value of what we choose, because we can never choose evil. We always choose the good, and nothing can be good for us without being good for all.

If, on the other hand, existence precedes essence, and if we grant that we exist and fashion our image at one and the same time, the image is valid for everybody and for our whole age. Thus, our responsibility is much greater than we might have supposed, because it involves all mankind. If I am a workingman and choose to join a Christian trade-union rather than be a communist, and if by being a member I want to show that the best thing for man is resignation, that the kingdom of man is not of this world, I am not only involving my own case – I want to be resigned for everyone. As a result, my action has involved all humanity. To take a more individual matter, if I want to marry, to have children; even if this marriage depends solely on my own circumstances or passion or wish, I am involving all humanity in monogamy and not merely myself. Therefore, I am responsible for myself and for everyone else. I am creating a certain image of man of my own choosing. In choosing myself, I choose man.

This helps us understand what the actual content is of such rather grandiloquent words as anguish, forlornness, despair. As you will see, it's all quite simple.

First, what is meant by anguish?[i] The existentialists say at once that man is anguish. What that means is this: the man who involves himself and who realizes that he is not only the person he chooses to be, but also a lawmaker who is, at the same time, choosing all mankind as well as himself, can not help escape the feeling of his total and deep responsibility. Of course, there are many people who are not anxious; but we claim that

---

[i] Sartre is here discussing the famous existentialist theme of anxiety or dread (in German, *Angst*).

they are hiding their anxiety, that they are fleeing from it. Certainly, many people believe that when they do something, they themselves are the only ones involved, and when someone says to them, "What if everyone acted that way?" they shrug their shoulders and answer, "Everyone doesn't act that way." But really, one should always ask himself, "What would happen if everybody looked at things that way?" There is no escaping this disturbing thought except by a kind of double-dealing. A man who lies and makes excuses for himself by saying "not everybody does that," is someone with an uneasy conscience, because the act of lying implies that a universal value is conferred upon the lie.

Anguish is evident even when it conceals itself. This is the anguish that Kierkegaard called the anguish of Abraham. You know the story: an angel has ordered Abraham to sacrifice his son; if it really were an angel who has come and said, "You are Abraham, you shall sacrifice your son," everything would be all right. But everyone might first wonder, "Is it really an angel, and am I really Abraham? What proof do I have?"

There was a madwoman who had hallucinations; someone used to speak to her on the telephone and give her orders. Her doctor asked her, "Who is it who talks to you?" She answered, "He says it's God." What proof did she really have that it was God? If an angel comes to me, what proof is there that it's an angel? And if I hear voices, what proof is there that they come from heaven and not from hell, or from the subconscious, or a pathological condition? What proves that they are addressed to me? What proof is there that I have been appointed to impose my choice and my conception of man on humanity? I'll never find any proof or sign to convince me of that. If a voice addresses me, it is always for me to decide that this is the angel's voice; if I consider that such an act is a good one, it is I who will choose to say that it is good rather than bad.

Now, I'm not being singled out as an Abraham, and yet at every moment I'm obliged to perform exemplary acts. For every man, everything happens as if all mankind had its eyes fixed on him and were guiding itself by what he does. And every man ought to say to himself, "Am I really the kind of man who has the right to act in such a way that humanity might guide itself by my actions?" And if he does not say that to himself, he is masking his anguish.

There is no question here of the kind of anguish which would lead to quietism, to inaction. It is a matter of a simple sort of anguish that anybody who has had responsibilities is familiar with. For example, when a military officer takes the responsibility for an attack and sends a certain number of men to death, he chooses to do so, and in the main he alone makes the choice. Doubtless, orders come from above, but they are too broad; he interprets them, and on this interpretation depend the lives of ten or fourteen or twenty men. In making a decision he can not help having a certain anguish. All leaders know this anguish. That doesn't keep them from acting; on the contrary, it is the very condition of their action. For it implies that they envisage a number of possibilities, and when they choose one, they realize that it has value only because it is chosen. We shall see that this kind of anguish, which is the kind that existentialism describes, is explained, in addition, by a direct responsibility to the other men whom it involves. It is not a curtain separating us from action, but is part of action itself.

When we speak of forlornness,[ii] a term Heidegger was fond of, we mean only that God does not exist and that we have to face all the consequences of this. The existentialist is strongly opposed to a certain kind of secular ethics which would like to abolish God with the least possible expense. About 1880, some French teachers tried to set up a secular ethics which went something like this: God is a useless and costly hypothesis; we are discarding it; but, meanwhile, in order for there to be an ethics, a society, a civilization, it is essential that certain values be taken seriously and that they be considered as having an *a priori* existence. It must be obligatory, *a priori*, to be honest, not to lie, not to beat your wife, to have children, etc., etc. So we're going to try a little device which will make it possible to show that values exist all the same, inscribed in a heaven of ideas, though otherwise God does not exist. In other words – and this, I believe, is the tendency of everything called reformism in France – nothing will be changed if God does not exist. We shall find ourselves with the same norms of honesty, progress, and humanism, and we shall have made of God an outdated hypothesis which will peacefully die off by itself.

The existentialist, on the contrary, thinks it very distressing that God does not exist, because all possibility of finding values in a heaven of ideas disappears along with Him; there can no longer be an *a priori* Good, since there is no infinite and perfect consciousness to think it. Nowhere is it written that the Good exists, that we must be honest, that we must not lie; because the fact is we are on a plane where there are only men. Dostoievsky said, "If God didn't exist, everything would be possible." That is the very starting point of existentialism. Indeed, everything is permissible if God does not exist, and as a result man is forlorn, because neither within him nor without does he find anything to cling to. He can't start making excuses for himself.

If existence really does precede essence, there is no explaining things away by reference to a fixed and given human nature. In other words, there is no determinism, man is free, man is freedom. On the other hand,

---

[ii] For Heidegger, a human being finds itself forlorn or abandoned (*verlassen*), thrown into (*geworfen*) the world, and so must live with *unheimlichkeit*, uncanniness (more literally, not-at-home-ness).

if God does not exist, we find no values or commands to turn to which legitimize our conduct. So, in the bright realm of values, we have no excuse behind us, nor justification before us. We are alone, with no excuses.

That is the idea I shall try to convey when I say that man is condemned to be free. Condemned, because he did not create himself, yet, in other respects is free; because, once thrown into the world, he is responsible for everything he does. The existentialist does not believe in the power of passion. He will never agree that a sweeping passion is a ravaging torrent which fatally leads a man to certain acts and is therefore an excuse. He thinks that man is responsible for his passion.

The existentialist does not think that man is going to help himself by finding in the world some omen by which to orient himself. Because he thinks that man will interpret the omen to suit himself. Therefore, he thinks that man, with no support and no aid, is condemned every moment to invent man. Ponge, in a very fine article, has said, "Man is the future of man." That's exactly it. But if it is taken to mean that this future is recorded in heaven, that God sees it, then it is false, because it would really no longer be a future. If it is taken to mean that, whatever a man may be, there is a future to be forged, a virgin future before him, then this remark is sound. But then we are forlorn. . . .

Therefore, in the name of this will for freedom, which freedom itself implies, I may pass judgment on those who seek to hide from themselves the complete arbitrariness and the complete freedom of their existence. Those who hide their complete freedom from themselves out of a spirit of seriousness or by means of deterministic excuses, I shall call cowards; those who try to show that their existence was necessary, when it is the very contingency of man's appearance on earth, I shall call stinkers. But cowards or stinkers can be judged only from a strictly unbiased point of view.

Therefore though the content of ethics is variable, a certain form of it is universal. Kant says that freedom desires both itself and the freedom of others. Granted. But he believes that the formal and the universal are enough to constitute an ethics. We, on the other hand, think that principles which are too abstract run aground in trying to decide action. Once again, take the case of the student. In the name of what, in the name of what great moral maxim do you think he could have decided, in perfect peace of mind, to abandon his mother or to stay with her? There is no way of judging. The content is always concrete and thereby unforeseeable; there is always the element of invention. The one thing that counts is knowing whether the inventing that has been done, has been done in the name of freedom.

For example, let us look at the following two cases. You will see to what extent they correspond, yet differ. Take *The Mill on the Floss*. We find a certain young girl, Maggie Tulliver, who is an embodiment of the value of passion and who is aware of it. She is in love with a young man, Stephen, who is engaged to an insignificant young girl. This Maggie Tulliver, instead of heedlessly preferring her own happiness, chooses, in the name of human solidarity, to sacrifice herself and give up the man she loves. On the other hand, Sanseverina, in *The Charterhouse of Parma*, believing that passion is man's true value, would say that a great love deserves sacrifices; that it is to be preferred to the banality of the conjugal love that would tie Stephen to the young ninny he had to marry. She would choose to sacrifice the girl and fulfill her happiness; and, as Stendhal shows, she is even ready to sacrifice herself for the sake of passion, if this life demands it. Here we are in the presence of two strictly opposed moralities. I claim that they are much the same thing; in both cases what has been set up as the goal is freedom.

You can imagine two highly similar attitudes: one girl prefers to renounce her love out of resignation; another prefers to disregard the prior attachment of the man she loves out of sexual desire. On the surface these two actions resemble those we've just described. However, they are completely different. Sanseverina's attitude is much nearer that of Maggie Tulliver, one of heedless rapacity.

Thus, you see that the second charge is true and, at the same time, false. One may choose anything if it is on the grounds of free involvement.

The third objection is the following: "You take something from one pocket and put it into the other. That is, fundamentally, values aren't serious, since you choose them." My answer to this is that I'm quite vexed that that's the way it is; but if I've discarded God the Father, there has to be someone to invent values. You've got to take things as they are. Moreover, to say that we invent values means nothing else but this: life has no meaning a *priori*. Before you come alive, life is nothing, it's up to you to give it a meaning, and value is nothing else but the meaning that you choose. In that way, you see, there is a possibility of creating a human community.

I've been reproached for asking whether existentialism is humanistic. It's been said, "But you said in *Nausea* that the humanists were all wrong. You made fun of a certain kind of humanist. Why come back to it now?" Actually, the word humanism has two very different meanings. By humanism one can mean a theory which takes man as an end and as a higher value. Humanism in this sense can be found in Cocteau's tale *Around the World in Eighty Hours* when a character, because he is flying over some mountains in an airplane, declares "Man is simply amazing." That means that I, who did not build the airplanes, shall personally benefit from these particular inventions, and that I, as man, shall personally consider myself responsible for, and honored by, acts of a few particular men. This would imply that we ascribe a value to man on the basis of the highest deeds of certain men. This humanism is absurd, because only the dog or the horse would be able to make such an over-all judgment about man, which they are careful not to do, at least to my knowledge.

But it can not be granted that a man may make a judgment about man. Existentialism spares him from any such judgment. The existentialist will never consider man as an end because he is always in the making. Nor should we believe that there is a mankind to which we might set up a cult in the manner of Auguste Comte.[iii] The cult of mankind ends in the self-enclosed humanism of Comte, and, let it be said, of fascism. This kind of humanism we can do without.

But there is another meaning of humanism. Fundamentally it is this: man is constantly outside of himself; in projecting himself, in losing himself outside of himself, he makes for man's existing; and, on the other hand, it is by pursuing transcendent goals that he is able to exist; man, being this state of passing-beyond, and seizing upon things only as they bear upon this passing-beyond, is at the heart, at the center of this passing-beyond. There is no universe other than a human universe, the universe of human subjectivity. This connection between transcendency, as a constituent element of man – not in the sense that God is transcendent, out in the sense of passing beyond – and subjectivity, in the sense that man is not closed in on himself but is always present in a human universe, is what we call existentialism humanism. Humanism, because we remind man that there is no law-maker other than himself, and that in his forlornness he will decide by himself; because we point out that man will fulfill himself as man, not in turning toward himself, but in seeking outside of himself a goal which is just this liberation, just this particular fulfillment.

From these few reflections it is evident that nothing is more unjust than the objections that have been raised against us. Existentialism is nothing else than an attempt to draw all the consequences of a coherent atheistic position. It isn't trying to plunge man into despair at all. But if one calls every attitude of unbelief despair, like the Christians, then the word is not being used in its original sense. Existentialism isn't so atheistic that it wears itself out showing that God doesn't exist. Rather, it declares that even if God did exist, that would change nothing. There you've got our point of view. Not that we believe that God exists, but we think that the problem of His existence is not the issue. In this sense existentialism is optimistic, a doctrine of action, and it is plain dishonesty for Christians to make no distinction between their own despair and ours and then to call us despairing.

---

iii Auguste Comte (1798–1857), most famous for his scientific philosophy of "positivism," developed the idea of a non-theistic religion of humanity, to be led by a scientific priesthood.

Part III

Postmodernism and the Revaluation of Modernity

Perhaps ironically, it was the relative stability and unprecedented prosperity of the period following the defeat of German fascism and Japanese militarism that became the background for the Western tradition's deepest self-criticism. To be sure, the tense nuclear stand-off of the Cold War, the various hot wars of the period, especially for the French in Algeria and the United States in Vietnam, together with vast social changes, made the post-World War II period anything but calm. Nevertheless, it is perhaps inevitable that the deepest self-criticism emerges only from periods of relative security. It is hard to imagine postmodernism thriving while Hitler was alive. Fighting the devil makes for fear and hatred, not uncertainty.

Along with the enormous expansion of the North American, Western European, and Japanese economies, their seeming political stability, their unprecedented rise in living standards, came an increasingly insistent list of debits: the expansion of governmental bureaucracy to manage the growing welfare state, new technologies, and a permanent military deterrent; the increasing technical and organizational control of social life by corporate institutions as well as government; the progressive replacement of traditional and local cultures by the universal network of television and instantaneous communications, creating the new universe of mass popular culture; the dissolution of the extended family and local community by social and geographical mobility; the environmental impact of technological modernization; and the psychic costs of life in the new economy of permanent change. Add to this the virtual end of the Western colonial empires, the domestic social rebellion of previously disenfranchised ethnic groups, economic classes, and women, and an apparent loss of public confidence in religious and secular authority, and the result was a sense of on-going crisis amidst plenty.

Whatever the precise list of reasons, in the 1960s something in the juggernaut of modern Western culture broke. Not that it had ever been untroubled, or that it had not been assailed by far greater crises (namely, two devastating wars and a world economic depression). But at the very least, its post-World War II confidence, its *Pax Americana*, was shaken. As an historian friend who taught at an East Coast American university during the period once said to me: "In 1968 the world changed." By this he meant the world of the university, the students, the faculty, and, by inference, the greater world. Of course, human nature and the laws of physics did not change, but some other things did: attitudes, styles, beliefs, hopes seemed to swing away from one pole and toward another. By no means were all overcome with radical, counter-cultural fervor; but even the defenders of the status quo seemed to lose their earlier idealism and certainty. Less and less could anyone regard this as the best of all possible worlds – an idea not far-fetched to many in the 1950s. This loss of confidence was as pervasive in the intellectual world as outside of it. And while it may be true that the spirit of radical innovation has been rolled back since the mid-1970s, the loss of confidence has not. The rise of political conservatism since the late 1970s, marked especially by the personalities of Ronald Reagan and Margaret Thatcher, did not mend what had been broken. It did not restore faith in modernity (since conservatives are as disturbed by modernity as liberals, although each is disturbed by different parts of it). At its best this period gave conservatives the confidence to raise their voices and contribute to the debate over modernity, which is to the good. But at its worst it offered only a grimly self-serving realism, made palatable by a willful inattention to the increasing problems of the public sphere, problems to which neither liberals nor conservatives have posed adequate answers. It is in this atmosphere of conservative reaction and uncertain repose during the late 1970s and the 1980s that postmodernism emerged as a formidable player in the English-speaking academic world.

Four of the following selections serve as background for the rest. Heidegger's attack on Western humanism and the domination of nature by the "subject" is crucial to later postmodernism, which would also accept his rejection of subjective representation as the center of thought, and his willingness to bend philosophical language in an attempt to say the unsayable. In analytic philosophy and philosophy of science, Thomas Kuhn's famous account of scientific progress as proceeding through revolutions and non-rational decisions, rather than as a purely rational and cumulative process, was crucial for Rorty and other antifoundationalists, as well as for the widespread uncertainty about foundationalism apparent today. Postmodern architecture received one of its most famous statements from Robert Venturi, who saw the eclectic glitz of Las Vegas and the hodgepodge of overgrown Main Street, USA, and asked, "What's wrong with that?" Daniel Bell authored the most well-known version of the thesis that advanced Western societies are passing out of the modern industrial age into a post-industrial information age, with profound cultural and political implications.

The basis for membership in the postmodern family differs among our remaining contributors. The work of Jacques Derrida, Michel Foucault, Gilles Deleuze, Jean-François Lyotard, Luce Irigaray, and Mark Taylor illustrates

270

poststructuralist methodology. Jean Baudrillard gives a poststructuralist analysis of popular culture. Charles Jencks and Ihab Hassan are diagnosing – and applauding – postmodernism throughout high and low culture. David Griffin makes a positive application of postmodernism to cosmology. Henry Giroux applies postmodernism to education, in effect endorsing what is sometimes called "multiculturalism." Rorty is above all a philosophical antifoundationalist.[1] All of these are part of the postmodern family.

Many contemporary philosophers, while resistant to postmodernism, are sensitive to its critique of the philosophical search for foundations. Best termed *non*foundationalists, rather than *anti*foundationalists, they include our selected authors Bordo, Harding, MacIntyre, Jameson, and Habermas – although what they regard as a successful avoidance of foundationalism may differ. Nonfoundationalism is the very widespread attempt to continue philosophy without recourse to the kind of foundationalism found in classical modern philosophers. Nonfoundationalist philosophers would largely agree with Wittgenstein, Heidegger, and Rorty that philosophy cannot achieve Cartesian certainty, but they feel that philosophy does not need such certainty, that it can turn to some kind of pragmatism or common sense or some other method, thereby avoiding both foundationalism and postmodern excess. In a sense, this is the great surgical problem of contemporary philosophy: Given that the disease of foundationalism must be cut out, how deep must we cut, and what shape will the patient be in once the surgery is over? Antifoundationalists say that the patient will be dead, because the diseased tissue is so deep as to be inseparable from what keeps the patient alive; nonfoundationalists disagree, and believe the patient can go on to lead a full, albeit non-transcendental, life.[2]

Speculative postmodernism, represented in this volume by David Griffin and in a different way by Mark Taylor, is at variance with many of the other postmodernists. Speculative postmodernists do not accept that methodological postmodernism forces a renunciation of speculative philosophy. Rather, they apply postmodern strategies to modern philosophical conceptions of God and nature in order either to introduce positive conceptions in tune with the anti-dualistic tenor of postmodernism (as Griffin does in cosmology), or to generate an ambiguous possibility for thought in an area that postmodernism might have seemed to foreclose (as Taylor does for theology).

As mentioned earlier, the most well-known political manifestation of postmodernism is the attempt to make contemporary culture acknowledge and respond to "*difference*," or *otherness*, under the names of feminism and multiculturalism, which overlap with postmodernism. In this volume, Irigaray represents feminist postmodernism, while Susan Bordo and Sandra Harding endorse a feminism that finds much of postmodernism alien. Henry Giroux's multiculturalism is explicitly postmodern. However, even those

271

multiculturalists and feminists who hesitate to endorse postmodernism share many of its enemies, namely its rejection of the modernist sense of unity, foundationalism, the transcendental status of norms, the strict division of types of knowledge, and the normative status of an integral, cogent rationality. They contribute to the widespread critique of the past, modern and premodern, as does postmodernism.

The volume then includes a small number of postmodernism's most important critics, who could loosely be divided into *promodernists* and *premodernists*. Promodernists believe in some kind of continuation of modern philosophy and liberal society as both justified by a universal reason. Two cases in point are Marxism, represented here by Frederic Jameson, and egalitarian or participatory liberalism, represented by Jürgen Habermas. Jameson faults postmodernism for its in effect apolitical stance, its "totalizing" critique of all social relations and social theories which removes the possibility of any philosophical justification for positive social change in the direction of equality or justice. Habermas, while influenced by the Marxist critique of capitalism, is most at home in the American liberal democratic tradition (e.g. of John Dewey). He believes that the problems of modernity can be fixed with modernity's own tools, in particular, by a reinvigoration of participatory democracy. Habermas thinks that freedom and reason can be legitimated immanently through an analysis of communication, without recourse to metaphysical or epistemic foundations. Our premodernist critic is Alasdair MacIntyre, who calls for a reincorporation of traditional, preliberal modes of thought. Both Habermas and MacIntyre are concerned to legitimate rationality, to prevent what they regard as the postmodern equation of validity and power. But MacIntyre insists that only cultural traditions can provide this legitimacy. He is a major contributor to communitarianism, a contemporary movement calling for a reincorporation of tradition in order to reinvigorate moral community, which often takes the philosophical form of a return to Aristotle or Hegel. MacIntyre's strongest claim is that rational discourse itself has no existence outside of particular cultural traditions.

Lastly, there is the non-Western response to modernity and postmodernism. This is a very complex affair, to which this anthology can do no justice. For in the greater world there are many distinct relations to the discussion of modernity, modernization, and postmodernism. Some non-Western philosophers are mainly concerned to evaluate their own culture's modernization, often critically, sometimes linking their critique to an attack on Western imperialism through Marxist categories. Others, in a move particularly influenced by Western postmodernism, analyze *the representation of* their own culture either by Western society or by their own (e.g. in film, literature, advertising, etc.). Others give a critical evaluation of Western modernity and postmodernism in general using their own traditional sources. Of course, there is no dearth of non-Western critical responses to the encroachment of modernity within traditional societies; Gandhi's response to modern industry being one of the most famous. In fact, the very term 'post-industrial' first emerged from this kind of criticism, since it was formulated by the Indian writer Ananda K. Coomaraswamy in 1914 to mean the end of industrialism and a return to local, village-centered economic activity.[3] It is possible to argue that non-Western experience points to another way of being modern, an alternative (e.g. non-individualistic) version of modernity, as Peter Berger has claimed for the economically advanced East Asian societies.[4] Recently, some have argued that certain non-Western traditional philosophies are implicitly postmodern, that is, they do not fall prey to the postmodern critique of modernity, and so might point the way for the West to transcend modernity without recourse to postmodernism. This is the claim of David Hall, who in the essay selected here suggests that the Chinese tradition may serve as an example for Western philosophy in its struggle to respond to the challenge of postmodernism.

Notes

1 Rorty is a postmodernist despite the fact that he has renounced the term (see his *Essays on Heidegger and Others* [Cambridge: Cambridge University Press, 1991], p. 1). The reason for that renunciation is his skepticism regarding any ascription of a culture-wide change to contemporary art, philosophy, literature, etc., as "postmodern" seems to him to imply. But if postmodernism does not have to be interpreted in this way, and I believe it does not, Rorty's objection cannot obscure his thematic affinity with postmodern philosophy.
2 This is a description of the views of many contemporary philosophers, not necessarily the view of the editor. I think it is far from clear that foundationalism really is a disease and must be removed.
3 See note 11 to the Introduction to this volume.
4 See Peter Berger and Hsin-Huang Michael Hsiao (eds), *In Search of an East Asian Development Model* (New Brunswick, NJ: Transaction Books, 1988).

chapter
twenty-one

"Letter on Humanism"

Martin Heidegger

Martin Heidegger (1889–1976), Husserl's replacement at the University of Freiburg, took phenomenology in an existentialist direction in his great early work, *Being and Time* (1927). In it he sought to investigate nothing less than the meaning of Being itself (crucially distinct from *beings* or things) through an analysis of the mode of Being characteristic of human being (*Dasein*, as he called us), an analysis marked by the theme of resoluteness in the face of Being-towards-death and historical destiny. His philosophy subsequently moved in an increasingly anti-humanist direction, for which the task of thinking Being meant a rejection of the subjectivism and anthropocentrism characteristic of modern thought and the modern technological domination of the world. In 1933 these philosophical themes took embodied form when Heidegger agreed to give his loyalty to the new National Socialist regime by becoming a party member in order to assume the rectorship of the university, and by publicly identifying Hitler and the Nazi Party with Germany's special destiny. Even after the war Heidegger never recanted these views, but merely ceased to speak of them. His "Letter on Humanism" (1947), written in response to a letter from a young French philosopher, is a direct repudiation of Sartre's existentialism. Heidegger insists that a true humanism, which can arise only when we abandon traditional philosophical thinking, would understand man's essence as his "proximity" to Being, would make man the "shepherd" of Being rather than its engineer or overseer.

We are still far from pondering the essence of action decisively enough. We view action only as causing an effect. The actuality of the effect is valued according to its utility. But the essence of action is accomplishment. To accomplish means to unfold something into the fullness of its essence, to

Martin Heidegger, "Letter on Humanism," in David Farrell Krell (ed.), *Martin Heidegger: Basic Writings*, trans. Frank A. Capuzzi, with J. Glenn Gray and David Farrell Krell (New York: Harper and Row, 1977), pp. 193–242.

274

lead it forth into this fullness – *producere*. Therefore only what already is can really be accomplished. But what "is" above all is Being.[i] Thinking accomplishes the relation of Being to the essence of man. It does not make or cause the relation. Thinking brings this relation to Being solely as something handed over to it from Being. Such offering consists in the fact that in thinking Being comes to language: Language is the house of Being. In its home man dwells. Those who think and those who create with words are the guardians of this home. Their guardianship accomplishes the manifestation of Being insofar as they bring the manifestation to language and maintain it in language through their speech. Thinking does not become action only because some effect issues from it or because it is applied. Thinking acts insofar as it thinks. Such action is presumably the simplest and at the same time the highest, because it concerns the relation of Being to man. But all working or effecting lies in Being and is directed toward beings. Thinking, in contrast, lets itself be claimed by Being so that it can say the truth of Being. Thinking accomplishes this letting. Thinking is *l'engagement par l'Être pour l'Être*.[ii] I do not know whether it is linguistically possible to say both of these ("*par*" and "*pour*") at once, in this way: *penser, c'est l'engagement de l'Être*.[iii] Here the possessive form "*de l'* . . ." is supposed to express both subjective and objective genitive. In this regard "subject" and "object" are inappropriate terms of metaphysics, which very early on in the form of Occidental "logic" and "grammar" seized control of the interpretation of language. We today can only begin to descry what is concealed in that occurrence. The liberation of language from grammar into a more original essential framework is reserved for thought and poetic creation. Thinking is not merely *l'engagement dans l'action*[iv] for and by beings, in the sense of the actuality of the present situation. Thinking is *l'engagement* by and for the truth of Being. The history of Being is never past but stands ever before; it sustains and defines every *condition et situation humaine*.[v] In order to learn how to experience the aforementioned essence of thinking purely, and that means at the same time to carry it through, we must free ourselves from the technical interpretation of thinking. The beginnings of that interpretation reach back to Plato and Aristotle. They take thinking itself to be a *technē*, a process of reflection in service to doing and making. But here reflection is already seen from the

---

[i] Being (*Sein*) is to be contrasted with beings (*seiende*) or entities. Heidegger's aim, since his early work *Being and Time* (*Sein und Zeit*, 1927) is to think the meaning of Being without reducing Being to beings.

[ii] Engagement by Being for Being.

[iii] Thinking is the engagement of Being.

[iv] Engagement in action.

[v] Human condition and situation.

perspective of *praxis* and *poiēsis*.[vi] For this reason thinking, when taken for itself, is not "practical." The characterization of thinking as *theōria* and the determination of knowing as "theoretical" behavior occur already within the "technical" interpretation of thinking. Such characterization is a reactive attempt to rescue thinking and preserve its autonomy over against acting and doing. Since then "philosophy" has been in the constant predicament of having to justify its existence before the "sciences." It believes it can do that most effectively by elevating itself to the rank of a science. But such an effort is the abandonment of the essence of thinking. Philosophy is hounded by the fear that it loses prestige and validity if it is not a science. Not to be a science is taken as a failing which is equivalent to being unscientific. Being, as the element of thinking, is abandoned by the technical interpretation of thinking. "Logic," beginning with the Sophists and Plato, sanctions this explanation. Thinking is judged by a standard that does not measure up to it. Such judgment may be compared to the procedure of trying to evaluate the nature and powers of a fish by seeing how long it can live on dry land. For a long time now, all too long, thinking has been stranded on dry land. Can then the effort to return thinking to its element be called "irrationalism"?

Surely the questions raised in your letter would have been better answered in direct conversation. In written form thinking easily loses its flexibility. But in writing it is difficult above all to retain the multidimensionality of the realm peculiar to thinking. The rigor of thinking, in contrast to that of the sciences, does not consist merely in an artificial, that is, technical-theoretical exactness of concepts. It lies in the fact that speaking remains purely in the element of Being and lets the simplicity of its manifold dimensions rule. On the other hand, written composition exerts a wholesome pressure toward deliberate linguistic formulation. Today I would like to grapple with only one of your questions. Perhaps its discussion will also shed some light on the others.

You ask: *Comment redonner un sens au mot "Humanisme"?*[vii] This question proceeds from your intention to retain the word "humanism." I wonder whether that is necessary. Or is the damage caused by all such terms still not sufficiently obvious? True, "-isms" have for a long time now been suspect. But the market of public opinion continually demands new ones. We are always prepared to supply the demand. Even such names as "logic," "ethics," and "physics" begin to flourish only when original thinking comes to an end. During the time of their greatness the Greeks thought without such headings. They did not even call thinking "philosophy." Thinking

---

vi *Praxis* is Greek for "action," *poiesis* for "making," and below, *theōria* for "theoretical cognition."

vii How can we restore meaning to the word "humanism"?

comes to an end when it slips out of its element. The element is what enables thinking to be a thinking. The element is what properly enables: the enabling. It embraces thinking and so brings it into its essence. Said plainly, thinking is the thinking of Being. The genitive says something twofold. Thinking is of Being inasmuch as thinking, coming to pass from Being, belongs to Being. At the same time thinking is of Being insofar as thinking, belonging to Being, listens to Being. As the belonging to Being that listens, thinking is what it is according to its essential origin. Thinking *is* – this says: Being has fatefully embraced its essence. To embrace a "thing" or a "person" in its essence means to love it, to favor it. Thought in a more original way such favoring means to bestow essence as a gift. Such favoring is the proper essence of enabling, which not only can achieve this or that but also can let something essentially unfold in its provenance, that is, let it be. It is on the "strength" of such enabling by favoring that something is properly able to be. This enabling is what is properly "possible," that whose essence resides in favoring. From this favoring Being enables thinking. The former makes the latter possible. Being is the enabling-favoring, the "may be." As the element, Being is the "quiet power" of the favoring-enabling, that is, of the possible. Of course, our words *möglich* and *Möglichkeit*,[viii] under the dominance of "logic" and "metaphysics," are thought solely in contrast to "actuality"; that is, they are thought on the basis of a definite – the metaphysical – interpretation of Being as *actus* and *potentia*, a distinction identified with the one between *existentia* and *essentia*.[ix] When I speak of the "quiet power of the possible" I do not mean the *possibile* of a merely represented *possibilitas*, nor *potentia* as the *essentia* of an *actus* of *existentia*; rather, I mean Being itself, which in its favoring presides over thinking and hence over the essence of humanity, and that means over its relation to Being. To enable something here means to preserve it in its essence, to maintain it in its element.

When thinking comes to an end by slipping out of its element it replaces this loss by procuring a validity for itself as *technē*,[x] as an instrument of education and therefore as a classroom matter and later a cultural concern. By and by philosophy becomes a technique for explaining from highest causes. One no longer thinks; one occupies himself with "philosophy." In competition with one another, such occupations publicly offer themselves as "-isms" and try to offer more than the others. The dominance of such terms is not accidental. It rests above all in the modern age upon the peculiar dictatorship of the public realm. However, so-called "private existence" is not really essential, that is to say free, human being. It simply

---

[viii] Possible and possibility, respectively.
[ix] These Latin terms mean, respectively, act or actuality, potentiality, existence, and essence.
[x] Greek term for productive art or skill.

insists on negating the public realm. It remains an offshoot that depends upon the public and nourishes itself by a mere withdrawal from it. Hence it testifies, against its own will, to its subservience to the public realm. But because it stems from the dominance of subjectivity the public realm itself is the metaphysically conditioned establishment and authorization of the openness of individual beings in their unconditional objectification. Language thereby falls into the service of expediting communication along routes where objectification – the uniform accessibility of everything to everyone – branches out and disregards all limits. In this way language comes under the dictatorship of the public realm which decides in advance what is intelligible and what must be rejected as unintelligible. What is said in *Being and Time* (1927), sections 27 and 35, about the "they" in no way means to furnish an incidental contribution to sociology. Just as little does the "they" mean merely the opposite, understood in an ethical-existentiell way, of the selfhood of persons. Rather, what is said there contains a reference, thought in terms of the question of the truth of Being, to the word's primordial belongingness to Being. This relation remains concealed beneath the dominance of subjectivity that presents itself as the public realm. But if the truth of Being has become thought-provoking for thinking, then reflection on the essence of language must also attain a different rank. It can no longer be a mere philosophy of language. That is the only reason *Being and Time* (section 34) contains a reference to the essential dimension of language and touches upon the simple question as to what mode of Being language as language in any given case has. The widely and rapidly spreading devastation of language not only undermines aesthetic and moral responsibility in every use of language; it arises from a threat to the essence of humanity. A merely cultivated use of language is still no proof that we have as yet escaped the danger to our essence. These days, in fact, such usage might sooner testify that we have not yet seen and cannot see the danger because we have never yet placed ourselves in view of it. Much bemoaned of late, and much too lately, the downfall of language is, however, not the grounds for, but already a consequence of, the state of affairs in which language under the dominance of the modern metaphysics of subjectivity almost irremediably falls out of its element. Language still denies us its essence: that it is the house of the truth of Being. Instead, language surrenders itself to our mere willing and trafficking as an instrument of domination over beings. Beings themselves appear as actualities in the interaction of cause and effect. We encounter beings as actualities in a calculative business-like way, but also scientifically and by way of philosophy, with explanations and proofs. Even the assurance that something is inexplicable belongs to these explanations and proofs. With such statements we believe that we confront the mystery. As if it were already decided that the truth of Being lets itself at all be established in causes and explanatory grounds or, what comes to the same, in their incomprehensibility.

But if man is to find his way once again into the nearness of Being he must first learn to exist in the nameless. In the same way he must recognize the seductions of the public realm as well as the impotence of the private. Before he speaks man must first let himself be claimed again by Being, taking the risk that under this claim he will seldom have much to say. Only thus will the preciousness of its essence be once more bestowed upon the word, and upon man a home for dwelling in the truth of Being.

But in the claim upon man, in the attempt to make man ready for this claim, is there not implied a concern about man? Where else does "care" tend but in the direction of bringing man back to his essence? What else does that in turn betoken but that man (*homo*) become human (*humanus*)? Thus *humanitas* really does remain the concern of such thinking. For this is humanism: meditating and caring, that man be human and not inhumane, "inhuman," that is, outside his essence. But in what does the humanity of man consist? It lies in his essence.

But whence and how is the essence of man determined? Marx demands that "man's humanity" be recognized and acknowledged. He finds it in "society." "Social" man is for him "natural" man. In "society" the "nature" of man, that is, the totality of "natural needs" (food, clothing, reproduction, economic sufficiency) is equably secured. The Christian sees the humanity of man, the *humanitas* of *homo*, in contradistinction to *Deitas*. He is the man of the history of redemption who as a "child of God" hears and accepts the call of the Father in Christ. Man is not of this world, since the "world," thought in terms of Platonic theory, is only a temporary passage to the beyond.

Humanitas, explicitly so called, was first considered and striven for in the age of the Roman Republic. *Homo humanus* was opposed to *homo barbarus*. *Homo humanus* here means the Romans, who exalted and honored Roman *virtus* through the "embodiment" of the *paideia*[xi] taken over from the Greeks. These were the Greeks of the Hellenistic age, whose culture was acquired in the schools of philosophy. It was concerned with *eruditio et institutio in bonas artes*.[xii] *Paideia* thus understood was translated as *humanitas*. The genuine *romanitas* of *homo romanus* consisted in such *humanitas*. We encounter the first humanism in Rome: it therefore remains in essence a specifically Roman phenomenon which emerges from the encounter of Roman civilization with the culture of late Greek civilization. The so-called Renaissance of the fourteenth and fifteenth centuries in Italy is a *renascentia romanitatis*. Because *romanitas* is what matters, it is concerned with *humanitas* and therefore with Greek *paideia*. But Greek civilization is always seen

[xi] Education.   [xii] Learning and training in good conduct.

in its later form and this itself is seen from a Roman point of view. The *homo romanus* of the Renaissance also stands in opposition to *homo barbarus*. But now the in-humane is the supposed barbarism of gothic Scholasticism in the Middle Ages. Therefore a *studium humanitatis*, which in a certain way reaches back to the ancients and thus also becomes a revival of Greek civilization, always adheres to historically understood humanism. For Germans this is apparent in the humanism of the eighteenth century supported by Winckelmann, Goethe, and Schiller. On the other hand, Hölderlin does not belong to "humanism" precisely because he thought the destiny of man's essence in a more original way than "humanism" could.[xiii]

But if one understands humanism in general as a concern that man become free for his humanity and find his worth in it, then humanism differs according to one's conception of the "freedom" and "nature" of man. So too are there various paths toward the realization of such conceptions. The humanism of Marx does not need to return to antiquity any more than the humanism which Sartre conceives existentialism to be. In this broad sense Christianity too is a humanism, in that according to its teaching everything depends on man's salvation (*salus aeterna*); the history of man appears in the context of the history of redemption. However different these forms of humanism may be in purpose and in principle, in the mode and means of their respective realizations, and in the form of their teaching, they nonetheless all agree in this, that the *humanitas* of *homo humanus* is determined with regard to an already established interpretation of nature, history, world, and the ground of the world, that is, of beings as a whole.

Every humanism is either grounded in a metaphysics or is itself made to be the ground of one. Every determination of the essence of man that already presupposes an interpretation of being without asking about the truth of Being, whether knowingly or not, is metaphysical. The result is that what is peculiar to all metaphysics, specifically with respect to the way the essence of man is determined, is that it is "humanistic." Accordingly, every humanism remains metaphysical. In defining the humanity of man humanism not only does not ask about the relation of Being to the essence of man; because of its metaphysical origin humanism even impedes the question by neither recognizing nor understanding it. On the contrary, the necessity and proper form of the question concerning the truth of Being, forgotten in and through metaphysics, can come to light only if the question "What is metaphysics?" is posed in the midst of metaphysics'

[xiii] Johann Christian Friedrich Hölderlin (1770–1843), German poet, regarded by Heidegger as a predecessor, in contrast to historian Johann Winkelmann (1717–68), poet Friedrich Schiller (1757–1805), and Goethe.

domination. Indeed every inquiry into Being, even the one into the truth of Being, must at first introduce its inquiry as a "metaphysical" one.

The first humanism, Roman humanism, and every kind that has emerged from that time to the present, has presupposed the most universal "essence" of man to be obvious. Man is considered to be an *animal rationale*. This definition is not simply the Latin translation of the Greek *zōon logon echon*[xiv] but rather a metaphysical interpretation of it. This essential definition of man is not false. But it is conditioned by metaphysics. The essential provenance of metaphysics, and not just its limits, became questionable in *Being and Time*. What is questionable is above all commended to thinking as what is to be thought, but not at all left to the gnawing doubts of an empty skepticism.

Metaphysics does indeed represent beings in their Being, and so it thinks the Being of beings. But it does not think the difference of both.[1] Metaphysics does not ask about the truth of Being itself. Nor does it therefore ask in what way the essence of man belongs to the truth of Being. Metaphysics has not only failed up to now to ask this question, the question is inaccessible to metaphysics as such. Being is still waiting for the time when it will become thought-provoking to man. With regard to the definition of man's essence, however one may determine the *ratio* of the *animal* and the reason of the living being, whether as a "faculty of principles," or a "faculty of categories," or in some other way, the essence of reason is always and in each case grounded in this: for every apprehending of beings in their Being, Being itself is already illumined and comes to pass in its truth. So too with *animal, zōon*, an interpretation of "life" is already posited which necessarily lies in an interpretation of beings as *zōē* and *physis*, within which what is living appears. Above and beyond everything else, however, it finally remains to ask whether the essence of man primordially and most decisively lies in the dimension of *animalitas* at all. Are we really on the right track toward the essence of man as long as we set him off as one living creature among others in contrast to plants, beasts, and God? We can proceed in that way; we can in such fashion locate man within being as one being among others. We will thereby always be able to state something correct about man. But we must be clear on this point, that when we do this we abandon man to the essential realm of *animalitas* even if we do not equate him with beasts but attribute a specific difference to him. In principle we are still thinking of *homo animalis* – even when *anima* is posited as *animus sive mens*,[xv] and this in turn is later posited as subject, person, or spirit. Such positing is the manner of metaphysics. But then the essence of man is too little heeded and not

[xiv] Literally, animal logical being.
[xv] *Anima* is Latin for "soul;" *animus sive mens* means "spirit or mind."

thought in its origin, the essential provenance that is always the essential future for historical mankind. Metaphysics thinks of man on the basis of *animalitas* and does not think in the direction of his *humanitas*.

Metaphysics closes itself to the simple essential fact that man essentially occurs only in his essence, where he is claimed by Being. Only from that claim "has" he found that wherein his essence dwells. Only from this dwelling "has" he "language" as the home that preserves the ecstatic for his essence. Such standing in the lighting of Being I call the ek-sistence of man.[xvi] This way of Being is proper only to man. Ek-sistence so understood is not only the ground of the possibility of reason, *ratio*, but is also that in which the essence of man preserves the source that determines him.

Ek-sistence can be said only of the essence of man, that is, only of the human way "to be." For as far as our experience shows, only man is admitted to the destiny of ek-sistence. Therefore ek-sistence can also never be thought of as a specific kind of living creature among others – granted that man is destined to think the essence of his Being and not merely to give accounts of the nature and history of his constitution and activities. Thus even what we attribute to man as *animalitas* on the basis of the comparison with "beast" is itself grounded in the essence of ek-sistence. The human body is something essentially other than an animal organism. Nor is the error of biologism overcome by adjoining a soul to the human body, a mind to the soul, and the existentiell to the mind, and then louder than before singing the praises of the mind – only to let everything relapse into "life-experience," with a warning that thinking by its inflexible concepts disrupts the flow of life and that thought of Being distorts existence. The fact that physiology and physiological chemistry can scientifically investigate man as an organism is no proof that in this "organic" thing, that is, in the body scientifically explained, the essence of man consists. That has as little validity as the notion that the essence of nature has been discovered in atomic energy. It could even be that nature, in the face she turns toward man's technical mastery, is simply concealing her essence. Just as little as the essence of man consists in being an animal organism can this insufficient definition of man's essence be overcome or offset by outfitting man with an immortal soul, the power of reason, or the character of a person. In each instance essence is passed over, and passed over on the basis of the same metaphysical projection.

What man is – or, as it is called in the traditional language of metaphysics, the "essence" of man – lies in his ek-sistence. But ek-sistence thought in this way is not identical with the traditional concept of

---

[xvi] Heidegger is playing on the relation of "existence" and the Greek *ekstasis*, meaning to be outside of oneself (as in "ecstasy"). For a human being, to exist is to be out in the world, not closed up inside a subjective Cartesian ego.

existentia, which means actuality in contrast to the meaning of *essentia* as possibility. In *Being and Time* this sentence is italicized: "The 'essence' of Dasein lies in its existence." However, here the opposition between *existentia* and *essentia* is not under consideration, because neither of these metaphysical determinations of Being, let alone their relationship, is yet in question. Still less does the sentence contain a universal statement about *Dasein*, since the word came into fashion in the eighteenth century as a name for "object," intending to express the metaphysical concept of the actuality of the actual. On the contrary, the sentence says: man occurs essentially in such a way that he is the "there", that is, the lighting of Being.[xvii] The "Being" of the *Da*, and only it, has the fundamental character of ek-sistence, that is, of an ecstatic inherence in the truth of Being. The ecstatic essence of man consists in ek-sistence, which is different from the metaphysically conceived *existentia*. Medieval philosophy conceives the latter as *actualitas*. Kant represents *existentia* as actuality in the sense of the objectivity of experience. Hegel defines *existentia* as the self-knowing Idea of absolute subjectivity. Nietzsche grasps *existentia* as the eternal recurrence of the same. Here it remains an open question whether through *existentia* – in these explanations of it as actuality, which at first seem quite different – the Being of a stone or even life as the Being of plants and animals is adequately thought. In any case living creatures are as they are without standing outside their Being as such and within the truth of Being, preserving in such standing the essential nature of their Being. Of all the beings that are, presumably the most difficult to think about are living creatures, because on the one hand they are in a certain way most closely related to us, and on the other are at the same time separated from our ek-sistent essence by an abyss. However, it might also seem as though the essence of divinity is closer to us than what is foreign in other living creatures, closer, namely, in an essential distance which however distant is nonetheless more familiar to our ek-sistent essence than is our appalling and scarcely conceivable bodily kinship with the beast. Such reflections cast a strange light upon the current and therefore always still premature designation of man as *animal rationale*. Because plants and animals are lodged in their respective environments but are never placed freely in the lighting of Being which alone is "world," they lack language. But in being denied language they are not thereby suspended worldlessly in their environment. Still, in this word "environment" converges all that is puzzling about living creatures. In its essence language is not the utterance

---

[xvii] *Dasein*, literally "there-being," is Heidegger's term for human being. It indicates that we are always *there*, thrown into and vulnerable to the world. He also describes this "there-ness" (or *Da*), as *lichtung*, a word meaning both light and a forest clearing. Dasein's there-ness is a place where things are lighted or revealed.

of an organism; nor is it the expression of a living thing. Nor can it ever be thought in an essentially correct way in terms of its symbolic character, perhaps not even in terms of the character of signification. Language is the lighting-concealing advent of Being itself.[xviii]

Ek-sistence, thought in terms of *ecstasis*, does not coincide with *existentia* in either form or content. In terms of content ek-sistence means standing out into the truth of Being. *Existentia* (*existence*) means in contrast *actualitas*, actuality as opposed to mere possibility as Idea. Ek-sistence identifies the determination of what man is in the destiny of truth. *Existentia* is the name for the realization of something that is as it appears in its Idea. The sentence "Man ek-sists" is not an answer to the question of whether man actually is or not; rather, it responds to the question concerning man's "essence." We are accustomed to posing this question with equal impropriety whether we ask what man is or who he is. For in the *Who?* or the *What?* we are already on the lookout for something like a person or an object. But the personal no less than the objective misses and misconstrues the essential unfolding of ek-sistence in the history of Being. That is why the sentence cited from *Being and Time* is careful to enclose the word "essence" in quotation marks. This indicates that "essence" is now being defined from neither *esse essentiae* nor *esse existentiae*[xix] but rather from the ek-static character of Dasein. As ek-sisting, man sustains Da-sein in that he takes the *Da*, the lighting of Being, into "care." But Da-sein itself occurs essentially as "thrown." It unfolds essentially in the throw of Being as the fateful sending.

But it would be the ultimate error if one wished to explain the sentence about man's ek-sistent essence as if it were the secularized transference to human beings of a thought that Christian theology expresses about God (*Deus est suum esse*);[xx] for ek-sistence is not the realization of an essence, nor does ek-sistence itself even effect and posit what is essential. If we understand what *Being and Time* calls "projection" as a representational positing, we take it to be an achievement of subjectivity and do not think it in the only way the "understanding of Being" in the context of the "existential analysis" of "being-in-the-world" can be thought – namely as the ecstatic relation to the lighting of Being. The adequate execution and completion of this other thinking that abandons subjectivity is surely made more difficult by the fact that in the publication of *Being and Time* the third division of the first part, "Time and Being," was held back.

[xviii] Rather than think of the mind as knowing or not knowing Being, Heidegger thinks of Being as revealing and concealing itself. Being grants unconcealment; it is not a passive object for the human subject.

[xix] Essential being and existing being, respectively.

[xx] God is His being.

Here everything is reversed. The section in question was held back because thinking failed in the adequate saying of this turning and did not succeed with the help of the language of metaphysics.[xxi] The lecture "On the Essence of Truth," thought out and delivered in 1930 but not printed until 1943, provides a certain insight into the thinking of the turning from "Being and Time" to "Time and Being." This turning is not a change of standpoint from *Being and Time*, but in it the thinking that was sought first arrives at the location of that dimension out of which *Being and Time* is experienced, that is to say, experienced from the fundamental experience of the oblivion of Being.

By way of contrast, Sartre expresses the basic tenet of existentialism in this way: Existence precedes essence. In this statement he is taking *existentia* and *essentia* according to their metaphysical meaning, which from Plato's time on has said that *essentia* precedes *existentia*. Sartre reverses this statement. But the reversal of a metaphysical statement remains a metaphysical statement. With it he stays with metaphysics in oblivion of the truth of Being. For even if philosophy wishes to determine the relation of *essentia* and *existentia* in the sense it had in medieval controversies, in Leibniz's sense, or in some other way, it still remains to ask first of all from what destiny of Being this differentiation in Being as *esse essentiae* and *esse existentiae* comes to appear to thinking! We have yet to consider why the question about the destiny of Being was never asked and why it could never be thought. Or is the fact that this is how it is with the differentiation of *essentia* and *existentia* not at all a sign of forgetfulness of Being? We must presume that this destiny does not rest upon a mere failure of human thinking, let alone upon a lesser capacity of early Western thinking. Concealed in its essential provenance, the differentiation of *essentia* (essentiality) and *existentia* (actuality) completely dominates the destiny of Western history and of all history determined by Europe.

Sartre's key proposition about the priority of *existentia* over *essentia* does, however, justify using the name "existentialism" as an appropriate title for a philosophy of this sort. But the basic tenet of "existentialism" has nothing at all in common with the statement from *Being and Time* – apart from the fact that in *Being and Time* no statement about the relation of *essentia* and *existentia* can yet be expressed since there it is still a question of preparing something precursory. As is obvious from what we have just said, that happens clumsily enough. What still today remains to be said could perhaps become an impetus for guiding the essence of man to the point where it thoughtfully attends to that dimension of the truth of Being which

---

[xxi] Heidegger is describing a major change ("turn") in his thinking. "On Time and Being" (below) was a late essay of Heidegger's.

thoroughly governs it. But even this could take place only to the honor of Being and for the benefit of Dasein which man eksistingly sustains; not, however, for the sake of man so that civilization and culture through man's doings might be vindicated.

But in order that we today may attain to the dimension of the truth of Being in order to ponder it, we should first of all make clear how Being concerns man and how it claims him. Such an essential experience happens to us when it dawns on us that man is in that he eksists. Were we now to say this in the language of the tradition, it would run: the ek-sistence of man is his substance. That is why in *Being and Time* the sentence often recurs, "The 'substance' of man is existence." But "substance," thought in terms of the history of Being, is already a blanket translation of *ousia*, a word that designates the presence of what is present and at the same time, with puzzling ambiguity, usually means what is present itself. If we think the metaphysical term "substance" in the sense already suggested in accordance with the "phenomenological destruction" carried out in *Being and Time*, then the statement "The 'substance' of man is ek-sistence" says nothing else but that the way that man in his proper essence becomes present to Being is ecstatic inherence in the truth of Being.[xxii] Through this determination of the essence of man the humanistic interpretations of man as *animal rationale*, as "person," as spiritual-en-souled-bodily being, are not declared false and thrust aside. Rather, the sole implication is that the highest determinations of the essence of man in humanism still do not realize the proper dignity of man. To that extent the thinking in *Being and Time* is against humanism. But this opposition does not mean that such thinking aligns itself against the humane and advocates the inhuman, that it promotes the inhumane and deprecates the dignity of man. Humanism is opposed because it does not set the *humanitas* of man high enough. Of course the essential worth of man does not consist in his being the substance of beings, as the "Subject" among them, so that as the tyrant of Being he may deign to release the beingness of beings into an all too loudly bruited "objectivity."

Man is rather "thrown" from Being itself into the truth of Being, so that ek-sisting in this fashion he might guard the truth of Being, in order that beings might appear in the light of Being as the beings they are. Man does not decide whether and how beings appear, whether and how God and the gods or history and nature come forward into the lighting of Being, come to presence and depart. The advent of beings lies in the destiny of Being. But for man it is ever a question of finding what is fitting in his essence which corresponds to such destiny; for in accord with this destiny man as

---

[xxii] "Truth" for Heidegger means "unconcealment" (the literal meaning of the ancient Greek word for truth, *aletheia*).

ek-sisting has to guard the truth of Being. Man is the shepherd of Being. It is in this direction alone that *Being and Time* is thinking when ecstatic existence is experienced as "care."

Yet Being – what is Being? It is It itself. The thinking that is to come must learn to experience that and to say it. "Being" – that is not God and not a cosmic ground. Being is farther than all beings and is yet nearer to man than every being, be it a rock, a beast, a work of art, a machine, be it an angel or God. Being is the nearest. Yet the near remains farthest from man. Man at first clings always and only to beings. But when thinking represents beings as beings it no doubt relates itself to Being. In truth, however, it always thinks only of beings as such; precisely not, and never, Being as such. The "question of Being" always remains a question about beings. It is still not at all what its elusive name indicates: the question in the direction of Being. Philosophy, even when it becomes "critical" through Descartes and Kant, always follows the course of metaphysical representation. It thinks from beings back to beings with a glance in passing toward Being. For every departure from beings and every return to them stands already in the light of Being.

But metaphysics recognizes the lighting of Being either solely as the view of what is present in "outward appearance" (*idea*) or critically as what is seen as a result of categorial representation on the part of subjectivity. This means that the truth of Being as the lighting itself remains concealed for metaphysics. However, this concealment is not a defect of metaphysics but a treasure withheld from it yet held before it, the treasure of its own proper wealth. But the lighting itself is Being. Within the destiny of Being in metaphysics the lighting first affords a view by which what is present comes into touch with man, who is present to it, so that man himself can in apprehending (*noein*) first touch upon Being (*thigein*, Aristotle, *Met.* IX, 10). This view first gathers the aspect to itself. It yields to such aspects when apprehending has become a setting-forth-before-itself in the *perceptio* of the *res cogitans* taken as the *subiectum* of *certitudo*.

But how – provided we really ought to ask such a question at all – how does Being relate to ek-sistence? Being itself is the relation to the extent that It, as the location of the truth of Being amid beings, gathers to itself and embraces ek-sistence in its existential, that is, ecstatic, essence. Because man as the one who ek-sists comes to stand in this relation that Being destines for itself, in that he ecstatically sustains it, that is, in care takes it upon himself, he at first fails to recognize the nearest and attaches himself to the next nearest. He even thinks that this is the nearest. But nearer than the nearest and at the same time for ordinary thinking farther than the farthest is nearness itself: the truth of Being.

Forgetting the truth of Being in favor of the pressing throng of beings unthought in their essence is what ensnarement means in *Being and*

Time.[xxiii] This word does not signify the Fall of Man understood in a "moral-philosophical" and at the same time secularized way; rather, it designates an essential relationship of man to Being within Being's relation to the essence of man. Accordingly, the terms "authenticity" and "inauthenticity," which are used in a provisional fashion, do not imply a moral-existentiell or an "anthropological" distinction but rather a relation which, because it has been hitherto concealed from philosophy, has yet to be thought for the first time, an "ecstatic" relation of the essence of man to the truth of Being. But this relation is as it is not by reason of ek-sistence; on the contrary, the essence of ek-sistence derives existentially–ecstatically from the essence of the truth of Being.

The one thing thinking would like to attain and for the first time tries to articulate in *Being and Time* is something simple. As such, Being remains mysterious, the simple nearness of an unobtrusive governance. The nearness occurs essentially as language itself. But language is not mere speech, insofar as we represent the latter at best as the unity of phoneme (or written character), melody, rhythm, and meaning (or sense). We think of the phoneme and written character as a verbal body for language, of melody and rhythm as its soul, and whatever has to do with meaning as its mind. We usually think of language as corresponding to the essence of man represented as *animal rationale*, that is, as the unity of body-soul-mind. But just as ek-sistence – and through it the relation of the truth of Being to man – remains veiled in the humanitas of *homo animalis*, so does the metaphysical-animal explanation of language cover up the essence of language in the history of Being. According to this essence language is the house of Being which comes to pass from Being and is pervaded by Being. And so it is proper to think the essence of language from its correspondence to Being and indeed as this correspondence, that is, as the home of man's essence.

But man is not only a living creature who possesses language along with other capacities. Rather, language is the house of Being in which man ek-sists by dwelling, in that he belongs to the truth of Being, guarding it.

So the point is that in the determination of the humanity of man as ek-sistence what is essential is not man but Being – as the dimension of the *ecstasis* of ek-sistence. However, the dimension is not something spatial in the familiar sense. Rather, everything spatial and all space-time occur essentially in the dimensionality which Being itself is.

Thinking attends to these simple relationships. It tries to find the right word for them within the long traditional language and grammar of metaphysics. But does such thinking – granted that there is something in

---

[xxiii] *Verfallen*, here translated as "ensnarement," has also been translated as "fallenness."

a name – still allow itself to be described as humanism? Certainly not so far as humanism thinks metaphysically. Certainly not if humanism is existentialism and is represented by what Sartre expresses: *précisément nous sommes sur un plan où il y a seulement des hommes.*[xxiv] Thought from *Being and Time*, this should say instead: *précisément nous sommes sur un plan où il y a principalement l'Être.*[xxv] But where does *le plan* come from and what is it? *L'Être et le plan* are the same. In *Being and Time* we purposely and cautiously say, *il y a l'Être*: "there is / it gives" Being.[xxvi] *Il y a* translates "it gives" imprecisely. For the "it" that here "gives" is Being itself. The "gives" names the essence of Being that is giving, granting its truth. The self-giving into the open, along with the open region itself, is Being itself.

At the same time "it gives" is used preliminarily to avoid the locution "Being is"; for "is" is commonly said of some thing which is. We call such a thing a being. But Being "is" precisely not "a being." If "is" is spoken without a closer interpretation of Being, then Being is all too easily represented as a "being" after the fashion of the familiar sort of beings which act as causes and are actualized as effects. And yet Parmenides, in the early age of thinking, says, *esti gar einai*, "for there is Being." The primal mystery for all thinking is concealed in this phrase. Perhaps "is" can be said only of Being in an appropriate way, so that no individual being ever properly "is." But because thinking should be directed only toward saying Being in its truth instead of explaining it as a particular being in terms of beings, whether and how Being is must remain an open question for the careful attention of thinking.

The *esti gar einai* of Parmenides is still unthought today. That allows us to gauge how things stand with the progress of philosophy. When philosophy attends to its essence it does not make forward strides at all. It remains where it is in order constantly to think the Same. Progression, that is, progression forward from this place, is a mistake that follows thinking as the shadow which thinking itself casts. Because Being is still unthought, *Being and Time* too says of it, "there is / it gives." Yet one cannot speculate about this *il y a* precipitously and without a foothold. This "there is / it gives" rules as the destiny of Being. Its history comes to language in the words of essential thinkers. Therefore the thinking that thinks into the truth of Being is, as thinking, historical. There is not a "systematic" thinking and next to it an illustrative history of past opinions. Nor is there, as Hegel thought, only a systematics which can fashion the law of its thinking into the law of history and simultaneously subsume history into

---

[xxiv] We are precisely in a situation where there are only human beings.
[xxv] We are precisely in a situation where there is principally Being.
[xxvi] In German *es gibt* means literally, "it gives," but is used to mean "there is."

the system. Thought in a more primordial way, there is the history of Being to which thinking belongs as recollection of this history that unfolds of itself. Such recollective thought differs essentially from the subsequent presentation of history in the sense of an evanescent past. History does not take place primarily as a happening. And its happening is not evanescence. The happening of history occurs essentially as the destiny of the truth of Being and from it.[2] Being comes to destiny in that It, Being, gives itself. But thought in terms of such destiny this says: it gives itself and refuses itself simultaneously. Nonetheless, Hegel's definition of history as the development of "Spirit" is not untrue. Neither is it partly correct and partly false. It is as true as metaphysics, which through Hegel first brings to language its essence – thought in terms of the absolute – in the system. Absolute metaphysics, with its Marxian and Nietzschean inversions, belongs to the history of the truth of Being. Whatever stems from it cannot be countered or even cast aside by refutations. It can only be taken up in such a way that its truth is more primordially sheltered in Being itself and removed from the domain of mere human opinion. All refutation in the field of essential thinking is foolish. Strife among thinkers is the "lovers' quarrel" concerning the matter itself. It assists them mutually toward a simple belonging to the Same, from which they find what is fitting for them in the destiny of Being.

Assuming that in the future man will be able to think the truth of Being, he will think from ek-sistence. Man stands ek-sistingly in the destiny of Being. The ek-sistence of man is historical as such, but not only or primarily because so much happens to man and to things human in the course of time. Because it must think the ek-sistence of Da-sein, the thinking of *Being and Time* is essentially concerned that the historicity of Dasein be experienced.

But does not *Being and Time* say, where the "there is / it gives" comes to language, "Only so long as Dasein is, is there Being"? To be sure. It means that only so long as the lighting of Being comes to pass does Being convey itself to man. But the fact that the *Da*, the lighting as the truth of Being itself, comes to pass is the dispensation of Being itself. This is the destiny of the lighting. But the sentence does not mean that the Dasein of man in the traditional sense of *existentia*, and thought in modern philosophy as the actuality of the *ego cogito*, is that being through which Being is first fashioned. The sentence does not say that Being is the product of man. The "Introduction" to *Being and Time* says simply and clearly, even in italics, "Being is the *transcendens* pure and simple." Just as the openness of spatial nearness seen from the perspective of a particular thing exceeds all things near and far, so is Being essentially broader than all beings, because it is the lighting itself. For all that, Being is thought on the basis of beings, a consequence of the approach – at first unavoidable – within a metaphysics that is still dominant. Only from such a perspective does Being show itself in and as a transcending.

The introductory definition, "Being is the *transcendens* pure and simple," articulates in one simple sentence the way the essence of Being hitherto has illumined man. This retrospective definition of the essence of Being from the lighting of beings as such remains indispensable for the prospective approach of thinking toward the question concerning the truth of Being. In this way thinking attests to its essential unfolding as destiny. It is far from the arrogant presumption that wishes to begin anew and declares all past philosophy false. But whether the definition of Being as the *transcendens* pure and simple really does express the simple essence of the truth of Being – this and this alone is the primary question for a thinking that attempts to think the truth of Being. That is why we also say that how Being *is* is to be understood chiefly from its "meaning", that is, from the truth of Being. Being is illumined for man in the ecstatic projection. But this projection does not create Being.

Moreover, the projection is essentially a thrown projection. What throws in projection is not man but Being itself, which sends man into the ek-sistence of Da-sein that is his essence. This destiny comes to pass as the lighting of Being, as which it is. The lighting grants nearness to Being. In this nearness, in the lighting of the *Da*, man dwells as the ek-sisting one without yet being able properly to experience and take over this dwelling. In the lecture on Hölderlin's elegy "Homecoming" (1943) this nearness "of" Being, which the *Da* of Dasein is, is thought on the basis of *Being and Time*; it is perceived as spoken from the minstrel's poem; from the experience of the oblivion of Being it is called the "homeland." The word is thought here in an essential sense, not patriotically or nationalistically but in terms of the history of Being. The essence of the homeland, however, is also mentioned with the intention of thinking the homelessness of contemporary man from the essence of Being's history. Nietzsche was the last to experience this homelessness. From within metaphysics he was unable to find any other way out than a reversal of metaphysics. But that is the height of futility. On the other hand, when Hölderlin composes "Homecoming" he is concerned that his "countrymen" find their essence. He does not at all seek that essence in an egoism of his nation. He sees it rather in the context of a belongingness to the destiny of the West. But even the West is not thought regionally as the Occident in contrast to the Orient, nor merely as Europe, but rather world-historically out of nearness to the source. We have still scarcely begun to think of the mysterious relations to the East which found expression in Hölderlin's poetry.[3] "German" is not spoken to the world so that the world might be reformed through the German essence; rather, it is spoken to the Germans so that from a fateful belongingness to the nations they might become world-historical

291

along with them.[4] The homeland of this historical dwelling is nearness to Being.

In such nearness, if at all, a decision may be made as to whether and how God and the gods withhold their presence and the night remains, whether and how the day of the holy dawns, whether and how in the upsurgence of the holy an epiphany of God and the gods can begin anew. But the holy, which alone is the essential sphere of divinity, which in turn alone affords a dimension for the gods and for God, comes to radiate only when Being itself beforehand and after extensive preparation has been illuminated and is experienced in its truth. Only thus does the overcoming of homelessness begin from Being, a homelessness in which not only man but the essence of man stumbles aimlessly about.

Homelessness so understood consists in the abandonment of Being by beings. Homelessness is the symptom of oblivion of Being. Because of it the truth of Being remains unthought. The oblivion of Being makes itself known indirectly through the fact that man always observes and handles only beings. Even so, because man cannot avoid having some notion of Being, it is explained merely as what is "most general" and therefore as something that encompasses beings, or as a creation of the infinite being, or as the product of a finite subject. At the same time "Being" has long stood for "beings" and, inversely, the latter for the former, the two of them caught in a curious and still unraveled confusion.

As the destiny that sends truth, Being remains concealed. But the world's destiny is heralded in poetry, without yet becoming manifest as the history of Being. The world-historical thinking of Hölderlin that speaks out in the poem "Remembrance" is therefore essentially more primordial and thus more significant for the future than the mere cosmopolitanism of Goethe. For the same reason Hölderlin's relation to Greek civilization is something essentially other than humanism. When confronted with death, therefore, those young Germans who knew about Hölderlin lived and thought something other than what the public held to be the typical German attitude.

Homelessness is coming to be the destiny of the world. Hence it is necessary to think that destiny in terms of the history of Being. What Marx recognized in an essential and significant sense, though derived from Hegel, as the estrangement of man has its roots in the homelessness of modern man. This homelessness is specifically evoked from the destiny of Being in the form of metaphysics and through metaphysics is simultaneously entrenched and covered up as such. Because Marx by experiencing estrangement attains an essential dimension of history, the Marxist view of history is superior to that of other historical accounts. But since neither Husserl nor – so far as I have seen till now – Sartre recognizes the essential importance of the historical in Being, neither phenomenology nor existentialism enters that dimension within which a productive dialogue with Marxism first becomes possible.

For such dialogue it is certainly also necessary to free oneself from naïve notions about materialism, as well as from the cheap refutations that are supposed to counter it. The essence of materialism does not consist in the assertion that everything is simply matter but rather in a metaphysical determination according to which every being appears as the material of labor. The modern metaphysical essence of labor is anticipated in Hegel's *Phenomenology of Spirit* as the self-establishing process of unconditioned production, which is the objectification of the actual through man experienced as subjectivity. The essence of materialism is concealed in the essence of technology, about which much has been written but little has been thought. Technology is in its essence a destiny within the history of Being and of the truth of Being, a truth that lies in oblivion. For technology does not go back to the *technē* of the Greeks in name only but derives historically and essentially from *technē* as a mode of *alētheuein*, a mode, that is, of rendering beings manifest. As a form of truth technology is grounded in the history of metaphysics, which is itself a distinctive and up to now the only perceptible phase of the history of Being. No matter which of the various positions one chooses to adopt toward the doctrines of communism and to their foundation, from the point of view of the history of Being it is certain that an elemental experience of what is world-historical speaks out in it. Whoever takes "communism" only as a "party" or a "Weltanschauung" is thinking too shallowly, just as those who by the term "Americanism" mean, and mean derogatorily, nothing more than a particular lifestyle. The danger into which Europe as it has hitherto existed is ever more clearly forced consists presumably in the fact above all that its thinking – once its glory – is falling behind in the essential course of a dawning world destiny which nevertheless in the basic traits of its essential provenance remains European by definition. No metaphysics, whether idealistic, materialistic, or Christian, can in accord with its essence, and surely not in its own attempts to explicate itself, "get a hold on" this destiny yet, and that means thoughtfully to reach and gather together what in the fullest sense of Being now is.

In the face of the essential homelessness of man, man's approaching destiny reveals itself to thought on the history of Being in this, that man find his way into the truth of Being and set out on this find. Every nationalism is metaphysically an anthropologism, and as such subjectivism. Nationalism is not overcome through mere internationalism; it is rather expanded and elevated thereby into a system. Nationalism is as little brought and raised to *humanitas* by internationalism as individualism is by an ahistorical collectivism. The latter is the subjectivity of man in totality. It completes subjectivity's unconditioned self-assertion, which refuses to yield. Nor can it be even adequately experienced by a thinking that

293

mediates in a one-sided fashion. Expelled from the truth of Being, man everywhere circles round himself as the *animal rationale.*

But the essence of man consists in his being more than merely human, if this is represented as "being a rational creature." "More" must not be understood here additively as if the traditional definition of man were indeed to remain basic, only elaborated by means of an existentiell postscript. The "more" means: more originally and therefore more essentially in terms of his essence. But here something enigmatic manifests itself: man is in throwness. This means that man, as the ek-sisting counter-throw of Being, is more than *animal rationale* precisely to the extent that he is less bound up with man conceived from subjectivity. Man is not the lord of beings. Man is the shepherd of Being. Man loses nothing in this "less"; rather, he gains in that he attains the truth of Being. He gains the essential poverty of the shepherd, whose dignity consists in being called by Being itself into the preservation of Being's truth. The call comes as the throw from which the thrownness of Da-sein derives. In his essential unfolding within the history of Being, man is the being whose Being as ek-sistence consists in his dwelling in the nearness of Being. Man is the neighbor of Being.

But – as you no doubt have been wanting to rejoin for quite a while now – does not such thinking think precisely the *humanitas* of *homo humanus*? Does it not think *humanitas* in a decisive sense, as no metaphysics has thought it or can think it? Is this not "humanism" in the extreme sense? Certainly. It is a humanism that thinks the humanity of man from nearness to Being. But at the same time it is a humanism in which not man but man's historical essence is at stake in its provenance from the truth of Being. But then doesn't the ek-sistence of man also stand or fall in this game of stakes? So it does.

In *Being and Time* it is said that every question of philosophy "recoils upon existence." But existence here is not the actuality of the *ego cogito*. Neither is it the actuality of subjects who act with and for each other and so become who they are. "Ek-sistence," in fundamental contrast to every *existentia* and "*existence*," is ecstatic dwelling in the nearness of Being. It is the guardianship, that is, the care for Being. Because there is something simple to be thought in this thinking it seems quite difficult to the representational thought that has been transmitted as philosophy. But the difficult is not a matter of indulging in a special sort of profundity and of building complicated concepts; rather, it is concealed in the step back that lets thinking enter into a questioning that experiences – and lets the habitual opining of philosophy fall away.

It is everywhere supposed that the attempt in *Being and Time* ended in a blind alley. Let us not comment any further upon that opinion. The thinking that hazards a few steps in *Being and Time* has even today not advanced beyond that publication. But perhaps in the meantime it has in one respect come farther into its own matter. However, as long as philosophy merely busies itself with continually obstructing the possibility of admittance into the matter for thinking, i.e. into the truth of Being, it stands safely beyond any danger of shattering against the hardness of that matter. Thus to "philosophize" about being shattered is separated by a chasm from a thinking that is shattered. If such thinking were to go fortunately for a man no misfortune would befall him. He would receive the only gift that can come to thinking from Being.

But it is also the case that the matter of thinking is not achieved in the fact that talk about the "truth of Being" and the "history of Being" is set in motion. Everything depends upon this alone, that the truth of Being come to language and that thinking attain to this language. Perhaps, then, language requires much less precipitous expression than proper silence. But who of us today would want to imagine that his attempts to think are at home on the path of silence? At best, thinking could perhaps point toward the truth of Being, and indeed toward it as what is to be thought. It would thus be more easily weaned from mere supposing and opining and directed to the now rare handicraft of writing. Things that really matter, although they are not defined for all eternity, even when they come very late still come at the right time.

Whether the realm of the truth of Being is a blind alley or whether it is the free space in which freedom conserves its essence is something each one may judge after he himself has tried to go the designated way, or even better, after he has gone a better way, that is, a way befitting the question. On the penultimate page of *Being and Time* stand the sentences: "The *conflict* with respect to the interpretation of Being (that is, therefore, not the interpretation of beings or of the Being of man) cannot be settled, *because it has not yet been kindled.* And in the end it is not a question of 'picking a quarrel,' since the kindling of the conflict does demand some preparation. To this end alone the foregoing investigation is under way." Today after two decades these sentences still hold. Let us also in the days ahead remain as wanderers on the way into the neighborhood of Being. The question you pose helps to clarify the way.

You ask, *Comment redonner un sens au mot 'Humanisme'?* "How can some sense be restored to the word 'humanism'?" Your question not only presupposes a desire to retain the word "humanism" but also contains an admission that this word has lost its meaning.

It has lost it through the insight that the essence of humanism is metaphysical, which now means that metaphysics not only does not pose the question concerning the truth of Being but also obstructs the question, insofar as metaphysics persists in the oblivion of Being. But the same thinking that has led us to this insight into the questionable essence of humanism has likewise compelled us to think the essence of man more primordially. With regard to this more essential *humanitas* of *homo humanus* there arises the possibility of restoring to the word "humanism" a historical sense that is older than its oldest meaning chronologically reckoned. The restoration is not to be understood as though the word "humanism" were wholly without meaning and a mere *flatus vocis*.[xxvii] The "*humanum*" in the word points to *humanitas*, the essence of man; the "-ism" indicates that the essence of man is meant to be taken essentially. This is the sense that the word "humanism" has as such. To restore a sense to it can only mean to redefine the meaning of the word. That requires that we first experience the essence of man more primordially; but it also demands that we show to what extent this essence in its own way becomes fateful. The essence of man lies in ek-sistence. That is what is essentially – that is, from Being itself – at issue here, insofar as Being appropriates man as ek-sisting for guardianship over the truth of Being into this truth itself. "Humanism" now means, in case we decide to retain the word, that the essence of man is essential for the truth of Being, specifically in such a way that the word does not pertain to man simply as such. So we are thinking a curious kind of "humanism." The word results in a name that is a *lucus a non lucendo*.[xxviii]

Should we still keep the name "humanism" for a "humanism" that contradicts all previous humanism – although it in no way advocates the inhuman? And keep it just so that by sharing in the use of the name we might perhaps swim in the predominant currents, stifled in metaphysical subjectivism and submerged in oblivion of Being? Or should thinking, by means of open resistance to "humanism," risk a shock that could for the first time cause perplexity concerning the *humanitas* of *homo humanus* and its basis? In this way it could awaken a reflection – if the world-historical moment did not itself already compel such a reflection – that thinks not only about man but also about the "nature" of man, not only about his nature but even more primordially about the dimension in which the essence of man, determined by Being itself, is at home. Should we not rather suffer a little while longer those inevitable misinterpretations to which the path of thinking in the element of Being and Time has hitherto been exposed and let them slowly dissipate? These misinterpretations are natural reinterpretations of what was read, or simply mirrorings of what one believes he knows already before he reads. They all betray the same structure and the same foundation.

Because we are speaking against "humanism" people fear a defense of the inhuman and a glorification of barbaric brutality. For what is more "logical" than that for somebody who negates humanism nothing remains but the affirmation of inhumanity?

[xxvii] Empty sound.   [xxviii] A grove that no light reaches.

Because we are speaking against "logic" people believe we are demanding that the rigor of thinking be renounced and in its place the arbitrariness of drives and feelings be installed and thus that "irrationalism" be proclaimed as true. For what is more "logical" than that whoever speaks against the logical is defending the alogical?

Because we are speaking against "values" people are horrified at a philosophy that ostensibly dares to despise humanity's best qualities. For what is more "logical" than that a thinking that denies values must necessarily pronounce everything valueless?

Because we say that the Being of man consists in "being-in-the-world" people find that man is downgraded to a merely terrestrial being, where-upon philosophy sinks into positivism. For what is more "logical" than that whoever asserts the worldliness of human being holds only this life as valid, denies the beyond, and renounces all "Transcendence"?

Because we refer to the word of Nietzsche on the "death of God" people regard such a gesture as atheism. For what is more "logical" than that whoever has experienced the death of God is godless?

Because in all the respects mentioned we everywhere speak against all that humanity deems high and holy our philosophy teaches an irrespon-sible and destructive "nihilism." For what is more "logical" than that whoever roundly denies what is truly in being puts himself on the side of nonbeing and thus professes the pure nothing as the meaning of reality?

What is going on here? People hear talk about "humanism," "logic," "values," "world," and "God." They hear something about opposition to these. They recognize and accept these things as positive. But with hearsay – in a way that is not strictly deliberate – they immediately assume that what speaks against something is automatically its negation and that this is "negative" in the sense of destructive. And somewhere in *Being and Time* there is explicit talk of "the phenomenological destruction." With the assistance of logic and *ratio* – so often invoked – people come to believe that whatever is not positive is negative and thus that it seeks to degrade reason – and therefore deserves to be branded as depravity. We are so filled with "logic" that anything that disturbs the habitual somnolence of prevailing opinion is automatically registered as a despicable contradiction. We pitch everything that does not stay close to the familiar and beloved positive into the previously excavated pit of pure negation which negates everything, ends in nothing, and so consummates nihilism. Following this logical course we let everything expire in a nihilism we invented for ourselves with the aid of logic.

But does the "against" which a thinking advances against ordinary opinion necessarily point toward pure negation and the negative? This happens – and then, to be sure, happens inevitably and conclusively, that is, without a clear prospect of anything else – only when one posits in advance what is meant by the "positive" and on this basis makes an absolute and absolutely negative decision about the range of possible opposition to it. Concealed in such a procedure is the refusal to subject to reflection this presupposed "positive" in which one believes himself saved, together with its position and opposition. By continually appealing to the logical one conjures up the illusion that he is entering straightforwardly into thinking when in fact he has disavowed it.

It ought to be somewhat clearer now that opposition to "humanism" in no way implies a defense of the inhuman but rather opens other vistas.

"Logic" understands thinking to be the representation of beings in their Being, which representation proposes to itself in the generality of the concept. But how is it with meditation on Being itself, that is, with the thinking that thinks the truth of Being? This thinking alone reaches the primordial essence of *logos* which was already obfuscated and lost in Plato and in Aristotle, the founder of "logic." To think against "logic" does not mean to break a lance for the illogical but simply to trace in thought the *logos* and its essence which appeared in the dawn of thinking, that is, to exert ourselves for the first time in preparing for such reflection. Of what value are even far-reaching systems of logic to us if, without really knowing what they are doing, they recoil before the task of simply inquiring into the essence of *logos*? If we wished to bandy about objections, which is of course fruitless, we could say with more right: irrationalism, as a denial of *ratio*, rules unnoticed and uncontested in the defense of "logic," which believes it can eschew meditation on *logos* and on the essence of *ratio* which has its ground in *logos*.

To think against "values" is not to maintain that everything interpreted as "a value" – "culture," "art," "science," "human dignity," "world," and "God" – is valueless. Rather, it is important finally to realize that precisely through the characterization of something as "a value" what is so valued is robbed of its worth. That is to say, by the assessment of something as a value what is valued is admitted only as an object for man's estimation. But what a thing is in its Being is not exhausted by its being an object, particularly when objectivity takes the form of value. Every valuing, even where it values positively, is a subjectivizing. It does not let beings: be. Rather, valuing lets beings: be valid – solely as the objects of its doing. The bizarre effort to prove the objectivity of values does not know what it is doing. When one proclaims "God" the altogether "highest value," this is a degradation of God's essence. Here as elsewhere thinking in values is the greatest blasphemy imaginable against Being. To think against values therefore does not mean to beat the drum for the valuelessness and nullity of beings. It means rather to bring the lighting of the truth of Being before thinking, as against subjectivizing beings into mere objects.

The reference to "being-in-the-world" as the basic trait of the *humanitas* of *homo humanus* does not assert that man is merely a "worldly" creature understood in a Christian sense, thus a creature turned away from God and so cut loose from "Transcendence." What is really meant by this word could be more clearly called "the transcendent." The transcendent is supersensible being. This is considered the highest being in the sense of the first cause of all beings. God is thought as this first cause. However, in the name "being-in-the-world," "world" does not in any way imply earthly as opposed to heavenly being, nor the "worldly" as opposed to the "spiritual." For us "world" does not at all signify beings or any realm of beings but the openness of Being. Man is, and is man, insofar as he is the ek-sisting one. He stands out into the openness of Being. Being itself, which as the throw has projected the essence of man into "care," is as this openness. Thrown in such fashion, man stands "in" the openness of Being. "World" is the lighting of Being into which man stands out on the basis of his thrown essence. "Being-in-the-world" designates the essence of ek-sistence with regard to the lighted dimension out of which the "ek-" of ek-sistence essentially unfolds. Thought in terms of ek-sistence, "world" is in a certain sense precisely "the beyond" within existence and for it. Man is never first and foremost man on the hither side of the world, as a "subject," whether this is taken as "I" or "We." Nor is he ever simply a mere subject which always simultaneously is related to objects, so that his essence lies in the subject-object relation. Rather, before all this, man in his essence is ek-sistent into the openness of Being, into the open region that lights the "between" within which a "relation" of subject to object can "be."

The statement that the essence of man consists in being-in-the-world likewise contains no decision about whether man in a theologico-metaphysical sense is merely a this-worldly or an other-worldly creature.

With the existential determination of the essence of man, therefore, nothing is decided about the "existence of God" or his "nonbeing," no more than about the possibility or impossibility of gods. Thus it is not only rash but also an error in procedure to maintain that the interpretation of the essence of man from the relation of his essence to the truth of Being is atheism. And what is more, this arbitrary classification betrays a lack of careful reading. No one bothers to notice that in the article *Vom Wesen des Grundes*[xxix] the following appears: "Through the ontological interpretation of Dasein as being-in-the-world no decision, whether positive or negative, is made concerning a possible being toward God. It is, however, the case that through an illumination of transcendence we first achieve an *adequate concept of Dasein*, with respect to which it can now be asked how the relationship of Dasein to God is ontologically ordered."[5] If we think about this remark too quickly, as is usually the case, we will declare that such a philosophy does not decide either for or against the existence of God. It

---

[xxix] Heidegger's 1929 essay, *On the Essence of Reasons*.

299

remains stalled in indifference. Thus it is unconcerned with the religious question. Such indifferentism ultimately falls prey to nihilism.

But does the foregoing observation teach indifferentism? Why then are particular words in the note italicized – and not just random ones? For no other reason than to indicate that the thinking that thinks from the question concerning the truth of Being questions more primordially than metaphysics can. Only from the truth of Being can the essence of the holy be thought. Only from the essence of the holy is the essence of divinity to be thought. Only in the light of the essence of divinity can it be thought or said what the word "God" is to signify. Or should we not first be able to hear and understand all these words carefully if we are to be permitted as men, that is, as eksistent creatures, to experience a relation of God to man? How can man at the present stage of world history ask at all seriously and rigorously whether the god nears or withdraws, when he has above all neglected to think into the dimension in which alone that question can be asked? But this is the dimension of the holy, which indeed remains closed as a dimension if the open region of Being is not lighted and in its lighting is near man. Perhaps what is distinctive about this world-epoch consists in the closure of the dimension of the hale.[xxx] Perhaps that is the sole malignancy.

But with this reference the thinking that points toward the truth of Being as what is to be thought has in no way decided in favor of theism. It can be theistic as little as atheistic. Not, however, because of an indifferent attitude, but out of respect for the boundaries that have been set for thinking as such, indeed set by what gives itself to thinking as what is to be thought, by the truth of Being. Insofar as thinking limits itself to its task it directs man at the present moment of the world's destiny into the primordial dimension of his historical abode. When thinking of this kind speaks the truth of Being it has entrusted itself to what is more essential than all values and all types of beings. Thinking does not overcome metaphysics by climbing still higher, surmounting it, transcending it somehow or other; thinking overcomes metaphysics by climbing back down into the nearness of the nearest. The descent, particularly where man has strayed into subjectivity, is more arduous and more dangerous than the ascent. The descent leads to the poverty of the ek-sistence of *homo humanus*. In ek-sistence the region of *homo animalis*, of metaphysics, is abandoned. The dominance of that region is the mediate and deeply rooted basis for the blindness and arbitrariness of what is called "biologism," but also of what is known under the heading "pragmatism." To think the truth of Being at the same time means to think the humanity of *homo humanus*. What counts

---

[xxx] *Hale* means fortunate, graced, or even lucky. The German is *des Heilen*, which shares a common root with "holy" (*das Heilig*) and "malignancy" (*Unheil*).

is *humanitas* in the service of the truth of Being, but without humanism in the metaphysical sense.

But if *humanitas* must be viewed as so essential to the thinking of Being, must not "ontology" therefore be supplemented by "ethics"? Is not that effort entirely essential which you express in the sentence "*Ce que je cherche à faire, depuis longtemps déjà, c'est préciser le rapport de l'ontologie avec une éthique possible*"?[xxxi]

Soon after *Being and Time* appeared a young friend asked me, "When are you going to write an ethics?" Where the essence of man is thought so essentially, i.e. solely from the question concerning the truth of Being, but still without elevating man to the center of beings, a longing necessarily awakens for a peremptory directive and for rules that say how man, experienced from ek-sistence toward Being, ought to live in a fitting manner. The desire for an ethics presses ever more ardently for fulfilment as the obvious no less than the hidden perplexity of man soars to immeasurable heights. The greatest care must be fostered upon the ethical bond at a time when technological man, delivered over to mass society, can be kept reliably on call only by gathering and ordering all his plans and activities in a way that corresponds to technology.

Who can disregard our predicament? Should we not safeguard and secure the existing bonds even if they hold human beings together ever so tenuously and merely for the present? Certainly. But does this need ever release thought from the task of thinking what still remains principally to be thought and, as Being prior to all beings, is their guarantor and their truth? Even further, can thinking refuse to think Being after the latter has lain hidden so long in oblivion but at the same time has made itself known in the present moment of world history by the uprooting of all beings?

Before we attempt to determine more precisely the relationship between "ontology" and "ethics" we must ask what "ontology" and "ethics" themselves are. It becomes necessary to ponder whether what can be designated by both terms still remains near and proper to what is assigned to thinking, which as such has to think above all the truth of Being.

Of course if both "ontology" and "ethics," along with all thinking in terms of disciplines, become untenable, and if our thinking therewith becomes more disciplined, how then do matters stand with the question about the relation between these two philosophical disciplines?

Along with "logic" and "physics," "ethics" appeared for the first time in the school of Plato. These disciplines arose at a time when thinking was becoming "philosophy," philosophy, *epistēmē* (science), and science itself a matter for schools and academic pursuits. In the course of a philosophy so

---

[xxxi] "What I have been trying to do for a long time already is to specify the relation of ontology to a possible ethics."

understood, science waxed and thinking waned. Thinkers prior to this period knew neither a "logic" nor an "ethics" nor "physics." Yet their thinking was neither illogical nor immoral. But they did think *physis*[xxxii] in a depth and breadth that no subsequent "physics" was ever again able to attain. The tragedies of Sophocles – provided such a comparison is at all permissible – preserve the *ēthos* in their sagas more primordially than Aristotle's lectures on "ethics." A saying of Heraclitus which consists of only three words says something so simply that from it the essence of the *ēthos* immediately comes to light.

The saying of Heraclitus (Frag. 119) goes: *ēthos anthrōpōi daimōn*. This is usually translated, "A man's character is his daimon." This translation thinks in a modern way, not a Greek one. *Ēthos* means abode, dwelling place. The word names the open region in which man dwells. The open region of his abode allows what pertains to man's essence, and what in thus arriving resides in nearness to him, to appear. The abode of man contains and preserves the advent of what belongs to man in his essence. According to Heraclitus' phrase this is *daimōn*, the god. The fragment says: Man dwells, insofar as he is man, in the nearness of god. A story that Aristotle reports (*De parte animalium*, 1, 5, 645a 17) agrees with this fragment of Heraclitus.

> The story is told of something Heraclitus said to some strangers who wanted to come visit him. Having arrived, they saw him warming himself at a stove. Surprised, they stood there in consternation – above all because he encouraged them, the astounded ones, and called for them to come in with the words, "For here too the gods are present."

The story certainly speaks for itself, but we may stress a few aspects.

The group of foreign visitors, in their importunate curiosity about the thinker, are disappointed and perplexed by their first glimpse of his abode. They believe they should meet the thinker in circumstances which, contrary to the ordinary round of human life, everywhere bear traces of the exceptional and rare and so of the exciting. The group hopes that in their visit to the thinker they will find things that will provide material for entertaining conversation – at least for a while. The foreigners who wish to visit the thinker expect to catch sight of him perchance at that very moment when, sunk in profound meditation, he is thinking. The visitors want this "experience" not in order to be overwhelmed by thinking but simply so they can say they saw and heard someone everybody says is a thinker.

Instead of this the sightseers find Heraclitus by a stove. That is surely a common and insignificant place. True enough, bread is baked here. But

---

[xxxii] Nature, physical processes.

Heraclitus is not even busy baking at the stove. He stands there merely to warm himself. In this altogether everyday place he betrays the whole poverty of his life. The vision of a shivering thinker offers little of interest. At this disappointing spectacle even the curious lose their desire to come any closer. What are they supposed to do here? Such an everyday and unexciting occurrence – somebody who is chilled warming himself at a stove – anyone can find any time at home. So why look up a thinker? The visitors are on the verge of going away again. Heraclitus reads the frustrated curiosity in their faces. He knows that for the crowd the failure of an expected sensation to materialize is enough to make those who have just arrived leave. He therefore encourages them. He invites them explicitly to come in with the words *Einai gar kai entautha theous*, "Here too the gods are present."

This phrase places the abode (*ēthos*) of the thinker and his deed in another light. Whether the visitors understood this phrase at once – or at all – and then saw everything differently in this other light the story doesn't say. But the story was told and has come down to us today because what it reports derives from and characterizes the atmosphere surrounding this thinker. *Kai entautha*, "even here," at the stove, in that ordinary place where every thing and every condition, each deed and thought is intimate and commonplace, that is, familiar [*geheuer*], "even there" in the sphere of the familiar, *einai theous*, it is the case that "the gods are present."

Heraclitus himself says, *ēthos anthrōpōi daimōn*, "The (familiar) abode is for man the open region for the presencing of god (the unfamiliar one)."

If the name "ethics," in keeping with the basic meaning of the word *ēthos*, should now say that "ethics" ponders the abode of man, then that thinking which thinks the truth of Being as the primordial element of man, as one who ek-sists, is in itself the original ethics. However, this thinking is not ethics in the first instance, because it is ontology. For ontology always thinks solely the being (*on*) in its Being. But as long as the truth of Being is not thought all ontology remains without its foundation. Therefore the thinking which in *Being and Time* tries to advance thought in a preliminary way into the truth of Being characterizes itself as "fundamental ontology." It strives to reach back into the essential ground from which thought concerning the truth of Being emerges. By initiating another inquiry this thinking is already removed from the "ontology" of metaphysics (even that of Kant). "Ontology" itself, however, whether transcendental or precritical, is subject to criticism, not because it thinks the Being of beings and thereby reduces Being to a concept, but because it does not think the truth of Being and so fails to recognize that there is a thinking more rigorous than the conceptual. In the poverty of its first breakthrough, the thinking that tries to advance thought into the truth of Being brings only a small part of that wholly other dimension to language. This language is still faulty insofar as

303

it does not yet succeed in retaining the essential help of phenomenological seeing and in dispensing with the inappropriate concern with "science" and "research." But in order to make the attempt at thinking recognizable and at the same time understandable for existing philosophy, it could at first be expressed only within the horizon of that existing philosophy and its use of current terms.

In the meantime I have learned to see that these very terms were bound to lead immediately and inevitably into error. For the terms and the conceptual language corresponding to them were not rethought by readers from the matter particularly to be thought; rather, the matter was conceived according to the established terminology in its customary meaning. The thinking that inquiries into the truth of Being and so defines man's essential abode from Being and toward Being is neither ethics nor ontology. Thus the question about the relation of each to the other no longer has any basis in this sphere. Nonetheless, your question, thought in a more original way, retains a meaning and an essential importance.

For it must be asked: If the thinking that ponders the truth of Being defines the essence of *humanitas* as ek-sistence from the latter's belongingness to Being, then does thinking remain only a theoretical representation of Being and of man, or can we obtain from such knowledge directives that can be readily applied to our active lives?

The answer is that such thinking is neither theoretical nor practical. It comes to pass before this distinction. Such thinking is, insofar as it is, recollection of Being and nothing else. Belonging to Being, because thrown by Being into the preservation of its truth and claimed for such preservation, it thinks Being. Such thinking has no result. It has no effect. It satisfies its essence in that it is. But it is by saying its matter. Historically, only one Saying [*Sage*] belongs to the matter of thinking, the one that is in each case appropriate to its matter. Its material relevance is essentially higher than the validity of the sciences, because it is freer. For it lets Being – be.

Thinking builds upon the house of Being, the house in which the jointure of Being fatefully enjoins the essence of man to dwell in the truth of Being. This dwelling is the essence of "being-in-the-world." The reference in *Being and Time* (p. 54) to "being-in" as "dwelling" is no etymological game. The same reference in the 1936 essay on Hölderlin's verse, "Full of merit, yet poetically, man dwells on this earth," is no adornment of a thinking that rescues itself from science by means of poetry. The talk about the house of Being is no transfer of the image "house" to Being. But one day we will, by thinking the essence of Being in a way appropriate to its matter, more readily be able to think what "house" and "to dwell" are.

And yet thinking never creates the house of Being. Thinking conducts historical eksistence, that is, the *humanitas of homo humanus*, into the realm of the upsurgence of the healing.

With healing, evil appears all the more in the lighting of Being. The essence of evil does not consist in the mere baseness of human action but rather in the malice of rage. Both of these, however, healing and the raging, can essentially occur only in Being, insofar as Being itself is what is contested. In it is concealed the essential provenance of nihilation. What nihilates illuminates itself as the negative. This can be addressed in the "no." The "not" in no way arises from the no-saying of negation. Every "no" that does not mistake itself as willful assertion of the positing power of subjectivity, but rather remains a letting-be of ek-sistence, answers to the claim of the nihilation illumined. Every "no" is simply the affirmation of the "not." Every affirmation consists in acknowledgment. Acknowledgment lets that toward which it goes come toward it. It is believed that nihilation is nowhere to be found in beings themselves. This is correct as long as one seeks nihilation as some kind of being, as an existing quality in beings. But in so seeking, one is not seeking nihilation. Neither is Being any existing quality which allows itself to be fixed among beings. And yet Being is more in being than any being. Because nihilation occurs essentially in Being itself we can never discern it as a being among beings. Reference to this impossibility never in any way proves that the origin of the not is no-saying. This proof appears to carry only if one posits beings as what is objective for subjectivity. From this alternative it follows that every "not," because it never appears as something objective, must inevitably be the product of a subjective act. But whether no-saying first posits the "not" as something merely thought, or whether nihilation first requires the "no" as what is to be said in the letting-be of beings – this can never be decided at all by a subjective reflection of a thinking already posited as subjectivity. In such a reflection we have not yet reached the dimension where the question can be appropriately formulated. It remains to ask, granting that thinking belongs to ek-sistence, whether every "yes" and "no" are not themselves already dependent upon Being. As these dependents, they can never first posit the very thing to which they themselves belong.

Nihilation unfolds essentially in Being itself, and not at all in the existence of man – so far as this is thought as the subjectivity of the *ego cogito*. Dasein in no way nihilates as a human subject who carries out nihilation in the sense of denial; rather, Da-sein nihilates inasmuch as it belongs to the essence of Being as that essence in which man ek-sists. Being nihilates – as Being. Therefore the "not" appears in the absolute Idealism of Hegel and Schelling as the negativity of negation in the essence of Being. But there Being is thought in the sense of absolute actuality as unconditioned will that wills itself and does so as the will of knowledge and of love. In this willing Being as will to power is still concealed. But just why the negativity of absolute subjectivity is "dialectical," and why nihilation comes to the fore through this dialectic but at the same time is veiled in its essence, cannot be discussed here.

The nihilating in Being is the essence of what I call the nothing. Hence because it thinks Being, thinking thinks the nothing.

To healing Being first grants ascent into grace; to raging its compulsion to malignancy.

Only so far as man, ek-sisting into the truth of Being, belongs to Being can there come from Being itself the assignment of those directions that must become law and rule for man. In Greek to assign is *nemein*. *Nomos* is not only law but more originally the assignment contained in the dispensation of Being. Only the assignment is capable of dispatching man into Being. Only such dispatching is capable of supporting and obligating. Otherwise all law remains merely something fabricated by human reason. More essential than instituting rules is that man find the way to his abode in the truth of Being. This abode first yields the experience of something we can hold on to. The truth of Being offers a hold for all conduct. "Hold" in our language means protective heed. Being is the protective heed that holds man in his ek-sistent essence to the truth of such protective heed – in such a way that it houses ek-sistence in language. Thus language is at once the house of Being and the home of human beings. Only because language is the home of the essence of man can historical mankind and human beings not be at home in their language, so that for them language becomes a mere container for their sundry preoccupations.

But now in what relation does the thinking of Being stand to theoretical and practical behavior? It exceeds all contemplation because it cares for the light in which a seeing, as *theoria*, can first live and move. Thinking attends to the lighting of Being in that it puts its saying of Being into language as the home of eksistence. Thus thinking is a deed. But a deed that also surpasses all *praxis*. Thinking towers above action and production, not through the grandeur of its achievement and not as a consequence of its effect, but through the humbleness of its inconsequential accomplishment.

For thinking in its saying merely brings the unspoken word of Being to language.

The usage "bring to language" employed here is now to be taken quite literally. Being comes, lighting itself, to language. It is perpetually under way to language. Such arriving in its turn brings ek-sisting thought to language in a saying. Thus language itself is raised into the lighting of Being. Language *is* only in this mysterious and yet for us always pervasive way. To the extent that language which has thus been brought fully into its essence is historical, Being is entrusted to recollection. Ek-sistence thoughtfully dwells in the house of Being. In all this it is as if nothing at all happens through thoughtful saying.

But just now an example of the inconspicuous deed of thinking manifested itself. For to the extent that we expressly think the usage "bring to language," which was granted to language, think only that and nothing further, to the extent that we retain this thought in the heedfulness of saying as what in the future continually has to be thought, we have brought something of the essential unfolding of Being itself to language.

What is strange in the thinking of Being is its simplicity. Precisely this keeps us from it. For we look for thinking – which has its world-historical prestige under the name "philosophy" – in the form of the unusual, which is accessible only to initiates. At the same time we conceive of thinking on the model of scientific knowledge and its research projects. We measure deeds by the impressive and successful achievements of *praxis*. But the deed of thinking is neither theoretical nor practical, nor is it the conjunction of these two forms of behavior.

Through its simple essence the thinking of Being makes itself unrecognizable to us. But if we become acquainted with the unusual character of the simple, then another plight immediately befalls us. The suspicion arises that such thinking of Being falls prey to arbitrariness; for it cannot cling to beings. Whence does thinking take its measure? What law governs its deed?

Here the third question of your letter must be entertained: *Comment sauver l'élément d'aventure que comporte toute recherche sans faire de la philosophie une simple aventurière?*[xxxiii] I shall mention poetry now only in passing. It is confronted by the same question, and in the same manner, as thinking. But Aristotle's words in the *Poetics*, although they have scarcely been pondered, are still valid – that poetic composition is truer than exploration of beings.

But thinking is an *aventure* not only as a search and an inquiry into the unthought. Thinking, in its essence as thinking of Being, is claimed by Being. Thinking is related to Being as what arrives (*l'avenant*). Thinking as such is bound to the advent of Being, to Being as advent, Being has already been dispatched to thinking. Being *is* as the destiny of thinking. But destiny is in itself historical. Its history has already come to language in the saying of thinkers.

To bring to language ever and again this advent of Being which remains, and in its remaining waits for man, is the sole matter of thinking. For this reason essential thinkers always say the Same. But that does not mean the identical. Of course they say it only to him who undertakes to think back on them. Whenever thinking, in historical recollection, attends to the destiny of Being, it has already bound itself to what is fitting for it, in accord with its destiny. To flee into the identical is not dangerous. To risk

---

[xxxiii] How can we preserve the element of adventure that all research contains without making philosophy into a mere adventuress?

discord in order to say the Same is the danger. Ambiguity threatens, and mere quarreling.

The fittingness of the saying of Being, as of the destiny of truth, is the first law of thinking – not the rules of logic which can become rules only on the basis of the law of Being. To attend to the fittingness of thoughtful saying does not only imply, however, that we contemplate at every turn *what* is to be said of Being and *how* it is to be said. It is equally essential to ponder *whether* what is to be thought is to be said – to what extent, at what moment of the history of Being, in what sort of dialogue with this history, and on the basis of what claim, it ought to be said. The threefold thing mentioned in an earlier letter is determined in its cohesion by the law of the fittingness of thought on the history of Being: rigor of meditation, carefulness in saying, frugality with words.

It is time to break the habit of overestimating philosophy and of thereby asking too much of it. What is needed in the present world crisis is less philosophy, but more attentiveness in thinking; less literature, but more cultivation of the letter.

The thinking that is to come is no longer philosophy, because it thinks more originally than metaphysics – a name identical to philosophy. However, the thinking that is to come can no longer, as Hegel demanded, set aside the name "love of wisdom" and become wisdom itself in the form of absolute knowledge. Thinking is on the descent to the poverty of its provisional essence. Thinking gathers language into simple saying. In this way language is the language of Being, as clouds are the clouds of the sky. With its saying, thinking lays inconspicuous furrows in language. They are still more inconspicuous than the furrows that the farmer, slow of step, draws through the field.

Notes

1 Cf. Martin Heidegger, *Vom Wesen des Grundes* (1929) [*The Essence of Reasons*, trans. Terrence Malick (Evanston, IL: Norweston University Press, 1969)], p.8; *Kant and the Problem of Metaphysics*, trans. J. Churchill (Bloomington, Ind.: Indiana University Press, 1962), p. 243; and *Being and Time*, section 44, p. 230.

2 See the lecture on Hölderlin's hymn, "Wie wenn am Feiertage . . ." in Martin Heidegger, *Erläuterungen zu Hölderlins Dichtung*, fourth, expanded edn (Frankfurt am Main: V. Klostermann, 1971), p. 76.

3 Cf. "The Ister" and "The Journey" [*Die Wanderung*], third stanza and ff. [In the translations by Michael Hamburger (Ann Arbor: University of Michigan Press, 1966), pp. 492 ff. and 392 ff.]

4 Cf. Hölderlin's poem "Remembrance" [*Andenken*] in the *Tübingen Memorial* (1943), p. 322. [Hamburger, pp. 488 ff.]

5 Martin Heidegger, *Vom Wesen des Grundes*, p. 28 n. 1.

chapter twenty-two

"The Nature and Necessity of Scientific Revolutions"

Thomas Kuhn

American historian of science Thomas Kuhn (1922–96) has had an enormous impact on the history and philosophy of science through his *The Structure of Scientific Revolutions* (1962). Kuhn famously argued that science proceeds not primarily by patient accretion of facts, but by revolutionary interpretive shifts in which one scientific "paradigm" displaces another. The history of science is thus marked by discontinuity. This raises the troubling question of whether the decision between paradigms is a rational, justifiable one, since paradigms appear to be so distinct – as some would say, "incommensurable" – that the evaluative criteria operative in one paradigm would seem logically unable to recognize the superiority of another paradigm. Indeed, it is not clear whether the meanings of the terms of one paradigm can even be translated into the terms of another. While Kuhn's aims were primarily historical and not philosophical, his work necessarily raised the question of the rationality of science. Much has been said to answer and clarify these issues since Kuhn first raised them, but few philosophers have been able to view science in quite the same terms since his book.

These remarks [in the previous chapter] permit us at last to consider the problems that provide this essay with its title. What are scientific revolutions, and what is their function in scientific development? Much of the answer to these questions has been anticipated in earlier sections. In particular, the preceding discussion has indicated that scientific revolutions are here taken to be those non-cumulative developmental episodes in which an older paradigm is replaced in whole or in part by an incompatible new one. There is more to be said, however, and an essential part of it can be introduced by asking one further question. Why should a change of

Thomas Kuhn, "The Nature and Necessity of Scientific Revolutions,"chapter ix of *The Structure of Scientific Revolutions* (Chicago: University of Chicago Press, 1962), pp. 92–110.

paradigm be called a revolution?[i] In the face of the vast and essential differences between political and scientific development, what parallelism can justify the metaphor that finds revolutions in both?

One aspect of the parallelism must already be apparent. Political revolutions are inaugurated by a growing sense, often restricted to a segment of the political community, that existing institutions have ceased adequately to meet the problems posed by an environment that they have in part created. In much the same way, scientific revolutions are inaugurated by a growing sense, again often restricted to a narrow subdivision of the scientific community, that an existing paradigm has ceased to function adequately in the exploration of an aspect of nature to which that paradigm itself had previously led the way. In both political and scientific development the sense of malfunction that can lead to crisis is prerequisite to revolution. Furthermore, though it admittedly strains the metaphor, that parallelism holds not only for the major paradigm changes, like those attributable to Copernicus and Lavoisier, but also for the far smaller ones associated with the assimilation of a new sort of phenomenon, like oxygen or X-rays.[ii] Scientific revolutions, as we noted at the end of Section V, need seem revolutionary only to those whose paradigms are affected by them. To outsiders they may, like the Balkan revolutions of the early twentieth century, seem normal parts of the developmental process. Astronomers, for example, could accept X-rays as a mere addition to knowledge, for their paradigms were unaffected by the existence of the new radiation. But for men like Kelvin, Crookes, and Roentgen, whose research dealt with radiation theory or with cathode ray tubes, the emergence of X-rays necessarily violated one paradigm as it created another. That is why these rays could be discovered only through something's first going wrong with normal research.

This genetic aspect of the parallel between political and scientific development should no longer be open to doubt. The parallel has, however, a second and more profound aspect upon which the significance of the first depends. Political revolutions aim to change political institutions in ways that those institutions themselves prohibit. Their success therefore necessitates the partial relinquishment of one set of institutions in favor of another, and in the interim, society is not fully governed by institutions at all. Initially it is crisis alone that attenuates the role of political institutions as we have already seen it attenuate the role of paradigms. In increasing

---

[i] Central to Kuhn's argument, the term "paradigm" refers to the fundamental concepts and aims of a science in an historical period. A scientific revolution involves the replacement of one paradigm by another.

[ii] Antoine Laurent Lavoisier (1743–94), father of modern chemistry. Below, William Kelvin (1824–1907), William Crookes (1832–1919), and Wilhelm Roentgen (1845–1923).

numbers individuals become increasingly estranged from political life and behave more and more eccentrically within it. Then, as the crisis deepens, many of these individuals commit themselves to some concrete proposal for the reconstruction of society in a new institutional framework. At that point the society is divided into competing camps or parties, one seeking to defend the old institutional constellation, the others seeking to institute some new one. And, once that polarization has occurred, *political recourse fails*. Because they differ about the institutional matrix within which political change is to be achieved and evaluated, because they acknowledge no supra-institutional framework for the adjudication of revolutionary difference, the parties to a revolutionary conflict must finally resort to the techniques of mass persuasion, often including force. Though revolutions have had a vital role in the evolution of political institutions, that role depends upon their being partially extrapolitical or extrainstitutional events.

The remainder of this essay aims to demonstrate that the historical study of paradigm change reveals very similar characteristics in the evolution of the sciences. Like the choice between competing political institutions, that between competing paradigms proves to be a choice between incompatible modes of community life. Because it has that character, the choice is not and cannot be determined merely by the evaluative procedures characteristic of normal science, for these depend in part upon a particular paradigm, and that paradigm is at issue. When paradigms enter, as they must, into a debate about paradigm choice, their role is necessarily circular. Each group uses its own paradigm to argue in that paradigm's defense.

The resulting circularity does not, of course, make the arguments wrong or even ineffectual. The man who premises a paradigm when arguing in its defense can nonetheless provide a clear exhibit of what scientific practice will be like for those who adopt the new view of nature. That exhibit can be immensely persuasive, often compellingly so. Yet, whatever its force, the status of the circular argument is only that of persuasion. It cannot be made logically or even probabilistically compelling for those who refuse to step into the circle. The premises and values shared by the two parties to a debate over paradigms are not sufficiently extensive for that. As in political revolutions, so in paradigm choice – there is no standard higher than the assent of the relevant community. To discover how scientific revolutions are effected, we shall therefore have to examine not only the impact of nature and of logic, but also the techniques of persuasive argumentation effective within the quite special groups that constitute the community of scientists.

To discover why this issue of paradigm choice can never be unequivocally settled by logic and experiment alone, we must shortly examine the nature of the differences that separate the proponents of a traditional paradigm from their revolutionary successors. That examination is the principal object of this section and the next. We have, however, already noted numerous examples of such differences, and no one will doubt that history can supply many others. What is more likely to be doubted than their existence – and what must therefore be considered first – is that such examples provide essential information about the nature of science. Granting that paradigm rejection has been a historic fact, does it illuminate more than human credulity and confusion? Are there intrinsic reasons why the assimilation of either a new sort of phenomenon or a new scientific theory must demand the rejection of an older paradigm?

First notice that if there are such reasons, they do not derive from the logical structure of scientific knowledge. In principle, a new phenomenon might emerge without reflecting destructively upon any part of past scientific practice. Though discovering life on the moon would today be destructive of existing paradigms (these tell us things about the moon that seem incompatible with life's existence there), discovering life in some less well-known part of the galaxy would not. By the same token, a new theory does not have to conflict with any of its predecessors. It might deal exclusively with phenomena not previously known, as the quantum theory deals (but, significantly, not exclusively) with subatomic phenomena unknown before the twentieth century. Or again, the new theory might be simply a higher level theory than those known before, one that linked together a whole group of lower level theories without substantially changing any. Today, the theory of energy conservation provides just such links between dynamics, chemistry, electricity, optics, thermal theory, and so on. Still other compatible relationships between old and new theories can be conceived. Any and all of them might be exemplified by the historical process through which science has developed. If they were, scientific development would be genuinely cumulative. New sorts of phenomena would simply disclose order in an aspect of nature where none had been seen before. In the evolution of science new knowledge would replace ignorance rather than replace knowledge of another and incompatible sort.

Of course, science (or some other enterprise, perhaps less effective) might have developed in that fully cumulative manner. Many people have believed that it did so, and most still seem to suppose that cumulation is at least the ideal that historical development would display if only it had not so often been distorted by human idiosyncrasy. There are important reasons for that belief. In Section X we shall discover how closely the view of science-as-cumulation is entangled with a dominant epistemology that takes knowledge to be a construction placed directly upon raw sense data by the mind. And in Section XI we shall examine the strong support provided to the same historiographic schema by the techniques of effective science pedagogy. Nevertheless, despite the immense plausibility of that ideal image, there is increasing reason to wonder whether it can possibly be an image of *science*. After the pre-paradigm period the assimilation of all new theories and of almost all new sorts of phenomena has in fact demanded the destruction of a prior paradigm and a consequent conflict between competing schools of scientific thought. Cumulative acquisition of unanticipated novelties proves to be an almost non-existent exception to the rule of scientific development. The man who takes historic fact seriously must suspect that science does not tend toward the ideal that our image of its cumulativeness has suggested. Perhaps it is another sort of enterprise.

If, however, resistant facts can carry us that far, then a second look at the ground we have already covered may suggest that cumulative acquisition of novelty is not only rare in fact but improbable in principle. Normal research, which *is* cumulative, owes its success to the ability of scientists regularly to select problems that can be solved with conceptual and instrumental techniques close to those already in existence. (That is why an excessive concern with useful problems, regardless of their relation to existing knowledge and technique, can so easily inhibit scientific development.) The man who is striving to solve a problem defined by existing knowledge and technique is not, however, just looking around. He knows what he wants to achieve, and he designs his instruments and directs his thoughts accordingly. Unanticipated novelty, the new discovery, can emerge only to the extent that his anticipations about nature and his instruments prove wrong. Often the importance of the resulting discovery will itself be proportional to the extent and stubbornness of the anomaly that foreshadowed it. Obviously, then, there must be a conflict between the paradigm that discloses anomaly and the one that later renders the anomaly lawlike. The examples of discovery through paradigm destruction examined in Section VI did not confront us with mere historical accident.[iii] There is no other effective way in which discoveries might be generated.

The same argument applies even more clearly to the invention of new theories. There are, in principle, only three types of phenomena about which a new theory might be developed. The first consists of phenomena already well explained by existing paradigms, and these seldom provide either motive or point of departure for theory construction. When they do, as with the three famous anticipations discussed at the end of Section VII, the theories that result are seldom accepted, because nature provides no

---

[iii] The three cases Kuhn discussed were the discoveries of oxygen, X-rays, and the Leyden jar.

ground for discrimination.[iv] A second class of phenomena consists of those whose nature is indicated by existing paradigms but whose details can be understood only through further theory articulation. These are the phenomena to which scientists direct their research much of the time, but that research aims at the articulation of existing paradigms rather than at the invention of new ones. Only when these attempts at articulation fail do scientists encounter the third type of phenomena, the recognized anomalies whose characteristic feature is their stubborn refusal to be assimilated to existing paradigms. This type alone gives rise to new theories. Paradigms provide all phenomena except anomalies with a theory-determined place in the scientist's field of vision.

But if new theories are called forth to resolve anomalies in the relation of an existing theory to nature, then the successful new theory must somewhere permit predictions that are different from those derived from its predecessor. That difference could not occur if the two were logically compatible. In the process of being assimilated, the second must displace the first. Even a theory like energy conservation, which today seems a logical superstructure that relates to nature only through independently established theories, did not develop historically without paradigm destruction. Instead, it emerged from a crisis in which an essential ingredient was the incompatibility between Newtonian dynamics and some recently formulated consequences of the caloric theory of heat. Only after the caloric theory had been rejected could energy conservation become part of science.[1] And only after it had been part of science for some time could it come to seem a theory of a logically higher type, one not in conflict with its predecessors. It is hard to see how new theories could arise without these destructive changes in beliefs about nature. Though logical inclusiveness remains a permissible view of the relation between successive scientific theories, it is a historical implausibility.

A century ago it would, I think, have been possible to let the case for the necessity of revolutions rest at this point. But today, unfortunately, that cannot be done because the view of the subject developed above cannot be maintained if the most prevalent contemporary interpretation of the nature and function of scientific theory is accepted. That interpretation, closely associated with early logical positivism and not categorically rejected by its successors, would restrict the range and meaning of an accepted theory so that it could not possibly conflict with any later theory that made predictions about some of the same natural phenomena. The best-known

[iv] The three anticipations were: the heliocentric cosmology of the ancient Greek philosopher Aristarchus of Samos (310–230 BC); seventeenth-century theories of combustion; and the relativistic view of space adopted by Newton's critics. These early "discoveries" preceded the historical crises that would only later legitimate them.

314

and the strongest case for this restricted conception of a scientific theory emerges in discussions of the relation between contemporary Einsteinian dynamics and the older dynamical equations that descend from Newton's *Principia*.[v] From the viewpoint of this essay these two theories are fundamentally incompatible in the sense illustrated by the relation of Copernican to Ptolemaic astronomy: Einstein's theory can be accepted only with the recognition that Newton's was wrong. Today this remains a minority view.[2] We must therefore examine the most prevalent objections to it.

The gist of these objections can be developed as follows. Relativistic dynamics cannot have shown Newtonian dynamics to be wrong, for Newtonian dynamics is still used with great success by most engineers and, in selected applications, by many physicists. Furthermore, the propriety of this use of the older theory can be proved from the very theory that has, in other applications, replaced it. Einstein's theory can be used to show that predictions from Newton's equations will be as good as our measuring instruments in all applications that satisfy a small number of restrictive conditions. For example, if Newtonian theory is to provide a good approximate solution, the relative velocities of the bodies considered must be small compared with the velocity of light. Subject to this condition and a few others, Newtonian theory seems to be derivable from Einsteinian, of which it is therefore a special case.

But, the objection continues, no theory can possibly conflict with one of its special cases. If Einsteinian science seems to make Newtonian dynamics wrong, that is only because some Newtonians were so incautious as to claim that Newtonian theory yielded entirely precise results or that it was valid at very high relative velocities. Since they could not have had any evidence for such claims, they betrayed the standards of science when they made them. In so far as Newtonian theory was ever a truly scientific theory supported by valid evidence, it still is. Only extravagant claims for the theory – claims that were never properly parts of science – can have been shown by Einstein to be wrong. Purged of these merely human extravagances, Newtonian theory has never been challenged and cannot be.

Some variant of this argument is quite sufficient to make any theory ever used by a significant group of competent scientists immune to attack. The much-maligned phlogiston theory, for example, gave order to a large number of physical and chemical phenomena. It explained why bodies burned – they were rich in phlogiston – and why metals had so many more properties in common than did their ores. The metals were all compounded from different elementary earths combined with phlogiston, and the latter,

---

[v] Isaac Newton's *Mathematical Principles of Natural Philosophy* (Latin orig., 1687). Below, the 2nd-century BC Alexandrian Ptolemy formulated the geocentric model of the universe later overturned by Copernicus.

common to all metals, produced common properties. In addition, the phlogiston theory accounted for a number of reactions in which acids were formed by the combustion of substances like carbon and sulphur. Also, it explained the decrease of volume when combustion occurs in a confined volume of air – the phlogiston released by combustion "spoils" the elasticity of the air that absorbed it, just as fire "spoils" the elasticity of a steel spring.[3] If these were the only phenomena that the phlogiston theorists had claimed for their theory, that theory could never have been challenged. A similar argument will suffice for any theory that has ever been successfully applied to any range of phenomena at all.

But to save theories in this way, their range of application must be restricted to those phenomena and to that precision of observation with which the experimental evidence in hand already deals.[4] Carried just a step further (and the step can scarcely be avoided once the first is taken), such a limitation prohibits the scientist from claiming to speak "scientifically" about any phenomenon not already observed. Even in its present form the restriction forbids the scientist to rely upon a theory in his own research whenever that research enters an area or seeks a degree of precision for which past practice with the theory offers no precedent. These prohibitions are logically unexceptionable. But the result of accepting them would be the end of the research through which science may develop further.

By now that point too is virtually a tautology. Without commitment to a paradigm there could be no normal science. Furthermore, that commitment must extend to areas and to degrees of precision for which there is no full precedent. If it did not, the paradigm could provide no puzzles that had not already been solved. Besides, it is not only normal science that depends upon commitment to a paradigm. If existing theory binds the scientist only with respect to existing applications, then there can be no surprises, anomalies, or crises. But these are just the signposts that point the way to extraordinary science. If positivistic restrictions on the range of a theory's legitimate applicability are taken literally, the mechanism that tells the scientific community what problems may lead to fundamental change must cease to function. And when that occurs, the community will inevitably return to something much like its pre-paradigm state, a condition in which all members practice science but in which their gross product scarcely resembles science at all. Is it really any wonder that the price of significant scientific advance is a commitment that runs the risk of being wrong?

More important, there is a revealing logical lacuna in the positivist's argument, one that will reintroduce us immediately to the nature of revolutionary change. Can Newtonian dynamics really be *derived* from relativistic dynamics? What would such a derivation look like? Imagine a set of statements, $E_1, E_2, \ldots, E_n$, which together embody the laws of relativity theory. These statements contain variables and parameters representing spatial position, time, rest mass, etc. From them, together with the apparatus of logic and mathematics, is deducible a whole set of further statements including some that can be checked by observation. To prove the adequacy of Newtonian dynamics as a special case, we must add to the E_i's additional statements, like $(v/c)^2 \ll 1$, restricting the range of the parameters and variables. This enlarged set of statements is then manipulated to yield a new set, $N_1, N_2, \ldots, N_m$ which is identical in form with Newton's laws of motion, the law of gravity, and so on. Apparently Newtonian dynamics has been derived from Einsteinian, subject to a few limiting conditions.

Yet the derivation is spurious, at least to this point. Though the N_i's are a special case of the laws of relativistic mechanics, they are not Newton's Laws. Or at least they are not unless those laws are reinterpreted in a way that would have been impossible until after Einstein's work. The variables and parameters that in the Einsteinian E_i's represented spatial position, time, mass, etc., still occur in the N_i's; and they there still represent Einsteinian space, time, and mass. But the physical referents of these Einsteinian concepts are by no means identical with those of the Newtonian concepts that bear the same name. (Newtonian mass is conserved; Einsteinian is convertible with energy. Only at low relative velocities may the two be measured in the same way, and even then they must not be conceived to be the same.) Unless we change the definitions of the variables in the N_i's, the statements we have derived are not Newtonian. If we do change them, we cannot properly be said to have *derived* Newton's Laws, at least not in any sense of "derive" now generally recognized. Our argument has, of course, explained why Newton's Laws ever seemed to work. In doing so it has justified, say, an automobile driver in acting as though he lived in a Newtonian universe. An argument of the same type is used to justify teaching earth-centered astronomy to surveyors. But the argument has still not done what it purported to do. It has not, that is, shown Newton's Laws to be a limiting case of Einstein's. For in the passage to the limit it is not only the forms of the laws that have changed. Simultaneously we have had to alter the fundamental structural elements of which the universe to which they apply is composed.

This need to change the meaning of established and familiar concepts is central to the revolutionary impact of Einstein's theory. Though subtler than the changes from geocentrism to heliocentrism, from phlogiston to oxygen, or from corpuscles to waves, the resulting conceptual transformation is no less decisively destructive of a previously established paradigm. We may even come to see it as a prototype for revolutionary reorientations in the sciences. Just because it did not involve the introduction of additional objects or concepts, the transition from Newtonian to Einsteinian

317

mechanics illustrates with particular clarity the scientific revolution as a displacement of the conceptual network through which scientists view the world.

These remarks should suffice to show what might, in another philosophical climate, have been taken for granted. At least for scientists, most of the apparent differences between a discarded scientific theory and its successor are real. Though an out-of-date theory can always be viewed as a special case of its up-to-date successor, it must be transformed for the purpose. And the transformation is one that can be undertaken only with the advantages of hindsight, the explicit guidance of the more recent theory. Furthermore, even if that transformation were a legitimate device to employ in interpreting the older theory, the result of its application would be a theory so restricted that it could only restate what was already known. Because of its economy, that restatement would have utility, but it could not suffice for the guidance of research.

Let us, therefore, now take it for granted that the differences between successive paradigms are both necessary and irreconcilable. Can we then say more explicitly what sorts of differences these are? The most apparent type has already been illustrated repeatedly. Successive paradigms tell us different things about the population of the universe and about that population's behavior. They differ, that is, about such questions as the existence of subatomic particles, the materiality of light, and the conservation of heat or of energy. These are the substantive differences between successive paradigms, and they require no further illustration. But paradigms differ in more than substance, for they are directed not only to nature but also back upon the science that produced them. They are the source of the methods, problem-field, and standards of solution accepted by any mature scientific community at any given time. As a result, the reception of a new paradigm often necessitates a redefinition of the corresponding science. Some old problems may be relegated to another science or declared entirely "unscientific." Others that were previously non-existent or trivial may, with a new paradigm, become the very archetypes of significant scientific achievement. And as the problems change, so, often, does the standard that distinguishes a real scientific solution from a mere metaphysical speculation, word game, or mathematical play. The normal-scientific tradition that emerges from a scientific revolution is not only incompatible but often actually incommensurable with that which has gone before.

The impact of Newton's work upon the normal seventeenth-century tradition of scientific practice provides a striking example of these subtler effects of paradigm shift. Before Newton was born the "new science" of the century had at last succeeded in rejecting Aristotelian and scholastic explanations expressed in terms of the essences of material bodies. To say

318

that a stone fell because its "nature" drove it toward the center of the universe had been made to look a mere tautological word-play, something it had not previously been. Henceforth the entire flux of sensory appearances, including color, taste, and even weight, was to be explained in terms of the size, shape, position, and motion of the elementary corpuscles of base matter. The attribution of other qualities to the elementary atoms was a resort to the occult and therefore out of bounds for science. Molière caught the new spirit precisely when he ridiculed the doctor who explained opium's efficacy as a soporific by attributing to it a dormitive potency.[vi] During the last half of the seventeenth century many scientists preferred to say that the round shape of the opium particles enabled them to sooth the nerves about which they moved.[5]

In an earlier period explanations in terms of occult qualities had been an integral part of productive scientific work. Nevertheless, the seventeenth century's new commitment to mechanico-corpuscular explanation proved immensely fruitful for a number of sciences, ridding them of problems that had defied generally accepted solution and suggesting others to replace them. In dynamics, for example, Newton's three laws of motion are less a product of novel experiments than of the attempt to reinterpret well-known observations in terms of the motions and interactions of primary neutral corpuscles. Consider just one concrete illustration. Since neutral corpuscles could act on each other only by contact, the mechanico-corpuscular view of nature directed scientific attention to a brand-new subject of study, the alteration of particulate motions by collisions. Descartes announced the problem and provided its first putative solution. Huyghens, Wren, and Wallis carried it still further, partly by experimenting with colliding pendulum bobs, but mostly by applying previously well-known characteristics of motion to the new problem. And Newton embedded their results in his laws of motion. The equal "action" and "reaction" of the third law are the changes in quantity of motion experienced by the two parties to a collision. The same change of motion supplies the definition of dynamical force implicit in the second law. In this case, as in many others during the seventeenth century, the corpuscular paradigm bred both a new problem and a large part of that problem's solution.[6]

Yet, though much of Newton's work was directed to problems and embodied standards derived from the mechanico-corpuscular world view, the effect of the paradigm that resulted from his work was a further and partially destructive change in the problems and standards legitimate for science. Gravity, interpreted as an innate attraction between every pair of

---

[vi] In Molière's play, La Malade imaginaire (The Hypochondriac), Interlude III (following Act III), see the first response of Bachelierus.

particles of matter, was an occult quality in the same sense as the scholastics' "tendency to fall" had been. Therefore, while the standards of corpuscularism remained in effect, the search for a mechanical explanation of gravity was one of the most challenging problems for those who accepted the *Principia* as paradigm. Newton devoted much attention to it and so did many of his eighteenth-century successors. The only apparent option was to reject Newton's theory for its failure to explain gravity, and that alternative, too, was widely adopted. Yet neither of these views ultimately triumphed. Unable either to practice science without the *Principia* or to make that work conform to the corpuscular standards of the seventeenth century, scientists gradually accepted the view that gravity was indeed innate. By the mid-eighteenth century that interpretation had been almost universally accepted, and the result was a genuine reversion (which is not the same as a retrogression) to a scholastic standard. Innate attractions and repulsions joined size, shape, position, and motion as physically irreducible primary properties of matter.[7]

The resulting change in the standards and problem-field of physical science was once again consequential. By the 1740's, for example, electricians could speak of the attractive "virtue" of the electric fluid without thereby inviting the ridicule that had greeted Molière's doctor a century before. As they did so, electrical phenomena increasingly displayed an order different from the one they had shown when viewed as the effects of a mechanical effluvium that could act only by contact. In particular, when electrical action-at-a-distance became a subject for study in its own right, the phenomenon we now call charging by induction could be recognized as one of its effects. Previously, when seen at all, it had been attributed to the direct action of electrical "atmospheres" or to the leakages inevitable in any electrical laboratory. The new view of inductive effects was, in turn, the key to Franklin's analysis of the Leyden jar and thus to the emergence of a new and Newtonian paradigm for electricity. Nor were dynamics and electricity the only scientific fields affected by the legitimization of the search for forces innate to matter. The large body of eighteenth-century literature on chemical affinities and replacement series also derives from this supramechanical aspect of Newtonianism. Chemists who believed in these differential attractions between the various chemical species set up previously unimagined experiments and searched for new sorts of reactions. Without the data and the chemical concepts developed in that process, the later work of Lavoisier and, more particularly, of Dalton[vii] would be incomprehensible.[8] Changes in the standards governing permissible problems, concepts, and explanations can transform a science. In

---

[vii] John Dalton (1766–1844) was an English chemist and physicist.

the next section I shall even suggest a sense in which they transform the world.

Other examples of these nonsubstantive differences between successive paradigms can be retrieved from the history of any science in almost any period of its development. For the moment let us be content with just two other and far briefer illustrations. Before the chemical revolution, one of the acknowledged tasks of chemistry was to account for the qualities of chemical substances and for the changes these qualities underwent during chemical reactions. With the aid of a small number of elementary "principles" – of which phlogiston was one – the chemist was to explain why some substances are acidic, others metalline, combustible, and so forth. Some success in this direction had been achieved. We have already noted that phlogiston explained why the metals were so much alike, and we could have developed a similar argument for the acids. Lavoisier's reform, however, ultimately did away with chemical "principles," and thus ended by depriving chemistry of some actual and much potential explanatory power. To compensate for this loss, a change in standards was required. During much of the nineteenth century failure to explain the qualities of compounds was no indictment of a chemical theory.[9]

Or again, Clerk Maxwell shared with other nineteenth-century proponents of the wave theory of light the conviction that light waves must be propagated through a material ether. Designing a mechanical medium to support such waves was a standard problem for many of his ablest contemporaries. His own theory, however, the electromagnetic theory of light, gave no account at all of a medium able to support light waves, and it clearly made such an account harder to provide than it had seemed before. Initially, Maxwell's theory was widely rejected for those reasons. But, like Newton's theory, Maxwell's proved difficult to dispense with, and as it achieved the status of a paradigm, the community's attitude toward it changed. In the early decades of the twentieth century Maxwell's insistence upon the existence of a mechanical ether looked more and more like lip service, which it emphatically had not been, and the attempts to design such an ethereal medium were abandoned. Scientists no longer thought it unscientific to speak of an electrical "displacement" without specifying what was being displaced. The result, again, was a new set of problems and standards, one which, in the event, had much to do with the emergence of relativity theory.[10]

These characteristic shifts in the scientific community's conception of its legitimate problems and standards would have less significance to this essay's thesis if one could suppose that they always occurred from some methodologically lower to some higher type. In that case their effects, too, would seem cumulative. No wonder that some historians have argued that the history of science records a continuing increase in the maturity and

321

refinement of man's conception of the nature of science.[11] Yet the case for cumulative development of science's problems and standards is even harder to make than the case for cumulation of theories. The attempt to explain gravity, though fruitfully abandoned by most eighteenth-century scientists, was not directed to an intrinsically illegitimate problem; the objections to innate forces were neither inherently unscientific nor metaphysical in some pejorative sense. There are no external standards to permit a judgment of that sort. What occurred was neither a decline nor a raising of standards, but simply a change demanded by the adoption of a new paradigm. Furthermore, that change has since been reversed and could be again. In the twentieth century Einstein succeeded in explaining gravitational attractions, and that explanation has returned science to a set of canons and problems that are, in this particular respect, more like those of Newton's predecessors than of his successors. Or again, the development of quantum mechanics has reversed the methodological prohibition that originated in the chemical revolution. Chemists now attempt, and with great success, to explain the color, state of aggregation, and other qualities of the substances used and produced in their laboratories. A similar reversal may even be underway in electromagnetic theory. Space, in contemporary physics, is not the inert and homogenous substratum employed in both Newton's and Maxwell's theories; some of its new properties are not unlike those once attributed to the ether; we may someday come to know what an electric displacement is.

By shifting emphasis from the cognitive to the normative functions of paradigms, the preceding examples enlarge our understanding of the ways in which paradigms give form to the scientific life. Previously, we had principally examined the paradigm's role as a vehicle for scientific theory. In that role it functions by telling the scientist about the entities that nature does and does not contain and about the ways in which those entities behave. That information provides a map whose details are elucidated by mature scientific research. And since nature is too complex and varied to be explored at random, that map is as essential as observation and experiment to science's continuing development. Through the theories they embody, paradigms prove to be constitutive of the research activity. They are also, however, constitutive of science in other respects, and that is now the point. In particular, our most recent examples show that paradigms provide scientists not only with a map but also with some of the directions essential for map-making. In learning a paradigm the scientist acquires theory, methods, and standards together, usually in an inextricable mixture. Therefore, when paradigms change, there are usually significant shifts in the criteria determining the legitimacy both of problems and of proposed solutions.

That observation returns us to the point from which this section began, for it provides our first explicit indication of why the choice between competing paradigms regularly raises questions that cannot be resolved by the criteria of normal science. To the extent, as significant as it is incomplete, that two scientific schools disagree about what is a problem and what a solution, they will inevitably talk through each other when debating the relative merits of their respective paradigms. In the partially circular arguments that regularly result, each paradigm will be shown to satisfy more or less the criteria that it dictates for itself and to fall short of a few of those dictated by its opponent. There are other reasons, too, for the incompleteness of logical contact that consistently characterizes paradigm debates. For example, since no paradigm ever solves all the problems it defines and since no two paradigms leave all the same problems unsolved, paradigm debates always involve the question: Which problems is it more significant to have solved? Like the issue of competing standards, that question of values can be answered only in terms of criteria that lie outside of normal science altogether, and it is that recourse to external criteria that most obviously makes paradigm debates revolutionary. . . .

Notes

1   Silvanus P. Thompson, *Life of William Thomson Baron Kelvin of Largs* (London, 1910), I, 266–81.

2   See, for example, the remarks by P. P. Wiener in *Philosophy of Science*, XXV (1958), pp. 298.

3   James B. Conant, *Overthrow of the Phlogiston Theory* (Cambridge, 1950), pp. 13–16; and J. R. Partington, *A Short History of Chemistry* (2d edn; London, 1951), pp. 85–8. The fullest and most sympathetic account of the phlogiston theory's achievements is by H. Metzger, *Newton, Stahl, Boerhaave et la doctrine chimique* (Paris, 1930), Part II.

4   Compare the conclusions reached through a very different sort of analysis by R. B. Braithwaite, *Scientific Explanation* (Cambridge, 1953), pp. 50–87, esp. p. 76.

5   For corpuscularism in general, see Marie Boas, "The Establishment of the Mechanical Philosophy," *Osiris*, X (1952), pp. 412–541. For the effect of particle-shape on taste, see ibid., p. 483.

6   R Dugas, *La mécanique au XVIIᵉ siècle* (Neuchatel, 1954), pp. 177–85, 284–98, 345–56.

7   I. B. Cohen, *Franklin and Newton: An Inquiry into Speculative Newtonian Experimental Science and Franklin's Work in Electricity as an Example Thereof* (Philadelphia, 1956), chs vi–vii.

8   For electricity, see ibid., chs viii–ix. For chemistry, see Metzger, *Newton, Stahl, Boerhaave*, Part I.

9   E. Meyerson, *Identity and Reality* (New York, 1930), ch. x.

10 E. T. Whittaker, *A History of the Theories of Aether and Electricity*, II (London, 1953), pp. 28–30.

11 For a brilliant and entirely up-to-date attempt to fit scientific development into this Procrustean bed, see C. C. Gillispie, *The Edge of Objectivity: An Essay in the History of Scientific Ideas* (Princeton, NJ, 1960).

chapter twenty-three

Complexity and Contradiction in Architecture

Robert Venturi

Philadelphia-based architect Robert Venturi (1925–) galvanized the growing rejection of the International Style of modernist architecture with his 1966 book *Complexity and Contradiction in Architecture*. It has been called the most important work on architecture since Le Corbusier's *Vers une Architecture*. Venturi famously responds to Mies van der Rohe's slogan that "Less is more" – that ornament and diversity of style are to be eliminated – with the playful, "Less is a bore." Venturi's architecture is marked by eclecticism and the refusal to reject popular commercial architecture as inherently vulgar. His aim is not to replace unity of style with pluralism, but to argue for less simple, more complex forms of unity, which constitute what he calls "the difficult whole," buildings that thrive on inner tension rather than trying to overcome it. It is this approach that later came to be called "postmodernism." Venturi further applied his principles in the book, *Learning from Las Vegas* (1972).

Nonstraightforward Architecture: A Gentle Manifesto

I like complexity and contradiction in architecture. I do not like the incoherence or arbitrariness of incompetent architecture nor the precious intricacies of picturesqueness or expressionism. Instead, I speak of a complex and contradictory architecture based on the richness and ambiguity of modern experience, including that experience which is inherent in art. Everywhere, except in architecture, complexity and contradiction have

From Robert Venturi, *Complexity and Contradiction in Architecture* (New York: Museum of Modern Art, 1966), pp. 16–17, 23–5, 38–41, 88 and 102–4.

been acknowledged, from Gödel's proof of ultimate inconsistency in mathematics to T. S. Eliot's analysis of "difficult" poetry and Joseph Albers' definition of the paradoxical quality of painting.[i]

But architecture is necessarily complex and contradictory in its very inclusion of the traditional Vitruvian elements of commodity, firmness, and delight. And today the wants of program, structure, mechanical equipment, and expression, even in single buildings in simple contexts, are diverse and conflicting in ways previously unimaginable. The increasing dimension and scale of architecture in urban and regional planning add to the difficulties. I welcome the problems and exploit the uncertainties. By embracing contradiction as well as complexity, I aim for vitality as well as validity.

Architects can no longer afford to be intimidated by the puritanically moral language of orthodox Modern architecture. I like elements which are hybrid rather than "pure," compromising rather than "clean," distorted rather than "straightforward," ambiguous rather than "articulated," perverse as well as impersonal, boring as well as "interesting," conventional rather than "designed," accommodating rather than excluding, redundant rather than simple, vestigial as well as innovating, inconsistent and equivocal rather than direct and clear. I am for messy vitality over obvious unity. I include the non sequitur and proclaim the duality.

I am for richness of meaning rather than clarity of meaning; for the implicit function as well as the explicit function. I prefer "both-and" to "either-or," black and white, and sometimes gray, to black or white. A valid architecture evokes many levels of meaning and combinations of focus: its space and its elements become readable and workable in several ways at once.

But an architecture of complexity and contradiction has a special obligation toward the whole: its truth must be in its totality or its implications of totality. It must embody the difficult unity of inclusion rather than the easy unity of exclusion. More is not less.

Complexity and Contradiction vs Simplification or Picturesqueness

Orthodox Modern architects have tended to recognize complexity insufficiently or inconsistently. In their attempt to break with tradition and start all over again, they idealized the primitive and elementary at the expense of the diverse and the sophisticated. As participants in a revolutionary

[i] Logician Kurt Gödel (1906–78), poet and critic T. S. Eliot (1888–1965), and painter Joseph Albers (1888–1976).

movement, they acclaimed the newness of modern functions, ignoring their complications. In their role as reformers, they puritanically advocated the separation and exclusion of elements, rather than the inclusion of various requirements and their juxtapositions. As a forerunner of the Modern movement, Frank Lloyd Wright,[ii] who grew up with the motto "Truth against the World," wrote: "Visions of simplicity so broad and far-reaching would open to me and such building harmonies appear that . . . would change and deepen the thinking and culture of the modern world. So I believed."[1] And Le Corbusier, co-founder of Purism, spoke of the "great primary forms" which, he proclaimed, were "distinct . . . and without ambiguity."[2] Modern architects with few exceptions eschewed ambiguity.

But now our position is different: "At the same time that the problems increase in quantity, complexity, and difficulty they also change faster than before,"[3] and require an attitude more like that described by August Heckscher: "The movement from a view of life as essentially simple and orderly to a view of life as complex and ironic is what every individual passes through in becoming mature. But certain epochs encourage this development; in them the paradoxical or dramatic outlook colors the whole intellectual scene. . . . Amid simplicity and order rationalism is born, but rationalism proves inadequate in any period of upheaval. Then equilibrium must be created out of opposites. Such inner peace as men gain must represent a tension among contradictions and uncertainties. . . . A feeling for paradox allows seemingly dissimilar things to exist side by side, their very incongruity suggesting a kind of truth."[4]

Rationalizations for simplification are still current, however, though subtler than the early arguments. They are expansions of Mies van der Rohe's magnificent paradox, "less is more."[iii] Paul Rudolph has clearly stated the implications of Mies' point of view: "All problems can never be solved. . . . Indeed it is a characteristic of the twentieth century that architects are highly selective in determining which problems they want to solve. Mies, for instance, makes wonderful buildings only because he ignores many aspects of a building. If he solved more problems, his buildings would be far less potent."[5]

The doctrine "less is more" bemoans complexity and justifies exclusion for expressive purposes. It does, indeed, permit the architect to be "highly selective in determining which problems [he wants] to solve." But if the architect must be "committed to his particular way of seeing the universe,"[6] such a commitment surely means that the architect determines how problems should be solved, not that he can determine which of the

---

[ii] Great American architect (1867–1959).

[iii] Ludwig Mies van der Rohe (1886–1969), German architect, one of the leaders of the modern International Style and director of the Bauhaus school.

problems he will solve. He can exclude important considerations only at the risk of separating architecture from the experience of life and the needs of society. If some problems prove insoluble, he can express this: in an inclusive rather than an exclusive kind of architecture there is room for the fragment, for contradiction, for improvisation, and for the tensions these produce. Mies' exquisite pavilions have had valuable implications for architecture, but their selectiveness of content and language is their limitation as well as their strength.

I question the relevance of analogies between pavilions and houses, especially analogies between Japanese pavilions and recent domestic architecture. They ignore the real complexity and contradiction inherent in the domestic program – the spatial and technological possibilities as well as the need for variety in visual experience. Forced simplicity results in oversimplification. In the Wiley House, for instance, in contrast to his glass house, Philip Johnson attempted to go beyond the simplicities of the elegant pavilion.[iv] He explicitly separated and articulated the enclosed "private functions" of living on a ground floor pedestal, thus separating them from the open social functions in the modular pavilion above. But even here the building becomes a diagram of an oversimplified program for living – an abstract theory of either-or. Where simplicity cannot work, simpleness results. Blatant simplification means bland architecture. Less is a bore. . . .

Contradictory Levels:
The Phenomenon of "Both-And" in Architecture

. . . Cleanth Brooks refers to Donne's art as "having it both ways" but, he says, "most of us in this latter day, cannot.[v] We are disciplined in the tradition either-or, and lack the mental agility – to say nothing of the maturity of attitude – which would allow us to indulge in the finer distinctions and the more subtle reservations permitted by the tradition of both-and."[7] The tradition "either-or" has characterized orthodox modern architecture: a sun screen is probably nothing else; a support is seldom an enclosure; a wall is not violated by window penetrations but is totally interrupted by glass; program functions are exaggeratedly articulated into wings or segregated separate pavilions. Even "flowing space" has implied being outside when inside, and inside when outside, rather than both at

---

[iv] Two buildings by contemporary American architect Philip Johnson in New Canaan, Connecticut.

[v] The great English poet John Donne (1572–1631).

the same time. Such manifestations of articulation and clarity are foreign to an architecture of complexity and contradiction, which tends to include "both-and" rather than exclude "either-or."

If the source of the both-and phenomenon is contradiction, its basis is hierarchy, which yields several levels of meanings among elements with varying values. It can include elements that are both good and awkward, big and little, closed and open, continuous and articulated, round and square, structural and spatial. An architecture which includes varying levels of meaning breeds ambiguity and tension.

Most of the examples will be difficult to "read," but abstruse architecture is valid when it reflects the complexities and contradictions of content and meaning. Simultaneous perception of a multiplicity of levels involves struggles and hesitations for the observer, and makes his perception more vivid. . . .

Conventional elements in architecture represent one stage in an evolutionary development, and they contain in their changed use and expression some of their past meaning as well as their new meaning. What can be called the vestigial element parallels the double-functioning element. It is distinct from a superfluous element because it contains a double meaning. This is the result of a more or less ambiguous combination of the old meaning, called up by associations, with a new meaning created by the modified or new function, structural or programmatic, and the new context. The vestigial element discourages clarity of meaning; it promotes richness of meaning instead. It is a basis for change and growth in the city as manifest in remodeling which involves old buildings with new uses both programmatic and symbolic (like palazzi which become museums or embassies), and old street patterns with new uses and scales of movement. The paths of medieval fortification walls in European cities became boulevards in the nineteenth century; a section of Broadway is a piazza and a symbol rather than an artery to upper New York state. The ghost of Dock Street in Philadelphia's Society Hill, however, is a meaningless vestige rather than a working element resulting from a valid transition between the old and the new. I shall later refer to the vestigial element as it appears in Michelangelo's architecture and in what might be called Pop architecture.

The rhetorical element, like the double-functioning element, is infrequent in recent architecture. If the latter offends through its inherent ambiguity, rhetoric offends orthodox Modern architecture's cult of the minimum. But the rhetorical element is justified as a valid if outmoded means of expression. An element can seem rhetorical from one point of view, but if it is valid, at another level it enriches meaning by underscoring. In the project for a gateway at Bourneville by Ledoux, the columns in the arch are structurally rhetorical if not redundant.[vi] Expressively, however, they underscore the abstractness of the opening as a semicircle more than an

329

arch, and they further define the opening as a gateway. As I have said, the stairway at the Pennsylvania Academy of the Fine Arts by Furness is too big in its immediate context, but appropriate as a gesture towards the outside scale and a sense of entry.[vii] The Classical portico is a rhetorical entrance. The stairs, columns, and pediment are juxtaposed upon the other-scale, real entrance behind. Paul Rudolph's entrance in the Art and Architecture Building at Yale is at the scale of the city; most people use the little door at the side in the stair tower.[viii]

Much of the function of ornament is rhetorical – like the use of Baroque pilasters for rhythm, and Vanbrugh's disengaged pilasters at the entrance to the kitchen court at Blenheim which are an architectural fanfare.[ix] The rhetorical element which is also structural is rare in Modern architecture, although Mies has used the rhetorical I-beam with an assurance that would make Bernini envious.[x]

Accommodation and the Limitations of Order: The Conventional Element

In short, that contradictions must be accepted.[8]

A valid order accommodates the circumstantial contradictions of a complex reality. It accommodates as well as imposes. It thereby admits "control *and* spontaneity," "correctness *and* ease" – improvisation within the whole. It tolerates qualifications and compromise. There are no fixed laws in architecture, but not everything will work in a building or a city. The architect must decide, and these subtle evaluations are among his principal functions. He must determine what must be made to work and what it is possible to compromise with, what will give in, and where and how. He does not ignore or exclude inconsistencies of program and structure within the order.

I have emphasized that aspect of complexity and contradiction which grows out of the medium more than the program of the building. Now I

[vi] Gateway in Bourneville, France, by French architect Claude-Nicolas Ledoux (1736–1806).

[vii] American architect Frank Furness's (1839–1912) work on the Pennsylvania Academy of Fine Arts, Philadelphia.

[viii] Contemporary American architect Paul Rudolph.

[ix] English architect John Vanbrugh's (1664–1726) work on Blenheim Palace in Oxfordshire, England.

[x] Gian Lorenzo Bernini (1598–1680), great Italian Renaissance sculptor.

shall emphasize the complexity and contradiction that develops from the program and reflects the inherent complexities and contradictions of living. It is obvious that in actual practice the two must be interrelated. Contradictions can represent the exceptional inconsistency that modifies the otherwise consistent order, or they can represent inconsistencies throughout the order as a whole. In the first case, the relationship between inconsistency and order accommodates circumstantial exceptions to the order, or it juxtaposes particular with general elements of order. Here you build an order up and then break it down, but break it from strength rather than from weakness. I have described this relationship as "contradiction accommodated." The relationship of inconsistency within the whole I consider a manifestation of "the difficult whole," which is discussed in the last chapter.

Mies refers to a need to "create order out of the desperate confusion of our times." But Kahn has said "by order I do not mean orderliness."[xi] Should we not resist bemoaning confusion? Should we not look for meaning in the complexities and contradictions of our times and acknowledge the limitations of systems? These, I think, are the two justifications for breaking order: the recognition of variety and confusion inside and outside, in program and environment, indeed, at all levels of experience; and the ultimate limitation of all orders composed by man. When circumstances defy order, order should bend or break: anomalies and uncertainties give validity to architecture.

Meaning can be enhanced by breaking the order; the exception points up the rule. A building with no "imperfect" part can have no perfect part, because contrast supports meaning. An artful discord gives vitality to architecture. You can allow for contingencies all over, but they cannot prevail all over. If order without expediency breeds formalism, expediency without order, of course, means chaos. Order must exist before it can be broken. No artist can belittle the role of order as a way of seeing a whole relevant to its own characteristics and context. "There is no work of art without a system" is Le Corbusier's dictum. . . .

Ironic convention is relevant both for the individual building and the townscape. It recognizes the real condition of our architecture and its status in our culture. Industry promotes expensive industrial and electronic research but not architectural experiments, and the Federal government diverts subsidies toward air transportation, communication, and the vast enterprises of war or, as they call it, national security, rather than toward the forces for the direct enhancement of life. The practicing architect must admit this. In simple terms, the budgets, techniques, and programs for his buildings must relate more to 1866 than 1966. Architects should accept

---

[xi] American architect Louis Kahn (1901–74).

their modest role rather than disguise it and risk what might be called an electronic expressionism, which might parallel the industrial expressionism of early Modern architecture. The architect who would accept his role as combiner of significant old clichés – valid banalities – in new contexts as his condition within a society that directs its best efforts, its big money, and its elegant technologies elsewhere, can ironically express in this indirect way a true concern for society's inverted scale of values.

I have alluded to the reasons why honky-tonk elements in our architecture and townscape are here to stay, especially in the important short-term view, and why such a fate should be acceptable. Pop Art has demonstrated that these commonplace elements are often the main source of the occasional variety and vitality of our cities, and that it is not their banality or vulgarity as elements which make for the banality or vulgarity of the whole scene, but rather their contextual relationships of space and scale.

Another significant implication from Pop Art involves method in city planning. Architects and planners who peevishly denounce the conventional townscape for its vulgarity or banality promote elaborate methods for abolishing or disguising honky-tonk elements in the existing landscape, or, for excluding them from the vocabulary of their new townscapes. But they largely fail either to enhance or to provide a substitute for the existing scene because they attempt the impossible. By attempting too much they flaunt their impotence and risk their continuing influence as supposed experts. Cannot the architect and planner, by slight adjustments to the conventional elements of the townscape, existing or proposed, promote significant effects? By modifying or adding conventional elements to still other conventional elements they can, by a twist of context, gain a maximum of effect through a minimum of means. They can make us see the same things in a different way.

Finally, standardization, like convention, can be another manifestation of the strong order. But unlike convention it has been accepted in Modern architecture as an enriching product of our technology, yet dreaded for its potential domination and brutality. But is it not standardization that is without circumstantial accommodation and without a creative use of context that is to be feared more than standardization itself? The ideas of order and circumstance, convention and context – of employing standardization in an unstandard way – apply to our continuing problem of standardization versus variety. Giedion has written of Aalto's[xii] unique "combination of standardization with irrationality so that standardization is no longer master but servant."[9] I prefer to think of Aalto's art as contradictory rather than irrational – an artful recognition of the circum-

---

[xii] Finnish architect Alvar Aalto (1898–1976).

stantial and the contextual and of the inevitable limits of the order of standardization.

The Obligation Toward the Difficult Whole

. . . Toledo [Ohio] was very beautiful.[10]

An architecture of complexity and accommodation does not forsake the whole. In fact, I have referred to a special obligation toward the whole because the whole is difficult to achieve. And I have emphasized the goal of unity rather than of simplification in an art "whose . . . truth [is] in its totality."[11] It is the difficult unity through inclusion rather than the easy unity through exclusion. Gestalt psychology considers a perceptual whole the result of, and yet more than, the sum of its parts. The whole is dependent on the position, number, and inherent characteristics of the parts. A complex system in Herbert A. Simon's definition includes "a large number of parts that interact in a non-simple way."[12] The difficult whole in an architecture of complexity and contradiction includes multiplicity and diversity of elements in relationships that are inconsistent or among the weaker kinds perceptually. . . .

Inherent in an architecture of opposites is the inclusive whole. The unity of the interior of the Imatra church or the complex at Wolfsburg is achieved not through suppression or exclusion but through the dramatic inclusion of contradictory or circumstantial parts.[xiii] Aalto's architecture acknowledges the difficult and subtle conditions of program, while "serene" architecture, on the other hand, works simplifications.

However, the obligation toward the whole in an architecture of complexity and contradiction does not preclude the building which is unresolved. Poets and playwrights acknowledge dilemmas without solutions. The validity of the questions and vividness of the meaning are what make their works art more than philosophy. A goal of poetry can be unity of expression over resolution of content. Contemporary sculpture is often fragmentary, and today we appreciate Michelangelo's unfinished Pietàs more than his early work, because their content is suggested, their expression more immediate, and their forms are completed beyond themselves. A building can also be more or less incompleted in the expression of its program and its form.

[xiii] Two projects by Aalto: Vooksenniska church in Imatra, Finland, and the Cultural Centre, Wolfsburg, Germany.

The Gothic cathedral, like Beauvais, for instance, of which only the enormous choir was built, is frequently unfinished in relation to its program, yet it is complete in the effect of its form because of the motival consistency of its many parts.[xiv] The complex program which is a process, continually changing and growing in time yet at each stage at some level related to a whole, should be recognized as essential at the scale of city planning. The incomplete program is valid for a complex single building as well.

Each of the fragmental twin churches on the Piazza del Popolo,[xv] however, is complete at the level of program but incomplete in the expression of form. The uniquely assymmetrically placed tower, as we have seen, inflects each building toward a greater whole outside itself. The very complex building, which in its open form is incomplete, in itself relates to Maki's "group form;" it is the antithesis of the "perfect single building"[13] or the closed pavilion. As a fragment of a greater whole in a greater context this kind of building relates again to the scope of city planning as a means of increasing the unity of the complex whole. An architecture that can simultaneously recognize contradictory levels should be able to admit the paradox of the whole fragment: the building which is a whole at one level and a fragment of a greater whole at another level.

In *God's Own Junkyard* Peter Blake has compared the chaos of commercial Main Street with the orderliness of the University of Virginia.[xvi] Besides the irrelevancy of the comparison, is not Main Street almost all right? Indeed, is not the commercial strip of a Route 66 almost all right? As I have said, our question is: what slight twist of context will make them all right? Perhaps more signs more contained. Illustrations in *God's Own Junkyard* of Times Square and roadtown are compared with illustrations of New England villages and arcadian countrysides. But the pictures in this book that are supposed to be bad are often good. The seemingly chaotic juxtapositions of honky-tonk elements express an intriguing kind of vitality and validity, and they produce an unexpected approach to unity as well.

It is true that an ironic interpretation such as this results partly from the change in scale of the subject matter in photographic form and the change in context within the frames of the photographs. But in some of these compositions there is an inherent sense of unity not far from the surface. It is not the obvious or easy unity derived from the dominant binder or the motival order of simpler, less contradictory compositions, but that derived from a complex and illusive order of the difficult whole. It is the taut

---

[xiv] Gothic cathedral in Beauvais, France.

[xv] In Rome.

[xvi] Peter Blake, *God's Own Junkyard: The Planned Deterioration of America's Landscape* (New York: Holt, Rinehart & Winston, 1964).

composition which contains contrapuntal relationships, equal combinations, inflected fragments, and acknowledged dualities. It is the unity which "maintains, but only just maintains, a control over the clashing elements which compose it. Chaos is very near; its nearness, but its avoidance, gives ... force."[14] In the validly complex building or cityscape, the eye does not want to be too easily or too quickly satisfied in its search for unity within a whole.

Some of the vivid lessons of Pop Art, involving contradictions of scale and context, should have awakened architects from prim dreams of pure order, which, unfortunately, are imposed in the easy Gestalt unities of the urban renewal projects of establishment Modern architecture and yet, fortunately are really impossible to achieve at any great scope. And it is perhaps from the everyday landscape, vulgar and disdained, that we can draw the complex and contradictory order that is valid and vital for our architecture as an urbanistic whole.

Notes

1 Frank Lloyd Wright, in *An American Architecture*, ed. Edgar Kaufmann (Horizon Press, New York, 1955), p. 207.
2 Le Corbusier, *Towards a New Architecture* (Architectural Press, London, 1927), p. 31.
3 Christopher Alexander, *Notes on the Synthesis of Form* (Harvard University Press, Cambridge, 1964), p. 4.
4 August Heckscher, *The Public Happiness* (Atheneum Publishers, New York, 1962), p. 102.
5 Paul Rudolph, in *Perspecta 7, The Yale Architectural Journal* (New Haven, 1961), p. 51.
6 Kenneth Burke: *Permanence and Change* (Hermes Publications, Los Altos, 1954), p. 107.
7 Cleanth Brooks, *The Well Wrought Urn* (Harcourt, Brace and World, New York, 1947), p. 81.
8 David Jones, *Epoch and Artist* (Chilmark Press, New York, 1959).
9 Siegfried Giedion, *Space, Time and Architecture* (Harvard University Press, Cambridge, 1963), p. 565.
10 Gertrude Stein, *Gertrude Stein's America*, ed. Gilbert A. Harrison (Robert B. Luce, Washington, DC, 1965).
11 Heckscher, *Public Happiness*, p. 287.
12 Herbert A. Simon, *Proceedings of the American Philosophical Society*, 106, no. 6 (December 12, 1962), p. 468.
13 Fumihiko Maki, *Investigations in Collective Form*, Special Publication No. 2, Washington University, St Louis (1964), p. 5.
14 Heckscher, *Public Happiness*, p. 289.

chapter
twenty-four

"The End of the Book and the Beginning of Writing"

Jacques Derrida

Algerian-born French philosopher Jacques Derrida (1930–) is one of the two most famous instigators of what is called postmodernism in contemporary philosophy (the other being Foucault). More accurately labelled a poststructuralist, he made his reputation in the late 1960s with a series of books remarkable for their careful analysis of texts, their novel critical perspective, and their difficult style. His work began as an analysis of Husserlian phenomenology that called attention to deep paradoxes and undecidable problems implicit in Husserl's fundamental distinctions. But the significance of this work extended far beyond phenomenology. In the selection below, from perhaps his most systematic work, *Of Grammatology* (1967), Derrida discovers in the philosophical tradition a search for presentation in representation, an attempt to grasp the ungraspable origin of meaning. This is especially evident in philosophy's "phonocentrism" or privileging the spoken word, with the latter's apparent immediacy of meaning and connection to the living presence of the human speaker, over the written word, which is always marked by mediation, distance, plurality, and uncertainty of meaning, or what Derrida called *différance*.

> *Socrates, he who does not write*
> Nietzsche

However the topic is considered, the *problem of language* has never been simply one problem among others. But never as much as at present has it invaded, *as such*, the global horizon of the most diverse researches and the

Jacques Derrida, "The End of the Book and the Beginning of Writing," Chapter 1, *Of Grammatology*, trans. Gayatri Chakravorty Spivak (Baltimore: Johns Hopkins University Press, 1974), pp. 6–26.

most heterogeneous discourses, diverse and heterogeneous in their intention, method, and ideology. The devaluation of the word "language" itself,
and how, in the very hold it has upon us, it betrays a loose vocabulary, the
temptation of a cheap seduction, the passive yielding to fashion, the
consciousness of the avant-garde, in other words – ignorance – are
evidences of this effect. This inflation of the sign "language" is the inflation
of the sign itself, absolute inflation, inflation itself. Yet, by one of its aspects
or shadows, it is itself still a sign: this crisis is also a symptom. It indicates,
as if in spite of itself, that a historico-metaphysical epoch *must* finally
determine as language the totality of its problematic horizon. It must do so
not only because all that desire had wished to wrest from the play of
language finds itself recaptured within that play but also because, for the
same reason, language itself is menaced in its very life, helpless, adrift in
the threat of limitlessness, brought back to its own finitude at the very
moment when its limits seem to disappear, when it ceases to be self-
assured, contained, and *guaranteed* by the infinite signified which seemed to
exceed it.

The Program

By a slow movement whose necessity is hardly perceptible, everything that
for at least some twenty centuries tended toward and finally succeeded in
being gathered under the name of language is beginning to let itself be
transferred to, or at least summarized under, the name of writing. By a
hardly perceptible necessity, it seems as though the concept of writing – no
longer indicating a particular, derivative, auxiliary form of language in
general (whether understood as communication, relation, expression, signification, constitution of meaning or thought, etc.), no longer designating
the exterior surface, the insubstantial double of a major signifier, *the
signifier of the signifier* – is beginning to go beyond the extension of
language. In all senses of the word, writing thus *comprehends* language. Not
that the word "writing" has ceased to designate the signifier of the signifier,
but it appears, strange as it may seem, that "signifier of the signifier" no
longer defines accidental doubling and fallen secondarity. "Signifier of the
signifier" describes on the contrary the movement of language: in its origin,
to be sure, but one can already suspect that an origin whose structure can
be expressed as "signifier of the signifier" conceals and erases itself in its
own production. There the signified always already functions as a signifier.
The secondarity that it seemed possible to ascribe to writing alone affects
all signifieds in general, affects them always already, the moment they *enter
the game*. There is not a single signified that escapes, even if recaptured, the

337

play of signifying references that constitute language. The advent of writing is the advent of this play; today such a play is coming into its own, effacing the limit starting from which one had thought to regulate the circulation of signs, drawing along with it all the reassuring signifieds, reducing all the strongholds, all the out-of-bounds shelters that watched over the field of language. This, strictly speaking, amounts to destroying the concept of "sign" and its entire logic. Undoubtedly it is not by chance that this *overwhelming* supervenes at the moment when the extension of the concept of language effaces all its limits. We shall see that this overwhelming and this effacement have the same meaning, are one and the same phenomenon. It is as if the Western concept of language (in terms of what, beyond its plurivocity and beyond the strict and problematic opposition of speech and language,[i] attaches it *in general* to phonematic or glossematic production, to language, to voice, to hearing, to sound and breadth, to speech) were revealed today as the guise or disguise of a primary writing:[1] more fundamental than that which, before this conversion, passed for the simple "supplement to the spoken word" (Rousseau). Either writing was never a simple "supplement," or it is urgently necessary to construct a new logic of the "supplement." It is this urgency which will guide us further in reading Rousseau.

These disguises are not historical contingencies that one might admire or regret. Their movement was absolutely necessary, with a necessity which cannot be judged by any other tribunal. The privilege of the *phone*[ii] does not depend upon a choice that could have been avoided. It responds to a moment of *economy* (let us say of the "life" of "history" or of "being as self-relationship"). The system of "hearing (understanding) oneself-speak" through the phonic substance – which *presents itself* as the nonexterior, nonmundane, therefore nonempirical or noncontingent signifier – has necessarily dominated the history of the world during an entire epoch, and has even produced the idea of the world, the idea of world-origin, that arises from the difference between the worldly and the non-worldly, the outside and the inside, ideality and nonideality, universal and nonuniversal, transcendental and empirical, etc.[2]

With an irregular and essentially precarious success, this movement would apparently have tended, as toward its *telos*, to confine writing to a secondary and instrumental function: translator of a full speech that was fully *present* (present to itself, to its signified, to the other, the very condition of the theme of presence in general), technics in the service of language, *spokesman*, interpreter of an originary speech itself shielded from interpretation.

[i] This is the distinction between *parole* and *langue*, earlier made by Saussure.
[ii] Sound, or the spoken.

Technics in the service of language: I am not invoking a general essence of technics which would be already familiar to us and would help us in *understanding* the narrow and historically determined concept of writing as an example. I believe on the contrary that a certain sort of question about the meaning and origin of writing precedes, or at least merges with, a certain type of question about the meaning and origin of technics. That is why the notion of technique can never simply clarify the notion of writing.

It is therefore as if what we call language could have been in its origin and in its end only a moment, an essential but determined mode, a phenomenon, an aspect, a species of writing. And as if it had succeeded in making us forget this, and *in wilfully misleading us*, only in the course of an adventure: as that adventure itself. All in all a short enough adventure. It merges with the history that has associated technics and logocentric metaphysics for nearly three millennia. And it now seems to be approaching what is really its own *exhaustion*; under the circumstances – and this is no more than one example among others – of this death of the civilization of the book, of which so much is said and which manifests itself particularly through a convulsive proliferation of libraries. All appearances to the contrary, this death of the book undoubtedly announces (and in a certain sense always has announced) nothing but a death of speech (of a *so-called* full speech) and a new mutation in the history of writing, in history as writing. Announces it at a distance of a few centuries. It is on that scale that we must reckon it here, being careful not to neglect the quality of a very heterogeneous historical duration: the acceleration is such, and such its qualitative meaning, that one would be equally wrong in making a careful evaluation according to past rhythms. "Death of speech" is of course a metaphor here: before we speak of disappearance, we must think of a new situation for speech, of its subordination within a structure of which it will no longer be the archon.

To affirm in this way that the concept of writing exceeds and comprehends that of language, presupposes of course a certain definition of language and of writing. If we do not attempt to justify it, we shall be giving in to the movement of inflation that we have just mentioned, which has also taken over the word "writing," and that not fortuitously. For some time now, as a matter of fact, here and there, by a gesture and for motives that are profoundly necessary, whose degradation is easier to denounce than it is to disclose their origin, one says "language" for action, movement, thought, reflection, consciousness, unconsciousness, experience, affectivity, etc. Now we tend to say "writing" for all that and more: to designate not only the physical gestures of literal pictographic or ideographic inscription, but also the totality of what makes it possible; and also, beyond the signifying face, the signified face itself. And thus we say "writing" for all that gives rise to an inscription in general, whether it is literal or not and even if what it distributes in space is alien to the order of the voice: cinematography, choreography, of course, but also pictorial, musical, sculptural "writing."[iii] One might also speak of athletic writing, and with even greater certainty of military or political writing in view of the techniques that govern those domains today. All this to describe not only the system of notation secondarily connected with these activities but the essence and the content of these activities themselves. It is also in this sense that the contemporary biologist speaks of writing and *pro-gram* in relation to the most elementary processes of information within the living cell. And, finally, whether it has essential limits or not, the entire field covered by the cybernetic *program* will be the field of writing. If the theory of cybernetics is by itself to oust all metaphysical concepts – including the concepts of soul, of life, of value, of choice, of memory – which until recently served to separate the machine from man,[3] it must conserve the notion of writing, trace, grammè [written mark], or grapheme, until its own historico-metaphysical character is also exposed. Even before being determined as human (with all the distinctive characteristics that have always been attributed to man and the entire system of significations that they imply) or nonhuman, the *grammè* – or the *grapheme* – would thus name the element.[iv] An element without simplicity. An element, whether it is understood as the medium or as the irreducible atom, of the arche-synthesis in general, of what one must forbid oneself to define within the system of oppositions of metaphysics, of what consequently one should not even call *experience* in general, that is to say the origin of *meaning* in general.

This situation has always already been announced. Why is it today in the process of making itself known *as such* and *after the fact*? This question would call forth an interminable analysis. Let us simply choose some points of departure in order to introduce the limited remarks to which I shall confine myself. I have already alluded to *theoretical* mathematics; its writing – whether understood as a sensible *graphie* [manner of writing] (and that already presupposes an identity, therefore an ideality, of its form, which in principle renders absurd the so easily admitted notion of the "sensible signifier"), or understood as the ideal synthesis of signifieds or a trace operative on another level, or whether it is understood, more profoundly, as the *passage* of the one to the other – has never been absolutely linked with a phonetic production. Within cultures practicing so-called phonetic writing, mathematics is not just an enclave. That is mentioned by all historians of writing; they recall at the same time the imperfections of alphabetic writing, which passed for so long as the most

---

[iii] Derrida is making "writing" coextensive with all use of signs or semiotics.
[iv] Mark, or the written.

convenient and "the most intelligent"[4] writing. This enclave is also the place where the practice of scientific language challenges intrinsically and with increasing profundity the ideal of phonetic writing and all its implicit metaphysics (metaphysics *itself*), particularly, that is, the philosophical idea of the *epistémè*;[v] also of *istoria*,[vi] a concept profoundly related to it in spite of the dissociation or opposition which has distinguished one from the other during one phase of their common progress. History and knowledge, *istoria* and *epistémè* have always been determined (and not only etymologically or philosophically) as detours *for the purpose of* the reappropriation of presence.

But beyond theoretical mathematics, the development of the *practical methods* of information retrieval extends the possibilities of the "message" vastly, to the point where it is no longer the "written" translation of a language, the transporting of a signified which could remain spoken in its integrity. It goes hand in hand with an extension of phonography and of all the means of conserving the spoken language, of making it function without the presence of the speaking subject. This development, coupled with that of anthropology and of the history of writing, teaches us that phonetic writing, the medium of the great metaphysical, scientific, technical, and economic adventure of the West, is limited in space and time and limits itself even as it is in the process of imposing its laws upon the cultural areas that had escaped it. But this nonfortuitous conjunction of cybernetics and the "human sciences" of writing leads to a more profound reversal.

The Signifier and Truth

The "rationality" – but perhaps that word should be abandoned for reasons that will appear at the end of this sentence – which governs a writing thus enlarged and radicalized, no longer issues from a logos. Further, it inaugurates the destruction, not the demolition but the de-sedimentation, the de-construction, of all the significations that have their source in that of the logos. Particularly the signification of *truth*. All the metaphysical determinations of truth, and even the one beyond metaphysical ontotheology that Heidegger reminds us of, are more or less immediately inseparable from the instance of the logos, or of a reason thought within the lineage of the logos, in whatever sense it is understood: in the pre-Socratic or the philosophical sense, in the sense of God's infinite understanding or in the anthropological sense, in the pre-Hegelian or the post-Hegelian sense.

[v] "Knowledge" in Greek.
[vi] History.

Jacques Derrida

Within this logos, the original and essential link to the *phonè* has never been broken. It would be easy to demonstrate this and I shall attempt such a demonstration later. As has been more or less implicitly determined, the essence of the *phonè* would be immediately proximate to that which within "thought" as logos relates to "meaning," produces it, receives it, speaks it, "composes" it. If, for Aristotle, for example, "spoken words (ta en tē phonē) are the symbols of mental experience (pathēmata tes psychēs) and written words are the symbols of spoken words" (*De interpretatione*, 1, 16a 3) it is because the voice, producer of *the first symbols*, has a relationship of essential and immediate proximity with the mind. Producer of the first signifier, it is not just a simple signifier among others. It signifies "mental experiences" which themselves reflect or mirror things by natural resemblance. Between being and mind, things and feelings, there would be a relationship of translation or natural signification; between mind and logos, a relationship of conventional symbolization. And the *first* convention, which would relate immediately to the order of natural and universal signification, would be produced as spoken language. Written language would establish the conventions, interlinking other conventions with them.

> Just as all men have not the same writing so all men have not the same speech sounds, but mental experiences, of which these are the *primary symbols* (*semeîa prótos*), are the same for all, as also are those things of which our experiences are the images. (*De interpretatione*, 1, 16a. Italics added)

The feelings of the mind, expressing things naturally, constitute a sort of universal language which can then efface itself. It is the stage of transparence. Aristotle can sometimes omit it without risk.[5] In every case, the voice is closest to the signified whether it is determined strictly as sense (thought or lived) or more loosely as thing. All signifiers, and first and foremost the written signifier, are derivative with regard to what would wed the voice indissolubly to the mind or to the thought of the signified sense, indeed to the thing itself (whether it is done in the Aristotelian manner that we have just indicated or in the manner of medieval theology, determining the *res* as a thing created from its *eidos*, from its sense thought in the logos or in the infinite understanding of God).[vii] The written signifier is always technical and representative. It has no constitutive meaning. This derivation is the very origin of the notion of the "signifier." The notion of the sign always implies within itself the distinction between signifier and signified, even if, as Saussure argues, they are distinguished simply as the two faces of one and the same leaf. This notion remains therefore within

[vii] *Res* in Latin is "thing," sometimes translated "substance;" *eidos* in Greek is "form;" *logos* in Greek can mean "discourse" or "logic".

342

the heritage of that logocentrism which is also a phonocentrism: absolute proximity of voice and being, of voice and the meaning of being, of voice and the ideality of meaning. Hegel demonstrates very clearly the strange privilege of sound in idealization, the production of the concept and the self-presence of the subject.

> This ideal motion, in which through the sound what is as it were the simple subjectivity, the soul of the material thing expresses itself, the ear receives also in a theoretical way, just as the eye shape and colour, thus allowing the interiority of the object to become interiority itself (*Esthétique*, III. I tr. fr. p. 16). . . . The ear, on the contrary, perceives the result of that interior vibration of material substance without placing itself in a practical relation toward the objects, a result by means of which it is no longer the material form in its repose, but the first, more ideal activity of the soul itself which is manifested (p. 296).

What is said of sound in general is a fortiori valid for the *phonè* by which, by virtue of hearing (understanding) oneself-speak – an indissociable system – the subject affects itself and is related to itself in the element of ideality.

We already have a foreboding that phonocentrism merges with the historical determination of the meaning of being in general as *presence*, with all the subdeterminations which depend on this general form and which organize within it their system and their historical sequence (presence of the thing to the sight as *eidos*, presence as substance/essence/existence, temporal presence as point of the now or of the moment, the self-presence of the cogito, consciousness, subjectivity, the co-presence of the other and of the self, intersubjectivity as the intentional phenomenon of the ego, and so forth). Logocentrism would thus support the determination of the being of the entity as presence. To the extent that such a logocentrism is not totally absent from Heidegger's thought, perhaps it still holds that thought within the epoch of onto-theology, within the philosophy of presence, that is to say within philosophy *itself*. This would perhaps mean that one does not leave the epoch whose closure one can outline. The movements of belonging or not belonging to the epoch are too subtle, the illusions in that regard are too easy, for us to make a definite judgment.

The epoch of the logos thus debases writing considered as mediation of mediation and as a fall into the exteriority of meaning. To this epoch belongs the difference between signified and signifier, or at least the strange separation of their "parallelism," and the exteriority, however extenuated, of the one to the other. This appurtenance is organized and hierarchized in a history. The difference between signified and signifier belongs in a profound and implicit way to the totality of the great epoch covered by the history of metaphysics, and in a more explicit and more systematically articulated way to the narrower epoch of Christian creationism and infinitism when these appropriate the resources of Greek conceptuality. This appurtenance is essential and irreducible; one cannot retain the convenience or the "scientific truth" of the Stoic and later medieval opposition between *signans* and *signatum*[viii] without also bringing with it all its metaphysico-theological roots. To these roots adheres not only the distinction between the sensible and the intelligible – already a great deal – with all that it controls, namely, metaphysics in its totality. And this distinction is generally accepted as self-evident by the most careful linguists and semiologists, even by those who believe that the scientificity of their work begins where metaphysics ends. Thus, for example:

> As modern structural thought has clearly realized, language is a system of signs and linguistics is part and parcel of the science of signs, or *semiotics* (Saussure's *sémiologie*). The mediaeval definition of sign – "*aliquid stat pro aliquo*" – has been resurrected and put forward as still valid and productive. Thus the constitutive mark of any sign in general and of any linguistic sign in particular is its twofold character: every linguistic unit is bipartite and involves both aspects – one sensible and the other intelligible, or in other words, both the *signans* "signifier" (Saussure's *signifiant*) and the *signatum* "signified" (*signifié*). These two constituents of a linguistic sign (and of sign in general) necessarily suppose and require each other.[6]

But to these metaphysico-theological roots many other hidden sediments cling. The semiological or, more specifically, linguistic "science" cannot therefore hold on to the difference between signifier and signified – the very idea of the sign – without the difference between sensible and intelligible, certainly, but also not without retaining, more profoundly and more implicitly, and by the same token the reference to a signified able to "take place" in its intelligibility, before its "fall," before any expulsion into the exteriority of the sensible here below. As the face of pure intelligibility, it refers to an absolute logos to which it is immediately united. This absolute logos was an infinite creative subjectivity in medieval theology: the intelligible face of the sign remains turned toward the word and the face of God.

Of course, it is not a question of "rejecting" these notions; they are necessary and, at least at present, nothing is conceivable for us without them. It is a question at first of demonstrating the systematic and historical solidarity of the concepts and gestures of thought that one often believes can be innocently separated. The sign and divinity have the same place and time of birth. The age of the sign is essentially theological. Perhaps it will never *end*. Its historical *closure* is, however, outlined.

[viii] Signifier and signified, respectively.

Since these concepts are indispensable for unsettling the heritage to which they belong, we should be even less prone to renounce them. Within the closure, by an oblique and always perilous movement, constantly risking falling back within what is being deconstructed, it is necessary to surround the critical concepts with a careful and thorough discourse – to mark the conditions, the medium, and the limits of their effectiveness and to designate rigorously their intimate relationship to the machine whose deconstruction they permit; and, in the same process, designate the crevice through which the yet unnameable glimmer beyond the closure can be glimpsed. The concept of the sign is here exemplary. We have just marked its metaphysical appurtenance. We know, however, that the thematics of the sign have been for about a century the agonized labor of a tradition that professed to withdraw meaning, truth, presence, being, etc., from the movement of signification. Treating as suspect, as I just have, the difference between signified and signifier, or the idea of the sign in general, I must state explicitly that it is not a question of doing so in terms of the instance of the present truth, anterior, exterior or superior to the sign, or in terms of the place of the effaced difference. Quite the contrary. We are disturbed by that which, in the concept of the sign – which has never existed or functioned outside the history of (the) philosophy (of presence) – remains systematically and genealogically determined by that history. It is there that the concept and above all the work of deconstruction, its "style," remain by nature exposed to misunderstanding and nonrecognition.

The exteriority of the signifier is the exteriority of writing in general, and I shall try to show later that there is no linguistic sign before writing.[ix] Without that exteriority, the very idea of the sign falls into decay. Since our entire world and language would collapse with it, and since its evidence and its value keep, to a certain point of derivation, an indestructible solidity, it would be silly to conclude from its placement within an epoch that it is necessary to "move on to something else," to dispose of the sign, of the term and the notion. For a proper understanding of the gesture that we are sketching here, one must understand the expressions "epoch," "closure of an epoch," "historical genealogy" in a new way; and must first remove them from all relativism.

Thus, within this epoch, reading and writing, the production or interpretation of signs, the text in general as fabric of signs, allow themselves to be confined within secondariness. They are preceded by a truth, or a meaning already constituted by and within the element of the logos. Even when the thing, the "referent," is not immediately related to the logos of a creator God where it began by being the spoken/thought sense, the signified has at

[ix] By "exteriority" Derrida means the material, external, physical mark of any written sign.

345

any rate an immediate relationship with the logos in general (finite or infinite), and a mediated one with the signifier, that is to say with the exteriority of writing. When it seems to go otherwise, it is because a metaphoric mediation has insinuated itself into the relationship and has simulated immediacy; the writing of truth in the soul, opposed by *Phaedrus*[x] (278a) to bad writing (writing in the "literal" and ordinary sense, "sensible" writing, "in space"), the book of Nature and God's writing, especially in the Middle Ages; all that functions as *metaphor* in these discourses confirms the privilege of the logos and founds the "literal" meaning then given to writing: a sign signifying a signifier itself signifying an eternal verity, eternally thought and spoken in the proximity of a present logos. The paradox to which attention must be paid is this: natural and universal writing, intelligible and nontemporal writing, is thus named by metaphor. A writing that is sensible, finite, and so on, is designated as writing in the literal sense; it is thus thought on the side of culture, technique, and artifice; a human procedure, the ruse of a being accidentally incarnated or of a finite creature. Of course, this metaphor remains enigmatic and refers to a "literal" meaning of writing as the first metaphor. This "literal" meaning is yet unthought by the adherents of this discourse. It is not, therefore, a matter of inverting the literal meaning and the figurative meaning but of determining the "literal" meaning of writing as metaphoricity itself.

In "The Symbolism of the Book," that excellent chapter of *European Literature and the Latin Middle Ages*, E. R. Curtius describes with great wealth of examples the evolution that led from the *Phaedrus* to Calderon, until it seemed to be "precisely the reverse" (tr. fr. p. 372) by the "newly attained position of the book" (p. 374). But it seems that this modification, however important in fact it might be, conceals a fundamental continuity. As was the case with the Platonic writing of the truth in the soul, in the Middle Ages too it is a writing understood in the metaphoric sense, that is to say a *natural*, eternal, and universal writing, the system of signified truth, which is recognized in its dignity. As in the *Phaedrus*, a certain fallen writing continues to be opposed to it. There remains to be written a history of this metaphor, a metaphor that systematically contrasts divine or natural writing and the human and laborious, finite and artificial inscription. It remains to articulate rigorously the stages of that history, as marked by the quotations below, and to follow the theme of God's book (nature or law, indeed natural law) through all its modifications.

---

[x] *Phaedrus* is a dialogue of Plato's, and also a character in that dialogue.

Rabbi Eliezer said: "If all the seas were of ink, and all ponds planted with reeds, if the sky and the earth were parchments and if all human beings practised the art of writing – they would not exhaust the Torah I have learned, just as the Torah itself would not be diminished any more than is the sea by the water removed by a paint brush dipped in it."[7]

Galileo: "It [the book of Nature] is written in a mathematical language."

Descartes: ". . . to read in the great book of Nature . . ."

Demea, in the name of natural religion, in the *Dialogues*, . . . of Hume: "And this volume of nature contains a great and inexplicable riddle, more than any intelligible discourse or reasoning."

Bonnet: "It would seem more philosophical to me to presume that our earth is a book that God has given to intelligences far superior to ours to read, and where they study in depth the infinitely multiplied and varied characters of His adorable wisdom."

G. H. von Schubert: "This language made of images and hieroglyphs, which supreme Wisdom uses in all its revelations to humanity – which is found in the inferior [*nieder*] language of poetry – and which, in the most inferior and imperfect way [*auf der allerniedrigsten und unvollkommensten*], is more like the metaphorical expression of the dream than the prose of wakefulness, . . . we may wonder if this language is not the true and wakeful language of the superior regions. If, when we consider ourselves awakened, we are not plunged in a millennial slumber, or at least in the echo of its dreams, where we only perceive a few isolated and obscure words of God's language, as a sleeper perceives the conversation of the people around him."

Jaspers: "The world is the manuscript of an other, inaccessible to a universal reading, which only existence deciphers."

Above all, the profound differences distinguishing all these treatments of the same metaphor must not be ignored. In the history of this treatment, the most decisive separation appears at the moment when, at the same time as the science of nature, the determination of absolute presence is constituted as self-presence, as subjectivity. It is the moment of the great rationalisms of the seventeenth century. From then on, the condemnation of fallen and finite writing will take another form, within which we still live: it is non-self-presence that will be denounced. Thus the exemplariness of the "Rousseauist" moment, which we shall deal with later, begins to be explained. Rousseau repeats the Platonic gesture by referring to another model of presence: self-presence in the senses, in the sensible cogito, which simultaneously carries in itself the inscription of divine law. On the one hand, *representative*, fallen, secondary, instituted writing, writing in the literal and strict sense, is condemned in *The Essay on the Origin of Languages* (it "enervates" speech; to "judge genius" from books is like "painting a man's portrait from his corpse," etc.).[xi] Writing in the common sense is the dead letter, it is the carrier of death. It exhausts life. On the other hand, on the other face of the same proposition, writing in the metaphoric sense, natural, divine, and living writing, is venerated; it is equal in dignity to the origin of value, to the voice of conscience as divine law, to the heart, to sentiment, and so forth.

> The Bible is the most sublime of all books, . . . but it is after all a book. . . . It is not at all in a few sparse pages that one should look for God's law, but in the human heart where His hand deigned to write (*Lettre à Vernes*).

> If the natural law had been written only in the human reason, it would be little capable of directing most of our actions. But it is also engraved in the heart of man in ineffacable characters. . . . There it cries to him (*L'état de guerre.*)

Natural writing is immediately united to the voice and to breath. Its nature is not grammatological but pneumatological. It is hieratic, very close to the interior holy voice of the *Profession of Faith*, to the voice one hears upon retreating into oneself: full and truthful presence of the divine voice to our inner sense: "The more I retreat into myself, the more I consult myself, the more plainly do I read these words written in my soul: be just and you will be happy. . . . I do not derive these rules from the principles of the higher philosophy, I find them in the depths of my heart written by nature in characters which nothing can efface."

There is much to say about the fact that the native unity of the voice and writing is *prescriptive*. Arche-speech is writing because it is a law. A natural law. The beginning word is understood, in the intimacy of self-presence, as the voice of the other and as commandment.

There is therefore a good and a bad writing: the good and natural is the divine inscription in the heart and the soul; the perverse and artful is technique, exiled in the exteriority of the body. A modification well within the Platonic diagram: writing of the soul and of the body, writing of the interior and of the exterior, writing of conscience and of the passions, as there is a voice of the soul and a voice of the body. "Conscience is the voice of the soul, the passions are the voice of the body". One must constantly go back toward the "voice of nature," the "holy voice of nature," that merges with the divine inscription and prescription; one must encounter oneself within it, enter into a dialogue within its signs, speak and respond to oneself in its pages.

[xi] *The Essay on the Origin of Language*, like each of the works referred to below, was authored by Jean-Jacques Rousseau.

> It was as if nature had spread out all her magnificence in front of our eyes to offer its text for our consideration. . . . I have therefore closed all the books. Only one is open to all eyes. It is the book of Nature. In this great and sublime book I learn to serve and adore its author.

The good writing has therefore always been *comprehended*. Comprehended as that which had to be comprehended: within a nature or a natural law, created or not, but first thought within an eternal presence. Comprehended, therefore, within a totality, and enveloped in a volume or a book. The idea of the book is the idea of a totality, finite or infinite, of the signifier; this totality of the signifier cannot be a totality, unless a totality constituted by the signified preexists it, supervises its inscriptions and its signs, and is independent of it in its ideality. The idea of the book, which always refers to a natural totality, is profoundly alien to the sense of writing. It is the encyclopedic protection of theology and of logocentrism against the disruption of writing, against its aphoristic energy, and, as I shall specify later, against difference in general. If I distinguish the text from the book, I shall say that the destruction of the book, as it is now under way in all domains, denudes the surface of the text. That necessary violence responds to a violence that was no less necessary.

The Written Being/The Being Written

The reassuring evidence within which Western tradition had to organize itself and must continue to live would therefore be as follows: the order of the signified is never contemporary, is at best the subtly discrepant inverse or parallel – discrepant by the time of a breath – from the order of the signifier. And the sign must be the unity of a heterogeneity, since the signified (sense or thing, noeme or reality) is not in itself a signifier, a *trace*: in any case is not constituted in its sense by its relationship with a possible trace. The formal essence of the signified is *presence*, and the privilege of its proximity to the logos as *phonè* is the privilege of presence. This is the inevitable response as soon as one asks: "what is the sign?," that is to say, when one submits the sign to the question of essence, to the "ti esti." The "formal essence" of the sign can only be determined in terms of presence. One cannot get around that response, except by challenging the very form of the question and beginning to think that the sign is that ill-named thing, the only one, that escapes the instituting question of philosophy: "what is . . .?"[8]

Radicalizing the concepts of *interpretation, perspective, evaluation, difference*, and all the "empiricist" or nonphilosophical motifs that have constantly tormented philosophy throughout the history of the West, and besides, have had nothing but the inevitable weakness of being produced in the field of philosophy, Nietzsche, far from remaining *simply* (with Hegel and as Heidegger wished) *within* metaphysics, contributed a great deal to the liberation of the signifier from its dependence or derivation with respect to the logos and the related concept of truth or the primary signified in whatever sense that is understood. Reading, and therefore writing, the text were for Nietzsche "originary"[9] operations (I put that word within quotation marks for reasons to appear later) with regard to a sense that they do not first have to transcribe or discover, which would not therefore be a truth signified in the original element and presence of the logos, as *topos noetos*, divine understanding, or the structure of a priori necessity. To save Nietzsche from a reading of the Heideggerian type, it seems that we must above all not attempt to restore or make explicit a less naïve "ontology," composed of profound ontological intuitions acceding to some originary truth, an entire fundamentality hidden under the appearance of an empiricist or metaphysical text. The virulence of Nietzschean thought could not be more competely misunderstood. On the contrary, one must *accentuate* the "naïveté" of a breakthrough which cannot attempt a step outside of metaphysics, which cannot *criticize* metaphysics radically without still utilizing in a certain way, in a certain type or a certain style of *text*, propostions that, read within the philosophic corpus, that is to say according to Nietzsche ill-read or unread, have alwaysbeen and will always be "naïvetés," incoherent signs of an absolute appurtenance. Therefore, rather than protect Nietzsche from the Heideggerian reading, we should perhaps offer him up to it completely, underwriting that interpretation without reserve; in a *certain way* and up to the point where, the content of the Nietzschean discourse being almost lost for the question of being, its form regains its absolute strangeness, where his text finally invokes a different type of reading, more faithful to his type of writing: Nietzsche has *written what* he has written. He has written that writing – and first of all his own – is not originarily subordinate to the logos and to truth. And that this subordination has *come into being* during an epoch whose meaning we must deconstruct. Now in this direction (but only in this direction, for read otherwise, the Nietzschean demolition remains dogmatic and, like all reversals, a captive of that metaphysical edifice which it professes to overthrow. On that point and in that *order of reading*, the conclusions of Heidegger and Fink are irrefutable), Heideggerian thought would reinstate rather than destroy the instance of the logos and of the truth of being as primum signatum:" the "transcendental" signified ("transcendental" in a certain sense, as in the Middle Ages the transcendental – *ens, unum, verum, bonum*[xii] – was said to be the "primum cognitum") implied by all categories

---

[xii] In Latin, respectively: being, unity, truth, goodness.

or all determined significations, by all lexicons and all syntax, and therefore by all linguistic signifiers, though not to be identified simply with any one of those signifiers, allowing itself to be precomprehended through each of them, remaining irreducible to all the epochal determinations that it nonetheless makes possible, thus opening the history of the logos, yet itself being only through the logos; that is, *being nothing* before the logos and outside of it. The logos of being, "Thought obeying the Voice of Being,"[10] is the first and the last resource of the sign, of the difference between *signans* and *signatum*. There has to be a transcendental signified for the difference between signifier and signified to be somewhere absolute and irreducible. It is not by chance that the thought of being, as the thought of this transcendental signified, is manifested above all in the voice: in a language of words. The voice is *heard* (understood) – that undoubtedly is what is called conscience – closest to the self as the absolute effacement of the signifier: pure auto-affection that necessarily has the form of time and which does not borrow from outside of itself, in the world or in "reality," any accessory signifier, any substance of expression foreign to its own spontaneity. It is the unique experience of the signified producing itself spontaneously, from within the self, and nevertheless, as signified concept, in the element of ideality or universality. The unworldly character of this substance of expression is constitutive of this ideality. This experience of the effacement of the signifier in the voice is not merely one illusion among many – since it is the condition of the very idea of truth – but I shall elsewhere show in what it does delude itself. This illusion is the history of truth and it cannot be dissipated so quickly. Within the closure of this experience, the word [*mot*] is lived as the elementary and undecomposable unity of the signified and the voice, of the concept and a transparent substance of expression. This experience is considered in its greatest purity – and at the same time in the condition of its possibility – as the experience of "being." The word "being," or at any rate the words designating the sense of being in different languages, is, with some others, an "originary word" ("*Urwort*"),[11] the transcendental word assuring the possibility of being-word to all other words. As such, it is precomprehended in all language and – this is the opening of *Being and Time* – only this precomprehension would permit the opening of the question of the sense of being in general, beyond all regional ontologies and all metaphysics: a question that broaches philosophy (for example, in the *Sophist*)[xiii] and lets itself be taken over by philosophy, a question that Heidegger repeats by submitting the history of metaphysics to it. Heidegger reminds us constantly that the sense of being is neither the word "being" nor the concept of being. But as that sense is nothing outside of language and the language

---

[xiii] A dialogue of Plato's.

of words, it is tied, if not to a particular word or to a particular system of language (concesso non dato), at least to the possibility of the word in general. And to the possibility of its irreducible simplicity. One could thus think that it remains only to choose between two possibilities. (1) Does a modern linguistics, a science of signification breaking the unity of the word and breaking with its alleged irreducibility, still have anything to do with "language?" Heidegger would probably doubt it. (2) Conversely, is not all that is profoundly meditated as the thought or the question of being enclosed within an old linguistics of the word which one practices here unknowingly? Unknowingly because such a lingiustics, whether spontaneous or systematic, has always had to share the presuppositions of metaphysics. The two operate on the same grounds.

It goes without saying that the alternatives cannot be so simple.

On the one hand, if modern linguistics remains completely enclosed within a classical conceptuality, if especially it naively uses the word *being* and all that it presupposes, that which, within this linguistics, deconstructs the unity of the word in general can no longer, according to the model of the Heideggerian question, as it functions powerfully from the very opening of *Being and Time*, be circumscribed as ontic science or regional ontology. In as much as the question of being unites indisolubly with the precomprehension of the *word being*, without being reduced to it, the linguistics that works for the deconstruction of the constituted unity of that word has only, in fact or in principle, to have the question of being posed in order to define its field and the order of its dependence.

Not only is its field no longer simply ontic, but the limits of ontology that correspond to it no longer have anything regional about them. And can what I say here of linguistics, or at least of a certain work that may be undertaken within it and thanks to it, not be said of all research *in as much as and to the strict extent that* it would finally deconstitute the founding concept-words of ontology, of being in its privilege? Outside of linguistics, it is in psychoanalytic research that this breakthrough seems at present to have the greatest likelihood of being expanded.

Within the strictly limited space of this breakthrough, these "sciences" are no longer *dominated* by the questions of a transcendental phenomenology or a fundamental ontology. One may perhaps say, following the order of questions inaugurated by *Being and Time* and radicalizing the questions of Husserlian phenomenology, that this breakthrough does not belong to science itself, that what thus seems to be produced within an ontic field or within a regional ontology, does not belong to them by rights and leads back to the question of being itself.

Because it is indeed the *question* of being that Heidegger asks metaphysics. And with it the question of truth, of sense, of the logos. The incessant meditation upon that question does not restore confidence. On the contrary, it dislodges the confidence at its own depth, which, being a matter of the meaning of being, is more difficult than is often believed. In examining the state just before all determinations of being, destroying the securities of onto-theology, such a meditation contributes, quite as much as the most contemporary linguistics, to the dislocation of the unity of the sense of being, that is, in the last instance, the unity of the word.

It is thus that, after evoking the "voice of being," Heidegger recalls that it is silent, mute, insonorous, wordless, originally *a-phonic* (*die Gewähr der lautlosen Stimme verborgener Quellen . . .*).[xiv] The voice of the sources is not heard. A rupture between the originary meaning of being and the word, between meaning and the voice, between "the voice of being" and the "*phonè*," between "the call of being," and articulated sound; such a rupture, which at once confirms a fundamental metaphor, and renders it suspect by accentuating its metaphoric discrepancy, translates the ambiguity of the Heideggerian situation with respect to the metaphysics of presence and logocentrism. It is at once contained within it and transgresses it. But it is impossible to separate the two. The very movement of transgression sometimes holds it back short of the limit. In opposition to what we suggested above, it must be remembered that, for Heidegger, the sense of being is never simply and rigorously a "signified." It is not by chance that that word is not used; that means that being escapes the movement of the sign, a proposition that can equally well be understood as a repetition of the classical tradition and as a caution with respect to a technical or metaphysical theory of signification. On the other hand, the sense of being is literally neither "primary," nor "fundamental," nor "transcendental," whether understood in the scholastic, Kantian, or Husserlian sense. The restoration of being as "transcending" the categories of the entity, the opening of the fundamental ontology, are nothing but necessary yet provisional moments. From *The Introduction to Metaphysics* onward, Heidegger renounces the project of and the word ontology. The necessary, originary, and irreducible dissimulation of the meaning of being, its occultation within the very blossoming forth of presence, that retreat without which there would be no history of being which was completely *history* and history of *being*, Heidegger's insistence on noting that being is produced as history only through the logos, and is nothing outside of it, the difference between being and the entity – all this clearly indicates that fundamentally nothing escapes the movement of the signifier and that, in the last instance, the difference between signified and signifier *is nothing*. This proposition of transgression, not yet integrated into a careful discourse, runs the risk of formulating regression itself. One must therefore *go by way of* the question of being as it is directed by Heidegger and by him

---

[xiv] The testimony of the soundless voice of hidden origins . . .

alone, at and beyond onto-theology, in order to reach the rigorous thought of that strange nondifference and in order to determine it correctly. Heidegger occasionally reminds us that "being," as it is fixed in its general syntactic and lexicological forms within linguistics and Western philosophy, is not a primary and absolutely irreducible signified, that it is still rooted in a system of languages and an historically determined "significance," although strangely privileged as the virtue of disclosure and dissimulation; particularly when he invites us to meditate on the "privilege" of the "third person singular of the present indicative" and the "infinitive." Western metaphysics, as the limitation of the sense of being within the field of presence, is produced as the domination of a linguistic form.[12] To question the origin of that domination does not amount to hypostatizing a transcendental signified, but to a questioning of what constitutes our history and what produced transcendentality itself. Heidegger brings it up also when in *Zur Seinsfrage*,[xv] for the same reason, he lets the word "being" be read only if it is crossed out (*kreuzweise Durchstreichung*). That mark of deletion is not, however, a "merely negative symbol" (p. 31). That deletion is the final writing of an epoch. Under its strokes the presence of a transcendental signified is effaced while still remaining legible. Is effaced while still remaining legible, is destroyed while making visible the very idea of the sign. In as much as it de-limits onto-theology, the methaphysics of presence and logocentrism, this last writing is also the first writing.

To come to recognize, not within but on the horizon of the Heideggerian paths, and yet in them, that the sense of being is not a transcendental or trans-epochal signified (even if it was always dissimulated within the epoch) but already, in a truly *unheard of* sense, a determined signifying trace, is to affirm that within the decisive concept of ontico-ontological difference, *all is not to be thought at one go*; entity and being, ontic and ontological, "ontico-ontological," are, in an original style, *derivative* with regard to difference; and with respect to what I shall later call *differance*, an economic concept designating the production of differing / deferring. The ontico-ontological difference and its ground (*Grund*) in the "transcendence of Dasein" (*Vom Wesen des Grundes*, p. 16)[xvi] are not absolutely originary. Difference by itself would be more "originary," but one would no longer be able to call it "origin" or "ground," those notions belonging essentially to the history of onto-theology, to the system functioning as the effacing of difference. It can, however, be thought of in the closest proximity to itself only on one condition: that one begins by determining it as the ontico-ontological difference before erasing that determination. The necessity of passing through that erased determination, the necessity of that *trick of*

xv   *On the Question of Being.*
xvi   *On the Essence of Reasons.*

writing is irreducible. An unemphatic and difficult thought that, through much unperceived meditation, must carry the entire burden of our question, a question that I shall provisionally call *historical*. It is with its help that I shall later be able to attempt to relate difference and writing.

The hestitation of these thoughts (here Nietzsche's and Heidegger's) is not an "incoherence": it is a trembling proper to all post-Hegelian attempts and to this passage between two epochs. The movements of deconstruction do not destroy structures from the outside. They are not possible and effective, nor can they take accurate aim, except by inhabiting those structures. Inhabiting them *in a certain way*, because one always inhabits, and all the more when one does not suspect it. Operating necessarily from the inside, borrowing all the strategic and economic resources of subversion from the old structure, borrowing them structurally, that is to say without being able to isolate their elements and atoms, the enterprise of deconstruction always in a certain way falls prey to its own work. This is what the person who has begun the same work in another area of the same habitation does not fail to point out with zeal. No exercise is more widespread today and one should be able to formalize its rules.

Hegel was already caught up in this game. *On the one hand*, he undoubtedly *summed up* the entire philosophy of the logos. He determined ontology as absolute logic; he assembled all the delimitations of philosophy as presence; he assigned to presence the eschatology of parousia, of the self-proximity of infinite subjectivity. And for the same reason he had to debase or subordinate writing. When he criticizes the Leibnizian characteristic, the formalism of the understanding, and mathematical symbolism, he makes the same gesture: denouncing the being-outside-of-itself of the logos in the sensible or the intellectual abstraction. Writing is that forgetting of the self, that exteriorization, the contrary of the interiorizing memory, of the *Erinnerung*[xvii] that opens the history of the spirit. It is this that the *Phaedrus* said: writing is at once mnemotechnique and the power of forgetting. Naturally, the Hegelian critique of writing stops at the alphabet. As phonetic writing, the alphabet is at the same time more servile, more contemptible, more secondary ("alphabetic writing expresses *sounds* which are themselves signs. It consists therefore of the signs of signs but it is also the best writing, the mind's writing; its effacement before the voice, that in it which respects the ideal interiority of phonic signifiers, all that by which it sublimates space and sight, all that makes of it the writing of history, the writing, that is, of the infinite spirit relating to itself in its discourse and its culture:

> It follows that to learn to read and write an alphabetic writing should be regarded as a means to infinite culture (*unendliches Bildungsmittel*) that is not

[xvii] Remembering.

enough appreciated; because thus the mind, distancing itself from the concrete sense-perceptible, directs its attention on the more formal moment, the
sonorous word and its abstract elements, and contributes essentially to the
founding and purifying of the ground of interiority within the subject.

In that sense it is the *Aufhebung*[xviii] of other writings, particularly of
hieroglyphic script and of the Leibnizian characteristic that had been
criticized previously through one and the same gesture. (*Aufhebung* is, more
or less implicitly, the dominant concept of nearly all histories of writing,
even today. It is *the* concept of history and of teleology.) In fact, Hegel
continues: "Acquired habit later also suppresses the specificity of alphabetic
writing, which consists in seeming to be, in the interest of sight, a detour
through hearing to arrive at representations, and makes it into a hieroglyphic script for us, such that in using it, we do not need to have present to
our consciousness the mediation of sounds."

It is on this condition that Hegel subscribes to the Leibnizian praise of
nonphonetic writing. It can be produced by deaf mutes, Leibniz had said.
Hegel:

> Beside the fact that, by the practice which transforms this alphabetic script
> into hieroglyphics, the aptitude for abstraction acquired through such an
> exercise *is conserved*,[xix] the reading of hieroglyphs is for itself a deaf reading
> and a mute writing (*ein taubes Lesen und ein stummes Schreiben*). What is
> audible or temporal, visible or spatial, has each its proper basis and in the
> first place they are of equal value; but in alphabetic script there is only *one*
> basis and that following a specific relation, namely, that the visible language
> is related only as a sign to the audible language; intelligence expresses itself
> immediately and unconditionally through speech. (ibid.)

What writing itself, in its nonphonetic moment, betrays, is life. It
menaces at once the breath, the spirit, and history as the spirit's relationship with itself. It is their end, their finitude, their paralysis. Cutting breath
short, sterilizing or immobilizing spiritual creation in the repetition of the
letter, in the commentary or the *exegesis*, confined in a narrow space,
reserved for a minority, it is the principle of death and of difference in the
becoming of being. It is to speech what China is to Europe: "It is only to
the exegeticism[13] of Chinese spiritual culture that their hieroglyphic writing
is suited. This type of writing is, besides, the part reserved for a very small
section of a people, the section that possesses the exclusive domain of
spiritual culture. . . . A hieroglyphic script would require a philosophy as
exegetical as Chinese culture generally is" (ibid.).

[xviii] "Sublation," or simultaneous fulfillment and cancellation.
[xix] Italics added by the translator.

If the nonphonetic moment menaces the history and the life of the spirit as self-presence in the breath, it is because it menaces substantiality, that other metaphysical name of presence and of *ousia*.[xx] First in the form of the substantive. Nonphonetic writing breaks the noun apart. It describes relations and not apellations. The noun and the word, those unities of breath and concept, are effaced within pure writing. In that regard, Leibniz is as disturbing as the Chinese in Europe: "This situation, the analytic notation of representations in hieroglyphic script, which seduced Leibniz to the point of wrongly preferring this script to the alphabetic, rather contradicts the fundamental exigency of language in general, namely the noun. . . . All difference in analysis would produce another formation of the written substantive."

The horizon of absolute knowledge is the effacement of writing in the logos, the retrieval of the trace in parousia, the reappropriation of difference, the accomplishment of what I have elsewhere called[14] the *metaphysics of the proper*.

Yet, all that Hegel thought within this horizon, all, that is, except eschatology, may be reread as a meditation on writing. Hegel is *also* the thinker of irreducible difference. He rehabilitated thought as the *memory productive* of signs. And he reintroduced, as I shall try to show elsewhere, the essential necessity of the written trace in a philosophical – that is to say Socratic – discourse that had always believed it possible to do without it; the last philosopher of the book and the first thinker of writing.

[xx] *Ousia* is "being" in Greek.

Notes

1 To speak of a primary writing here does not amount to affirming a chronological priority of fact. That debate is well-known; is writing, as affirmed, for example, by Metchaninov and Marr, then Loukotka, "anterior to phonetic language?" (A conclusion assumed by the first edition of the Great Soviet Encyclopedia, later contradicted by Stalin. On this debate, cf. V. Istrine, "Langue et écriture," *Linguistique*, pp. 35, 60. This debate also forms around the theses advanced by P. van Ginneken. On the discussion of these propositions, cf. James Février, *Histoire de l'écriture*. pp. 5 f.). I shall try to show below why the terms and premises of such a debate are suspicious.

2 I shall deal with this problem more directly in *La voix et le phénomène* (Paris, 1967). [*Speech and Phenomena*, trans. David Allison (Evanston, IL: Northwestern University Press, 1973).]

3 Wiener, for example, while abandoning "semantics," and the opposition, judged by him as too crude and too general, between animate and inanimate etc., nevertheless continues to use expressions like "organs of sense," "motor organs," etc. to qualify the parts of the machine.

357

4 Cf., e.g. *L'écriture et la psychologie des peuples*, pp. 126, 148, 355, etc. From another point of view, cf. Roman Jakobson, *Essais de linguistique générale* (tr. fr. [Nicolas Ruwet, Paris, 1963], p. 116).

5 This is shown by Pierre Aubenque (*Le problème de l'être chez Aristotle* [Paris, 1966], pp. 106 f.). In the course of a provocative analysis, to which I am here indebted, Aubenque remarks: "In other texts, to be sure, Aristotle designates as symbol the relationship between language and things: 'It is not possible to bring the things themselves to the discussion, but, instead of things, we can use their names as symbols.' The intermediary constituted by the mental experience is here suppressed or at least neglected, but this suppression is legitimate, since, mental experiences behaving like things, things can be substituted for them immediately. On the other hand, one cannot by any means substitute names for things" (pp. 107–8).

6 Roman Jakobson, *Essais de linguistique générale*, tr. fr., p. 162. On this problem, on the tradition of the concept of the sign, and on the originality of Saussure's contribution within this continuity, cf. Edmond Ortigues, *Le discours et le symbole* (Aubier, 1962), pp. 54 f.

7 Cited by Emmanuel Levinas, in *Difficile liberté* (Paris, 1963), p. 44.

8 I attempt to develop this theme elsewhere (*Speech and Phenomena*).

9 This does not, by simple inversion, mean that the signifier is fundamental or primary. The "primacy" or "priority" of the signifier would be an expression untenable and absurd to formulate illogically within the very logic that it would legitimately destroy. The signifier will never by rights precede the signified, in which case it would no longer be a signifier and the "signifying" signifier would no longer have a possible signified. The thought that is announced in this impossible formula without being successfully contained therein should therefore be stated in another way; it will clearly be impossible to do so without putting the very idea of the sign into suspicion, the "sign-of" which will always remain attached to what is here put in question. At the limit therefore, that thought would destroy the entire conceptuality organized around the concept of the sign (signifier and signified, expression and content, and so on).

10 Postface to *Was ist Metaphysik?* (Frankfurt am Main, 1960), p. 46. [*What is Metaphysics?*, trans. David Krell in *Basic Writings* (New York: Harper & Row, 1977).] The insistence of the voice also dominates the analysis of *Gewissen* [conscience] in *Sein und Zeit* (pp. 267 f.).

11 Cf. *Das Wesen der Sprache*, and *Das Wort*, in *Unterwegs zur Sprache* (Pfüllingen, 1959). ["The Nature of Language" and "words" in *On the Way to Language*, trans. Peter Hertz (New York: Harper & Row, 1971).]

12 *Introduction à la métaphysique*, tr. fr. p. 103. "All this points in the direction of what we encountered when we characterized the Greek experience and interpretation of being. If we retain the usual interpretation of being, the word 'being' takes its meaning from the unity and determinateness of the horizon which guided our understanding. In short: we understand the verbal substantive 'Sein' through the infinitive, which in turn is related to the 'is' and its diversity that we have described. The definite and particular verb form 'is,' the

third person singular of the present indicative, has here a pre-eminent rank. We understand 'being' not in regard to the 'thou art,' 'you are,' 'I am,' or 'they would be,' though all of these, just as much as 'is,' represent verbal inflections of 'to be.' . . . And involuntarily, almost as though nothing else were possible, we explain the infinitive 'to be' to ourselves through the 'is.'

"Accordingly, 'being' has the meaning indicated above, recalling the Greek view of the essence of being, hence a determinateness which has not just dropped on us accidentally from somewhere but has dominated our historical being-there since antiquity. At one stroke our search for the definition of the meaning of the word 'being' becomes explicitly what it is, namely a reflection on the source of our hidden history." I should, of course, cite the entire analysis that concludes with these words.

13 *dem Statarischen*, an old German word that one has hitherto been tempted to translate as "immobile" or "static" (see [Jean] Gibelin, [tr. *Leçons sur la philosophie de la religion* (Paris, 1959),] pp. 255–7.

14 "La parole soufflée," *L'écriture et la différence*. [*Writing and Difference*, trans. Alan Bass (Chicago: University of Chicago, 1978).]

chapter
twenty-five

"Nietzsche, Genealogy, History"
"Truth and Power"

Michel Foucault

With Derrida, Michel Foucault (1926–84) was the most influential of postmodernist thinkers. Unlike Derrida, however, his work is explicitly sociological, political, and historical. Much of it entails an historical analysis of the "discursive practises" that have constituted social life and ideology, with special attention to the maintenance of normal social life through the control and marginalization of some groups or some features of life (the insane, criminals, sexual deviance). In Nietzschean fashion, Foucault accepts that all life is power; rather than endorsing an impossible renunciation of power and repression, he seeks their modification into less static and less concentrated forms. In the first selection, Foucault distinguishes Nietzsche's method of "genealogy" from traditional historical research, which eschews the latter's implicit metaphysical search for origins. Foucault regards himself as a Nietzschean genealogist. In the second selection, he famously denies that truth as a norm can be understood to be separate from social and political power.

"Nietzsche, Genealogy, History"

1. Genealogy is gray, meticulous, and patiently documentary. It operates on a field of entangled and confused parchments, on documents that have been scratched over and recopied many times.

Michel Foucault, "Nietzsche, Genealogy, History," trans. Donald Bouchard and Sherry Simon, in *Language, Counter-Memory, Practise*, ed. Donald Bouchard (Ithaca, NY: Cornell University Press, 1977), pp. 139–64; and, from "Truth and Power," interview by Alessandro Fontana and Pasquale Pasquino, trans. Colin Gordon, in *Power/Knowledge: Selected Interviews and Other Writings 1972–77*, ed. Colin Gordon (New York: Pantheon Books, 1972), answer to final question, pp. 131–3.

On this basis, it is obvious that Paul Ree[i] was wrong to follow the English tendency in describing the history of morality in terms of a linear development – in reducing its entire history and genesis to an exclusive concern for utility. He assumed that words had kept their meaning, that desires still pointed in a single direction, and that ideas retained their logic; and he ignored the fact that the world of speech and desires has known invasions, struggles, plundering, disguises, ploys. From these elements, however, genealogy retrieves an indispensable restraint: it must record the singularity of events outside of any monotonous finality; it must seek them in the most unpromising places, in what we tend to feel is without history – in sentiments, love, conscience, instincts; it must be sensitive to their recurrence, not in order to trace the gradual curve of their evolution, but to isolate the different scenes where they engaged in different roles. Finally, genealogy must define even those instances where they are absent, the moment when they remained unrealized (Plato, at Syracuse, did not become Mohammed).[ii]

Genealogy, consequently, requires patience and a knowledge of details and it depends on a vast accumulation of source material. Its "cyclopean monuments"[1] are constructed from "discreet and apparently insignificant truths and according to a rigorous method"; they cannot be the product of "large and well-meaning errors."[2] In short, genealogy demands relentless erudition. Genealogy does not oppose itself to history as the lofty and profound gaze of the philosopher might compare to the molelike perspective of the scholar; on the contrary, it rejects the metahistorical deployment of ideal significations and indefinite teleologies. It opposes itself to the search for "origins."

2. In Nietzsche, we find two uses of the word *Ursprung*.[iii] The first is unstressed, and it is found alternately with other terms such as *Entstehung, Herkunft, Abkunft, Geburt*. In *The Genealogy of Morals*, for example, *Entstehung* or *Ursprung* serve equally well to denote the origin of duty or guilty conscience;[3] and in the discussion of logic or knowledge in *The Gay Science*, their origin is indiscriminately referred to as *Ursprung, Entstehung*, or *Herkunft*.[4]

The other use of the word is stressed. On occasion, Nietzsche places the term in opposition to another: in the first paragraph of *Human, All Too Human* the miraculous origin (*Wunderursprung*) sought by metaphysics is

---

[i] French moral philosopher and friend of Nietzsche, whose relationship with Nietzsche ended when Ree won the love of Nietzsche's life, Lou Salomé.

[ii] Plato visited Syracuse, in Sicily, at the invitation of its tyrant but declined to support him and thereby gain political power.

[iii] Foucault is distinguishing a series of overlapping German terms: *Ursprung* (source, origin); *Entstehung* (genesis); *Herkunft* (descent); *Abkunft* (lineage); and *Geburt* (birth).

set against the analyses of historical philosophy, which poses questions *über Herkunft und Anfang*.[iv] *Ursprung* is also used in an ironic and deceptive manner. In what, for instance, do we find the original basis (*Ursprung*) of morality, a foundation sought after since Plato? "In detestable, narrow-minded conclusions. *Pudenda origo*."[v] Or in a related context, where should we seek the origin of religion (*Ursprung*), which Schopenhauer located in a particular metaphysical sentiment of the hereafter? It belongs, very simply, to an invention (*Erfindung*), a sleight-of-hand, an artifice (*Kunststück*), a secret formula, in the rituals of black magic, in the work of the *Schwarzkünstler*.[vi]

One of the most significant texts with respect to the use of all these terms and to the variations in the use of *Ursprung* is the preface to the *Genealogy*. At the beginning of the text, its objective is defined as an examination of the origin of moral preconceptions and the term used is *Herkunft*. Then, Nietzsche proceeds by retracing his personal involvement with this question: he recalls the period when he "calligraphied" philosophy, when he questioned if God must be held responsible for the origin of evil. He now finds this question amusing and properly characterizes it as a search for *Ursprung* (he will shortly use the same term to summarize Paul Ree's activity).[5] Further on, he evokes the analyses that are characteristically Nietzschean and that began with *Human, All Too Human*. Here, he speaks of *Herkunfthypothesen*.[vii] This use of the word *Herkunft* cannot be arbitrary, since it serves to designate a number of texts, beginning with *Human, All Too Human*, which deal with the origin of morality, asceticism, justice, and punishment. And yet, the word used in all these works had been *Ursprung*.[6] It would seem that at this point in the *Genealogy* Nietzsche wished to validate an opposition between *Herkunft* and *Ursprung* that did not exist ten years earlier. But immediately following the use of the two terms in a specific sense, Nietzsche reverts, in the final paragraphs of the preface, to a usage that is neutral and equivalent.[7]

Why does Nietzsche challenge the pursuit of the origin (*Ursprung*), at least on those occasions when he is truly a genealogist? First, because it is an attempt to capture the exact essence of things, their purest possibilities, and their carefully protected identities, because this search assumes the existence of immobile forms that precede the external world of accident and succession. This search is directed to "that which was already there," the image of a primordial truth fully adequate to its nature, and it necessitates the removal of every mask to ultimately disclose an original identity.

[iv] *Anfang* means "beginning."
[v] Shameful origin.
[vi] Black magician.
[vii] Hypotheses of descent.

However, if the genealogist refuses to extend his faith in metaphysics, if he listens to history, he finds that there is "something altogether different" behind things: not a timeless and essential secret, but the secret that they have no essence or that their essence was fabricated in a piecemeal fashion from alien forms. Examining the history of reason, he learns that it was born in an altogether "reasonable" fashion – from chance;[8] devotion to truth and the precision of scientific methods arose from the passion of scholars, their reciprocal hatred, their fanatical and unending discussions, and their spirit of competition – the personal conflicts that slowly forged the weapons of reason.[9] Further, genealogical analysis shows that the concept of liberty is an "invention of the ruling classes"[10] and not fundamental to man's nature or at the root of his attachment to being and truth. What is found at the historical beginning of things is not the inviolable identity of their origin; it is the dissension of other things. It is disparity.

History also teaches how to laugh at the solemnities of the origin. The lofty origin is no more than "a metaphysical extension which arises from the belief that things are most precious and essential at the moment of birth."[11] We tend to think that this is the moment of their greatest perfection, when they emerged dazzling from the hands of a creator or in the shadowless light of a first morning. The origin always precedes the Fall. It comes before the body, before the world and time; it is associated with the gods, and its story is always sung as a theogony. But historical beginnings are lowly: not in the sense of modest or discreet like the steps of a dove, but derisive and ironic, capable of undoing every infatuation. "We wished to awaken the feeling of man's sovereignty by showing his divine birth: this path is now forbidden, since a monkey stands at the entrance."[12] Man originated with a grimace over his future development; and Zarathustra himself is plagued by a monkey who jumps along behind him, pulling on his coattails.[viii]

The final postulate of the origin is linked to the first two in being the site of truth. From the vantage point of an absolute distance, free from the restraints of positive knowledge, the origin makes possible a field of knowledge whose function is to recover it, but always in a false recognition due to the excesses of its own speech. The origin lies at a place of inevitable loss, the point where the truth of things corresponded to a truthful discourse, the site of a fleeting articulation that discourse has obscured and finally lost. It is a new cruelty of history that compels a reversal of this relationship and the abandonment of "adolescent" quests: behind the always recent, avaricious, and measured truth, it posits the ancient proliferation of errors. It is now impossible to believe that "in the rending

---

[viii] Zarathustra is the prophetic main character of Nietzsche's *Thus Spoke Zarathustra*.

of the veil, truth remains truthful; we have lived long enough not to be taken in."[13] Truth is undoubtedly the sort of error that cannot be refuted because it was hardened into an unalterable form in the long baking process of history.[14] Moreover, the very question of truth, the right it appropriates to refute error and oppose itself to appearance, the manner in which it developed (initially made available to the wise, then withdrawn by men of piety to an unattainable world where it was given the double role of consolation and imperative, finally rejected as a useless notion, superfluous, and contradicted on all sides) – does this not form a history, the history of an error we call truth? Truth, and its original reign, has had a history within history from which we are barely emerging "in the time of the shortest shadow," when light no longer seems to flow from the depths of the sky or to arise from the first moments of the day.[15]

A genealogy of values, morality, asceticism, and knowledge will never confuse itself with a quest for their "origins," will never neglect as inaccessible the vicissitudes of history. On the contrary, it will cultivate the details and accidents that accompany every beginning; it will be scrupulously attentive to their petty malice; it will await their emergence, once unmasked, as the face of the other. Wherever it is made to go, it will not be reticent – in "excavating the depths," in allowing time for these elements to escape from a labyrinth where no truth had ever detained them. The genealogist needs history to dispel the chimeras of the origin, somewhat in the manner of the pious philosopher who needs a doctor to exorcise the shadow of his soul. He must be able to recognize the events of history, its jolts, its surprises, its unsteady victories and unpalatable defeats – the basis of all beginnings, atavisms, and heredities. Similarly, he must be able to diagnose the illnesses of the body, its conditions of weakness and strength, its breakdown and resistances, to be in a position to judge philosophical discourse. History is the concrete body of a development, with its moments of intensity, its lapses, its extended periods of feverish agitation, its fainting spells; and only a metaphysician would seek its soul in the distant ideality of the origin.

3. *Entstehung* and *Herkunft* are more exact than *Ursprung* in recording the true objective of genealogy; and, while they are ordinarily translated as "origin," we must attempt to reestablish their proper use.

Herkunft is the equivalent of stock or *descent*; it is the ancient affiliation to a group, sustained by the bonds of blood, tradition, or social class. The analysis of *Herkunft* often involves a consideration of race[16] or social type.[17] But the traits it attempts to identify are not the exclusive generic characteristics of an individual, a sentiment, or an idea, which permit us to qualify them as "Greek" or "English"; rather, it seeks the subtle, singular, and subindividual marks that might possibly intersect in them to form a network that is difficult to unravel. Far from being a category of resemblance, this origin allows the sorting out of different traits: the Germans imagined that they had finally accounted for their complexity by saying they possessed a double soul; they were fooled by a simple computation, or rather, they were simply trying to master the racial disorder from which they had formed themselves.[18] Where the soul pretends unification or the self fabricates a coherent identity, the genealogist sets out to study the beginning – numberless beginnings whose faint traces and hints of color are readily seen by an historical eye. The analysis of descent permits the dissociation of the self, its recognition and displacement as an empty synthesis, in liberating a profusion of lost events.

An examination of descent also permits the discovery, under the unique aspect of a trait or a concept, of the myriad events through which – thanks to which, against which – they were formed. Genealogy does not pretend to go back in time to restore an unbroken continuity that operates beyond the dispersion of forgotten things; its duty is not to demonstrate that the past actively exists in the present, that it continues secretly to animate the present, having imposed a predetermined form to all its vicissitudes. Genealogy does not resemble the evolution of a species and does not map the destiny of a people. On the contrary, to follow the complex course of descent is to maintain passing events in their proper dispersion; it is to identify the accidents, the minute deviations – or conversely, the complete reversals – the errors, the false appraisals, and the faulty calculations that gave birth to those things that continue to exist and have value for us; it is to discover that truth or being do not lie at the root of what we know and what we are, but the exteriority of accidents.[19] This is undoubtedly why every origin of morality from the moment it stops being pious – and *Herkunft* can never be – has value as a critique.[20]

Deriving from such a source is a dangerous legacy. In numerous instances, Nietzsche associates the terms *Herkunft* and *Erbschaft*.[ix] Nevertheless, we should not be deceived into thinking that this heritage is an acquisition, a possession that grows and solidifies; rather, it is an unstable assemblage of faults, fissures, and heterogeneous layers that threaten the fragile inheritor from within or from underneath: "injustice or instability in the minds of certain men, their disorder and lack of decorum, are the final consequences of their ancestors' numberless logical inaccuracies, hasty conclusions, and superficiality."[21] The search for descent is not the erecting of foundations: on the contrary, it disturbs what was previously considered immobile; it fragments what was thought unified; it shows the heterogeneity of what was imagined consistent with itself. What convictions and, far more decisively, what knowledge can resist it? If a genealogical analysis

---

[ix] *Erbschaft* means "legacy".

of a scholar were made – of one who collects facts and carefully accounts for them – his *Herkunft* would quickly divulge the official papers of the scribe and the pleadings of the lawyer – their father[22] – in their apparently disinterested attention, in the "pure" devotion to objectivity.

Finally, descent attaches itself to the body.[22] It inscribes itself in the nervous system, in temperament, in the digestive apparatus; it appears in faulty respiration, in improper diets, in the debilitated and prostrate body of those whose ancestors committed errors. Fathers have only to mistake effects for causes, believe in the reality of an "afterlife," or maintain the value of eternal truths, and the bodies of their children will suffer. Cowardice and hypocrisy, for their part, are the simple offshoots of error: not in a Socratic sense, not that evil is the result of a mistake, not because of a turning away from an original truth, but because the body maintains, in life as in death, through its strength or weakness, the sanction of every truth and error, as it sustains, in an inverse manner, the origin – descent. Why did men invent the contemplative life? Why give a supreme value to this form of existence? Why maintain the absolute truth of those fictions which sustain it? "During barbarous ages . . . if the strength of an individual declined, if he felt himself tired or sick, melancholy or satiated and, as a consequence, without desire or appetite for a short time, he became relatively a better man, that is, less dangerous. His pessimistic ideas could only take form as words or reflections. In this frame of mind, he either became a thinker and prophet or used his imagination to feed his superstitions."[24] The body – and everything that touches it: diet, climate, and soil – is the domain of the *Herkunft*. The body manifests the stigmata of past experience and also gives rise to desires, failings, and errors. These elements may join in a body where they achieve a sudden expression, but as often, their encounter is an engagement in which they efface each other, where the body becomes the pretext of their insurmountable conflict.

The body is the inscribed surface of events (traced by language and dissolved by ideas), the locus of a dissociated Self (adopting the illusion of a substantial unity), and a volume in perpetual disintegration. Genealogy, as an analysis of descent, is thus situated within the articulation of the body and history. Its task is to expose a body totally imprinted by history and the process of history's destruction of the body.

4. *Entstehung* designates *emergence*, the moment of arising. It stands as the principle and the singular law of an apparition. As it is wrong to search for descent in an uninterrupted continuity, we should avoid thinking of emergence as the final term of an historical development; the eye was not always intended for contemplation, and punishment has had other purposes than setting an example. These developments may appear as a culmination, but they are merely the current episodes in a series of subjugations: the eye initially responded to the requirements of hunting

and warfare; and punishment has been subjected, throughout its history, to a variety of needs – revenge, excluding an aggressor, compensating a victim, creating fear. In placing present needs at the origin, the metaphysician would convince us of an obscure purpose that seeks its realization at the moment it arises. Genealogy, however, seeks to reestablish the various systems of subjection: not the anticipatory power of meaning, but the hazardous play of dominations.

Emergence is always produced through a particular stage of forces. The analysis of the *Entstehung* must delineate this interaction, the struggle these forces wage against each other or against adverse circumstances, and the attempt to avoid degeneration and regain strength by dividing these forces against themselves. It is in this sense that the emergence of a species (animal or human) and its solidification are secured "in an extended battle against conditions which are essentially and constantly unfavorable." In fact, "the species must realize itself as a species, as something – characterized by the durability, uniformity, and simplicity of its form – which can prevail in the perpetual struggle against outsiders or the uprising of those it oppresses from within." On the other hand, individual differences emerge at another stage of the relationship of forces, when the species has become victorious and when it is no longer threatened from outside. In this condition, we find a struggle "of egoisms turned against each other, each bursting forth in a splintering of forces and a general striving for the sun and for the light."[25] There are also times when force contends against itself, and not only in the intoxication of an abundance, which allows it to divide itself, but at the moment when it weakens. Force reacts against its growing lassitude and gains strength; it imposes limits, inflicts torments and mortifications; it masks these actions as a higher morality, and, in exchange, regains its strength. In this manner, the ascetic ideal was born, "in the instinct of a decadent life which ... struggles for its own existence."[26] This also describes the movement in which the Reformation arose, precisely where the church was least corrupt,[27] German Catholicism, in the sixteenth century, retained enough strength to turn against itself, to mortify its own body and history, and to spiritualize itself into a pure religion of conscience.

Emergence is thus the entry of forces; it is their eruption, the leap from the wings to center stage, each in its youthful strength. What Nietzsche calls the *Entstehungsherd*[28] of the concept of goodness is not specifically the energy of the strong or the reaction of the weak,[x] but precisely this scene where they are displayed superimposed or face-to-face. It is nothing but the space that divides them, the void through which they exchange their threatening gestures and speeches. As descent qualifies the strength or

[x] *Entstehungdsherd* means roughly "original home."

367

weakness of an instinct and its inscription on a body, emergence designates a place of confrontation but not as a closed field offering the spectacle of a struggle among equals. Rather, as Nietzsche demonstrates in his analysis of good and evil, it is a "non-place," a pure distance, which indicates that the adversaries do not belong to a common space. Consequently, no one is responsible for an emergence; no one can glory in it, since it always occurs in the interstice.

In a sense, only a single drama is ever staged in this "non-place," the endlessly repeated play of dominations. The domination of certain men over others leads to the differentiation of values;[29] class domination generates the idea of liberty;[30] and the forceful appropriation of things necessary to survival and the imposition of a duration not intrinsic to them account for the origin of logic.[31] This relationship of domination is no more a "relationship" than the place where it occurs is a place; and, precisely for this reason, it is fixed, throughout its history, in rituals, in meticulous procedures that impose rights and obligations. It establishes marks of its power and engraves memories on things and even within bodies. It makes itself accountable for debts and gives rise to the universe of rules, which is by no means designed to temper violence, but rather to satisfy it. Following traditional beliefs, it would be false to think that total war exhausts itself in its own contradictions and ends by renouncing violence and submitting to civil laws. On the contrary, the law is a calculated and relentless pleasure, delight in the promised blood, which permits the perpetual instigation of new dominations and the staging of meticulously repeated scenes of violence. The desire for peace, the serenity of compromise, and the tacit acceptance of the law, far from representing a major moral conversion or a utilitarian calculation that gave rise to the law, are but its result and, in point of fact, its perversion: "guilt, conscience, and duty had their threshold of emergence in the right to secure obligations; and their inception, like that of any major event on earth, was saturated in blood."[32] Humanity does not gradually progress from combat to combat until it arrives at universal reciprocity, where the rule of law finally replaces warfare; humanity installs each of its violences in a system of rules and thus proceeds from domination to domination.

The nature of these rules allows violence to be inflicted on violence and the resurgence of new forces that are sufficiently strong to dominate those in power. Rules are empty in themselves, violent and unfinalized; they are impersonal and can be bent to any purpose. The successes of history belong to those who are capable of seizing these rules, to replace those who had used them, to disguise themselves so as to pervert them, invert their meaning, and redirect them against those who had initially imposed them; controlling this complex mechanism, they will make it function so as to overcome the rulers through their own rules.

The isolation of different points of emergence does not conform to the successive configurations of an identical meaning; rather, they result from substitutions, displacements, disguised conquests, and systematic reversals. If interpretation were the slow exposure of the meaning hidden in an origin, then only metaphysics could interpret the development of humanity. But if interpretation is the violent or surreptitious appropriation of a system of rules, which in itself has no essential meaning, in order to impose a direction, to bend it to a new will, to force its participation in a different game, and to subject it to secondary rules, then the development of humanity is a series of interpretations. The role of genealogy is to record its history: the history of morals, ideals, and metaphysical concepts, the history of the concept of liberty or of the ascetic life; as they stand for the emergence of different interpretations, they must be made to appear as events on the stage of historical process.

5. How can we define the relationship between genealogy, seen as the examination of *Herkunft* and *Entstehung*, and history in the traditional sense? We could, of course, examine Nietzsche's celebrated apostrophes against history, but we will put these aside for the moment and consider those instances when he conceives of genealogy as "wirkliche Historie,"[xi] or its more frequent characterization as historical "spirit" or "sense."[33] In fact, Nietzsche's criticism, beginning with the second of the *Untimely Meditations*, always questioned the form of history that reintroduces (and always assumes) a suprahistorical perspective: a history whose function is to compose the finally reduced diversity of time into a totality fully closed upon itself; a history that always encourages subjective recognitions and attributes a form of reconciliation to all the displacements of the past; a history whose perspective on all that precedes it implies the end of time, a completed development. The historian's history finds its support outside of time and pretends to base its judgments on an apocalyptic objectivity. This is only possible, however, because of its belief in eternal truth, the immortality of the soul, and the nature of consciousness as always identical to itself. Once the historical sense is mastered by a suprahistorical perspective, metaphysics can bend it to its own purpose and, by aligning it to the demands of objective science, it can impose its own "Egyptianism." On the other hand, the historical sense can evade metaphysics and become a privileged instrument of genealogy if it refuses the certainty of absolutes. Given this, it corresponds to the acuity of a glance that distinguishes, separates, and disperses, that is capable of liberating divergence and marginal elements – the kind of dissociating view that is capable of decomposing itself, capable of shattering the unity of man's being through

---

[xi] Usually translated as "effective history".

369

which it was thought that he could extend his sovereignty to the events of his past.

Historical meaning becomes a dimension of "wirkliche Historie" to the extent that it places within a process of development everything considered immortal in man. We believe that feelings are immutable, but every sentiment, particularly the noblest and most disinterested, has a history. We believe in the dull constancy of instinctual life and imagine that it continues to exert its force indiscriminately in the present as it did in the past. But a knowledge of history easily disintegrates this unity, depicts its wavering course, locates its moments of strength and weakness, and defines its oscillating reign. It easily seizes the slow elaboration of instincts and those movements where, in turning upon themselves, they relentlessly set about their self-destruction.[34] We believe, in any event, that the body obeys the exclusive laws of physiology and that it escapes the influence of history, but this too is false. The body is molded by a great many distinct regimes; it is broken down by the rhythms of work, rest, and holidays; it is poisoned by food or values, through eating habits or moral laws; it constructs resistances.[35] "Effective" history differs from traditional history in being without constants. Nothing in man – not even his body – is sufficiently stable to serve as the basis for self-recognition or for understanding other men. The traditional devices for constructing a comprehensive view of history and for retracing the past as a patient and continuous development must be systematically dismantled. Necessarily, we must dismiss those tendencies that encourage the consoling play of recognitions. Knowledge, even under the banner of history, does not depend on "rediscovery," and it emphatically excludes the "rediscovery of ourselves." History becomes "effective" to the degree that it introduces discontinuity into our very being – as it divides our emotions, dramatizes our instincts, multiplies our body and sets it against itself. "Effective" history deprives the self of the reassuring stability of life and nature, and it will not permit itself to be transported by a voiceless obstinacy toward a millenial ending. It will uproot its traditional foundations and relentlessly disrupt its pretended continuity. This is because knowledge is not made for understanding; it is made for cutting.

From these observations, we can grasp the particular traits of historical meaning as Nietzsche understood it – the sense which opposes "wirkliche Historie" to traditional history. The former transposes the relationship ordinarily established between the eruption of an event and necessary continuity. An entire historical tradition (theological or rationalistic) aims at dissolving the singular event into an ideal continuity – as a teleological movement or a natural process. "Effective" history, however, deals with events in terms of their most unique characteristics, their most acute manifestations. An event, consequently, is not a decision, a treaty, a reign, or a battle, but the reversal of a relationship of forces, the usurpation of power, the appropriation of a vocabulary turned against those who had once used it, a feeble domination that poisons itself as it grows lax, the entry of a masked "other." The forces operating in history are not controlled by destiny or regulative mechanisms, but respond to haphazard conflicts.[36] They do not manifest the successive forms of a primordial intention and their attraction is not that of a conclusion, for they always appear through the singular randomness of events. The inverse of the Christian world, spun entirely by a divine spider, and different from the world of the Greeks, divided between the realm of will and the great cosmic folly, the world of effective history knows only one kingdom, without providence or final cause, where there is only "the iron hand of necessity shaking the dice-box of chance."[37] Chance is not simply the drawing of lots, but raising the stakes in every attempt to master chance through the will to power, and giving rise to the risk of an even greater chance.[38] The world we know is not this ultimately simple configuration where events are reduced to accentuate their essential traits, their final meaning, or their initial and final value. On the contrary, it is a profusion of entangled events. If it appears as a "marvelous motley, profound and totally meaning-ful," this is because it began and continues its secret existence through a "host of errors and phantasms."[39] We want historians to confirm our belief that the present rests upon profound intentions and immutable necessities. But the true historical sense confirms our existence among countless lost events, without a landmark or a point of reference.

Effective history can also invert the relationship that traditional history, in its dependence on metaphysics, establishes between proximity and distance. The latter is given to a contemplation of distances and heights: the noblest periods, the highest forms, the most abstract ideas, the purest individualities. It accomplishes this by getting as near as possible, placing itself at the foot of its mountain peaks, at the risk of adopting the famous perspective of frogs. Effective history, on the other hand, shortens its vision to those things nearest to it – the body, the nervous system, nutrition, digestion, and energies; it unearths the periods of decadence and if it chances upon lofty epochs, it is with the suspicion – not vindictive but joyous – of finding a barbarous and shameful confusion. It has no fear of looking down, so long as it is understood that it looks from above and descends to seize the various perspectives, to disclose dispersions and dif-ferences, to leave things undisturbed in their own dimension and intensity. It reverses the surreptitious practice of historians, their pretension to examine things furthest from themselves, the grovelling manner in which they approach this promising distance (like the metaphysicians who proclaim the existence of an afterlife, situated at a distance from this world, as a promise of their reward). Effective history studies what is closest, but in an abrupt dispossession, so as to seize it at a distance (an approach similar to that of a doctor who looks closely, who plunges to make a diagnosis and to state its difference). Historical sense has more in common with medicine than philosophy; and it should not surprise us that Nietzsche occasionally employs the phrase "historically and physiologically,"[40] since among the philosopher's idiosyncrasies is a complete denial of the body. This includes, as well, "the absence of historical sense, a hatred for the idea of development, Egyptianism," the obstinate "placing of conclusions at the beginning," of "making last things first."[41] History has a more important task than to be a handmaiden to philosophy, to recount the necessary birth of truth and values; it should become a differential knowledge of energies and failings, heights and degenerations, poisons and antidotes. Its taks is to become a curative science.[42]

The final trait of effective history is its affirmation of knowledge as perspective. Historians take unusual pains to erase the elements in their work which reveal their grounding in a particular time and place, their preferences in a controversy – the unavoidable obstacles of their passion. Nietzsche's version of historical sense is explicit in its perspective and acknowledges its system of injustice. Its perception is slanted, being a deliberate appraisal, affirmation, or negation; it reaches the lingering and poisonous traces in order to prescribe the best antidote. It is not given to a discreet effacement before the objects it observes and does not submit itself to their processes; nor does it seek laws, since it gives equal weight to its own sight and to its objects. Through this historical sense, knowledge is allowed to create its own genealogy in the act of cognition; and "wirkliche Historie" composes a genealogy of history as the vertical projection of its position.

6. In this context, Nietzsche links historical sense to the historian's history. They share a beginning that is similarly impure and confused, share the same sign in which the symptoms of sickness can be recognized as well as the seed of an exquisite flower.[43] They arose simultaneously to follow their separate ways, but our task is to trace their common genealogy.

The descent (*Herkunft*) of the historian is unequivocal: he is of humble birth. A characteristic of history is to be without choice: it encourages thorough understanding and excludes qualitative judgments – a sensitivity to all things without distinction, a comprehensive view excluding differences. Nothing must escape it and, more importantly, nothing must be excluded. Historians argue that this proves their tact and discretion. After all, what right have they to impose their tastes and preferences when they seek to determine what actually occurred in the past? Their mistake is to exhibit a total lack of taste, the kind of crudeness that becomes smug in the presence of the loftiest elements and finds satisfaction in reducing them to size. The historian is insensitive to the most disgusting things; or rather, he especially enjoys those things that should be repugnant to him. His apparent serenity follows from his concerted avoidance of the exceptional and his reduction of all things to the lowest common denominator. Nothing is allowed to stand above him; and underlying his desire for total knowledge is his search for the secrets that belittle everything: "base curiosity." What is the source of history? It comes from the plebs.[xii] To whom is it addressed? To the plebs. And its discourse strongly resembles the demagogue's refrain: "No one is greater than you and anyone who presumes to get the better of you – you who are good – is evil." The historian, who functions as his double, can be heard to echo: "No past is greater than your present, and, through my meticulous erudition, I will rid you of your infatuations and transform the grandeur of history into pettiness, evil, and misfortune." The historian's ancestry goes back to Socrates.

This demagogy, of course, must be masked. It must hide its singular malice under the cloak of universals. As the demagogue is obliged to invoke truth, laws of essences, and eternal necessity, the historian must invoke objectivity, the accuracy of facts, and the permanence of the past. The demagogue denies the body to secure the sovereignty of a timeless idea and the historian effaces his proper individuality so that others may enter the stage and reclaim their own speech. He is divided against himself: forced to silence his preferences and overcome his distaste, to blur his own perspective and replace it with the fiction of a universal geometry, to mimic death in order to enter the kingdom of the dead, to adopt a faceless anonymity. In this world where he has conquered his individual will, he becomes a guide to the inevitable law of a superior will. Having curbed the demands of his individual will in his knowledge, he will disclose the form of an eternal will in his object of study. The objectivity of historians inverts the relationships of will and knowledge and it is, in the same stroke, a necessary belief in Providence, in final causes and teleology – the beliefs that place the historian in the family of ascetics. "I can't stand these lustful eunuchs of history, all the seductions of an ascetic ideal; I can't stand these blanched tombs producing life or those tired and indifferent beings who dress up in the part of wisdom and adopt an objective point of view."[44]

The *Entstehung* of history is found in nineteenth-century Europe: the land of interminglings and bastardy, the period of the "man-of-mixture." We have become barbarians with respect to those rare moments of high civilization: cities in ruin and enigmatic monuments are spread out before us; we stop before gaping walls; we ask what gods inhabited these empty temples. Great epochs lacked this curiosity, lacked our excessive deference; they ignored their predecessors: the classical period ignored Shakespeare.

[xii] "Plebs" is short for plebians, an ancient Roman term for the lower class.

The decadence of Europe presents an immense spectacle (while stronger periods refrained from such exhibitions), and the nature of this scene is to represent a theater; lacking monuments of our own making, which properly belong to us, we live among crowded scenes. But there is more. Europeans no longer know themselves; they ignore their mixed ancestries and seek a proper role. They lack individuality: We can begin to understand the spontaneous historical bent of the nineteenth century: the anemia of its forces and those mixtures that effaced all its individual traits produced the same results as the mortifications of asceticism; its inability to create, its absence of artistic works, and its need to rely on past achievements forced it to adopt the base curiosity of plebs.

If this fully represents the genealogy of history, how could it become, in its own right, a genealogical analysis? Why did it not continue as a form of demagogic or religious knowledge? How could it change roles on the same stage? Only by being seized, dominated, and turned against its birth. And it is this movement which properly describes the specific nature of the *Entstehung:* it is not the unavoidable conclusion of a long preparation, but a scene where forces are risked in the chance of confrontations, where they emerge triumphant, where they can also be confiscated. The locus of emergence for metaphysics was surely Athenian demagogy, the vulgar spite of Socrates and his belief in immortality, and Plato could have seized this Socratic philosophy to turn it against itself. Undoubtedly, he was often tempted to do so, but his defeat lies in its consecration. The problem was similar in the nineteenth century: to avoid doing for the popular asceticism of historians what Plato did for Socrates. This historical trait should not be founded upon a philosophy of history, but dismantled beginning with the things it produced; it is necessary to master history so as to turn it to genealogical uses, that is, strictly anti-Platonic purposes. Only then will the historical sense free itself from the demands of a suprahistorical history.

7. The historical sense gives rise to three uses that oppose and correspond to the three Platonic modalities of history. The first is parodic, directed against reality, and opposes the theme of history as reminiscence or recognition; the second is dissociative, directed against identity, and opposes history given as continuity or representative of a tradition; the third is sacrificial, directed against truth, and opposes history as knowledge. They imply a use of history that severs its connection to memory, its metaphysical and anthropological model, and constructs a counter-memory – a transformation of history into a totally different form of time.

First, the parodic and farcical use. The historian offers this confused and anonymous European, who no longer knows himself or what name he should adopt, the possibility of alternate identities, more individualized and substantial than his own. But the man with historical sense will see that this substitution is simply a disguise. Historians supplied the Revolution with Roman prototypes, romanticism with knight's armor, and the Wagnerian era was given the sword of a German hero – ephemeral props that point to our own unreality. No one kept them from venerating these religions, from going to Bayreuth[xiii] to commemorate a new afterlife; they were free, as well, to be transformed into street-vendors of empty identities. The new historian, the genealogist, will know what to make of this masquerade. He will not be too serious to enjoy it; on the contrary, he will push the masquerade to its limit and prepare the great carnival of time where masks are constantly reappearing. No longer the identification of our faint individuality with the solid identities of the past, but our "unrealization" through the excessive choice of identities – Frederick of Hohenstaufen, Caesar, Jesus, Dionysus, and possibly Zarathustra. Taking up these masks, revitalizing the buffoonery of history, we adopt an identity whose unreality surpasses that of God who started the charade. "Perhaps, we can discover a realm where originality is again possible as parodists of history and buffoons of God."[45] In this, we recognize the parodic double of what the second of the *Untimely Meditations* called "monumental history": a history given to reestablishing the high points of historical development and their maintenance in a perpetual presence, given to the recovery of works, actions, and creations through the monogram of their personal essence. But in 1874, Nietzsche accused this history, one totally devoted to veneration, of barring access to the actual intensities and creations of life. The parody of his last texts serves to emphasize that "monumental history" is itself a parody. Genealogy is history in the form of a concerted carnival.

The second use of history is the systematic dissociation of identity. This is necessary because this rather weak identity, which we attempt to support and to unify under a mask, is in itself only a parody: it is plural; countless spirits dispute its possession; numerous systems intersect and compete. The study of history makes one "happy, unlike the metaphysicians, to possess in oneself not an immortal soul but many mortal ones."[46] And in each of these souls, history will not discover a forgotten identity, eager to be reborn, but a complex system of distinct and multiple elements, unable to be mastered by the powers of synthesis: "it is a sign of superior culture to maintain, in a fully conscious way, certain phases of its evolution which lesser men pass through without thought. The initial result is that we can understand those who resemble us as completely determined systems and as representative of diverse cultures, that is to say, as necessary and capable of modification. And in return, we are able to separate the phases

[xiii] Bayreuth was the home of German composer Richard Wagner from 1872 until his death in 1883, and the center of the cult that surrounded him.

375

of our own evolution and consider them individually."[47] The purpose of history, guided by genealogy, is not to discover the roots of our identity but to commit itself to its dissipation. It does not seek to define our unique threshold of emergence, the homeland to which metaphysicians promise a return; it seeks to make visible all of those discontinuities that cross us. "Antiquarian history," according to the *Untimely Meditations*, pursues opposite goals. It seeks the continuities of soil, language, and urban life in which our present is rooted and, "by cultivating in a delicate manner that which existed for all time, it tries to conserve for posterity the conditions under which we were born."[48] This type of history was objected to in the *Meditations* because it tended to block creativity in support of the laws of fidelity. Somewhat later – and already in *Human, All Too Human* – Nietzsche reconsiders the task of the antiquarian, but with an altogether different emphasis. If genealogy in its own right gives rise to questions concerning our native land, native language, or the laws that govern us, its intention is to reveal the heterogenous systems which, masked by the self, inhibit the formation of any form of identity.

The third use of history is the sacrifice of the subject of knowledge. In appearance, or rather, according to the mask it bears, historical consciousness is neutral, devoid of passions, and committed solely to truth. But if it examines itself and if, more generally, it interrogates the various forms of scientific consciousness in its history, it finds that all these forms and transformations are aspects of the will to knowledge: instinct, passion, the inquisitor's devotion, cruel subtlety, and malice. It discovers the violence of a position that sides against those who are happy in their ignorance, against the effective illusions by which humanity protects itself, a position that encourages the dangers of research and delights in disturbing discoveries.[49] The historical analysis of this rancorous will to knowledge reveals that all knowledge rests upon injustice (that there is no right, not even in the act of knowing, to truth or a foundation for truth) and that the instinct for knowledge is malicious (something murderous, opposed to the happiness of mankind). Even in the greatly expanded form it assumes today, the will to knowledge does not achieve a universal truth; man is not given an exact and serene mastery of nature. On the contrary, it ceaselessly multiplies the risks, creates dangers in every area; it breaks down illusory defences; it dissolves the unity of the subject; it releases those elements of itself that are devoted to its subversion and destruction. Knowledge does not slowly detach itself from its empirical roots, the initial needs from which it arose, to become pure speculation subject only to the demands of reason; its development is not tied to the constitution and affirmation of a free subject; rather, it creates a progressive enslavement to its instinctive violence. Where religions once demanded the sacrifice of bodies, knowledge now calls for experimentation on ourselves,[50] calls us to the sacrifice of the subject of knowledge. "The desire for knowledge has been transformed among us into a passion which fears no sacrifice, which fears nothing but its own extinction. It may be that mankind will eventually perish from this passion for knowledge. If not through passion, then through weakness. We must be prepared to state our choice: do we wish humanity to end in fire and light or to end on the sands?"[51] We should now replace the two great problems of nineteenth-century philosophy, passed on by Fichte and Hegel (the reciprocal basis of truth and liberty and the possibility of absolute knowledge), with the theme that "to perish through absolute knowledge may well form a part of the basis of being."[52] This does not mean, in terms of a critical procedure, that the will to truth is limited by the intrinsic finitude of cognition, but that it loses all sense of limitations and all claim to truth in its unavoidable sacrifice of the subject of knowledge. "It may be that there remains one prodigious idea which might be made to prevail over every other aspiration, which might overcome the most victorious: the idea of humanity sacrificing itself. It seems indisputable that if this new constellation appeared on the horizon, only the desire for truth, with its enormous prerogatives, could direct and sustain such a sacrifice. For to knowledge, no sacrifice is too great. Of course, this problem has never been posed."[53]

The *Untimely Meditations* discussed the critical use of history: its just treatment of the past, its decisive cutting of the roots, its rejection of traditional attitudes of reverence, its liberation of man by presenting him with other origins than those in which he prefers to see himself. Nietzsche, however, reproached critical history for detaching us from every real source and for sacrificing the very movement of life to the exclusive concern for truth. Somewhat later, as we have seen, Nietzsche reconsiders this line of thought he had at first refused, but directs it to altogether different ends. It is no longer a question of judging the past in the name of a truth that only we can possess in the present; but risking the destruction of the subject who seeks knowledge in the endless deployment of the will to knowledge.

In a sense, genealogy returns to the three modalities of history that Nietzsche recognized in 1874. It returns to them in spite of the objections that Nietzsche raised in the name of the affirmative and creative powers of life. But they are metamorphosized; the veneration of monuments becomes parody; the respect for ancient continuities becomes systematic dissociation; the critique of the injustices of the past by a truth held by men in the present becomes the destruction of the man who maintains knowledge by the injustice proper to the will to knowledge.

Notes

1   *The Gay Science*, 7.
2   *Human All Too Human*, 3.
3   *The Genealogy [of Morals]*, II, 6, 8.
4   *The Gay Science*, 110, 111, 300.
5   Paul Ree's text was entitled *Ursprung der Moralischen Empfindungen* [*Origin of the Moral Sentiments*].
6   In *Human, All Too Human*, aphorism 92 was entitled *Ursprung der Gerechtigkeit* [*Origin of Justice*].
7   In the main body of *The Genealogy*, *Ursprung* and *Herkunpt* are used interchangeably in numerous instances (I, 2; II, 8, 11, 12, 16, 17).
8   *The Dawn*, 123.
9   *Human, All Too Human*, 34.
10 *The Wanderer and his Shadow*, 9.
11 The *Wanderer and his Shadow*, 3.
12 *The Dawn*, 49.
13 *Nietzsche contra Wagner*, p. 99.
14 *The Gay Science*, 265 and 110.
15 *Twilight of the Idols*, "How the world of truth becomes a fable."
16 For example, *The Gay Science*, 135; *Beyond Good and Evil*, 200, 242, 244; *The Genealogy*, I, 5.
17 *The Gay Science*, 348–9; *Beyond Good and Evil*, 260.
18 *Beyond Good and Evil*, 244.
19 *The Genealogy*, III, 17. The *abkunft* of feelings of depression.
20 *Twilight*, "Reasons for philosophy."
21 *The Dawn*, 247.
22 *The Gay Science*, 348–9.
23 Ibid., 200.
24 *The Dawn*, 42.
25 *Beyond Good and Evil*, 262.
26 *The Genealogy*, III, 13.
27 *The Gay Science*, 148. It is also to an anemia of the will that one must attribute the *Entstehung* of Buddhism and Christianity, 347.
28 *The Genealogy*, I, 2.
29 *Beyond Good and Evil*, 260; cf. also *The Genealogy*, II, 12.
30 *The Wanderer*, 9.
31 *The Gay Science*, 111.
32 *The Genealogy*, II, 6.
33 *The Genealogy*, Preface, 7; and I, 2. *Beyond Good and Evil*, 224.
34 *The Gay Science*, 7.
35 Ibid.
36 *The Genealogy*, II, 12.
37 *The Dawn*, 130.
38 *The Genealogy*, II, 12.

39   *Human, All Too Human*, 16.
40   *Twilight*, 44.
41   *Twilight*, "Reason within philosophy," 1 and 4.
42   *The Wanderer*, 188.
43   *The Gay Science*, 337.
44   *The Genealogy*, III, 26.
45   *Beyond Good and Evil*, 223.
46   *The Wanderer* (Opinions and Mixed Statements), 17.
47   *Human, All Too Human*, 274.
48   *Untimely Meditations*, II, 3.
49   Cf. *The Dawn*, 429 and 432; *The Gay Science*, 333; *Beyond Good and Evil*, 229–30.
50   *The Dawn*, 501.
51   Ibid., 429.
52   *Beyond Good and Evil*, 39.
53   *The Dawn*, 45.

"Truth and Power"

. . . The important thing here, I believe, is that truth isn't outside power, or lacking in power: contrary to a myth whose history and functions would repay further study, truth isn't the reward of free spirits, the child of protracted solitude, nor the privilege of those who have succeeded in liberating themselves. Truth is a thing of this world: it is produced only by virtue of multiple forms of constraint. And it induces regular effects of power. Each society has its regime of truth, its 'general politics' of truth: that is, the types of discourse which it accepts and makes function as true; the mechanisms and instances which enable one to distinguish true and false statements, the means by which each is sanctioned; the techniques and procedures accorded value in the acquisition of truth; the status of those who are charged with saying what counts as true.

In societies like ours, the 'political economy' of truth is characterised by five important traits. 'Truth is centred on the form of scientific discourse and the institutions which produce it; it is subject to constant economic and political incitement (the demand for truth, as much for economic production as for political power); it is the object, under diverse forms, of immense diffusion and consumption (circulating through apparatuses of education and information whose extent is relatively broad in the social body, not withstanding certain strict limitations); it is produced and transmitted under the control, dominant if not exclusive, of a few great political and economic apparatuses (university, army, writing, media);

lastly, it is the issue of a whole political debate and social confrontation ('ideological' struggles).

It seems to me that what must now be taken into account in the intellectual is not the 'bearer of universal values'. Rather, it's the person occupying a specific position – but whose specificity is linked, in a society like ours, to the general functioning of an apparatus of truth. In other words, the intellectual has a three-fold specificity: that of his class position (whether as petty-bourgeois[xiv] in the service of capitalism or 'organic' intellectual of the proletariat); that of his conditions of life and work, linked to his condition as an intellectual (his field of research, his place in a laboratory, the political and economic demands to which he submits or against which he rebels, in the university, the hospital, etc.); lastly, the specificity of the politics of truth in our societies. And it's with this last factor that his position can take on a general significance and that his local, specific struggle can have effects and implications which are not simply professional or sectoral. The intellectual can operate and struggle at the general level of that regime of truth which is so essential to the structure and functioning of our society. There is a battle 'for truth', or at least 'around truth' – it being understood once again that by truth I do not mean 'the ensemble of truths which are to be discovered and accepted', but rather 'the ensemble of rules according to which the true and the false are separated and specific effects of power attached to the true', it being understood also that it's not a matter of a battle 'on behalf' of the truth, but of a battle about the status of truth and the economic and political role it plays. It is necessary to think of the political problems of intellectuals not in terms of 'science' and 'ideology', but in terms of 'truth' and 'power'. And thus the question of the professionalisation of intellectuals and the division between intellectual and manual labour can be envisaged in a new way.

All this must seem very confused and uncertain. Uncertain indeed, and what I am saying here is above all to be taken as a hypothesis. In order for it to be a little less confused, however, I would like to put forward a few 'propositions' – not firm assertions, but simply suggestions to be further tested and evaluated.

'Truth' is to be understood as a system of ordered procedures for the production, regulation, distribution, circulation and operation of statements.

'Truth' is linked in a circular relation with systems of power which produce and sustain it, and to effects of power which it induces and which extend it. A regime of truth.

[xiv] The "little bourgeoisie," a Marxist term for small capitalists, civil servants, professionals, etc.

This regime is not merely ideological or superstructural; it was a condition of the formation and development of capitalism. And it's this same regime which, subject to certain modifications, operates in the socialist countries (I leave open here the question of China, about which I know little).

The essential political problem for the intellectual is not to criticise the ideological contents supposedly linked to science, or to ensure that his own scientific practice is accompanied by a correct ideology, but that of ascertaining the possibility of constituting a new politics of truth. The problem is not changing people's consciousnesses – or what's in their heads – but the political, economic, institutional regime of the production of truth.

It's not a matter of emancipating truth from every system of power (which would be a chimera, for truth is already power) but of detaching the power of truth from the forms of hegemony, social, economic and cultural, within which it operates at the present time.

The political question, to sum up, is not error, illusion, alienated consciousness or ideology; it is truth itself. Hence the importance of Nietzsche.

chapter twenty-six

"POSTmodernISM: A Paracritical Bibliography"

Ihab Hassan

> Professor of literature, Ihab Hassan (1925–) was one of the earliest advocates of postmodernism. In the following 1971 essay, his first on the subject, he presents a listing of the elements and influences that suggest a turn from modernism to postmodernism, and does so in a particularly postmodern style, an eclectic, non-linear, virtually anarchic listing of cultural elements, along with graphic textual anomalies that have become familiar to readers of postmodern literature. In addition to the intentional playfulness of this kind of writing (versus modernist seriousness), the unmistakable implication is that inquiry (in this case, Hassan's essay) cannot systematically exhaust or enclose the cultural phenomena it seeks to understand, but must make its way nonetheless with whatever devices and insights it can muster. Yet, Hassan's postmodernism is not primarily negative, not simply a recognition of the limits of human inquiry. It is positive and ecstatic; for Hassan, postmodernism is an attempt to write the unwritable. "Truly," he remarks, "we dwell happily in the Unimaginable."

1 Change

Dionysus and Cupid are both agents of change. First, *The Bacchae*, destruction of the city, then *The Metamorphoses*, mischievous variations of nature.[i]

Ihab Hassan, "POSTmodernISM: A Paracritical Bibliography," in *Paracriticisms: Seven Speculations of the Times* (Urbana: University of Illinois Press, 1975), pp. 39–59.

[i] Dionysus was a character in Euripedes' *The Bacchae*, as was Cupid, god of love, in Ovid's *Metamorphoses*. Note that this essay employs an abundance of cultural and literary references, making it impractical to annotate them all.

Some might say that change is violence, and violence is continuous whether it be Horror or High Camp. But sly Ovid simply declares:

> My intention is to tell of bodies changed
> To different forms; the gods, who made the changes,
> Will help me – or I hope so – with a poem
> That runs from the world's beginning to our own days.

To our own days, the bodies natural or politic wax and wane, *carpen perpetuam*.[ii] Something warms Galatea[iii] out of ivory; even rock turns into spiritual forms. Perhaps love is one way we experience change.

How then can we live without love of change?

> Evolution has its enemies, that quiet genius Owen Barfield knows. In Unancestral Voices he calls them by name: Lucifer and Ahriman. Most often they coexist in us. Lucifer preserves the past utterly from dissolution. Ahriman destroys the past utterly for the sake of his own inventions.

a. Thus in one kind of history, chronicles of continuity, we deny real change. Even endings become part of a history of endings. From schism to paradigm; from apocalypse to archetype. Warring empires, catastrophe and famine, immense hopes, faraway names – Cheops, Hammurabi, David, Darius, Alcibiades, Hannibal, Caesar – all fall into place on numbered pages.

Yet continuities, "the glory that was Greece, the grandeur that was Rome," must prevail in Story, on a certain level of narrative abstraction, obscuring change.

b. Thus, too, in another kind of history, we reinvent continually the past. Without vision, constant revision, the Party chronicles of *Nineteen Eighty-Four*. Or individually, each man dreams his ancestors to remake himself. The Black Muslim takes on a new name, ignoring the deadly dawn raids, cries of Allah among slave traders, journeys across Africa in Arab chains.

Yet relevances must persist in Story, on a certain level of fictional selectivity, veiling change.

Behind all history, continuous or discrete, abstract or autistic, lurks the struggle of identity with death. Is history often the secret biography of historians? The recorded imagination of our own mortality?

> Thou, silent form, dost tease us out of thought
> As doth eternity: Cold Pastoral.

[ii] "Seize the perpetual," a play on *carpe diem* (seize the day).
[iii] Pygmalion's beloved statue, granted life by Aphrodite.

Ihab Hassan

2 Periods

When will the Modern Period end?

Has ever a period waited so long? Renaissance? Baroque? Neo-Classical? Romantic? Victorian? Perhaps only the Dark Middle Ages.

When will Modernism cease and what comes thereafter?

What will the twenty-first century call us? and will its voice come from the same side of our graves?

Does Modernism stretch merely to stretch out our lives? Or, ductile, does it give a new sense of time? The end of periodicization? The slow arrival of simultaneity?

If change changes ever more rapidly and the future jolts us now, do men, more than ever, resist both endings and beginnings?

> Childhood is huge and youth golden. Few recover. Critics are no exception. Like everyone else, they recall the literature of their youth brilliantly; they do not think it can ever tarnish.
>
> "Let us consider where the great men are
> Who will obsess the child when he can read."
>
> So Delmore Schwartz wrote, naming Joyce, Eliot, Pound, Rilke, Yeats, Kafka, Mann. He could have added: Proust, Valéry, Gide, Conrad, Lawrence, Woolf, Faulkner, Hemingway, O'Neill. . . .
>
> A walker in the city of that literature will not forget. Nor will he forgive. How can contemporaries of Ellison, Pinter, or Grass dare breathe in this ancestral air? Yet it is possible that we will all remain Invisible Men until each becomes his own father.

3 Innovation

All of us devise cunning ceremonies of ancester worship. Yet there is a fable for us in the lives of two men: Proteus and Picasso, mentors of shapes. Their forms are self-transformations. They know the secret of Innovation: Motion.

> Masters of possibility, ponder this. They used to say: the kingdom of the dead is larger than any kingdom. But the earth has now exploded. Soon the day may come when there will be more people alive than ever lived.
>
> When the quick are more populous than all the departed, will history reverse itself? End?

384

We resist the new under the guise of judgment. "We must have standards." But standards apply only where they are applicable. This has been the problem with the Tradition of the New (Harold Rosenberg).

Standards are inevitable, and the best of these will create themselves to meet, to *create*, new occasions. Let us, therefore, admit standards. But let us also ask how many critics of literature espouse, even selectively, the new, speak of it with joyous intelligence? Taking few risks, the best known among them wait for reviewers to clear the way.

Reaction to the new has its own reasons that reason seldom acknowledges. It also has its rhetoric of dismissal.

a. The Fad
  – "It's a passing fashion, frivolous; if we ignore it now, it will quietly go away."
  – This implies permanence as absolute value. It also implies the ability to distinguish between fashion and history without benefit of time or creative intuition. How many judgments of this kind fill the Purgatorio of Letters?
b. The Old Story
  – "It's been done before, there's nothing new in it; you can find it in Euripides, Sterne, or Whitman."
  – This implies prior acquaintance, rejection on the basis of dubious similitude. It also implies that nothing really changes. Therefore, why unsettle things, re-quire a fresh response?
c. The Safe Version
  – "Yes, it seems new, but in the same genre, I prefer Duchamp; he really did it better."
  – This implies a certain inwardness with innovation. The entrance fee has been paid, once and forever. Without seeming in the least Philistine, one can disdain the intrusions of the present.
d. The Newspeak of Art
  – "The avant-garde is just the new academicism."
  – This may imply that art which seems conventional can be more genuinely innovative: this is sometimes true. It may also imply mere irritation: the oxymoron as means of discreditation.

> About true innovation we can have no easy preconceptions. Prediction is mere extrapolation, the cool whisper of RAND.[iv] But prophecy is akin to madness, or the creative imagination; its path, seldom linear, breaks, turns, disappears in mutations or quantum jumps.

[iv] Presumably a reference to the Rand Corporation and its futuristic technological predictions.

Ihab Hassan

Therefore, we cannot expect the avant-garde of past, present, and future to obey the same logic, assume the same forms. For instance, the new avant-garde need not have a historical consciousness, express recognizable values, or endorse radical politics. It need not shock, surprise, protest. The new avant-garde may not be an " avant-garde"at all: simply an agent of yet-invisible change.

Note: Consult Renato Poggioli, The Theory of the Avant-Garde (Cambridge, Mass., 1968).

And yet everything I have said here can lend itself to abuse. The rage for change can be a form of self-hatred or spite. Look deep into any revolutionary.
Look also into extremes of the recent avant-garde. Vito Hannibal Acconci creates his "body sculptures" by biting, mutilating, himself in public. Rudolph Schwarzkogler slowly amputates his penis, and expires. In a world no longer linear, we must wonder: which way is forward? which way is life? Action often acquires the logic of the boomerang.

4 Distinctions

The change in Modernism may be called Postmodernism. Viewing the former with later eyes, we begin to discern fringe figures closer to us now than the great Moderns who "will obsess the child" someday.

Thus the classic text of Modernism is Edmund Wilson's *Axel's Castle: A Study in the Imaginative Literature of 1870–1930* (1931). Contents: Symbolism, Yeats, Valéry, Eliot, Proust, Joyce, Stein.

Thus, forty years later, my alternate view, *The Dismemberment of Orpheus: Toward a Postmodern Literature* (1971). Contents: Sade, 'Pataphysics to Surrealism, Hemingway, Kafka, Existentialism to Aliterature, Genet, Beckett.

Erratum: Gertrude Stein should have appeared in the latter work, for she contributed to both Modernism and Postmodernism.

But without a doubt, the crucial text is

If we can arbitrarily state that literary Modernism includes certain works between Jarry's *Ubu Roi* (1896) and Joyce's *Finnegans Wake* (1939), where will we arbitrarily say that Postmodernism begins? A year earlier than the *Wake*? With Sartre's *La Nausée* (1938) or Beckett's *Murphy* (1938)? In any case Postmodernism includes works by writers as different as Barth, arthelme, ecker, eckett, ense, lanchot, orges, recht, urroughs, utor.

Query: But is not *Ubu Roi* itself as Postmodern as it is Modern?

5 Critics

The assumptions of Modernism elaborated by formalist and mythopoeic critics especially, by the intellectual culture of the first half of the century as a whole, still define the dominant perspective on the study of literature.

> Exception: Karl Shapiro's *Beyond Criticism* (1953), *In Defence of Ignorance* (1960). Too "cranky" and "cantankerous" for academic *biens pensants*?

In England as in America, the known critics, different as they may seem in age, persuasion, or distinction, share the broad Modernist view: Blackmur, Brooks, Connolly, Empson, Frye, Howe, Kazin, Kermode, Leavis, Levin, Pritchett, Ransom, Rahv, Richards, Schorer, Tate, Trilling, Warren, Wellek, Wilson, Winters, etc.

No doubt there are many passages in the writings of these critics – of Leavis, say, or of Wilson – which will enlighten minds in every age. Yet it was Herbert Read[v] who possessed the most active sympathy for the avant-garde. His generosity of intuition enabled him to sponsor the new, rarely embracing the trivial. He engaged the Postmodern spirit in his anarchic affinities, in his concern for the prevalence of suffering, in his sensuous apprehension of renewed being. He cried: behold the Child! To him, education through art meant a salutation to Eros. Believing that the imagination serves the purpose of moral good, Read hoped to implicate art into existence so fully that their common substance became as simple, as necessary, as bread and water. This is a sacramental hope, still alive though mute in our midst, which recalls Tolstoy's *What Is Art?* I can hardly think of another critic, younger even by several decades, who might have composed that extraordinary romance, *The Green Child.*[vi]

---

[v] (1893–1968), English poet and critic.
[vi] A work of Herbert Read's.

The culture of literary criticism is still ruled by Modernist assumptions. This is particularly true within the academic profession, excepting certain linguistic, structuralist, and hermeneutic schools. But it is also true within the more noisy culture of our media. *The New York Review of Books, Time* (the literary sections), and *The New York Times Book Review* share a certain aspiration to wit or liveliness, to intelligence really, concealing resistance to the new. All the more skeptical in periods of excess, the culture of the Logos insists on old orders in clever or current guises, and, with the means of communication at hand, inhibits and restrains.

> *Self-Admonition:* Beware of glib condemnations of the media. They are playing a national role as bold, as crucial, as the Supreme Court played in the Fifties. Willful and arbitrary as they may be in their creation of public images – which preempt our selves – they are still custodians of some collective sanity. Note, too, the rising quality of the very publications you cited. [This was written in 1971.][vii]

6 Bibliography

Here is a curious chronology of some Postmodern criticism:

1 George Steiner, "The Retreat from the Word," *Kenyon Review*, 23 (Spring 1961). See also his *Language and Silence* (New York, 1967), and *Extraterritorial* (New York, 1971).
2 Ihab Hassan, "The Dismemberment of Orpheus," *American Scholar*, 23 (Summer 1963). See also his *Literature of Silence* (New York, 1967).
3 Hugh Kenner, "Art in a Closed Field," in *Learners and Discerners*, ed. Robert Scholes (Charlottesville, Va., 1964). See also his *Samuel Beckett* (New York, 1961; Berkeley and Los Angeles, 1968), and *The Counterfeiters* (Bloomington, Ind., 1968).
4 Leslie Fiedler, "The New Mutants," *Partisan Review*, 32 (Fall 1965). See also his "The Children's Hour; or, The Return of the Vanishing Longfellow," in *Liberations*, ed. Ihab Hassan (Middletown, Conn., 1971), and *Collected Essays* (New York, 1971).
5 Susan Sontag, "The Aesthetics of Silence," *Aspen*, nos. 5 & 6 (1967). See also her *Against Interpretation* (New York, 1966), and *Styles of Radical Will* (New York, 1969).
6 Richard Poirier, "The Literature of Waste," *New Republic*, 20 May

---

[vii] Author's addition.

1967. See also his "The Politics of Self-Parody," *Partisan Review*, 35 (Summer 1968), and *The Performing Self* (New York, 1971).
7   John Barth, "The Literature of Exhaustion," *Atlantic Monthly*, August 1967. See also his *Lost in the Funhouse* (New York, 1968).

And here are some leitmotifs of that criticism: the literary act in quest and question of itself; self-subversion or self-transcendence of forms; popular mutations; languages of silence.

7   ReVisions

A revision of Modernism is slowly taking place, and this is another evidence of Postmodernism. In *The Performing Self*, Richard Poirier tries to mediate between these two movements. We need to recall the doctrines of formalist criticism, the canons of classroom and quarterly in the last three decades, to savor such statements:

> Three of the great and much used texts of twentieth-century criticism, *Moby Dick, Ulysses, The Waste Land*, are written in mockery of system, written against any effort to harmonize discordant elements, against any mythic or metaphoric scheme. . . . But while this form of the literary imagination is radical in its essentially parodistic treatment of systems, its radicalism is in the interest of essentially conservative feelings.
>
> .   .   .
>
> The most complicated examples of twentieth-century literature, like *Ulysses* and *The Waste Land*, the end of which seems parodied by the end of *Giles* [*Goat-Boy* by Barth], are more than contemptuous of their own formal and stylistic elaborateness.

Certainly some profound philosophic minds of our century have concerned themselves with the disease of verbal systems: Heidegger, Wittgenstein, Sartre. And later writers as different as John Cage, Norman O. Brown, and Elie Wiesel have listened intently to the sounds of silence in art or politics, sex, morality, or religion. In this context the statements of Poirier do not merely display a revisionist will; they strain toward an aesthetic of Postmodernism.

We are still some way from attaining such an aesthetic; nor is it clear that Postmodern art gives high priority to that end. Perhaps we can start by revisioning Modernism as well as revising the pieties we have inherited about it. In *Continuities* Frank Kermode cautiously attempts that task. A critic of great civility, he discriminates well between types of modernism – what he calls "palaeo- and neo-modern" correspond perhaps to Modern and

Postmodern – and takes note of the new "anti-art," which he rightly traces back to Duchamp. But his preference for continuities tempts him to assimilate current to past things. Kermode, for instance, writes: "Aleatory art is accordingly, for all its novelty, an extension of past art, indeed the hypertrophy of one aspect of that art." Does not this statement close more possibilities than it opens? There is another perspective of things that Goethe described: "The most important thing is always the contemporary element, because it is most purely reflected in ourselves, as we are in it." I think that we will not grasp the cultural experience of our moment if we insist that the new arts are "marginal developments of older modernism," or that distinctions between "art" and "joke" are crucial to any future aesthetic.

Whether we tend to revalue Modernism in terms of Postmodernism (Poirier) or to reverse that procedure (Kermode), we will end by doing something of both since relations, analogies, enable our thought. Modernism does not suddenly cease so that Postmodernism may begin: they now *coexist*. New lines emerge from the past because our eyes every morning open anew. In a certain frame of mind, Michelangelo or Rembrandt, Goethe or Hegel, Nietzsche or Rilke, can reveal to us something about Postmodernism, as Erich Heller incidentally shows. Consider this marvelous passage from *The Artist's Journey to the Interior*:

> Michelangelo spent the whole of his last working day, six days before his death, trying to finish the Pietà which is known as the "Pietà Rondanini." He did not succeed. Perhaps it lies in the nature of stone that he had to leave unfinished what Rembrandt completed in paint: the employment of the material in the service of its own negation. For this sculpture seems to intimate that its maker was in the end determined to use only as much marble as was necessary to show that matter did not matter; what alone mattered was the pure inward spirit.

Here Michelangelo envisions, past any struggle with the obdurate material of existence, a state of gnostic consciousness to which we may be tending. Yet can we justifiably call him Postmodern?

Where Modern and Postmodern May Meet: or, Make Your Own List
1. Blake, Sade, Lautréamont, Rimbaud, Mallarmé, Whitman, etc.
2. daDaDA
3. SURrealism
4. KAFKA
5. Finnegans Wake
6. The Cantos
7. ???

8   Modernism

This is no place to offer a comprehensive definition of Modernism. From Apollinaire and Arp to Valéry, Woolf, and Yeats – I seem to miss the letters X and Z – runs the alphabet of authors who have delivered themselves memorably on the subject; and the weighty work of Richard Ellmann and Charles Feidelson, Jr., *The Modern Tradition*, still stands as the best compendium of that "large spiritual enterprise including philosophic, social, and scientific thought, and aesthetic and literary theories and manifestoes, as well as poems, novels, dramas."

Expectations of agreement, let alone of definition, seem superlatively naïve. This is true among stately and distinguished minds, not only rowdy critical tempers. Here, for instance, is Lionel Trilling, "On the Modern Element in Modern Literature":

> I can identify it by calling it the disenchantment of our culture with culture itself . . . the bitter line of hostility to civilization that runs through it [modern literature]. . . . I venture to say that the idea of losing oneself up to the point of self-destruction, of surrendering oneself to experience without regard to self-interest or conventional morality, of escaping wholly from the societal bonds, is an "element" somewhere in the mind of every modern person.

To this, Harry Levin counters in "What Was Modernism?":[1]

> Insofar as we are still moderns, I would argue, we are the children of Humanism and the Enlightenment. To identify and isolate the forces of unreason, in a certain sense, has been a triumph for the intellect. In another sense, it has reinforced that anti-intellectual undercurrent which, as it comes to the surface, I would prefer to call post-modern.

Yet the controversy of Modernism has still wider scope, as Monroe K. Spears, in *Dionysus and the City*, with bias beneath his Apollonian lucidity, shows. Released as energy from the contradictions of history, Modernism makes contradiction its own.

> For my purpose, let Modernism stand for X: a window on human madness, the shield of Perseus against which Medusa glances, the dream of some frowning, scholarly muse. I offer, instead, some rubrics and spaces. Let readers fill them with their own queries or grimaces. We value what we choose.

a. *Urbanism:* Nature put in doubt, from Baudelaire's *"cité fourmillante"*[viii] to Proust's Paris, Joyce's Dublin, Eliot's London, Dos Passos' New York,

---

viii Swarming city.

Döblin's Berlin. It is not a question of locale but of presence. The sanatorium of *The Magic Mountain* and the village of *The Castle* are still enclosed in an urban spiritual space. Exceptions, Faulkner's Yoknapatawpha or Lawrence's Midlands, recognize the City as pervasive threat.

b. *Technologism:* City and Machine make and remake one another. Extension, diffusion, and alienation of the human will. Yet technology does not feature simply as a theme of Modernism; it is also a form of its artistic struggle. Witness Cubism, Futurism, Dadaism. Other *reactions* to technology: primitivism, the occult, Bergsonian time, the dissociation of sensibility, etc. (See Wylie Sypher, *Literature and Technology*.)

c. *"Dehumanization"*: Ortega y Gasset really means Elitism, Irony, and Abstraction (*The Dehumanization of Art*). Style takes over; let life and the masses fend for themselves. "Poetry has become the higher algebra of metaphor." Instead of Vitruvian man, Leonardo's famous image of the human measure, we have Picasso's beings splintered on many planes. Not less human, just another idea of man.

Elitism:	Aristocratic or crypto-fascist: Rilke, Proust, Yeats, Eliot, Lawrence, Pound, d'Annunzio, Wyndham Lewis, etc.
Irony:	Play, complexity, formalism. The aloofness of art but also sly hints of its radical incompleteness. *Dr Faustus* and *Confessions of Felix Krull*. Irony as awareness of Non-being.
Abstraction:	Impersonality, sophistical simplicity, reduction and construction, time decomposed or spatialized. Thus Mondrian on Reductionism:

"To create pure reality plastically, it is necessary to reduce natural forms to the *constant elements* of form and natural colour to *primary colour.*" Gabo on Constructivism: "It has revealed a universal law that the elements of a visual art such as lines, colours, shapes, possess their own forces of expression, independent of any association with the external aspects of the world. . . ." The literary equivalent of these ideas may be "spatial time." (See Joseph Frank, "Spatial Form in Modern Literature," in *The Widening Gyre.*)

An Addendum: There is more to "dehumanization" than "another idea of man," there is also an incipient revulsion against the human, sometimes a renewal of the sense of the superhuman. Rilke's "Angels." Lawrence's "Fish":

And my heart accused itself
Thinking: I am not the measure of creation
This is beyond me, this fish.
His God stands outside my God.

d. *Primitivism:* The archetypes behind abstraction, beneath ironic civilization. An African mask, a beast slouching toward Bethlehem. Structure as ritual or myth, metaphors from the collective dream of mankind. Cunning palimpsests of literary time and space, knowing palingenesis of literary souls. Also Dionysus and the violent return of the repressed. (See Northrop Frye, *The Modern Century.*)

e. *Eroticism:* All literature is erotic but Modernist sex scratches the skin from within. It is not merely the liberation of the libido, a new language of anger or desire; love now becomes an intimate of disease. Sadomasochism, solipsism, nihilism, anomie. Consciousness seeks desperately to discharge itself in the world. A new and darker stage in the struggle between Eros and Thanatos.[ix] (See Lionel Trilling, "The Fate of Pleasure," in *Beyond Culture.*)

[ix] Eros and Thanatos are Freud's Greek terms for the opposed instincts of Love and Death, respectively.

————————————
————————————
————————————

f. *Antinomianism:* Beyond law, dwelling in paradox. Also discontinuity, alienation, *non serviam!*[x] The pride of art, of the self, defining the conditions of its own grace. Iconoclasm, schism, excess. Beyond antinomianism, toward apocalypse. Therefore, decadence and renovation. (See Nathan A. Scott, Jr., *The Broken Center.*)

————————————
————————————
————————————

g. *Experimentalism:* Innovation, dissociation, the brilliance of change in all its aesthetic shapes. New languages, new concepts of order. Also, the Word beginning to put its miracle to question in the midst of an artistic miracle. Poem, novel, or play henceforth can never really bear the same name.

————————————
————————————
————————————

In those seven rubrics, I seek not so much to define Modernism as to carry certain elements which I consider crucial, carry them forward toward Postmodernism.

9 The Unimaginable

The unimaginable lies somewhere between the Kingdom of Complacence and the Sea of Hysteria. It balks all geographies; bilks the spirit of the traveler who passes unwittingly through its space-realm; boggles time. Yet anyone who can return from it to tell his tale may also know how to spell the destiny of man.

I know the near-infinite resources of man, and that his imagination may still serve as the teleological organ of his evolution. Yet I am possessed by the feeling that in the next few decades, certainly within half a century, the earth and all that inhabits it may be wholly other, perhaps ravaged,

[x] I will not serve.

perhaps on the way to some strange utopia indistinguishable from nightmare. I have no language to articulate this feeling with conviction, nor imagination to conceive this special destiny. To live from hour to hour seems as maudlin as to invoke every hour the Last Things. In this feeling I find that I am not alone.

The litany of our disasters is all too familiar, and we recite it in the name of that unholy trinity, Population, Pollution, Power (read genocide), hoping to appease our furies, turn our fate inside out. But soon our minds lull themselves to sleep again on this song of abstractions, and a few freak out. The deathly dreariness of politics brings us ever closer to death. Neither is the alteration of human consciousness at hand. And the great promise of technology? Which technology? Fuller's? Skinner's? Dr Strangelove's and Dr No's? Engineers of liberation or of control? The promise is conditional on everything that we are, in this our ambiguous state.

Truly, we dwell happily in the Unimaginable. We also dwell at our task: Literature. I could learn to do pushups in a prison cell, but I cannot bring myself to "study literature" as if the earth were still in the orbit of our imagination. I hope this is Hope.

10 Postmodernism

Postmodernism may be a response, direct or oblique, to the Unimaginable that Modernism glimpsed only in its most prophetic moments. Certainly it is not the Dehumanization of the Arts that concerns us now; it is rather the Denaturalization of the Planet and the End of Man. We are, I believe, inhabitants of another Time and another Space, and we no longer know what response is adequate to our reality. In a sense we have all learned to become minimalists – of that time and space we can call our own – though the globe may have become our village. That is why it seems bootless to compare Modern with Postmodern artists, range "masters" against "epigones." The latter are closer to "zero in the bone," to silence or exhaustion, and the best of them brilliantly display the resources of the void. Thus the verbal omnipotence of Joyce yields to the impotence of Beckett, heir and peer, no less genuine, only more austere. Yet moving into the void, these artists sometimes pass to the other side of silence. The consummation of their art is a work that, remaining art, pretends to abolish itself (Beckett, Tinguely, Robert Morris), or else to become indistinguishable from life (Cage, Rauschenberg, Mailer). Duchamp coolly pointed the way.

> Nihilism is a word we often use, when we use it unhistor-
> ically, to designate values we dislike. It is sometimes applied
> to the children of Marcel Duchamp.
>
> When John Cage, in "HPSCHD" for instance, insists on
> Quantity rather than Quality, he does not surrender to nihil-
> ism – far, far from it – he requires:
> – affluence and permission of being, generosity
> – discovery in multitude, confusion of prior judgment
> – mutation of perception, of consciousness, through ran-
> domness and diversity
>
> Cage knows how to praise Duchamp: "The rest of them
> were artists. Duchamp collects dust."

I have not defined Modernism; I can define Postmodernism less. No
doubt, the more we ponder, the more we will need to qualify all we say.
Perhaps elisions may serve to qualify these notes.

Modernist Rubrics	Postmodernist Notes
a. Urbanism	– The City and also the Global Village (McLuhan) and Spaceship Earth (Fuller). The City as Cosmos. Therefore, Science Fiction.
	– Meanwhile, the world breaks up into untold blocs, nations, tribes, clans, parties, languages, sects. Anarchy and fragmentation everywhere. A new diversity or prelude to world totalitarianism? Or to world unification?
	– Nature recovered partly in ecological activism, the green revolution, urban renewal, health foods, etc.
	– Meanwhile, Dionysus has entered the City: prison riots, urban crime, pornography, etc. Worse, the City as holocaust or death camp: Hiroshima, Dresden, Auschwitz.
b. Technologism	– Runaway technology, from genetic engineering and thought control to the conquest of space. Futurists and Technophiles vs. Arcadians and Luddites.
	– All the physical materials of the arts changed. New media, art forms. The problematics of the book as artifact.
	– Boundless dispersal by media. The sensuous object becoming "anxious," then "de-defined" (Rosenberg). Matter disappearing into a concept?

c. "Dehumanization"

– The computer as substitute consciousness, or as extension of consciousness? Will it prove tautological, increasing reliance on prior orders? Or will it help to create novel forms?

– Antielitism, antiauthoritarianism. Diffusion of the ego. Participation. Art becomes communal, optional, anarchic. Acceptance.

– At the same time, Irony becomes radical, self-consuming play, entropy of meaning. Also comedy of the absurd, black humor, insane parody and slapstick, Camp. Negation.

– Abstraction taken to the limit and coming back as New Concreteness: the found object, the signed Brillo box or soup can, the nonfiction novel, the novel as history. The range is from Concept Art (abstract) to Environmental Art (concrete).

– Warhol's wanting to be a machine, Cioran's ambivalent temptation to exist. Humanism yields to infrahumanism or posthumanism. But yields also to a cosmic humanism, as in Science Fiction, as in Fuller, Castaneda, N. O. Brown, Ursula LeGuin.

"Dehumanization," both in Modernism and Postmodernism, finally means the end of the old Realism. Increasingly, Illusionism takes its place, not only in art but also in life. The media contribute egregiously to this process in Postmodern society. In *Act and the Actor Making the Self*, Harold Rosenberg says: "History has been turned inside out; writing takes place in advance of its occurrence, and every statesman is an author in embryo." Thus the Illusionism of politics matches that of Pop Art or Neo-Realism. An Event need never have happened.

The end of the old Realism also affects the sense of the Self. Thus "Dehumanization," both in Modernism and Postmodernism, requires a revision of the literary and authorial Self evidenced:

in Modernism – by doctrines of Surrealism (Breton), by ideas of impersonality in art (the masks of Yeats, the tradition of Eliot), by modes of hyperpersonality (the stream of consciousness of Joyce, Proust, Faulkner, Nin, or the allotropic ego of Lawrence). (See Robert

	Langbaum, *The Modern Spirit,* 164–84.)
In Postmodernism	– by authorial self-reflexiveness, by the fusion of fact and fiction (Capote, Wolfe, Mailer), phenomenology (Husserl, Sartre, Merleau-Ponty), Beckett's fiction of consciousness, varieties of the *nouveau roman* (Sarraute, Butor, Robbe-Grillet), and the linguistic novel of *Tel Quel* (Sollers, Thibaudeau). (See Vivian Mercier, *The New Novel,* 3–42.)
d. Primitivism	– Away from the mythic, toward the existential. Beat and Hip. Energy and spontaneity of the White Negro (Mailer). – Later, the post-existential ethos, psychedelics (Leary), the Dionysian ego (Brown), Pranksters (Kesey), madness (Laing), animism and magic (Castaneda). – The Hippie movement. Woodstock, rock music and poetry, communes. The culture of *The Whole Earth Catalog.* Pop. – The primitive Jesus. The new Rousseauism and Deweyism: Human Potential movement, Open Classroom (Goodman, Rogers, Leonard).
e. Eroticism	– Beyond the trial of *Lady Chatterley's Lover.* The repeal of censorship. Grove Press and *Evergreen Review.* – The new sexuality, from Reichian orgasm to polymorphous perversity and Esalen body consciousness. – The homosexual novel (Burroughs, Vidal, Selby, Rechy). From feminism to lesbianism. Toward a new androgyny? – Camp and comic pornography. Sex as solipsist play.
f. Antinomianism	– The Counter Cultures, political and otherwise. Free Speech Movement, S.D.S., Weathermen, Church Militants, Women's Lib, J.D.L., Black, Red, and Chicano Power, etc. Rebellion and Reaction!

– Beyond alienation from the whole culture, acceptance of discreteness and discontinuity. Evolution of radical empiricism in art as in politics or morality.

– Counter Western "ways" or metaphysics, Zen, Buddhism, Hinduism. But also Western mysticism, transcendentalism, witchcraft, the occult. (See "Primitivism" above.)

– The widespread cult of apocalyptism, sometimes as renovation, sometimes as annihilation – often both.

g. Experimentalism

– Open, discontinuous, improvisational, indeterminate, or aleatory structures. End-game strategies and neosurrealist modes. Both reductive, minimalist forms and lavish extravaganzas. In general, antiformalism. (See Calvin Tomkins, *The Bride and the Bachelors*.)

– Simultaneism. Now. The impermanence of art (scupture made of dry ice or a hole in Central Park filled with earth), the transcience of man. Absurd time.

– Fantasy, play, humor, happening, parody, "dreck" (Barthelme). Also, increasing self-reflexiveness. (See Irony under "Dehumanization" above.)

– Intermedia, the fusion of forms, the confusion of realms. An end to traditional aesthetics focused on the "beauty" or "uniqueness" of the art work? Against interpretation (Sontag).

In *Man's Rage for Chaos*, Morse Peckham argues "that art is a disjunctive category, established by convention, and that art is not a category of perceptual fields, but of role-playing". And in *The Art of Time*, Michael Kirby says: "Traditional aesthetics asks a particular hermetic attitude or state of mind that concentrates on the sensory perception of the work. . . . [Postmodern] aesthetics makes use of no special attitude or set, and art is viewed just as anything else in life." When art is viewed like "anything else in life," Fantasy is loosened from its "objective correlatives"; Fantasy becomes supreme.

Is this why Postmodern art, viewed in a Modernist perspective, creates more anxiety than it appeases? Or is the tendency toward a new gnosticism?

Ihab Hassan

11 Alternatives

The reader, no doubt, will want to judge for himself how much Modernism permeates the present and how much the latter contains elements of a new reality. The judgment is not always made rationally; self-love and the fear of dissolution may enter into it as much as the conflict of literary generations. Yet it is already possible to note that whereas Modernism – excepting Dada and Surrealism – created its own forms of artistic Authority precisely because the center no longer held, Postmodernism has tended toward artistic Anarchy in deeper complicity with things falling apart – or has tended toward Pop.

Speculating further, we may say that the Authority of Modernism – artistic, cultural, personal – rests on intense, elitist, self-generated orders in times of crisis, of which the Hemingway Code is perhaps the starkest exemplar, and Eliot's Tradition or Yeats's Ceremony is a more devious kind. Such elitist orders, perhaps the last of the world's Eleusinian mysteries,[xi] may no longer have a place amongst us, threatened as we are, at the same instant, by extermination and totalitarianism.

Yet is the Anarchy or Pop of Postmodernism, or its Fantasy, a deeper response, somehow more inward with destiny? Though my sympathies are in the present, I cannot believe this to be entirely so. True, there is enhancement of life in certain anarchies of the spirit, in humor and play, in love released and freedom of the imagination to overreach itself, in a cosmic consciousness of variousness as of unity. I recognize these as values intended by Postmodern art, and see the latter as closer, not only in time, but even more in tenor, to the transformation of hope itself. Still, I wonder if any art can help to engender the motives we must now acquire; or if we can long continue to value an art that fails us in such endeavor.

Note

1 More accurately, the quotation appears in a note preceding the essay. See Harry Levin, *Refractions* (New York: 1966), 271–3.

[xi] A mystery cult centered in the ancient Greek City of Eleusis.

chapter twenty-seven

Anti-Oedipus: Capitalism and Schizophrenia

Gilles Deleuze and Félix Guattari

Philosopher Gilles Deleuze (1925–95) and radical psychotherapist Félix Guattari (1930–) brought together poststructuralism and political radicalism in their controversial *Anti-Oedipus: Capitalism and Schizophrenia* (vol. 1, 1972). They connected their neo-Marxist rejection of capitalism to an analogous rejection of Freudian psychoanalysis as itself a bourgeois attempt to repress instinctual life ("desire") through encoding it with the language of the family (i.e. the Oedipus complex) in the name of social control. Their criticism goes as far as to undermine the notion of the self as authoritative, unified, rationally controllable. The ultimate human realities, they say, are desire and the *socius* (society), hence the self is a secondary, derivative entity. Whereas Freud concentrated on the analysis of the neuroses, Deleuze and Guattari view schizophrenia as a better window on the human nature that is normally obscured by social control. It allows us to see the chaotic life of desire which is, *à la* Nietzsche's concept of the will to power, the fundamental human process.

Desiring-Production

It is at work everywhere, functioning smoothly at times, at other times in fits and starts. It breathes, it heats, it eats. It shits and fucks. What a mistake to have ever said *the* id. Everywhere *it* is machines – real ones, not figurative ones: machines driving other machines, machines being driven by other machines, with all the necessary couplings and connections. An

Gilles Deleuze and Félix Guattari, *Anti-Oedipus: Capiltalism and Schizophrenia*, trans. Helen Lane, Mark Seem, and Robert Hurley (New York: Viking Penguin, 1977), chapter 1, Introduction, sections one and four, pp. 1–8 and 22–35.

organ-machine is plugged into an energy-source-machine: the one produces a flow that the other interrupts. The breast is a machine that produces milk, and the mouth a machine coupled to it. The mouth of the anorexic wavers between several functions: its possessor is uncertain as to whether it is an eating-machine, an anal machine, a talking-machine, or a breathing-machine (asthma attacks). Hence we are all handymen: each with his little machines. For every organ-machine, an energy-machine: all the time, flows and interruptions. Judge Schreber has sunbeams in his ass.[i] *A solar anus.* And rest assured that it works: Judge Schreber feels something, produces something, and is capable of explaining the process theoretically. Something is produced: the effects of a machine, not mere metaphors.

A schizophrenic out for a walk is a better model than a neurotic lying on the analyst's couch. A breath of fresh air, a relationship with the outside world. Lenz's stroll, for example, as reconstructed by Büchner. This walk outdoors is different from the moments when Lenz finds himself closeted with his pastor, who forces him to situate himself socially, in relationship to the God of established religion, in relationship to his father, to his mother. While taking a stroll outdoors, on the other hand, he is in the mountains, amid falling snowflakes, with other gods or without any gods at all, without a family, without a father or a mother, with nature. "What does my father want? Can he offer me more than that? Impossible. Leave me in peace.[1] Everything is a machine. Celestial machines, the stars or rainbows in the sky, alpine machines – all of them connected to those of his body. The continual whirr of machines." He thought that it must be a feeling of endless bliss to be in contact with the profound life of every form, to have a soul for rocks, metals, water, and plants, to take into himself, as in a dream, every element of nature, like flowers that breathe with the waxing and waning of the moon." To be a chlorophyll-or a photosynthesis-machine, or at least slip his body into such machines as one part among the others. Lenz has projected himself back to a time before the man-nature dichotomy, before all the co-ordinates based on this fundamental dichotomy have been laid down. He does not live nature as nature, but as a process of production. There is no such thing as either man or nature now, only a process that produces the one within the other and couples the machines together. Producing-machines, desiring-machines everywhere, schizophrenic machines, all of species life: the self and the non-self, outside and inside, no longer have any meaning whatsoever.

Now that we have had a look at this stroll of a schizo, let us compare what happens when Samuel Beckett's characters decide to venture out-

---

[i] Daniel Paul Schreber (1842–1911), a German judge whose memoirs of his psychosis were analyzed by Freud. Among various delusions, Schreber believed his bowels served a divine function connected with the sun.

doors. Their various gaits and methods of self-locomotion constitute, in and of themselves, a finely tuned machine. And then there is the function of the bicycle in Beckett's works: what relationship does the bicycle-horn machine have with the mother-anus machine? "What a rest to speak of bicycles and horns. Unfortunately it is not of them I have to speak, but of her who brought me into the world, through the hole in her arse if my memory is correct."[ii] It is often thought that Oedipus is an easy subject to deal with, something perfectly obvious, a "given" that is there from the very beginning. But that is not so at all: Oedipus presupposes a fantastic repression of desiring-machines. And why are they repressed? To what end? Is it really necessary or desirable to submit to such repression? And what means are to be used to accomplish this? What ought to go inside the Oedipal triangle, what sort of thing is required to construct it? Are a bicycle horn and my mother's arse sufficient to do the job? Aren't there more important questions than these, however? Given a certain effect, what machine is capable of producing it? And given a certain machine, what can it be used for? Can we possibly guess, for instance, what a knife rest is used for if all we are given is a geometrical description of it? Or yet another example: on being confronted with a complete machine made up of six stones in the right-hand pocket of my coat (the pocket that serves as the source of the stones), five stones in the right-hand pocket of my trousers, and five in the left-hand pocket (transmission pockets), with the remaining pocket of my coat receiving the stones that have already been handled, as each of the stones moves forward one pocket, how can we determine the effect of this circuit of distribution in which the mouth, too, plays a role as a stone-sucking machine? Where in this entire circuit do we find the production of sexual pleasure? At the end of *Malone Dies*, Lady Pedal takes the schizophrenics out for a ride in a van and a rowboat, and on a picnic in the midst of nature: an infernal machine is being assembled. "Under the skin the body is an over-heated factory,/ and outside,/ the invalid shines,/ glows,/ from every burst pore."[2]

This does not mean that we are attempting to make nature one of the poles of schizophrenia. What the schizophrenic experiences, both as an individual and as a member of the human species, is not at all any one specific aspect of nature, but nature as a process of production. What do we mean here by process? It is probable that at a certain level nature and industry are two separate and distinct things: from one point of view, industry is the opposite of nature; from another, industry extracts its raw materials from nature; from yet another, it returns its refuse to nature; and so on. Even within society, this characteristic man-nature, industry-nature,

---

[ii] Samuel Beckett, *Molloy*, in *Three Plays by Samuel Beckett* (New York: Grove Press, 1959), p. 16. The other plays are *Malone Dies* and *The Unnamable*.

society-nature relationship is responsible for the distinction of relatively autonomous spheres that are called production, distribution, consumption. But in general this entire level of distinctions, examined from the point of view of its formal developed structures, presupposes (as Marx has demonstrated) not only the existence of capital and the division of labor, but also the false consciousness that the capitalist being necessarily acquires, both of itself and of the supposedly fixed elements within an over-all process. For the real truth of the matter – the glaring, sober truth that resides in delirium – is that there is no such thing as relatively independent spheres or circuits: production is immediately consumption and a recording process without any sort of mediation, and the recording process and consumption directly determine production, though they do so within the production process itself. Hence everything is production: *production of productions*, of actions and of passions; *productions of recording processes*, of distributions and of co-ordinates that serve as points of reference; *productions of consumptions*, of sensual pleasures, of anxieties, and of pain. Everything is production, since the recording processes are immediately consumed, immediately consummated, and these consumptions directly reproduced.[3] This is the first meaning of process as we use the term: incorporating recording and consumption within production itself, thus making them the productions of one and the same process.

Second, we make no distinction between man and nature: the human essence of nature and the natural essence of man become one within nature in the form of production or industry, just as they do within the life of man as a species. Industry is then no longer considered from the extrinsic point of view of utility, but rather from the point of view of its fundamental identity with nature as production of man and by man.[4] Not man as the king of creation, but rather as the being who is in intimate contact with the profound life of all forms or all types of beings, who is responsible for even the stars and animal life, and who ceaselessly plugs an organ-machine into an energy-machine, a tree into his body, a breast into his mouth, the sun into his asshole: the eternal custodian of the machines of the universe. This is the second meaning of process as we use the term: man and nature are not like two opposite terms confronting each other – not even in the sense of bipolar opposites within a relationship of causation, ideation, or expression (cause and effect, subject and object, etc.); rather, they are one and the same essential reality, the producer-product. Production as process overtakes all idealistic categories and constitutes a cycle whose relationship to desire is that of an immanent principle. That is why desiring-production is the principal concern of a materialist psychiatry, which conceives of and deals with the schizo as *Homo natura*.[iii] This will be the case, however, only

[iii] Natural man.

on one condition, which in fact constitutes the third meaning of process as we use the term: it must not be viewed as a goal or an end in itself, nor must it be confused with an infinite perpetuation of itself. Putting an end to the process or prolonging it indefinitely – which, strictly speaking, is tantamount to ending it abruptly and prematurely – is what creates the artificial schizophrenic found in mental institutions: a limp rag forced into autistic behavior, produced as an entirely separate and independent entity. D.H. Lawrence says of love: "We have pushed a process into a goal. The aim of any process is not the perpetuation of that process, but the completion thereof. . . . The process should work to a completion, not to some horror of intensification and extremity wherein the soul and body ultimately perish."[5] Schizophrenia is like love: there is no specifically schizophrenic phenomenon or entity; schizophrenia is the universe of productive and reproductive desiring machines, universal primary production as "the essential reality of man and nature."

Desiring-machines are binary machines, obeying a binary law or set of rules governing associations: one machine is always coupled with another. The productive synthesis, the production of production, is inherently connective in nature: "and . . ." "and then . . ." This is because there is always a flow-producing machine, and another machine connected to it that interrupts or draws off part of this flow (the breast – the mouth). And because the first machine is in turn connected to another whose flow it interrupts or partially drains off, the binary series is linear in every direction. Desire constantly couples continuous flows and partial objects that are by nature fragmentary and fragmented. Desire causes the current to flow, itself flows in turn, and breaks the flows. "I love everything that flows, even the menstrual flow that carries away the seed unfecund."[6] Amniotic fluid spilling out of the sac and kidney stones; flowing hair; a flow of spittle, a flow of sperm, shit, or urine that are produced by partial objects and constantly cut off by other partial objects, which in turn produce other flows, interrupted by other partial objects. Every "object" presupposes the continuity of a flow; every flow, the fragmentation of the object. Doubtless each organ-machine interprets the entire world from the perspective of its own flux, from the point of view of the energy that flows from it: the eye interprets everything – speaking, understanding, shitting, fucking – in terms of seeing. But a connection with another machine is always established, along a transverse path, so that one machine interrupts the current of the other or "sees" its own current interrupted.

Hence the coupling that takes place within the partial object–flow connective synthesis also has another form: product/producing. Producing is always something "grafted onto" the product; and for that reason desiring-production is production of production, just as every machine is a machine connected to another machine. We cannot accept the idealist category of "expression" as a satisfactory or sufficient explanation of this phenomenon. We cannot, we must not attempt to describe the schizophrenic object without relating it to the process of production. The *Cahiers de l'art brut*[iv] are a striking confirmation of this principle, since by taking such an approach they deny that there is any such thing as a specific, identifiable schizophrenic entity. Or to take another example, Henri Michaux describes a schizophrenic table in terms of a process of production which is that of desire: "Once noticed, it continued to occupy one's mind. It even persisted, as it were, in going about its own business. . . . The striking thing was that it was neither simple nor really complex, initially or intentionally complex, or constructed according to a complicated plan. Instead, it had been desimplified in the course of its carpentering. . . . As it stood, it was a table of additions, much like certain schizophrenics' drawings, described as 'overstuffed,' and if finished it was only in so far as there was no way of adding anything more to it, the table having become more and more an accumulation, less and less a table. . . . It was not intended for any specific purpose, for anything one expects of a table. Heavy, cumbersome, it was virtually immovable. One didn't know how to handle it (mentally or physically). Its top surface, the useful part of the table, having been gradually reduced, was disappearing, with so little relation to the clumsy framework that the thing did not strike one as a table, but as some freak piece of furniture, an unfamiliar instrument . . . for which there was no purpose. A dehumanized table, nothing cozy about it, nothing 'middle-class,' nothing rustic, nothing countrified, not a kitchen table or a work table. A table which lent itself to no function, self-protective, denying itself to service and communication alike. There was something stunned about it, something petrified. Perhaps it suggested a stalled engine."[7]

The schizophrenic is the universal producer. There is no need to distinguish here between producing and its product. We need merely note that the pure "thisness" of the object produced is carried over into a new act of producing. The table continues to "go about its business." The surface of the table, however, is eaten up by the supporting framework. The nontermination of the table is a necessary consequence of its mode of production. When Claude Lévi-Strauss defines *bricolage*,[v] he does so in terms of a set of closely related characteristics: the possession of a stock of materials or of rules of thumb that are fairly extensive, though more or less a hodge-podge – multiple and at the same time limited; the ability to rearrange fragments continually in new and different patterns or configurations; and

---

[iv] A series publishing art works by psychiatric inmates.

[v] Proposed by Lévi-Strauss as a method for the human sciences, the term literally refers to the tinkering of a handyman, who patches various kinds of materials together.

as a consequence, an indifference toward the act of producing and toward the product, toward the set of instruments to be used and toward the over-all result to be achieved.[8] The satisfaction the handyman experiences when he plugs something into an electric socket or diverts a stream of water can scarcely be explained in terms of "playing mommy and daddy," or by the pleasure of violating a taboo. The rule of continually producing production, of grafting producing onto the product, is a characteristic of desiring-machines or of primary production: the production of production. A painting by Richard Lindner, "Boy with Machine," shows a huge, pudgy, bloated boy working one of his little desiring-machines, after having hooked it up to a vast technical social machine – which, as we shall see, is what even the very young child does.

Producing, a product: a producing/product identity. It is this identity that constitutes a third term in the linear series: an enormous undifferentiated object. Everything stops dead for a moment, everything freezes in place – and then the whole process will begin all over again. From a certain point of view it would be much better if nothing worked, if nothing functioned. Never being born, escaping the wheel of continual birth and rebirth, no mouth to suck with, no anus to shit through. Will the machines run so badly, their component pieces fall apart to such a point that they will return to nothingness and thus allow us to return to nothingness? It would seem, however, that the flows of energy are still too closely connected, the partial objects still too organic, for this to happen. What would be required is a pure fluid in a free state, flowing without interruption, streaming over the surface of a full body. Desiring-machines make us an organism; but at the very heart of this production, within the very production of this production, the body suffers from being organized in this way, from not having some other sort of organization, or no organization at all. "An incomprehensible, absolutely rigid stasis" in the very midst of process, as a third stage: "*No mouth. No tongue. No teeth. No larynx. No esophagus. No belly. No anus.*" The automata stop dead and set free the unorganized mass they once served to articulate. The full body without organs is the unproductive, the sterile, the unengendered, the unconsumable. Antonin Artaud discovered this one day, finding himself with no shape or form whatsoever, right there where he was at that moment. The death instinct: that is its name, and death is not without a model. For desire desires death also, because the full body of death is its motor, just as it desires life, because the organs of life are the *working machine*. We shall not inquire how all this fits together so that the machine will run: the question itself is the result of a process of abstraction.

Desiring-machines work only when they break down, and by continually breaking down. Judge Schreber "lived for a long time without a stomach, without intestines, almost without lungs, with a torn oesophagus, without a bladder, and with shattered ribs; he used sometimes to swallow part of his own larynx with his food, etc." The body without organs is nonproductive; nonetheless it is produced, at a certain place and a certain time in the connective synthesis, as the identity of producing and the product: the schizophrenic table is a body without organs. The body without organs is not the proof of an original nothingness, nor is it what remains of a lost totality. Above all, it is not a projection; it has nothing whatsoever to do with the body itself, or with an image of the body. It is the body without an image. This imageless, organless body, the nonproductive, exists right there where it is produced, in the third stage of the binary-linear series. It is perpetually reinserted into the process of production. The catatonic body is produced in the water of the hydrotherapy tub. The full body without organs belongs to the realm of antiproduction; but yet another characteristic of the connective or productive synthesis is the fact that it couples production with antiproduction, with an element of antiproduction.

A Materialist Psychiatry

The famous hypothesis put forward by the psychiatrist G. de Clerambault seems well founded: delirium, which is by nature global and systematic, is a secondary phenomenon, a consequence of partial and local automatistic phenomena. Delirium is in fact characteristic of the recording that is made of the process of production of the desiring-machines; and though there are syntheses and disorders (*affections*) that are peculiar to this recording process, as we see in paranoia and even in the paranoid forms of schizophrenia, it does not constitute an autonomous sphere, for it depends on the functioning and the breakdowns of desiring-machines. Nonetheless Clerambault used the term "(mental) automatism" to designate only athematic phenomena – echolalia, the uttering of odd sounds, or sudden irrational outbursts – which he attributed to the mechanical effects of infections or intoxications. Moreover, he explained a large part of delirium in turn as an effect of automatism; as for the rest of it, the "personal" part, in his view it was of the nature of a reaction and had to do with "character," the manifestations of which might well precede the automatism (as in the paranoiac character, for instance).[9] Hence Clerambault regarded automatism as merely a neurological mechanism in the most general sense of the word, rather than a process of economic production involving desiring-machines. As for history, he was content merely to mention its innate or acquired nature. Clerambault is the Feuerbach of psychiatry, in the sense in which Marx remarks: "Whenever Feuerbach looks at things as a materialist, there is no history in his works, and whenever he takes history into account, he no longer is a materialist." A truly materialist psychiatry can be defined, on the contrary, by the twofold task it sets itself: introducing desire into the mechanism, and introducing production into desire.

There is no very great difference between false materialism and typical forms of idealism. The theory of schizophrenia is formulated in terms of three concepts that constitute its trinary schema: dissociation (Kraepelin), autism (Bleuler), and space-time or being-in-the-world (Binswanger). The first of these is an explanatory concept that supposedly locates the specific dysfunction or primary deficiency. The second is an ideational concept indicating the specific nature of the effect of the disorder: the delirium itself or the complete withdrawal from the outside world, "the detachment from reality, accompanied by a relative or an absolute predominance of [the schizophrenic's] inner life." The third concept is a descriptive one, discovering or rediscovering the delirious person in his own specific world. What is common to these three concepts is the fact that they all relate the problem of schizophrenia to the ego through the intermediary of the "body image" – the final avatar of the soul, a vague conjoining of the requirements of spiritualism and positivism.

The ego, however, is like daddy-mommy: the schizo has long since ceased to believe in it. He is somewhere else, beyond or behind or below these problems, rather than immersed in them. And wherever he is, there are problems, insurmountable sufferings, unbearable needs. But why try to bring him back to what he has escaped from, why set him back down amid problems that are no longer problems to him, why mock his truth by believing that we have paid it its due by merely figuratively taking our hats off to it? There are those who will maintain that the schizo is incapable of uttering the word *I*, and that we must restore his ability to pronounce this hallowed word. All of which the schizo sums up by saying: they're fucking me over again. "I won't say *I* any more, I'll never utter the word again; it's just too damn stupid. Every time I hear it, I'll use the third person instead, if I happen to remember to. If it amuses them. And it won't make one bit of difference."[vi] And if he does chance to utter the word *I* again, that won't make any difference either. He is too far removed from these problems, too far past them.

Even Freud never went beyond this narrow and limited conception of the ego. And what prevented him from doing so was his own tripartite formula – the Oedipal, neurotic one: daddy-mommy-me. We may well ponder the possibility that the analytic imperialism of the Oedipus complex led Freud to rediscover, and to lend all the weight of his authority to, the unfortunate misapplication of the concept of autism to schizophrenia. For we must not delude ourselves: Freud doesn't like schizophrenics. He doesn't like their resistance to being oedipalized, and tends to treat them more or

[vi] Samuel Beckett, *The Unnamable*.

less as animals. They mistake words for things, he says. They are apathetic, narcissistic, cut off from reality, incapable of achieving transference; they resemble philosophers – "an undesirable resemblance."

The question as to how to deal analytically with the relationship between drives (*pulsions*) and symptoms, between the symbol and what is symbolized, has arisen again and again. Is this relationship to be considered *causal?* Or is it a relationship of *comprehension?* A mode of *expression?* The question, however, has been posed too theoretically. The fact is, from the moment that we are placed within the framework of Oedipus – from the moment that we are measured in terms of Oedipus – the cards are stacked against us, and the only real relationship, that of production, has been done away with. The great discovery of psychoanalysis was that of the production of desire, of the productions of the unconscious. But once Oedipus entered the picture, this discovery was soon buried beneath a new brand of idealism: a classical theater was substituted for the unconscious as a factory; representation was substituted for the units of production of the unconscious; and an unconscious that was capable of nothing but expressing itself – in myth, tragedy, dreams – was substituted for the productive unconscious.

Every time that the problem of schizophrenia is explained in terms of the ego, all we can do is "sample" a supposed essence or a presumed specific nature of the schizo, regardless of whether we do so with love and pity or disgustedly spit out the mouthful we have tasted. We have "sampled" him once as a dissociated ego, another time as an ego cut off from the world, and yet again – most temptingly – as an ego that had not ceased to be, who was there in the most specific way, but in his very own world, though he might reveal himself to a clever psychiatrist, a sympathetic superobserver – in short, a phenomenologist. Let us remember once again one of Marx's caveats: we cannot tell from the mere taste of wheat who grew it; the product gives us no hint as to the system and the relations of production. The product appears to be all the more specific, incredibly specific and readily describable, the more closely the theoretician relates it to *ideal forms of causation, comprehension, or expression,* rather than to *the real process of production on which it depends.* The schizophrenic appears all the more specific and recognizable as a distinct personality if the process is halted, or if it is made an end and a goal in itself, or if it is allowed to go on and on endlessly in a void, so as to provoke that "horror of . . . extremity wherein the soul and body ultimately perish"[vii] (the autist). Kraepelin's celebrated terminal state . . . But the moment that one describes, on the contrary, the material process of production, the specificity of the product tends to evaporate, while at the same time the possibility of another outcome,

---

[vii] D. H. Lawrence, *Aaron's Rod*, p. 162.

another end result of the process appears. Before being a mental state of the schizophrenic who has made himself into an artificial person through autism, schizophrenia is the process of the production of desire and desiring-machines. How does one get from one to the other, and is this transition inevitable? This remains the crucial question. Karl Jaspers has given us precious insights, on this point as on so many others, because his "idealism" was remarkably atypical. Contrasting the concept of process with those of reaction formation or development of the personality, he views process as a rupture or intrusion, having nothing to do with an imaginary relationship with the ego; rather, it is a relationship with the "demoniacal" in nature. The one thing Jaspers failed to do was to view process as material economic reality, as the process of production wherein Nature = Industry, Nature = History.

To a certain degree, the traditional logic of desire is all wrong from the very outset: from the very first step that the Platonic logic of desire forces us to take, making us choose between *production* and *acquisition*. From the moment that we place desire on the side of acquisition, we make desire an idealistic (dialectical, nihilistic) conception, which causes us to look upon it as primarily a lack: a lack of an object, a lack of the real object. It is true that the other side, the "production" side, has not been entirely ignored. Kant, for instance, must be credited with effecting a critical revolution as regards the theory of desire, by attributing to it "the faculty of being, through its representations, the cause of the reality of the objects of these representations."[10] But it is not by chance that Kant chooses superstitious beliefs, hallucinations, and fantasies as illustrations of this definition of desire: as Kant would have it, we are well aware that the real object can be produced only by an external causality and external mechanisms; nonetheless this knowledge does not prevent us from believing in the intrinsic power of desire to create its own object – if only in an unreal, hallucinatory, or delirious form – or from representing this causality as stemming from within desire itself. The reality of the object, insofar as it is produced by desire, is thus a *psychic reality*. Hence it can be said that Kant's critical revolution changes nothing essential: this way of conceiving of productivity does not question the validity of the classical conception of desire as a lack; rather, it uses this conception as a support and a buttress, and merely examines its implications more carefully.

In point of fact, if desire is the lack of the real object, its very nature as a real entity depends upon an "essence of lack" that produces the fantasized object. Desire thus conceived of as production, though merely the production of fantasies, has been explained perfectly by psychoanalysis. On the very lowest level of interpretation, this means that the real object that desire lacks is related to an extrinsic natural or social production, whereas desire intrinsically produces an imaginary object that functions as a double

411

of reality, as though there were a "dreamed-of object behind every real object," or a mental production behind all real productions. This conception does not necessarily compel psychoanalysis to engage in a study of gadgets and markets, in the form of an utterly dreary and dull psychoanalysis of the object: psychoanalytic studies of packages of noodles, cars, or "thingumajigs." But even when the fantasy is interpreted in depth, not simply as an object, but as a specific machine that brings desire itself front and center, this machine is merely theatrical, and the complementarity of what it sets apart still remains: it is now need that is defined in terms of a relative lack and determined by its own object, whereas desire is regarded as what produces the fantasy and produces itself by detaching itself from the object, though at the same time it intensifies the lack by making it absolute: an "incurable insufficiency of being," an "inability-to-be that is life itself." Hence the presentation of desire as something *supported* by needs, while these needs, and their relationship to the object as something that is lacking or missing, continue to be the basis of the productivity of desire (theory of an underlying support). In a word, when the theoretician reduces desiring-production to a production of fantasy, he is content to exploit to the fullest the idealist principle that defines desire as a lack, rather than a process of production, of "industrial" production. Clément Rosset puts it very well: every time the emphasis is put on a lack that desire supposedly suffers from as a way of defining its object, "the world acquires as its double some other sort of world, in accordance with the following line of argument: there is an object that desire feels the lack of; hence the world does not contain each and every object that exists; there is at least one object missing, the one that desire feels the lack of; hence there exists some other place that contains the key to desire (missing in this world)."[11]

If desire produces, its product is real. If desire is productive, it can be productive only in the real world and can produce only reality. Desire is the set of *passive syntheses* that engineer partial objects, flows, and bodies, and that function as units of production. The real is the end product, the result of the passive syntheses of desire as autoproduction of the unconscious. Desire does not lack anything; it does not lack its object. It is, rather, the *subject* that is missing in desire, or desire that lacks a fixed subject; there is no fixed subject unless there is repression. Desire and its object are one and the same thing: the machine, as a machine of a machine. Desire is a machine, and the object of desire is another machine connected to it. Hence the product is something removed or deducted from the process of producing: between the act of producing and the product, something becomes detached, thus giving the vagabond, nomad subject a residuum. The objective being of desire is the Real in and of itself.[12] There is no particular form of existence that can be labeled "psychic reality." As Marx notes, what exists in fact is not lack, but passion, as a "natural and sensuous object."

412

Desire is not bolstered by needs, but rather the contrary; needs are derived from desire: they are counterproducts within the real that desire produces. Lack is a countereffect of desire; it is deposited, distributed, vacuolized within a real that is natural and social. Desire always remains in close touch with the conditions of objective existence; it embraces them and follows them, shifts when they shift, and does not outlive them. For that reason it so often becomes the desire to die, whereas need is a measure of the withdrawal of a subject that has lost its desire at the same time that it loses the passive syntheses of these conditions. This is precisely the significance of need as a search in a void: hunting about, trying to capture or become a parasite of passive syntheses in whatever vague world they may happen to exist in. It is no use saying: We are not green plants; we have long since been unable to synthesize chlorophyll, so it's necessary to eat. . . . Desire then becomes this abject fear of lacking something. But it should be noted that this is not a phrase uttered by the poor or the dispossessed. On the contrary, such people know that they are close to grass, almost akin to it, and that desire "needs" very few things – *not those leftovers that chance to come their way, but the very things that are continually taken from them* – and that what is missing is not things a subject feels the lack of somewhere deep down inside himself, but rather the objectivity of man, the objective being of man, for whom to desire is to produce, to produce within the realm of the real.

The real is not impossible; on the contrary, within the real everything is possible, everything becomes possible. Desire does not express a molar lack within the subject; rather, the molar organization deprives desire of its objective being. Revolutionaries, artists, and seers are content to be objective, merely objective: they know that desire clasps life in its powerfully productive embrace, and reproduces it in a way that is all the more intense because it has few needs. And never mind those who believe that this is very easy to say, or that it is the sort of idea to be found in books. "From the little reading I had done I had observed that the men who were most *in* life, who were moulding life, who were life itself, ate little, slept little, owned little or nothing. They had no illusions about duty, or the perpetuation of their kith and kin, or the preservation of the State. . . . The phantasmal world is the world which has never been fully conquered over. It is the world of the past, never of the future. To move forward clinging to the past is like dragging a ball and chain."[13] The true visionary is a Spinoza in the garb of a Neapolitan revolutionary. We know very well where lack – and its subjective correlative – come from. Lack is created, planned, and organized in and through social production. It is counterproduced as a result of the pressure of antiproduction; the latter falls back on (*se rabat sur*) the forces of production and appropriates them. It is never primary; production is never organized on the basis of a pre-existing need or lack

413

(*manque*). It is lack that infiltrates itself, creates empty spaces or vacuoles, and propagates itself in accordance with the organization of an already existing organization of production.[14] The deliberate creation of lack as a function of market economy is the art of a dominant class. This involves deliberately organizing wants and needs amid an abundance of production; making all of desire teeter and fall victim to the great fear of not having one's needs satisfied; and making the object dependent upon a real production that is supposedly exterior to desire (the demands of rationality), while at the same time the production of desire is categorized as fantasy and nothing but fantasy.

There is no such thing as the social production of reality on the one hand, and a desiring-production that is mere fantasy on the other. The only connections that could be established between these two productions would be secondary ones of introjection and projection, as though all social practices had their precise counterpart in introjected or internal mental practices, or as though mental practices were projected upon social systems, without either of the two sets of practices ever having any real or concrete effect upon the other. As long as we are content to establish a perfect parallel between money, gold, capital, and the capitalist triangle on the one hand, and the libido, the anus, the phallus, and the family triangle on the other, we are engaging in an enjoyable pastime, but the mechanisms of money remain totally unaffected by the anal projections of those who manipulate money. The Marx–Freud parallelism between the two remains utterly sterile and insignificant as long as it is expressed in terms that make them introjections or projections of each other without ceasing to be utterly alien to each other, as in the famous equation money = shit. The truth of the matter is that *social production is purely and simply desiring-production itself under determinate conditions*. We maintain that the social field is immediately invested by desire, that it is the historically determined product of desire, and that libido has no need of any mediation or sublimation, any psychic operation, any transformation, in order to invade and invest the productive forces and the relations of production. *There is only desire and the social, and nothing else.*

Even the most repressive and the most deadly forms of social reproduction are produced by desire within the organization that is the consequence of such production under various conditions that we must analyze. That is why the fundamental problem of political philosophy is still precisely the one that Spinoza saw so clearly, and that Wilhelm Reich rediscovered: "Why do men fight *for* their servitude as stubbornly as though it were their salvation?"[viii] How can people possibly reach the point of shouting: "More

---

[viii] Wilhelm Reich (1897–1957), maverick Viennese psychiatrist who died in an American prison, charged with contempt of court.

taxes! Less bread!"? As Reich remarks, the astonishing thing is not that some people steal or that others occasionally go out on strike, but rather that all those who are starving do not steal as a regular practice, and all those who are exploited are not continually out on strike: after centuries of exploitation, why do people still tolerate being humiliated and enslaved, to such a point, indeed, that they *actually want* humiliation and slavery not only for others but for themselves? Reich is at his profoundest as a thinker when he refuses to accept ignorance or illusion on the part of the masses as an explanation of fascism, and demands an explanation that will take their desires into account, an explanation formulated in terms of desire: no, the masses were not innocent dupes; at a certain point, under a certain set of conditions, they *wanted* fascism, and it is this perversion of the desire of the masses that needs to be accounted for.[15]

Yet Reich himself never manages to provide a satisfactory explanation of this phenomenon, because at a certain point he reintroduces precisely the line of argument that he was in the process of demolishing, by creating a distinction between rationality as it is or ought to be in the process of social production, and the irrational element in desire, and by regarding only this latter as a suitable subject for psychoanalytic investigation. Hence the sole task he assigns psychoanalysis is the explanation of the "negative," the "subjective," the "inhibited" within the social field. He therefore necessarily returns to a dualism between the real object rationally produced on the one hand, and irrational, fantasizing production on the other.[16] He gives up trying to discover the *common denominator or the coextension of the social field and desire*. In order to establish the basis for a genuinely materialistic psychiatry, there was a category that Reich was sorely in need of: that of desiring-production, which would apply to the real in both its so-called rational and irrational forms.

The fact there is massive social repression that has an enormous effect on desiring-production in no way vitiates our principle: desire produces reality, or stated another way, desiring-production is one and the same thing as social production. It is not possible to attribute a special form of existence to desire, a mental or psychic reality that is presumably different from the material reality of social production. Desiring-machines are not fantasy-machines or dream-machines, which supposedly can be distinguished from technical and social machines. Rather, fantasies are secondary expressions, deriving from the identical nature of the two sorts of machines in any given set of circumstances. Thus fantasy is never individual: it is *group fantasy* – as institutional analysis has successfully demonstrated. And if there is such a thing as two sorts of group fantasy, it is because two different readings of this identity are possible, depending upon whether the desiring-machines are regarded from the point of view of the great gregarious masses that they form, or whether social machines are considered from the point of view of

415

the elementary forces of desire that serve as a basis for them. Hence in group fantasy the libido may invest all of an existing social field, including the latter's most repressive forms; or on the contrary, it may launch a counterinvestment whereby revolutionary desire is plugged into the existing social field as a source of energy. (The great socialist utopias of the nineteenth century function, for example, not as ideal models but as group fantasies – that is, as agents of the real productivity of desire, making it possible to disinvest the current social field, to "deinstitutionalize" it, to further the revolutionary institution of desire itself.) But there is never any difference in nature between the desiring-machines and the technical social machines. There is a certain distinction between them, but it is merely a distinction of *régime*,[ix] depending on *their* relationships of size. Except for this difference in regime, they are the same machines, as group fantasies clearly prove.

When in the course of our discussion above, we laid down the broad outlines of a parallelism between social production and desiring-production, in order to show that in both cases there is a strong tendency on the part of the forces of antiproduction to operate retroactively on productive forms and appropriate them, this parallelism was in no way meant as an exhaustive description of the relationship between the two systems of production. It merely enables us to point to certain phenomena having to do with the difference in regime between them. In the first place, technical machines obviously work only if they are not out of order; they ordinarily stop working not because they break down but because they wear out. Marx makes use of this simple principle to show that the regime of technical machines is characterized by a strict distinction between the means of production and the product; thanks to this distinction, the machine transmits value to the product, but only the value that the machine itself loses as it wears out. Desiring-machines, on the contrary, continually break down as they run, and in fact run only when they are not functioning properly: the product is always an offshoot of production, implanting itself upon it like a graft, and at the same time the parts of the machine are the fuel that makes it run.

Art often takes advantage of this property of desiring-machines by creating veritable group fantasies in which desiring-production is used to short-circuit social production, and to interfere with the reproductive function of technical machines by introducing an element of dysfunction. Arman's charred violins, for instance, or César's compressed car bodies. More generally, Dali's method of critical paranoia assures the explosion of a desiring-machine within an object of social production.[x] But even earlier,

---

ix The French word can mean government, laws, speed (of a motor), flow rate (of current).

x French sculptors Armand Fernandez and César Baldaccini; Salvador Dali (1904–89), surrealist painter.

Ravel preferred to throw his inventions entirely out of gear rather than let them simply run down, and chose to end his compositions with abrupt breaks, hesitations, tremolos, discordant notes, and unresolved chords, rather than allowing them to slowly wind down to a close or gradually die away into silence.[17] The artist is the master of objects; he puts before us shattered, burned, broken-down objects, converting them to the regime of desiring-machines, breaking down is part of the very functioning of desiring-machines; the artist presents paranoiac machines, miraculating-machines, and celibate machines as so many technical machines, so as to cause desiring-machines to undermine technical machines. Even more important, the work of art is itself a desiring-machine. The artist stores up his treasures so as to create an immediate explosion, and that is why, to his way of thinking, destructions can never take place as rapidly as they ought to.

From this, a second difference in regime results: desiring-machines produce antiproduction all by themselves, whereas the antiproduction characteristic of technical machines takes place only within the extrinsic conditions of the reproduction of the process (even though these conditions do not come into being at some "later stage"). That is why technical machines are not an economic category, and always refer back to a socius or a social machine that is quite distinct from these machines, and that conditions this reproduction. A technical machine is therefore not a cause but merely an index of a general form of social production: thus there are manual machines and primitive societies, hydraulic machines and "Asiatic" forms of society, industrial machines and capitalism. Hence when we posited the socius as the analogue of a full body without organs, there was nonetheless one important difference. For desiring-machines are the fundamental category of the economy of desire; they produce a body without organs all by themselves, and make no distinction between agents and their own parts, or between the relations of production and their own relations, or between the social order and technology. Desiring-machines are both technical and social. It is in this sense that desiring-production is the locus of a primal psychic repression, whereas social production is where social repression takes place, and it is between the former and the latter that there occurs something that resembles secondary psychic repression in the "strictest" sense: the situation of the body without organs or its equivalent is the crucial factor here, depending on whether it is the result of an internal process or of an extrinsic condition (and thus affects the role of the death instinct in particular).

But at the same time they are the same machines, despite the fact that they are governed by two different regimes – and despite the fact that it is admittedly a strange adventure for desire to desire repression. There is only one kind of production, the production of the real. And doubtless we can express this identity in two different ways, even though these two ways together constitute the autoproduction of the unconscious as a cycle. We can say that social production, under determinate conditions, derives primarily from desiring-production: which is to say that *Homo natura* comes first. But we must also say, more accurately, that desiring-production is first and foremost social in nature, and tends to free itself only at the end: which is to say that *Homo historia*[xi] comes first. The body without organs is not an original primordial entity that later projects itself into different sorts of socius, as though it were a raving paranoiac, the chieftain of the primitive horde, who was initially responsible for social organization. The social machine or socius may be the body of the Earth, the body of the Despot, the body of Money. It is never a projection, however, of the body without organs. On the contrary: the body without organs is the ultimate residuum of a deterritorialized socius. The prime function incumbent upon the socius has always been to codify the flows of desire, to inscribe them, to record them, to see to it that no flow exists that is not properly dammed up, channeled, regulated. When the primitive *territorial machine* proved inadequate to the task, the *despotic machine* set up a kind of overcoding system. But the *capitalist machine*, insofar as it was built on the ruins of a despotic State more or less far removed in time, finds itself in a totally new situation: it is faced with the task of decoding and deterritorializing the flows. Capitalism does not confront this situation from the outside, since it experiences it as the very fabric of its existence, as both its primary determinant and its fundamental raw material, its form and its function, and deliberately perpetuates it, in all its violence, with all the powers at its command. Its sovereign production and repression can be achieved in no other way. Capitalism is in fact born of the encounter of two sorts of flows: the decoded flows of production in the form of money-capital, and the decoded flows of labor in the form of the "free worker." Hence, unlike previous social machines, the capitalist machine is incapable of providing a code that will apply to the whole of the social field. By substituting money for the very notion of a code it has created an axiomatic of abstract quantities that keeps moving further and further in the direction of the deterritorialization of the socius. Capitalism tends toward a threshold of decoding that will destroy the socius in order to make it a body without organs and unleash the flows of desire on this body as a deterritorialized field. Is it correct to say that in this sense schizophrenia is the product of the capitalist machine, as manic-depression and paranoia are the product of the despotic machine, and hysteria the product of the territorial machine?[18]

The decoding of flows and the deterritorialization of the socius thus constitutes the most characteristic and the most important tendency of

---

[xi] Historical man.

418

capitalism. It continually draws near to its limit, which is a genuinely schizophrenic limit. It tends, with all the strength at its command, to produce the schizo as the subject of the decoded flows on the body without organs – more capitalist than the capitalist and more proletarian than the proletariat. This tendency is being carried further and further, to the point that capitalism with all its flows may dispatch itself straight to the moon: we really haven't seen anything yet! When we say that schizophrenia is our characteristic malady, the malady of our era, we do not merely mean to say that modern life drives people mad. It is not a question of a way of life, but of a process of production. Nor is it merely a question of a simple parallelism, even though from the point of view of the failure of codes, such a parallelism is a much more precise formulation of the relationship between, for example, the phenomena of shifting of meaning in the case of schizophrenics and the mechanisms of ever increasing disharmony and discord at every level of industrial society.

What we are really trying to say is that capitalism, through its process of production, produces an awesome schizophrenic accumulation of energy or charge, against which it brings all its vast powers of repression to bear, but which nonetheless continues to act as capitalism's limit. For capitalism constantly counteracts, constantly inhibits this inherent tendency while at the same time allowing it free rein; it continually seeks to avoid reaching its limit while simultaneously tending toward that limit. Capitalism institutes or restores all sorts of residual and artificial, imaginary, or symbolic territorialities, thereby attempting, as best it can, to recode, to rechannel persons who have been defined in terms of abstract quantities. Everything returns or recurs: States, nations, families. That is what makes the ideology of capitalism "a motley painting of everything that has ever been believed." The real is not impossible; it is simply more and more artificial. Marx termed the twofold movement of the tendency to a falling rate of profit, and the increase in the absolute quantity of surplus value, the law of the counteracted tendency. As a corollary of this law, there is the twofold movement of decoding or deterritorializing flows on the one hand, and their violent and artificial reterritorialization on the other. The more the capitalist machine deterritorializes, decoding and axiomatizing flows in order to extract surplus value from them, the more its ancillary apparatuses, such as government bureaucracies and the forces of law and order, do their utmost to reterritorialize, absorbing in the process a larger and larger share of surplus value.

There is no doubt that at this point in history the neurotic, the pervert, and the psychotic cannot be adequately defined in terms of drives, for drives are simply the desiring-machines themselves. They must be defined in terms of modern territorialities. The neurotic is trapped within the residual or artificial territorialities of our society, and reduces all of them to Oedipus as the ultimate territoriality – as reconstructed in the analyst's office and projected upon the full body of the psychoanalyst (yes, my boss is my father, and so is the Chief of State, and so are you, Doctor). The pervert is someone who takes the artifice seriously and plays the game to the hilt: if you want them, you can have them – territorialities infinitely more artificial than the ones that society offers us, totally artificial new families, secret lunar societies. As for the schizo, continually wandering about, migrating here, there, and everywhere as best he can, he plunges further and further into the realm of deterritorialization, reaching the furthest limits of the decomposition of the socius on the surface of his own body without organs. It may well be that these peregrinations are the schizo's own particular way of rediscovering the earth. The schizophrenic deliberately seeks out the very limit of capitalism: he is its inherent tendency brought to fulfillment, its surplus product, its proletariat, and its exterminating angel. He scrambles all the codes and is the transmitter of the decoded flows of desire. The real continues to flow. In the schizo, the two aspects of *process* are conjoined: the metaphysical process that puts us in contact with the "demoniacal" element in nature or within the heart of the earth, and the historical process of social production that restores the autonomy of desiring-machines in relation to the deterritorialized social machine. Schizophrenia is desiring-production as the limit of social production. Desiring-production, and its difference in regime as compared to social production, are thus end points, not points of departure. Between the two there is nothing but an ongoing process of becoming that is the becoming of reality. And if materialist psychiatry may be defined as the psychiatry that introduces the concept of production into consideration of the problem of desire, it cannot avoid posing in eschatological terms the problem of the ultimate relationship between the analytic machine, the revolutionary machine, and desiring-machines.

Notes

1 See Georg Büchner, *Lenz*, in *Complete Plays and Prose*, trans. Carl Richard Mueller (New York: Hill & Wang, 1963), p. 141.

2 Antonin Artaud, *Van Gogh, the Man Suicided by Society*, trans. Mary Beach and Lawrence Ferlinghetti, in *Artaud Anthology* (San Francisco: City Lights Books, 1965), p. 158.

3 When Georges Bataille speaks of sumptuary, nonproductive expenditures or consumptions in connection with the energy of nature, these are expenditures or consumptions that are not part of the supposedly independent sphere of human production, insofar as the latter is determined by "the useful." They therefore have to do with what we call the production of consumption. See Georges Bataille, *La part maudite, précédé de la notion de dépense* (Paris: Editions

de Minuit) [*La Parte maudite* was published in English as *The Accursed Share*: *An Essay on General Economy*, trans. Robert Hurley (New York: Zone, 1989)].

4   On the identity of nature and production, and species life in general, according to Marx, see the commentaries of Gérard Granel, "L'ontologie marxiste de 1844 et la question de la coupure," in *L'endurance de la pensée* (Paris: Plon, 1968), pp. 301–10.

5   D.H. Lawrence, *Aaron's Rod* (New York: Penguin, 1976), ppl 200–1.

6   Henry Miller, *Tropic of Cancer*, ch. 13. See in this same chapter the celebration of desire-as-flux expressed in the phrase: "... and my guts spilled out in a grand schizophrenic rush, an evacuation that leaves me face to face with the Absolute."

7   Henri Michaux, *The Major Ordeals of the Mind*, trans. Richard Howard (New York: Harcourt Brace Jovanovich, 1974), pp. 125–7.

8   Claude Lévi-Strauss, The Savage Mind (Chicago: University of Chicago Press, 1966), p. 17.

9   G. de Clerambault, *Oeuvre psychiatrique* (Paris: Presses Universitaires de France).

10   Immanuel Kant, *The Critique of Judgment*, Introduction, §3.

11   Clément Rosset, *Logique du pire* (Paris: Presses Universitaries de France, 1970), p. 37.

12   Lacan's admirable theory of desire appears to us to have two poles: one related to "the object small *a*" as a desiring-machine, which defines desire in terms of a real production, thus going beyond both any idea of need and any idea of fantasy; and the other related to the "great Other" as a signifier, which reintroduces a certain notion of lack. In Serge Leclaire's article "La réalité du désir" (*Sexualité humaine* [Aubier, 1970]), the oscillation between these two poles can be seen quite clearly.

13   Henry Miller, *Sexus* (New York: Grove Press, 1965), pp. 262, 430.

14   Maurice Clavel remarks, apropos of Jean-Paul Sartre, that a Marxist philosophy cannot allow itself to introduce the notion of scarcity as its initial premise: "Such a scarcity antedating exploitation makes of the law of supply and demand a reality that will remain forever independent, since it is situated at a primordial level. Hence it is no longer a question of including or deducing this law within Marxism since it is immediately evident at a prior stage, at a level from which Marxism itself derives. Being a rigorous thinker, Marx refuses to employ the notion of scarcity, and is quite correct to do so, for this category would be his undoing." In *Qui est aliéné?* (Paris: Flammarion, 1970), p. 330.

15   Wilhelm Reich, *The Mass Psychology of Fascism*, trans. Vincent R. Carfagno (London: Souvenir Press, 1970).

16   We find in the case of culturalists a distinction between rational systems and projective systems, with psychoanalysis applying only to these latter (as for example in Abram Kardiner). Despite their hostility to culturalism, we find in both Wilhelm Reich and Herbert Marcuse certain traces of this same dualism, even though they define the rational and the irrational in a completely different way and assign them quite different roles.

17   Vladimir Jankelevitch, *Ravel*, trans. Margaret Crosland (New York: Grove Press, 1959), pp. 73–80.

18 On hysteria, schizophrenia, and their relationships with social structures, see
the analyses by Georges Devereux in his *Essais d'ethnopsychiatrie générale*
(Paris: Gallimard), p. 67 ff., and the wonderful pages in Karl Jaspers' *Strindberg
und Van Gogh* (Berlin: J. Springer, 1926). (English translation, *Strindberg and
Van Gogh*, trans. Oskar Grunow [Tucson, Arizona: University of Arizona
Press.]) The question has been asked: is madness in our time "a state of total
sincerity, in areas where in less chaotic times one would have been capable of
honest experience and expression without it?" Jaspers reformulates this question by adding: "We have seen that in former times human beings attempted
to drive themselves into hysteria; and we might say that today many human
beings attempt to drive themselves into madness in much the same way. But
if the former attempt was to a certain extent psychologically possible, the latter
is not possible at all, and can lead only to inauthenticity."

chapter twenty-eight

The Coming of Post-Industrial Society

Daniel Bell

The influential American sociologist Daniel Bell (1919–   ) was well known for his controversial analysis of the post-World War II environment in *The End of Ideology* (1960). A decade later he ventured again into prognostication with the timely, *The Coming of Post-Industrial Society* (1973). While Bell invented neither the term 'post-industrial' nor the idea of a post-industrial society, his book is the most famous and cogent expression of this insight into contemporary history. Bell attempted to show that the nature of the post-war economy was fundamentally changing, and with it, our social arrangements, our culture, and our politics. The idea was later taken up by many writers, including Lyotard, and is now a commonplace of socio-economic analysis. In the following Introduction to his book (written three years after its original publication), he explains that in a post-industrial society *knowledge* replaces material goods as the most important commodity for production and exchange.

The phrase "post-industrial society" has passed quickly into the socio-logical literature – whether for better or worse remains to be seen. In one sense, the reception was logical and understandable. Once it was clear that countries with diverse social systems could be defined commonly as "industrial societies," it was inevitable that societies which were primarily extractive rather than fabricating would be classified as "pre-industrial," and, as significant changes in the character of technology took place, one could think about "post-industrial" societies as well. Given, too, the vogue of "future schlock," in which breathless prose is mistaken for the pace of change, a hypothesis about the lineaments of a new society is

Daniel Bell, *The Coming of Post-Industrial Society* (New York: Basic Books, 1976), "Foreword: 1976," pp.ix–xxii.

bound to provoke interest. If I have been a beneficiary of fashion, I regret it.

As I indicate in the book, the idea of a post-industrial society is not a point-in-time prediction of the future but a speculative construct, an *as if* based on emergent features, against which the sociological reality could be measured decades hence, so that, in comparing the two, one might seek to determine the operative factors in effecting societal change. Equally, I rejected the temptation to label these emergent features as the "service society" or the "information society" or the "knowledge society," even though all these elements are present, since such terms are only partial, or they seek to catch a fashionable wind and twist it for modish purposes.[1]

I employed the term "post-industrial" for two reasons. First, to emphasize the interstitial and transitory nature of these changes. And second, to underline a major axial principle, that of an intellectual technology. But such emphasis does not mean that technology is the primary determinant of all other societal changes. No conceptual scheme ever exhausts a social reality. Each conceptual scheme is a prism which selects *some* features, rather than others, in order to highlight historical change or, more specifically, to answer certain questions.

One can see this by relating the concept of post-industrial society to that of capitalism. Some critics have argued that post-industrial society will not "succeed" capitalism. But this sets up a false confrontation between two *different* conceptual schemata organized along two different axes. The post-industrial schema refers to the socio-technical dimension of a society, capitalism to the socio-economic dimension.

The confusion between the two arose in the first place because Marx thought that the mode of production (the sub-structure of a society) determines and encompasses *all* other dimensions of a society. Since capitalism is the prevailing mode of production in Western society, Marxists sought to use that concept to explain all realms of social conduct, from economics through politics to culture. And since Marx felt that industrialization as the advanced feature of capitalist production would spread throughout the world, there would be, ultimately, global uniformity in the mode of production, and a uniformity in the conditions of life. National differences would disappear, and in the end only the two classes, capitalists and proletariat, would be left in stark, final confrontation.

I think this is demonstrably not so. Societies are not unified entities. The nature of the polity – whether a nation is democratic or not – rests not on the economic "foundation" but on historic traditions, on value systems, and on the way in which power is concentrated or dispersed throughout the society. Democracy cannot be easily "discarded," even when it begins to hobble the economic power of capitalists.[2] Equally, contemporary Western culture is not the "bourgeois" culture of the eighteenth or nineteenth century, but a modernism, hostile to the economizing mode, that has been absorbed by a "cultural mass" and transformed into a materialistic hedonism which is promoted, paradoxically, by capitalism itself.

For Marx, the mode of production united *social relations* and *forces* of production under a single historical rubric. The social relations were primarily property relations; the forces of production, technological. Yet the same forces of production (i.e. technology) exist within a wide variety of different systems of social relations. One cannot say that the technology (or chemistry or physics) of the Soviet Union is different from the technology (or chemistry or physics) of the capitalist world.

Rather than assume a single linkage between the social relations and the forces of production, if we *uncouple* the two dimensions, we can get different "answers" to the question of the relation between different social systems. Thus, if one asks: Is there a "convergence" between the Soviet Union and the United States? the answer would depend on the axis specified. This can be indicated, graphically, by Figure 1.

Thus, if one divides the countries by the horizontal axis of technology, both the United States and the USSR are industrial societies, whereas Indonesia and China are not. Yet if one divides the countries along the

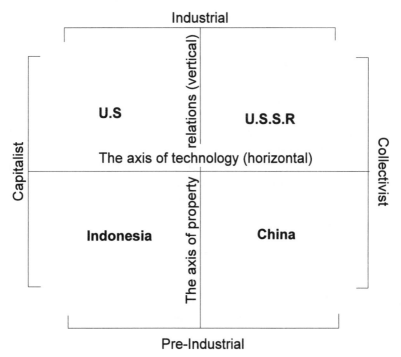

Figure 1

425

vertical axis of property relations, there is a divergence, in that the United States and Indonesia are capitalist while the Soviet Union and China are both "socialist" or state collectivist. (Yet *that* congruence does not explain why there is such fierce rivalry and tension between the two communist countries.)

And if we uncouple the concepts, we can also specify different schemata of social development: feudal, capitalist, and socialist; or pre-industrial, industrial, and post-industrial; or, within the Weberian[i] framework of political authority, that of patriarchical, patrimonial, and legal-rational bureaucracy – so long as one does not claim that the particular conceptual scheme is exhaustive, and subsumes all others. Within a given historical period, it may well be that a specific axial principle is so important that it becomes determinative of most other social relations. I think it is quite evident that in the nineteenth century the capitalist mode of social relations (i.e. private property, commodity production, etc.) became the prevailing ethos and substantially shaped much of character and culture. But that is different from the claim that the mode of production always determines the "superstructure" of a society.

The mode of production does not unify a society. National differences have not disappeared. There are no unilineal sequences of societal change, no "laws of social development." The most grievous mistake in the social sciences is to read the character of a society through a single overriding concept, whether it be *capitalism* or *totalitarianism*, and to mislead one as to the complex (overlapping and even contradictory) features of any modern society, or to assume that there are "laws of social development" in which one social system succeeds another by some inexorable necessity. Any society, since it mingles different kinds of economic, technological, political, and cultural systems (some features of which are common to all, some of which are historical and idiosyncratic), has to be analyzed from different vantage points, depending on the question one has in mind. My focus has been on the influence of technology, not as an autonomous factor but as an analytical element, in order to see what social changes come in the wake of new technologies, and what problems the society, and its political system, must then attempt to solve.

The concept "post-industrial" is counterposed to that of "pre-industrial" and "industrial." A pre-industrial sector is primarily *extractive*, its economy based on agriculture, mining, fishing, timber, and other resources such as natural gas or oil. An industrial sector is primarily *fabricating*, using energy and machine technology, for the manufacture of goods. A post-industrial

---

[i] This refers to Max Weber. Any additions in brackets are the editor's.

sector is one of *processing* in which telecommunications and computers are strategic for the exchange of information and knowledge.

In recent years, the world has become dramatically aware of the strategic role of energy and natural resources as limiting factors of industrial growth, and the question is raised whether these limitations do not modify the onset of a post-industrial sector.

To this, there is an empirical and a theoretical answer. As a practical fact, the introduction of post-industrial elements, which are capital intensive, does depend – in the timing, rate of diffusion, and extensivity of use – on the productivity of the other sectors. The development of an industrial sector depends in considerable measure on the economic surplus of an agrarian sector; yet once industrialization is under way, the productivity of the agrarian sector itself is increased through the use of fertilizer and other petro-chemical products. Similarly, the introduction of new information and processing devices may be delayed by rising costs in the industrial sector or lagging productivity, but once introduced they may be the very means of raising that productivity.

Theoretically, one can say that post-industrial society is, *in principle*, different from the other two. As a theoretical principle, the idea of industrialism did not derive from an agrarian mode. And similarly, the strategic role of theoretical knowledge as the new basis of technological innovation, or the role of information in re-creating social processes, does not derive from the role of energy in creating a manufacturing or fabricating society. In short, these are, *analytically*, independent principles.

Broadly speaking, if industrial society is based on machine technology, post-industrial society is shaped by an intellectual technology. And if capital and labor are the major structural features of industrial society, information and knowledge are those of the post-industrial society.[3] For this reason, the social organization of a post-industrial sector is vastly different from an industrial sector, and one can see this by contrasting the economic features of the two.

Industrial commodities are produced in discrete, identifiable units, exchanged and sold, consumed and used up, as are a loaf of bread or an automobile. One buys the products from a seller and takes physical possession of it. The exchange is governed by specific legal rules of contract. But information and knowledge are not consumed or "used up." Knowledge is a *social* product and the question of its costs, price, or value is vastly different from that of industrial items.

In the manufacture of industrial goods, one can set up a "production function," (i.e. the relative proportions of capital and labor to be employed) and determine the appropriate mix, at the relative costs, of each factor. If capital is embodied labor, one can talk of a labor theory of value.

427

But a post-industrial society is characterized not by a labor theory but by a knowledge theory of value.[4] It is the codification of knowledge that becomes directive of innovation. Yet knowledge, even when it is sold, remains also with the producer. It is a "collective good" in that, once it has been created, it is by its character available to all, and thus there is little incentive for any single person or enterprise to pay for the production of such knowledge unless they can obtain a proprietary advantage, such as a patent or a copyright. But, increasingly, patents no longer guarantee exclusiveness, and many firms lose out by spending money on research only to find that a competitor can quickly modify the product and circumvent the patent; similarly, the question of copyright becomes increasingly difficult to police when individuals or libraries can Xerox whatever pages they need from technical journals or books, or individuals and schools can tape music off the air or record a television performance on video disks.

If there is less and less incentive for individual persons or private enterprises to produce knowledge without particular gain, then the need and effort falls increasingly on some social unit, be it university or government, to underwrite the costs. And since there is no ready market test (how does one estimate the value of "basic research?") there is a challenge to economic theory to design a socially optimal policy of investment in knowledge (e.g., how much money should be spent for basic research; what allocations should be made for education, and for what fields; in what areas do we obtain the "better returns" in health; and so on), and how to "price" information and knowledge to users.[5]

In a narrower, technical sense, the major problem for the post-industrial society will be the development of an appropriate "infra-structure" for the developing *compunications* networks (the phrase is Anthony Oettinger's) of digital information technologies that will tie the post-industrial society together. The first infra-structure in society is transportation – roads, canals, rail, air – for the movement of people and goods. The second infra-structure has been the energy utilities – oil pipeline, gas, electricity – for the transmission of power. The third infra-structure has been telecommunications, principally the voice telephone, radio, and television. But now with the explosive growth of computers and terminals for data (the number of data terminals in use in the United States went from 185,000 in 1970 to 800,000 in 1976) and the rapid decrease in the costs of computation and information storage, the question of hitching together the varied ways information is transmitted in the country becomes a major issue of economic and social policy.

The "economics of information" is not the same character as the "economics of goods," and the social relations created by the new networks of information (from an interactive research group communicating through computer terminals to the large cultural homogenization created by national television) are not the older social patterns – or work relations – of industrial society.[6] We have here – if this kind of society develops – the foundations of a vastly different kind of social structure than we have previously known.

The post-industrial society, as I have implied, does not *displace* the industrial society, just as an industrial society has not done away with the agrarian sectors of the economy. Like palimpsests, the new developments overlie the previous layers, erasing some features and thickening the texture of society as a whole. In orienting a reader to the detailed arguments in this book, therefore, it might be useful to highlight some of the new dimensions of post-industrial society.

1 *The centrality of theoretical knowledge.* Every society has always existed on the basis of knowledge, but only now has there been a change whereby the codification of theoretical knowledge and materials science becomes the basis of innovations in technology. One sees this primarily in the new science-based industries – computers, electronics, optics, polymers – that mark the last third of the century.

2 *The creation of a new intellectual technology.* Through new mathematical and economic techniques – based on the computer linear programming, Markov chains, stochastic processes and the like – we can utilize modeling, simulation and other tools of system analysis and decision theory in order to chart more efficient, "rational" solutions to economic and engineering, if not social, problems.

3 *The spread of a knowledge class.* The fastest growing group in society is the technical and professional class. In the United States this group, together with managers, made up 25 percent of a labor force of eight million persons in 1975. By the year 2000, the technical and professional class will be the largest single group in the society.

4 *The change from goods to services.* In the United States today more than 65 out of every 100 persons are engaged in services. By 1980, the figure will be about 70 in every 100. A large service sector exists in every society. In a pre-industrial society this is mainly a household and domestic class. (In England, it was the single largest class in the society until about 1870.) In an industrial society, the services are transportation utilities, and finance, which are auxiliary to the production of goods, and personal service (beauticians, restaurant employees, and so forth). But in a post-industrial society, the new services are primarily human services (principally in health, education and social services) and professional and technical services (e.g. research, evaluation, computers, and systems analysis). The expansion of these services becomes a constraint on economic growth and a source of persistent inflation.

429

Daniel Bell

5   *A change in the character of work.* In a pre-industrial world, life is a game against nature in which men wrest their living from the soil, the waters, or the forests, working usually in small groups, subject to the vicissitudes of nature. In an industrial society, work is a game against fabricated nature, in which men become dwarfed by machines as they turn out goods and things. But in a post-industrial world, work is primarily a "game between persons" (between bureaucrat and client, doctor and patient, teacher and student, or within research groups, office groups, service groups). Thus in the experience of work and the daily routine, nature is excluded, artifacts are excluded, and persons have to learn how to live with one another. In the history of human society, this is a completely new and unparalleled state of affairs.

6   *The role of women.* Work in the industrial sector (e.g. the factory) has largely been men's work, from which women have been usually excluded. Work in the post-industrial sector (e.g. human services) provides expanded employment opportunities for women. For the first time, one can say that women have a secure base for economic independence. One sees this in the steadily rising curve of women's participation in the labor force, in the number of families (now 60 percent of the total) that have more than one regular wage earner, and in the rising incidence of divorce as women increasingly feel less dependent, economically, on men.

7   *Science as the imago.* The scientific community, going back to the seventeenth century, has been a unique institution in human society. It has been charismatic, in that it has been revolutionary in its quest for truth and open in its methods and procedures; it derives its legitimacy from the credo that knowledge itself, not any specific instrumental ends, is the goal of science. Unlike other charismatic communities (principally religious groups and messianic political movements), it has not "routinized" its creeds and enforced official dogmas. Yet until recently, science did not have to deal with the bureaucratization of research, the subordination of its inquiries to state-directed goals, and the "test" of its results on the basis of some instrumental payoff. Now science has become inextricably intertwined not only with technology but with the military and with social technologies and social needs. In all this – a central feature of the post-industrial society – the character of the new scientific institutions – will be crucial for the future of free inquiry and knowledge.

8   *Situses as political units.* Most of sociological analysis has focused its attention on classes or strata, horizontal units of society that exist in superior – subordinate relation to each other. Yet for the post-industrial sectors, it may well be that *situses* (from the Latin *situ*, location), a set of vertical orders, will be the more important loci of political attachment. [Later in the book] I sketch the possible situses of the post-industrial order.

430

There are four *functional* situses – scientific, technological (i.e. applied skills: engineering, economics, medicine), administrative and cultural – and five *institutional* situses – economic enterprises, government bureaus, universities and research complexes, social complexes (e.g. hospitals, social-service centers), and the military. My argument is that the major interest conflicts will be between the situs groups, and that the attachments to these situses might be sufficiently strong to prevent the organization of the new professional groups into a coherent class in society.[7]

9 *Meritocracy.* A post-industrial society, being primarily a technical society, awards place less on the basis of inheritance or property (though these can command wealth or cultural advantage) than on education and skill. Inevitably the question of a meritocracy becomes a crucial normative question. In this book I attempt to define the character of meritocracy and defend the idea of a "just meritocracy," or of place based on achievement, through the respect of peers.

10 *The end of scarcity?* Most socialist and utopian theories of the nineteenth century ascribed almost all the ills of society to the scarcity of goods and the competition of men for these scarce goods. In fact, one of the most common definitions of economics characterized it as the art of efficient allocation of scarce goods among competing ends. Marx and other socialists argued that abundance was the precondition for socialism and claimed, in fact, that under socialism there would be no need to adopt normative rules of just distribution, since there would be enough for everyone's needs. In that sense, the definition of communism was the abolition of economics, or the "material embodiment" of philosophy. Yet it is quite clear that scarcity will always be with us. I mean not just the question of scarce resources (for this is still a moot point) but that a post-industrial society, by its nature, brings new scarcities which nineteenth-and early-twentieth-century writers had never thought of. The socialists and liberals had talked of the scarcities of goods; but in the post-industrial society, as I point out, there will be scarcities of information and of time. And the problems of allocation inevitably remain, in the crueler form, even, of man becoming *homo economicus* in the disposition of his leisure time.

11 *The economics of information.* As I pointed out earlier, information is by its nature a collective, not a private, good (i.e. a property). In the marketing of individual goods, it is clear that a "competitive" strategy between producers is to be preferred lest enterprise become slothful or monopolistic. Yet for the optimal social investment in knowledge, we have to follow a "cooperative" strategy in order to increase the spread and use of knowledge in society. This new problem regarding information poses the most fascinating challenges to economists and decision makers in respect to both theory and policy in the post-industrial society.

431

Most of the examples in this book are taken from the United States. The question that arises is whether other industrial nations in Western Europe, Japan, and the Soviet Union will become post-industrial as well. . . . I do not believe that any social system is subject to such a causal trajectory. Yet the very features of post-industrial society indicate that, *as tendencies*, they are emergent in all industrial societies, and the extent to which they do appear depends upon a host of economic and political factors that have to do with the balance of world power, the ability of "third world" countries to organize effectively for a political and economic redistribution of wealth, the tensions between the major powers which might erupt into war or not. But it is clear that, as a theoretical construct, the continuing economic growth of all these societies necessarily involves the introduction of post-industrial elements.

The two large dimensions of a post-industrial society, as they are elaborated in this book, are the centrality of theoretical knowledge and the expansion of the service sector as against a manufacturing economy. The first means an increasing dependence on science as the means of innovating and organizing technological change. Most of the industrial societies are highly sensitive to the need for access to scientific knowledge, the organization of research, and the increasing importance of information as the strategic resource in the society. And to that extent a shift in the sociological weight of the sectors within the advanced societies, and the increasing role of science-based industries, are a crescive fact.[8]

The second change – the expansion of services in the economic sector – has been most striking in the United States, but has occurred in Western Europe as well. In 1960, a total of 39.5 percent of the workers in the enlarged Common Market area were in services (defined broadly as transport, trade, insurance, banking, public administration, personal service). Thirteen years later, in 1973, the proportion had risen to 47.6 percent. A change of this kind usually goes in two phases. The first – the observation of Colin Clark who first described the phenomenon thirty years ago – was a shift to services at the expense of agriculture, but with industrial employment growing as well. But in Denmark, Sweden, Belgium and the United Kingdom, the service-oriented sectors have now grown at the relative expense of *industrial* employment (since agriculture has reached almost rock-bottom), and this is beginning to take place throughout Europe as well.[9]

The Soviet Union is an industrial society, and it is likely that post-industrial features will appear in that country as well. The striking fact, however, is that this book, *The Coming of Post-Industrial Society*, has been the object of an extraordinary range of attacks in the Soviet press, from serious discussions in academic journals, such as *Problems of Philosophy*, or intellectual weeklies such as the *Literary Gazette*, to ideological polemics in the official Party theoretical magazine *Kommunist* and vulgar and highly distorted accounts in *Pravda*. It would seem as if a decision had been made by the Party's ideological committee to attack this book as an ideological threat to Party doctrine. The reasons are quite clear. From the Soviet point of view there is a "historic" conflict between capitalism and communism in which the "objective laws of history" prove the ultimate victory of communism. And this is still a central tenet of the faith – at least for export purposes. On a theoretical level, my discussion denies the idea that one can use monolithic concepts such as capitalism or socialism to explain the complex structure of modern societies. More directly, since the Party doctrine bases its view of history on the inevitable victory of the proletariat (and justifies the repressive rule of the Party in the name of the "dictatorship of the proletariat"), how can one sustain that dogma when the proletariat is no longer the major occupational class of a post-industrial society?

This was precisely the problem of a remarkable book by some members of the Czechoslovak Academy of Science, *Civilization at the Crossroads: Social and Human Implications of the Scientific and Technological Revolution*, which appeared during the "Prague Spring," in 1967, under the sponsorship of the social-science director Radovan Richta. In this book, the Czechoslovak sociologists explored the possibility of new "interest conflicts," if not "class conflicts," between the new scientific and professional strata and the working class in socialist society. Clearly, such a discussion was highly embarrassing to Marxist doctrine, and the theme a threat to the ideological justification of the Party. After 1968, Richta, who remained in Czechoslovakia after the Soviet occupation, abjectly and ignominiously repudiated the implications of his work.

The theme of post-industrialism applies primarily to changes in *the social structure* (the techno-economic order) and only indirectly to those in the polity and the culture, which comprise the other major realms of societal structure. One consequence of this is to widen the disjunction between the realms, since each now operates under axial principles that are contrary to the other.

When capitalism arose as a socio-economic system, it had a tenuous unity: an ethos (individualism), a political philosophy (liberalism), a culture (a bourgeois conception of utility and realism), and a character structure (respectability, delayed gratification, and the like). Many of these elements have withered or remain as pale ideologies. What is left is a technological engine, geared to the idea of functional rationality and efficiency, which promises a rising standard of living and promotes a hedonistic way of life. A post-industrial change begins to rework the stratification system of the society, to provide a more sophisticated technology, and to harness science more directly to instrumental purposes. Yet it is not at all clear that science, as a "republic of virtue," has the power to provide a new ethos for the society; more likely it is science itself that may become subverted. What this means is that the society is left with no transcendent ethos to provide some appropriate sense of purpose, no anchorages that can provide stable meanings for people.

In effect, what a post-industrial transformation means is the enhancement of *instrumental* powers, powers over nature and powers, even, over people. In the nineteenth century, utopian and socialist thinkers believed that any enhancement of man's power would necessarily be progressive, since it would mean the decline of religion and superstition and a proof of the greater powers and self-consciousness of Man. Yet this has proved to be a delusion. Instruments can be put to varied use. The kinds of use depend upon the values of a society, the entrenched nature of a privileged class, the openness of the society, its sense of decency or – as we have learned so viciously in the twentieth century – its bestiality.

A post-industrial transformation provides no "answers." It only establishes new promises and new powers, new constraints and new questions – with the difference that these are now on a *scale* that had never been previously imagined in world history.

Notes

1   Perhaps the major misconception is to identify the idea of the post-industrial society with the expansion of the service (or tertiary) sector of the economy and dispute its importance. Some writers using the term (e.g. Herman Kahn) have emphasized this feature. To the extent that some critics identify me with the centrality of a service sector, it is either ignorance or a willful misreading of my book.

2   For Marxists, fascism was the "last" stage of monopoly capitalism. While many capitalists did support fascism, the character of the system derived from the déclassé who led the movement, and the lower middle class which formed its mass base. Fascism is a cultural-political phenomenon. Curiously, we still have no comprehensive Marxist analysis of fascism, nor even a "Marxist analysis" of the new class structure of the Soviet Union itself.

3   By information I mean, broadly, the storing, retrieval, and processing of data, as the basis of all economic and social exchanges. This would include:

    1   Records: payrolls, government benefits (e.g., social security), bank clearances, credit clearances, and the like.

    2   Scheduling: airline reservations, production scheduling, inventory analysis, product-mix information, and so forth.

    3   Demographic and library: census data, opinion surveys, market research, knowledge storage, election data, and so forth.

    By knowledge, I mean an organized set of statements, of facts or ideas, presenting a reasoned judgment or an experimental result that is transmitted to others through communication media in some systematic form.

4   A parallel argument has been made by the German Marxist scholar Jurgen Habermas, who has written:

> . . . technology and science [have] become a leading productive force, rendering inoperative the conditions for Marx's labor theory of value. It is no longer meaningful to calculate the amount of capital investment in research and development on the basis of the value of unskilled (simple) labor power, when scientific-technical progress has become an independent source of surplus value, in relation to which the only source of surplus value considered by Marx, namely the labor power of the immediate producers, plays an ever smaller role. Jurgen Habermas, *Toward a Rational Society* (Boston: Beacon Press, 1970), p. 104.

To that extent, too, one can say that *knowledge*, not labor, is a social product, and that Marx's analysis of the social character of production applies more fully to knowledge than to the production of goods.

5   The seminal work on this question of collective goods is Mancur Olson's *The Logic of Collective Action* (Cambridge: Harvard University Press, 1965). The question of the "economics of information" has come to absorb the attention of the Harvard economists Kenneth Arrow and Michael Spence. For some initial reflections, see, Kenneth Arrow, "Limited Knowledge and Economic Analysis," *American Economic Review* (March 1974), and Michael A. Spence, "An Economist's View of Information," in *Annual Review of Information Science and Technology*, 9, edited by Carlos A. Cuadra and Ann W. Luke (Washington, DC, 1974, American Society for Information Science).

6   One intriguing way in which cheap communications technology creates new social patterns is the use of citizens' band radio as a form of coordinated action. In 1974, independent truckers could create vast slowdowns on a thousand-mile chain of roads in the midwest by radio communication from selected blockade points. In one sense, this is little different from the pattern of riverboat pilots exchanging information which Mark Twain described so hilariously in *Life on the Mississippi*, but in this, as in so many instances, the characteristic of modernity is not the nature of the action but its scale, rapidity, and coordination.

For an authoritative elaboration of these technical questions, see the monograph *The Medium and the Telephone: The Politics of Information Resources*, by Paul J. Berman and Anthony Oettinger, Working Paper 75–8, Harvard Program on Information Technology and Public Policy. For this and other materials on information technology I am indebted to my colleague Professor Oettinger.

7   What is striking is that in the communist world, it is quite clear that *situses* play the major role in politics. One analyzes the play of power, not in class terms, but on the basis of the rivalries among the party, the military, the planning ministries, the industrial enterprises, the collective farms, the cultural institutions – all of which are *situses*.

8 As I indicated in the text, the national power of industrial societies was once rated on the basis of steel capacity. Two years ago, the Soviet Union passed the United States in the steel tonnage it produces, a fact that received only passing mention in the business pages of the *New York Times*. Yet in the development of computers, both in degree of sophistication and numbers, the Soviet Union is far, far behind the United States, a fact that was made vividly clear when the Soyuz and Apollo capsules were linked and the quality of their equipment could be compared.

9 It is striking that Italy, Germany and France are the countries where industrial employment has increased; the largest increase was in Italy, which had lagged furthest in industrialization in Europe. But in the other countries, the proportion of those in industry has begun to shrink in relation to services. (For some detailed statistics on these occupational shifts, see *The Economist* [London], November 29, 1975, p. 17.)

Japan too, has been following a similar trajectory in which the expansion in services has been at the expense of industry. For a detailed discussion, see Henry Rosovsky, "Japan's Economic Future," *Challenge*, July/August, 1973. In this essay Rosovsky develops a definition of "economic maturity" which is interesting in the light of sector changes that have taken place in the industrializing countries in the last fifty years. He writes: "Economic maturity is a difficult term to define but as used here it has a narrow meaning. Let us call it that state in which the incentives of sectoral labor force reallocation have become minimal – in the extreme case, impossible" (p. 16).

chapter twenty-nine

Symbolic Exchange and Death

Jean Baudrillard

Controversial sociologist Jean Baudrillard (1929–) has produced a unique analysis of contemporary culture, indebted to Marx, to structuralism, and to Marshall
McLuhan's work on electronic media. Having earlier applied a Marxist analysis to
the use of symbols in capitalist mass culture, Baudrillard came to regard Marxism
itself as such a symbol, or ideology, produced by modern culture. The modern
image of representation as rooted in production is evident in the Marxist distinction
between the epiphenomenal "superstructure" (culture, ideology, the "symbolic")
and the fundamental reality of the "infrastructure" (economy, or material production). But an analysis unprejudiced by this view reveals that in contemporary
culture representation or the symbolic is primary. Like a number of writers
associated with Pop Art and Camp literature, Baudrillard came to regard his
formerly oppositionist views of mass culture as untenable. In perhaps his most
pivotal book, *Symbolic Exchange and Death* (1976), he argues that the culture of
electronic media replaces earlier senses of reality with a new "hyperreality."

The Structural Revolution of Value

Saussure located two dimensions to the exchange of terms of the *langue*,
which he assimilated to money. A given coin must be exchangeable against
a real good of some value, while on the other hand it must be possible to
relate it to all the other terms in the monetary system. More and more,
Saussure reserves the term *value* for this second aspect of the system: every
term can be related to every other, their *relativity*, internal to the system and
constituted by binary oppositions. This definition is opposed to the other

---

Jean Baudrillard, *Symbolic Exchange and Death*, trans. Iain H. Grant (London: Sage, 1993):
from chapter 1, pp. 6–12; from chapter 2, pp. 50, 55–61, 70–6.

437

possible definition of value: the relation of every term to what it designates, of each signifier to its signified, like the relation of every coin with what it can be exchanged against. The first aspect corresponds to the structural dimension of language, the second to its functional dimension. Each dimension is separate but linked, which is to say that they mesh and cohere. This coherence is characteristic of the 'classical' configuration of the linguistic sign, under the rule of the commodity law of value, where designation always appears as the finality of the structural operation of the *langue*. The parallel between this 'classical' stage of signification and the mechanics of value in material production is absolute, as in Marx's analysis: use-value plays the role of the horizon and finality of the system of exchange-values. The first qualifies the concrete operation of the commodity in consumption (a moment parallel to designation in the sign), the second relates to the exchangeability of any commodity for any other under the law of equivalence (a moment parallel to the structural organisation of the sign). Both are dialectically linked throughout Marx's analyses and define a rational configuration of production, governed by political economy.

A revolution has put an end to this 'classical' economics of value, a revolution of value itself, which carries value beyond its commodity form into its radical form.

This revolution consists in the dislocation of the two aspects of the law of value, which were thought to be coherent and eternally bound as if by a natural law. *Referential value is annihilated, giving the structural play of value the upper hand.* The structural dimension becomes autonomous by excluding the referential dimension, and is instituted upon the death of reference. The systems of reference for production, signification, the affect, substance and history, all this equivalence to a 'real' content, loading the sign with the burden of 'utility', with gravity – its form of representative equivalence – all this is over with. Now the other stage of value has the upper hand, a total relativity, general commutation, combination and simulation – simulation, in the sense that, from now on, signs are exchanged against each other rather than against the real (it is not that they just happen to be exchanged against each other, they do so *on condition* that they are no longer exchanged against the real). The emancipation of the sign: remove this 'archaic' obligation to designate something and it finally becomes free, indifferent and totally indeterminate, in the structural or combinatory play which succeeds the previous rule of determinate equivalence. The same operation takes place at the level of labour power and the production process: the annihilation of any goal as regards the contents of production allows the latter to function as a code, and the monetary sign, for example, to escape into infinite speculation, beyond all reference to a real of production, or even to a gold-standard. The flotation of money and signs, the flotation of 'needs' and ends of production, the

438

flotation of labour itself – the commutability of every term is accompanied by speculation and a limitless inflation (and we really have *total liberty* – no duties, disaffection and general disenchantment; but this remains a magic, a sort of magical obligation which keeps the sign chained up to the real, capital has freed signs from this 'naïvety' in order to deliver them into pure circulation). Neither Saussure nor Marx had any presentiment of all this: they were still in the golden age of the dialectic of the sign and the real, which is at the same time the 'classical' period of capital and value. Their dialectic is in shreds, and the real has died of the shock of value acquiring this fantastic autonomy. Determinacy is dead, indeterminacy holds sway. There has been an extermination (in the literal sense of the word) of the real of production and the real of signification.[1]

I indicated this structural revolution of the law of value in the term 'political economy of the sign'. This term, however, can only be regarded as makeshift, for the following reasons:

1   Does this remain a political-economic question? Yes, in that it is always a question of value and the law of value. However, the mutation that affects it is so profound and so decisive, the content of political economy so thoroughly changed, indeed annihilated, that the term is nothing more than an allusion. Moreover, it is precisely *political* to the extent that it is always the *destruction* of social relations governed by the relevant value. For a long time, however, it has been a matter of something entirely different from economics.

2   The term 'sign' has itself only an allusive value. Since the structural law of value affects signification as much as it does everything else, its form is not that of the sign in general, but that of a certain organisation which is that of the code. The code only governs certain signs however. Just as the commodity law of value does not, at a given moment, signify just any determinant instance of material production, neither, conversely, does the structural law of value signify any pre-eminence of the sign whatever. This illusion derives from the fact that Marx developed the one in the shadow of the commodity, while Saussure developed the other in the shadow of the linguistic sign. But this illusion must be shattered. The commodity law of value is a law of equivalences, and this law operates throughout every sphere: it equally designates the equivalence in the configuration of the sign, where one signifier and one signified facilitate the regulated exchange of a referential content (the other parallel modality being the linearity of the signifier, contemporaneous with the linear and cumulative time of production).

The classical law of value then operates simultaneously in every instance (language, production, etc.), despite these latter remaining distinct according to their sphere of reference.

Conversely, the structural law of value signifies the indeterminancy of every sphere in relation to every other, and to their proper content (also therefore the passage from the *determinant* sphere of signs to the *indeterminacy* of the code). To say that the sphere of material production and that of signs exchange their respective contents is still too wide of the mark: they literally disappear as such and lose their specificity along with their determinacy, to the benefit of a form of value, of a much more general assemblage, where designation and production are annihilated.

The 'political economy of the sign' was also consequent upon an extension of the commodity law of value and its confirmation at the level of signs, whereas the structural configuration of value simply and simultaneously puts an end to the regimes of production, political economy, representation and signs. With the code, all this collapses into simulation. Strictly speaking, neither the 'classical' economy nor the political economy of the sign ceases to exist: they lead a secondary existence, becoming a sort of phantom principle of dissuasion.

The end of labour. The end of production. The end of political economy. The end of the signifier/signified dialectic which facilitates the accumulation of knowledge and meaning, the linear syntagma of cumulative discourse. And at the same time, the end of the exchange-value/use-value dialectic which is the only thing that makes accumulation and social production possible. The end of the linear dimension of discourse. The end of the linear dimension of the commodity. The end of the classical era of the sign. The end of the era of production.

It is not *the* revolution which puts an end to all this, it is *capital itself* which abolishes the determination of the social according to the means of production, substitutes the structural form for the commodity form of value, and currently controls every aspect of the system's strategy.

This historical and social mutation is legible at every level. In this way the era of simulation is announced everywhere by the commutability of formerly contradictory or dialectically opposed terms. Everywhere we see the same 'genesis of simulacra': the commutability of the beautiful and the ugly in fashion, of the left and the right in politics, of the true and the false in every media message, the useful and the useless at the level of objects, nature and culture at every level of signification. All the great humanist criteria of value, the whole civilisation of moral, aesthetic and practical judgement are effaced in our system of images and signs. Everything becomes undecidable, the characteristic effect of the domination of the code, which everywhere rests on the principle of neutralisation, of indifference.[2] This is the generalised brothel of capital, a brothel not for prostitution, but for substitution and commutation.

This process, which has for a long time been at work in culture, art, politics, and even in sexuality (in the so-called 'superstructural' domains), today affects the economy itself, the whole so-called 'infrastructural' field. Here the same indeterminacy holds sway. And, of course, with the loss of determination of the economic, we also lose any possibility of conceiving it as the determinant agency.

Since for two centuries historical determination has been built up around the economic (since Marx in any case), it is there that it is important to grasp the interruption of the code.

The End of Production

We are at the end of production. In the West, this form coincides with the proclamation of the commodity law of value, that is to say, with the reign of political economy. First, nothing is *produced*, strictly speaking: everything is *deduced*, from the grace (God) or beneficence (nature) of an agency which releases or withholds its riches. Value emanates from the reign of divine or natural qualities (which for us have become retrospectively confused). The Physiocrats still saw the cycles of land and labour in this way, as having no value of their own.[i] We may wonder, then, whether there is a genuine *law* of value, since this law is *dispatch* without attaining rational expression. Its form cannot be separated from the inexhaustible referential substance to which it is bound. If there is a law here, it is, in contrast to the commodity law, a *natural* law of value.

A mutation shakes this edifice of a natural distribution or dispensing of wealth as soon as value is *produced*, as its reference becomes labour, and its law of equivalence is generalised to every type of labour. Value is now assigned to the distinct and rational operation of human (social) labour. It is measurable, and, in consequence, so is surplus-value.

The critique of political economy begins with social production or the mode of production as its reference. The concept of production alone allows us, by means of an analysis of that unique commodity called labour power, to extract a *surplus* (a surplus-value) which controls the rational dynamics of capital as well as its beyond, the revolution.

Today everything has changed again. Production, the commodity form, labour power, equivalence and surplus-value, which together formed the outline of a quantitative, material and measurable configuration, are now things of the past. Productive forces outlined another reference which, although in contradiction with the relations of production, remained a

---

[i] The Physiocrats were an eighteenth-century school of economic thinkers.

reference, that of social wealth. An aspect of production still supports both a social form called capital and its internal critique called Marxism. Now, revolutionary demands are based on the abolition of the *commodity* law of value.

Now we have passed from the commodity law of value to the structural law of value, and this coincides with the obliteration of the social form known as production. Given this, are we still within a capitalist mode? It may be that we are in a hyper-capitalist mode, or in a very different order. Is the form of capital bound to the law of value in general, or to some specific form of the law of value (perhaps we are really already within a socialist mode? Perhaps this metamorphosis of capital under the sign of the structural law of value is merely its socialist outcome? Oh dear . . .)? If the life and death of capital are staked on the *commodity* law of value, if the revolution is staked on the mode of production, then we are within neither capital nor revolution. If this latter consists in a liberation of the social and generic production of man, then there is no longer any prospect of a revolution since there is no more production. If, on the other hand, capital is a *mode of domination*, then we are always in its midst. This is because the structural law of value is the purest, most illegible form of social domination, like surplus-value. It no longer has any references within a dominant class or a relation of forces, it works without violence, entirely reabsorbed without any trace of bloodshed into the signs which surround us, operative everywhere in the code in which capital finally holds its purest discourses, beyond the dialects of industry, trade and finance, beyond the dialects of class which it held in its 'productive' phase – a symbolic violence inscribed everywhere in signs, even in the signs of the revolution.

The structural revolution of value eliminated the basis of the 'Revolution'. The loss of reference fatally affected first the revolutionary systems of reference, which can no longer be found in any social substance of production, nor in the certainty of a reversal in any truth of labour power. This is because labour is not a *power*, it has become one *sign* amongst many. Like every other sign, it produces and consumes itself. It is exchanged against non-labour, leisure, in accordance with a total equivalence, it is commutable with every other sector of everyday life. No more or less 'alienated', it is no longer a unique, historical 'praxis' giving rise to unique social relations. Like most practices, it is now only a set of signing operations. It becomes part of contemporary life in general, that is, it is framed by signs. It is no longer even the suffering of historical prostitution which used to play the role of the contrary promise of final emancipation (or, as in Lyotard, as the space of the workers' enjoyment which fulfils an unremitting desire in the abjection of value and the rule of capital). None of this remains true. Sign-form seizes labour and rids it of every historical or libidinal significance, and absorbs it in the process of its own reproduction: the operation of the *sign*, behind the empty allusion to what it designates, is to replicate itself. In the past, labour was used to designate the reality of a social production and a social objective of accumulating wealth. Even capital and surplus-value exploited it – precisely where it retained a use-value for the expanded reproduction of capital and its final destruction. It was shot through with finality anyway – if the worker is absorbed in the pure and simple reproduction of his labour power, it is not true that the process of production is experienced as senseless repetition. Labour revolutionises society through its very abjection, as a commodity whose potential always exceeds pure and simple reproduction of value.

Today this is no longer the case since labour is no longer productive but has become reproductive of the *assignation to labour* which is the general habit of a society which no longer knows whether or not it wishes to produce. No more myths of production and no more contents of production: national balance sheets now merely retrace a numerical and statistical growth devoid of meaning, an inflation of the signs of accountancy over which we can no longer even project the phantasy of the collective will. The pathos of growth itself is dead, since no-one believes any longer in the pathos of production, whose final, paranoid and panic-stricken tumescence it was. Today these codes are detumescent. It remains, however, more necessary than ever to reproduce labour as a social ritual as a reflex, as morality, as consensus, as regulation, as the reality principle. The reality principle *of the code*, that is: an immense *ritual of the signs of labour* extends over society in general – since it *reproduces* itself, it matters little whether or not it *produces*. It is much more effective to socialise by means of rituals and signs than by the bound energies of production. You are asked only to become socialised, not to produce or to excel yourself (this classical ethic now arouses suspicion instead). You are asked only to consider value, according to the structural definition which here takes on its full social significance, as one term in relation to others, to function as a sign in the general scenario of production, just as labour and production now function only as signs, as terms commutable with non-labour, consumption, communication, etc. – a multiple, incessant, twisting relation across the entire network of other signs. Labour, once voided of its energy and substance (and generally disinvested), is given a new role as the model of social simulation, bringing all the other categories along with it into the aleatory sphere of the code.

An unnervingly strange state of affairs: this sudden plunge into a sort of secondary existence, separated from you by all the opacity of a previous life, where there was a familiarity and an intimacy in the traditional process of labour. Even the concrete reality of exploitation, the violent sociality of

443

labour, is familiar. This has all gone now, and is due not so much to the *operative* abstraction of the *process* of labour, so often described, as to the passage of every *signification* of labour into an *operational* field where it becomes a floating variable, dragging the whole imaginary of a previous life along with it.

Beyond the autonomisation of production as *mode* (beyond the convulsions, contradictions and revolutions inherent in the mode), the *code* of production must re-emerge. This is the dimension things are taking on today, at the end of a 'materialist' history which has succeeded in authenticating it as the real movement of society. (Art, religion and duty have no real history for Marx – only production has a history, or, rather, it *is* history, it grounds history. An incredible fabrication of labour and production as historical reason and the generic model of fulfilment.)

The end of this religious autonomisation of production allows us to see that all of this could equally have been *produced* (this time in the sense of a stage-production and a scenario) fairly recently, with totally different goals than the internal finalities (that is, the revolution) secreted away within production.

To analyse production as a code cuts across both the material evidence of machines, factories, labour time, the product, salaries and money, and the more formal, but equally 'objective', evidence of surplus-value, the market, capital, to discover the rule of the game which is to destroy the logical network of the agencies of capital, and even the critical network of the Marxian categories which analyse it (which categories are again only an appearance at the second degree of capital, its *critical* appearance), in order to discover the elementary signifiers of production, the social relations it establishes, buried away forever beneath the historical illusion of the producers (and the theoreticians).

The Three Orders of Simulacra

There are three orders of simulacra, running parallel to the successive mutations of the law of value since the Renaissance:

- The *counterfeit* is the dominant schema in the 'classical' period, from the Renaissance to the Industrial Revolution.
- *Production* is the dominant schema in the industrial era.
- Simulation is the dominant schema in the current code-governed phase.

The first-order simulacrum operates on the natural law of value, the second-order simulacrum on the market law of value, and the third-order simulacrum on the structural law of value.

The Industrial Simulacrum

A new generation of signs and objects arises with the Industrial Revolution – signs with no caste tradition that will never have known restrictions on their status, and which will never have to be *counterfeits*, since from the outset they will be *products* on a gigantic scale. The problem of their specificity and their origin is no longer posed: technics is their origin, they have meaning only within the dimension of the industrial simulacrum.

That is, the series: the very possibility of two or *n* identical objects. The relation between them is no longer one of an original and its counterfeit, analogy or reflection, but is instead one of equivalence and indifference. In the series, objects become indistinct simulacra of one another and, along with objects, of the men that produce them. The extinction of the original reference alone facilitates the general law of equivalences, that is to say, *the very possibility of production*.

The entire analysis of production will be swept aside if we stop regarding it as an original process, as *the* process at the origin of all the others, but conversely as *a* process which reabsorbs every original being and introduces a series of identical beings. Up to this point, we have considered production and labour as potential, as force and historical process, as a generic activity: an energetic-economic myth proper to modernity. We must ask ourselves whether production is not rather an intervention, a *particular* phase, *in the order of signs* – whether it is basically only one episode in the line of simulacra, that episode of producing an infinite series of potentially identical beings (object-signs) by means of technics.

The fabulous energies at work in technics, industry and economics should not hide the fact that it is at bottom only a matter of attaining this indefinite reproducibility, which is a definite challenge to the 'natural' order, and ultimately only a 'second-order' simulacrum and a somewhat weak imaginary solution to the question of world mastery. In relation to the era of the counterfeit, the double, the mirror and the theatre, games of masks and appearances, the serial and technical era of reproduction is basically an era of less ambitious scope (the following era of simulation models and third-order simulacra is of much more considerable dimensions).

Walter Benjamin, in 'The Work of Art in the Age of Mechanical Reproduction', was the first to draw out the essential implications of the

445

principle of reproduction.[ii] He shows that reproduction absorbs the process of production, changes its goals, and alters the status of the product and the producer. He shows this in the fields of art, cinema and photography, because it is there that new territories are opened up in the twentieth century, with no 'classical' tradition of productivity, placed from the outset under the sign of reproduction. Today, however, we know that all material production remains within the same sphere. Today we know that it is at the level of reproduction (fashion, the media, advertising, information and communications networks), at the level of what Marx rather carelessly used to call the *faux frais* of capital (immense historical irony!), that is, in the sphere of simulacra and the code, that the unity of the whole process of capital is formed. Benjamin was also the first (with McLuhan after him)[iii] to grasp technology as a medium rather than a 'productive force' (at which point the Marxian analysis retreats), as the form and principle of an entirely new generation of meaning. The mere fact that any given thing can simply be reproduced, as such, in an exemplary double is already a revolution: one need only think of the stupefaction of the Black boy seeing two identical books for the first time. That these two technical products are *equivalent* under the sign of necessary social labour is less important in the long term than the *serial* repetition of the same object (which is also the serial repetition of individuals as labour power). Technique as a medium gains the upper hand not only over the product's 'message' (its use-value) but also over labour power, which Marx wanted to turn into the revolutionary message of production. Benjamin and McLuhan saw more clearly than Marx, they saw that the real message, *the real ultimatum, lay in reproduction itself.* Production itself has no meaning: its social finality is lost in the series. Simulacra prevail over history.

Moreover, the stage of serial reproduction (that of the industrial mechanism, the production line, the growth of reproduction, etc.) is ephemeral. As soon as dead labour gains the upper hand over living labour (that is to say, since the end of primitive accumulation), serial production gives way to generation through models. In this case it is a matter of a reversal of origin and end, since all forms change from the moment that they are no longer mechanically reproduced, but *conceived according to their very reproducibility,* their diffraction from a generative core called a 'model'. We are dealing with third-order simulacra here. There is no more counterfeiting of an original, as there was in the first order, and no more pure series as there were in the second; there are models from which all forms proceed according to modulated differences. Only affiliation to the model has any meaning, since nothing proceeds in accordance with its end any more, but

[ii] In Walter Benjamin, *Illuminations*, trans. Harry Zohn (New York: Schocken, 1969).
[iii] Marshall McLuhan, contemporary Canadian analyst of communications media.

issues instead from the model, the 'signifier of reference', functioning as a foregone, and the only credible, conclusion. We are dealing with simulation in the modern sense of the term, where industrialisation is only its initial form. Modulation is ultimately more fundamental than serial reproducibility, distinct oppositions more than quantitative equivalences, and the commutation of terms more than the law of equivalences; the structural, not the market, law of value. Not only do we not need to search for the secrets of the code in technique or economics, it is on the contrary the very possibility of industrial production that we must seek in the genesis of the code and the simulacrum. Every order subsumes the previous order. Just as the order of the counterfeit was captured by the order of serial reproduction (look at how art passed entirely into 'machinality'), so the entire order of production is in the process of toppling into operational simulation.

The analyses of both Benjamin and McLuhan stand on the borders of reproduction and simulation, at the point where referential reason disappears and production is seized by vertigo. These analyses mark a decisive advance over Veblen and Goblot, who, describing, for example, the signs of fashion still refer to a classical configuration where signs constitute a distinct material having a finality and are used for prestige, status and social differentiation. The strategy they deploy is contemporaneous with Marx's strategy of profit and commodity, at a moment where they could still speak of a use-value of the sign, or quite simply of economics at all, because there was still a Reason of the sign and a Reason of production.

The Metaphysics of the Code

> The mathematically minded Leibniz saw in the mystical elegance of the binary system where only the zero and the one count, the very image of creation. The unity of the Supreme Being, operating by means of a binary function against the nothing, was sufficient ground, he thought, from which all things could be made.
>
> Marshall McLuhan

The great man-made simulacra pass from a universe of natural laws into a universe of forces and tensions, and today pass into a universe of structures and binary oppositions. After the metaphysics of being and appearance, after energy and determinacy, the metaphysics of indeterminacy and the code. Cybernetic control, generation through models, differential modulation, feedback, question/answer, etc.: this is the new *operational* configuration (industrial simulacra being *mere operations*). Digitality is its metaphysical principle (Leibniz's God), and DNA is its prophet. In fact, it is in the genetic

447

code that the 'genesis of simulacra' today finds its completed form. At the limits of an ever more forceful extermination of references and finalities, of a loss of semblances and designators, we find the digital, programmatic sign, which has a purely *tactical* value, at the intersection of other signals ('bits' of information/tests) and which has the structure of a micro-molecular code of command and control.

At this level, the question of signs and their rational destinations, their 'real' and their 'imaginary', their repression, reversal, the illusions they form of what they silence or of their parallel significations, is completely effaced. We have already seen the signs of the first order, complex signs with a wealth of illusion, change with the advent of machines into crude, dull, industrial, repetitive, echoless, functional and efficient signs. There is a still more radical mutation as regards the code's signals, which become illegible, and for which no possible interpretation can be provided, buried like programmatic matrices, light years, ultimately, from the 'biological' body, black boxes where every command and response are in ferment. End of the theatre of representation, the space of the conflicts and silences of the sign: only the black box of the code remains, the molecule emitting signals which irradiate us, networking questions/answers through us as identifying signals, and continuously tested by the programme we have hardwired into our own cells. Whether it is prison cells, electronic cells, party cells or microbiological cells we are dealing with, we are always searching for the smallest indivisible element, the organic synthesis of which will follow in accordance with the givens of the code. The code itself is nothing other than a genetic, generative cell where the myriad intersections produce all the questions and all the possible solutions from which to select (for whom?). There is no finality to these 'questions' (informational signals, impulses) other than the response which is either genetic and immutable or inflected with minuscule and aleatory differences. Even space is no longer linear or unidimensional but *cellular*, indefinitely generating the same signals like the lonely and repetitive habits of a stir-crazy prisoner. The genetic code is the perpetual jump in a floppy disk, and we are nothing more than VDUs. The whole aura of the sign and signification itself is determinately resolved: everything is resolved into inscription and decoding.

Such is our third-order simulacrum, such is the 'mystical elegance of the binary system of zero and one', from which all beings issue. Such also is the status of the sign at the end of signification: DNA or operational simulation.

This is all perfectly summed up by Thomas Sebeok in 'Genetics and Semiotics' (*Versus*):

> Innumerable observations confirm the hypothesis that the internal world of the organic descends directly from the primordial forms of life. The most remarkable fact is the omnipresence of the DNA molecule. The genetic

material of all the earth's known organisms is in large part composed of the nucleic acids DNA and RNA, whose structure contains information transmitted through reproduction from one generation to the next, and furthermore endowed with the capacity to reproduce itself and to imitate. In short, the genetic code is universal, or almost. Decoding it was an immense discovery to the extent that it showed that 'the two languages of the great polymers, the languages of nucleic acid and protein, correlate directly' . . . The Soviet mathematician Liapunov demonstrated in 1963 that every living system transmits a small but precise quantity of energy or matter containing a great volume of information through channels laid down in advance. This information is responsible for the subsequent control of large quantities of energy and matter. From this perspective numerous biological and cultural phenomena (storing, feedback, channelling messages and so on) can be conceived as manifestations of information processing. In the final analysis, information appears in large part to be the repetition of information, but still another kind of information, a kind of control which seems to be a universal property of terrestrial life, irrespective of its form or substance.

Five years ago I drew attention to the convergence of genetics and linguistics as autonomous but parallel disciplines in the larger field of the science of communication (which is also a part of zoosemiotics). The terminology of genetics is full of expressions taken from linguistics and communication theory . . ., which emphasised both the principal similarities and the important differences in the structure and function of genetic and verbal codes . . . Today it is clear that the genetic code must be considered as the most basic semiotic network, and therefore as the prototype of all the other systems of signification used by the animals, including man. From this point of view, molecules, which are systems of quanta of, and which act as stable vehicles of physical information, zoosemiotic and cultural systems including language, constitute a continuous chain of stages, with ever more complex energy levels, in the context of a unique and universal evolution. It is therefore possible to describe both language or living systems from a unifying cybernetic point of view. For the moment, this is only a useful and provisional analogy. . . . A reciprocal rapprochement between genetics, animal communication and linguistics may lead to a complete science of the dynamics of semiosis, which science may turn out, in the final analysis, to be nothing other than a definition of life.

So the outline of the current strategic model emerges, everywhere taking over from the great ideological model which political economy was in its time.

We find this again, under the rigorous sign of 'science', in Jacques Monod's *Chance and Necessity*. The end of dialectical evolution. Life is now ruled by the discontinuous indeterminacy of the genetic code, by the *teleonomic* principle.[iv] Finality is no longer at the end, there is no more

---

[iv] For Monod, all living beings are "teleonomic," attempting to transmit the information necessary for preservation of the species to the next generation.

finality, nor any determinacy. Finality is there in advance, inscribed in the code. We can see that nothing has changed – the order of ends has ceded its place to molecular play, as the order of signifieds has yielded to the play of infinitesimal signifies, condensed into their aleatory commutation. All the transcendental finalities are reduced to an instrument panel. This is still to make recourse to nature however, to an inscription in a 'biological' nature; a phantasm of nature in fact, as it has always been, no longer a metaphysical sanctuary for the origin and substance, but this time, for the code. The code must have an 'objective' basis. What better than molecules and genetics? Monod is the strict theologian of this molecular transcendence, Edgar Morin its ecstatic supporter (DNA = ADoNaï!). In each of them, however, the phantasm of the code, which is equivalent to the reality of power, is confused with the idealism of the molecule.

Again we find the hallucination or illusion of a world reunited under a single principle – a homogeneous substance according to the Counter-Reformation Jesuits. With Leibniz and his binary deity as their precursor, the technocrats of the biological (as well as the linguistic) sciences opt for the genetic code, for their intended programme has nothing to do with genetics, but is a social and historical programme. Biochemistry hypostatises the ideal of a social order governed by a kind of genetic code, a macromolecular calculus by the PPBS (Planning Programming Budgeting System), its operational circuits radiating over the social body. Here techno-cybernetics finds its 'natural philosophy', as Monod said. The biological and the biochemical have always exerted a fascination, ever since the beginnings of science. In Spencer's organicism (bio-sociologism)[v] it was operative at the level of second and third order structures (following Jacob's classification in *The Logic of Life*), while today, in modern biochemistry, this applies to the level of fourth-order structures.

Coded similarities and dissimilarities: the exact image of cyberneticised social exchange. We need only add the 'stereospecific complex' to reinject the intracellular communication that Morin will transform into a molecular Eros.

Practically and historically, this means that social control by means of the *end* (and the more or less dialectical *providence* that ministers to the fulfilment of this end) is replaced with social control by means of prediction, simulation, programmed anticipation and indeterminate mutation, all governed, however, by the code. Instead of a process finalised in accordance with its ideal development, we are dealing with generative *models*. Instead of prophecy, we fall subject to 'inscription'. There is no radical difference between the two. Only the schemata of control change and, it has to be

---

[v] Herbert Spencer (1820–1903) made Darwinian evolution the basis of a social philosophy.

said, reach a fantastic degree of perfection. From a capitalist productivist society to a neo-capitalist cybernetic order, aiming this time at absolute control: the biological theory of the code has taken up arms in the service of this mutation. Far from 'indeterminate', this mutation is the outcome of an entire history where God, Man, Progress and even History have successively passed away to the advantage of the code, where the death of transcendence benefits immanence, which corresponds to a far more advanced phase of the vertiginous manipulation of social relations.

In its infinite reproduction, the system puts an end to the myth of its origin and to all the referential values it has itself secreted in the course of its process. By putting an end to the myth of its origin, it puts an end to its internal contradictions (there is no longer a real or a referential to which to oppose them) and also puts an end to the myth of its end, the revolution itself. With the revolution you could still make out the outline of a victorious human and generic reference, the original potential of man. But what if capital wiped generic man himself off the map (in favour of genetic man)? The revolution's golden age was the age of capital, where myths of the origin and the end were still in circulation. Once these myths were short-circuited (the only threat that capital had ever faced historically came from this *mythical* demand for rationality which pervaded it from the start) in a *de facto* operationality, a non-discursive operationality – once it became its own myth, or rather an indeterminate, aleatory machine, something like a *social genetic code* – capital no longer left the slightest opportunity for a determinate reversal. This is the real violence of capital. However, it remains to be seen whether this operationality is itself a myth, whether DNA is itself a *myth*.

This effectively poses the problem of the discursive status of science once and for all. In Monod, this discourse is so candidly absolutised that it provides a perfect opportunity for posing the problem:

> Plato, Heraclitus, Hegel, Marx . . .: these ideological edifices, represented as a priori, were in reality a posteriori constructions designed to justify preconceived ethico-political theories. . . . For science, objectivity is the only a priori postulate of objectivity, which spares, or rather forbids it from taking part in this debate.

However, this postulate is itself a result of the never innocent decision to objectify the world and the 'real'. In fact, it postulates the coherence of a specific *discourse*, and scientificity is doubtless only the space of this discourse, never manifest as such, whose simulacrum of 'objectivity' covers over this political and strategic speech. Besides, Monod clearly expresses the arbitrariness of this discourse a little further on:

> It may be asked, of course, whether all the invariants, conservations and symmetries that make up the texture of scientific discourse are not fictions

451

substituted for reality in order to obtain a workable image. . . . A logic itself founded upon a purely abstract, perhaps 'conventional', principle of identity – a convention with which, however, human reason seems to be incapable of doing without.

We couldn't put it more clearly: science itself determines its generative formula and its discourse model on the basis of a faith in a conventional order (and moreover not just any order, but the order of a total reduction). But Monod quickly glosses over this dangerous hypothesis of 'conventional' identity. A rigid basis would serve science better, an 'objective' reality for example. Physics will testify that identity is not only a postulate, but that it is *in things*, since there is an 'absolute identity of two atoms when they are found to be in the same quantitative state'. So, is it convention or is it objective reality? The truth is that science, like any other discourse, is organised on the basis of a conventional logic, but, like any other ideological discourse, requires a real, 'objective' reference within the processes of substance in order to justify it. If the principle of identity is in any way 'true', even if this is at the infinitesimal level of two atoms, then the entire conventional edifice of science which draws its inspiration from it is also 'true'. The hypothesis of the genetic code DNA is also true and cannot be defeated. The same goes for metaphysics. Science explains things which have been defined and formalised in advance and which subsequently conform to these explanations, that's all that 'objectivity' is. The ethics that come to sanction this objective knowledge are just systems of defence and misconstrual that aim to preserve this vicious circle.[3]

As Nietzsche said: 'Down with all hypotheses that have allowed belief in a real world.'

The Hyperrealism of Simulation

We have just defined a digital space, a magnetic field of the code with its modelled polarisations, diffractions and gravitations, with the insistent and perpetual flux of the smallest disjunctive units (the question/answer cell operates like the cybernetic atom of *signification*). We must now measure the disparity between this field of control and the traditional field of repression, the police-space which used to correspond to a violence of signification. This space was one of reactionary conditioning, inspired by the Pavlovian apparatus of programmed and repetitive aggression which we also saw scaled up in 'hard sell' advertising and the political propaganda of the thirties. A crafted but industrial violence that aimed to produce terrified behaviour and animal obedience. This no longer has any meaning. Totalitarian, bureaucratic concentration is a schema dating from the era of the market law of value. The schema of equivalences effectively imposes the form of a general equivalent, and hence the centralisation of a global process. This is an archaic rationality compared to simulation, in which it is no longer a single general equivalent but a diffraction of models that plays the regulative role: no longer the form of the general equivalent, but the form of distinct oppositions. We pass from injunction to disjunction through the code, from the ultimatum to solicitation, from obligatory passivity to models constructed from the outset on the basis of the subject's 'active response', and this subject's involvement and 'ludic' participation, towards a total environment model made up of incessant spontaneous responses, joyous feedback and irradiated contacts. According to Nicolas Schöffer, this is a 'concretisation of the general ambience': the great festival of Participation is made up of myriad stimuli, miniaturised tests, and infinitely divisible question/answers, all magnetised by several great models in the luminous field of the code.

Here comes the great Culture of tactile communication, under the sign of techno-lumino-kinetic space and total spatio-dynamic theatre!

A whole imaginary based on contact, a sensory mimicry and a tactile mysticism, basically ecology in its entirety, comes to be grafted on to this universe of operational simulation, multi-stimulation and multi-response. This incessant test of successful adaptation is naturalised by assimilating it to animal mimicry ('the phenomenon of animals' adaptation to the colours and forms of their habitat also holds for man' – Nicolas Schöffer), and even to the Indians with their 'innate sense of ecology'! Tropisms, mimicry and empathy: the ecological evangelism of open systems, with positive or negative feedback, will be engulfed in this breach, with an ideology of regulation through information that is only the avatar, in accordance with a more flexible rationality, of the Pavlov reflex. Hence electro-shock is replaced by body attitude as the condition of mental health. When notions of need, perception, desire, etc., become operational, then the apparatuses of force and forcing yield to ambient apparatuses. A generalised, mystical ecology of the 'niche' and the context, a simulated environment eventually including the 'Centres for Cultural and Aesthetic Re-animation' planned for the Left Bank (why not?) and the Centre for Sexual Leisure, which, built in the form of a breast, will offer 'a superlative euphoria thanks to a pulsating ambience. . . . Workers from all classes will be able to enter these stimulating centres.' A spatio-dynamic fascination, just like 'total theatre', set up 'according to a hyperbolic, circular apparatus turning around a cylindrical spindle'. No more scenes, no more cuts, no more 'gaze', the end of the spectacle and the spectacular, towards the total, fusional, tactile and aesthesic (and no longer the aesthetic) etc., environment. We can only think of Artaud's total theatre, his Theatre of Cruelty, of which this spatio-dynamic simulation is the abject, black-humour caricature. Here

453

cruelty is replaced by minimum and maximum 'stimulus thresholds', by the invention of 'perceptual codes calculated on the basis of saturation thresholds'. Even the good old 'catharsis' of the classical theatre of the passions has today become a homeopathy by means of simulation.

The end of the spectacle brings with it the collapse of reality into hyperrealism, the meticulous reduplication of the real, preferably through another reproductive medium such as advertising or photography. Through reproduction from one medium into another the real becomes volatile, it becomes the allegory of death, but it also draws strength from its own destruction, becoming the real for its own sake, a fetishism of the lost object which is no longer the object of representation, but the ecstasy of denegation and its own ritual extermination: the hyperreal.

Realism had already inaugurated this tendency. The rhetoric of the real already signals that its status has been radically altered (the golden age of the innocence of language where what is said need not be doubled in an effect of reality). Surrealism was still in solidarity with the realism it contested, but which it doubled and ruptured in the imaginary. The hyperreal represents a much more advanced phase insofar as it effaces the contradiction of the real and the imaginary. Irreality no longer belongs to the dream or the phantasm, to a beyond or a hidden interiority, but to *the hallucinatory resemblance of the real to itself*. To gain exit from the crisis of representation, the real must be sealed off in a pure repetition. Before emerging in pop art and painterly neo-realism, this tendency can already be discerned in the *nouveau roman*.[vi] Here the project is to construct a void around the real, to eradicate all psychology and subjectivity from it in order to give it a pure objectivity. In fact, this is only the objectivity of the pure gaze, an objectivity finally free of the object, but which merely remains a blind relay of the gaze that scans it. It is easy to detect the unconscious trying to remain hidden in this circular seduction.

This is indeed the impression made by the *nouveau roman*, a wild elision of meaning in a meticulous but blind reality. Syntax and semantics have disappeared: the object now only appears in court, where its scattered fragments are subjected to unremitting cross-examination. There is neither metaphor nor metonymy, only a successive immanence under the law enforcing authority of the gaze. This 'objective' microscopy incites reality to vertiginous motion, the vertiginous death of representation within the confines of representation. The old illusions of relief, perspective and depth (both spatial and psychological) bound up with the perception of the object are over with: optics in its entirety, scopics, has begun to operate on the surface of things – the gaze has become the object's molecular code.

[vi] Literally, "new novel," referring to the avant-garde French "antinovels" of the 1950s and 1960s.

There are several possible modalities of this vertigo of realistic simulation:

1. The detailed deconstruction of the real, the paradigmatic close 'reading' of the object: the flattening out, linearity and seriality of part-objects.

2. Abyssal vision: all the games of splitting the object in two and duplicating it in every detail. This reduction is taken to be a depth, indeed a critical metalanguage, and doubtless this was true of a reflective configuration of the sign in a dialectics of the mirror. From now on this infinite refraction is nothing more than another type of seriality in which the real is no longer reflected, but folds in on itself to the point of exhaustion.

3. The properly serial form (Andy Warhol). Here the paradigmatic dimension is abolished along with the syntagmatic dimension, since there is no longer a flexion of forms, nor even an internal reflexion, only a contiguity of the same: zero degree flexion and reflexion. Take this erotic photograph of twin sisters where the fleshy reality of their bodies is annihilated by their similarity. How do you invest when the beauty of the one is immediately duplicated in the other? The gaze can only go from one to the other, and these poles enclose all vision. This is a subtle means of murdering the original, but it is also a singular seduction, where the total extent of the object is intercepted by its infinite diffraction into itself (this scenario reverses the Platonic myth of the reunion of two halves separated by a symbol. In the series, signs subdivide like protozoa). Perhaps this is the seduction of death, in the sense that, for we sexually differentiated beings, death is perhaps not nothingness, but quite simply the mode of reproduction prior to sexual differentiation. The models that generate in infinite chains effectively bring us closer to the generation of protozoa; sex, which for us is confused with life, being the only remaining difference.

4. This pure machinality is doubtless only a paradoxical limit, however. Binarity and digitality constitute the true generative formula which encompasses all the others and is, in a way, the stabilised form of the code. This does not mean pure repetition, but minimal difference, the minimal inflexion between two terms, that is, the 'smallest common paradigm' that can sustain the fiction of meaning. A combinatory of differentiation internal to the painterly object as well as to the consumer object, this simulation contracts, in contemporary art, to the point of being nothing more than the infinitesimal difference that still separates hyper-reality from hyperpainting. Hyperpainting claims to exhaust itself to the point of its sacrificial eclipse in the face of the real, but we know how all painting's prestige is revived in this infinitesimal difference: painting

retreats into the border that separates the painted surface and the wall. It also hides in the signature, the metaphysical sign of painting and the metaphysics of representation at the limit, where it takes itself as its own model (the 'pure gaze') and turns around itself in the compulsive repetition of the code.

The very definition of the real is *that of which it is possible to provide an equivalent reproduction*. It is a contemporary of science, which postulates that a process can be reproduced exactly within given conditions, with an industrial rationality which postulates a universal system of equivalences (classical representation is not equivalence but transcription, interpretation and commentary). At the end of this process of reproducibility, the real is not only that which can be reproduced, but *that which is always already reproduced*: the hyperreal.

So are we then at the end of the real and the end of art due to a total mutual reabsorption? No, since at the level of simulacra, hyperrealism is the apex of both art and the real, by means of a mutual exchange of the privileges and prejudices that found them. The hyperreal is beyond representation (cf. Jean-François Lyotard, 'Esquisse d'une économique de l'hyperrealisme', *L'Art vivant*, 36, 1973) only because it is entirely within simulation, in which the barriers of representation rotate crazily, an implosive madness which, far from being ex-centric, keeps its gaze fixed on the centre, on its own abyssal repetition. Analogous to the effect of an internal distance from the dream, allowing us to say that we are dreaming, hyperrealism is only the play of censorship and the perpetuation of the dream, becoming an integral part of a coded reality that it perpetuates and leaves unaltered.

In fact, hyperrealism must be interpreted in inverse manner: *today reality itself is hyperrealist*. The secret of surrealism was that the most everyday reality could become surreal, but only at privileged instants which again arose out of art and the imaginary. Today everyday, political, social, historical, economic, etc., reality has already incorporated the hyperrealist dimension of simulation so that we are now living entirely within the 'aesthetic' hallucination of reality. The old slogan 'reality is stranger than fiction', which still corresponded to the surrealist stage in the aestheticisation of life, has been outrun, since there is no longer any fiction that life can possibly confront, even as its conqueror. Reality has passed completely into the game of reality. Radical disaffection, the cool and cybernetic stage, replaces the hot, phantasmatic phase.

The consummate enjoyment [*jouissance*] of the signs of guilt, despair, violence and death are replacing guilt, anxiety and even death in the total euphoria of simulation. This euphoria aims to abolish cause and effect, origin and end, and replace them with reduplication. Every closed system protects itself in this way from the referential and the anxiety of the referential, as well as from all metalanguage that the system wards off by operating its own metalanguage, that is, by duplicating itself as its own critique. In simulation, the metalinguistic illusion reduplicates and completes the referential illusion (the pathetic hallucination of the sign and the pathetic hallucination of the real).

'It's a circus', 'it's a theatre', 'it's a movie'; all these old adages are ancient naturalist denunciations. This is no longer what is at issue. What is at issue this time is *turning the real into a satellite*, putting an undefinable reality with no common measure into orbit with the phantasma that once illustrated it. This satellisation has subsequently been materialised as the two-room-kitchen-shower which we really have sent into orbit, to the 'spatial power' you could say, with the latest lunar module. The most everyday aspect of the terrestrial environment raised to the rank of a cosmic value, an absolute decor, hypostatised in space. This is the end of metaphysics and the beginning of the era of hyperreality.[4] The spatial transcendence of the banality of the two-room apartment by a cool, machinic figuration in hyperrealism[5] tells us only one thing, however: this module, such as it is, participates in a hyperspace of representation where everyone is already in possession of the technical means for the instant reproduction of his or her own life. Thus the *Tupolev*'s pilots who crashed in Bourget were able, by means of their cameras, to see themselves dying at first hand. This is nothing other than the short-circuit of the response by the question in the test, a process of instant renewal whereby reality is immediately contaminated by its simulacrum.

A specific class of allegorical and somewhat diabolical objects used to exist, made up of mirrors, images, works of art (concepts?). Although simulacra, they were transparent and manifest (you could distinguish craftsmanship from the counterfeit) with their own characteristic style and *savoir-faire*. Pleasure, then, consisted in locating what was 'natural' within what was artificial and counterfeit. Today, where the real and the imaginary are intermixed in one and the same operational totality, aesthetic fascination reigns supreme: with subliminal perception (a sort of sixth sense) of special effects, editing and script, reality is overexposed to the glare of models. This is no longer a space of production, but a reading strip, a coding and decoding strip, magnetised by signs. Aesthetic reality is no longer achieved through art's premeditation and distancing, but by its elevation to the second degree, to the power of two, by the anticipation and immanence of the code. A kind of unintentional parody hovers over everything, a tactical simulation, a consummate aesthetic enjoyment, is attached to the indefinable play of reading and the rules of the game. Travelling signs, media, fashion and models, the blind but brilliant ambience of simulacra.

Art has for a long time prefigured this turn, by veering towards what today is a turn to everyday life. Very early on the work of art produced a double of itself as the manipulation of the signs of art, bringing about an oversignification of art, or, as Lévi-Strauss said, an 'academicisation of the signifier', irreversibly introducing art to the form of the sign.[vii] At this point art entered into infinite *reproduction*, with everything that doubles itself, even the banal reality of the everyday, falling by the same token under the sign of art and becoming aesthetic. The same goes for production, which we might say has today entered into aesthetic reduplication, the phase where, expelling all content and all finality, it becomes somehow abstract and non-figurative. In this way it expresses the pure form of production, taking upon itself, as art does, the value of the finality without end. Art and industry may then exchange their signs: art can become a reproductive machine (Andy Warhol) without ceasing to be art, since the machine is now nothing but a sign.[viii] Production can also lose all its social finality as its means of verification, and finally glorify in the prestigious, hyperbolic and aesthetic signs that the great industrial complexes are, 400 m high towers or the numerical mysteries of the Gross National Product.

So art is everywhere, since artifice lies at the heart of reality. So art is dead, since not only is its critical transcendence dead, but reality itself, entirely impregnated by an aesthetic that holds onto its very structurality, has become inseparable from its own image. It no longer even has the time to take on the effect of reality. Reality is no longer stranger than fiction: it captures every dream before it can take on the dream effect. A schizophrenic vertigo of serial signs that have no counterfeit, no possible sublimation, and are immanent to their own repetition – who will say where the reality they simulate now lies? They no longer even repress anything (which, if you like, keeps simulation from entering the sphere of psychosis): even the primary processes have been annihilated. The cool universe of digitality absorbs the universe of metaphor and metonymy. The simulation principle dominates the reality principle as well as the pleasure principle.

[vii] Claude Lévi-Strauss, a contemporary French anthropologist, led the introduction of structuralism into the human sciences after World War II.

[viii] Designer, painter and personality Andy Warhol (1928–87) was the most famous representative of Pop Art.

Notes

1 If it were only a question of the ascendancy of exchange-value over use-value (or the ascendancy of the structural over the functional dimension of language), then Marx and Saussure have already signalled it. Marx almost turns use-value into the medium or the alibi, pure and simple, of exchange-value. His entire analysis is based on the principle of equivalence at the core of the system of exchange-value. But if *equivalence* is at the core of the system, there is no *indeterminacy* in the global system (there is always a dialectical determinacy and finality of the mode of production). The current system, however, is itself based on indeterminacy, and draws impetus from it. Conversely, it is haunted by the death of all determinacy.

2 Theoretical production, like material production, loses its determinacy and begins to turn around itself, slipping abyssally towards a reality that cannot be found. This is where we are today: undecidability, the era of *floating theories*, as much as floating money. No matter what perspective they come from (the psychoanalytic included), no matter with what violence they struggle and claim to rediscover an immanence, or a movement without systems of reference (Deleuze, Lyotard, etc.), all contemporary theories are floating and have no meaning other than to serve as signs for one another. It is pointless to insist on their coherence with some 'reality', whatever that might be. The system has removed every secure reference from theory as it has from any other labour power. Theory no longer has any use-value, the theoretical mirror of production has also cracked. So much the better. What I mean is that the very undecidability of theory is an effect of the code. Let there be no illusions: there is no schizophrenic 'drift' about this flotation of theories, where flows pass freely over the body without organs (of what, capital?). It merely signifies that any theory can from now on be exchanged against any other according to variable exchange rates, but without any longer being invested anywhere, unless it is the mirror of their writing.

3 Furthermore, there is a flagrant contradiction in Monod's book, reflecting the ambiguity of all contemporary science: its discourse is directed at the code, that is, at third-order simulacra, but it still follows second-order 'scientific' schemata such as objectivity, the scientific 'ethic' of knowledge, the truth-principle and the transcendence of science, and so on. These things are all incompatible with third-order models of indeterminacy.

4 The coefficient of reality is proportionate to the reserve of the imaginary that gives it its specific weight. This is true of terrestrial as well as space exploration: when there is no more virgin, and hence available to the imaginary, territory, when the map covers the whole territory, something like the reality principle disappears. In this sense, the conquest of space constitutes an irreversible threshold on the way to the loss of terrestrial references. Reality haemorrhages to the precise extent that the limits of an internally coherent universe are infinitely pushed back. The conquest of space comes after the conquest of the planet, as the last phantasmatic attempt to extend

the jurisdiction of the real (for example, when the flag, technology and two-room apartments are carried to the moon); it is even an attempt to substantiate concepts or territorialise the unconscious, which is equivalent to the derealisation of human space, or its reversal into a hyperreality of simulation.

5 What about the cool figuration of the metallic caravan and the supermarket so beloved of the hyperrealists, or the Campbell's soup cans dear to Andy Warhol, or even that of the Mona Lisa when it was satellited into planetary orbit as the absolute model of the earth's art. The Mona Lisa was not even sent as a work of art, but as a planetary simulacrum where a whole world bears testimony to its existence (testifying, in reality, to its own death) for the gaze of a future universe.

chapter thirty

"The Sex Which is Not One"

Luce Irigaray

Luce Irigaray (1930–) is a key figure in French feminist thought, which has integrated feminism, postmodern theories of signs, and psychoanalysis. Expelled from the Paris psychoanalytic association and the University of Paris after publication of her book, *Speculum of the Other Woman* (1974), she continued to work as a practising psychoanalyst, and remained associated with the *Centre Nationale de la Recherche Scientifique*. For Irigaray, female experience, marginalized by traditional philosophical inquiry, registers plurality and difference more deeply than does male experience. Rather than minimize gender difference Irigaray insists on its importance, denying that the categories and ideals of the dominant philosophical tradition can capture the characteristic experience and thought of women. One effect of this view is a radical denial of the Enlightenment conception of universal reason.

Female sexuality has always been theorized within masculine parameters. Thus, the opposition "viril"[i] clitoral activity/"feminine" vaginal passivity which Freud – and many others – claims are alternative behaviors or steps in the process of becoming a sexually normal woman, seems prescribed more by the practice of masculine sexuality than by anything else. For the clitoris is thought of as a little penis which is pleasurable to masturbate, as long as the anxiety of castration does not exist (for the little boy), while the vagina derives its value from the "home" it offers the male penis when the now forbidden hand must find a substitute to take its place in giving pleasure.

According to these theorists, woman's erogenous zones are no more than a clitoris-sex, which cannot stand up in comparison with the valued phallic organ; or a hole-envelope, a sheath which surrounds and rubs the penis

---

Luce Irigaray, "The Sex Which is Not One," trans. Claudia Reeder, in *New French Feminisms*, ed. Elaine Marks and Isabelle de Courtivron (New York: Schoken, 1981), pp. 99–106.

[i] Virile, masculine.

461

during coition; a nonsex organ or a masculine sex organ turned inside out in order to caress itself.

Woman and her pleasure are not mentioned in this conception of the sexual relationship. Her fate is one of "lack," "atrophy" (of her genitals), and "penis envy,"[ii] since the penis is the only recognized sex organ of any worth. Therefore she tries to appropriate it for herself, by all the means at her disposal: by her somewhat servile love of the father-husband capable of giving it to her; by her desire of a penis-child, preferably male; by gaining access to those cultural values which are still "by right" reserved for males alone and are therefore always masculine, etc. Woman lives her desire only as an attempt to possess at long last the equivalent of the male sex organ.

All of that seems rather foreign to her pleasure however, unless she remains within the dominant phallic economy. Thus, for example, woman's autoeroticism is very different from man's. He needs an instrument in order to touch himself: his hand, woman's genitals, language – And this self-stimulation requires a minimum of activity. But a woman touches herself by and within herself directly, without mediation, and before any distinction between activity and passivity is possible. A woman "touches herself" constantly without anyone being able to forbid her to do so, for her sex is composed of two lips which embrace continually. Thus, within herself she is already two – but not divisible into ones – who stimulate each other.

This autoeroticism, which she needs in order not to risk the disappearance of her pleasure in the sex act, is interrupted by a violent intrusion: the brutal spreading of these two lips by a violating penis. If, in order to assure an articulation between autoeroticism and heteroeroticism in coition (the encounter with the absolute other which always signifies death), the vagina must also, but not only, substitute for the little boy's hand, how can woman's autoeroticism possibly be perpetuated in the classic representation of sexuality? Will she not indeed be left the impossible choice between defensive virginity, fiercely turned back upon itself, or a body open for penetration, which no longer recognizes in its "hole" of a sex organ the pleasure of retouching itself? The almost exclusive, and ever so anxious, attention accorded the erection in Occidental sexuality proves to what extent the imaginary[iii] that commands it is foreign to everything female. For the most part, one finds in Occidental sexuality nothing more than imperatives dictated by rivalry among males: the "strongest" being the one who "gets it up the most," who has the longest, thickest, hardest penis or

[ii] Freud attributed to girls a disappointment over not having a penis.

[iii] A concept originally formulated by French psychoanalyst Jacques Lacan (1901–81). The "imaginary" refers to the psychological images held by a person or a culture, contrasted by Lacan to the "symbolic," the impersonal code or language that structures social life. I thank Tina Chanter for advising me on Irigaray's use of this concept.

indeed the one who "pisses the farthest" (cf. little boys' games). These imperatives can also be dictated by sado-masochist fantasies, which in turn are ordered by the relationship between man and mother: his desire to force open, to penetrate, to appropriate for himself the mystery of the stomach in which he was conceived, the secret of his conception, of his "origin." Desire-need, also, once again, to make blood flow in order to revive a very ancient – intrauterine, undoubtedly, but also prehistoric – relation to the maternal.

Woman, in this sexual imaginary, is only a more or less complacent facilitator for the working out of man's fantasies. It is possible, and even certain, that she experiences vicarious pleasure there, but this pleasure is above all a masochistic prostitution of her body to a desire that is not her own and that leaves her in her well-known state of dependency. Not knowing what she wants, ready for anything, even asking for more, if only he will "take" her as the "object" of *his* pleasure, she will not say what *she* wants. Moreover, she does not know, or no longer knows, what she wants. As Freud admits, the beginnings of the sexual life of the little girl are so "obscure," so "faded by the years," that one would have to dig very deep in order to find, behind the traces of this civilization, this history, the vestiges of a more archaic civilization which could give some indication as to what woman's sexuality is all about. This very ancient civilization undoubtedly would not have the same language, the same alphabet – Woman's desire most likely does not speak the same language as man's desire, and it probably has been covered over by the logic that has dominated the West since the Greeks.

In this logic, the prevalence of the gaze, discrimination of form, and individualization of form is particularly foreign to female eroticism. Woman finds pleasure more in touch than in sight and her entrance into a dominant scopic economy signifies, once again, her relegation to passivity: she will be the beautiful object. Although her body is in this way eroticized and solicited to a double movement between exhibition and pudic retreat in order to excite the instincts of the "subject," her sex organ represents the horror of having nothing to see. In this system of representation and desire, the vagina is a flaw, a hole in the representation's scoptophilic objective. It was admitted already in Greek statuary that this "nothing to be seen" must be excluded, rejected, from such a scene of representation. Woman's sexual organs are simply absent from this scene: they are masked and her "slit" is sewn up.

In addition, this sex organ which offers nothing to the view has no distinctive form of its own. Although woman finds pleasure precisely in this incompleteness of the form of her sex organ, which is why it retouches itself indefinitely, her pleasure is denied by a civilization that privileges phallomorphism. The value accorded to the only definable form excludes the form

463

involved in female autoeroticism. The *one* of form, the individual sex, proper name, literal meaning – supersedes, by spreading apart and dividing, this touching of *at least two* (lips) which keeps woman in contact with herself, although it would be impossible to distinguish exactly what "parts" are touching each other.

Whence the mystery that she represents in a culture that claims to enumerate everything, cipher everything by units, inventory everything by individualities. *She is neither one nor two.* She cannot, strictly speaking, be determined either as one person or as two. She renders any definition inadequate. Moreover she has no "proper" name. And her sex organ, which is not *a* sex organ, is counted as *no* sex organ. It is the negative, the opposite, the reverse, the counterpart, of the only visible and morphologically designatable sex organ (even if it does pose a few problems in its passage from erection to detumescence): the penis.

But woman holds the secret of the "thickness" of this "form," its many-layered volume, its metamorphosis from smaller to larger and vice versa, and even the intervals at which this change takes place. Without even knowing it. When she is asked to maintain, to revive, man's desire, what this means in terms of the value of her own desire is neglected. Moreover, she is not aware of her desire, at least not explicitly. But the force and continuity of her desire are capable of nurturing all the "feminine" masquerades that are expected of her for a long time.

It is true that she still has the child, with whom her appetite for touching, for contact, is given free reign, unless this appetite is already lost, or alienated by the taboo placed upon touching in a largely obsessional civilization. In her relation to the child she finds compensatory pleasure for the frustrations she encounters all too often in sexual relations proper. Thus maternity supplants the deficiencies of repressed female sexuality. Is it possible that man and woman no longer even caress each other except indirectly through the mediation between them represented by the child? Preferably male. Man, identified with his son, rediscovers the pleasure of maternal coddling; woman retouches herself in fondling that part of her body: her baby-penis-clitoris.

What that entails for the amorous trio has been clearly spelled out. The Oedipal interdict seems, however, a rather artificial and imprecise law – even though it is the very means of perpetuating the authoritarian discourse of fathers – when it is decreed in a culture where sexual relations are impracticable, since the desire of man and the desire of woman are so foreign to each other. Each of them is forced to search for some common meeting ground by indirect means: either an archaic, sensory relation to the mother's body, or a current, active or passive prolongation of the law of the father. Their attempts are characterized by regressive emotional behavior and the exchange of words so far from the realm of the sexual that they are completely exiled from it. "Mother" and "father" dominate the couple's functioning, but only as social roles. The division of labor prevents them from making love. They produce or reproduce. Not knowing too well how to use their leisure. If indeed they have any, if moreover they want to have any leisure. For what can be done with leisure? What substitute for amorous invention can be created?

We could go on and on – but perhaps we should return to the repressed female imaginary? Thus woman does not have a sex. She has at least two of them, but they cannot be identified as ones. Indeed she has many more of them than that. Her sexuality, always at least double, is in fact *plural*. Plural as culture now wishes to be plural? Plural as the manner in which current texts are written, with very little knowledge of the censorship from which they arise? Indeed, woman's pleasure does not have to choose between clitoral activity and vaginal passivity, for example. The pleasure of the vaginal caress does not have to substitute itself for the pleasure of the clitoral caress. Both contribute irreplaceably to woman's pleasure but they are only two caresses among many to do so. Caressing the breasts, touching the vulva, opening the lips, gently stroking the posterior wall of the vagina, lightly massaging the cervix, etc., evoke a few of the most specifically female pleasures. They remain rather unfamiliar pleasures in the sexual difference as it is currently imagined, or rather as it is currently ignored: the other sex being only the indispensable complement of the only sex.

But *woman has sex organs just about everywhere*. She experiences pleasure almost everywhere. Even without speaking of the hysterization of her entire body, one can say that the geography of her pleasure is much more diversified, more multiple in its differences, more complex, more subtle, than is imagined – in an imaginary centered a bit too much on one and the same.

"She" is indefinitely other in herself. That is undoubtedly the reason she is called temperamental, incomprehensible, perturbed, capricious – not to mention her language in which "she" goes off in all directions and in which "he" is unable to discern the coherence of any meaning. Contradictory words seem a little crazy to the logic of reason, and inaudible for him who listens with ready-made grids, a code prepared in advance. In her statements – at least when she dares to speak out – woman retouches herself constantly. She just barely separates from herself some chatter, an exclamation, a half-secret, a sentence left in suspense – When she returns to it, it is only to set out again from another point of pleasure or pain. One must listen to her differently in order to hear an *"other meaning" which is constantly in the process of weaving itself, at the same time ceaselessly embracing words and yet casting them off to avoid becoming fixed, immobilized.* For when "she" says something, it is already no longer identical to what

465

she means. Moreover, her statements are never identical to anything. Their distinguishing feature is one of contiguity. They touch (*upon*). And when they wander too far from this nearness, she stops and begins again from "zero": her body-sex organ.

It is therefore useless to trap women into giving an exact definition of what they mean, to make them repeat (themselves) so the meaning will be clear. They are already elsewhere than in this discursive machinery where you claim to take them by surprise. They have turned back within themselves, which does not mean the same thing as "within yourself." They do not experience the same interiority that you do and which perhaps you mistakenly presume they share. "Within themselves" means *in the privacy of this silent, multiple, diffuse tact.* If you ask them insistently what they are thinking about, they can only reply: nothing. Everything.

Thus they desire at the same time nothing and everything. It is always more and other than this *one* – of sex, for example – that you give them, that you attribute to them and which is often interpreted, and feared, as a sort of insatiable hunger, a voracity which will engulf you entirely. While in fact it is really a question of another economy which diverts the linearity of a project, undermines the target-object of a desire, explodes the polarization of desire on only one pleasure, and disconcerts fidelity to only one discourse –

Must the multiple nature of female desire and language be understood as the fragmentary, scattered remains of a raped or denied sexuality? This is not an easy question to answer. The rejection, the exclusion of a female imaginary undoubtedly places woman in a position where she can experience herself only fragmentarily as waste or as excess in the little structured margins of a dominant ideology, this mirror entrusted by the (masculine) "subject" with the task of reflecting and redoubling himself. The role of "femininity" is prescribed moreover by this masculine specula(riza)tion and corresponds only slightly to woman's desire, which is recuperated only secretly, in hiding, and in a disturbing and unpardonable manner.

But if the female imaginary happened to unfold, if it happened to come into play other than as pieces, scraps, deprived of their assemblage, would it present itself for all that as *a* universe? Would it indeed be volume rather than surface? No. Unless female imaginary is taken to mean, once again, the prerogative of the maternal over the female. This maternal would be phallic in nature however, closed in upon the jealous possession of its valuable product, and competing with man in his esteem for surplus. In this race for power, woman loses the uniqueness of her pleasure. By diminishing herself in volume, she renounces the pleasure derived from the nonsuture of her lips: she is a mother certainly, but she is a virgin mother. Mythology long ago assigned this role to her in which she is allowed a certain social power as long as she is reduced, with her own complicity, to sexual impotence.

Thus a woman's (re) discovery of herself can only signify the possibility of not sacrificing any of her pleasures to another, of not identifying with anyone in particular, of never being simply one. It is a sort of universe in expansion for which no limits could be fixed and which, for all that, would not be incoherency. Nor would it be the polymorphic perversion of the infant during which its erogenous zones await their consolidation under the primacy of the phallus.

Woman would always remain multiple, but she would be protected from dispersion because the other is a part of her, and is autoerotically familiar to her. That does not mean that she would appropriate the other for herself, that she would make it her property. Property and propriety are undoubtedly rather foreign to all that is female. At least sexually. *Nearness*, however, is not foreign to woman, a nearness so close that any identification of one or the other, and therefore any form of property, is impossible. Woman enjoys a closeness with the other that is *so near she cannot possess it, any more than she can possess herself*. She constantly trades herself for the other without any possible identification of either one of them. Woman's pleasure, which grows indefinitely from its passage in/through the other, poses a problem for any current economy in that all computations that attempt to account for woman's incalculable pleasure are irremediably destined to fail.

However, in order for woman to arrive at the point where she can enjoy her pleasure as a woman, a long detour by the analysis of the various systems of oppression which affect her is certainly necessary. By claiming to resort to pleasure alone as the solution to her problem, she runs the risk of missing the reconsideration of a social practice upon which *her* pleasure depends.

For woman is traditionally use-value for man, exchange-value among men.[iv] Merchandise, then. This makes her the guardian of matter whose price will be determined by "subjects": workers, tradesmen, consumers, according to the standard of their work and their need-desire. Women are marked phallically by their fathers, husbands, procurers. This stamp(ing) determines their value in sexual commerce. Woman is never anything more than the scene of more or less rival exchange between two men, even when they are competing for the possession of mother-earth.

How can this object of transaction assert a right to pleasure without extricating itself from the established commercial system? How can this merchandise relate to other goods on the market other than with aggressive

---

[iv] Irigaray is employing the Marxist distinction between value for actual use and value as exchangeable commodity.

jealousy? How can raw materials possess themselves without provoking in the consumer fear of the disappearance of his nourishing soil? How can this exchange in nothingness that can be defined in "proper" terms of woman's desire not seem to be pure enticement, folly, all too quickly covered over by a more sensible discourse and an apparently more tangible system of values?

A woman's evolution, however radical it might seek to be, would not suffice then to liberate woman's desire. Neither political theory nor political practice have yet resolved nor sufficiently taken into account this historical problem, although Marxism has announced its importance. But women are not, strictly speaking, a class and their dispersion in several classes makes their political struggle complex and their demands sometimes contradictory.

Their underdeveloped condition stemming from their submission by/to a culture which oppresses them, uses them, cashes in on them, still remains. Women reap no advantage from this situation except that of their quasi-monopoly of masochistic pleasure, housework, and reproduction. The power of slaves? It is considerable since the master is not necessarily well served in matters of pleasure. Therefore, the inversion of the relationship, especially in sexual economy, does not seem to be an enviable objective.

But if women are to preserve their auto-eroticism, their homo-sexuality, and let it flourish, would not the renunciation of heterosexual pleasure simply be another form of this amputation of power that is traditionally associated with women? Would this renunciation not be a new incarceration, a new cloister that women would willingly build? Let women tacitly go on strike, avoid men long enough to learn to defend their desire notably by their speech, let them discover the love of other women protected from that imperious choice of men which puts them in a position of rival goods, let them forge a social status which demands recognition, let them earn their living in order to leave behind their condition of prostitute – These are certainly indispensable steps in their effort to escape their proletarization on the trade market. But, if their goal is to reverse the existing order – even if that were possible – history would simply repeat itself and return to phallocratism, where neither women's sex, their imaginary, nor their language can exist.

chapter thirty-one

"The Death of Modern Architecture"
"What Is Post-Modernism?"

Charles Jencks

Charles Jencks (1939–   ), architect and architectural writer, was in 1975 the first to use the term "post-modern" in architecture to mean a departure from modernism. His 1977 book, *The Language of Post-Modern Architecture*, made him the most well-known expositor and analyst of postmodernism and related developments in architecture. In the selection from that book which follows, Jencks famously dates the death of architectural modernism; it expired July 15, 1972, at 3:32 p.m. His subsequent work, *What Is Post-Modernism?* (1986) developed the broader cultural and intellectual meaning of postmodernism. Jencks defines postmodern architecture in terms of "double coding." A postmodern structure exhibits at least two different codes or languages, one that is modernist and one that is not. His view of postmodernism as a general cultural movement, evident in contemporary science as well as in art, links him to the positive, "revisionary" postmodernism of David Griffin.

The Death of Modern Architecture

Happily, we can date the death of modern architecture to a precise moment in time. Unlike the legal death of a person, which is becoming a complex affair of brain waves versus heartbeats, modern architecture went out with

From Charles Jencks, *The Language of Post-Modern Architecture* (New York: Rizzoli, 1984), Part One, "The Death of Modern Architecture," pp. 9–10; and *What Is Post-Modernism?* (London: Academy Editions, 1986), from chapter 2, pp. 14–20, and from chapter 7, pp. 57–9.

469

a bang. That many people didn't notice, and no one was seen to mourn, does not make the sudden extinction any less of a fact, and that many designers are still trying to administer the kiss of life does not mean that it has been miraculously resurrected. No, it expired finally and completely in 1972, after having been flogged to death remorselessly for ten years by critics such as Jane Jacobs; and the fact that many so-called modern architects still go around practising a trade as if it were alive can be taken as one of the great curiosities of our age (like the British Monarchy giving life-prolonging drugs to 'The Royal Company of Archers' or 'The Extra Women of the Bedchamber').

Modern Architecture died in St Louis, Missouri on July 15, 1972 at 3.32 p.m. (or thereabouts) when the infamous Pruitt-lgoe scheme, or rather several of its slab blocks, were given the final *coup de grâce* by dynamite. Previously it had been vandalised, mutilated and defaced by its black inhabitants, and although millions of dollars were pumped back, trying to keep it alive (fixing the broken elevators, repairing smashed windows, repainting), it was finally put out of its misery. Boom, boom, boom.

Without doubt, the ruins should be kept, the remains should have a preservation order slapped on them, so that we keep a live memory of this failure in planning and architecture. Like the folly or artificial ruin – constructed on the estate of an eighteenth-century English eccentric to provide him with instructive reminders of former vanities and glories – we should learn to value and protect our former disasters. As Oscar Wilde said, 'experience is the name we give to our mistakes', and there is a certain health in leaving them judiciously scattered around the landscape as continual lessons.

Pruitt-lgoe was constructed according to the most progressive ideals of CIAM (the Congress of International Modern Architects) and it won an award from the American Institute of Architects when it was designed in 1951. It consisted of elegant slab blocks fourteen storeys high with rational 'streets in the air' (which were safe from cars, but as it turned out, not safe from crime); 'sun, space and greenery', which Le Corbusier called the 'three essential joys of urbanism' (instead of conventional streets, gardens and semi-private space, which he banished). It had a separation of pedestrian and vehicular traffic, the provision of play space, and local amenities such as laundries, crèches and gossip centres – all rational substitutes for traditional patterns. Moreover, its Purist style, its clean, salubrious hospital metaphor, was meant to instil, by good example, corresponding virtues in the inhabitants. Good form was to lead to good content, or at least good conduct; the intelligent planning of abstract space was to promote healthy behaviour.

Alas, such simplistic ideas, taken over from philosophic doctrines of Rationalism, Behaviourism and Pragmatism, proved as irrational as the

philosophies themselves. Modern Architecture, as the son of the Enlightenment, was an heir to its congenital naïvities too great and awe-inspiring to
warrant refutation in a book on mere building. I will concentrate here, in
this first part, on the demise of a very small branch of a big bad tree; but
to be fair it should be pointed out that modern architecture is the offshoot
of modern painting, the modern movements in all the arts. Like rational
schooling, rational health and rational design of women's bloomers, it has
the faults of an age trying to reinvent itself totally on rational grounds.
These shortcomings are now well known, thanks to the writings of Ivan
Illich, Jacques Ellul, E. F. Schumacher, Michael Oakshott and Hannah
Arendt, and the overall misconceptions of Rationalism will not be dwelt
upon. They are assumed for my purposes. Rather than a deep extended
attack on modern architecture, showing how its ills relate very closely to
the prevailing philosophies of the modern age, I will attempt a caricature,
a polemic. The virtue of this genre (as well as its vice) is its license to cut
through the large generalities with a certain abandon and enjoyment,
overlooking all the exceptions and subtleties of the argument. Caricature is
of course not the whole truth. Daumier's drawings didn't really show what
nineteenth-century poverty was about, but rather gave a highly selective
view of *some* truths. Let us then romp through the desolation of modern
architecture, and the destruction of our cities, like some Martian tourist out
on an earthbound excursion, visiting the archaeological sites with a
superior disinterest, bemused by the sad but instructive mistakes of a
former architectural civilisation. After all, since it is fairly dead, we might
as well enjoy picking over the corpse.

What Is Post-Modernism?

Post-Modernism, like Modernism, varies for each art both in its motives and
time-frame, and here I shall define it just in the field with which I am most
involved – architecture. The responsibility for introducing it into the
architectural subconscious lies with Joseph Hudnut who, at Harvard with
Walter Gropius, may have wished to give this pioneer of the Modern
Movement a few sleepless nights. At any rate, he used the term in the title
of an article published in 1945 called 'the post-modern house' (all lower
case, as was Bauhaus practice),[i] but didn't mention it in the body of the
text or define it polemically. Except for an occasional slip here and there,

---

[i] The Bauhaus school (*Staatliches Bauhaus*, or Public House of Building), a German School
  of design from 1919 to 1933, founded by Walter Gropius, was part of the Modernist
  movement in architecture.

by Philip Johnson or Nikolaus Pevsner, it wasn't used until my own writing on the subject which started in 1975.[1] In that first year of lecturing and polemicising in Europe and America, I used it as a temporising label, as a definition to describe where we had left rather than where we were going. The observable fact was that architects as various as Ralph Erskine, Robert Venturi, Lucien Kroll, the Krier brothers and Team Ten had all departed from Modernism and set off in different directions which *kept a trace of their common departure.* To this day I would define Post-Modernism as I did in 1978 as *double coding: the combination of Modern techniques with something else (usually traditional building) in order for architecture to communicate with the public and a concerned minority, usually other architects.* The point of this double coding was itself double. Modern architecture had failed to remain credible partly because it didn't communicate effectively with its ultimate users – the main argument of my book *The Language of Post-Modern Architecture* – and partly because it didn't make effective links with the city and history. Thus the solution I perceived and defined as Post-Modern: an architecture that was professionally based *and* popular as well as one that was based on new techniques *and* old patterns. Double coding to simplify means both elite/popular and new/old and there are compelling reasons for these opposite pairings. Today's Post-Modern architects were trained by Modernists, and are committed to using contemporary technology as well as facing current social reality. These commitments are enough to distinguish them from revivalists or traditionalists, a point worth stressing since it creates their hybrid language, the style of Post-Modern architecture. The same is not completely true of Post-Modern artists and writers who may use traditional techniques of narrative and representation in a more straightforward way. Yet all the creators who could be called Post-Modern keep something of a Modern sensibility – some intention which distinguishes their work from that of revivalists – whether this is irony, parody, displacement, complexity, eclecticism, realism or any number of contemporary tactics and goals. As I mentioned in the foreword, Post-Modernism has the essential double meaning: the continuation of Modernism and its transcendence.

The main motive for Post-Modern architecture is obviously the social failure of Modern architecture, its mythical 'death' announced repeatedly over ten years. In 1968, an English tower block of housing, Ronan Point, suffered what was called 'cumulative collapse' as its floors gave way after an explosion. In 1972, many slab blocks of housing were intentionally blown up at Pruitt-Igoe in St Louis. By the mid 1970s, these explosions were becoming a quite frequent method of dealing with the failures of Modernist building methods: cheap prefabrication, lack of personal 'defensible' space and the alienating housing estate. The 'death' of Modern architecture and its ideology of progress which offered technical solutions to social problems was seen by everyone in a vivid way. The destruction of the central city and historical fabric was almost equally apparent to the populace and again these popular, social motives should be stressed because they aren't quite the same in painting, film, dance or literature. There is no similar, vivid 'death' of Modernism in these fields, nor perhaps the same social motivation that one finds in Post-Modern architecture. But even in Post-Modern literature there is a social motive for using past forms in an ironic way. Umberto Eco has described this irony or double coding: 'I think of the postmodern attitude as that of a man who loves a very cultivated woman and knows he cannot say to her, "I love you madly", because he knows that she knows (and that she knows that he knows) that these words have already been written by Barbara Cartland. Still, there is a solution. He can say, "As Barbara Cartland would put it, I love you madly". At this point, having avoided false innocence, having said clearly that it is no longer possible to speak innocently, he will nevertheless have said what he wanted to say to the woman: that he loves her, but he loves her in an age of lost innocence. If the woman goes along with this, she will have received a declaration of love all the same. Neither of the two speakers will feel innocent, both will have accepted the challenge of the past, of the already said, which cannot be eliminated, both will consciously and with pleasure play the game of irony . . . But both will have succeeded, once again, in speaking of love.'[2]

Thus Eco underlines the lover's use of Post-Modern double coding and extends it, of course, to the novelist's and poet's social use of previous forms. Faced with a restrictive Modernism, a minimalism of means and ends, writers such as John Barth have felt just as restricted as architects forced to build in the International Style,[ii] or using only glass and steel. The most notable, and perhaps the best, use of this double coding in architecture is James Stirling's addition to the Staatsgalerie in Stuttgart. Here one can find the fabric of the city and the existing museum extended in amusing and ironic ways. The U-shaped palazzo form of the old gallery is echoed and placed on a high plinth, or 'Acropolis', above the traffic. But this classical base holds a very real and necessary parking garage, one that is ironically indicated by stones which have 'fallen', like ruins, to the ground. The resultant holes show the real construction – not the thick marble blocks of the real Acropolis, but a steel frame holding stone cladding which allows the air ventilation required by law. One can sit on these false ruins and ponder the truth of our lost innocence: that we live in an age which can build with beautiful, expressive masonry as long as we make it skin-deep and hang it on a steel skeleton. A Modernist would of course

---

[ii] The dominant style of world architecture which grew out of the modernism of Walter Gropius, Ludwig Mies van der Rohe, and Le Corbusier.

deny himself and us this pleasure for a number of reasons: 'truth to materials', 'logical consistency', 'straightforwardness', 'simplicity' – all the values and rhetorical tropes celebrated by such Modernists as Le Corbusier and Mies van der Rohe.

Stirling, by contrast and like the lovers of Umberto Eco, wants to communicate more and different values. To signify the permanent nature of the museum, he has used traditional rustication and classical forms including an Egyptian cornice, an open-air Pantheon, and segmental arches. These are beautiful in an understated and conventional way, but they aren't revivalist either because of small distortions, or the use of a modern material such as reinforced concrete. They say, 'We are beautiful like the Acropolis or Pantheon, but we are also based on concrete technology and deciet.' The extreme form of this double coding is visible at the entry points: a steel temple outline which announces the taxi drop-off point, and the Modernist steel canopies which tell the public where to walk in. These forms and colours are reminiscent of De Stijl, that quintessentially modern language, but they are collaged onto the traditional background.[iii] Thus Modernism confronts Classicism to such an extent that both Modernists and Classicists would be surprised, if not offended. There is not the simple harmony and consistency of either language or world view. It's as if Stirling were saying through his hybrid language and uneasy confrontations that we live in a complex world where we can't deny either the past and conventional beauty, or the present and current technical and social reality. Caught between this past and present, unwilling to oversimplify our situation, Stirling has produced the most 'real' beauty of Post-Modern architecture to date.

As much of this reality has to do with taste as it does with technology. Modernism failed as mass-housing and city building partly because it failed to communicate with its inhabitants and users who might not have liked the style, understood what it meant or even known how to use it. Hence the double coding, the essential definition of Post-Modernism, has been used as a strategy of communicating on various levels at once. Virtually every Post-Modern architect – Robert Venturi, Hans Hollein, Charles Moore, Robert Stern, Michael Graves, Arata Isozaki are the notable examples – use popular *and* elitist signs in their work to achieve quite different ends, and their styles are essentially hybrid. To simplify, at Stuttgart the blue and red handrails and vibrant polychromy fit in with the youth that uses the museum – they literally resemble their dayglo hair and anoraks – while the Classicism appeals more to the lovers of Schinkel. This is a very popular building with young and old and when I interviewed people

[iii] De Stijl ("The Style") was an Amsterdam group of abstract painters that thrived between the world wars, most notably represented by Piet Mondrian.

there – a group of *plein air*^{iv} painters, schoolchildren and businessmen – I found their different perceptions and tastes were accommodated and stretched. The pluralism which is so often called on to justify Post-Modernism is here a tangible reality.

This is not the place to recount the history of Post-Modern architecture, but I want to stress the ideological and social intentions which underlie this history because they are so often overlooked in the bitter debate with Modernists.[3] Even traditionalists often reduce the debate to matters of style, and thus the symbolic intentions and morality are overlooked. If one reads the writings of Robert Venturi, Denise Scott Brown, Christian Norberg-Schulz, or myself, one will find the constant notion of pluralism, the idea that the architect must design for different 'taste cultures' (in the words of the sociologist Herbert Gans) and for differing views of the good life. In any complex building, in any large city building such as an office, there will be varying tastes and functions that have to be articulated and these will inevitably lead, if the architect follows these hints, towards an eclectic style. He may pull this heterogeneity together under a Free-Style Classicism, as do many Post-Modernists today, but a trace of the pluralism will and should remain. I would even argue that 'the true and proper style' is not as they said Gothic, but some form of eclecticism, because only this can adequately encompass the pluralism that is our social and metaphysical reality. . . .

The feeling that we are living through a turning point in history is widespread. But this mood has been pervasive for the last two hundred years, a period of continuous transition. Nevertheless the types of change that affect us seem more radical and thoroughgoing than in previous years, with deep social and political consequences. Perhaps the most momentous shift of some thirty under way is the breakup of the Modernist paradigm of Marxism and centralised economic planning in socialist countries (some of which could be called State Capitalist). If Eastern Europe is turned into a neutral zone (or 'Austrianised'), if Russia and China successfully introduce 'market socialism' – a hybridisation typical of Post-Modernism – then these changes in economics and ideology of one third of humanity will be the most fundamental shift in our time.

The short-lived student movement in China shows some of the characteristic changes in style and practice. Motivated by a minority appeal for social justice and increased freedom, it was essentially a spontaneous, self-organising event dependent on decentralising technologies such as the fax, two-way radio, motor-bike, TV and telephone. These allowed instant communication locally and globally. Its style and content were quintessen-

---

^{iv} Open air, outdoor.

tially hybrid, mixing quotes from Mao with phrases taken from the French and American Revolutions and their Bills of Rights. Indeed its symbol, the Goddess of Democracy, was a mixture of French *Liberté* and the American Statue of Liberty, and it was erected across from the large portrait of Mao on the Tiananmen square. The music during the long hours of waiting varied from Chinese singing to broadcasting, on makeshift loudspeakers, the 'Ode to Joy' from Beethoven's *Ninth Symphony* with its message of global brotherhood.

Whenever an international television crew swung its cameras over the crowds, up went the two-finger salute of Winston Churchill. (Did it have some specific Chinese overtone beyond 'V for Victory'?) Headbands had dual-language slogans: 'Glasnost' above its Chinese translation (again so TV could beam the instant message around China and the English-speaking world). When the final debacle came at Tiananmen Square its impact was immediate throughout the globe because of television, and it even had some influence on the vote for democracy that was taking place in Poland at the time.[4] Just after the students were crushed, on June 4, 1989, Solidarity won an extraordinary landslide victory that neither they nor the Polish Communist Party had foreseen: all 161 seats that were open to it in the lower house, the Sejm, and 99 out of a hundred seats in the upper house, the Senate.[v] In twenty-four hours the Dictatorship of the Proletariat had taken a Leninist two-step: one back, one forward. Never had political events in these parts of the world been seen, communicated, analysed and judged so quickly by the globe. And this quick reaction of the information world had a feedback effect on the events themselves – for the most part positive.[5]

But if there really is a shift to 'post-socialism' under way (and the term has been used of Britain since the early eighties) then it, like so many other turns in direction, will take twenty to thirty years to be completed. The previous shift to a new paradigm – that from the Medieval to the Modern – was very uneven and different for each nation, field of work and specialisation. And it took more than a hundred years. This might be the time it takes to shift to a Post-Modern world, except that today because of the information flow all change is much faster. If we date the beginning of Post-Modern movements to 1960, then we might imagine the paradigm as a whole starting to dominate the competing ones – the Traditional and Modern – by the year 2000. But the Modern world view hangs on tenaciously and, as Max Planck said of disputes in theoretical physics, one can never manage to convince one's opponents, only aim to outlive them. Already there has been a strong Modernist backlash against Post-Modern-

[v] Solidarity is the labor union that led the struggle against communist control in Poland in the 1980s.

476

ism in architecture, led by the RIBA[vi] in Britain, Deconstructionsts in America and assorted Neo-Modernists everywhere, and similar reactions can probably be found in all the arts and sciences.[vii]

Many physicists still won't accept the fundamental reality of the uncertainty principle, chaos theory and the many manifestations of Post-Modern science. With Einstein, who didn't want to give up the Modern world view of an ordered, deterministic and certain cosmos, they insist that God doesn't play dice with the universe. The prevailing paradigms in the science departments of many universities will favour modified Newtonian mechanics and Darwinian evolution in their highly elaborated 'Neo' forms, and such orthodoxies are bound to last because they still describe, quite adequately, the everyday world. The fact that Post-Newtonian and Post- Darwinian theories, of a higher order, can explain a wider range of phenomena and encompass the former theories, is not regarded as particularly significant.

For analogous reasons we can predict that much of the world will carry on happily for the next twenty years modernising and following the ideology of Modernism. After all much of it, like China, is still rural and not yet industrialised. Post-Modernism is a *stage of growth*, not an anti-Modern reaction, and before one country or people can reach it, the various stages of urbanisation, industrialisation and post-industrialisation have to occur.

However, there are developments that lead one to believe the world might shift to the paradigm by the year 2000: above all the crisis of the ecosphere. If conservative estimates of the greenhouse effect are right, by that time much of the world will be involved in a rearguard action, trying to hold back the unintended consequences of modernisation, engaged in a desperate attempt to slow down – or reverse – the inertia of long-term warming and pollution. It may just be that this common problem, or 'enemy', unites the globe in an ethical battle which some philosophers have called 'the moral equivalent of war'. Conversely some scenarios predict that the greenhouse effect may lead to autocratic repression and war. Either way it will make the world hyperconscious of the limits of modernisation, Modernism and all their cognate practices and ideas. Also it will force a consciousness of what that essential Post-Modern science, ecology, has been saying now for more than thirty years: all living and non-living things on the globe are interconnected, or capable of being linked. Indeed Modern scientists have granted such points for many years, although the paradigm they have worked with – favouring analysis, reductivism and specialisation – has not followed the implications.

[vi] The Royal Institute of British Architects.

[vii] Deconstruction is the method of critical reading developed by Jacques Derrida; "Neo-Modernism" is Jencks' own term for attempts to modify but retain Modernism.

Modern sciences have triumphed through specialising on limited parts of reality: extremely few of them, like ecology and ethology, have been holistic. Modern knowledge has progressed by analysing problems into their parts, dividing to conquer, hence the multiple branching of university departments and investigative disciplines over the last two hundred years. Only a few fields, such as philosophy, theology and sociology have made their purview the whole of knowledge, or the interconnection of disciplines, and on these rare occasions only imperfectly so. Perhaps in the future with the environmental crises and the increasing globalisation of the economy, communications and virtually every specialisation, we will be encouraged – even forced – to emphasise the things which interact, the connections between a growing economy, an ideology of constant change and waste. Those who don't realise the world is a whole are doomed to pollute it.

So one of the key shifts to the Post-Modern world will be a change in epistemology, the understanding of knowledge and how it grows and relates to other assumptions. Not only will it emphasise the continuities of nature, but the time-bound, cultural nature of knowledge. Instead of regarding the world and nature as simply there, working according to immutable laws that are eternally true, the Post-Modern view will emphasise the developmental nature of science – its perspectival distortion in time, space and culture. It will not embrace an absolute relativism and contend that one scientific hypothesis is as good as another, or as Jean-François Lyotard has argued, a complete scepticism and an end to all master narratives and beliefs. Rather, it will support relative absolutism, or fragmental holism, which insists on the developing and jumping nature of scientific growth, and the fact that all propositions of truth are time- and context-sensitive.

If the truths of Post-Modernism are culture-dependent and grow in time, this helps explain the hybrid nature of its philosophy and world view; why it is so continuously mixed, mongrel and dialectically involved with Modernism. Among the thirty or so shifts that have the prefix 'post', look at Post-Fordism. Like all the other 'posties' this concept implicates its forerunner in a complicated way. It doesn't contend that Fordism (the large corporation with central planning and mass-production) is dead, or completely transcended, or unimportant, or no longer powerful. Rather it asserts that a new level of small businesses has grown – fast-changing, creative, and networked by computer and an array of communicational systems – which has a complementary existence to large organisations. Post-Fordist enterprises may have accounted for more than 50 per cent of the new jobs in Italy and the United States during the eighties, and now they exist in a symbiotic relationship to transnationals and big companies, forming an economy that is more flexible and creative than one based simply on the Modernist and Fordist model.[6]

478

Notes

1   My own writing and lecturing on Post-Modernism in architecture started in
    1975 and 'The Rise of Post-Modern Architecture' was published in a Dutch
    book and a British magazine, *Architecture – Inner Town Government*, Eindhoven,
    July 1975, and *Architecture Association Quarterly*, No. 4, 1975. Subsequently
    Eisenman and Stern started using the term and by 1977 it had caught on. For
    a brief history see the 'Footnote on the Term' in *The Language of Post-Modern
    Architecture*, fourth edition (Academy Editions, London/Rizzoli, New York
    1984), p. 8.
2   Umberto Eco, *Postscript to The Name of the Rose* (Harcourt Brace Jovanovich,
    New York, 1984), pp. 67–8.
3   Besides my own *The Language of Post-Modern Architecture* and *Current Architec-
    ture* (Academy Editions, London/Rizzoli, New York, 1982), and *Modern
    Movements in Architecture*, second edition (Penguin Books, Harmondsworth,
    1985), see Paolo Portoghesi, *After Modern Architecture* (Rizzoli, New York,
    1982), and its updated version, *Postmodern* (Rizzoli (New York, 1983), and
    Immagini del Post-Moderno (Edizioni Chiva, Venice 1983). See also Heinrich
    Klotz, *Die Revision der Moderne, Postmoderne Architektur, 1960–1980* and
    Moderne und Postmoderne Architektur der Gegenwart 1960–1980 (Friedr. Vieweg
    & Sohn, Braunschweig/Wiesbaden, 1984). We have debated his notion of
    Post-Modern architecture as 'fiction' and this has been published in *Architec-
    tural Design*, 7/8 (1984), *Revision of the Modern*. See also my discussion of users
    and abusers of Post-Modern in 'La Bataille des étiquettes', *Nouveaux plaisirs
    d'architecture* (Centre Georges Pompidou, Paris, 1985), pp. 25–33.
4   See Timothy Garton Ash, 'Revolution in Hungary and Poland', *New York
    Review of Books*, August 17, 1989, p 10.
5   It is of course impossible to accurately measure the feedback effect of the
    information world on events in China and Poland, but effect it undoubted-
    ly had as can be judged by the authorities' attempts to counteract and
    distort it, especially in China. It appears that the Chinese sought to reas-
    sure the international business community and convey a picture of nor-
    mality and reasonableness in all dealing with foreigners *partly in reaction to*
    the televised massacre and this may, in turn, have had a restraining effect
    on their suppression. I think it's more obvious that the instant, wide-
    spread knowledge of the vote in Poland (especially in Russia) immediately
    de-legitimised the Polish Communist Party and led directly to the change
    in government on August 24th – the election of Tadeusz Mazowiecki,
    etc.
6   The phrase 'Post-Fordist' starts some time in the early 1980s in juxtaposition
    to the large corporation based on the model of Henry Ford. For a discussion of
    it within a Post-Modern context see the impressively argued book *The Condition
    of Post-Modernity*, David Harvey (Blackwell, Oxford, 1989). For a critical
    discussion of where new jobs came from – and their percentages – see 'The

Disciples of David Birch', John Chase, *Inc.*, January, 1989, pp 39–45. Companies with fewer than 100 employees, from 1969 to 1986, have in the USA created an average of 65% of the new jobs – according to the most reliable statistics. But these statistics can be questioned.

chapter thirty-two

The Postmodern Condition: A Report on Knowledge

Jean-François Lyotard

Professor of philosophy, Jean-François Lyotard (1926–) published the most famous philosophical formulation of postmodernism in 1979. His short book, actually a report to the Province of Quebec's *Conseil des Universitiés*, defines postmodernism as "incredulity regarding metanarratives," grand stories about the world and the place of inquiry in it. Lyotard claims that in the postmodern era our social "language games" – borrowing Wittgenstein's term – no longer require metanarratives to justify the utterances made in them. Simply put, postmodern culture no longer needs any form of legitimation beyond expediency or "performativity." Lyotard analyzes the production of knowledge by science, as well as the discourse of everyday social life, in terms of discontinuity, plurality, and "paralogy" (logically unjustified conclusions). The modernist notions of justification, system, proof, and the unity of science no longer hold.

The object of this study is the condition of knowledge in the most highly developed societies. I have decided to use the word *postmodern* to describe that condition. The word is in current use on the American continent among sociologists and critics; it designates the state of our culture following the transformations which, since the end of the nineteenth century, have altered the game rules for science, literature, and the arts. The present study will place these transformations in the context of the crisis of narratives.

Science has always been in conflict with narratives. Judged by the yardstick of science, the majority of them prove to be fables. But to the

Jean-François Lyotard, *The Postmodern Condition: A Report on Knowledge*, trans. Geoff Bennington and Brian Massumi (Minneapolis: University of Minnesota Press, 1984), Introduction and Sections 9 to 11, and 14, pp. xxiii–xxv, 31–47, 64–7.

extent that science does not restrict itself to stating useful regularities and seeks the truth, it is obliged to legitimate the rules of its own game. It then produces a discourse of legitimation with respect to its own status, a discourse called philosophy. I will use the term modern to designate any science that legitimates itself with reference to a metadiscourse of this kind making an explicit appeal to some grand narrative, such as the dialectics of Spirit, the hermeneutics of meaning, the emancipation of the rational or working subject, or the creation of wealth.[i] For example, the rule of consensus between the sender and addresse of a statement with truth-value is deemed acceptable if it is cast in terms of a possible unanimity between rational minds: this is the Enlightenment narrative, in which the hero of knowledge works toward a good ethico-political end – universal peace. As can be seen from this example, if a metanarrative implying a philosophy of history is used to legitimate knowledge, questions are raised concerning the validity of the institutions governing the social bond: these must be legitimated as well. Thus justice is consigned to the grand narrative in the same way as truth.

Simplifying to the extreme, I define *postmodern* as incredulity toward metanarratives. This incredulity is undoubtedly a product of progress in the sciences: but that progress in turn presupposes it. To the obsolescence of the metanarrative apparatus of legitimation corresponds, most notably, the crisis of metaphysical philosophy and of the university institution which in the past relied on it. The narrative function is losing its functors, its great hero, its great dangers, its great voyages, its great goal. It is being dispersed in clouds of narrative language elements – narrative, but also denotative, prescriptive, descriptive, and so on. Conveyed within each cloud are pragmatic valencies specific to its kind. Each of us lives at the intersection of many of these. However, we do not necessarily establish stable language combinations, and the properties of the ones we do establish are not necessarily communicable.

Thus the society of the future falls less within the province of a Newtonian anthropology (such as stucturalism or systems theory) than a pragmatics of language particles. There are many different language games – a heterogeneity of elements. They only give rise to institutions in patches – local determinism.

The decision makers, however, attempt to manage these clouds of sociality according to input/output matrices, following a logic which implies that their elements are commensurable and that the whole is determinable. They allocate our lives for the growth of power. In matters of social justice and of scientific truth alike, the legitimation of that power

---

[i] These grand narratives are what Lyotard calls "metanarratives," philosophical stories which legitimate all other discourse.

is based on its optimizing the system's performance – efficiency. The application of this criterion to all of our games necessarily entails a certain level of terror, whether soft or hard: be operational (that is, commensurable) or disappear.

The logic of maximum performance is no doubt inconsistent in many ways, particularly with respect to contradiction in the socio-economic field: it demands both less work (to lower production costs) and more (to lessen the social burden of the idle population). But our incredulity is now such that we no longer expect salvation to rise from these inconsistencies, as did Marx.

Still, the postmodern condition is as much a stranger to disenchantment as it is to the blind positivity of delegitimation. Where, after the metanarratives, can legitimacy reside? The operativity criterion is technological; it has no relevance for judging what is true or just. Is legitimacy to be found in consensus obtained through discussion, as Jürgen Habermas thinks? Such consensus does violence to the heterogeneity of language games. And invention is always born of dissension. Postmodern knowledge is not simply a tool of the authorities; it refines our sensitivity to differences and reinforces our ability to tolerate the incommensurable. Its principle is not the expert's homology, but the inventor's paralogy.

Here is the question: is a legitimation of the social bond, a just society, feasible in terms of a paradox analogous to that of scientific activity? What would such a paradox be? . . .

Narratives of the Legitimation of Knowledge

We shall examine two major versions of the narrative of legitimation. One is more political, the other more philosophical; both are of great importance in modern history, in particular in the history of knowledge and its institutions.

The subject of the first of these versions is humanity as the hero of liberty. All peoples have a right to science. If the social subject is not already the subject of scientific knowledge, it is because that has been forbidden by priests and tyrants. The right to science must be reconquered. It is understandable that this narrative would be directed more toward a politics of primary education, rather than of universities and high schools.[1] The educational policy of the French Third Republic[ii] powerfully illustrates these presuppositions.

It seems that this narrative finds it necessary to de-emphasize higher education. Accordingly, the measures adopted by Napoleon regarding

[ii] 1871–1940.

higher education are generally considered to have been motivated by the desire to produce the administrative and professional skills necessary for the stability of the State.[2] This overlooks the fact that in the context of the narrative of freedom, the State receives its legitimacy not from itself but from the people. So even if imperial politics designated the institutions of higher education as a breeding ground for the officers of the State and secondarily, for the managers of civil society, it did so because the nation as a whole was supposed to win its freedom through the spread of new domains of knowledge to the population, a process to be effected through agencies and professions within which those cadres would fulfill their functions. The same reasoning is a fortiori valid for the foundation of properly scientific institutions. The State resorts to the narrative of freedom every time it assumes direct control over the training of the "people," under the name of the "nation," in order to point them down the path of progress.[3]

With the second narrative of legitimation, the relation between science, the nation, and the State develops quite differently. It first appears with the founding, between 1807 and 1810, of the University of Berlin,[4] whose influence on the organization of higher education in the young countries of the world was to be considerable in the nineteenth and twentieth centuries.

At the time of the University's creation, the Prussian ministry had before it a project conceived by Fichte and counterproposals by Schleiermacher. Wilhelm von Humboldt had to decide the matter and came down on the side of Schleiermacher's more "liberal" option.[iii]

Reading Humboldt's report, one may be tempted to reduce his entire approach to the politics of the scientific institution to the famous dictum: "Science for its own sake." But this would be to misunderstood the ultimate aim of his policies, which is guided by the principle of legitimation we are discussing and is very close to the one Schleiermacher elucidates in a more thorough fashion.

Humboldt does indeed declare that science obeys its own rules, that the scientific institution "lives and continually renews itself on its own, with no constraint or determined goal whatsoever." But he adds that the University should orient its constituent element, science, to "the spiritual and moral training of the nation."[5] How can this *Bildung*-effect result from the disinterested pursuit of learning? Are not the State, the nation, the whole of humanity indifferent to knowledge for its own sake? What interests them, as Humboldt admits, is not learning, but "character and action."

[iii] Three German intellectuals: philosopher Johann Gottlieb Fichte; theologian Friedrich Schleiermacher (1768–1834), and philosopher and linguist Wilhelm von Humboldt (1767–1835).

The minister's adviser thus faces a major conflict, in some ways reminiscent of the split introduced by the Kantian critique between knowing and willing: it is a conflict between a language game made of denotations answerable only to the criterion of truth, and a language game governing ethical, social, and political practice that necessarily involves decisions and obligations, in other words, utterances expected to be just rather than true and which in the final analysis lie outside the realm of scientific knowledge.

However, the unification of these two sets of discourse is indispensable to the *Bildung* aimed for by Humboldt's project, which consists not only in the acquisition of learning by individuals, but also in the training of a fully legitimated subject of knowledge and society. Humboldt therefore invokes a Spirit (what Fichte calls Life), animated by three ambitions, or better, by a single, threefold aspiration: "that of deriving everything from an original principle" (corresponding to scientific activity), "that of relating everything to an ideal" (governing ethical and social practice), and "that of unifying this principle and this ideal in a single Idea" (ensuring that the scientific search for true causes always coincides with the pursuit of just ends in moral and political life). This ultimate synthesis constitutes the legitimate subject.

Humboldt adds in passing that this triple aspiration naturally inheres in the "intellectual character of the German nation."[6] This is a concession, but a discreet one, to the other narrative, to the idea that the subject of knowledge is the people. But in truth this idea is quite distant from the narrative of the legitimation of knowledge advanced by German idealism. The suspicion that men like Schleiermacher, Humboldt, and even Hegel harbor towards the State is an indication of this. If Schleiermacher fears the narrow nationalism, protectionism, utilitarianism, and positivism that guide the public authorities in matters of science, it is because the principle of science does not reside in those authorities, even indirectly. The subject of knowledge is not the people, but the speculative spirit. It is not embodied, as in France after the Revolution, in a State, but in a System. The language game of legitimation is not state-political, but philosophical.

The great function to be fulfilled by the universities is to "lay open the whole body of learning and expound both the principles and the foundations of all knowledge." For "there is no creative scientific capacity without the speculative spirit."[7] "Speculation" is here the name given the discourse on the legitimation of scientific discourse. Schools are functional; the University is speculative, that is to say, philosophical.[8] Philosophy must restore unity to learning, which has been scattered into separate sciences in laboratories and in preuniversity education; it can only achieve this in a language game that links the sciences together as moments in the becoming of spirit, in other words, which links them in a rational narration, or rather metanarration. Hegel's *Encyclopedia* (1817–27) attempts to realize this project of totalization, which was already present in Fichte and Schelling in the form of the idea of the System.

It is here, in the mechanism of developing a Life that is simultaneously Subject, that we see a return of narrative knowledge. There is a universal "history" of spirit, spirit is "life," and "life" is its own self-presentation and formulation in the ordered knowledge of all of its forms contained in the empirical sciences. The encyclopedia of German idealism is the narration of the "(hi)story" of this life-subject. But what it produces is a metanarrative, for the story's narrator must not be a people mired in the particular positivity of its traditional knowledge, nor even scientists taken as a whole, since they are sequestered in professional frameworks corresponding to their respective specialities.

The narrator must be a metasubject in the process of formulating both the legitimacy of the discourses of the empirical sciences and that of the direct institutions of popular cultures. This metasubject, in giving voice to their common grounding, realizes their implicit goal. It inhabits the speculative University. Positive science and the people are only crude versions of it. The only valid way for the nation-state itself to bring the people to expression is through the mediation of speculative knowledge.

It has been necessary to elucidate the philosophy that legitimated the foundation of the University of Berlin and was meant to be the motor both of its development and the development of contemporary knowledge. As I have said, many countries in the nineteenth and twentieth centuries adopted this university organization as a model for the foundation or reform of their own system of higher education, beginning with the United States.[9] But above all, this philosophy – which is far from dead, especially in university circles[10] – offers a particularly vivid representation of one solution to the problem of the legitimacy of knowledge.

Research and the spread of learning are not justified by invoking a principle of usefulness. The idea is not at all that science should serve the interests of the State and/or civil society. The humanist principle that humanity rises up in dignity and freedom through knowledge is left by the wayside. German idealism has recourse to a metaprinciple that simultaneously grounds the development of learning, of society, and of the State in the realization of the "life" of a Subject, called "divine Life" by Fichte and "Life of the spirit" by Hegel. In this perspective, knowledge first finds legitimacy within itself, and it is knowledge that is entitled to say what the State and what Society are.[11] But it can only play this role by changing levels, by ceasing to be simply the positive knowledge of its referent (nature, society, the State, etc.), becoming in addition to that the knowledge of the knowledge of the referent – that is, by becoming speculative. In the names "Life" and "Spirit," knowledge names itself.

A noteworthy result of the speculative apparatus is that all of the discourses of learning about every possible referent are taken up not from the point of view of their immediate truth-value, but in terms of the value they acquire by virtue of occupying a certain place in the itinerary of Spirit or Life – or, if preferred, a certain position in the Encyclopedia recounted by speculative discourse. That discourse cites them in the process of expounding for itself what it knows, that is, in the process of self-exposition. True knowledge, in this perspective, is always indirect knowledge; it is composed of reported statements that are incorporated into the metanarrative of a subject that guarantees their legitimacy.

The same thing applies for every variety of discourse, even if it is not a discourse of learning; examples are the discourse of law and that of the State. Contemporary hermeneutic discourse[12] is born of this presupposition, which guarantees that there is meaning to know and thus confers legitimacy upon history (and especially the history of learning). Statements are treated as their own autonyms[13] and set in motion in a way that is supposed to render them mutually engendering: these are the rules of speculative language. The University, as its name indicates, is its exclusive institution.

But, as I have said, the problem of legitimacy can be solved using the other procedures as well. The difference between them should be kept in mind: today, with the status of knowledge unbalanced and its speculative unity broken, the first version of legitimacy is gaining new vigor.

According to this version, knowledge finds its validity not within itself, not in a subject that develops by actualizing its learning possibilities, but in a practical subject – humanity. The principle of the movement animating the people is not the self-legitimation of knowledge, but the self-grounding of freedom or, if preferred, its self-management. The subject is concrete, or supposedly so, and its epic is the story of its emancipation from everything that prevents it from governing itself. It is assumed that the laws it makes for itself are just, not because they conform to some outside nature, but because the legislators are, constitutionally, the very citizens who are subject to the laws. As a result, the legislator's will – the desire that the laws be just – will always coincide with the will of the citizen, who desires the law and will therefore obey it.

Clearly, this mode of legitimation through the autonomy of the will[14] gives priority to a totally different language game, which Kant called imperative and is known today as prescriptive. The important thing is not, or not only, to legitimate denotative utterances pertaining to the truth, such as "The earth revolves around the sun," but rather to legitimate prescriptive utterances pertaining to justice, such as "Carthage must be destroyed" or "The minimum wage must be set at x dollars." In this context, the only role positive knowledge can play is to inform the practical subject about the reality within which the execution of the prescription is to be inscribed. It allows the subject to circumscribe the executable, or what it is possible to do. But the executory, what should be done, is not within the purview of positive knowledge. It is one thing for an undertaking to be possible and another for it to be just. Knowledge is no longer the subject, but in the service of the subject: its only legitimacy (though it is formidable) is the fact that it allows morality to become reality.

This introduces a relation of knowledge to society and the State which is in principle a relation of the means to the end. But scientists must cooperate only if they judge that the politics of the State, in other words the sum of its prescriptions, is just. If they feel that the civil society of which they are members is badly represented by the State, they may reject its prescriptions. This type of legitimation grants them the authority, as practical human beings, to refuse their scholarly support to a political power they judge to be unjust, in other words, not grounded in a real autonomy. They can even go so far as to use their expertise to demonstrate that such autonomy is not in fact realized in society and the State. This reintroduces the critical function of knowledge. But the fact remains that knowledge has no final legitimacy outside of serving the goals envisioned by the practical subject, the autonomous collectivity.[15]

This distribution of roles in the enterprise of legitimation is interesting from our point of view because it assumes, as against the system-subject theory, that there is no possibility that language games can be unified or totalized in any metadiscourse. Quite to the contrary, here the priority accorded prescriptive statements – uttered by the practical subject – renders them independent in principle from the statements of science, whose only remaining function is to supply this subject with information.

Two remarks:

1 It would be easy to show that Marxism has wavered between the two models of narrative legitimation I have just described. The Party takes the place of the University, the proletariat that of the people or of humanity, dialectical materialism that of speculative idealism, etc. Stalinism may be the result, with its specific relationship with the sciences: in Stalinism, the sciences only figure as citations from the metanarrative of the march towards socialism, which is the equivalent, of the life of the spirit. But on the other hand Marxism can, in conformity to the second version, develop into a form of critical knowledge by declaring that socialism is nothing other than the constitution of the autonomous subject and that the only justification for the sciences is if they give the empirical subject (the proletariat) the means to emancipate itself from alienation and repression: this was, briefly, the position of the Frankfurt School.

2 The speech Heidegger gave on May 27, 1933, on becoming rector of the university of Freiburg-in-Breisgau,[16] can be read as an unfortunate

episode in the history of legitimation.[iv] Here, speculative science has become the questioning of being. This questioning is the "destiny" of the German people, dubbed an "historico-spiritual people." To this subject are owed the three services of labor, defense, and knowledge. The University guarantees a metaknowledge of the three services, that is to say, science. Here, as in idealism, legitimation is achieved through a metadiscourse called science, with ontological pretensions. But here the metadiscourse is questioning, not totalizing. And the University, the home of this metadiscourse, owes its knowledge to a people whose "historic mission" is to bring that metadiscourse to fruition by working, fighting, and knowing. The calling of this people-subject is not to emancipate humanity, but to realize its "true world of the spirit," which is "the most profound power of conservation to be found within its forces of earth and blood." This insertion of the narrative of race and work into that of the spirit as a way of legitimating knowledge and its institutions is doubly unfortunate: theoretically inconsistent, it was compelling enough to find disastrous echoes in the realm of politics.

Delegitimation

In contemporary society and culture – postindustrial society, postmodern culture[17] – the question of the legitimation of knowledge is formulated in different terms. The grand narrative has lost its credibility, regardless of what mode of unification it uses, regardless of whether it is a speculative narrative or a narrative of emancipation.

The decline of narrative can be seen as an effect of the blossoming of techniques and technologies since the Second World War, which has shifted emphasis from the ends of action to its means; it can also be seen as an effect of the redeployment of advanced liberal capitalism after its retreat under the protection of Keynesianism during the period 1930–60, a renewal that has eliminated the communist alternative and valorized the individual enjoyment of goods and services.

Anytime we go searching for causes in this way we are bound to be disappointed. Even if we adopted one or the other of these hypotheses, we would still have to detail the correlation between the tendencies mentioned and the decline of the unifying and legitimating power of the grand narratives of speculation and emancipation.

It is, of course, understandable that both capitalist renewal and prosperity and the disorienting upsurge of technology would have an impact on

[iv] Heidegger became rector after joining the Nazi Party, as was required by law. He openly supported National Socialism.

the status of knowledge. But in order to understand how contemporary science could have been susceptible to those effects long before they took place, we must first locate the seeds of "delegitimation"[18] and nihilism that were inherent in the grand narratives of the nineteenth century.

First of all, the speculative apparatus maintains an ambigious relation to knowledge. It shows that knowledge is only worthy of that name to the extent that it reduplicates itself ("lifts itself up," *hebt sich auf*; is sublated) by citing its own statements in a second-level discourse (autonymy) that functions to legitimate them. This is as much as to say that, in its immediacy, denotative discourse bearing on a certain referent (a living organism, a chemical property, a physical phenomenon, etc.) does not really know what it thinks it knows. Positive science is not a form of knowledge. And speculation feeds on its suppression. The Hegelian speculative narrative thus harbors a certain skepticism toward positive learning, as Hegel himself admits.[19]

A science that has not legitimated itself is not a true science; if the discourse that was meant to legitimate it seems to belong to a prescientific form of knowledge, like a "vulgar" narrative, it is demoted to the lowest rank, that of an ideology or instrument of power. And this always happens if the rules of the science game that discourse denounces as empirical are applied to science itself.

Take for example the speculative statement: "A scientific statement is knowledge if and only if it can take its place in a universal process of engendering." The question is: Is this statement knowledge as it itself defines it? Only if it can take its place in a universal process of engendering. Which it can. All it has to do is to presuppose that such a process exists (the Life of spirit) and that it is itself an expression of that process. This presupposition, in fact, is indispensable to the speculative language game. Without it, the language of legitimation would not be legitimate; it would accompany science in a nosedive into nonsense, at least if we take idealism's word for it.

But this presupposition can also be understood in a totally different sense, one which takes us in the direction of postmodern culture: we could say, in keeping with the perspective we adopted earlier, that this presupposition defines the set of rules one must accept in order to play the speculative game.[20] Such an appraisal assumes first that we accept that the "positive" sciences represent the general mode of knowledge and second, that we understand this language to imply certain formal and axiomatic presuppositions that it must always make explicit. This is exactly what Nietzsche is doing, though with a different terminology, when he shows that "European nihilism" resulted from the truth requirement of science being turned back against itself.[21]

There thus arises an idea of perspective that is not far removed, at least in this respect, from the idea of language games. What we have here is a process of delegitimation fueled by the demand for legitimation itself. The "crisis" of scientific knowledge, signs of which have been accumulating since the end of the nineteenth century, is not born of a chance proliferation of sciences, itself an effect of progress in technology and the expansion of capitalism. It represents, rather, an internal erosion of the legitimacy principle of knowledge. There is erosion at work inside the speculative game, and by loosening the weave of the encyclopedic net in which each science was to find its place, it eventually sets them free.

The classical dividing lines between the various fields of science are thus called into question – disciplines disappear, overlappings occur at the borders between sciences, and from these new territories are born. The speculative hierarchy of learning gives way to an immanent and, as it were, "flat" network of areas of inquiry, the respective frontiers of which are in constant flux. The old "faculties" splinter into institutes and foundations of all kinds, and the universities lose their function of speculative legitimation. Stripped of the responsibility for research (which was stifled by the speculative narrative), they limit themselves to the transmission of what is judged to be established knowledge, and through didactics they guarantee the replication of teachers rather than the production of researchers. This is the state in which Nietzsche finds and condemns them.[22]

The potential for erosion intrinsic to the other legitimation procedure, the emancipation apparatus flowing from the *Aufklärung*,[v] is no less extensive than the one at work within speculative discourse. But it touches a different aspect. Its distinguishing characteristic is that it grounds the legitimation of science and truth in the autonomy of interlocutors involved in ethical, social, and political praxis. As we have seen, there are immediate problems with this form of legitimation: the difference between a denotative statement with cognitive value and a prescriptive statement with practical value is one of relevance therefore of competence. There is nothing to prove that if a statement describing a real situation is true, it follows that a prescriptive statement based upon it (the effect of which will necessarily be a modification of that reality) will be just.

Take, for example, a closed door. Between "The door is closed" and "Open the door" there is no relation of consequence as defined in propositional logic. The two statements belong to two autonomous sets of rules defining different kinds of relevance, and therefore of competence. Here, the effect of dividing reason into cognitive or theoretical reason on the one hand, and practical reason on the other, is to attack the legitimacy of the discourse of science. Not directly, but indirectly, by revealing that it is a language game

---

[v] Enlightenment.

with its own rules (of which the a priori conditions of knowledge in Kant provide a first glimpse) and that it has no special calling to supervise the game of praxis (nor the game of aesthetics, for that matter). The game of science is thus put on a par with the others.

If this "delegitimation" is pursued in the slightest and if its scope is widened (as Wittgenstein does in his own way, and thinkers such as Martin Buber and Emmanuel Lévinas in theirs)[23] the road is then open for an important current of postmodernity: science plays its own game; it is incapable of legitimating the other language games. The game of prescription, for example, escapes it. But above all, it is incapable of legitimating itself, as speculation assumed it could.

The social subject itself seems to dissolve in this dissemination of language games. The social bond is linguistic, but is not woven with a single thread. It is a fabric formed by the intersection of at least two (and in reality an indeterminate number) of language games, obeying different rules. Wittgenstein writes: "Our language can be seen as an ancient city: a maze of little streets and squares, of old and new houses, and of houses with additions from various periods; and this surrounded by a multitude of new boroughs with straight regular streets and uniform houses."[24] And to drive home that the principle of unitotality – or synthesis under the authority of a metadiscourse of knowledge – is inapplicable, he subjects the "town" of language to the old sorites paradox by asking: "how many houses or streets does it take before a town begins to be a town?"[25]

New languages are added to the old ones, forming suburbs of the old town: "the symbolism of chemistry and the notation of the infinitesimal calculus."[26] Thirty-five years later we can add to the list: machine languages, the matrices of game theory, new systems of musical notation, systems of notation for nondenotative forms of logic (temporal logics, deontic logics, modal logics), the language of the genetic code, graphs of phonological structures, and so on.

We may form a pessimistic impression of this splintering: nobody speaks all of those languages, they have no universal metalanguage, the project of the system-subject is a failure, the goal of emancipation has nothing to do with science, we are all stuck in the positivism of this or that discipline of learning, the learned scholars have turned into scientists, the diminished tasks of research have become compartmentalized and no one can master them all.[27] Speculative or humanistic philosophy is forced to relinquish its legitimation duties,[28] which explains why philosophy is facing a crisis wherever it persists in arrogating such functions and is reduced to the study of systems of logic or the history of ideas where it has been realistic enough to surrender them.

Turn-of-the-century Vienna was weaned on this pessimism: not just artists such as Musil, Kraus, Hofmannsthal, Loos, Schönberg, and Broch,

492

but also the philosophers Mach and Wittgenstein.[30] They carried awareness of and theoretical and artistic responsibility for delegitimation as far as it could be taken. We can say today that the mourning process has been completed. There is no need to start all over again. Wittgenstein's strength is that he did not opt for the positivism that was being developed by the Vienna Circle,[31] but outlined in his investigation of language games a kind of legitimation not based on performativity. That is what the postmodern world is all about. Most people have lost the nostalgia for the lost narrative. It in no way follows that they are reduced to barbarity. What saves them from it is their knowledge that legitimation can only spring from their own linguistic practice and communicational interaction. Science "smiling into its beard" at every other belief has taught them the harsh austerity of realism.[32]

Research and Its Legitimation through Performativity

Let us return to science and begin by examining the pragmatics of research. Its essential mechanisms are presently undergoing two important changes: a multiplication in methods of argumentation and a rising complexity level in the process of establishing proof.

Aristotle, Descartes, and John Stuart Mill, among others, attempted to lay down the rules governing how a denotative utterance can obtain its addressee's assent.[33] Scientific research sets no great store by these methods. As already stated, it can and does use methods the demonstrative properties of which seem to challenge classical reason. Bachelard compiled a list of them, and it is already incomplete.[34]

These languages are not employed haphazardly, however. Their use is subject to a condition we could call pragmatic: each must formulate its own rules and petition the addressee to accept them. To satisfy this condition, an axiomatic is defined that includes a definition of symbols to be used in the proposed langauge, a description of the form expressions in the language must take in order to gain acceptance (well-formed expressions), and an enumeration of the operations that may be performed on the accepted expressions (axioms in the narrow sense).[35]

But how do we know what an axiomatic should, or does in fact, contain? The conditions listed above are formal conditions. There has to be a metalanguage to determine whether a given language satisfies the formal conditions of an axiomatic; that metalanguage is logic.

At this point a brief clarification is necessary. The alternative between someone who begins by establishing an axiomatic and then uses it to produce what are defined as acceptable statements, and a scientist who begins by establishing and stating facts and then tries to discover the axiomatics of the language he used in making his statements, is not a logical alternative, but only an empirical one. It is certainly of great importance for the researcher, and also for the philosopher, but in each case the question of the validation of statements is the same.[36]

The following question is more pertinent to legitimation: By what criteria does the logician define the properties required of an axiomatic? Is there a model for scientific languages? If so, is there just one? Is it verifiable? The properties generally required of the syntax of a formal system[37] are consistency (for example, a system inconsistent with respect to negation would admit both a proposition and its opposite), syntactic completeness (the system would lose its consistency if an axiom were added to it), decidability (there must be an effective procedure for deciding whether a given proposition belongs to the system or not), and the independence of the axioms in relation to one another. Now Gödel has effectively established the existence in the arithmetic system of a proposition that is neither demonstrable nor refutable within that system; this entails that the arithmetic system fails to satisfy the condition of completeness.[38]

Since it is possible to generalize this situation, it must be accepted that all formal systems have internal limitations.[39] This applies to logic: the metalanguage it uses to describe an artificial (axiomatic) language is "natural" or "everyday" language; that language is universal, since all other languages can be translated into it, but it is not consistent with respect to negation – it allows the formation of paradoxes.[40]

This necessitates a reformulation of the question of the legitimation of knowledge. When a denotative statement is declared true, there is a presupposition that the axiomatic system within which it is decidable and demonstrable has already been formulated, that it is known to the interlocutors, and that they have accepted that it is as formally satisfactory as possible. This was the spirit in which the mathematics of the Bourbaki group[vi] was developed.[41] But analogous observations can be made for the other sciences: they owe their status to the existence of a language whose rules of functioning cannot themselves be demonstrated but are the object of a consensus among experts. These rules, or at least some of them, are requests. The request is a modality of prescription.

The argumentation required for a scientific statement to be accepted is thus subordinated to a "first" acceptance (which is in fact constantly renewed by virtue of the principle of recursion) of the rules defining the allowable means of argumentation. Two noteworthy properties of scientific

---

[vi] "Nicolas Bourbaki" was the fanciful name of a group of French mathematicians in the 1930s.

knowledge result from this: the flexibility of its means, that is, the plurality of its languages; and its character as a pragmatic game – the acceptability of the "moves" (new propositions) made in it depends on a contract drawn between the partners. Another result is that there are two different kinds of "progress" in knowledge: one corresponds to a new move (a new argument) within the established rules; the other, to the invention of new rules, in other words, a change to a new game.[42]

Obviously, a major shift in the notion of reason accompanies this new arrangement. The principle of a universal metalanguage is replaced by the principle of a plurality of formal and axiomatic systems capable of arguing the truth of denotative statements; these systems are described by a metalanguage that is universal but not consistent. What used to pass as paradox, and even paralogism, in the knowledge of classical and modern science can, in certain of these systems, acquire a new force of conviction and win the acceptance of the community of experts.[43] The language game method I have followed here can claim a modest place in this current of thought.

The other fundamental aspect of research, the production of proof, takes us in quite a different direction. It is in principle part of an argumentation process designed to win acceptance for a new statement (for example, giving testimony or presenting an exhibit in the case of judicial rhetoric).[44] But it presents a special problem: it is here that the referent ("reality") is called to the stand and cited in the debate between scientists.

I have already made the point that the question of proof is problematical since proof needs to be proven. One can begin by publishing a description of how the proof was obtained, so other scientists can check the result by repeating the same process. But the fact still has to be observed in order to stand proven. What constitutes a scientific observation? A fact that has been registered by an eye, an ear, a sense organ?[45] Senses are deceptive, and their range and powers of discrimination are limited.

This is where technology comes in. Technical devices originated as prosthetic aids for the human organs or as physiological systems whose function it is to receive data or condition the context.[46] They follow a principle, and it is the principle of optimal performance: maximizing output (the information or modifications obtained) and minimizing input (the energy expended in the process).[47] Technology is therefore a game pertaining not to the true, the just, or the beautiful, etc., but to efficiency: a technical "move" is "good" when it does better and/or expends less energy than another.

This definition of technical competence is a late development. For a long time inventions came in fits and starts, the products of chance research, or research as much or more concerned with the arts (*technai*) than with knowledge: the Greeks of the Classical period, for example, established no close relationship between knowledge and technology.[48] In the sixteenth and seventeenth centuries, the work of "perspectors" was still a matter of curiosity and artistic innovation.[49] This was the case until the end of the eighteenth century.[50] And it can be maintained that even today "wildcat" activities of technical invention, sometimes related to *bricolage*,[vii] still go on outside the imperatives of scientific argumentation.[51]

Nonetheless, the need for proof becomes increasingly strong as the pragmatics of scientific knowledge replaces traditional knowledge or knowledge based on revelation. By the end of the *Discourse on Method*, Descartes is already asking for laboratory funds. A new problem appears: devices that optimize the performance of the human body for the purpose of producing proof require additional expenditures. No money, no proof – and that means no verification of statements and no truth. The games of scientific language become the games of the rich, in which whoever is wealthiest has the best chance of being right. An equation between wealth, efficiency, and truth is thus established.

What happened at the end of the eighteenth century, with the first industrial revolution, is that the reciprocal of this equation was discovered: no technology without wealth, but no wealth without technology. A technical apparatus requires an investment; but since it optimizes the efficiency of the task to which it is applied, it also optimizes the surplus-value derived from this improved performance. All that is needed is for the surplus-value to be realized, in other words, for the product of the task performed to be sold. And the system can be sealed in the following way: a portion of the sale is recycled into a research fund dedicated to further performance improvement. It is at this precise moment that science becomes a force of production, in other words, a moment in the circulation of capital.

It was more the desire for wealth than the desire for knowledge that initially forced upon technology the imperative of performance improvement and product realization. The "organic" connection between technology and profit preceded its union with science. Technology became important to contemporary knowledge only through the mediation of a generalized spirit of performativity. Even today, progress in knowledge is not totally subordinated to technological investment.[52]

Capitalism solves the scientific problem of research funding in its own way: directly by financing research departments in private companies, in which demands for performativity and recommercialization orient research first and foremost toward technological "applications"; and indirectly by creating private, state, or mixed-sector research foundations that grant

[vii] The technique of the handyman, who uses whatever diverse materials are at hand, suggested for the human sciences by Claude Lévi-Strauss.

program subsidies to university departments, research laboratories, and independent research groups with no expectation of an immediate return on the results of the work – this is done on the theory that research must be financed at a loss for certain length of time in order to increase the probability of its yielding a decisive, and therefore highly profitable, innovation.[53] Nation-states, especially in their Keynesian period,[viii] follow the same rule: applied research on the one hand, basic research on the other. They collaborate with corporations through an array of agencies.[54] The prevailing corporate norms of work management spread to the applied science laboratories: hierarchy, centralized decision making, teamwork, calculation of individual and collective returns, the development of saleable programs, market research, and so on.[55] Centers dedicated to "pure" research suffer from this less, but also receive less funding.

The production of proof, which is in principle only part of an argumentation process designed to win agreement from the addressees of scientific messages, thus falls under the control of another language game, in which the goal is no longer truth, but performativity – that is, the best possible input/output equation. The State and/or company must abandon the idealist and humanist narratives of legitimation in order to justify the new goal: in the discourse of today's financial backers of research, the only credible goal is power. Scientists, technicians, and instruments are purchased not to find truth, but to augment power.

The question is to determine what the discourse of power consists of and if it can constitute a legitimation. At first glance, it is prevented from doing so by the traditional distinction between force and right, between force and wisdom – in other words, between what is strong, what is just, and what is true. I referred to this incommensurability earlier in terms of the theory of language games, when I distinguished the denotative game (in which what is relevant is the true/false distinction) from the prescriptive game (in which the just/unjust distinction pertains) from the technical game (in which the criterion is the efficient/inefficient distinction). "Force" appears to belong exclusively to the last game, the game of technology. I am excluding the case in which force operates by means of terror. This lies outside the realm of language games, because the efficacy of such force is based entirely on the threat to eliminate the opposing player, not on making a better "move" than he. Whenever efficiency (that is, obtaining the desired effect) is derived from a "Say or do this, or else you'll never speak again," then we are in the realm of terror, and the social bond is destroyed.

But the fact remains that since performativity increases the ability to produce proof, it also increases the ability to be right: the technical

viii John Maynard Keynes (1883–1946), English economist, proposed increased government spending to stimulate economic activity.

criterion, introduced on a massive scale into scientific knowledge, cannot fail to influence the truth criterion. The same has been said of the relationship between justice and performance: the probability that an order would be pronounced just was said to increase with its chances of being implemented, which would in turn increase with the performance capability of the prescriber. This led Luhmann[ix] to hypothesize that in postindustrial societies the normativity of laws is replaced by the performativity of procedures.[56] "Context control," in other words, performance improvement won at the expense of the partner or partners constituting that context (be they "nature" or men), can pass for a kind of legitimation.[57] De facto legitimation.

This procedure operates within the following framework: since "reality" is what provides the evidence used as proof in scientific argumentation, and also provides prescriptions and promises of a juridical, ethical, and political nature with results, one can master all of these games by mastering "reality." That is precisely what technology can do. By reinforcing technology, one "reinforces" reality, and one's chances of being just and right increase accordingly. Reciprocally, technology is reinforced all the more effectively if one has access to scientific knowledge and decision-making authority.

This is how legitimation by power takes shape. Power is not only good performativity, but also effective verification and good verdicts. It legitimates science and the law on the basis of their efficiency, and legitimates this efficiency on the basis of science and law. It is self-legitimating, in the same way a system organized around performance maximization seems to be.[58] Now it is precisely this kind of context control that a generalized computerization of society may bring. The performativity of an utterance, be it denotative or prescriptive, increases proportionally to the amount of information about its referent one has at one's disposal. Thus the growth of power, and its self-legitimation, are now taking the route of data storage and accessibility, and the operativity of information.

The relationship between science and technology is reversed. The complexity of the argumentation becomes relevant here, especially because it necessitates greater sophistication in the means of obtaining proof, and that in turn benefits performativity. Research funds are allocated by States, corporations, and nationalized companies in accordance with this logic of power growth. Research sectors that are unable to argue that they contribute even indirectly to the optimization of the system's performance are abandoned by the flow of capital and doomed to senescence. The criterion of performance is explicitly invoked by the authorities to justify their refusal to subsidize certain research centers.[59]

[ix] Niklas Luhmann, contemporary German sociologist.

Legitimation by Paralogy

Let us say at this point that the facts we have presented concerning the problem of the legitimation of knowledge today are sufficient for our purposes. We no longer have recourse to the grand narratives – we can resort neither to the dialectic of Spirit nor even to the emancipation of humanity as a validation for postmodern scientific discourse. But as we have just seen, the little narrative remains the quintessential form of imaginative invention, most particularly in science.[60] In addition, the principle of consensus as a criterion of validation seems to be inadequate. It has two formulations. In the first, consensus is an agreement between men, defined as knowing intellects and free wills, and is obtained through dialogue. This is the form elaborated by Habermas, but his conception is based on the validity of the narrative of emancipation. In the second, consensus is a component of the system, which manipulates it in order to maintain and improve its performance.[61] It is the object of administrative procedures, in Luhmann's sense. In this case, its only validity is as an instrument to be used toward achieving the real goal, which is what legitimates the system – power.

The problem is therefore to determine whether it is possible to have a form of legitimation based solely on paralogy. Paralogy must be distinguished from innovation: the latter is under the command of the system, or at least used by it to improve its efficiency; the former is a move (the importance of which is often not recognized until later) played in the pragmatics of knowledge. The fact that it is in reality frequently, but not necessarily, the case that one is transformed into the other presents no difficulties for the hypothesis.

Returning to the description of scientific pragmatics, it is now dissension that must be emphasized. Consensus is a horizon that is never reached. Research that takes place under the aegis of a paradigm[62] tends to stabilize; it is like the exploitation of a technological, economic, or artistic "idea." It cannot be discounted. But what is striking is that someone always comes along to disturb the order of "reason." It is necessary to posit the existence of a power that destabilizes the capacity for explanation, manifested in the promulgation of new norms for understanding or, if one prefers, in a proposal to establish new rules circumscribing a new field of research for the language of science. This, in the context of scientific discussion, is the same process Thom calls morphogenesis. It is not without rules (there are classes of catastrophes), but it is always locally determined. Applied to scientific discussion and placed in a temporal framework, this property implies that "discoveries" are unpredictable. In terms of the idea of transparency, it is a factor that generates blind spots and defers consensus.[63]

This summary makes it easy to see that systems theory and the kind of legitimation it proposes have no scientific basis whatsoever; science itself does not function according to this theory's paradigm of the system, and contemporary science excludes the possibility of using such a paradigm to describe society.

In this context, let us examine two important points in Luhmann's argument. On the one hand, the system can only function by reducing complexity, and on the other, it must induce the adaptation of individual aspirations to its own ends.[64] The reduction in complexity is required to maintain the system's power capability. If all messages could circulate freely among all individuals, the quantity of the information that would have to be taken into account before making the correct choice would delay decisions considerably, thereby lowering performativity. Speed, in effect, is a power component of the system.

The objection will be made that these molecular opinions must indeed be taken into account if the risk of serious disturbances is to be avoided. Luhmann replies – and this is the second point – that it is possible to guide individual aspirations through a process of "quasi-apprenticeship," "free of all disturbance," in order to make them compatible with the system's decisions. The decisions do not have to respect individuals' aspirations: the aspirations have to aspire to the decisions, or at least to their effects. Administrative procedures should make individuals "want" what the system needs in order to perform well.[65] It is easy to see what role telematics technology could play in this.

It cannot be denied that there is persuasive force in the idea that context control and domination are inherently better than their absence. The performativity criterion has its "advantages." It excludes in principle adherence to a metaphysical discourse; it requires the renunciation of fables; it demands clear minds and cold wills; it replaces the definition of essences with the calculation of interactions; it makes the "players" assume responsibility not only for the statements they propose, but also for the rules to which they submit those statements in order to render them acceptable. It brings the pragmatic functions of knowledge clearly to light, to the extent that they seem to relate to the criterion of efficiency: the pragmatics of argumentation, of the production of proof, of the transmission of learning, and of the apprenticeship of the imagination.

It also contributes to elevating all language games to self-knowledge, even those not within the realm of canonical knowledge. It tends to jolt everyday discourse into a kind of metadiscourse: ordinary statements are now displaying a propensity for self-citation, and the various pragmatic posts are tending to make an indirect connection even to current messages concerning them.[66] Finally, it suggests that the problems of internal communication experienced by the scientific community in the course of its work of dismantling and remounting its languages are comparable in nature to the problems experienced by the social collectivity when, deprived of its narrative culture, it must reexamine its own internal communication and in the process question the nature of the legitimacy of the decisions made in its name.

At risk of scandalizing the reader, I would also say that the system can count severity among its advantages. Within the framework of the power criterion, a request (that is, a form of prescription) gains nothing in legitimacy by virtue of being based on the hardship of an unmet need. Rights do not flow from hardship, but from the fact that the alleviation of hardship improves the system's performance. The needs of the most underprivileged should not be used as a system regulator as a matter of principle: since the means of satisfying them is already known, their actual satisfaction will not improve the system's performance, but only increase its expenditures. The only counterindication is that not satisfying them can destabilize the whole. It is against the nature of force to be ruled by weakness. But it is in its nature to induce new requests meant to lead to a redefinition of the norms of "life."[67] In this sense, the system seems to be a vanguard machine dragging humanity after it, dehumanizing it in order to rehumanize it at a different level of normative capacity. The technocrats declare that they cannot trust what society designates as its needs; they "know" that society cannot know its own needs since they are not variables independent of the new technologies.[68] Such is the arrogance of the decision makers – and their blindness.

What their "arrogance" means is that they identify themselves with the social system conceived as a totality in quest of its most performative unity possible. If we look at the pragmatics of science, we learn that such an identification is impossible: in principle, no scientist embodies knowledge or neglects the "needs" of a research project, or the aspirations of a researcher, on the pretext that they do not add to the performance of "science" as a whole. The response a researcher usually makes to a request is: "We'll have to see, tell me your story."[69] In principle, he does not prejudge that a case has already been closed or that the power of "science" will suffer if it is reopened. In fact, the opposite is true.

Of course, it does not always happen like this in reality. Countless scientists have seen their "move" ignored or repressed, sometimes for decades, because it too abruptly destabilized the accepted positions, not only in the university and scientific hierarchy, but also in the problematic.[70] The stronger the "move," the more likely it is to be denied the minimum consensus, precisely because it changes the rules of the game upon which consensus had been based. But when the institution of knowledge functions in this manner, it is acting like an ordinary power center whose behavior is governed by a principle of homeostasis.

Such behavior is terrorist, as is the behavior of the system described by Luhmann. By terror I mean the efficiency gained by eliminating, or threatening to eliminate, a player from the language game one shares with him. He is silenced or consents, not because he has been refuted, but because his ability to participate has been threatened (there are many ways to prevent someone from playing). The decision makers' arrogance, which in principle has no equivalent in the sciences, consists in the exercise of terror. It says: "Adapt your aspirations to our ends – or else."[71]

Even permissiveness toward the various games is made conditional on performativity. The redefinition of the norms of life consists in enhancing the system's competence for power. That this is the case is particularly evident in the introduction of telematics technology: the technocrats see in telematics a promise of liberalization and enrichment in the interactions between interlocutors; but what makes this process attractive for them is that it will result in new tensions in the system, and these will lead to an improvement in its performativity.[72]

To the extent that science is differential, its pragmatics provides the antimodel of a stable system. A statement is deemed worth retaining the moment it marks a difference from what is already known, and after an argument and proof in support of it has been found. Science is a model of an "open system,"[73] in which a statement becomes relevant if it "generates ideas," that is, if it generates other statements and other game rules. Science possesses no general metalanguage in which all other languages can be transcribed and evaluated. This is what prevents its identification with the system and, all things considered, with terror. If the division between decision makers and executors exists in the scientific community (and it does), it is a fact of the socioeconomic system and not of the pragmatics of science itself. It is in fact one of the major obstacles to the imaginative development of knowledge.

The general question of legitimation becomes: What is the relationship between the antimodel of the pragmatics of science and society? Is it applicable to the vast clouds of language material consituting a society? Or is it limited to the game of learning? And if so, what role does it play with respect to the social bond? Is it an impossible ideal of an open community? Is it an essential component for the subset of decision makers, who force on society the performance criterion they reject for themselves? Or, conversely, is it a refusal to cooperate with the authorities, a move in the direction of counterculture, with the attendant risk that all possibility for research will be foreclosed due to lack of funding?[74]

From the beginning of this study, I have emphasized the differences (not only formal, but also pragmatic) between the various language games, especially between denotative, or knowledge, games and prescriptive, or action, games. The pragmatics of science is centered on denotative utterances, which are the foundation upon which it builds institutions of learning (institutes, centers, universities, etc.). But its postmodern development brings a decisive "fact" to the fore: even discussions of denotative statements need to have rules. Rules are not denotative but prescriptive utterances, which we are better off calling metaprescriptive utterances to avoid confusion (they prescribe what the moves of language games must be in order to be admissible). The function of the differential or imaginative or paralogical activity of the current pragmatics of science is to point out these metaprescriptives (science's "presuppositions")[75] to petition the players to accept different ones. The only legitimation that can make this kind of request admissible is that it will generate ideas, in other words, new statements.

Social pragmatics does not have the "simplicity" of scientific pragmatics. It is a monster formed by the interweaving of various networks of heteromorphous classes of utterances (denotative, prescriptive, performative, technical, evaluative, etc.). There is no reason to think that it would be possible to determine metaprescriptives common to all of these language games or that a revisable consensus like the one in force at a given moment in the scientific community could embrace the totality of metaprescriptions regulating the totality of statements circulating in the social collectivity. As a matter of fact, the contemporary decline of narratives of legitimation – be they traditional or "modern" (the emancipation of humanity, the realization of the Idea) – is tied to the abandonment of this belief. It is its absence for which the ideology of the "system," with its pretensions to totality, tries to compensate and which it expresses in the cynicism of its criterion of performance.

For this reason, it seems neither possible, nor even prudent, to follow Habermas in orienting our treatment of the problem of legitimation in the direction of a search for universal consensus[76] through what he calls *Diskurs*, in other words, a dialogue of argumentation.[77]

This would be to make two assumptions. The first is that it is possible for all speakers to come to agreement on which rules or metaprescriptions are universally valid for language games, when it is clear that language games are heteromorphous, subject to heterogeneous sets of pragmatic rules.

The second assumption is that the goal of dialogue is consensus. But as I have shown in the analysis of the pragmatics of science, consensus is only a particular state of discussion, not its end. Its end, on the contrary, is paralogy. This double observation (the heterogeneity of the rules and the search for dissent) destroys a belief that still underlies Habermas's research, namely, that humanity as a collective (universal) subject seeks its common emancipation through the regularization of the "moves" permitted in all

503

language games and that the legitimacy of any statement resides in its contributing to that emancipation.[78]

It is easy to see what function this recourse plays in Habermas's argument against Luhmann. *Diskurs* is his ultimate weapon against the theory of the stable system. The cause is good, but the argument is not.[79] Consensus has become an outmoded and suspect value. But justice as a value is neither outmoded nor suspect. We must thus arrive at an idea and practice of justice that is not linked to that of consensus.

A recognition of the heteromorphous nature of language games is a first step in that direction. This obviously implies a renunciation of terror, which assumes that they are isomorphic and tries to make them so. The second step is the principle that any consensus on the rules defining a game and the "moves" playable within it *must* be local, in other words, agreed on by its present players and subject to eventual cancellation. The orientation then favors a multiplicity of finite meta-arguments, by which I mean argumentation that concerns metaprescriptives and is limited in space and time.

This orientation corressponds to the course that the evolution of social interaction is currently taking; the temporary contract is in practice supplanting permanent institutions in the professional, emotional, sexual, cultural, family, and international domains, as well as in political affairs. This evolution is of course ambiguous: the temporary contract is favored by the system due to its greater flexibility, lower cost, and the creative turmoil of its accompanying motivations – all of these factors contribute to increased operativity. In any case, there is no question here of proposing a "pure" alternative to the system: we all now know, as the 1970s come to a close, that an attempt at an alternative of that kind would end up resembling the system it was meant to replace. We should be happy that the tendency toward the temporary contract is ambiguous: it is not totally subordinated to the goal of the system, yet the system tolerates it. This bears witness to the existence of another goal within the system: knowledge of language games as such and the decision to assume responsibility for their rules and effects. Their most significant effect is precisely what validates the adoption of rules – the quest for paralogy.

We are finally in a position to understand how the computerization of society affects this problematic. It could become the "dream" instrument for controlling and regulating the market system, extended to include knowledge itself and governed exclusively by the performativity principle. In that case, it would inevitably involve, the use of terror. But it could also aid groups discussing metaprescriptives by supplying them with the information they usually lack for making knowledgeable decisions. The line to follow for computerization to take the second of these two paths is, in principle, quite simple: give the public free access to the memory and data banks.[80] Language games would then be games of perfect information at any given moment. But they would also be non-zero-sum games, and by virtue of that fact discussion would never risk fixating in a position of minimax equilibrium because it had exhausted its stakes. For the stakes would be knowledge (or information, if you will), and the reserve of knowledge – language's reserve of possible utterances – is inexhaustible. This sketches the outline of a politics that would respect both the desire for justice and the desire for the unknown.

Notes

1 A trace of this politics is to be found in the French institution of a philosophy class at the end of secondary studies, and in the proposal by the Groupe de recherches sur l'enseignement de la philosophie (GREPH) to teach "some" philosophy starting at the beginning of secondary studies: see their *Qui a peur de la philosophie?* (Paris: Flammarion, 1977), sec. 2, "La Philosophie déclassée." This also seems to be the orientation of the curriculum of the CEGEP's in Quebec, especially of the philosophy courses (see for example the *Cabiers de l'enseignement collégial* (1975–76) for philosophy).

2 See H. Janne, "L'Université et les besoins de la société contemporaine," *Cabiers de l'Association internationale des Universités*, 10 (1970): 5; quoted by the Commission d'étude sur les universités, *Document de consultation* (Montréal, 1978).

3 A "hard," almost mystico-military expression of this can be found in Julio de Mesquita Filho, *Discorso de Paraninfo da primeiro turma de licenciados pela Faculdade de Filosofia, Ciêncas e Letras da Universidade de Saô Paulo* (25 January 1937), and an expression of it adapted to the modern problems of Brazilian development in the *Relatorio do Grupo de Rabalho, Reforma Universitaria* (Brasilia: Ministries of Education and Culture, etc., 1968). These documents are part of a dossier on the university in Brazil, kindly sent to me by Helena C. Chamlian and Martha Ramos de Carvalho of the University of São Paulo.

4 The documents are available in French thanks to Miguel Abensour and the Collège de philosophie: *Philosophes de l'Université: L'Idéalisme allemand et la question de l'université* (Paris: Payot, 1979). The collection includes texts by Schelling, Fichte, Schleiermacher, Humboldt, and Hegel.

5 "Über die innere und äussere Organisation der höheren wissenschaftlichen Anstalten in Berlin" (1810), in *Wilhelm von Humboldt* (Frankfurt, 1957), p. 126.

6 Ibid., p. 128.

7 Friedrich Schleiermacher, "Gelegentliche Gedanken über Universitäten in deutschen Sinn, nebst einem Anhang über eine neu zu errichtende" (1808), in E. Spranger, (ed.), *Fichte, Schleiermacher, Steffens über das Wesen der Universität* (Leipzig, 1910), p. 126 ff.

505

8 "The teaching of philosophy is generally recognized to be the basis of all university activity" (ibid., p. 128).

9 Alain Touraine has analyzed the contradictions involved in this transplanation in *Université et société aux Etats-Unis* (Paris: Seuil, 1972), pp. 32–40 [Eng. trans. *The Academic System in American Society* (New York: McGraw-Hill, 1974)].

10 It is present even in the conclusions of Robert Nisbet, *The Degradation of the Academic Dogma: The University in America, 1945–70* (London: Heinemann, 1971). The author is a professor at the University of California, Riverside.

11 See G. W. F. Hegel, *Philosophie des Rechts* (1821) [Eng. trans. T. M. Knox, *Hegel's Philosophy of Right* (Oxford: Oxford University Press, 1967)].

12 See Paul Ricoeur, *Le Conflit des interprétations. Essais d'herméneutique* (Paris: Seuil, 1969) [Eng. trans. Don Ihde, *The Conflict of Interpretations* (Evanston, Ill.: North-western University Press, 1974)]; Hans Georg Gadamer, *Warheit und Methode* 2d edn (Tübingen: Mohr, 1965) [Eng. trans. Garrett Barden and John Cumming, *Truth and Method* (New York: Seabury Press, 1975)].

13 Take two statements: (1) "The moon has risen"; (2) "The statement/ The moon has risen/ is a denotative statement". The syntagm /The moon has risen / in statement 2 is said to be the autonym of statement 1. See Josette Rey-Debove, *Le Métalangage* (Paris: Le Robert, 1978), pt. 4.

14 Its principle is Kantian, at least in matters of transcendental ethics – see the *Critique of Practical Reason*. When it comes to politics and empirical ethics, Kant is prudent: since no one can identify himself with the transcendental normative subject, it is theoretically more exact to compromise with the existing authorities. See for example, "Antwort an der Frage: 'Was ist "Aufklärung"?' " (1784) [Eng. trans. Lewis White Beck, in *Critique of Practical Reason and Other Writings in Moral Philosophy* (Chicago: Chicago University Press, 1949)].

15 See Kant, "Antwort"; Jürgen Habermas, *Strukturwandel der Öffentlichkeit* (Frankfort: Luchterhand, 1962) [*The Structural Transformation of the Public Sphere: An Inquiry into a Category of Bourgeois Society*, trans. Thomas Burger and Frederick Lawrence (Cambridge, Mass.: MIT, 1989)]. The principle of Öffentlichkeit ("public" or "publicity" in the sense of "making public a private correspondence" or "public debate") guided the action of many groups of scientists at the end of the 1960s, especially the group "Survivre" (France), the group "Scientists and Engineers for Social and Political Action" (USA), and the group "British Society for Social Responsibility in Science."

16 A French translation of this text by G. Granel can be found in *Phi*, supplement to the *Annales de l'université de Toulouse – Le Mirail* (Toulouse: January 1977).

17 Certain scientific aspects of postmodernism are inventoried by Ihab Hassan in "Culture, Indeterminacy, and Immanence: Margins of the (Postmodern) Age," *Humanities in Society*, 1 (1978): 51–85.

18 Claus Mueller uses the expression "a process of delegitimation" in *The Politics of Communication* (New York: Oxford University Press, 1973), p. 164.

19 "Road of doubt . . . road of despair . . . skepticism," writes Hegel in the preface to the *Phenomenology of Spirit* to describe the effect of the speculative drive on natural knowledge.

20 For fear of encumbering this account, I have postponed until a later study the exposition of this group of rules.

21 Nietzsche, "Der europäische Nihilismus" (MS. N VII 3); "der Nihilism, ein normaler Zustand" (MS. W II 1); "Kritik der Nihilism" (MS. W VII 3); "Zum Plane" (MS. W II 1), in *Nietzshes Werke kritische Gesamtausgabe*, vol. 7, pts. 1 and 2 (1887–89) (Berlin: De Gruyter, 1970). These texts have been the object of a commentary by K. Ryjik, *Nietzsche, le manuscrit de Lenzer Heide* (typescript, Départment de philosophie, Université de Paris VIII [Vincennes]).

22 "On the future of our educational institutions," in *Complete Works*, vol. 3.

23 Martin Buber, *Ich und Du* (Berlin: Schocken Verlag, 1922) [Eng. trans. Ronald G. Smith, *I and Thou* (New York: Charles Scribner's Sons, 1937)]. and *Dialogisches Leben* (Zürich: Müller, 1947); Emmanuel Lévinas, *Totalité et Infinité* (La Haye: Nijhoff, 1961) [Eng. trans. Alphonso Lingis, *Totality and Infinity: An Essay on Exteriority* (Pittsburgh: Duquesne University Press, 1969)], and "Martin Buber und die Erkenntnish theorie" (1958), in *Philosophen des 20. Jahrhunderts* (Stuttgart: Kohlhammer, 1963).

24 *Philosophical Investigations*, sec. 18, p. 8 [by Ludwig Wittgenstein, trans. G. E. M. Anscombe (New York: Macmillan, 1958)].

25 Ibid.

26 Ibid.

27 See for example, "La taylorisation de la recherche," in *(Auto) critique de la science*, pp. 291–3, And especially D. J. de Solla Price, *Little Science, Big Science* (New York: Columbia University Press, 1963), who emphasizes the split between a small number of highly productive researches (evaluated in terms of publication) and a large mass of researchers with low productivity. The number of the latter grows as the square of the former, so that the number of high productivity researchers only really increases every twenty years. Price concludes that science considered as a social entity is "undemocratic" (p. 59) and that "the eminent scientist" is a hundred years ahead of "the minimal one" (p. 56).

28 See J. T. Desanti, "Sur le rapport traditional des sciences et de la philosophie," in *La Philosophie silencieuse, ou critique des philosophies de la science* (Paris: Seuil, 1975).

29 The reclassification of academic philosophy as one of the human sciences in this respect has a significant far beyond simply professional concerns. I do not think that philosophy as legitimation is condemned to disappear, but it is possible that it will not be able to carry out this work, or at least advance it, without revising its ties to the university institution. See on this matter the preamble to the *Projet d'un institut polytechnique de philosophie* (typescript, Départment de philosophie, Université de Paris VIII, 1979).

30 See Allan Janik and Stephan Toulmin, *Wittgenstein's Vienna* (New York: Simon & Schuster, 1973), and J. Piel (ed.), "Vienne début d'un siècle," *Critique*, 339–40 (1975).

31 See Jürgen Habermas, "Dogmatismus, Vernunft unt Entscheidung – Zu Theorie und Praxis in der verwissenschaftlichen Zivilisation" (1963), in *Theorie und Praxis [Theory and Practice*, abr. edn of 4th German edn, trans. John Viertel (Boston: Beacon Press, 1971)].

32 "Science Smiling into its Beard" is the title of chap. 72, vol. 1 of Musil's *The Man Without Qualities*. Cited and discussed by J. Bouveresse, "La Problématique du sujet".

33 Aristotle in the *Analytics* (ca. 330 BC), Descartes in the *Regulae ad directionem ingenii* (1641) [Rules for the Direction of the Mind] and the *Principes de la philosophie* (1644), John Stuart Mill in the *System of Logic* (1843).

34 Gaston Bachelard, *Le Rationalisme appliqué* (Paris: Presses Universitaires de France, 1949); Michel Serres, "La Réforme et les sept péchés," *L'Arc*, 42, Bachelard special issue (1970).

35 David Hilbert, *Grundlagen der Geometrie* (1899) [Eng. trans. Leo Unger, *Foundations of Geometry* (La Salle: Open Court, 1971)]. Nicolas Bourbaki, "L'architecture des mathématiques," in Le Lionnais, ed., *Les Grands Courants de la pensée mathématique* (Paris: Hermann, 1948); Robert Blanché, *L'Axiomatique* (Paris: Presses Universitaires de France, 1955) [Eng. trans. G. B. Keene, *Axiomatics* (New York: Free Press of Glencoe, 1962)].

36 See Blanché, *L'Axiomatique*, chap. 5.

37 I am here following Robert Martin, *Logique contemporaine et formalisation* (Paris: Presses Universitaires de France, 1964), pp. 33–41 and 122ff.

38 Kurt Gödel, "Über formal unentscheidbare Sätze der Principia Mathematica und verwandter Systeme," *Monatshefte für Mathematik, und Physik*, 38 (1931) [Eng. trans. B. Bletzer, *On Formally Undecidable Propositions of Principia Mathematica and Related Systems* (New York: Basic Books, 1962)].

39 Jean Ladrière, *Les Limitations internes des formalismes* (Louvain: E. Nauwelaerts, 1957).

40 Alfred Tarski, *Logic, Semantics, Metamathematics*, trans. J. H. Woodger (Oxford: Clarendon Press, 1956); J. P. Desclès and Z. Guentcheva-Desclès, "Métalangue, métalangage, métalinguistique," *Documents de travail*, 60–1 (Università di Urbino, January–February 1977).

41 *Les Eléments des mathématiques* (Paris: Hermann, 1940–). The distant points of departure of this work are to be found in the first attempts to demonstrate certain "postulates" of Euclidian geometry. See Léon Brunschvicg, *Les Etapes de la philosophie mathématique*, 3d edn (Paris: Presses Universitaires de France, 1947).

42 Thomas Kuhn, *Structure of Scientific Revolutions*.

43 A classification of logico-mathematical paradoxes can be found in F. P. Ramsey, *The Foundations of Mathematics and Other Logical Essays* (New York: Harcourt & Brace, 1931).

44 See Aristotle, *Rhetoric*, 2, 1393a ff.

45 The problem is that of the witness and also of the historical source: is the fact known from hearsay or *de visu*? The distinction is made by Herodotus. See F. Hartog, "Hérodote rapsode et arpenteur," *Hérodote*, 9 (1977): 55–65.

46 A. Gehlen, "Die Technik in der Sichtweise der Anthropologie," *Anthropologische Forschung* (Hamburg: Rowohlt, 1961).

47 André Leroi-Gourhan, *Milieu et techniques* (Paris: Albin-Michel, 1945), and *Le Geste et la parole, I, Technique et langage* (Paris: Albin-Michel, 1964).

48 Jean Pierre Vernant, *Mythe et pensée chez les Grecs* (Paris: Maspero, 1965),

especially sec. 4, "Le travail et la pensée technique" [Eng. trans. Janet Lloyd, *Myth and Society in Ancient Greece* (Brighton, Eng.: Harvester Press, 1980)].

49 Jurgis Baltrusaitis, *Anamorphoses, ou magie artificielle des effets merveilleux* (Paris: O. Perrin, 1969) [Eng. trans. W. J. Strachan, *Anamorphic Art* (New York: Abrams, 1977)].

50 Lewis Mumford, *Technics and Civilization* New York: Harcourt, Brace, 1963); Bertrand Gille, *Historie des Techniques* (Paris: Gallimard, Pléiade, 1978).

51 A striking example of this, the use of amateur radios to verify certain implications of the theory of relativity, is studied by M. J. Mulkay and D. O. Edge, "Cognitive, Technical, and Social Factors in the Growth of Radio-Astronomy," *Social Science Information*, 12, no. 6 (1973): 25–61.

52 Mulkay elaborates a flexible model for the relative independence of technology and scientific knowledge in "The Model of Branching," *The Sociological Review*, 33 (1976): 509–26. H. Brooks, president of the Science and Public Committee of the National Academy of Sciences, and coauthor of the "Brooks Report" (OCDE, June 1971), criticizing the method of investment in research and development during the 1960s, declares: "One of the effects of the race to the moon has been to increase the cost of technological innovation to the point where it becomes quite simply too expensive. . . . Research is properly speaking a long-term activity: rapid acceleration or deceleration imply concealed expenditure and a great deal of incompetence. Intellectual production cannot go beyond a certain pace" ("Les Etats-Unis ont-ils une politique de la science?" *La Recherche*, 14:611). In March 1972, E. E. David, Jr, scientific adviser to the White House, proposing the idea of a program of Research Applied to National Needs (RANN), came to similar conclusions: a broad and flexible strategy for research and more restrictive tactics for development (*La Recherche*, 21 (1972): 211).

53 This was one of the Lazarsfeld's conditions for agreeing to found what was to become the Mass Communication Research Center at Princeton in 1937. This produced some tension: the radio industries refused to invest in the project; people said that Lazarsfeld started things going but finished nothing. Lazarsfeld himself said to Morrison, "I usually put things together and hoped they worked." Quoted by D. Morrison, "The Beginning of Modern Mass Communication Research," *Archives européennes de sociologie*, 19, no. 2 (1978): 347–59.

54 In the United States, the funds allocated to research and development by the federal government were, in 1956, equal to the funds coming from private capital; they have been higher since that time (OCDE, 1956).

55 Robert Nisbet, *Degradation*, chap. 5, provides a bitter description of the penetration of "higher capitalism" into the university in the form of research centers independent of departments. The social relations in such centers disturb the academic tradition. See too in *(Auto)critique de la science*, the chapters "Le prolétariat scientifique," "Les chercheurs," "La Crise des mandarins."

56 Niklas Luhmann, *Legitimation durch Verfahren* (Neuweid: Luchterhand, 1969).

57 Commenting on Luhmann, Mueller writes, "In advanced industrial society, legal-rational legitimation is replaced by a technocratic legitimation that does

not accord any significance to the beliefs of the citizen or to morality per se" (*Politics of Communication*, p. 135). There is a bibliography of German material on the technocratic question in Habermas, *Theory and Practice*.

58 Gilles Fauconnier gives a linguistic analysis of the control of truth in "Comment contrôler la vérité? Remarques illustrées par des assertions dangereuses et pernicieuses en tout genre," *Actes de la recherche en sciences sociales*, 25 (1979): 1–22.

59 Thus in 1970 the British University Grants Committee was "persuaded to take a much more positive role in productivity, specialization, concentration of subjects, and control of building through cost limits" [*The Politics of Education: Edward Boyle and Anthony Crosland in Conversation with Maurice Kogan* (Harmondsworth, Eng.: Penguin, 1971), p. 196]. This may appear to contradict declarations such as that of Brooks, quoted above (note 52). But (1) the "strategy" may be liberal and the "tactics" authoritarian, as Edwards says elsewhere; (2) responsibility within the hierarchy of public authorities is often taken in its narrowest sense, namely the capacity to answer for the calculable performance of a project; (3) public authorities are not always free from pressures from private groups whose performance criterion is immediately binding. If the chances of innovation in research cannot be calculated, then public interest seems to lie in aiding all research, under conditions other than that of efficiency assessment after a fixed period.

60 It has not been possible within the limits of this study to analyze the form assumed by the return of narrative in discourses of legitimation. Examples are: the study of open systems, local determinism, antimethod – in general, everything that I group under the name *paralogy*.

61 Nora and Minc, for example, attribute Japan's success in the field of computers to an "intensity of social consensus" that they judge to be specific to Japanese society (*L'Informatisation de la Société*, p. 4). They write in their conclusion: "The dynamics of extended social computerization leads to a fragile society: such a society is constructed with a view to facilitating consensus, but already presupposes its existence, and comes to a standstill if that consensus cannot be realized" (p. 125). Y. Stourdzé, "Les Etats-Unis", emphasizes the fact that the current tendency to deregulate, destabilize, and weaken administration is encouraged by society's loss of confidence in the State's performance capability.

62 In Kuhn's sense.

63 Pomian ("Catastrophes") shows that this type of functioning bears no relation to Hegelian dialectics.

64 "What the legitimation of decisions accordingly entails is fundamentally an effective learning process, with a minimum of friction, within the social system. This is an aspect of the more general question, "how do aspirations change, how can the political-administrative subsystem, itself only part of society, nevertheless structure expectations in society through its decisions?' The effectiveness of the activity of what is only a part, for the whole, will in large measure depend on how well it succeeds in integrating new expectations into already existing systems – whether these are persons or social systems –

without thereby provoking considerable functional disturbances" (Niklas Luhmann, *Legitimation durch Verfahren*, p. 35).

65 This hypothesis is developed in David Riesman's earlier studies. See Riesman, *The Lonely Crowd* (New Haven: Yale University Press, 1950); W. H. Whyte, *The Organization Man* (New York: Simon & Schuster, 1956); Herbert Marcuse, *One Dimensional Man* (Boston: Beacon, 1966).

66 Josette Rey-Debove (*Le Métalangage*, pp. 228ff.) notes the proliferation of marks of indirect discourse or autonymic connotation in contemporary daily language. As she reminds us, "indirect discourse cannot be trusted."

67 As Georges Canguilhem says, "man is only truly healthy when he is capable of a number of norms, when he is more than normal" ("Le Normal et la pathologique", in *La Connaissance de la vie* [Paris: Hachette, 1952], p. 210) [Eng. trans. Carolyn Fawcett, *On the Normal and the Pathological* (Boston: D. Reidel, 1978)].

68 E. E. David comments that society can only be aware of the needs it feels in the present state of its technological milieu. It is of the nature of the basic sciences to discover unknown properties which remodel the technical milieu and create unpredictable needs. He cites as examples the use of solid materials as amplifiers and the rapid development of the physics of solids. This "negative regulation" of social interactions and needs by the object of contemporary techniques is critiqued by R. Jaulin, "Le Mythe technologique," *Revue de l'entreprise*, 26, special "Ethnotechnology" issue (March 1979): 49–55. This is a review of A. G. Haudricourt, "La Technologie culturelle, essai de méthodologie," in Gille, *Historie des techniques*.

69 Medawar (*Art of the Soluble*, pp. 151–2) compares scientists' written and spoken styles. The former must be "inductive" or they will not be considered; as for the second, Medawar makes a list of expressions often heard in laboratories, including, "My results don't make a story yet." He concludes, "Scientists are building explanatory structures, *telling stories . . .*"

70 For a famous example, see Lewis S. Feuer, *Einstein and the Generations of Science* (New York: Basic Books, 1974). As Moscovici emphasizes in his introduction to the French translation [trans. Alexandre, *Einstein et le conflit des générations* (Bruxelles' Complexe, 1979)], "Relativity was born in a makeshift 'academy' formed by friends, not one of whom was a physicist; all were engineers or amateur philosophers."

71 Orwell's paradox. The bureaucrat speaks: "We are not content with negative obedience, nor even with the most abject submission. When finally you do surrender to us, it must be of your own free will" (*1984* [New York: Harcourt, Brace, 1949], p. 258). In language game terminology the paradox would be expressed as a "Be free," or a "Want what you want," and is analyzed by Watzlawick et al., *Pragmatics of Human Communication*, pp. 203–7. On these paradoxes, see J. M. Salanskis, "Genèses 'actuelles' et genèses 'sérielles' de l'inconsistant et de l'hétérogeme," *Critique*, 379 (1978): 1155–73.

72 See Nora and Minc's description of the tensions that mass computerization will inevitably produce in French society (*L'informatisation de la société*, introduction).

73 Cf. the discussion of open systems in Watzlawick et al., *Pragmatics of Human Communication*, pp. 117–48. The concept of open systems theory is the subject of a study by J. M. Salanskis, *Le Systématique ouvert* (forthcoming).

74 After the separation of Church and State, Paul Feyerabend (*Against Method*), demands in the same "lay" spirit the separation of Science and State. But what about Science and Money?

75 This is at least one way of understanding this term, which comes from Ducrot's problematic, *Dire*.

76 *Legitimationsprobleme*, passim, especially pp. 21–2: "Language functions in the manner of a transformer . . . changing cognitions into propositions, needs and feelings into normative expectations (commands, values). This transformation produces the far-reaching distinction between the subjectivity of intention, willing, of pleasure and unpleasure on the one hand, and expressions and norms with a *pretension to universality* on the other. Universality signifies the objectivity of knowledge and the legitimacy of prevailing norms; both assure the community constitutive of lived social experience." We see that by formulating the problematic in this way, the question of legitimacy is fixated on one type of reply, universality. This on the one hand presupposes that the legitimation of the subject of knowledge is identical to that of the subject of action (in opposition to Kant's critique, which dissociates conceptual universality, appropriate to the former, and ideal universality, or "suprasensible nature," which forms the horizon of the latter, and on the other hand it maintains that consensus (*Gemeinschaft*) is the only possible horizon for the life of humanity.

77 Ibid., p. 20. The subordination of the metaprescriptives of prescription (i.e. the normalization of laws) to *Diskurs* [Discourse] is explicit, for example, on p. 144: "The normative pretension to validity is itself cognitive in the sense that it always assumes it could be accepted in a rational discussion."

78 Garbis Kortian, *Métacritique* (Paris: Editions de Minuit, 1979) [Eng. trans. John Raffan, *Metacritique: The Philosophical Argument of Jürgen Habermas* (Cambridge: Cambridge University Press, 1980)], pt. 5, examines this enlightenment aspect of Habermas's thought. See by the same author, "Le Discours philosophique et son objet," *Critique*, 384 (1979): 407–19.

79 See J. Poulain ("Vers une pragmatique nucléaire"), and for a more general discussion of the pragmatics of Searle and Gehlen, see J. Poulain, "Pragmatique de la parole et pragmatique de la vie," *Phi zéro* 7, no. 1 (Université de Montréal, September 1978): 5–50.

80 See Tricot et al., *Informatique et libertés*, government report (La Documentation française, 1975); L. Joinet, "Les 'pièges liberaticides' de l'informatique," *Le Monde diplomatique*, 300 (March 1979): these traps (*pièges*) are "the application of the technique of 'social profiles' to the management of the mass of the population; the logic of security produced by the automatization of society." See too the documents and analysis in *Interférences*, 1 and 2 (Winter 1974– Spring 1975), the theme of which is the establishment of popular networks of multimedia communication. Topics treated include: amateur radios (especially their role in Quebec during the FLQ affair of October 1970 and that of the

"Front commun" in May 1972); community radios in the United States and Canada; the impact of computers on editorial work in the press; pirate radios (before their development in Italy); administrative files, the IBM monopoly, computer sabotage. The municipality of Yverdon (Canton of Vaud), having voted to buy a computer (operational in 1981), enacted a certain number of rules: exclusive authority of the municipal council to decide which data are collected, to whom and under what conditions they are communicated; access for all citizens to all data (on payment); the right of every citizen to see the entries on his file (about 50), to correct them and address a complaint about them to the municipal council and if need be to the Council of State; the right of all citizens to know (on request) which data concerning them is communicated and to whom (*La Semaine media* 18, 1 March 1979, 9).

chapter
thirty-three

Erring: A Postmodern A/theology
Mark C. Taylor

Professor of religion, Mark Taylor (1945–) is the primary exponent of what might seem an impossible combination: postmodern theology. It has roots in the so-called "death of God theology" of the 1960s which tried to reconceive Christianity in the light of Nietzsche's announcement of God's demise. In this spirit, Taylor rejects any traditional substantive or personal notion of divinity, and any teleological view of human history. His work is heavily indebted to Derrida. He regards Derrida's strategy of critical reading, deconstruction, as pointing out the utterly marginal or "liminal" nature of experience. Just as Derrida gives primacy to writing, Taylor sees religion as essentially based in scripture, not in the sense of ancient books, but as the process of generating, reading, and rewriting "the word." In this process, every human judgment is limited, transitory, uncertain, never able to grasp or adequately represent what it seeks. Any writing, or living, which recognizes this fact admits that its very nature is "erring." Taylor interprets this erring context of all becoming, the "nonoriginal origin of everything that is," as the "divine milieu."

In many ways, deconstruction might seem an unlikely partner for religious reflection. As a form of thought it appears avowedly atheistic. Derrida speaks for others as well as himself when he adamantly maintains that deconstruction "blocks every relationship to theology."[1] Paradoxically, it is just this antithetical association with theology that lends deconstruction[i] its "religious" significance for marginal thinkers. By reflecting and recasting the pathos of so much contemporary art, literature, and philosophy,

From Mark C. Taylor, *Erring: A Postmodern A/theology* (Chicago: University of Chicago Press, 1984), pp. 6–13, 103–7, and 115–20.

[i] Deconstruction is Derrida's method of critical reading which displays the undecidable, self-undermining elements in a text.

deconstruction expresses greater appreciation for the significance of the death of God than most contemporary philosophers of religion and theologians. Though anticipated in Hegel's speculative philosophy and Kierkegaard's attack on Christendom[ii] and proclaimed by Nietzsche's madman, the death of God is not concretely actualized until the emergence of the twentieth-century industrial state. And yet, as Nietzsche realized, "This tremendous event is," in an important sense, "still on its way, still wandering; it has not yet reached the ears of men."[2] This deafness is all too evident among many contemporary philosophers of religion and theologians. Too often they attempt to solve difficult religious problems by simply trying to recapture a past that now seems decisively gone. This attitude is no longer defensible.

Postmodernism opens with the sense of *irrevocable* loss and *incurable* fault. This wound is inflicted by the overwhelming awareness of death – a death that "begins" with the death of God and "ends" with the death of our selves. We are in a time between times and a place which is no place. Here our reflection must "begin." In this liminal[iii] time and space, deconstructive philosophy and criticism offer rich, though still largely untapped, resources for religious reflection. One of the distinctive features of deconstruction is its willingness to confront the problem of the death of God squarely even if not always directly. The insights released by deconstructive criticism suggest the ramifications of the death of God for areas as apparently distinct as contemporary psychology, linguistics, and historical analysis. In view of its remarkable grasp of the far-reaching significance of the dissolution of the Western theological and philosophical tradition, it would not be too much to suggest that *deconstruction is the "hermeneutic" of the death of God.* As such, it provides a possible point of departure for a postmodern a/theology. Given the marginality of its site, an a/theology that draws on deconstructive philosophy will invert established meaning and subvert everything once deemed holy. It will thus be utterly transgressive.

The failure (or refusal) to come to terms with the radical implications of the death of God has made it impossible for most Western theology to approach postmodernism. This shortcoming results, at least in part, from the lack of a clear recognition that concepts are not isolated entities. Rather, they form intricate networks or complex webs of interrelation and coimplication. As a result of this interconnection, notions mutually condition and reciprocally define each other. Such thoroughgoing corelativity implies that no *single* concept is either absolutely primary or exclusively

---

[ii] Søren Kierkegaard (1813–55), Danish Christian philosopher, attacked the Christianity of his day as inauthentically religious.
[iii] Marginal, transitional, at the border. "Limen" means threshold.

foundational. Clusters of coordinated notions form the matrix of any coherent conceptual system. It would, of course, be a vast oversimplification to insist that all Western theology can be made to fit a single system. Efforts to totalize the tradition inevitably leave a remainder and consequently always negate themselves. It is, nonetheless, possible to identify a set of interrelated concepts that have been particularly persistent in theological reflection. This network includes at least four terms: God, self, history, and book. In order to anticipate the course of the argument that follows, it might be helpful to indicate briefly the interplay of these important notions and to suggest some of the assumptions and consequences of the closely knit network that they form.

According to the tenets of classical theism, God, who is One, is the supreme Creator, who, through the mediation of His divine Logos, brings the world into being and providentially directs its course. This Primal Origin (First Cause or *Archē*) is also the Ultimate End (Final Goal or *Telos*) of the world. Utterly transcendent and thoroughly eternal, God is represented as totally present to Himself [*sic*]. He is, in fact, the omnipresent fount, source, ground, and uncaused cause of presence itself. The self is made in the image of God and consequently is also one, i.e. a centered individual. Mirroring its Creator, the single subject is both self-conscious and freely active. Taken together, self-consciousness and freedom entail individual responsibility. History is the domain where divine guidance and human initiative meet. The temporal course of events is not regarded as a random sequence. It is believed to be plotted along a single line stretching from a definite beginning (creation) through an identifiable middle (incarnation) to an expected end (kingdom or redemption). Viewed in such ordered terms, history forms a purposeful process whose meaning can be coherently represented. Page by page and chapter by chapter, the Book weaves the unified story of the interaction between God and self. Since the logic of this narrative reflects the Logos of history, Scripture, in effect, rewrites the Word of God.

God, self, history, and book are, thus, bound in an intricate relationship in which each mirrors the other. No single concept can be changed without altering all of the others. As a result of this thorough interdependence, the news of the death of God cannot really reach our ears until its reverberations are traced in the notions of self, history and book. The echoes of the death of God can be heard in the disappearance of the self, the end of history, and the closure of the book. We can begin to unravel this web of conceptual relations by plotting the coordinates of a new a/theological network.

The Western theological tradition, in all its evident diversity, rests upon a polar or, more precisely, a dyadic foundation. Though consistently monotheistic, Christian theology is repeatedly inscribed in binary terms.

The history of religious thought in the West can be read as a pendular movement between seemingly exclusive and evident opposites.

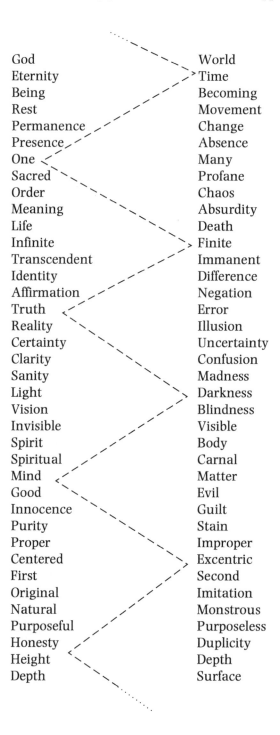

God	World
Eternity	Time
Being	Becoming
Rest	Movement
Permanence	Change
Presence	Absence
One	Many
Sacred	Profane
Order	Chaos
Meaning	Absurdity
Life	Death
Infinite	Finite
Transcendent	Immanent
Identity	Difference
Affirmation	Negation
Truth	Error
Reality	Illusion
Certainty	Uncertainty
Clarity	Confusion
Sanity	Madness
Light	Darkness
Vision	Blindness
Invisible	Visible
Spirit	Body
Spiritual	Carnal
Mind	Matter
Good	Evil
Innocence	Guilt
Purity	Stain
Proper	Improper
Centered	Excentric
First	Second
Original	Imitation
Natural	Monstrous
Purposeful	Purposeless
Honesty	Duplicity
Height	Depth
Depth	Surface

Mark C. Taylor

Interiority   Exteriority
Speech   Writing
Seriousness   Play

Like its intellectual twin, philosophy, theology does not regard these opposites as equivalent. It refuses to allow the possibility that oppositional terms can coexist peacefully. Invariably one term is privileged through the divestment of its relative. The resultant economy of privilege sustains an asymmetrical hierarchy in which one member governs or rules the other throughout the theological, logical, axiological, and even political domains.

It is against just this hierarchy that so many modern thinkers rebel. Indeed, modernism might be described as the struggle to overturn this structure of domination upon which Western thought and society traditionally have rested. Many theologians who have taken up the challenge of modernism have been inevitably driven to revolutionary radicalism. The theological radical learns from modern politics, painting, music, and literature that "true revolution is not simply an opening to the future but also a closing of the past. Yet the past which is negated by a revolutionary future cannot simply be negated or forgotten. It must be transcended by way of a reversal of the past, a reversal bringing a totally new light and meaning to everything which is manifest as the past, and therefore a reversal fully transforming the whole horizon of the present. Modern revolutionary assaults upon the whole movement of a profane or secular history can now serve not only as models but also as sources for a revolutionary theological assault upon the history of faith."[3] Even revolutionary thought, however, runs the risk of being *insufficiently* radical. If hierarchical oppression and repression are to be overcome, it is necessary to *pass through* a phase of inversion. But reversal can remain caught within the dyadic economy of conflictual opposition. Merely "To put a minus sign instead of a plus sign before the elements of Western culture is not to liberate oneself from them but to remain entirely bound within their net. To define God as the supreme evil is as much an act of homage and belief as to define him as the supreme good."[4] In place of a simple reversal, it is necessary to effect a dialectical inversion that does not leave contrasting opposites unmarked but dissolves their original identities. Inversion, in other words, must simultaneously be a perversion that is subversive. Unless theological transgression becomes genuinely subversive, nothing fundamental will change. What is needed is a critical lever with which the

518

entire inherited order can be creatively disorganized. It is at this point that deconstruction becomes a potential resource for the a/theologian.

Deconstructive criticism unravels the very fabric of most Western theology and philosophy. When subjected to a deconstructive critique, the structure of relationship that both joins and separates opposites is reformulated in such a way that contraries are not merely reversed but are recast to dissolve their original propriety and proper identity. Deconstruction, therefore, both affects specific concepts within a dyadic economy and calls into question the entire network of notions that traditionally have grounded theological reflection. Once terms undergo deconstructive analysis, they cannot simply be reinscribed within an oppositional system that previously had defined and constituted them. It is important to stress that this critique does not approach the theological network from without and thus does not involve a disjunctive epistemological break. Like any parasite, deconstruction attacks from within, using "the strengths of the field to turn its own stratagems against it, producing a force of dislocation that spreads itself throughout the entire system, fissuring it in every direction and thoroughly *delimiting* it."[5]

Deconstruction is irrevocably liminal or marginal. Its liminality marks an unstable border along which marginal thinkers wander. This novel and admittedly controversial form of criticism seems to me to be particularly well suited to address many of the issues that preoccupy people caught *between* belief and unbelief. Deconstruction itself is at one and the same time inside and outside the network that it questions. On the one hand, deconstruction's uncanny criticism pervades and subverts the hierarchical system of theological concepts. On the other hand, the survival of this parasitic discourse presupposes the continuing existence of its host. Hence deconstructive writing is always paradoxical, double, duplicitous, excentric, improper, . . . errant. Calling into question the very notion of propriety, the language of deconstruction can possess no final or proper meaning. It remains transitional. Its words cannot be completely fixed, mastered, or captured in the net of either/or. Instead, deconstructive criticism constantly errs along the / of neither/nor. Forever wavering and wandering, deconstruction is (re)inscribed betwixt 'n' between the opposites it inverts, perverts, and subverts. Consequently, deconstruction can be written only on the boundary, a boundary that, though always the "middest," knows no bounds. The time and space of this border form a middle age or middle kingdom that is not, in any ordinary sense, intermediate. The ceaseless play of opposites renders transition permanent and passage absolute. This interval is the medium or mean within which all extremes cross. While not reducible to or expressible in a traditional oppositional logic of extremes, this milieu is the "nonoriginal origin" of everything that is – and that is not.

In the following pages I shall be asking whether the scriptural network graphed in deconstruction can be read as the eternal cross(ing) of the word that repeatedly inscribes and reinscribes the infinite play of the divine milieu. In a sense, this query implies the possibility of deconstructing deconstruction. As I have noted, proponents of deconstruction insist that their practice blocks every relationship to theology. Insofar as theology remains bound to or caught in its traditional systematic form, this claim of deconstructive critics is, of course, correct. I have, however, briefly suggested that deconstruction calls into question the coherence, integrity, and intelligibility of this network of oppositions. By inverting and subverting the poles between which Western theology has been suspended, deconstruction reverses itself and creates a new opening for the religious imagination.

Thought that wanders into this interstitial space will, of necessity, be unsettled and unsettling. Repeatedly slipping through the holes in the system within which it must, nevertheless, be registered, such thought is perpetually transitory and forever nomadic. It is neither simply this nor that, here nor there, inside nor outside. To follow the ways of such vagrant thought is inevitably to err. Writing that attempts to trace the border and retrace the margin can, therefore, be described as *erring*. *Err* is an uncommonly rich word whose many (perhaps bottomless) layers suggest multiple dimensions of the argument I shall be developing. By roaming through the labyrinth of this word, we catch an initial glimpse of the wiles and ways of postmodern a/theology.

Err appears to derive from the Latin *errāre* (whose "prehistoric" form is *ersāre*) by way of Middle English *erre*, French *errer*, Provençal and Spanish *errar*, and Italian *errare*.[6] *Errāre* ("to wander, or stray about, to rove") is cognate with the Gothic *aírzjan*, which means "to lead astray." To err is to ramble, roam, stray, wander, like Chaucer's "weary ghost that errest to and fro." Such wandering inevitably leads one astray – away from one's path or line of direction. To err, therefore, is to "fail, miss, go wrong in judgment or opinion; to make a mistake, blunder, or commit a fault; to be incorrect; to go astray morally"; even "to sin." *Err* drifts toward: *Errable* ("fallible, liable to error"); *Errabund* ("random"); *Errancy* ("the condition of erring or being in error"); *Errand* ("a message, a verbal communication to be repeated to a third party; a petition or prayer presented through another; a short journey on which an inferior – e.g. a servant, a child – is sent to convey a message or perform some simple business on behalf of the sender"); *Errantly* ("wandering, prone to wander; wandering from place to place, vagrant, nomadic; irregular or uncertain in movement, having no fixed course; irregular or eccentric in conduct, habit, or opinion"); *Erratum* ("an error in writing or printing"); *Erre* ("wound, scar"); *Erre* ("wrath"); *Erroneous* ("wandering, roving, moving aimlessly, vagrant; straying from the ways of wisdom or prudence; misguided; of doctrines, opinions, statements: incorrect, mistaken, wrong"); *Error* ("the action of roaming or wandering; hence a devious or winding course, a roving, winding; chagrin, fury, vexation; extravagance of passion; the condition of erring in opinion; holding of mistaken notions or beliefs; a delusion, trick; something incorrectly done through ignorance or inadvertance; a departure from moral rectitude; a transgression"); and, of course, *Errant*. "Errant" subdivides into three branches. I. Old French *errer*, which is from the Latin *iterāre* ("to journey, travel"): "Itinerant, traveling; said of knights who traveled about in quest of adventure; in chess, a traveling pawn, one that has been advanced from its original square; and *Errant juif* – the Wandering Jew." II. "The primary notion of branch II is uncertain:"A notorious, 'common' thief." III. French *errār*, which is from the Latin *errāre* ("to stray, wander, err"): "Astray, wandering, roving; straying from the proper course or place; having no fixed course." *Erring*, then, is "wandering, roaming; deviating from the right or intended course; missing the mark." The semantic branches of *err* spread to errancy, erratic, erratum, erre, erroneous, and errant.

The erring a/theologian is driven to consider and reconsider errant notions: transgression, subversion, mastery, utility, consumption, domination, narcissism, nihilism, possession, uncanniness, repetition, tropes, writing, dissemination, dispossession, expropriation, impropriety, anonymity, spending, sacrifice, death, desire, delight, wandering, aberrance, carnival, comedy, superficiality, carnality, duplicity, shiftiness, undecidability, and spinning. In view of these preoccupations, it should be clear that erring thought is neither *properly* theological nor nontheological, theistic nor atheistic, religious nor secular, believing nor nonbelieving. A/theology represents the liminal thinking of marginal thinkers. The / of a / theology (which, it is important to note, can be written but not spoken) marks the *limen* that signifies *both* proximity and distance, similarity and difference, interiority and exteriority. This strangely permeable membrane forms a border where fixed boundaries disintegrate. Along this boundless boundary the traditional polarities between which Western theology has been suspended are inverted and subverted. Since it is forever *entre-deux*,[iv] a/theology is undeniably ambiguous. The a/theologian asks errant questions and suggests responses that often seem erratic or even erroneous. Since his reflection wanders, roams, and strays from the "proper" course, it tends to deviate from well-established ways. To traditional eyes, a/theology doubtless appears to be irregular, eccentric, and vagrant. At best it seems aimless, at worst devious. Within this framework, a/theology is, in fact, heretical. For the a/theologian, however, heresy and aimlessness are unavoidable. Ideas are never fixed but are always in transition; thus they are irrepress-

---

[iv] Intermediate, in-between.

ibly transitory. For this reason, a/theology might be labeled "Nomad Thought."[7] The erring nomad neither looks back to an absolute beginning nor ahead to an ultimate end. His writing, therefore, remains unfinished. His work is less a complete book than an open (perhaps broken) text that never really begins or actually ends. The words of a/theology fall in between; they are *always* in the middle. The a/theological text is a tissue woven of threads that are produced by endless spinning. This vertiginous wordplay points to the paradoxical nonbinary (a)logic of the cross. I am persuaded that along the middle way traced by deconstruction there lies a revolutionary reading of writing that reveals scripture anew. The way of the word, of course, is also the tortuous path to Golgotha.[v] As the threshold of absolute passage, the cross marks the intersection of ascent and descent that is the "marriage of heaven and hell." . . .

The main contours of deconstructive a/theology begin to emerge with the realization of the necessary interrelation between the death of God and radical christology.[vi] Radical christology is *thoroughly* incarnational – the divine "*is*" the incarnate word. Furthermore, this embodiment of the divine is the death of God. With the appearance of the divine that is not only itself but is at the same time other, the God who alone is God disappears. The death of God is the sacrifice of the transcendent Author/Creator/Master who governs from afar. Incarnation *irrevocably* erases the disembodied logos and inscribes a word that becomes the script enacted in the infinite play of interpretation. To understand incarnation as inscription is to discover the word. Embodied word is script(ure), the writing in which we are inscribed and which we inscribe. Like all writing, the carnal word is transgressive. Inscription inverts the traditional understanding of the God-world relationship and subverts all forms of transcendence. A/theology is, in large measure, a critique of the notion of the transcendent God, who is "self-clos'd, all-repelling."[8] In this case, however, the struggle against the omnipotent Father does not simply repeat the undialectical inversion of God and self enacted in humanistic atheism. As a result of the recognition of the necessary interplay between patricide and suicide, the death of God does not issue in the deification of the individual ego. Far from resisting the unsettling currents that circulate throughout postmodern worlds, the a/theologian welcomes the death of God and embraces the disappearance of the self.

In order to avoid unnecessary confusion, it is important to realize that in radical christology the divine is *forever* embodied. The word is *always already* inscribed. Incarnation, therefore, is not a once-and-for-all event,

---

[v] The place where Christ was crucified.
[vi] Christology is the subfield of Christian theology that seeks to understand Christ.

restricted to a specific time and place and limited to a particular individual. Rather, inscription is a continual (though not necessarily a continuous) process. To insist that God "is" eternally embodied in *word* or that the divine "*is*" incarnate *word* is to imply that "there is a sense in which the word 'God' refers to the word 'word' and the word 'word' refers to the word 'God'."[9] God is what word means, and word is what "God" means. To interpret God as word is to understand the divine as scripture or writing. In order to develop the far-reaching implications of this suggestion, it is necessary to consider different ways of reading the word "word."

According to traditional Occidental wisdom, the notion of the word is inextricably tied to the structure of signification. As remarks scattered throughout earlier chapters imply, signification at the most basic level presupposes a distinction between signifier and signified. In this binary relationship, the signifier points beyond itself to that which it represents (i.e. the signified). Insofar as word is sign, it appears to be essentially ostensive or fundamentally referential. I have already indicated that the referent of the sign can be interpreted in different ways. In general, the signified tends to be viewed as either "real" or "ideal." Accordingly, a sign is believed to designate something conceptual, like an idea, image, or mental construct, or is held to denote an actual object in the world. Common sense and reasoning based upon it frequently try to mediate ideality and reality by insisting that, while every sign carries an "ideal" meaning, signified meaning always points to a "real" referent, which remains extramental. This analysis of words appears to rest on the assumption that nouns and the activity of naming are normative for all uses of language. The relationship between named/signified and name/signifier is not symmetrical. The former is traditionally regarded as primary, the latter as secondary. The meaning of any word is that to which it refers. Conversely, the signified grounds (and thus lends weight to) the signifier. The word, therefore, remains obediently subservient to the signified.

Although not immediately evident, this pattern of signification is tied up in the ontotheological network. God, or His substitute, appears either overtly or covertly to be the final meaning of the word. Put differently, God is, in effect, the "transcendental signified" that grounds the structure of signification. Since the "sign and divinity have the same place and time of birth," the "age of the sign is essentially theological."[10] This does not mean, of course, that every sign refers directly or even indirectly to God. The point to be stressed is that some notion of the transcendental signified is required by any referential system that gives priority to the signified over the signifier. While not always explicitly named God, the transcendental signified *functions* as the purported locus of truth that is supposed to stabilize all meaningful words.

A closer examination of this structure of signification discloses inherent contradictions that call into question the fundamental opposition between signifier and signified. Whether the referent of the sign is taken to be "real" or "ideal," the distinction between signifier and signified is actually a product of *consciousness itself*. Though not always aware of its own activity, consciousness attempts to *give itself* a criterion by which to judge itself. The signified is distinguished from the signifier and serves as the standard by which all signs are measured. For the most part, consciousness regards its criterion as external to, independent of, and imposed upon itself. But this interpretation of experience fails to do justice to the creativity and productivity of consciousness. That to which consciousness points is always already within consciousness itself. This analysis of the relationship between signifier and signified overturns the traditional understanding of signification. The signified is neither independent of nor superior to the signifier. To the contrary, the signified is a signifier. Consciousness, therefore, deals *only* with signs and never reaches the thing itself. More precisely, the thing itself is not an independent entity (be it "real" or "ideal") to which all signs refer but is itself a *sign*.

Armed with this insight, it is possible to reinterpret the claim that the word "God" refers to the word "word" and that the word "word" refers to the word "God." Although the word is a sign, the signified is not independent of, and qualitatively different from, the signifier. Inasmuch as the signified is a signifier, the sign is a sign of a sign. Since a word is a sign, it is always about another word. In different terms, the word stages a drama whose script is the interplay of signs. When the word is understood in this way, it appears as *writing* or *scripture*. Simultaneously inside and outside the traditional structure of signification, "writing is not *about* something; it *is that something itself*."[11]

It should be clear that writing inscribes the disappearance of the transcendental signified. In this way, scripture embodies and enacts the death of God, even as the death of God opens and releases writing. The disappearance of the transcendental signified closes the theological age of the sign and makes possible the free play of a/theological writing. Within the classical economy of signification, "*Logos* is a son . . . a son that would be destroyed in his very *presence* without the present attendance of his father.[vii] His father who answers. His father who speaks for him and answers for him. Without his father, he would be nothing but, in fact, writing. At least that is what is said by the one who says: it is the father's thesis. The specificity of writing would thus be intimately bound to the absence of the father. Such an absence can of course exist along very diverse modalities, distinctly or confusedly, successively or simultaneously: to have lost one's

---

[vii] *Logos* is the Greek term meaning "word," discourse, or reason. It is also the term with which John famously began his Gospel ("In the beginning was the Word [*Logos*] . . .").

father, through natural or violent death, through random violence or patricide."[12] By enacting the death of the transcendent(al) Father/signified, the word becomes the wayward, rebellious, errant "son." "Writing, the lost son . . . writes (itself): (that) the father *is not*, that is to say, is not present."[13] The word marks the closure of all presence that is not at the same time absence and marks the end of identity that is not also difference. In this way, the incarnate word spells the death of the God who alone is God. The death of God, however, is the birth of the divine that is not only itself but is always at the same time other. . . .

This account of scripture cannot, of course, be reduced to the common-place view of writing as the simple transcription of antecedent thoughts, ideas, or images from immaterial interior form to material exterior expression. It is precisely this view of writing that is negated by the disappearance of the transcendental signified. The death of the father opens the reign of the word that is embodied in scripture. Since this word enacts absolute passage, it is forever liminal and eternally playful. The play of the word is writing, and the drama of writing is word. In writing, fixed boundaries break down. Scripture, therefore, is always marginal. The/A word is nothing in itself; it is a play within a play, a play that is forever an interplay. This play is a play of differences that forms and reforms the word itself. The specificity of any signifier is a function of its entwinement within a complex signifying web. This differential network of signs is "the functional condition, the condition of possibility, for every sign."[14] Its "name" is *writing*.

Within a scriptural economy, writing is the articulation of (the) word(s). To articulate is to joint. A joint (where only outlaws and the errant hang out) joins by separating and separates by joining. This joint, this threshold, is neither here nor there, neither present nor absent. And yet, without articulation there is only an inarticulateness, which is not merely silence but, simply, nothing. *Everything hinges on scripture*. . . .

Mitte designates not only center but also middle, midst, mean, and medium. For example, *die goldene Mitte* is the golden mean and *das Reich der Mitte* is the Middle Kingdom. Closely related to *Mitte*, *Mittel* refers to measure, mean, and medium. A suggestive extension of this word prompts further reflection. *Mittel* can also "mean" remedy or medicine. The French *milieu* captures various nuances of the German *Mitte*. *Le milieu* is the middle, midst, heart, center, medium, and mean. In addition to this cluster of meanings, *milieu* refers to one's environment, habitat, or surroundings. Through a curious twist of meaning, *le milieu* is sometimes used to designate the criminal underworld, the world of gangsters. Two English words closely related to *Mitte* and *milieu* are mean and medium. Mean derives from the Latin *medianus*, which is defined as "the middle." In this context, mean is that which is in the middle. This intermediate position can be both spatial and temporal. "Mean," of course, also designates an intermediary agent, i.e. one who acts as a mediator or go-between, who intercedes on behalf of one of the parties in a conflict. In view of issues yet to be considered, it is important to recall that the sacraments are labeled "the *means* of grace." "Medium" (*medius*, middle, midst, mid) likewise means something intermediate. Furthermore, medium refers to any intervening substance through which a force acts on objects at a distance, e.g. air or ether. This sense of the word gives rise to the notion of a pervading or enveloping substance or element in which an organism lives, i.e. its environment or the conditions of its life. By drawing on this fund of associations, it is possible to suggest that *Mitte*, or *milieu*, is "medium in the sense of middle, neither/nor, what is between extremes, and [a] medium in the sense of element, ether, matrix, means."[15]

This milieu marks a middle way that is thoroughly liminal. At this threshold, opposites cross. The margin itself, however, is not reducible to the extremes whose mean it forms. The medium, in other words, can never be contained, captured, or caught by any fixed pair of terms. Consequently, the milieu is always para-doxical. As we have seen elsewhere, a "thing in 'para' . . . is not only simultaneously on both sides of the boundary line between inside and out. It is also the boundary itself, the screen which is a permeable membrane connecting inside and outside. It confuses them with one another, allowing the outside in, making the inside out, dividing them and joining them. It also forms an ambiguous transition between one and the other."[16] This paradoxical limen or permeable membrane can be described as something like a *hymen*.[viii] By undermining the simplicity of oppositions and distinctions, "the hymen, the confusion between the present and the nonpresent, along with all the indifferences it entails within the whole series of opposites . . . produces the effect of a medium (a medium as element enveloping both terms at once; a medium located between the two terms). It is an operation that *both* sows confusion *between* opposites *and* stands *between* opposites 'at once.' What counts here is the *between*, the in-between-ness of the hymen. The hymen 'takes place' in the 'inter-,' in the spacing between desire and fulfillment, between penetration and its recollection. But this medium of the *entre* has nothing to do with a center."[17]

If *die Mitte ist überall*,[ix] *die Mitte* is not so much the center as it is the milieu. Moreover, this milieu is not restricted to a particular spatial or temporal point. It is everywhere and everytime. The universality of the

---

viii A membrane partly covering the opening of the vagina, broken during heterosexual intercourse. Derrida uses "hymen" as a sign for the "between" in his essay, "The Double Session."

ix The middle is everywhere.

medium implies that what is intermediate is not transitory and that what is interstitial is "permanent." Though always betwixt 'n' between, the "eternal" time of the middle neither begins nor ends. This universal and eternal milieu marks the (para)site where the word plays freely. Along this boundless boundary, the word appears divine. Scripture *is* the divine milieu, and the divine milieu *is* writing. The milieu embodied in word and inscribed in/by writing is divine insofar as it is the creative/destructive medium of everything that is and all that is not. Writing, as I have emphasized, is the "structured and differing origin of differences." This play of differences or differential web of interrelation is universally constitutive. When understood as scripture, the divine milieu is "what at the same time renders possible and impossible, probable and improbable oppositions such as"[18] eternity/time, infinitude/finitude, being/becoming, good/evil, etc. Writing is "originary" (though not original) inasmuch as it "grounds" or "founds" the differences that form and deform identity. Though the divine milieu is never simply present or absent, it is the *medium* of all presence and absence. In this complex mean, opposites, that do not remain themselves, cross over into each other and thus dissolve all original identity.

By disclosing the formative force of negativity, writing inverts and subverts the dyadic structure of the Western theological network. Through the enactment of an unending dialectic of transgression, the divine milieu effects "a total negation of everything which is manifest and real in consciousness and experience as God, so as to make possible a radically new form of consciousness and experience. Thereby a new form of God appears, but precisely because it is a radically new form it no longer can be given the name or image of God."[9] This negation of God appears as the word incarnate in writing. In the embodied word, the God of writing is manifested as the writing of God. The "figure of Thoth[x] is opposed to its other (father, sun, life, speech, origin or orient, etc.), but as that which at once supplements and supplants it. Thoth extends or opposes by repeating or replacing. By the same token, the figure of Thoth takes shape and takes its shape from the very thing it resists and substitutes for. But it thereby opposes *itself*, passes into its other, and this messenger-god is truly a god of the absolute passage between opposites. If he had any identity – but he is precisely the god of nonidentity – he would be that *coincidentia oppositorum* to which we shall soon have recourse again. In distinguishing himself from his opposite, Thoth also imitates it, becomes its sign and representative, obeys it and *conforms* to it, replaces it, by violence if need be. He is thus the father's other, the father, and the subversive movement of replacement.

---

[x] The Egyptian god, "Hermes" to the Greeks, whose name means "word," was the inventor of writing. Derrida writes of Thoth in his essay, "Plato's Pharmacy."

The god of writing is thus at once his father, his son, and himself. He cannot be assigned a fixed spot in the play of differences."[20]

It is, of course, impossible to *master* Thoth by the logic of exclusion. In the liminal time-space of scripture, hard-and-fast oppositions are shattered and every seemingly stable either-or is perpetually dislocated. The divine milieu is neither fully present nor absent but is present only to the extent that it is at the same time absent. It neither is nor is not; it is insofar as it is not and is not insofar as it is. It is not totally positive or completely negative but affirms in negating and negates in affirming. According to traditional logic, which rests on the correlative principles of identity and noncontradiction, such claims are not only improper, they are actually absurd. The paradoxical divine milieu presupposes a "logic of contamination and the contamination of logic."[21] The eternally errant medium in which all differentiation is produced and destroyed cannot be re-presented in distinct categories and clear concepts. For this reason, the divine milieu "is not thinkable within the terms of classical logic but only within the graphics . . . of the *pharmakon*."[22]

Transgressive scripture engenders incurable disease by violating propriety and infecting purity. In this case, dis-ease need not be destructive and can actually be productive. Insofar as writing is parasitical, it is both nourishing and debilitating. This ambiguity lends scripture its pharmacological character. The Greek word from which *pharmaco-* and all its variants derive is *pharmakon*, which can mean "drug, medicine, or poison." Interestingly enough, the god of writing is also the god of medicine, who is supposed to restore health. A medicine man, however, is always something of a magician and trickster. The drug he prescribes is both a medicine and a poison – both gift and *Gift*.[xi] This generative/destructive *prescription* is a *pharmakon*. "If the *pharmakon* is 'ambivalent,' it is because it constitutes the medium in which opposites are opposed, the movement and the play that link them among themselves, reverses them or makes one side cross over into the other. . . . The *pharmakon* is the movement, the locus, and the play: (the production of) difference."[23] Though it is supposed to fix, the *pharmakon* itself cannot be fixed. Its shape is always changing, its form forever reforming. The *pharmakon* seems to be a liquid medium whose play is completely fluid. Like ink, wine, and semen, the *pharmakon* always manages to penetrate. "[I]t is absorbed, drunk, introduced into the inside, which it first marks with the hardness of the type, soon to invade and inundate it with its medicine, its brew, its drink, its potion, its poison."[24]

Such a strange potion can be concocted only by a physician who knows the magic (of) word(s): Hocus-pocus – *Hoc est corpus meum*.[xii] In the(se)

[xi] "Gift" in German means poison.

[xii] This is my body.

extraordinary word(s), the physician himself appears as a *pharmakos*. Like every uncanny guest, this unsettling trickster is never permitted to pass beyond the threshold. Responsible authorities and distinguished authors attempt to keep the *pharmakos* behind bars. For this reason, the "site" of the word is always marked by an X and forever bears the sign of a cross. Since the *pharmakos* is irreducibly marginal, the ceremony in which it (or rather "he") is imbibed and inscribed must be "played out on the boundary line between inside and outside, which it has as its function ceaselessly to trace and retrace. *Intra muros/extra muros*.[xiii] The origin of differences and division, the *pharmakos* represents evil both introjected and projected. Beneficial insofar as he cures – and for that, venerated and cared for – harmful insofar as he incarnates the powers of evil – and for that, feared and treated with caution. Alarming and calming. Sacred and accursed."[25]

In the ambiguous figure of the *pharmakos*, the intercourse of Terminus and Dionysus is manifest in the body and blood of the Crucified.[xiv] The Crucified is the cruciform word that is always already inscribed in the eternally recurring play of the divine milieu. Scripture marks the *via crucis* in which all creation involves dismemberment and every solution presupposes dissolution.[xv] When *die Mitte ist überall*, transitoriness and passage no longer need to be repressed. Arising and passing can be welcomed as "productive and destructive force, as *continual creation*."

The incarnate word inscribed in writing spells the closure of all presence that is not at the same time absence and the end of all identity that is not also difference. Writing is an unending play of differences that establishes the thoroughgoing relativity of all "things." This complex web of interrelations is the divine milieu. Within this nontotalizable totality, nothing is itself by itself, for all things emerge and fade through the interplay of forces. Insofar as the embodied word "is the name of the eternal perishing of eternal presence,"[26] scripture marks the death of God. In different terms, writing is a kenotic process; it empties everything of absolute self-identity and complete self-presence. In the eternal play of the divine milieu, nothing is fully autonomous or solely sovereign. Thus there is no *causa sui*,[xvi] antecedent to and the ultimate origin of everything else. The absolute relativity of the divine milieu renders all other things completely co-relative. As a consequence of the eternal cross(ing) of scripture, nothing stands alone and everything "originates" codependently. "Codependent

---

[xiii] *Intra muros/extra muros* means "within the walls" (e.g. of a town)/"outside the walls."

[xiv] Terminus was the Roman god of boundaries and endings (e.g. of the year). Dionysus was the Greek god of fertility, wine and sensual ecstasy ("Bacchus" to the Romans).

[xv] *Via crucis* means "way of the cross."

[xvi] *Causa sui* means "self-cause."

origination"[27] is nothing other than the nonoriginal origin that erases absolute originality.

As the nonoriginal origin that "founds" the differences constitutive of relative identity, writing inverts and subverts the notion of origin itself. The generative movement of scripture rifts all seemingly immovable foundations and keeps everything in motion. The incarnate word is neither transcendent nor self-derived. To the contrary, the divine milieu is a/the grounded ground that, nonetheless, "grounds." In writing's unending play of differences, neither ground nor grounded is absolutely prior or undeniably primal. Ground and grounded are separated and joined in a relation that is characterized by radical codependence. "{T}here is nothing in the ground that is not in the grounded, and there is nothing in the grounded that is not in the ground."[28] Since writing empties every causa sui of total self-possession, the divine milieu cannot be an absolute origin. It must be a nonoriginal "origin" or a grounded "ground." Contrary to common sense, writing is "founded" by the differences it "founds." In other words, writing is always in other words. The word is never disembodied; it is forever inscribed in writing. Since the word incarnates the coincidence of presence and absence and of identity and difference, it appears only by disappearing. This unstoppable interplay shows that the Logos is always the Logos Spermatikos, endlessly propagated by dissemination.[xvii] Dissemination inscribes the way from the eternal recurrence of the divine milieu to the free play of marks and traces.

"To disseminate" (disseminare: dis + semen, gen. seminis, seed) is to scatter abroad, as in sowing seed. By extension, dissemination refers to the action of dispersing, diffusing, broadcasting, or promulgating. When translated into the present context, these verbal affiliations suggest that the dissemination of the word can be understood as its spreading, scattering, diffusion, or publication. The notion of the dissemination of the word is not, of course, new. Consider, for example, the following parabolic formulation:

> A sower went out to sow. And as he sowed, some seed fell along the path, and the birds came and devoured it. Other seed fell on rocky ground, where it had not much soil, and immediately it sprang up, since it had no depth of soil; and when the sun rose it was scorched, and since it had no root it withered away. Other seed fell among thorns and the thorns grew up and choked it, and it yielded no grain. And other seeds fell into good soil and brought forth grain, growing up and increasing and yielding thirtyfold and sixtyfold and a hundredfold.[29]

[xvii] Derrida writes of "Logos Spermatikos," or "word seed," meaning that Logos is usually conceived by the Western tradition as reproductive (and male). "Dissemination" is the name of an essay, and a book, by Derrida.

Like any text, these lines can be read in many ways. In this context, it is important to recognize that, according to this parable, the word is seed that appears with the disappearance of the sower. The "sower, mentioned only at the start of the story, immediately disappears. It would have been quite possible to leave him out completely: 'at the time of sowing, some seed fell. . . .' It would also have been easy to have retained him consistently: 'and some of the sower's seed fell. . . .' Instead, he is mentioned at the start and thereafter ignored. The parable is about seed and about the inevitable polyvalence of failure and success in sowing. . . . Or, if one prefers, it is about the absence and departure, the necessary self-negation of the sower."[30] By negating the sower in order to concentrate on the seed, this parable implies that dispersal is neither accidental nor secondary to a primordial, self-contained word. Quite the opposite, dissemination is necessary if any word is to be fertile. The seminal/seminary word *must* flow freely in liquid media like ink, semen, and wine. Because of its fluency, the embodied word cannot be contained within fixed boundaries or inscribed in straight lines. It is always dispersed and diffused. Furthermore, this scattering is not a temporary aberration, eventually overcome. Dissemination "can be led back neither to a present of simple origin . . . nor to an eschatological presence. It marks an irreducible *generative* multiplicity."[31] By figuring what cannot return to the father, the dissemination of the word replaces sterile stability and univocacy with creative instability and equivocacy.

To the extent that the embodied word enacts the *kenōsis* of all absolute self-presence and total self-identity, it can be itself only in and through the process of *its own* self-emptying. Like the transcendent father, the incarnate son must also pass away. Having displaced the Lord of Hosts, word becomes host. The word, which itself is a transgressor, is at the same time a victim who invites transgression. The patricidal act of transgression manifests the host-ility of the word. Not only is parasite host; sacrificer is also sacrifice. The word turns out to be a hospitable host who asks everyone to sit down at his table and even offers *himself* for our nourishment.

> For my flesh is food indeed, and my blood is drink indeed. He who eats my flesh and drinks my blood abides in me, and I in him.

Word becomes flesh: body and blood, bread and wine. Take, eat. Take, drink. To eat this bread and drink this wine is to extend the embodiment of the word and to expand the fluid play of the divine milieu. When freely enacted, the drama of the word proves to be self-consuming. While the incarnation of the divine is the death of God, the dissemination of the word is the crucifixion of the individual self. This dismemberment inflicts an incurable wound, which gives birth to erratic marks and erring traces.

Mark C. Taylor

Notes

1 Jacques Derrida, *Positions*, trans. A. Bass (Chicago: University of Chicago Press, 1981), p. 40.
2 Friedrich Nietzsche, *The Gay Science*, trans. Walten Kaufman (New York: Random House, 1974), p. 182.
3 Thomas J. J. Altizer, *The Descent into Hell: A Study of the Radical Reversal of the Christian Consciousness* (New York: Seabury Press, 1979), p. 53.
4 J. Hillis Millier, "Theology and Logology in Victorian Literature," in *Religion and Literature: The Convergence of Approaches*, supplement to *Journal of the American Academy of Religion*, 47 (1979): 354.
5 Jacques Derrida, *Writing and Difference*, trans. A. Bass (Chicago: University of Chicago Press, 1978), p. 20.
6 Unless otherwise indicated, I have drawn definitions and etymologies from the *Oxford English Dictionary* (New York: Oxford University Press, 1971).
7 Gilles Deleuze, "Nomad Thought," in *The New Nietzsche: Contemporary Styles of Interpretation*, ed. D. B. Allison (New York: Dell, 1977), pp. 142–9.
8 William Blake.
9 Robert Scharlemann, "The Being of God When God Is Not Being God: Deconstructing the History of Theism," in Altizer et al., *Deconstruction and Theology* (New York: Crossroad, 1982), p. 101.
10 Jacques Derrida, *Of Grammatology*, trans. G. C. Spivak (Baltimore: Johns Hopkins University Press, 1976), p. 14.
11 Samuel Beckett, quoted in Daniel Albright, *Representation and the Imagination: Beckett, Kafka, Nabokov, and Schoenberg* (Chicago: University of Chicago Press, 1981), p. 2.
12 Jacques Derrida, *Dissemination*, trans, B. Johnson (Chicago: University of Chicago Press, 1981), p. 77.
13 Ibid., p. 146.
14 Jacques Derrida, *Speech and Phenomena, and other Essays on Husserl's Theory of Signs*, trans. D. B. Allison, (Evanston, Ill.: Northwestern University, 1973), p. 134.
15 Derrida, *Dissemination*, p. 211.
16 J. Hillis Miller, "The Critic as Host," in Harold Bloom et al., *Deconstruction and Criticism* (New York: Seabury, 1979), p. 219.
17 Derrida, *Dissemination*, p. 212.
18 Jacques Derrida, "Limited Inc abc . . . ," *Glyph*, 7 (1980): 176–233, p. 225.
19 Altizer, *Descent into Hell*, pp. 56–7.
20 Derrida, *Dissemination*, pp. 92–3.
21 Ibid., p. 149.
22 Ibid., p. 153.
23 Ibid., p. 127.
24 Ibid., p. 152.
25 Ibid., p. 133.
26 Thomas J. Altizer, *The Self-Embodiment of God* (New York: Harper & Row, 1979), p. 36.

532

27 Nargarjuna.

28 G. W. F. Hegel, *Science of Logic* trans. A. V. Miller (New York: Humanities Press, 1969), p. 457.

29 Mark 4: 3–8.

30 John Dominic Crossan, *Cliffs of Fall: Paradox and Polyvalence in the Parables of Jesus* (New York: Crossroad, 1980), p. 50.

31 Derrida, *Positions*, p. 45.

chapter thirty-four

"The Virtues, the Unity of a Human Life and the Concept of a Tradition"

Alasdair MacIntyre

Philosopher Alasdair MacIntyre (1929–) presents a critique of modernity in the opposite direction from postmodernism, in effect defending the past against the present and the future. Modern liberalism has regarded cultural tradition as dispensable. But outside of tradition, he argues, there can be no conclusive rational deliberation. Traditions provide the ultimate vocabularies for the "narratives" that any self can tell about its life and thereby achieve self-understanding. Man, according to MacIntyre, is a story-telling animal. By denying legitimacy to such traditional narratives, liberalism has led to nihilism and the end of rational discourse regarding conduct. In advanced liberal society all moral deliberation ends in pronouncements of unjustifiable preferences that cannot be adjudicated. MacIntyre's hope lies in a return to the "virtue ethics" of Aristotle, a culture-bound account of the traits of the ideal moral personality, unlike the moral theories of Kant and Utilitarianism which ignore personality in a hopeless search for universal rules for action that transcend culture.

Any contemporary attempt to envisage each human life as a whole, as a unity, whose character provides the virtues with an adequate *telos* encounters two different kinds of obstacle, one social and one philosophical. The social obstacles derive from the way in which modernity partitions each human life into a variety of segments, each with its own norms and modes of behavior. So work is divided from leisure, private life from public, the corporate from the personal. So both childhood and old age have been wrenched away from the rest of human life and made over into distinct realms. And all these separations have been achieved so that it is the distinctiveness of each and not the unity of the life of the individual who

Alasdair MacIntyre, "The Virtues, the Unity of a Human Life and the Concept of a Tradition," chapter 15 of *After Virtue* (Notre Dame, Ind.: University of Notre Dame Press, 1984), pp. 204–25.

passes through those parts in terms of which we are taught to think and to feel.

The philosophical obstacles derive from two distinct tendencies, one chiefly, though not only, domesticated in analytical philosophy and one at home in both sociological theory and in existentialism. The former is the tendency to think atomistically about human action and to analyze complex actions and transactions in terms of simple components. Hence the recurrence in more than one context of the notion of "a basic action." That particular actions derive their character as parts of larger wholes is a point of view alien to our dominant ways of thinking and yet one which it is necessary at least to consider if we are to begin to understand how a life may be more than a sequence of individual actions and episodes.

Equally the unity of a human life becomes invisible to us when a sharp separation is made either between the individual and the roles that he or she plays – a separation characteristic not only of Sartre's existentialism, but also of the sociological theory of Ralf Dahrendorf – or between the different role – and quasi-role – enactments of an individual life so that life comes to appear as nothing but a series of unconnected episodes – a liquidation of the self characteristic, as I noticed earlier, of Goffman's sociological theory. I already, also suggested in Chapter 3 that both the Sartrian and the Goffmanesque[i] conceptions of selfhood are highly characteristic of the modes of thought and practice of modernity. It is perhaps therefore unsurprising to realize that the self as thus conceived cannot be envisaged as a bearer of the Aristotelian virtues.

For a self separated from its roles in the Sartrian mode loses that arena of social relationships in which the Aristotelian virtues function if they function at all. The patterns of a virtuous life would fall under those condemnations of conventionality which Sartre put into the mouth of Antoine Roquentin in *La Nausée* and which he uttered in his own person in *L'Etre et le néant*.[ii] Indeed the self's refusal of the inauthenticity of conventionalized social relationships becomes what integrity is diminished into in Sartre's account.

At the same time the liquidation of the self into a set of demarcated areas of role-playing allows no scope for the exercise of dispositions which could genuinely be accounted virtues in any sense remotely Aristotelian. For a virtue is not a disposition that makes for success only in some one particular type of situation. What are spoken of as the virtues of a good committee man or of a good administrator or of a gambler or a pool hustler

---

[i] Erving Goffman (1922–82), sociologist famous for studying the relation of personal identity to social roles.

[ii] Sartre's novel, *Nausea*, and his most important philosophical work, *Being and Nothingness*, respectively.

are professional skills professionally deployed in those situations where they can be effective, not virtues. Someone who genuinely possesses a virtue can be expected to manifest it in very different types of situation, many of them situations where the practice of a virtue cannot be expected to be effective in the way that we expect a professional skill to be. Hector exhibited one and the same courage in his parting from Andromache and on the battlefield with Achilles; Eleanor Marx exhibited one and the same compassion in her relationship with her father, in her work with trade unionists and in her entanglement with Aveling. And the unity of a virtue in someone's life is intelligible only as a characteristic of a unitary life, a life that can be conceived and evaluated as a whole. Hence just as in the discussion of the changes in and fragmentation of morality which accompanied the rise of modernity in the earlier parts of this book, each stage in the emergence of the characteristically modern views of the moral judgment was accompanied by a corresponding stage in the emergence of the characteristically modern conceptions of selfhood; so now, in defining the particular pre-modern concept of the virtues with which I have been preoccupied, it has become necessary to say something of the concomitant concept of selfhood, a concept of a self whose unity resides in the unity of a narrative which links birth to life to death as narrative beginning to middle to end.

Such a conception of the self is perhaps less unfamiliar than it may appear at first sight. Just because it has played a key part in the cultures which are historically predecessors of our own, it would not be surprising if it turned out to be still an unacknowledged presence in many of our ways of thinking and acting. Hence it is not inappropriate to begin by scrutinizing some of our most taken-for-granted, but clearly correct conceptual insights about human actions and selfhood in order to show how natural it is to think of the self in a narrative mode.

It is a conceptual commonplace, both for philosophers and for ordinary agents, that one and the same segment of human behavior may be correctly characterized in a number of different ways. To the question "What is he doing?" the answers may with equal truth and appropriateness be "Digging," "Gardening," "Taking exercise," "Preparing for winter" or "Pleasing his wife." Some of these answers will characterize the agent's intentions, others unintended consequences of his actions, and of these unintended consequences some may be such that the agent is aware of them and others not. What is important to notice immediately is that any answer to the questions of how we are to understand or to explain a given segment of behavior will presuppose some prior answer to the question of how these different correct answers to the question "What is he doing?" are related to each other. For if someone's primary intention is to put the garden in order before the winter and it is only incidentally the case that

536

in so doing he is taking exercise and pleasing his wife, we have one type of behavior to be explained; but if the agent's primary intention is to please his wife by taking exercise, we have quite another type of behavior to be explained and we will have to look in a different direction for under-standing and explanation.

In the first place the episode has been situated in an annual cycle of domestic activity, and the behavior embodies an intention which presup-poses a particular type of household-cum-garden setting with the peculiar narrative history of that setting in which this segment of behavior now becomes an episode. In the second instance the episode has been situated in the narrative history of a marriage, a very different, even if related, social setting. We cannot, that is to say, charcterize behavior independently of intentions, and we cannot characterize intentions independently of the settings which make those intentions intelligible both to agents themselves and to others.

I use the word 'setting' here as a relatively inclusive term. A social setting may be an institution, it may be what I have called a practice, or it may be a milieu of some other human kind. But it is central to the notion of a setting as I am going to understand it that a setting has a history, a history within which the histories of individual agents not only are, but have to be, situated, just because without the setting and its changes through time the history of the individual agent and his changes through time will be unintelligible. Of course one and the same piece of behavior may belong to more than one setting. There are at least two different ways in which this may be so.

In my earlier example the agent's activity may be part of the history both of the cycle of household activity and of his marriage, two histories which have happened to intersect. The household may have its own history stretching back through hundreds of years, as do the histories of some European farms, where the farm has had a life of its own, even though different families have in different periods inhabited it; and the marriage will certainly have its own history, a history which itself presupposes that a particular point has been reached in the history of the institution of marriage. If we are to relate some particular segment of behavior in any precise way to an agent's intentions and thus to the settings which that agent inhabits, we shall have to understand in a precise way how the variety of correct characterizations of the agent's behavior relate to each other first by identifying which characteristics refer us to an intention and which do not and then by classifying further the items in both categories.

Where intentions are concerned, we need to know which intention or intentions were primary, that is to say, of which it is the case that, had the agent intended otherwise, he would not have performed that action. Thus if we know that a man is gardening with the self-avowed purposes of

537

healthful exercise and of pleasing his wife, we do not yet know how to understand what he is doing until we know the answer to such questions as whether he would continue gardening if he continued to believe that gardening was healthful exercise, but discovered that his gardening no longer pleased his wife, *and* whether he would continue gardening, if he ceased to believe that gardening was healthful exercise, but continued to believe that it pleased his wife, *and* whether he would continue gardening if he changed his beliefs on both points. That is to say, we need to know both what certain of his beliefs are and which of them are causally effective; and, that is to say, we need to know whether certain contrary-to-fact hypothetical statements are true or false. And until we know this, we shall not know how to characterize correctly what the agent is doing.

Consider another equally trivial example of a set of compatibly correct answers to the question "What is he doing?" "Writing a sentence"; "Finishing his book"; "Contributing to the debate on the theory of action"; "Trying to get tenure." Here the intentions can be ordered in terms of the stretch of time to which reference is made. Each of the shorter-term intentions is, and can only be made, intelligible by reference to some longer-term intentions; and the characterization of the behavior in terms of the longer-term intentions can only be correct if some of the characterizations in terms of shorter-term intentions are also correct. Hence the behaviour is only characterized adequately when we know what the longer and longest-term intentions invoked are and how the shorter-term intentions are related to the longer. Once again we are involved in writing a narrative history.

Intentions thus need to be ordered both causally and temporally and both orderings will make references to settings, references already made obliquely by such elementary terms as "gardening," "wife," "book," and "tenure." Moreover the correct identification of the agent's beliefs will be an essential constituent of this task; failure at this point would mean failure in the whole enterprise. (The conclusion may seem obvious; but it already entails one important consequence. There is no such thing as 'behaviour', to be identified prior to and independently of intentions, beliefs and settings. Hence the project of a science of behavior takes on a mysterious and somewhat outré character. It is not that such a science is impossible; but there is nothing for it to be but a science of uninterpreted physical movement such as B.F. Skinner aspires to.[iii] It is no part of my task here to examine Skinner's problems; but it is worth noticing that it is not at all clear what a scientific experiment could be, if one were a Skinnerian; since the conception of an experiment is certainly one of intention- and belief-informed behavior. And what would be utterly doomed to failure would be

[iii] B. F. Skinner (1904–90), famous American behaviorist psychologist.

the project of a science of, say, *political* behavior, detached from a study of intentions, beliefs and settings. It is perhaps worth noting that when the expression "the behavioral sciences" was given its first influential use in a Ford Foundation Report of 1953, the term "behavior" was defined so as to include what were called "such subjective behavior as attitudes, beliefs, expectations, motivations and aspirations" as well as "overt acts." But what the Report's wording seems to imply is that it is cataloguing two distinct sets of items, available for independent study. If the argument so far is correct, then there is only one set of items.)

Consider what the argument so far implies about the interrelationships of the intentional, the social and the historical. We identify a particular action only by invoking two kinds of context, implicitly if not explicitly. We place the agent's intentions, I have suggested, in causal and temporal order with reference to their role in his or her history; and we also place them with reference to their role in the history of the setting or settings to which they belong. In doing this, in determining what causal efficacy the agent's intentions had in one or more directions, and how his short-term intentions succeeded or failed to be constitutive of long-term intentions, we ourselves write a further part of these histories. Narrative history of a certain kind turns out to be the basic and essential genre for the characterization of human actions.

It is important to be clear how different the standpoint presupposed by the argument so far is from that of those analytical philosophers who have constructed accounts of human actions which make central the notion of "a" human action. A course of human events is then seen as a complex sequence of individual actions, and a natural question is: How do we individuate human actions? Now there are contexts in which such notions are at home. In the recipes of a cookery book for instance actions are individuated in just the way that some analytical philosophers have supposed to be possible of all actions. "Take six eggs. Then break them into a bowl. Add flour, salt, sugar, etc." But the point about such sequences is that each element in them is intelligible as an action only as a- possible-element-in-a-sequence. Moreover even such a sequence requires a context to be intelligible. If in the middle of my lecture on Kant's ethics I suddenly broke six eggs into a bowl and added flour and sugar, proceeding all the while with my Kantian exegesis, I have *not*, simply in virtue of the fact that I was following a sequence prescribed by Fanny Farmer, performed an intelligible action.

To this it might be retorted that I certainly performed an action or a set of actions, if not an intelligible action. But to this I want to reply that the concept of an intelligible action. is a more fundamental concept than that of an action as such. Unintelligible actions are failed candidates for the status of intelligible action; and to lump unintelligible actions and intelligible actions together in a single class of actions and then to characterize action in terms of what items of both sets have in common is to make the mistake of ignoring this. It is also to neglect the central importance of the concept of intelligibility.

The importance of the concept of intelligibility is closely related to the fact that the most basic distinction of all embedded in our discourse and our practice in this area is that between human beings and other beings. Human beings can be held to account for that of which they are the authors; other beings cannot. To identify an occurrence as an action is in the paradigmatic instances to identify it under a type of description which enables us to see that occurrence as flowing intelligibly from a human agent's intentions, motives, passions and purposes. It is therefore to understand an action as something for which someone is accountable, about which it is always appropriate to ask the agent for an intelligible account. When an occurrence is apparently the intended action of a human agent, but nonetheless we cannot so identify it, we are both intellectually and practically baffled. We do not know how to respond; we do not know how to explain; we do not even know how to characterize minimally as an intelligible action; our distinction between the humanly accountable and the merely natural seems to have broken down. And this kind of bafflement does indeed occur in a number of different kinds of situation; when we enter alien cultures or even alien social structures within our own culture, in our encounters with certain types of neurotic or psychotic patient (it is indeed the unintelligibility of such pa-tients' actions that leads to their being treated as patients; actions unintel-ligible to the agent as well as to everyone else are understood – rightly – as a kind of suffering), but also in everyday situations. Consider an example.

I am standing waiting for a bus and the young man standing next to me suddenly says: "The name of the common wild duck is *Histrionicus histrioni-cus histrionicus*." There is no problem as to the meaning of the sentence he uttered: the problem is, how to answer the question, what was he doing in uttering it? Suppose he just uttered such sentences at random intervals; this would be one possible form of madness. We would render his action of utterance intelligible if one of the following turned out to be true. He has mistaken me for someone who yesterday had approached him in the library and asked: "Do you by any chance know the Latin name of the common wild duck?" *Or* he has just come from a session with his psychotherapist who has urged him to break down his shyness by talking to strangers. "But what shall I say?" "Oh, anything at all." *Or* he is a Soviet spy waiting at a prearranged rendez-vous and uttering the ill-chosen code sentence which will identify him to his contact. In each case the act of utterance becomes intelligible by finding its place in a narrative.

To this it may be replied that the supplying of a narrative is not necessary to make such an act intelligible. All that is required is that we can identify the relevant type of speech act (e.g. "He was answering a question") or some purpose served by his utterance (e.g. "He was trying to attract your attention"). But speech acts and purposes too can be intelligible or unintelligible. Suppose that the man at the bus stop explains his act of utterance by saying "I was answering a question." I reply: "But I never asked you any question to which that could have been the answer." He says, "Oh, I know *that*." Once again his action becomes unintelligible. And a parallel example could easily be constructed to show that the mere fact that an action serves some purposes of a recognized type is not sufficient to render an action intelligible. Both purposes and speech-acts require contexts.

The most familiar type of context in and by reference to which speech-acts and purposes are rendered intelligible is the conversation. Conversation is so all-pervasive a feature of the human world that it tends to escape philosophical attention. Yet remove conversation from human life and what would be left? Consider then what is involved in following a conversation and finding it intelligible or unintelligible. (To find a conversation intelligible is not the same as to understand it; for a conversation which I overhear may be intelligible, but I may fail to understand it.) If I listen to a conversation between two other people my ability to grasp the thread of the conversation will involve an ability to bring it under some one out of a set of descriptions in which the degree and kind of coherence in the conversation is brought out: "a drunken, rambling quarrel," "a serious intellectual disagreement," "a tragic misunderstanding of each other," "a comic, even farcial miscontrual of each other's motives," "a penetrating interchange of views," "a struggle to dominate each other," "a trivial exchange of gossip."

The use of words such as "tragic," "comic," and "farcial" is not marginal to such evaluations. We allocate conversations to genres, just as we do literary narratives. Indeed a conversation is a dramatic work, even if a very short one, in which the participants are not only the actors, but also the joint authors, working out in agreement or disagreement the mode of their production. For it is not just that conversations belong to genres in just the way that plays and novels do; but they have beginnings, middles and endings just as do literary works. They embody reversals and recognitions; they move towards and away from climaxes. There may within a longer conversation be digressions and subplots, indeed digressions within digressions and subplots within subplots.

But if this is true of conversations, it is true also *mutatis mutandis* of battles, chess games, courtships, philosophy seminars, families at the dinner table, businessmen negotiating contracts – that is, of human transactions in general. For conversation, understood widely enough, is the form of human transactions in general. Conversational behavior is not a special sort or aspect of human behavior, even though the forms of language-using and of human life are such that the deeds of others speak for them as much as do their words. For that is possible only because they are the deeds of those who have words.

I am presenting both conversations in particular then and human actions in general as enacted narratives. Narrative is not the work of poets, dramatists and novelists reflecting upon events which had no narrative order before one was imposed by the singer or the writer; narrative form is neither disguise nor decoration. Barbara Hardy has written that "we dream in narrative, day-dream in narrative, remember, anticipate, hope, despair, believe, doubt, plan, revise, criticize, construct, gossip, learn, hate and love by narrative" in arguing the same point.[iv]

At the beginning of this chapter I argued that in successfully identifying and understanding what someone else is doing we always move towards placing a particular episode in the context of a set of narrative histories, histories both of the individuals concerned and of the settings in which they act and suffer. It is now becoming clear that we render the actions of others intelligible in this way because action itself has a basically historical character. It is because we all live out narratives in our lives and because we understand our own lives in terms of the narratives that we live out that the form of narrative is appropriate for understanding the actions of others. Stories are lived before they are told – except in the case of fiction.

This has of course been denied in recent debates. Louis O. Mink, quarrelling with Barbara Hardy's view, has asserted: "Stories are not lived but told. Life has no beginnings, middles, or ends; there are meetings, but the start of an affair belongs to the story we tell ourselves later, and there are partings, but final partings only in the story. There are hopes, plans, battles and ideas, but only in retrospective stories are hopes unfulfilled, plans miscarried, battles decisive, and ideas seminal. Only in the story is it America which Columbus discovers and only in the story is the kingdom lost for want of a nail".[v]

What are we to say to this? Certainly we must agree that it is only retrospectively that hopes can be characterized as unfulfilled or battles as decisive and so on. But we so characterize them in life as much as in art. And to someone who says that in life there are no endings, or that final partings take place only in stories, one is tempted to reply, "But have you never heard of death?" Homer did not have to tell the tale of Hector before Andromache could lament unfulfilled hope and final parting.[vi] There are

[iv] Barbara Hardy, "Towards a Poetics of Fiction," *Novel*, 2, 1968: 5–14.

[v] Louis O. Mink, "History and Fiction as Modes of Comprehension," *New Literary History*, 1, 1970: 541–58.

[vi] In the *Iliad*.

countless Hectors and countless Andromaches whose lives embodied the form of their Homeric namesakes, but who never came to the attention of any poet. What is true is that in taking an event as a beginning or an ending we bestow a significance upon it which may be debatable. Did the Roman republic end with the death of Julius Caesar, or at Philippi, or with the founding of the principate? The answer is surely that, like Charles II, it was a long time a-dying; but this answer implies the reality of its ending as much as do any of the former. There is a crucial sense in which the principate of Augustus, or the taking of the oath in the tennis court, or the decision to construct an atomic bomb at Los Alamos constitute beginnings; the peace of 404 BC, the abolition of the Scottish Parliament and the battle of Waterloo equally constitute endings; while there are many events which are both endings and beginnings.[vii]

As with beginnings, middles and endings, so also with genres and with the phenomenon of embedding. Consider the question of to what genre the life of Thomas Becket belongs, a question which has to be asked and answered before we can decide how it is to be written. (On Mink's paradoxical view this question could not be asked until *after* the life had been written.) In some of the medieval versions, Thomas's career is presented in terms of the canons of medieval hagiography. In the Icelandic *Thomas Saga* he is presented as a saga hero. In Dom David Knowles's modern biography the story is a tragedy, the tragic relationship of Thomas and Henry II, each of whom satisfies Aristotle's demand that the hero be a great man with a fatal flaw. Now it clearly makes sense to ask who is right, if anyone: the monk William of Canterbury, the author of the saga, or the Cambridge Regius Professor Emeritus? The answer appears to be clearly the last. The true genre of the life is neither hagiography nor saga, but tragedy. So of such modern narrative subjects as the life of Trotsky or that of Lenin, of the history of the Soviet Communist Party or the American presidency, we may also ask: To what genre does their history belong? And this is the same question as: What type of account of their history will be both true and intelligible?

Or consider again how one narrative may be embedded in another. In both plays and novels there are well-known examples: the play within the play in *Hamlet*, Wandering Willie's Tale in *Redgauntlet*, Aeneas' narrative to Dido in book 2 of the *Aeneid*, and so on.[viii] But there are equally well-known examples in real life. Consider again the way in which the career of Becket as archbishop and chancellor is embedded within the reign

[vii] Augustus Caesar, Roman Emperor 27 BC–14 AD; in the French Revolution a republican National Assembly was first declared on a tennis court; the Peloponnesian War ended in 404 BC; the Scottish Parliament ended in 1707; in 1815 Napoleon was defeated at Waterloo.

[viii] *Redgauntlet* by Sir Walter Scott (1771–1832), *Aeneid* by Virgil (70–19 BC).

of Henry II, or the way in which the tragic life of Mary Stuart is embedded in that of Elizabeth I, or the history of the Confederacy within the history of the United States. Someone may discover (or not discover) that he or she is a character in a number of narratives at the same time, some of them embedded in others. Or again, what seemed to be an intelligible narrative in which one was playing a part may be transformed wholly or partly into a story of unintelligible episodes. This last is what happened to Kafka's character K. in both *The Trial* and *The Castle*. (It is no accident that Kafka could not end his novels, for the notion of an ending like that of a beginning has its sense only in terms of intelligible narrative.)

I spoke earlier of the agent as not only an actor, but an author. Now I must emphasize that what the agent is able to do and say intelligibly as an actor is deeply affected by the fact that we are never more (and sometimes less) than the co-authors of our own narratives. Only in fantasy do we live what story we please. In life, as both Aristotle and Engels noted, we are always under certain constraints. We enter upon a stage which we did not design and we find ourselves part of an action that was not of our making. Each of us being a main character in his own drama plays subordinate parts in the dramas of others, and each drama constrains the others. In my drama, perhaps, I am Hamlet or Iago or at least the swineherd who may yet become a prince, but to you I am only A Gentleman or at best Second Murderer, while you are my Polonius or my Gravedigger, but your own hero. Each of our dramas exerts constraints on each other's, making the whole different from the parts, but still dramatic.

It is considerations as complex as these which are involved in making the notion of intelligibility the conceptual connecting link between the notion of action and that of narrative. Once we have understood its importance the claim that the concept of an action is secondary to that of an intelligible action will perhaps appear less bizarre and so too will the claim that the notion of 'an' action, while of the highest practical importance, is always a potentially misleading abstraction. An action is a moment in a possible or actual history or in a number of such histories. The notion of a history is as fundamental a notion as the notion of an action. Each requires the other. But I cannot say this without noticing that it is precisely this that Sartre denies – as indeed his whole theory of the self, which captures so well the spirit of modernity, requires that he should. In *La Nausée*, Sartre makes Antoine Roquentin argue not just what Mink argues, that narrative is very different from life, but that to present human life in the form of a narrative is always to falsify it. There are not and there cannot be any true stories. Human life is composed of discrete actions which lead nowhere, which have no order; the story-teller imposes on human events retrospectively an order which they did not have while they were lived. Clearly if Sartre/Roquentin is right – I speak of Sartre/Roquentin to distinguish him from such other well-known characters as Sartre/Heidegger and Sartre/Marx – my central contention must be mistaken. There is nonetheless an important point of agreement between my thesis and that of Sartre/Roquentin. We agree in identifying the intelligibility of an action with its place in a narrative sequence. Only Sartre/Roquentin takes it that human actions are as such unintelligible occurrences: it is to a realization of the metaphysical implications of this that Roquentin is brought in the course of the novel and the practical effect upon him is to bring to an end his own project of writing an historical biography. This project no longer makes sense. Either he will write what is true or he will write an intelligible history, but the one possibility excludes the other. Is Sartre/Roquentin right?

We can discover what is wrong with Sartre's thesis in either of two ways. One is to ask: what would human actions deprived of any falsifying narrative order be like? Sartre himself never answers this question; it is striking that in order to show that there are no true narratives, he himself writes a narrative, albeit a fictional one. But the only picture that I find myself able to form of human nature *an-sich*,[ix] prior to the alleged misinterpretation by narrative, is the kind of dislocated sequence which Dr Johnson offers us in his notes of his travels in France: "There we waited on the ladies – Morville's. – Spain. Country towns all beggars. At Dijon he could not find the way to Orleans. – Cross roads of France very bad. – Five soldiers. – Women. – Soldiers escaped. – The Colonel would not lose five men for the sake of one woman. – The magistrate cannot seize a soldier but by the Colonel's permission, etc., etc."[x] What this suggests is what I take to be true, namely that the characterization of actions allegedly prior to any narrative form being imposed upon them will always turn out to be the presentation of what are plainly the disjointed parts of some possible narrative.

We can also approach the question in another way. What I have called a history is an enacted dramatic narrative in which the characters are also the authors. The characters of course never start literally *ab initio*; they plunge *in medias res*, the beginnings of their story already made for them by what and who has gone before. But when Julian Grenfell or Edward Thomas went off to France in the 1914–18 war they no less enacted a narrative than did Menelaus or Odysseus when *they* went off.[xi] The difference between imaginary characters and real ones is not in the

---

[ix] In-itself.

[x] See Philip Hobsbaum, *A Reader's Guide to Charles Dickens* (New York, 1973), p. 32.

[xi] English writers Julian Grenfell (1888–1915) and Edward Thomas (1878–1917) died in the war; Menelaus, King of Sparta, served Greece in the Trojan War, as did Odysseus, hero of Homer's *Odyssey*.

narrative form of what they do; it is in the degree of their authorship of that form and of their own deeds. Of course just as they do not begin where they please, they cannot go on exactly as they please either; each character is constrained by the actions of others and by the social settings presupposed in his and their actions, a point forcibly made by Marx in the classical, if not entirely satisfactory account of human life as enacted dramatic narrative, *The Eighteenth Brumaire of Louis Bonaparte*.

I call Marx's account less than satisfactory partly because he wishes to present the narrative of human social life in a way that will be compatible with a view of the life as law-governed and predictable in a particular way. But it is crucial that at any given point in an enacted dramatic narrative we do not know what will happen next. The kind of unpredictability for which I argued in Chapter 8 is required by the narrative structure of human life, and the empirical generalizations and explorations which social scientists discover provide a kind of understanding of human life which is perfectly compatible with that structure.

This unpredictability coexists with a second crucial characteristic of all lived narratives, a certain teleological character. We live out our lives, both individually and in our relationships with each other, in the light of certain conceptions of a possible shared future, a future in which certain possibilities beckon us forward and others repel us, some seem already foreclosed and others perhaps inevitable. There is no present which is not informed by some image of some future and an image of the future which always presents itself in the form of a *telos* – or of a variety of ends or goals – towards which we are either moving or failing to move in the present. Unpredictability and teleology therefore coexist as part of our lives; like characters in a fictional narrative we do not know what will happen next, but nonetheless our lives have a certain form which projects itself towards our future. Thus the narratives which we live out have both an unpredictable and a partially teleological character. If the narrative of our individual and social lives is to continue intelligibly – and either type of narrative may lapse into unintelligibility – it is always both the case that there are constraints on how the story can continue *and* that within those constraints there are indefinitely many ways that it can continue.

A central thesis then begins to emerge: man is in his actions and practice, as well as in his fictions, essentially a story-telling animal. He is not essentially, but becomes through his history, a teller of stories that aspire to truth. But the key question for men is not about their own authorship; I can only answer the question "What am I to do?" if I can answer the prior question "Of what story or stories do I find myself a part?" We enter human society, that is, with one or more imputed characters – roles into which we have been drafted – and we have to learn what they are in order to be able to understand how others respond to us and how our responses to them are apt to be construed. It is through hearing stories about wicked stepmothers, lost children, good but misguided kings, wolves that suckle twin boys, youngest sons who receive no inheritance but must make their own way in the world and eldest sons who waste their inheritance on riotous living and go into exile to live with the swine, that children learn or mislearn both what a child and what a parent is, what the cast of characters may be in the drama into which they have been born and what the ways of the world are. Deprive children of stories and you leave them unscripted, anxious stutterers in their actions as in their words. Hence there is no way to give us an understanding of any society, including our own, except through the stock of stories which constitute its initial dramatic resources. Mythology, in its original sense, is at the heart of things. Vico[xii] was right and so was Joyce. And so too of course is that moral tradition from heroic society to its medieval heirs according to which the telling of stories has a key part in educating us into the virtues.

I suggested earlier that "an" action is always an episode in a possible history: I would now like to make a related suggestion about another concept, that of personal identity. Derek Parfit and others have recently drawn our attention to the contrast between the criteria of strict identity, which is an all-or-nothing matter (*either* the Tichborne claimant *is* the last Tichborne heir *or* he is not; *either* all the properties of the last heir belong to the claimant *or* the claimant is not the heir – Leibniz's Law applies)[xiii] and the psychological continuities of personality which are a matter of more or less. (Am I the same man at fifty as I was at forty in respect of memory, intellectual powers, critical responses? More or less.) But what is crucial to human beings as characters in enacted narratives is that, possessing only the resources of psychological continuity, we have to be able to respond to the imputation of strict identity. I am forever whatever I have been at any time for others – and I may at any time be called upon to answer for it – no matter how changed I may be now. There is no way of *founding* my identity – or lack of it – on the psychological continuity or discontinuity of the self. The self inhabits a character whose unity is given as the unity of a character. Once again there is a crucial disagreement with empiricist or analytical philosophers on the one hand and with existentialists on the other.

Empiricists, such as Locke or Hume, tried to give an account of personal identity solely in terms of psychological states or events. Analytical philosophers, in so many ways their heirs as well as their critics, have wrestled with the connection between those states and events and strict identity

---

[xii] The Italian philosopher Giambattista Vico (1668–1744) argued against the rationalism of his day for the ineliminability of mythical thought.

[xiii] There was a false claim to the Tichborne estates in England in the nineteenth century; G. W. Leibniz held that two things are identical only if "indiscernible."

understood in terms of Leibniz's Law. Both have failed to see that a background has been omitted, the lack of which makes the problems insoluble. That background is provided by the concept of a story and of that kind of unity of character which a story requires. Just as a history is not a sequence of actions, but the concept of an action is that of a moment in an actual or possible history abstracted for some purpose from that history, so the characters in a history are not a collection of persons, but the concept of a person is that of a character abstracted from a history.

What the narrative concept of selfhood requires is thus twofold. On the one hand, I am what I may justifiably be taken by others to be in the course of living out a story that runs from my birth to my death; I am the *subject* of a history that is my own and no one else's, that has its own peculiar meaning. When someone complains – as do some of those who attempt or commit suicide – that his or her life is meaningless, he or she is often and perhaps characteristically complaining that the narrative of their life has become unintelligible to them, that it lacks any point, any movement towards a climax or a *telos*.[xiv] Hence the point of doing any one thing rather than another at crucial junctures in their lives seems to such a person to have been lost.

To be the subject of a narrative that runs from one's birth to one's death is, I remarked earlier, to be accountable for the actions and experiences which compose a narratable life. It is, that is, to be open to being asked to give a certain kind of account of what one did or what happened to one or what one witnessed at any earlier point in one's life than the time at which the question is posed. Of course someone may have forgotten or suffered brain damage or simply not attended sufficiently at the relevant time to be able to give the relevant account. But to say of someone under some one description ("The prisoner of the Chateau d'If") that he is the same person as someone characterized quite differently ("The Count of Monte Cristo") is precisely to say that it makes sense to ask him to give an intelligible narrative account enabling us to understand how he could at different times and different places be one and the same person and yet be so differently characterized. Thus personal identity is just that identity presupposed by the unity of the character which the unity of a narrative requires. Without such unity there would not be subjects of whom stories could be told.

The other aspect of narrative selfhood is correlative: I am not only accountable, I am one who can always ask others for an account, who can put others to the question. I am part of their story, as they are part of mine. The narrative of any one life is part of an interlocking set of narratives. Moreover this asking for and giving of accounts itself plays an important part in constituting narratives. Asking you what you did and why, saying

---

[ix] Goal.

what I did and why, pondering the differences between your account of what I did and my account of what I did, and *vice versa*, these are essential constituents of all but the very simplest and barest of narratives. Thus without the accountability of the self those trains of events that constitute all but the simplest and barest of narratives could not occur; and without that same accountability narratives would lack that continuity required to make both them and the actions that constitute them intelligible.

It is important to notice that I am not arguing that the concepts of narrative or of intelligibility or of accountability are *more* fundamental than that of personal identity. The concepts of narrative, intelligibility and accountability presuppose the applicability of the concept of personal identity, just as it presupposes their applicability and just as indeed each of these three presupposes the applicability of the two others. The relationship is one of mutual presupposition. It does follow of course that all attempts to elucidate the notion of personal identity independently of and in isolation from the notions of narrative, intelligibility and accountability are bound to fail. As all such attempts have.

It is now possible to return to the question from which this enquiry into the nature of human action and identity started: In what does the unity of an individual life consist? The answer is that its unity is the unity of a narrative embodied in a single life. To ask "What is the good for me?" is to ask how best I might live out that unity and bring it to completion. To ask "What is the good for man?" is to ask what all answers to the former question must have in common. But now it is important to emphasize that it is the systematic asking of these two questions and the attempt to answer them in deed as well as in word which provide the moral life with its unity. The unity of a human life is the unity of a narrative quest. Quests sometimes fail, are frustrated, abandoned or dissipated into distractions; and human lives may in all these ways also fail. But the only criteria for success or failure in a human life as a whole are the critieria of success or failure in a narrated or to-be-narrated quest. A quest for what?

Two key features of the medieval conception of a quest need to be recalled. The first is that without some at least partly determinate conception of the final *telos* there could not be any beginning to a quest. Some conception of the good for man is required. Whence is such a conception to be drawn? Precisely from those questions which led us to attempt to transcend that limited conception of the virtues which is available in and through practices. It is in looking for a conception of *the* good which will enable us to order other goods, for a conception of *the* good which will enable us to extend our understanding of the purpose and content of the virtues, for a conception of *the* good which will enable us to understand the place of integrity and constancy in life, that we initially define the kind of life which is a quest for the good. But secondly it is clear the medieval

549

conception of a quest is not at all that of a search for something already adequately characterized, as miners search for gold or geologists for oil. It is in the course of the quest and only through encountering and coping with the various particular harms, dangers, temptations and distractions which provide any quest with its episodes and incidents that the goal of the quest is finally to be understood. A quest is always an education both as to the character of that which is sought and in self-knowledge.

The virtues therefore are to be understood as those dispositions which will not only sustain practices and enable us to achieve the goods internal to practices, but which will also sustain us in the relevant kind of quest for the good, by enabling us to overcome the harms, dangers, temptations and distractions which we encounter, and which will furnish us with increasing self-knowledge and increasing knowledge of the good. The catalogue of the virtues will therefore include the virtues required to sustain the kind of households and the kind of political communities in which men and women can seek for the good together and the virtues necessary for philosophical enquiry about the character of the good. We have then arrived at a provisional conclusion about the good life for man: the good life for man is the life spent in seeking for the good life for man, and the virtues necessary for the seeking are those which will enable us to understand what more and what else the good life for man is. We have also completed the second stage in our account of the virtues, by situating them in realtion to the good life for man and not only in relation to practices. But our enquiry requires a third stage.

For I am never able to seek for the good or exercise the virtues only *qua* individual. This is partly because what it is to live the good life concretely varies from circumstance to circumstance even when it is one and the same conception of the good life and one and the same set of virtues which are being embodied in a human life. What the good life is for a fifth-century Athenian general will not be the same as what it was for a medieval nun or a seventeenth-century farmer. But it is not just that different individuals live in different social circumstances; it is also that we all approach our own circumstances as bearers of a particular social identity. I am someone's son or daughter, someone else's cousin or uncle, I am a citizen of this or that city, a member of this or that guild or profession; I belong to this clan, that tribe, this nation. Hence what is good for me has to be the good for one who inhabits these roles. As such, I inherit from the past of my family, my city, my tribe, my nation, a variety of debts, inheritances, rightful expectations and obligations. These constitute the given of my life, my moral starting point. This is in part what gives my life its own moral particularity.

This thought is likely to appear alien and even suprising from the standpoint of modern individualism. From the standpoint of individualism I am what I myself choose to be. I can always, if I wish to, put in question what are taken to be the merely contingent social features of my existence. I may biologically be my father's son; but I cannot be held responsible for what he did unless I choose implicitly or explicitly to assume such responsibility. I may legally be a citizen of a certain country; but I cannot be held responsible for what my country does or has done unless I choose implicitly or explicitly to assume such responsibility. Such individualism is expressed by those modern Americans who deny any responsibility for the effects of slavery upon black Americans, saying "I never owned any slaves." It is more subtly the standpoint of those other modern Americans who accept a nicely calculated responsibility for such effects measured precisely by the benefits they themselves as individuals have indirectly received from slavery. In both cases "being an American" is not in itself taken to be part of the moral identity of the individual. And of course there is nothing peculiar to modern Americans in this attitude: the Englishman who says, "*I* never did any wrong to Ireland; why bring up that old history as though it had something to do with *me?*" or the young German who believes that being born after 1945 means that what Nazis did to Jews has no moral relevance to his relationship to his Jewish contemporaries, exhibit the same attitude, that according to which the self is detachable from its social and historical roles and statuses. And the self so detached is of course a self very much at home in either Sartre's or Goffman's perspective, a self that can have no history. The contrast with the narrative view of the self is clear. For the story of my life is always embedded in the story of those communities from which I derive my identity. I am born with a past; and to try to cut myself off from that past, in the individualist mode, is to deform my present relationships. The possession of an historical identity and the possession of a social identity coincide. Notice that rebellion against my identity is always one possible mode of expressing it.

Notice also that the fact that the self has to find its moral identity in and through its membership in communities such as those of the family, the neighborhood, the city and the tribe does not entail that the self has to accept the moral *limitations* of the particularity of those forms of community. Without those moral particularities to begin from there would never be anywhere to begin; but it is in moving forward from such particularity that the search for the good, for the universal, consists. Yet particularity can never be simply left behind or obliterated. The notion of escaping from it into a realm of entirely universal maxims which belong to man as such, whether in its eighteenth-century Kantian form or in the presentation of some modern analytical moral philosophies, is an illusion and an illusion with painful consequences. When men and women identify what are in fact their partial and particular causes too easily and too completely with the cause of some universal principle, they usually behave worse than they would otherwise do.

What I am, therefore, is in key part what I inherit, a specific past that is present to some degree in my present. I find myself part of a history and that is generally to say, whether I like it or not, whether I recognize it or not, one of the bearers of a tradition. It was important when I characterized the concept of a practice to notice that practices always have histories and that at any given moment what a practice is depends on a mode of understanding it which has been transmitted often through many generations. And thus, insofar as the virtues sustain the relationships required for practices, they have to sustain relationships to the past – and to the future – as well as in the present. But the traditions through which particular practices are transmitted and reshaped never exist in isolation for larger social traditions. What constitutes such traditions?

We are apt to be misled here by the ideological uses to which the concept of a tradition has been put by conservative political theorists. Characteristically such theorists have followed Burke in contrasting tradition with reason and the stability of tradition with conflict. Both contrasts obfuscate. For all reasoning takes place within the context of some traditional mode of thought, transcending through criticism and invention the limitations of what had hitherto been reasoned in that tradition; this is as true of modern physics as of medieval logic. Moreover when a tradition is in good order it is always partially constituted by an argument about the goods the pursuit of which gives to that tradition its particular point and purpose.

So when an institution – a university, say, or a farm, or a hospital – is the bearer of a tradition of practice or practices, its common life will be partly, but in a centrally important way, constituted by a continuous argument as to what a university is and ought to be or what good farming is or what good medicine is. Traditions, when vital, embody continuities of conflict. Indeed when a tradition becomes Burkean, it is always dying or dead.

The individualism of modernity could of course find no use for the notion of tradition within its own conceptual scheme except as an adversary notion; it therefore all too willingly abandoned it to the Burkeans, who, faithful to Burke's own allegiance, tried to combine adherence in politics to a conception of tradition which would vindicate the oligarchical revolution of property of 1688 and adherence in economics to the doctrine and institutions of the free market. The theoretical incoherence of this mismatch did not deprive it of ideological usefulness. But the outcome has been that modern conservatives are for the most part engaged in conserving only older rather than later versions of liberal individualism. Their own core doctrine is as liberal and as individualist as that of self-avowed liberals.

A living tradition then is an historically extended, socially embodied argument and an argument precisely in part about the goods which constitute that tradition. Within a tradition the pursuit of goods extends through generations, sometimes through many generations. Hence the individual's search for his or her good is generally and characteristically conducted within a context defined by those traditions of which the individual's life is a part, and this is true both of those goods which are internal to practices and of the goods of a single life. Once again the narrative phenomenon of embedding is crucial: the history of a practice in our time is generally and characteristically embedded in and made intelligible in terms of the larger and longer history of the tradition through which the practice in its present form was conveyed to us; the history of each of our own lives is generally and characteristically embedded in and made intelligible in terms of the larger and longer histories of a number of traditions. I have to say 'generally and characteristically' rather than 'always', for traditions decay, disintegrate and disappear. What then sustains and strengthens traditions? What weakens and destroys them?

The answer in key part is: the exercise or the lack of exercise of the relevant virtues. The virtues find their point and purpose not only in sustaining those relationships necessary if the variety of goods internal to practices are to be achieved and not only in sustaining the form of an individual life in which that individual may seek out his or her good as the good of his or her whole life, but also in sustaining those traditions which provide both practices and individual lives with their necessary historical context. Lack of justice, lack of truthfulness, lack of courage, lack of the relevant intellectual virtues – these corrupt traditions, just as they do those institutions and practices which derive their life from the traditions of which they are the contemporary embodiments. To recognize this is of course also to recognize the existence of an additional virtue, one whose importance is perhaps most obvious when it is least present, the virtue of having an adequate sense of the traditions to which one belongs or which confront one. This virtue is not to be confused with any form of conservative antiquarianism; I am not praising those who choose the conventional conservative role of *laudator temporis acti*.[xv] It is rather the case that an adequate sense of tradition manifests itself in a grasp of those future possibilities which the past has made available to the present. Living traditions, just because they continue a not-yet-completed narrative, confront a future whose determinate and determinable character, so far as it possesses any, derives from the past.

In practical reasoning the possession of this virtue is not manifested so much in the knowledge of a set of generalizations or maxims which may provide our practical inferences with major premises; its presence or absence rather appears in the kind of capacity for judgment which the agent possesses in knowing how to select among the relevant stack of maxims and how to apply them in particular situations. Cardinal Pole

[xv] Eulogizer of times gone by.

possessed it, Mary Tudor did not; Montrose possessed it, Charles I did not. What Cardinal Pole and the Marquis of Montrose possessed were in fact those virtues which enable their possessors to pursue both their own good and the good of the tradition of which they are the bearers even in situations defined by the necessity of tragic, dilemmatic choice.[xvi] Such choices, understood in the context of the tradition of the virtues, are very different from those which face the modern adherents of rival and incommensurable moral premises in the debates about which I wrote in Chapter 2. Wherein does the difference lie?

It has often been suggested – by J. L. Austin, for example – that *either* we can admit the existence of rival and contingently incompatible goods which make incompatible claims to our practical allegiance *or* we can believe in some determinate conception of *the* good life for man, but that these are mutually exclusive alternatives. No one can consistently hold both these views. What this contention is blind to is that there may be better or worse ways for individuals to live through the tragic confrontation of good with good. And that to know what the good life for man is may require knowing what are the better and what are the worse ways of living in and through such situations. Nothing *a priori* rules out this possibility; and this suggests that within a view such as Austin's there is concealed an unacknowledged empirical premise about the character of tragic situations.

One way in which the choice between rival goods in a tragic situation differs from the modern choice between incommensurable moral premises is that *both* of the alternative courses of action which confront the individual have to be recognized as leading to some authentic and substantial good. By choosing one I do nothing to diminish or derogate from the claim upon me of the other; and therefore, whatever I do, I shall have left undone what I ought to have done. The tragic protagonist, unlike the moral agent as depicted by Sartre or Hare,[xvii] is not choosing between allegiance to one moral principle rather than another, nor is he or she deciding upon some principle of priority between moral principles. Hence the "ought" involved has a different meaning and force from that of the "ought" in moral principles understood in a modern way. For the tragic protagonist cannot do everything that he or she ought to do. This "ought", unlike Kant's, does not imply "can." Moreover any attempt to map the logic of such "ought" assertions on to some modal calculus so as to produce a version of deontic logic has to fail. (See, from a very different point of view, Bas C. Van Fraasen 1973.[xviii])

[xvi] Reginald Pole (1500–58) English cardinal in the reign of Mary Tudor (1553–8); Marquess of Montrose (1612–50), Scottish general who changed sides to support Charles I, King 1625–49.

[xvii] Rom Hare, contemporary moral philosopher.

[xviii] "Values and the Heart's Command," *Journal of Philosophy*, 70, 1973: 5–19.

Yet it is clear that the moral task of the tragic protagonist may be performed better or worse, independently of the choice between alternatives that he or she makes – *ex hypothesi* he or she has no *right* choice to make.[xix] The tragic protagonist may behave heroically or unheroically, generously or ungenerously, gracefully or gracelessly, prudently or imprudently. To perform his or her task better rather than worse will be to do both what is better for him or her *qua* individual and *qua* parent or child or *qua* citizen or member of a profession, or perhaps *qua* some or all of these. The existence of tragic dilemmas casts no doubt upon and provides no counter-examples to the thesis that assertions of the form "To do this in this way would be better for X and/or for his or her family, city or profession" are susceptible of objective truth and falsity, any more than the existence of alternative and contingently incompatible forms of medical treatment casts doubt on the thesis that assertions of the form "To undergo his medical treatment in this way would be better for X and/or his or her family" are susceptible of objective truth and falsity. (See, from a different point of view, the illuminating discussion in Samuel Guttenplan[xx]).

The presupposition of this objectivity is of course that we can understand the notion of "good for X" and cognate notions in terms of some conception of the unity of X's life. What is better or worse for X depends upon the character of that intelligible narrative which provides X's life with its unity. Unsurprisingly it is the lack of any such unifying conception of a human life which underlies modern denials of the factual character of moral judgments and more especially of those judgments which ascribe virtues or vices to individuals.

I argued earlier that every moral philosophy has some particular socio-logy as its counterpart. What I have tried to spell out in this chapter is the kind of understanding of social life which the tradition of the virtues requires, a kind of understanding very different from those dominant in the culture of bureaucratic individualism. Within that culture conceptions of the virtues become marginal and the tradition of the virtues remains central only in the lives of social groups whose existence is on the margins of the central culture. Within the central cultural of liberal or bureaucratic individualism new conceptions of the virtues emerge and the concept of a virtue is itself transformed. To the history of that transformation I therefore now turn; for we shall only understand the tradition of the virtues fully if we understand to what kinds of degeneration it has proved liable.

[xix] "*Ex hypothesi*" – according to what is assumed.
[xx] Samuel Guttenplan, "Moral Realism and Moral Dilemmas," *Proceedings of the Aristotelian Society*, 1979–80: 61–80.

chapter thirty-five

"The Cultural Logic of Late Capitalism"

Fredric Jameson

Professor of comparative literature, Fredric Jameson (1934–) has commented widely on contemporary literature, art, and culture. In the following essay, originally published in 1984, Jameson defends a Marxist interpretation of postmodernism as an expression of the current state of capitalist society, "late capitalism." The phenomena that postmodernists interpret as signaling a discontinuity with modernity, Jameson sees instead as symptoms of underlying political-economic realities that are continuous with earlier phases of capitalism. Far from treating cultural phenomena in the non-economic style of postmodernism, Jameson suggests that the hallmark of postmodern culture is the absorption of culture by multinational capital, the final overcoming of the partial independence that art and theory had been permitted by earlier forms of capitalism. He is a harsh critic of postmodern theory for celebrating, rather than criticizing, these developments.

The last few years have been marked by an inverted millenarianism in which premonitions of the future, catastrophic or redemptive, have been replaced by senses of the end of this or that (the end of ideology, art, or social class; the "crisis" of Leninism, social democracy, or the welfare state, etc., etc.); taken together, all of these perhaps constitute what is increasingly called postmodernism. The case for its existence depends on the hypothesis of some radical break or *coupure*, generally traced back to the end of the 1950s or the early 1960s.

As the word itself suggests, this break is most often related to notions of the waning or extinction of the hundred-year-old modern movement (or to its ideological or aesthetic repudiation). Thus abstract expressionism in painting, existentialism in philosophy, the final forms of representation in the novel, the films of the great *auteurs*, or the modernist school of poetry (as institutionalized and canonized in the works of Wallace Stevens) all are

Fredric Jameson, "The Cultural Logic of Late Capitalism," from chapter 1 of *Postmodernism, Or, The Cultural Logic of Late Capitalism* (Durham: Duke University Press, 1991), pp.1–6, 32–8, 45–51, 54.

now seen as the final, extraordinary flowering of a high-modernist impulse which is spent and exhausted with them. The enumeration of what follows, then, at once becomes empirical, chaotic, and heterogeneous: Andy Warhol and pop art, but also photorealism, and beyond it, the "new expressionism";[i] the moment, in music, of John Cage, but also the synthesis of classical and "popular" styles found in composers like Phil Glass and Terry Riley, and also punk and new wave rock (the Beatles and the Stones now standing as the high-modernist moment of that more recent and rapidly evolving tradition); in film, Godard, post-Godard, and experimental cinema and video, but also a whole new type of commercial film (about which more below); Burroughs, Pynchon, or Ishmael Reed, on the one hand, and the French *nouveau roman*[ii] and its succession, on the other, along with alarming new kinds of literary criticism based on some new aesthetic of textuality or *écriture* . . .[iii] The list might be extended indefinitely; but does it imply any more fundamental change or break than the periodic style and fashion changes determined by an older high-modernist imperative of stylistic innovation?

It is in the realm of architecture, however, that modifications in aesthetic production are most dramatically visible, and that their theoretical problems have been most centrally raised and articulated; it was indeed from architectural debates that my own conception of postmodernism – as it will be outlined in the following pages – initially began to emerge. More decisively than in the other arts or media, postmodernist positions in architecture have been inseparable from an implacable critique of architectural high modernism and of Frank Lloyd Wright or the so-called international style (Le Corbusier, Mies, etc), where formal criticism and analysis (of the high-modernist transformation of the building into a virtual sculpture, or monumental "duck,"[iv] as Robert Venturi puts it)[1] are at one with reconsiderations on the level of urbanism and of the aesthetic institution. High modernism is thus credited with the destruction of the fabric of the traditional city and its older neighborhood culture (by way of the radical disjunction of the new Utopian high-modernist building from its surrounding context), while the prophetic elitism and authoritarianism of the modern movement are remorselessly identified in the imperious gesture of the charismatic Master.

---

[i] Neo-Expressionism, a predominantly German style of painting from the 1960s to mid-1980s, e.g. see the work of Georg Baselitz.

[ii] Literally, "new novel," this refers to the French antinovel of the 1950s and 1960s.

[iii] Writing.

[iv] A category of building-as-sculpture, formulated by Robert Venturi in his *Learning from Las Vegas*. The term is taken from a photograph of a duck-shaped drive-in on Long Island in Peter Blake's *God's Own Junkyard: The Planned Deterioration of America's Landscape*.

557

Fredric Jameson

Postmodernism in architecture will then logically enough stage itself as a kind of aesthetic populism, as the very title of Venturi's influential manifesto, *Learning from Las Vegas*, suggests. However, we may ultimately wish to evaluate this populist rhetoric,[2] it has at least the merit of drawing our attention to one fundamental feature of all the postmodernisms enumerated above: namely, the effacement in them of the older (essentially high-modernist) frontier between high culture and so-called mass or commercial culture, and the emergence of new kinds of texts infused with the forms, categories, and contents of that very culture industry so passionately denounced by all the ideologues of the modern, from Leavis[v] and the American New Criticism[vi] all the way to Adorno and the Frankfurt School. The postmodernisms have, in fact, been fascinated precisely by this whole "degraded" landscape of schlock and kitsch, of TV series and *Reader's Digest* culture, of advertising and motels, of the late show and the grade-B Hollywood film, of so-called paraliterature, with its airport paperback categories of the gothic and the romance, the popular biography, the murder mystery, and the science fiction or fantasy novel: materials they no longer simply "quote," as a Joyce or a Mahler might have done, but incorporate into their very substance.

Nor should the break in question be thought of as a purely cultural affair: indeed, theories of the postmodern – whether celebratory or couched in the language of moral revulsion and denunciation – bear a strong family resemblance to all those more ambitious sociological generalizations which, at much the same time, bring us the news of the arrival and inauguration of a whole new type of society, most famously baptized "postindustrial society" (Daniel Bell) but often also designated consumer society, media society, information society, electronic society or high tech, and the like. Such theories have the obvious ideological mission of demonstrating, to their own relief, that the new social formation in question no longer obeys the laws of classical capitalism, namely, the primacy of industrial production and the omnipresence of class struggle. The Marxist tradition has therefore resisted them with vehemence, with the signal exception of the economist Ernest Mandel, whose book *Late Capitalism* sets out not merely to anatomize the historic originality of this new society (which he sees as a third stage or moment in the evolution of capital) but also to demonstrate that it is, if anything, a *purer* stage of capitalism than any of the moments that preceded it. I will return to this argument later; suffice it for the moment to anticipate a point that will be argued in chapter 2, namely, that every position on postmodernism in culture – whether apologia or

---

[v] Frank Leavis (1895–1978) advocated evaluating literature according to the author's moral standing.

[vi] Post-world War I critical school advocating purely internal analysis of literary texts.

stigmatization – is also at one and the same time, and *necessarily*, an implicitly or explicitly political stance on the nature of multinational capitalism today.

A last preliminary word on method: what follows is not to be read as stylistic description, as the account of one cultural style or movement among others. I have rather meant to offer a periodizing hypothesis, and that at a moment in which the very conception of historical periodization has come to seem most problematical indeed. I have argued elsewhere that all isolated or discrete cultural analysis always involves a buried or repressed theory of historical periodization; in any case, the conception of the "genealogy" largely lays to rest traditional theoretical worries about so-called linear history, theories of "stages," and teleological historiography. In the present context, however, lengthier theoretical discussion of such (very real) issues can perhaps be replaced by a few substantive remarks.

One of the concerns frequently aroused by periodizing hypotheses is that these tend to obliterate difference and to project an idea of the historical period as massive homogeneity (bounded on either side by inexplicable chronological metamorphoses and punctuation marks). This is, however, precisely why it seems to me essential to grasp postmodernism not as a style but rather as a cultural dominant: a conception which allows for the presence and coexistence of a range of very different, yet subordinate, features.

Consider, for example, the powerful alternative position that postmodernism is itself little more than one more stage of modernism proper (if not, indeed, of the even older romanticism); it may indeed be conceded that all the features of postmodernism I am about to enumerate can be detected, full-blown, in this or that preceding modernism (including such astonishing genealogical precursors as Gertrude Stein, Raymond Roussel, or Marcel Duchamp, who may be considered outright postmodernists, avant la lettre).[vii] What has not been taken into account by this view, however, is the social position of the older modernism, or better still, its passionate repudiation by an older Victorian and post-Victorian bourgeoisie for whom its forms and ethos are received as being variously ugly, dissonant, obscure, scandalous, immoral, subversive, and generally "antisocial." It will be argued here, however, that a mutation in the sphere of culture has rendered such attitudes archaic. Not only are Picasso and Joyce no longer ugly; they now strike us, on the whole, as rather "realistic," and this is the result of a canonization and academic institutionalization of the modern movement generally that can be traced to the late 1950s. This is surely one of the most plausible explanations for the emergence of postmodernism

[vii] "Before the word". Gertrude Stein (1874–1946), American writer and poet; Raymond Roussel (1877–1933), French writer; Marcel Duchamp (1887–1968), French painter.

itself, since the younger generation of the 1960s will now confront the formerly oppositional modern movement as a set of dead classics, which "weigh like a nightmare on the brains of the living," as Marx once said in a different context.

As for the postmodern revolt against all that, however, it must equally be stressed that its own offensive features – from obscurity and sexually explicit material to psychological squalor and overt expressions of social and political defiance, which transcend anything that might have been imagined at the most extreme moments of high modernism – no longer scandalize anyone and are not only received with the greatest complacency but have themselves become institutionalized and are at one with the official or public culture of Western society.

What has happened is that aesthetic production today has become integrated into commodity production generally: the frantic economic urgency of producing fresh waves of ever more novel-seeming goods (from clothing to airplanes), at ever greater rates of turnover, now assigns an increasingly essential structural function and position to aesthetic innovation and experimentation. Such economic necessities then find recognition in the varied kinds of institutional support available for the newer art, from foundations and grants to museums and other forms of patronage. Of all the arts, architecture, is the closest constitutively to the economic, with which, in the form of commissions and land values, it has a virtually unmediated relationship. It will therefore not be surprising to find the extraordinary flowering of the new postmodern architecture grounded in the patronage of multinational business, whose expansion and development is strictly contemporaneous with it. Later I will suggest that these two new phenomena have an even deeper dialectical interrelationship than the simple one-to-one financing of this or that individual project. Yet this is the point at which I must remind the reader of the obvious; namely, that this whole global, yet American, postmodern culture is the internal and superstructural expression of a whole new wave of American military and economic domination throughout the world: in this sense, as throughout class history, the underside of culture is blood, torture, death, and terror.

The first point to be made about the conception of periodization in dominance, therefore, is that even if all the constitutive features of postmodernism were identical with and coterminous to those of an older modernism – a position I feel to be demonstrably erroneous but which only an even lengthier analysis of modernism proper could dispel – the two phenomena would still remain utterly distinct in their meaning and social function, owing to the very different positioning of postmodernism in the economic system of late capital and, beyond that, to the transformation of the very sphere of culture in contemporary society.

560

This point will be further discussed at the conclusion of this book. I must now briefly address a different kind of objection to periodization, a concern about its possible obliteration of heterogeneity, one most often expressed by the Left. And it is certain that there is a strange quasi-Sartrean irony – a "winner loses" logic – which tends to surround any effort to describe a "system," a totalizing dynamic, as these are detected in the movement of contemporary society. What happens is that the more powerful the vision of some increasingly total system or logic – the Foucault of the prisons book is the obvious example – the more powerless the reader comes to feel. Insofar as the theorist wins, therefore, by constructing an increasingly closed and terrifying machine, to that very degree he loses, since the critical capacity of his work is thereby paralyzed, and the impulses of negation and revolt, not to speak of those of social transformation, are increasingly perceived as vain and trivial in the face of the model itself.

I have felt, however, that it was only in the light of some conception of a dominant cultural logic or hegemonic norm that genuine difference could be measured and assessed. I am very far from feeling that all cultural production today is "postmodern" in the broad sense I will be conferring on this term. The postmodern is, however, the force field in which very different kinds of cultural impulses – what Raymond Williams has usefully termed "residual" and "emergent" forms of cultural production – must make their way.[viii] If we do not achieve some general sense of a cultural dominant, then we fall back into a view of present history as sheer heterogeneity, random difference, a coexistence of a host of distinct forces whose effectivity is undecidable. At any rate, this has been the political spirit in which the following analysis was devised: to project some conception of a new systematic cultural norm and its reproduction in order to reflect more adequately on the most effective forms of any radical cultural politics today.

The exposition will take up in turn the following constitutive features of the postmodern: a new depthlessness, which finds its prolongation both in contemporary "theory" and in a whole new culture of the image or the simulacrum; a consequent weakening of historicity, both in our relationship to public History and in the new forms of our private temporality, whose "schizophrenic" structure (following Lacan[ix]) will determine new types of syntax or syntagmatic relationships in the more temporal arts; a whole new type of emotional ground tone – what I will call "intensities" – which can best be grasped by a return to older theories of the sublime; the

---

[viii] Prominent English critic and man of the left, Raymond Williams (1922–88) distinguished the *emergent* (or novel) and the *residual* (anachronistic) from the dominant cultural elements of a given historical period.

[ix] Jacques Lacan, innovative recent French psychoanalyst.

deep constitutive relationships of all this to a whole new technology, which is itself a figure for a whole new economic world system; and, after a brief account of postmodernist mutations in the lived experience of built space itself, some reflections on the mission of political art in the bewildering new world space of late or multinational capital.

Now we need to complete this exploratory account of postmodernist space and time with a final analysis of that euphoria or those intensities which seem so often to characterize the newer cultural experience. Let us reemphasize the enormity of a transition which leaves behind it the desolation of Hopper's buildings or the stark Midwest syntax of Sheeler's forms,[x] replacing them with the extraordinary surfaces of the photorealist cityscape, where even the automobile wrecks gleam with some new hallucinatory splendor. The exhilaration of these new surfaces is all the more paradoxical in that their essential content – the city itself – has deteriorated or disintegrated to a degree surely still inconceivable in the early years of the twentieth century, let alone in the previous era. How urban squalor can be a delight to the eyes when expressed in commodification, and how an unparalleled quantum leap in the alienation of daily life in the city can now be experienced in the form of a strange new hallucinatory exhilaration – these are some of the questions that confront us in this moment of our inquiry. Nor should the human figure be exempted from investigation, although it seems clear that for the newer aesthetic the representation of space itself has come to be felt as incompatible with the representation of the body: a kind of aesthetic division of labor far more pronounced than in any of the earlier generic conceptions of landscape, and a most ominous symptom indeed. The privileged space of the newer art is radically antianthropomorphic, as in the empty bathrooms of Doug Bond's work. The ultimate contemporary fetishization of the human body, however, takes a very different direction in the statues of Duane Hanson: what I have already called the simulacrum, whose peculiar function lies in what Sartre would have called the *derealization* of the whole surrounding world of everyday reality. Your moment of doubt and hesitation as to the breath and warmth of these polyester figures, in order words, tends to return upon the real human beings moving about you in the museum and to transform them also for the briefest instant into so many dead and flesh-colored simulacra in their own right. The world thereby momentarily loses its depth and threatens to become a glossy skin, a stereoscopic illusion, a rush of filmic images without density. But is this now a terrifying or an exhilarating experience?

[x] American artists Edward Hopper (1882–1967), painter of stark urban scenes, and Charles Sheeler (1883–1965), who abstractly rendered industrial forms.

It has proved fruitful to think of such experiences in terms of what Susan Sontag, in an influential statement, isolated as "camp." I propose a somewhat different cross-light on it, drawing on the equally fashionable current theme of the "sublime," as it has been rediscovered in the works of Edmund Burke and Kant; or perhaps one might want to yoke the two notions together in the form of something like a camp or "hysterical" sublime.[xi] The sublime was for Burke an experience bordering on terror, the fitful glimpse, in astonishment, stupor, and awe, of what was so enormous as to crush human life altogether: a description then refined by Kant to include the question of representation itself, so that the object of the sublime becomes not only a matter of sheer power and of the physical incommensurability of the human organism with Nature but also of the limits of figuration and the incapacity of the human mind to give representation to such enormous forces. Such forces Burke, in his historical moment at the dawn of the modern bourgeois state, was only able to conceptualize in terms of the divine, while even Heidegger continues to entertain a phantasmatic relationship with some organic precapitalist peasant landscape and village society, which is the final form of the image of Nature in our own time.

Today, however, it may be possible to think all this in a different way, at the moment of a radical eclipse of Nature itself: Heidegger's "field path" is, after all, irredeemably and irrevocably destroyed by late capital, by the green revolution, by neocolonialism and the megalopolis, which runs its superhighways over the older fields and vacant lots and turns Heidegger's "house of being" into condominiums, if not the most miserable unheated, rat-infested tenement buildings. The *other* of our society is in that sense no longer Nature at all, as it was in precapitalist societies, but something else which we must now identify.

I am anxious that this other thing not overhastily be grasped as technology per se, since I will want to show that technology is here itself a figure for something else. Yet technology may well serve as adequate shorthand to designate that enormous properly human and anti-natural power of dead human labor stored up in our machinery – an alienated power, what Sartre calls the counterfinality of the practico-inert, which turns back on and against us in unrecognizable forms and seems to constitute the massive dystopian horizon of our collective as well as our individual praxis.

Technological development is however on the Marxist view the result of the development of capital rather than some ultimately determining in-

---

[xi] The distinction between the beautiful and the sublime is traditional in aesthetic theory, the former often being understood as what is well-formed and pleasing, the latter as what is awesome, beyond comprehension.

stance in its own right. It will therefore be appropriate to distinguish several generations of machine power, several stages of technological revolution within capital itself. I here follow Ernest Mandel, who outlines three such fundamental breaks or quantum leaps in the evolution of machinery under capital:

> The fundamental revolutions in power technology – the technology of the production of motive machines by machines – thus appears as the determinant moment in revolutions of technology as a whole. Machine production of steam-driven motors since 1848; machine production of electric and combustion motors since the 90s of the 19th century; machine production of electronic and nuclear-powered apparatuses since the 40s of the 20th century – these are the three general revolutions in technology engendered by the capitalist mode of production since the "original" industrial revolution of the later 18th century.[3]

This periodization underscores the general thesis of Mandel's book *Late Capitalism*; namely, that there have been three fundamental moments in capitalism, each one marking a dialectical expansion over the previous stage. These are market capitalism, the monopoly stage or the stage of imperialism, and our own, wrongly called postindustrial, but what might better be termed multinational, capital. I have already pointed out that Mandel's intervention in the postindustrial debate involves the proposition that late or multinational or consumer capitalism, far from being inconsistent with Marx's great nineteenth-century analysis, constitutes, on the contrary, the purest form of capital yet to have emerged, a prodigious expansion of capital into hitherto uncommodified areas. This purer capitalism of our own time thus eliminates the enclaves of precapitalist organization it had hitherto tolerated and exploited in a tributary way. One is tempted to speak in this connection of a new and historically original penetration and colonization of Nature and the Unconscious: that is, the destruction of precapitalist Third World agriculture by the Green Revolution, and the rise of the media and the advertising industry. At any rate, it will also have been clear that my own cultural periodization of the stages of realism, modernism, and postmodernism is both inspired and confirmed by Mandel's tripartite scheme.

We may therefore speak of our own period as the Third Machine Age; and it is at this point that we must reintroduce the problem of aesthetic representation already explicitly developed in Kant's earlier analysis of the sublime, since it would seem only logical that the relationship to and the representation of the machine could be expected to shift dialectically with each of these qualitatively different stages of technological development.

It is appropriate to recall the excitement of machinery in the moment of capital preceding our own, the exhilaration of futurism, most notably, and of Marinetti's celebration of the machine gun and the motorcar. These are still visible emblems, sculptural nodes of energy which give tangibility and figuration to the motive energies of that earlier moment of modernization. The prestige of these great streamlined shapes can be measured by their metaphorical presence in Le Corbusier's buildings, vast Utopian structures which ride like so many gigantic steamship liners upon the urban scenery of an older fallen earth.[4] Machinery exerts another kind of fascination in the works of artists like Picabia and Duchamp,[xii] whom we have no time to consider here; but let me mention, for completeness' sake, the ways in which revolutionary or communist artists of the 1930s also sought to reappropriate this excitement of machine energy for a Promethean reconstruction of human society as a whole, as in Fernand Léger and Diego Rivera.

It is immediately obvious that the technology of our own moment no longer possesses this same capacity for representation: not the turbine, nor even Sheeler's grain elevators or smokestacks, not the baroque elaboration of pipes and conveyor belts, nor even the streamlined profile of the railroad train – all vehicles of speed still concentrated at rest – but rather the computer, whose outer shell has no emblematic or visual power, or even the casings of the various media themselves, as with that home appliance called television which articulates nothing but rather implodes, carrying its flattened image surface within itself.

Such machines are indeed machines of reproduction rather than of production, and they make very different demands on our capacity for aesthetic representation than did the relatively mimetic idolatry of the older machinery of the futurist moment, of some older speed-and-energy sculpture. Here we have less to do with kinetic energy than with all kinds of new reproductive processes; and in the weaker productions of postmodernism the aesthetic embodiment of such processes often tends to slip back more comfortably into a mere thematic representation of content – into narratives which are *about* the processes of reproduction and include movie cameras, video, tape recorders, the whole technology of the production and reproduction of the simulacrum. (The shift from Antonioni's modernist *Blow-Up* to DePalma's postmodernist *Blowout* is here paradigmatic.) When Japanese architects, for example, model a building on the decorative imitation of stacks of cassettes, then the solution is at best thematic and allusive, although often humorous.

Yet something else does tend to emerge in the most energetic postmodernist texts, and this is the sense that beyond all thematics or content the work seems somehow to tap the networks of the reproductive process and thereby to afford us some glimpse into a postmodern or technological

[xii] French painters Francis Picabia (1879–1953) and Marcel Duchamp were associated with abstraction, Surrealism, and Dadaism.

sublime, whose power or authenticity is documented by the success of such works in evoking a whole new postmodern space in emergence around us. Architecture therefore remains in this sense the privileged aesthetic language; and the distorting and fragmenting reflections of one enormous glass surface to the other can be taken as paradigmatic of the central role of process and reproduction in postmodernist culture.

As I have said, however, I want to avoid the implication that technology is in any way the "ultimately determining instance" either of our present-day social life or of our cultural production: such a thesis is, of course, ultimately at one with the post-Marxist notion of a postindustrial society. Rather, I want to suggest that our faulty representations of some immense communicational and computer network are themselves but a distorted figuration of something even deeper, namely, the whole world system of a present-day multinational capitalism. The technology of contemporary society is therefore mesmerizing and fascinating not so much in its own right but because it seems to offer some privileged representational shorthand for grasping a network of power and control even more difficult for our minds and imaginations to grasp: the whole new decentered global network of the third stage of capital itself. This is a figural process presently best observed in a whole mode of contemporary entertainment literature – one is tempted to characterize it as "high-tech paranoia" – in which the circuits and networks of some putative global computer hookup are narratively mobilized by labyrinthine conspiracies of autonomous but deadly interlocking and competing information agencies in a complexity often beyond the capacity of the normal reading mind. Yet conspiracy theory (and its garish narrative manifestations) must be seen as a degraded attempt – through the figuration of advanced technology – to think the impossible totality of the contemporary world system. It is in terms of that enormous and threatening, yet only dimly perceivable, other reality of economic and social institutions that, in my opinion, the postmodern sublime can alone be adequately theorized.

Such narratives, which first tried to find expression through the generic structure of the spy novel, have only recently crystallized in a new type of science fiction, called *cyberpunk*, which is fully as much an expression of transnational corporate realities as it is of global paranoia itself: William Gibson's representational innovations, indeed, mark his work as an exceptional literary realization within a predominantly visual or aural postmodern production.

The conception of postmodernism outlined here is a historical rather than a merely stylistic one. I cannot stress too greatly the radical distinction between a view for which the postmodern is one (optional) style among many others available and one which seeks to grasp it as the cultural dominant of the logic of late capitalism: the two approaches in fact generate two very different ways of conceptualizing the phenomenon as a whole: on the one hand, moral judgments (about which it is indifferent whether they are positive or negative), and, on the other, a genuinely dialectical attempt to think our present of time in History.

Of some positive moral evaluation of postmodernism little needs to be said: the complacent (yet delirious) camp-following celebration of this aesthetic new world (including its social and economic dimension, greeted with equal enthusiasm under the slogan of "postindustrial society") is surely unacceptable, although it may be somewhat less obvious that current fantasies about the salvational nature of high technology, from chips to robots – fantasies entertained not only by both left and right governments in distress but also by many intellectuals – are also essentially of a piece with more vulgar apologias for postmodernism.

But in that case it is only consequent to reject moralizing condemnations of the postmodern and of its essential triviality when juxtaposed against the Utopian "high seriousness" of the great modernisms: judgments one finds both on the Left and on the radical Right. And no doubt the logic of the simulacrum, with its transformation of older realities into television images, does more than merely replicate the logic of late capitalism; it reinforces and intensifies it. Meanwhile, for political groups which seek actively to intervene in history and to modify its otherwise passive momentum (whether with a view toward channeling it into a socialist transformation of society or diverting it into the regressive reestablishment of some simpler fantasy past), there cannot but be much that is deplorable and reprehensible in a cultural form of image addiction which, by transforming the past into visual mirages, stereotypes, or texts, effectively abolishes any practical sense of the future and of the collective project, thereby abandoning the thinking of future change to fantasies of sheer catastrophe and inexplicable cataclysm, from visions of "terrorism" on the social level to those of cancer on the personal. Yet if postmodernism is a historical phenomenon, then the attempt to conceptualize it in terms of moral or moralizing judgments must finally be identified as a category mistake. All of which becomes more obvious when we interrogate the position of the cultural critic and moralist; the latter, along with all the rest of us, is now so deeply immersed in postmodernist space, so deeply suffused and infected by its new cultural categories, that the luxury of the old-fashioned ideological critique, the indignant moral denunciation of the other, becomes unavailable.

The distinction I am proposing here knows one canonical form in Hegel's differentiation of the thinking of individual morality or moralizing (*Moralität*) from that whole very different realm of collective social values and practices (*Sittlichkeit*).[5] But it finds its definitive form in Marx's

567

demonstration of the materialist dialectic, most notably in those classic pages of the *Manifesto* which teach the hard lesson of some more genuinely dialectical way to think historical development and change. The topic of the lesson is, of course, the historical development of capitalism itself and the deployment of a specific bourgeois culture. In a well-known passage Marx powerfully urges us to do the impossible, namely, to think this development positively *and* negatively all at once; to achieve, in other words, a type of thinking that would be capable of grasping the demonstrably baleful features of capitalism along with its extraordinary and liberating dynamism simultaneously within a single thought, and without attenuating any of the force of either judgment. We are somehow to lift our minds to a point at which it is possible to understand that capitalism is at one and the same time the best thing that has ever happened to the human race, and the worst. The lapse from this austere dialectical imperative into the more comfortable stance of the taking of moral positions is inveterate and all too human: still, the urgency of the subject demands that we make at least some effort to think the cultural evolution of late capitalism dialectically, as catastrophe and progress all together.

Such an effort suggests two immediate questions, with which we will conclude these reflections. Can we in fact identify some "moment of truth" within the more evident "moments of falsehood" of postmodern culture? And, even if we can do so, is there not something ultimately paralyzing in the dialectical view of historical development proposed above; does it not tend to demobilize us and to surrender us to passivity and helplessness by systematically obliterating possibilities of action under the impenetrable fog of historical inevitability? It is appropriate to discuss these two (related) issues in terms of current possibilities for some effective contemporary cultural politics and for the construction of a genuine political culture.

To focus the problem in this way is, of course, immediately to raise the more genuine issue of the fate of culture generally, and of the function of culture specifically, as one social level or instance, in the postmodern era. Everything in the previous discussion suggests that what we have been calling postmodernism is inseparable from, and unthinkable without the hypothesis of, some fundamental mutation of the sphere of culture in the world of late capitalism, which includes a momentous modification of its social function. Older discussions of the space, function, or sphere of culture (mostly notably Herbert Marcuse's classic essay "The Affirmative Character of Culture") have insisted on what a different language would call the "semiautonomy" of the cultural realm: its ghostly, yet Utopian, existence, for good or ill, above the practical world of the existent, whose mirror image it throws back in forms which vary from the legitimations of flattering resemblance to the contestatory indictments of critical satire or Utopian pain.

What we must now ask ourselves is whether it is not precisely this semiautonomy of the cultural sphere which has been destroyed by the logic of late capitalism. Yet to argue that culture is today no longer endowed with the relative autonomy it once enjoyed as one level among others in earlier moments of capitalism (let alone in precapitalist societies) is not necessarily to imply its disappearance or extinction. Quite the contrary; we must go on to affirm that the dissolution of an autonomous sphere of culture is rather to be imagined in terms of an explosion: a prodigious expansion of culture throughout the social realm, to the point at which everything in our social life – from economic value and state power to practices and to the very structure of the psyche itself – can be said to have become "cultural" in some original and yet untheorized sense. This proposition is, however, substantively quite consistent with the previous diagnosis of a society of the image or the simulacrum and a transformation of the "real" into so many pseudoevents.

It also suggests that some of our most cherished and time-honored radical conceptions about the nature of cultural politics may thereby find themselves outmoded. However distinct those conceptions – which range from slogans of negativity, opposition, and subversion to critique and reflexivity – may have been, they all shared a single, fundamentally spatial, presupposition, which may be resumed in the equally time-honored formula of "critical distance." No theory of cultural politics current on the Left today has been able to do without one notion or another of a certain minimal aesthetic distance, of the possibility of the positioning of the cultural act outside the massive Being of capital, from which to assault this last. What the burden of our preceding demonstration suggests, however, is that distance in general (including "critical distance" in particular) has very precisely been abolished in the new space of postmodernism. We are submerged in its henceforth filled and suffused volumes to the point where our now postmodern bodies are bereft of spatial coordinates and practically (let alone theoretically) incapable of distantiation; meanwhile, it has already been observed how the prodigious new expansion of multinational capital ends up penetrating and colonizing those very precapitalist enclaves (Nature and the Unconscious) which offered extraterritorial and Archimedean footholds for critical effectivity. The shorthand language of co-optation is for this reason omnipresent on the left, but would now seem to offer a most inadequate theoretical basis for understanding a situation in which we all, in one way or another, dimly feel that not only punctual and local countercultural forms of cultural resistance and guerrilla warfare but also even overtly political interventions like those of *The Clash*[xiii] are all some-

---

[xiii] An English punk-based but mainstream rock band, active in the late 1970s and early 1980s.

569

how secretly disarmed and reabsorbed by a system of which they themselves might well be considered a part, since they can achieve no distance from it.

What we must now affirm is that it is precisely this whole extraordinarily demoralizing and depressing original new global space which is the "moment of truth" of postmodernism. What has been called the postmodernist "sublime" is only the moment in which this content has become most explicit, has moved the closest to the surface of consciousness as a coherent new type of space in its own right – even though a certain figural concealment or disguise is still at work here, most notably in the high-tech thematics in which the new spatial content is still dramatized and articulated. Yet the earlier features of the postmodern which were enumerated above can all now be seen as themselves partial (yet constitutive) aspects of the same general spatial object.

The argument for a certain authenticity in these otherwise patently ideological productions depends on the prior proposition that what we have been calling postmodern (or multinational) space is not merely a cultural ideology or fantasy but has genuine historical (and socioeconomic) reality as a third great original expansion of capitalism around the globe (after the earlier expansions of the national market and the older imperialist system, which each had their own cultural specificity and generated new types of space appropriate to their dynamics). The distorted and unreflexive attempts of newer cultural production to explore and to express this new space must then also, in their own fashion, be considered as so many approaches to the representation of (a new) reality (to use a more antiquated language). As paradoxical as the terms may seem, they may thus, following a classic interpretive option, be read as peculiar new forms of realism (or at least of the mimesis of reality), while at the same time they can equally well be analyzed as so many attempts to distract and divert us from that reality or to disguise its contradictions and resolve them in the guise of various formal mystifications.

As for that reality itself, however – the as yet untheorized original space of some new "world system" of multinational or late capitalism, a space whose negative or baleful aspects are only too obvious – the dialectic requires us to hold equally to a positive or "progressive" evaluation of its emergence, as Marx did for the world market as the horizon of national economies, or as Lenin did for the older imperialist global network. For neither Marx nor Lenin was socialism a matter of returning to smaller (and thereby less repressive and comprehensive) systems of social organization; rather, the dimensions attained by capital in their own times were grasped as the promise, the framework, and the precondition for the achievement of some new and more comprehensive socialism. Is this not the case with the yet more global and totalizing space of the new world system, which demands the intervention and elaboration of an internationalism of a radically new type? The disastrous realignment of socialist revolution with the older nationalisms (not only in Southeast Asia), whose results have necessarily aroused much serious recent left reflection, can be adduced in support of this position.

But if all this is so, then at least one possible form of a new radical cultural politics becomes evident, with a final aesthetic proviso that must quickly be noted. Left cultural producers and theorists – particularly those formed by bourgeois cultural traditions issuing from romanticism and valorizing spontaneous, instinctive, or unconscious forms of "genius," but also for very obvious historical reasons such as Zhdanovism[xiv] and the sorry consequences of political and party interventions in the arts – have often by reaction allowed themselves to be unduly intimidated by the repudiation, in bourgeois aesthetics and most notably in high modernism, of one of the age-old functions of art – the pedagogical and the didactic. The teaching function of art was, however, always stressed in classical times (even though it there mainly took the form of moral lessons), while the prodigious and still imperfectly understood work of Brecht reaffirms, in a new and formally innovative and original way, for the moment of modernism proper, a complex new conception of the relationship between culture and pedagogy. The cultural model I will propose similarly foregrounds the cognitive and pedagogical dimensions of political art and culture, dimensions stressed in very different ways by both Lukács and Brecht[xv] (for the distinct moments of realism and modernism, respectively).

We cannot, however, return to aesthetic practices elaborated on the basis of historical situations and dilemmas which are no longer ours. Meanwhile, the conception of space that has been developed here suggests that a model of political culture appropriate to our own situation will necessarily have to raise spatial issues as its fundamental organizing concern. I will therefore provisionally define the aesthetic of this new (and hypothetical) cultural form as an aesthetic of cognitive mapping. . . .

An aesthetic of cognitive mapping – a pedagogical political culture which seeks to endow the individual subject with some new heightened sense of its place in the global system – will necessarily have to respect this now enormously complex representational dialectic and invent radically new forms in order to do it justice. This is not then, clearly, a call for a return to some older kind of machinery, some older and more transparent national

---

[xiv] The USSR's policy of strict control of the arts following World War II, named after its executor, A. A. Zhdanov.

[xv] György Lukács (1885–1971), Hungarian philosopher who authored an idealist reinterpretation of Marxism, and Bertolt Brecht (1898–1956), radical German playwright, who employed "distancing-effects" to prevent suspension of disbelief.

space, or some more traditional and reassuring perspectival or mimetic enclave: the new political art (if it is possible at all) will have to hold to the truth of postmodernism, that is to say, to its fundamental object – the world space of multinational capital – at the same time at which it achieves a breakthrough to some as yet unimaginable new mode of representing this last, in which we may again begin to grasp our positioning as individual and collective subjects and regain a capacity to act and struggle which is at present neutralized by our spatial as well as our social confusion. The political form of postmodernism, if there ever is any, will have as its vocation the invention and projection of a global cognitive mapping, on a social as well as a spatial scale.

Notes

1 Robert Venturi and Denise Scott-Brown, *Learning from Las Vegas* (Cambridge, Mass., 1972).
2 The originality of Charles Jencks's pathbreaking *Language of Post-Modern Architecture* (1977) lay in its well-nigh dialectical combination of postmodern architecture and a certain kind of semiotics, each being appealed to to justify the existence of the other. Semiotics becomes appropriate as a mode of analysis of the newer architecture by virtue of the latter's populism, which does emit signs and messages to a spatial "reading public," unlike the monumentality of the high modern. Meanwhile, the newer architecture is itself thereby validated, insofar as it is accessible to semiotic analysis and thus proves to be an essentially aesthetic object (rather than the transaesthetic constructions of the high modern). Here, then, aesthetics reinforces an ideology of communication (about which more will be observed in the concluding chapter), and vice versa. Besides Jencks's many valuable contributions, see also Heinrich Klotz, *History of Postmodern Architecture* (Cambridge, Mass., 1988); Pier Paolo Portoghesi, *After Modern Architecture* (New York, 1982).
3 Ernest Mandel, *Late Capitalism* (London, 1978), p. 118.
4 See, particularly on such motifs in Le Corbusier, Gert Kähler, *Architektur als Symbolverfall: Das Dampfermotiv in der Baukunst* (Brunswick, 1981).
5 See my "Morality and Ethical Substance," in *The Ideologies of Theory*, vol. I (Minneapolis, 1988).

chapter thirty-six

"Solidarity or Objectivity?"

Richard Rorty

Philosopher Richard Rorty's (1931–) book, *Philosophy and the Mirror of Nature* (1979), created great controversy in American philosophy by criticizing recent analytic philosophy and suggesting that this tradition, with continental philosophy, was converging on pragmatism as a postfoundationalist philosophical method. In the succeeding decade Rorty became the most famous American philosopher to present a radical critique of philosophy, a denial that the traditional philosophical pursuit of ultimate, transcendental, foundational knowledge was a valid or desirable enterprise – which seemed to leave little for philosophy to do but, in his words, contribute to the continuing "conversation of culture." Unlike the French postmodernists, Rorty denied that this antifoundationalism can lead to any radical political conclusions, since it implies that philosophy can no more justify any program of political reform than it can legitimate the status quo. Once foundationalism is abandoned, all philosophical writing can do is engage in the rhetorical task of making different world descriptions or "vocabularies" look attractive. In the following essay, published in 1985, he criticizes the attempt to ground our interpretive vocabularies in an appeal to "objectivity," offering the pragmatic alternative that legitimation is always an appeal to "solidarity" or culture.

There are two principal ways in which reflective human beings try, by placing their lives in a larger context, to give sense to those lives. The first is by telling the story of their contribution to a community. This community may be the actual historical one in which they live, or another actual one, distant in time or place, or a quite imaginary one, consisting perhaps of a dozen heroes and heroines selected from history or fiction or both. The second way is to describe themselves as standing in immediate relation to a nonhuman reality. This relation is immediate in the sense that it does not derive from a relation between such a reality and their tribe, or their nation, or their imagined band of comrades. I shall say that stories of the former kind exemplify the desire for solidarity, and that stories of the

Richard Rorty, "Solidarity or Objectivity?" in *Objectivity, Relativism, and Truth* (Cambridge: Cambridge University Press, 1991), pp. 21–34.

573

latter kind exemplify the desire for objectivity. Insofar as a person is seeking solidarity, she does not ask about the relation between the practices of the chosen community and something outside that community. Insofar as she seeks objectivity, she distances herself from the actual persons around her not by thinking of herself as a member of some other real or imaginary group, but rather by attaching herself to something which can be described without reference to any particular human beings.

The tradition in Western culture which centers around the notion of the search for Truth, a tradition which runs from the Greek philosophers through the Enlightenment, is the clearest example of the attempt to find a sense in one's existence by turning away from solidarity to objectivity. The idea of Truth as something to be pursued for its own sake, not because it will be good for oneself, or for one's real or imaginary community, is the central theme of this tradition. It was perhaps the growing awareness by the Greeks of the sheer diversity of human communities which stimulated the emergence of this ideal. A fear of parochialism, of being confined within the horizons of the group into which one happens to be born, a need to see it with the eyes of a stranger, helps produce the skeptical and ironic tone characteristic of Euripides and Socrates. Herodotus' willingness to take the barbarians seriously enough to describe their customs in detail may have been a necessary prelude to Plato's claim that the way to transcend skepticism is to envisage a common goal of humanity – a goal set by human nature rather than by Greek culture. The combination of Socratic alienation and Platonic hope gives rise to the idea of the intellectual as someone who is in touch with the nature of things, not by way of the opinions of his community, but in a more immediate way.

Plato developed the idea of such an intellectual by means of distinctions between knowledge and opinion, and between appearance and reality. Such distinctions conspire to produce the idea that rational inquiry should make visible a realm to which nonintellectuals have little access, and of whose very existence they may be doubtful. In the Enlightenment, this notion became concrete in the adoption of the Newtonian physical scientist as a model of the intellectual. To most thinkers of the eighteenth century, it seemed clear that the access to Nature which physical science had provided should now be followed by the establishment of social, political, and economic institutions which were in accordance with Nature. Ever since, liberal social thought has centered around social reform as made possible by objective knowledge of what human beings are like – not knowledge of what Greeks or Frenchmen or Chinese are like, but of humanity as such. We are the heirs of this objectivist tradition, which centers around the assumption that we must step outside our community long enough to examine it in the light of something which transcends it, namely, that which it has in common with every other actual and possible human community. This tradition dreams of an ultimate community which will have transcended the distinction between the natural and the social, which will exhibit a solidarity which is not parochial because it is the expression of an ahistorical human nature. Much of the rhetoric of contemporary intellectual life takes for granted that the goal of scientific inquiry into man is to understand "underlying structures," or "culturally invariant factors," or "biologically determined patterns."

Those who wish to ground solidarity in objectivity – call them "realists" – have to construe truth as correspondence to reality. So they must construct a metaphysics which has room for a special relation between beliefs and objects which will differentiate true from false beliefs. They also must argue that there are procedures of justification of belief which are natural and not merely local. So they must construct an epistemology which has room for a kind of justification which is not merely social but natural, springing from human nature itself, and made possible by a link between that part of nature and the rest of nature. On their view, the various procedures which are thought of as providing rational justification by one or another culture may or may not really *be* rational. For to be truly rational, procedures of justification *must* lead to the truth, to correspondence to reality, to the intrinsic nature of things.

By contrast, those who wish to reduce objectivity to solidarity – call them "pragmatists" – do not require either a metaphysics or an epistemology. They view truth as, in William James' phrase, what is good for *us* to believe.[i] So they do not need an account of a relation between beliefs and objects called "correspondence," nor an account of human cognitive abilities which ensures that our species is capable of entering into that relation. They see the gap between truth and justification not as something to be bridged by isolating a natural and transcultural sort of rationality which can be used to criticize certain cultures and praise others, but simply as the gap between the actual good and the possible better. From a pragmatist point of view, to say that what is rational for us now to believe may not be *true*, is simply to say that somebody may come up with a better idea. It is to say that there is always room for improved belief, since new evidence, or new hypotheses, or a whole new vocabulary, may come along.[1] For pragmatists, the desire for objectivity is not the desire to escape the limitations of one's community, but simply the desire for as much intersubjective agreement as possible, the desire to extend the reference of "us" as far as we can. Insofar as pragmatists make a distinction between knowledge and opinion, it is simply the distinction between topics on which

---

[i] William James (1842–1910), pragmatic American philosopher and psychologist, a friend of Peirce.

such agreement is relatively easy to get and topics on which agreement is relatively hard to get.

"Relativism" is the traditional epithet applied to pragmatism by realists. Three different views are commonly referred to by this name. The first is the view that every belief is as good as every other. The second is the view that "true" is an equivocal term, having as many meanings as there are procedures of justification. The third is the view that there is nothing to be said about either truth or rationality apart from descriptions of the familiar procedures of justification which a given society – ours – uses in one or another area of inquiry. The pragmatist holds the ethnocentric third view. But he does not hold the self-refuting first view, nor the eccentric second view. He thinks that his views are better than the realists', but he does not think that his views correspond to the nature of things. He thinks that the very flexibility of the word "true" – the fact that it is merely an expression of commendation – insures its univocity. The term "true," on his account, means the same in all cultures, just as equally flexible terms like "here," "there," "good," "bad," "you," and "me" mean the same in all cultures. But the identity of meaning is, of course, compatible with diversity of reference, and with diversity of procedures for assigning the terms. So he feels free to use the term "true" as a general term of commendation in the same way as his realist opponent does – and in particular to use it to commend his own view.

However, it is not clear why "relativist" should be thought an appropriate term for the ethnocentric third view, the one which the pragmatist *does* hold. For the pragmatist is not holding a positive theory which says that something is relative to something else. He is, instead, making the purely *negative* point that we should drop the traditional distinction between knowledge and opinion, construed as the distinction between truth as correspondence to reality and truth as a commendatory term for well-justified beliefs. The reason that the realist calls this negative claim "relativistic" is that he cannot believe that anybody would seriously deny that truth has an intrinsic nature. So when the pragmatist says that there is nothing to be said about truth save that each of us will commend as true those beliefs which he or she finds good to believe, the realist is inclined to interpret this as one more positive theory about the nature of truth: a theory according to which truth is simply the contemporary opinion of a chosen individual or group. Such a theory would, of course, be self-refuting. But the pragmatist does not have a theory of truth, much less a relativistic one. As a partisan of solidarity, his account of the value of cooperative human inquiry has only an ethical base, not an epistemological or metaphysical one. Not having *any* epistemology, *a fortiori* he does not have a relativistic one.

The question of whether truth or rationality has an intrinsic nature, of whether we ought to have a positive theory about either topic, is just the question of whether our self-description ought to be constructed around a relation to human nature or around a relation to a particular collection of human beings, whether we should desire objectivity or solidarity. It is hard to see how one could choose between these alternatives by looking more deeply into the nature of knowledge, or of man, or of nature. Indeed, the proposal that this issue might be so settled begs the question in favor of the realist, for it presupposes that knowledge, man, and nature *have* real essences which are relevant to the problem at hand. For the pragmatist, by contrast, "knowledge" is, like "truth," simply a compliment paid to the beliefs which we think so well justified that, for the moment, further justification is not needed. An inquiry into the nature of knowledge can, on his view, only be a sociohistorical account of how various people have tried to reach agreement on what to believe.

The view which I am calling "pragmatism" is almost, but not quite, the same as what Hilary Putnam, in his recent *Reason, Truth, and History*, calls "the internalist conception of philosophy."[2] Putnam defines such a conception as one which gives up the attempt at a God's eye view of things, the attempt at contact with the nonhuman which I have been calling "the desire for objectivity." Unfortunately, he accompanies his defense of the antirealist views I am recommending with a polemic against a lot of the other people who hold these views – e.g. Kuhn, Feyerabend, Foucault, and myself.[ii] We are criticized as "relativists." Putnam presents "internalism" as a happy *via media* between realism and relativism. He speaks of "the plethora of relativistic doctrines being marketed today"[3] and in particular of "the French philosophers" as holding "some fancy mixture of cultural relativism and 'structuralism.' "[4] But when it comes to criticizing these doctrines all that Putnam finds to attack is the so-called "incommensurability thesis": viz., "terms used in another culture cannot be equated in meaning or reference with any terms or expressions *we* possess."[5] He sensibly agrees with Donald Davidson in remarking that this thesis is self-refuting. Criticism of this thesis, however, is destructive of, at most, some incautious passages in some early writings by Feyerabend. Once this thesis is brushed aside, it is hard to see how Putnam himself differs from most of those he criticizes.

Putnam accepts the Davidsonian point that, as he puts it, "the whole justification of an interpretative scheme . . . is that it renders the behavior of others at least minimally reasonable by *our* lights."[6] It would seem natural to go on from this to say that we cannot get outside the range of those lights, that we cannot stand on neutral ground illuminated only by the natural light of reason. But Putnam draws back from this conclusion. He does so because he construes the claim that we cannot do so as the

---

[ii] Contemporary philosopher of science Paul Feyerabend.

577

claim that the range of our thought is restricted by what he calls "institutionalized norms," publicly available criteria for settling all arguments, including philosophical arguments. He rightly says that there are no such criteria, arguing that the suggestion that there are is as self-refuting as the "incommensurability thesis." He is, I think, entirely right in saying that the notion that philosophy is or should become such an application of explicit criteria contradicts the very idea of philosophy.[7] One can gloss Putnam's point by saying that "philosophy" is precisely what a culture becomes capable of when it ceases to define itself in terms of explicit rules, and becomes sufficiently leisured and civilized to rely on inarticulate know-how, to substitute *phronesis*[iii] for codification, and conversation with foreigners for conquest of them.

But to say that we cannot refer every question to explicit criteria institutionalized by our society does not speak to the point which the people whom Putnam calls "relativists" are making. One reason these people are pragmatists is precisely that they share Putnam's distrust of the positivistic idea that rationality is a matter of applying criteria.

Such a distrust is common, for example, to Kuhn, Mary Hesse, Wittgenstein, Michael Polanyi, and Michael Oakeshott.[iv] Only someone who did think of rationality in this way would dream of suggesting that "true" means something different in different societies. For only such a person could imagine that there was anything to pick out to which one might make "true" relative. Only if one shares the logical positivists' idea that we all carry around things called "rules of language" which regulate what we say when, will one suggest that there is no way to break out of one's culture.

In the most original and powerful section of his book, Putnam argues that the notion that "rationality . . . is defined by the local cultural norms" is merely the demonic counterpart of positivism. It is, as he says, "a scientistic theory inspired by anthropology as positivism was a scientistic theory inspired by the exact sciences." By "scientism" Putnam means the notion that rationality consists in the application of criteria.[8] Suppose we drop this notion, and accept Putnam's own Quinean picture[v] of inquiry as the continual reweaving of a web of beliefs rather than as the application of criteria to cases. Then the notion of "local cultural norms" will lose its offensively parochial overtones. For now to say that we must work by our own lights, that we must be ethnocentric, is merely to say that beliefs suggested by another culture must be tested by trying to weave them together with beliefs we already have. It is a consequence of this holistic

---

iii Practical wisdom, a high ideal for Aristotle.

iv Austrian philosopher Michael Polanyi (1891–1976), contemporary American philosopher of science Mary B. Hesse and English political philosopher Michael Oakeshott (1901–90).

v Willard van Orman Quine and Hilary Putnam are contemporary American philosophers.

view of knowledge, a view *shared* by Putnam and those he criticizes as "relativists," that alternative cultures are not to be thought of on the model of alternative geometries. Alternative geometries are irreconcilable because they have axiomatic structures, and contradictory axioms. They are *designed* to be irreconcilable. Cultures are not so designed, and do not have axiomatic structures. To say that they have "institutionalized norms" is only to say, with Foucault, that knowledge is never separable from power – that one is likely to suffer if one does not hold certain beliefs at certain times and places. But such institutional backups for beliefs take the form of bureaucrats and policemen, not of "rules of language" and "criteria of rationality." To think otherwise is the Cartesian fallacy of seeing axioms where there are only shared habits, of viewing statements which summarize such practices as if they reported constraints enforcing such practices. Part of the force of Quine's and Davidson's attack on the distinction between the conceptual and the empirical is that the distinction between different cultures does not differ in kind from the distinction between different theories held by members of a single culture. The Tasmanian aborigines and the the British colonists had trouble communicating, but this trouble was different only in extent from the difficulties in communication experienced by Gladstone and Disraeli.[vi] The trouble in all such cases is just the difficulty of explaining why other people disagree with us, of reweaving our beliefs so as to fit the fact of disagreement together with the other beliefs we hold. The same Quinean arguments which dispose of the positivists' distinction between analytic and synthetic truth dispose of the anthropologists' distinction between the intercultural and the intracultural.

On this holistic account of cultural norms, however, we do not need the notion of a universal transcultural rationality which Putnam invokes against those whom he calls "relativists." Just before the end of his book, Putnam says that once we drop the notion of a God's-eye point of view we realize that:

> we can only hope to produce a more rational *conception* of rationality or a better *conception* of morality if we operate from *within* our tradition (with its echoes of the Greek agora, of Newton, and so on, in the case of rationality, and with its echoes of scripture, of the philosophers, of the democratic revolutions, and so on . . . in the case of morality.) We are invited to engage in a truly human dialogue.[9]

With this I entirely agree, and so, I take it, would Kuhn, Hesse, and most of the other so-called "relativists" – perhaps even Foucault. But Putnam then goes on to pose a further question.

[vi] Nineteenth-century politicians William Gladstone and Benjamin Disraeli battled as leaders of the Whig and Tory parties.

> Does this dialogue have an ideal terminus? Is there a *true* conception of rationality, an ideal morality, even if all we ever have are our conceptions of these?

I do not see the point of this question. Putnam suggests that a negative answer – the view that "there is only the dialogue" – is just another form of self-refuting relativism. But, once again, I do not see how a claim that something does not exist can be construed as a claim that something is relative to something else. In the final sentence of his book, Putnam says that "The very fact that we speak of our different conceptions as different conceptions of *rationality* posits a *Grenzbegriff*, a limit-concept of ideal truth." But what is such a posit supposed to do, except to say that from God's point of view the human race is heading in the right direction? Surely Putnam's "internalism" should forbid him to say anything like that. To say that *we* think we're heading in the right direction is just to say, with Kuhn, that we can, by hindsight, tell the story of the past as a story of progress. To say that we still have a long way to go, that our present views should not be cast in bronze, is too platitudinous to require support by positing limit-concepts. So it is hard to see what difference is made by the difference between saying "there is only the dialogue" and saying "there is also that to which the dialogue converges."

I would suggest that Putnam here, at the end of the day, slides back into the scientism he rightly condemns in others. For the root of scientism, defined as the view that rationality is a matter of applying criteria, is the desire for objectivity, the hope that what Putnam calls "human flourishing" has a transhistorical nature. I think that Feyerabend is right in suggesting that until we discard the metaphor of inquiry, and human activity generally, as converging rather than proliferating, as becoming more unified rather than more diverse, we shall never be free of the motives which once led us to posit gods. Positing *Grenzbegriffe* seems merely a way of telling ourselves that a nonexistent God would, if he did exist, be pleased with us. If we could ever be moved solely by the desire for solidarity, setting aside the desire for objectivity altogether, then we should think of human progress as making it possible for human beings to do more interesting things and be more interesting people, not as heading towards a place which has somehow been prepared for humanity in advance. Our self-image would employ images of making rather than finding, the images used by the Romantics to praise poets rather than the images used by the Greeks to praise mathematicians. Feyerabend seems to me right in trying to develop such a self-image for us, but his project seems misdescribed, by himself as well as by his critics, as "relativism."[10]

Those who follow Feyerabend in this direction are often thought of as necessarily enemies of the Enlightenment, as joining in the chorus which claims that the traditional self-descriptions of the Western democracies are bankrupt, that they somehow have been shown to be "inadequate" or "self-deceptive." Part of the instinctive resistance to attempts by Marxists, Sartreans, Oakeshottians, Gadamerians and Foucauldians to reduce objectivity to solidarity is the fear that our traditional liberal habits and hopes will not survive the reduction.[vii] Such feelings are evident, for example, in Habermas' criticism of Gadamer's position as relativistic and potentially repressive, in the suspicion that Heidegger's attacks on realism are somehow linked to his Nazism, in the hunch that Marxist attempts to interpret values as class interests are usually just apologies for Leninist takeovers, and in the suggestion that Oakeshott's skepticism about rationalism in politics is merely an apology for the status quo.

I think that putting the issue in such moral and political terms, rather than in epistemological or metaphilosophical terms, makes clearer what is at stake. For now the question is not about how to define words like "truth" or "rationality" or "knowledge" or "philosophy," but about what self-image our society should have of itself. The ritual invocation of the "need to avoid relativism" is most comprehensible as an expression of the need to preserve certain habits of contemporary European life. These are the habits nurtured by the Enlightenment, and justified by it in terms of an appeal of Reason, conceived as a transcultural human ability to correspond to reality, a faculty whose possession and use is demonstrated by obedience to explicit criteria. So the real question about relativism is whether these same habits of intellectual, social, and political life can be justified by a conception of rationality as criterionless muddling through, and by a pragmatist conception of truth.

I think that the answer to this question is that the pragmatist cannot justify these habits without circularity, but then neither can the realist. The pragmatists' justification of toleration, free inquiry, and the quest for undistorted communication can only take the form of a comparison between societies which exemplify these habits and those which do not, leading up to the suggestion that nobody who has experienced both would prefer the latter. It is exemplified by Winston Churchill's defense of democracy as the worst from of government imaginable, except for all the others which have been tried so far. Such justification is not by reference to a criterion, but by reference to various detailed practical advantages. It is circular only in that the terms of praise used to describe liberal societies will be drawn from the vocabulary of the liberal societies themselves. Such praise has to be in *some* vocabulary, after all, and the terms of praise current in primitive or theocratic or totalitarian societies will not produce

[vii] Contemporary German philosopher Hans-Georg Gadamer developed a "hermeneutic" theory of knowledge as interpretation, inspired by Heidegger's work.

the desired result. So the pragmatist admits that he has no ahistorical standpoint from which to endorse the habits of modern democracies he wishes to praise. These consequences are just what partisans of solidarity expect. But among partisans of objectivity they give rise, once again, to fears of the dilemma formed by ethnocentrism on the one hand and relativism on the other. Either we attach a special privilege to our own community, or we pretend an impossible tolerance for every other group.

I have been arguing that we pragmatists should grasp the ethnocentric horn of this dilemma. We should say that we must, in practice, privilege our own group, even though there can be no noncircular justification for doing so. We must insist that the fact that nothing is immune from criticism does not mean that we have a duty to justify everything. We Western liberal intellectuals should accept the fact that we have to start from where we are, and that this means that there are lots of views which we simply cannot take seriously. To use Neurath's familiar analogy,[viii] we can *understand* the revolutionary's suggestion that a sailable boat can't be made out of the planks which make up ours, and that we must simply abandon ship. But we cannot take his suggestion seriously. We cannot take it as a rule for action, so it is not a live option. For some people, to be sure, the option *is* live. These are the people who have always hoped to become a New Being, who have hoped to be converted rather than persuaded. But we – the liberal Rawlsian searchers for consensus, the heirs of Socrates, the people who wish to link their days dialectically each to each – cannot do so. Our community – the community of the liberal intellectuals of the secular modern West – wants to be able to give a *post factum* account of any change of view. We want to be able, so to speak, to justify ourselves to our earlier selves. This preference is not built into us by human nature. It is just the way *we* live now.[11]

This lonely provincialism, this admission that we are just the historical moment that we are, not the representatives of something ahistorical, is what makes traditional Kantian liberals like Rawls[ix] draw back from pragmatism.[12] "Relativism," by contrast, is merely a red herring. The realist is, once again, projecting his own habits of thought upon the pragmatist when he charges him with relativism. For the realist thinks that the whole point of philosophical thought is to detach oneself from any particular community and look down at it from a more universal standpoint. When he hears the pragmatist repudiating the desire for such a standpoint he cannot quite believe it. He thinks that everyone, deep down inside, *must* want such detachment. So he attributes to the pragmatist a perverse form

---

[viii] Austrian philosopher Otto Neurath (1882–1945) compared the task of philosophically analyzing knowledge to rebuilding a ship while at sea.

[ix] Contemporary American political philosopher, John Rawls.

of his own attempted detachment, and sees him as an ironic, sneering aesthete who refuses to take the choice between communities seriously, a mere "relativist." But the pragmatist, dominated by the desire for solidarity, can only be criticized for taking his own community *too* seriously. He can only be criticized for ethnocentrism, not for relativism. To be ethnocentric is to divide the human race into the people to whom one must justify one's beliefs and the others. The first group – one's *ethnos* – comprises those who share enough of one's beliefs to make fruitful conversation possible. In this sense, everybody is ethnocentric when engaged in actual debate, no matter how much realist rhetoric about objectivity he produces in his study.[13]

What is disturbing about the pragmatist's picture is not that it is relativistic but that it takes away two sorts of metaphysical comfort to which our intellectual tradition has become accustomed. One is the thought that membership in our biological species carries with it certain "rights," a notion which does not seem to make sense unless the biological similarities entail the possession of something nonbiological, something which links our species to a nonhuman reality and thus gives the species moral dignity. This picture of rights as biologically transmitted is so basic to the political discourse of the Western democracies that we are troubled by any suggestion that "human nature" is not a useful moral concept. The second comfort is provided by the thought that our community cannot wholly die. The picture of a common human nature oriented towards correspondence to reality as it is in itself comforts us with the thought that even if our civilization is destroyed, even if all memory of our political or intellectual or artistic community is erased, the race is fated to recapture the virtues and the insights and the achievements which were the glory of that community. The notion of human nature as an inner structure which leads all members of the species to converge to the same point, to recognize the same theories, virtues, and works of art as worthy of honor, assures us that even if the Persians had won, the arts and sciences of the Greeks would sooner or later have appeared elsewhere. It assures us that even if the Orwellian bureaucrats of terror rule for a thousand years the achievements of the Western democracies will someday be duplicated by our remote descendants. It assures us that "man will prevail," that something reasonably like *our* world-view, *our* virtues, *our* art, will bob up again whenever human beings are left alone to cultivate their inner natures. The comfort of the realist picture is the comfort of saying not simply that there is a place prepared for our race in our advance, but also that we now know quite a bit about what that place looks like. The inevitable ethnocentrism to which we are all condemned is thus as much a part of the realist's comfortable view as of the pragmatist's uncomfortable one.

The pragmatist gives up the first sort of comfort because he thinks that to say that certain people have certain rights is merely to say that we should treat them in certain ways. It is not to give a *reason* for treating them in those ways. As to the second sort of comfort, he suspects that the hope that something resembling *us* will inherit the earth is impossible to eradicate, as impossible as eradicating the hope of surviving our individual deaths through some satisfying transfiguration. But he does not want to turn this hope into a theory of the nature of man. He wants solidarity to be our *only* comfort, and to be seen not to require metaphysical support.

My suggestion that the desire for objectivity is in part a disguised form of the fear of the death of our community echoes Nietzsche's charge that the philosophical tradition which seems from Plato is an attempt to avoid facing up to contingency, to escape from time and chance. Nietzsche thought that realism was to be condemned not only by arguments from its theoretical incoherence, the sort of argument we find in Putnam and Davidson, but also on practical, pragmatic, grounds. Nietzsche thought that the test of human character was the ability to live with the thought that there was no convergence. He wanted us to be able to think of truth as:

> a mobile army of metaphors, metonyms, and anthromorphisms – in short a sum of human relations, which have been enhanced, transposed, and embellished poetically and rhetorically and which after long use seem firm, canonical, and obligatory to a people.[14]

Nietzsche hoped that eventually there might be human beings who could and did think of truth in this way, but who still liked themselves, who saw themselves as *good* people for whom solidarity was *enough*.[15]

I think that pragmatism's attack on the various structure-content distinctions which buttress the realist's notion of objectivity can best be seen as an attempt to let us think of truth in this Nietzschean way, as entirely a matter of solidarity. That is why I think we need to say, despite Putnam, that "there is only the dialogue," only *us*, and to throw out the last residues of the notion of "transcultural rationality." But this should not lead us to repudiate, as Nietzsche sometimes did, the elements in our movable host which embody the ideas of Socratic conversation, Christian fellowship, and Enlightenment science. Nietzsche ran together his diagnosis of philosophical realism as an expression of fear and resentment with his own resentful idiosyncratic idealizations of silence, solitude, and violence. Post-Nietzschean thinkers like Adorno and Heidegger and Foucault have run together Nietzsche's criticisms of the metaphysical tradition on the one hand with his criticisms of bourgeois civility, of Christian love, and of the nineteenth century's hope that science would make the world a better place to live, on the other. I do not think that there is any interesting connection between these two sets of criticisms. Pragmatism seems to me, as I have said, a philosophy of solidarity rather than of despair. From this point of view, Socrates' turn away from the gods, Christianity's turn from an Omnipotent Creator to the man who suffered on the Cross, and the Baconian turn from science as contemplation of eternal truth to science as instrument of social progress, can be seen as so many preparations for the act of social faith which is suggested by a Nietzschean view of truth.[16]

The best argument we partisans of solidarity have against the realistic partisans of objectivity is Nietzsche's argument that the traditional Western metaphysico-epistemological way of firming up our habits simply isn't working anymore. It isn't doing its job. It has become as transparent a device as the postulation of deities who turn out, by a happy coincidence, to have chosen *us* as their people. So the pragmatist suggestion that we substitute a "merely" ethical foundation for our sense of community – or, better, that we think of our sense of community as having no foundation except shared hope and the trust created by such sharing – is put forward on practical grounds. It is *not* put forward as a corollary of a metaphysical claim that the objects in the world contain no intrinsically action-guiding properties, nor of an epistemological claim that we lack a faculty of moral sense, nor of a semantical claim that truth is reducible to justification. It is a suggestion about how we might think of ourselves in order to avoid the kind of resentful belatedness – characteristic of the bad side of Nietzsche – which now characterizes much of high culture. This resentment arises from the realization, which I referred to at the beginning of this chapter, that the Enlightenment's search for objectivity has often gone sour.

The rhetoric of scientific objectivity, pressed too hard and taken too seriously, has led us to people like B. F. Skinner on the one hand and people like Althusser[x] on the other – two equally pointless fantasies, both produced by the attempt to be "scientific" about our moral and political lives. Reaction against scientism led to attacks on natural science as a sort of false god. But there is nothing wrong with science, there is only something wrong with the attempt to divinize it, the attempt characteristic of realistic philosophy. This reaction has also led to attacks on liberal social thought of the type common to Mill and Dewey and Rawls as a mere ideological superstructure, one which obscures the realities of our situation and represses attempts to change that situation. But there is nothing wrong with liberal democracy, nor with the philosophers who have tried to enlarge its scope. There is only something wrong with the attempt to see their efforts as failures to achieve something which they were not trying to achieve – a demonstration of the "objective" superiority of our way of life over all other alternatives. There is, in short, nothing wrong with the hopes of the Enlightenment, the hopes which created the Western democracies. The value of the ideals of the Enlightenment is, for us pragmatists, just the

[x] Louis Althusser (1918–90), French Marxist philosopher.

585

value of some of the institutions and practices which they have created. In this essay I have sought to distinguish these institutions and practices from the philosophical justifications for them provided by partisans of objectivity, and to suggest an alternative justification.

Notes

1   This attitude toward truth, in which the consensus of a community rather than a relation to a nonhuman reality is taken as central, is associated not only with the American pragmatic tradition but with the work of Popper and Habermas. Habermas' criticisms of lingering positivist elements in Popper parallel those made by Deweyan holists of the early logical empiricists. It is important to see, however, that the pragmatist notion of truth common to James and Dewey is not dependent upon either Peirce's notion of an "ideal end of inquiry" nor on Habermas' notion of an "ideally free community." For criticism of these notions, which in my view are insufficiently ethnocentric, see my "Pragmatism, Davidson and Truth" (below) and "Habermas and Lyotard on Postmodernity" in the second voilume of these papers [*Essays on Heidegger and Others* (Cambridge: Cambridge University Press, 1991)].

2   Hilary Putnam, *Reason, Truth, and History* (Cambridge: Cambridge University Press, 1981), pp. 49–50.

3   Ibid., p. 119.

4   Ibid., p. x.

5   Ibid., p. 114.

6   Ibid., p. 119. See Davidson's "On the very idea of a conceptual scheme," in his *Inquiries into Truth and Interpretation* (Oxford: Oxford University Press, 1984) for a more complete and systematic presentation of this point.

7   Putnam, p. 113.

8   Ibid., p. 126.

9   Ibid., p. 216.

10 See, e.g., Paul Feyerabend, *Science in a Free Society* (London: New Left Books, 1978), p. 9, where Feyerabend identifies his own view with "relativism (in the old and simple sense of Protagoras)." This identification is accompanied by the claim that " 'Objectively' there is not much to choose between anti-semitism and humanitarianism." I think Feyerabend would have served himself better by saying that the scare-quoted word "objectively" should simply be dropped from use, together with the traditional philosophical distinctions which buttress the subjective-objective distinction, than by saying that we may keep the word and use it to say the sort of thing Protagoras said. What Feyerabend is really against is the correspondence theory of truth, not the idea that some views cohere better than others.

11 This quest for consensus is opposed to the sort of quest for authenticity which wishes to free itself from the opinion of our community. See, for example, Vincent Descombes' account of Deleuze in *Modern French Philosophy*

(Cambridge: Cambridge University Press, 1980), p. 153: "Even if philosophy is essentially demystificatory, philosophers often fail to produce authentic critiques; they defend order, authority, institutions, 'decency,' everything in which the ordinary person believes." On the pragmatist or ethonocentric view I am suggesting, all that critique can or should do is play off elements in "what the ordinary person believes" against other elements. To attempt to do more than this is to fantasize rather than to converse. Fantasy may, to be sure, be an incentive to more fruitful conversation, but when it no longer fulfills this function it does not deserve the name of "critique."

12 In *A Theory of Justice* Rawls seemed to be trying to retain the authority of Kantian "practical reason" by imagining a social contract devised by choosers "behind a veil of ignorance" – using the "rational self-interest" of such choosers as a touchstone for the ahistorical validity of certain social institutions. Much of the criticism to which that book was subjected, e.g. by Michael Sandel in his *Liberalism and the Limits of Justice* (Cambridge: Cambridge University Press, 1982), has centered on the claim that one cannot escape history in this way. In the meantime, however, Rawls has put forward a meta-ethical view which drops the claim to ahistorical validity. Concurrently, T. M. Scanlon has urged that the essence of a "contractualist" account of moral motivation is better understood as the desire to justify one's action to others than in terms of "rational self-interest." See Scanlon, "Contractualism and Utilitarianism," in A. Sen and B. Williams (eds), *Utilitarianism and Beyond* (Cambridge: Cambridge University Press, 1982). Scanlon's emendation of Rawls leads in the same direction as Rawls' later work, since Scanlon's use of the notion of "justification to others on grounds they could not reasonably reject" chimes with the "constructivist" view that what counts for social philosophy is what can be justified to a particular historical community, not to "humanity in general." On my view, the frequent remark that Rawls' rational choosers look remarkably like twentieth-century American liberals is perfectly just, but not a criticism of Rawls. It is merely a frank recognition of the ethnocentrism which is essential to serious, nonfantastical, thought. I defend this view in "The Priority of Democracy to Philosophy" and "Postmodernist Bourgeois Liberalism" in Part III of this volume.

13 In an important paper called "The Truth in Relativism," included in his *Moral Luck* (Cambridge: Cambridge University Press, 1981), Bernard Williams makes a similar point in terms of a distinction between "genuine confrontation" and "notional confrontation." The latter is the sort of confrontation which occurs, asymmetrically, between us and primitive tribespeople. The belief-systems of such people do not present, as Williams puts it, "real options" for us, for we cannot imagine going over to their view without "self-deception or paranoia." These are the people whose beliefs on certain topics overlap so little with ours that their inability to agree with us raises no doubt in our minds about the correctness of our own beliefs. Williams' use of "real option" and "notional confrontation" seems to me very enlightening, but I think he turns these notions to purposes they will not serve. Williams wants to defend ethical relativism, defined as the claim that when ethical confrontations are merely

notional "questions of appraisal do not genuinely arise." He thinks they *do* arise in connection with notional confrontations between, e.g., Einsteinian and Amazonian cosmologies. (See Williams, p. 142.) This distinction between ethics and physics seems to me an awkward result to which Williams is driven by his unfortunate attempt to find *something* true in relativism, an attempt which is a corollary of his attempt to be "realistic" about physics. On my (Davidsonian) view, there is no point in distinguishing between true sentences which are "made true by reality" and true sentences which are "made by us," because the whole idea of "truth-makers" needs to be dropped. So I would hold that there is *no* truth in relativism, but this much truth in ethnocentrism: we cannot justify our beliefs (in physics, ethics, or any other area) to everybody, but only to those whose beliefs overlap ours to some appropriate extent. (This is not a theoretical problem about "untranslatability," but simply a practical problem about the limitations of argument; it is not that we live in different worlds than the Nazis or the Amazonians, but that conversion from or to their point of view, though possible, will not be a matter of inference from previously shared premises.)

14 Nietzsche, "On Truth and Lie in an Extra-Moral Sense," in *The Viking Portable Nietzsche*, Walter Kaufmann, ed. and trans., pp. 46–7.

15 See Sabina Lovibond, *Realism and Imagination in Ethics* (Minneapolis: University of Minnesota Press, 1983), p. 158: "An adherent of Wittgenstein's view of language should equate that goal with the establishment of a language-game in which we could participate ingenuously, while retaining our awareness of it as a specific historical formation. A community in which such a language-game was played would be one . . . whose members understood their own form of life and yet were not embarrassed by it."

16 See Hans Blumenberg, *The Legitimation of Modernity* (Cambridge, Mass.: MIT Press, 1982), for a story about the history of European thought which, unlike the stories told by Nietzsche and Heidegger, sees the Enlightenment as a definitive step forward. For Blumenberg, the attitude of "self-assertion," the kind of attitude which stems from a Baconian view of the nature and purpose of science, needs to be distinguished from "self-foundation," the Cartesian project of grounding such inquiry upon ahistorical criteria of rationality. Blumenberg remarks, pregnantly, that the "historicist" criticism of the optimism of the Enlightenment, criticism which began with the Romantics' turn back to the Middle Ages, undermines self-foundation but not self-assertion.

chapter thirty-seven

"An Alternative Way out of the Philosophy of the Subject: Communicative versus Subject-Centered Reason"

Jürgen Habermas

Perhaps the most important living German philosopher, Jürgen Habermas (1929–)
argues for the indispensability of the Enlightenment. Former assistant to Theodor
Adorno and heir to the Frankfurt School legacy, Habermas made a mammoth
contribution to the debate over modernity with his two-volume *Theory of Communicative Action* (German original, 1981; English, 1984 and 1987), based largely in
his notion of "communicative reason." Weber, Adorno and Horkeheimer had
neglected the communicative essence of rationality in favor of the purely instrumental rationality that led to the "Dialectic of Enlightenment." Habermas's
reformulation of modernity is based on the two insights that: (a) rationality is
inherently linguistic and discursive, hence social; and (b) discourse requires that
interlocutors assume the possibility of sincere, truth-governed speech. This means
that participants in discourse cannot regard all of discourse as merely a matter of
power and self-interest. Consequently, Habermas denies the pessimism of Adorno
and Horkheimer, as well as the postmodern denial of the transcendence of norms:
there remains, he claims, "a moment of unconditionality," of truth and freedom in
human relations, despite the inroads of the late modern "system" of money and
power. In the following selection from 1985, Habermas laments the traditional
dependence of both modern thought and its postmodern critics on a "subjectivist,"
non-social conception of rationality.

Jürgen Habermas, "An Alternative Way out of the Philosophy of the Subject: Communicative
versus Subject-Centered Reason," from *The Philosophical Discourse of Modernity*, trans.
Frederick Lawrence (Cambridge: MIT Press, 1987), pp. 294–326.

Jürgen Habermas

The aporias[i] of the theory of power leave their traces behind in the selective readings of genealogical historiography, whether of modern penal procedure or of sexuality in modern times. Unsettled methodological problems are reflected in empirical deficits. Foucault did indeed provide an illuminating critique of the entanglement of the human sciences in the philosophy of the subject: These sciences try to escape from the aporetic tangles of contradictory self-thematization by a subject seeking to know itself, but in doing so they become all the more deeply ensnared in the self-reifications of scientism. However, Foucault did not think through the aporias of his own approach well enough to see how his theory of power was overtaken by a fate similar to that of the human sciences rooted in the philosophy of the subject. His theory tries to rise above those pseudo-sciences to a more rigorous objectivity, and in doing so it gets caught all the more hopelessly in the trap of a presentist historiography, which sees itself compelled to a relativist self-denial and can give no account of the normative foundations of its own rhetoric. To the objectivism of self-mastery on the part of the human sciences there corresponds a subjectivism of self-forgetfulness on Foucault's part. Presentism, relativism, and cryptonormativism are the consequences of his attempt to preserve the transcendental moment proper to generative performances in the basic concept of power while driving from it every trace of subjectivity. This concept of power does not free the genealogist from contradictory self-thematizations.

Hence it would be a good idea to return once again to the unmasking of the human sciences through the critique of reason, but this time in full awareness of a fact that the successors of Nietzsche stubbornly ignore. They do not see that the philosophical counterdiscourse which, from the start, accompanied the philosophical discourse of modernity initiated by Kant already drew up a counterreckoning for subjectivity as the principle of modernity.[1] The basic conceptual aporias of the philosophy of consciousness, so acutely diagnosed by Foucault in the final chapter of *The Order of Things*, were already analyzed by Schiller, Fichte, Schelling,[ii] and Hegel in a similar fashion. To be sure, the solutions they offer are quite different. But if, now, the theory of power also fails to provide a way out of this problematic situation, it behooves us to retrace the path of the philosophical discourse of modernity back to its starting point – in order to examine once again the directions once suggested at the chief crossroads. This is the intention behind these lectures. You will recall that I marked the places where the young Hegel, the young Marx, and even the Heidegger of *Being and Time* and Derrida in his discussion with Husserl stood before alternative paths they did not choose.

[i] *Aporia* is a Greek term meaning an undecidable issue.
[ii] Three German idealist philosophers: Friedrich Schiller (1759–1805), Johann Fichte and Friedrich Schelling (1775–1854).

590

With Hegel and Marx, it would have been a matter of not swallowing the intuition concerning the ethical totality back into the horizon of the self-reference of the knowing and acting subject, but of explicating it in accord with the model of unconstrained consensus formation in a communication community standing under cooperative constraints. With Heidegger and Derrida it would have been a matter of ascribing the meaning-creating horizons of world interpretation not to a Dasein heroically projecting itself or to a background occurrence that shapes structures, but rather to communicatively structured lifewords that reproduce themselves via the palpable medium of action oriented to mutual agreement. At these places, I have already *suggested* that the paradigm of the knowledge of objects has to be replaced by the paradigm of mutual understanding between subjects capable of speech and action. Hegel and Marx did not achieve this paradigm-change; in their attempt to leave behind the metaphysics of subjectivity, Heidegger and Derrida likewise remain caught up in the intention of *Ursprungsphilosophie*.[iii] From the point where he gave a threefold analysis of the compulsion to an aporetic doubling on the part of the self-referential subject, Foucault veered off into a theory of power that has shown itself to be a dead end. He follows Heidegger and Derrida in the abstract negation of the self-referential subject, inasmuch as, put briefly, he declares "man" to be nonexistent. But unlike them, he no longer attempts to compensate, by way of temporalized originary powers, for the lost order of things that the metaphysically isolated and structurally overburdened subject tries in vain to renew from its own forces. In the end, the transcendental-historicist "power," the single constant in the ups and downs of overwhelming and overwhelmed discourses, proves to be only an equivalent for the "life" of the hoary *Lebensphilosophie*.[iv] A more viable solution suggests itself if we drop the somewhat sentimental presupposition of metaphysical homelessness, and if we understand the hectic to and fro between transcendental and empirical modes of dealing with issues, between radical self-reflection and an incomprehensible element that cannot be reflectively retrieved, between the productivity of a self-generating species and a primordial element prior to all production – that is to say, when we understand the puzzle of all these doublings for what it is: a symptom of exhaustion. The paradigm of the philosophy of consciousness is exhausted. If this is so, the symptoms of exhaustion should dissolve with the transition to the paradigm of mutual understanding.

If we can presuppose for a moment the model of action oriented to reaching understanding that I have developed elsewhere,[2] the objectifying attitude in which the knowing subject regards itself as it would entities in

---

[iii] Philosophy of origins.

[iv] Literally, "life-philosophy," a philosophical movement focusing on human spirit or vitality.

the external world is no longer privileged. Fundamental to the paradigm of mutual understanding is, rather, the performative attitude of participants in interaction, who coordinate their plans for action by coming to an understanding about something in the world. When ego carries out a speech act and alter takes up a position with regard to it, the two parties enter into an interpersonal relationship. The latter is structured by the system of reciprocally interlocked perspectives among speakers, hearers, and non-participants who happen to be present at the time. On the level of grammar, this corresponds to the system of personal pronouns. Whoever has been trained in this system has learned how, in the performative attitude, to take up and to transform into one another the perspectives of the first, second, and third persons.

Now this attitude of participants in linguistically mediated interaction makes possible a different relationship of the subject to itself from the sort of objectifying attitude that an observer assumes toward entities in the external world. The transcendental-empirical doubling of the relation to self is only unavoidable so long as there is no alternative to this observer perspective; only then does the subject have to view itself as the dominating counterpart to the world as a whole or as an entity appearing within it. No mediation is possible between the extramundane stance of the transcendental I and the intramundane stance of the empirical I. As soon as linguistically generated intersubjectivity gains primacy, this alternative no longer applies. Then ego stands within an interpersonal relationship that allows him to relate to himself as a participant in an interaction from the perspective of alter. And indeed this reflection undertaken from the perspective of the participant escapes the kind of objectification inevitable from the reflexively applied perspective of the observer. Everything gets frozen into an object under the gaze of the third person, whether directed inwardly or outwardly. The first person, who turns back upon himself in a performative attitude from the angle of vision of the second person, can *recapitulate* the acts it just carried out. In place of reflectively objectified knowledge – the knowledge proper to self-consciousness – we have a recapitulating reconstruction of knowledge already employed.

What earlier was relegated to transcendental philosophy, namely the intuitive analysis of self-consciousness, now gets adapted to the circle of reconstructive sciences that try to make explicit, from the perspective of those participating in discourses and interactions, and by means of analyzing successful or distorted utterances, the pretheoretical grasp of rules on the part of competently speaking, acting, and knowing subjects. Because such reconstructive attempts are no longer aimed at a realm of the intelligible beyond that of appearances, but at the actually exercised rule-knowledge that is deposited in correctly generated utterances, the ontological separation between the transcendental and the empirical is no longer applicable. As can be shown in connection with Jean Piaget's genetic structuralism, reconstructive and empirical assumptions can be brought together in one and the same theory.[3] In this way, the spell of an unresolved back-and-forth between two aspects of self-thematization that are as inevitable as they are incompatible is broken. Consequently, we do not need hybrid theories any more to close the gap between the transcendental and the empirical.

The same holds true for the doubling of the relation to self in the dimension of making the unconscious conscious. Here, according to Foucault, the thought of subject philosophy oscillates back and forth between heroic exertions bent on reflectively transforming what is in-itself into what is for-itself, and the recognition of an opaque background that stubbornly escapes the transparency of self-consciousness. If we make the transition to the paradigm of mutual understanding, these two aspects of self-thematization are no longer incompatible. Insofar as speakers and hearers straightforwardly achieve a mutual understanding about something in the world, they move within the horizon of their common lifeworld; this remains in the background of the participants – as an intuitively known, unproblematic, and unanalyzable, holistic background. The speech situation is the segment of a lifeworld[v] tailored to the relevant theme; it both forms a *context* and furnishes *resources* for the process of mutual understanding. The lifeworld forms a horizon and at the same time offers a store of things taken for granted in the given culture from which communicative participants draw consensual interpretative patterns in their efforts at interpretation. The solidarities of groups integrated by values and the competences of socialized individuals belong, as do culturally ingrained background assumptions, to the components of the lifeworld.

In order to be able to make these kinds of statements, we naturally have to undertake a change in perspective: We can only get insight into the lifeworld *a tergo*.[vi] From the straightforward perspective of acting subjects oriented to mutual understanding, the lifeworld that is always only "co-given" has to evade thematization. As a totality that makes possible the identities and biographical projects of groups and individuals, it is present only prereflectively. Indeed, the practically employed rule-knowledge sedimented in utterances can be reconstructed from the perspective of participants, but not the ever-receding context and the always-in-the-background resources of the lifeworld as a whole. We need a *theoretically constituted perspective* to be able to treat communicative action as the medium through which the lifeworld as a whole is reproduced. Even from this vantage point, only formal-pragmatic statements are possible, state-

---

[v] Husserl's notion of the pre-theoretical world of experience.
[vi] *A tergo* means "from the rear."

ments related to the structures of the lifeworld in general, and not to determinate lifeworlds in their concrete historical configurations. Of course, interaction participants then no longer appear as originators who master situations with the help of accountable actions, but as the products of the traditions in which they stand, of the solidary groups to which they belong, and of the socialization processes within which they grow up. This is to say that the lifeworld reproduces itself to the extent that these three functions, which transcend the perspectives of the actors, are fulfilled: the propagation of cultural traditions, the integration of groups by norms and values, and the socialization of succeeding generations. But what comes into view in this manner are the properties of communicatively structured lifeworlds *in general*.

Whoever wants to become reflectively aware of the individual totality of any individual biography or of a particular way of life has to recur to the perspective of the participants, give up the intention of rational reconstruction, and simply proceed historically. Narrative tools can, if necessary, be stylized into a dialogically conducted self-critique, for which the analytic conversation between doctor and patient offers a suitable model. This self-critique, which is aimed at eliminating pseudo-nature, that is, the pseudo-aprioris made up of unconsciously motivated perceptual barriers and compulsions to action, is related to the narratively recollected entirety of a course of life or way of life. The analytic dissolution of hypostatizations, of self-engendered objective illusions, is due to an experience of reflection. But its liberating force is directed toward *single* illusions: It cannot make transparent the *totality* of a course of life in the process of individuation or of a collective way of life.

The two heritages of self-reflection that get beyond the limits of the philosophy of consciousness, have different aims and scopes. *Rational reconstruction* subscribes to the program of heightening consciousness, but is directed toward anonymous rule systems and does not refer to totalities. In contrast, *methodically carried out self-critique* is related to totalities, and yet in the awareness that it can never completely illuminate the implicit, the prepredicative, the not focally present background of the lifeworld.[4] As can be shown through the example of psychoanalysis, as interpreted in terms of communication theory,[5] the two procedures of reconstruction and of self-critique can still be brought together within the framework of one and the same theory. These two aspects of self-thematization on the part of the knowing subject are also not irreconcilable; in this respect, too, hybrid theories that overcome contradictions by force are superfluous.

Something similar holds true of the third doubling of the subject as an originally creative actor simultaneously alienated from its origin. If the formal-pragmatic concept of the lifeworld is going to be made fruitful for the purposes of social theory, it has to be transformed into an empirically usable concept and integrated with the concept of a self-regulating system into a two-level concept of society. Furthermore, a careful separation between problems of developmental logic and those of developmental dynamics is necessary so that social evolution and social history can be methodically discriminated from each other and related to each other. Finally, social theory has to remain aware of the context of its own emergence and of its position in the contemporary context; even basic concepts that are starkly universalist have a temporal core.[6] If, with the aid of these operations, one succeeds in steering between the Scylla of absolutism and the Charybdis of relativism,[7] we are no longer faced with the alternatives of the conception of world history as a process of self-generation (whether of the spirit or of the species), on the one hand, and, on the other hand, the conception of an impenetrable dispensation that makes the power of lost origins felt through the negativity of withdrawal and deprival.

I cannot go into these complicated interconnections here. I only wanted to suggest how a paradigm-change can render objectless those dilemmas out of which Foucault explains the perilous dynamics of a subjectivity that is bent on knowledge and falls prey to pseudo-sciences. The change of paradigm from subject-centered to communicative reason also encourages us to resume once again the counterdiscourse that accompanied modernity from the beginning. Since Nietzsche's radical critique of reason cannot be consistently carried out along the lines of a critique of metaphysics or of a theory of power, we are directed toward a *different* way out of the philosophy of the subject. Perhaps the grounds for the self-critique of a modernity in collapse can be considered under other premises such that we can do justice to the motives, virulent since Nietzsche, for a precipitous leavetaking of modernity. It must be made clear that the purism of pure reason is not resurrected again in communicative reason.

During the last decade, the radical critique of reason has become fashionable. A study by Hartmut and Gernot Böhme, who take up Foucault's idea of the rise of the modern form of knowledge in connection with the work and biography of Kant, is exemplary in theme and execution. In the style of a historiography of science expanded by cultural and social history, the authors take a look, so to speak, at what goes on behind the back of the critique of pure and of practical reason. For example, they seek the real motives for the critique of reason in the debate with the spiritual clairvoyant, Swedenborg, in whom Kant is supposed to have recognized his dark twin, his repressed counterimage. They pursue these motives into the sphere of the personal, into the, as it were, abstract conduct (turned away from everything sexual, bodily, and imaginative) of a scholarly life marked by hypochondria, crotchetiness, and immobility. The authors marshal before our eyes the "costs of reason" in terms of psychohistory. They undertake this cost/benefit accounting ingenuously with psychoanalytic arguments and document it with historical data, though without being able to specify the place at which such arguments could claim any weight – if indeed the thesis they are concerned with is supposed to make sense.

Kant had carried out his critique of reason from reason's own perspective, that is to say, in the form of a rigorously argued self-limitation of reason. If, now, the production costs of this self-confining reason (which places anything metaphysical off limits) are to be made clear, we require a horizon of reason reaching beyond this drawing of boundaries in which the transcending discourse that adds up the bill can operate. This further radicalized critique of reason would have to postulate a more far-reaching and *comprehensive* reason. But the Böhme brothers do not intend to cast out the devil by Beelzebub; instead, with Foucault, they see in the transition from an exclusive reason (in the Kantian mold) to a comprehensive reason merely "the completion of the power-technique of exclusion by the power-technique of permeation."[8] If they were to be consistent, their own investigation of the other of reason would have to occupy a position utterly heterogeneous to reason – but what does consistency count for in a place that is a priori inaccessible to rational discourse? In this text, the paradoxes repeatedly played out since Nietzsche leave behind no recognizable traces of unrest. This methodological enmity toward reason may have something to do with the type of historical innocence with which studies of this kind today move in the no-man's-land between argumentation, narration, and fiction.[9] The New Critique of Reason suppresses that almost 200-year-old counterdiscourse inherent in modernity itself which I am trying to recall in these lectures.

The latter discourse set out from Kantian philosophy as an unconscious expression of the modern age and pursued the goal of enlightening the Enlightenment about its own narrow-mindedness. The New Critique of Reason denies the continuity with this counterdiscourse, within which it nevertheless still stands: "No longer can it be a matter of completing the project of modernity (Habermas); it has to be a matter of revising it. Also, the Enlightenment has not remained incomplete, but unenlightened."[10] The intention of revising the Enlightenment with the very tools of the Enlightenment is, however, what united the critics of Kant from the start – Schiller with Schlegel, Fichte with the Tübingen seminarians. Further on we read: "Kant's philosophy was initiated as the enterprise of drawing boundaries. But nothing was said about the fact that drawing boundaries is a dynamic process, that reason retreated to firm ground and abandoned other areas, that drawing boundaries means self-inclusion and exclusion of others." At the start of our lectures, we saw how Hegel, along with Schelling and Hölderlin, saw as so many provocations the philosophy of reflection's achievements of delimitation – the opposition of faith and knowledge, of infinite and finite, the separation of spirit and nature, of understanding and sensibility, of duty and inclination. We saw how they tracked the estrangement of an overblown subjective reason from internal and external nature right into the "positivities" of the demolished *Sittlichkeit*[vii] of everyday political and private life. Indeed, Hegel saw the vanishing of the power of reconciliation from the life of mankind as the source of an objective need for philosophy. At any rate, he interpreted the boundaries drawn by subject-centered reason not as exclusions from but as dichotomies within reason, and ascribed to philosophy an access to the totality *that encompasses within itself* subjective reason and its other. Our authors' distrust is directed against this, when they continue: "Whatever reason is, however, remains unclear as long as its other is not thought along with it (in its irreducibility). For reason can be deceived about itself, take itself to be the whole (Hegel), or pretend to comprehend the totality."

This is just the objection that the Young Hegelians once made good against the master. They brought a suit against absolute reason in which the other of reason, what is always prior to it, was supposed to be rehabilitated in its own proper right. The concept of a *situated reason* issued from this process of desublimation; its relationship to the historicity of time, to the facticity of external nature, to the decentered subjectivity of internal nature, and to the material character of society was defined neither by inclusion nor by exclusion, but by a praxis of projecting and developing essential powers that takes place under conditions "not themselves chosen." Society is portrayed as practices in which reason is embodied. This praxis takes place in the dimension of historical time; it mediates the inner nature of needful individuals with an external nature objectified by labor, within the horizon of a surrounding cosmic nature. This social practice is the place where a historically situated, bodily incarnated reason, confronted by external nature, is concretely mediated with its other. Whether this mediating practice is successful depends on its internal constitution, on the degrees of bifurcation and of reconciliation in the socially institutionalized context of life. What was called the system of egoism and divided ethical totality in Schiller and Hegel is transformed by Marx into a society split into social classes. Just as in Schiller and in the young Hegel, the social bond – that is, the community-forming and solidarity-building force of unalienated cooperation and living together – ultimately decides whether reason embodied in social practices is in touch with history and nature. It is the dichotomized society itself that exacts the repression of death, the leveling of historical consciousness, and the subjugation of both internal and external nature.

[vii] Community *mores* or customs.

Within the context of the philosophy of history, the praxis philosophy of the young Marx has the significance of disconnecting Hegel's model of diremption from an *inclusive* concept of reason that incorporated even the other of reason in its totality. The reason of praxis philosophy is understood as finite; nevertheless it remains tied to a *comprehensive* reason – in the form of a critical social theory – insofar as it realizes that it could not identify the historical limits of subject-centered reason – as embodied in bourgeois social relations – without transcending them. Whoever fastens obstinately upon the model of exclusion has to be closed to this Hegelian insight, which, as is evident in Marx, can be had without paying the price of abolutizing the spirit. From such a restricted perspective, the Hegelian defect attending the birth of post-Hegelian theory is still also effective "where reason is criticized as instrumental, repressive, narrow: in Horkheimer and Adorno. Their critique still takes place in the name of a superior reason, namely, the comprehensive reason, to which the intention of totality is conceded, though it was always disputed when it came to real reason. There is no comprehensive reason. One should have learned from Freud or even from Nietzsche that reason does not exist apart from its other and that – functionally considered – it becomes necessary in virtue of this other."[11]

With this assertion, the Böhme brothers call to mind the place where Nietzsche, having recourse to the Romantic heritage, once set a totalizing critique of reason in opposition to an intrinsically dialectical Enlightenment. The dialectic of enlightenment would indeed only have played itself out if reason were robbed of any transcendent force and, in virtual impotence, remained confined, in the madness of its autonomy, to those boundaries that Kant had defined for understanding and for any state based on understanding: "That the subject of reason wants to owe no one and nothing outside itself is its ideal and its insanity at once."[12] Only if reason shows itself to be essentially narcissistic – an identifying, only seemingly universal power, bent upon self-assertion and particular self-aggrandizement, subjugating everything around it as an object – can the other of reason be thought for its part as a spontaneous, creative power that is at the ground of Being, a power that is simultaneously vital and unperspicuous, that is no longer illuminated by any spark of reason. Only reason as reduced to the subjective faculty of understanding and purposive activity corresponds to the image of an *exclusive* reason that further uproots itself the more it strives triumphally for the heights, until, withered, it falls victim to the power of its concealed heterogeneous origin. The dynamism of self-destruction, in which the secret of the dialectic of enlightenment supposedly comes to light, can only function if reason cannot produce anything from itself except that naked power to which it actually hopes to provide an alternative, namely the unforced force of a better insight.

This move explains, moreover, the drastic leveling of Kant's architectonic of reason that results from the Nietzsche-inspired reading of Kant; it has to obliterate the connection of the critiques of pure and practical reason with the critique of judgment, so as to reduce the former to a theory of alienated, external nature and the latter to a theory of domination over internal nature.[13]

Whereas the *diremption model* of reason distinguishes solidary social practice as the locus of a historically situated reason in which the threads of outer nature, inner nature, and society converge, in the *exclusion model* of reason the space opened up by utopian thought gets completely filled in with an irreconcilable reason reduced to bare power. Here social practice only serves as the stage upon which disciplinary power finds ever new scenarios. It is haunted by a reason denied the power to gain access, without coercion, to what is prior to it. In its putative sovereignty, reason that has evaporated into subjectivity becomes the plaything of unmediated forces working upon it, as it were, mechanically – forces of the internal and external nature that have been excluded and rendered into objects.

The other of this self-inflated subjectivity is no longer the diremption totality, which makes itself felt primarily in the avenging power of destroyed reciprocities and in the fateful causality of distorted communicative relationships, as well as through suffering from the disfigured totality of social life, from alienated inner and outer nature. In the model of exclusion, this complicated structure of a subjective reason that is socially divided and thereby torn away from nature is peculiarly de-differentiated: "The other of reason is nature, the human body, fantasy, desire, the feelings – or better: all this insofar as reason has not been able to appropriate it."[4] Thus, it is directly the vital forces of a split-off and repressed subjective nature, it is the sorts of phenomena rediscovered by Romanticism – dreams, fantasies, madness, orgiastic excitement, ecstacy – it is the aesthetic, body-centered experiences of a decentered subjectivity that function as the placeholders for the other of reason. To be sure, early Romanticism still wanted to establish art, in the form of a new mythology, as a public institution in the midst of social life; it wanted to elevate the excitement radiating from this into an equivalent for the unifying power of religion. Nietzsche was the first to transfer this potential for excitement into the beyond of modern society and of history overall. The modern origin of aesthetic experience heightened in an avant-garde fashion remains concealed.

The potential for excitement, stylized into the other of reason, becomes at once esoteric and pseudonymous; it comes up under different names – as Being, as the heterogeneous, as power. The cosmic nature of the metaphysicians and the God of the philosophers become blurred into an enchanting reminiscence, a moving remembrance on the part of the metaphysically and religiously isolated subject. The order from which this

599

subject has emancipated himself – which is to say, internal and external nature in their unalienated form – appears now only in the past tense, as the archaic origin of metaphysics for Heidegger, as a turning point in the archeology of the human sciences for Foucault – and also, somewhat more fashionably, as follows: "Separated from the body, whose libidinous potencies could have supplied images of happiness, separated from a maternal nature, which embraced the archaic *image* of symbiotic wholeness and nurturing protection, separated from the feminine, mingling with which belonged to the primal images of happiness – the philosophy of a reason robbed of all images generated only a grandiose consciousness of the superiority in principle of the intelligible over nature and over the lowliness of the body and the woman. . . . Philosophy attributed to reason an omnipotence, infinity, and future perfection, whereas *the lost childlike relationship to nature* did not appear."[15]

Nonetheless, these recollections of origins by the modern subject serve as points of reference for responses to the question that the more consistent among Nietzsche's followers did not try to evade. As long as we speak in narrative form of the other of reason (whatever it might be called), and as long as this factor that is heterogeneous to discursive thought comes up in portrayals of the history of philosophy and science as a name without any further qualifications, the pose of innocence cannot make up for this underselling of the critique of reason inaugurated by Kant. In Heidegger and Foucault, subjective nature as the placeholder for the other has disappeared, because it can no longer be declared the other of reason once it is brought into scientific discourse as the individual or collective unconscious in the concepts of Freud or Jung, of Lacan or Lévi-Strauss.[viii] Whether in the form of meditative thought or of genealogy, Heidegger and Foucault want to initiate a *special discourse* that claims to operate *outside* the horizon of reason without being utterly irrational. To be sure, this merely shifts the paradox.

Reason is supposed to be criticizable in its historical forms from the perspective of the other that has been excluded from it; this requires, then, an ultimate act of self-reflection that surpasses itself, and indeed an act of reason for which the place of the *genitivus subjectivus*[ix] would have to be occupied by the other of reason. Subjectivity, as the relation-to-self of the knowing and acting subject, is represented in the bipolar relationship of self-reflection. This figure is retained, and yet subjectivity is supposed to appear only in the place reserved for the object. Heidegger and Foucault elaborate this paradox in a structurally similar way, inasmuch as they *generate* what is heterogeneous to reason by way of a self-exiling of reason,

[viii] Carl Jung (1875–1961), Swiss psychiatrist, modified Freud's theory.
[ix] Generating subject.

a banishing of reason from its own territory. This operation is understood as an unmasking reversal of the self-idolizing that subjectivity carries on and at the same time conceals from itself. In the process, it ascribes attributes to itself that it borrows from the shattered religious and metaphysical concepts of order. Conversely, the other they seek, which is heterogeneous to reason and still related to it as its heterogeneous factor, results from a radical finitizing of the absolute for which subjectivity had falsely substituted itself. As we have seen, Heidegger chooses time as the dimension of finitizing and conceives the other of reason as an anonymous, primordial power, set aflow temporally; Foucault chooses the dimension of spatial centering in the experience of one's own body and conceives the other of reason as the anonymous source of the empowerment of interactions tied to the body.

We have seen that this elaboration of the paradox by no means amounts to its solution; the paradox is withdrawn into the special status of extraordinary discourse. Just as meditative thought pertains to a mystified Being, genealogy pertains to power. Meditative thought is supposed to open up a privileged access to metaphysically buried truth; genealogy is supposed to take the place of the apparently degenerate human sciences. Whereas Heidegger remains reticent about the kind of privilege that is his – so that one is not sure of how the genre of his late philosophy could be judged in any sense – Foucault has carried out his work unpretentiously to the very last, in the awareness of being unable to dodge his methodological aporias.

The spatial metaphor of inclusive and exclusive reason reveals that the supposedly radical critique of reason remains tied to the presuppositions of the philosophy of the subject from which it wanted to free itself. Only a reason to which we ascribe a "power of the keys" could either include or exclude. Hence, inside and outside are linked with domination and subjugation; and the overcoming of reason-as-powerholder is linked with breaking open the prison gates and vouchsafing release into an indeterminate freedom. Thus, the other of reason remains the mirror image of reason in power. Surrender and letting-be remain as chained to the desire for control as the rebellion of counterpower does to the oppression of power. Those who would like to leave all paradigms behind along with the paradigm of the philosophy of consciousness, and go forth into the clearing of postmodernity, will just not be able to free themselves from the concepts of subject-centered reason and its impressively illustrated topography.

Since early Romanticism, limit experiences of an aesthetic and mystical kind have always been claimed for the purpose of a rapturous transcendence of the subject. The mystic is blinded by the light of the absolute and closes his eyes; aesthetic ecstasy finds expression in the stunning and dizzying effects of (the illuminating) shock. In both cases, the source of the experience of being shaken up evades any specification. In this indeterminacy, we can make out only the silhouette of the paradigm under attack – the outline of what has been deconstructed. In this constellation, which persists from Nietzsche to Heidegger and Foucault, there arises a readiness for excitement without any proper object; in its wake, subcultures are formed which simultaneously allay and keep alive their excitement in the face of future truths (of which they have been notified in an unspecified way) by means of cultic actions without any cultic object. This scurrilous game with religiously and aesthetically toned ecstasy finds an audience especially in circles of intellectuals who are prepared to make their *sacrificium intellectus*[x] on the altar of their needs of orientation.

But here, too, a paradigm only loses its force when it is negated in a *determinate* manner by a *different* paradigm, that is, when it is devalued in an *insightful* way; it is certainly resistant to any simple invocation of the extinction of the subject. Even the furious labor of deconstruction has identifiable consequences only when the paradigm of self-consciousness, of the relation-to-self of a subject knowing and acting in isolation, is replaced by a different one – by the paradigm of mutual understanding, that is, of the intersubjective relationship between individuals who are socialized through communication and reciprocally recognize one another. Only then does the critique of the domineering thought of subject-centered reason emerge in a *determinate* form – namely, as a critique of Western "logocentrism," which is diagnosed not as an excess but as a deficit of rationality. Instead of overtrumping modernity, it takes up again the counterdiscourse inherent in modernity and leads it away from the battle lines between Hegel and Nietzsche, from which there is no exit. This critique renounces the high-flown originality of a return to archaic origins; it unleashes the subversive force of modern thought itself against the paradigm of the philosophy of consciousness that was installed in the period from Descartes to Kant.

The critique of the Western emphasis on logos[xi] inspired by Nietzsche proceeds in a destructive manner. It demonstrates that the embodied, speaking and acting subject is not master in its own house; it draws from this the conclusion that the subject positing itself in knowledge is in fact dependent upon something prior, anonymous, and transsubjective – be it the dispensation of Being, the accident of structure-formation, or the generative power of some discourse formation. The logos of an omnipotent subject thus appears as a misadventure of misguided specialization, which

[x] Sacrifice of the intellect.
[xi] Rational discourse, logic.

is as rich in consequences as it is wrongheaded. The hope awakened by such post-Nietzschean analyses has constantly the same quality of expectant indeterminacy. Once the defenses of subject-centered reason are razed, the logos, which for so long had held together an interiority protected by power, hollow within and aggressive without, will collapse into itself. It has to be delivered over to its other, whatever that may be.

A different, less dramatic, but step-by-step testable critique of the Western emphasis on logos starts from an attack on the abstractions surrounding logos itself, as free of language, as universalist, and as disembodied. It conceives of intersubjective understanding as the telos inscribed into communication in ordinary language, and of the logocentrism of Western thought, heightened by the philosophy of consciousness, as a systematic *foreshortening* and *distortion* of a potential always already operative in the communicative practice of everyday life, but only selectively exploited. As long as Occidental self-understanding views human beings as distinguished in their relationship to the world by their monopoly on encountering entities, knowing and dealing with objects, making true statements, and implementing plans, reason remains confined ontologically, epistemologically, or in terms of linguistic analysis to only one of its dimensions. The relationship of the human being to the world is cognitivistically reduced: Ontologically, the world is reduced to the world of entities as a whole (as the totality of objects that can be represented and of existing states of affairs); epistemologically, our relationship to that world is reduced to the capacity to know existing states of affairs or to bring them about in a purposive-rational fashion; semantically, it is reduced to fact-stating discourse in which assertoric sentences are used – and no validity claim is admitted besides propositional truth, which is available *in foro interno*.[xi]

Language philosophy – from Plato to Popper – has concentrated this logocentrism into the affirmation that the linguistic function of representing states of affairs is the sole human monopoly.[xii] Whereas human beings share the so-called appellative and expressive functions (Bühler) with animals, only the representative function is supposed to be constitutive of reason.[16] However, evidence from more recent ethology, especially experiments with the artificially induced acquisition of language by chimpanzees, teaches us that it is not the use of propositions per se, but only the *communicative use* of propositionally differentiated language that is proper to our socio-cultural form of life and is constitutive for the level of a genuinely social reproduction of life. In terms of language philosophy, the

---

[xii] Karl Popper, contemporary English philosopher. Below, Karl Bühler (1879–1963) was a German psychologist.
[xiii] Before an inner tribunal.

equiprimordiality and equal value of the three fundamental linguistic functions come into view as soon as we abandon the analytic level of the judgment or the sentence and expand our analysis to speech acts, precisely to the communicative use of sentences. Elementary speech acts display a structure in which three components are mutually combined: the propositional component for representing (or mentioning) states of affairs; the illocutionary component for taking up interpersonal relationships; and finally, the linguistic components that bring the intention of the speaker to expression. The clarification, in terms of speech-act theory, of the complex linguistic functions of representation, the estbalishment of interpersonal relationships, and the expression of one's own subjective experiences has far-reaching consequences for (a) the theory of meaning, (b) the ontological presuppositions of the theory of communication, and (c) the concept of rationality itself. Here I will only point out these consequences to the extent that they are directly relevant to (d) a *new orientation* for the critique of instrumental reason.

(a) Truth-condition semantics,[xiv] as it has been developed from Frege to Dummett and Davidson,[xv] proceeds – as does the Husserlian theory of meaning – from the logocentric assumption that the truth reference of the assertoric sentence (and the indirect truth reference of intentional sentences related to the implementation of plans) offers a suitable point of departure for the explication of the linguistic accomplishment of mutual understanding generally. Thus, this theory arrives at the principle that we understand a sentence when we know the conditions under which it is true. (For understanding intentional and imperative sentences it requires a corresponding knowledge of "conditions for success."[17]) The pragmatically expanded theory of meaning overcomes this fixation on the fact-mirroring function of language. Like truth-condition semantics, it affirms an internal connection between meaning and validity, but it does not reduce this to the validity proper to truth. Correlative to the three fundamental functions of language, each elementary speech act as a whole can be contested under three different aspects of validity. The hearer can reject the utterance of a speaker *in toto* by either disputing the *truth* of the proposition asserted in it (or of the existential presuppositions of its propositional content), or the *rightness* of the speech act in view of the normative context of the utterance (or the legitimacy of the presupposed context itself), or the *truthfulness* of the intention expressed by the speaker (that is, the agreement of what is

---

[xiv] The study of the meanings of utterances that are either true or false.

[xv] German logician Gottlob Frege (1848–1925) was one of the inventors of modern, that is twentieth-century, logic; Michael Dummett and Donald Davidson are contemporary philosophers of language.

meant with what is stated). Hence, the internal connection of meaning and validity holds for the *entire spectrum* of linguistic meanings – and not just for the meaning of expressions that can be expanded into assertoric sentences. It holds true not only for constative[xiv] speech acts, but for any given speech act, that we understand its meaning when we know the conditions under which it can be accepted as valid.

(b) If, however, not just constative but also regulative and expressive speech acts can be connected with validity claims and accepted as valid or rejected as invalid, the basic, ontological framework of the philosophy of consciousness (which has remained normative for linguistic philosophy as well, with exceptions such as Austin)[xvii] proves to be too narrow. The "world" to which subjects can relate with their representations or propositions was hitherto conceived of as the totality of objects or existing states of affairs. The objective world is considered the correlative of all true assertoric sentences. But if normative rightness and subjective truthfulness are introduced as validity claims analogous to truth, "worlds" analogous to the world of facts have to be postulated for legitimately regulated interpersonal relationships and for attributable subjective experiences – a "world" not only for what is "objective," which appears to us in the attitude of the third person, but also one for what is normative, to which we feel obliged in the attitude of addresses, as well as one for what is subjective, which we either disclose or conceal to a public in the attitude of the first person. With any speech act, the speaker takes up a relation to something in the objective world, something in a common social world, and something in his own subjective world. The legacy of logocentrism is still noticeable in the terminological difficulty of expanding the ontological concept of "world" in this way.

The phenomenological concept (elaborated by Heidegger in particular) of a referential context, a lifeworld, that forms the unquestioned context for processes of mutual understanding – behind the backs of participants in interaction, so to speak – needs a corresponding expansion. Participants draw from this *lifeworld* not just consensual patterns of interpretation (the background knowledge from which propositional contents are fed), but also normatively reliable patterns of social relations (the tacitly presupposed solidarities on which illocutionary acts are based) and the competences acquired in socialization processes (the background of the speaker's intentions).

(c) "Rationality" refers in the first instance to the disposition of speaking and acting subjects to acquire and use fallible knowledge. As long as the basic concepts of the philosophy of consciousness lead us to understand

---

[xvi] Utterances intended to state what is true.
[xvii] English "ordinary language" philosopher John L. Austin (1911–60).

knowledge exclusively as knowledge of something in the objective world, rationality is assessed by how the isolated subject orients himself to representational and propositional contents. Subject-centered reason finds its criteria in standards of truth and success that govern the relationships of knowing and purposively acting subjects to the world of possible objects or states of affairs. By contrast, as soon as we conceive of knowledge as communicatively mediated, rationality is assessed in terms of the capacity of responsible participants in interaction to orient themselves in relation to validity claims geared to intersubjective recognition. Communicative reason finds its criteria in the argumentative procedures for directly or indirectly redeeming claims to propositional truth, normative rightness, subjective truthfulness, and aesthetic harmony.[18]

Thus, a procedural concept of rationality can be worked out in terms of the interdependence of various forms of argumentation, that is to say, with the help of a pragmatic logic of argumentation. This concept is richer than that of purposive rationality, which is tailored to the cognitive-instrumental dimension, because it integrates the moral-practical as well as the aesthetic-expressive domains; it is an explicitation of the rational potential built into the validity basis of speech. This communicative rationality recalls older ideas of logos, inasmuch as it brings along with it the connotations of a noncoercively unifying, consensus-building force of a discourse in which the participants overcome their at first subjectively biased views in favor of a rationally motivated agreement. Communicative reason is expressed in a decentered understanding of the world.

(d) From this perspective, both cognitive-instrumental mastery of an objectivated nature (and society) and narcissistically overinflated autonomy (in the sense of purposively rational self-assertion) are derivative moments that have been rendered independent from the communicative structures of the lifeworld, that is, from the intersubjectivity of relationships of mutual understanding and relationships of reciprocal recognition. Subject-centered reason is the *product of division and usurpation*, indeed of a social process in the course of which a subordinated moment assumes the place of the whole, without having the power to assimilate the structure of the whole. Horkheimer and Adorno have, like Foucault, described this process of a self-overburdening and self-reifying subjectivity as a world-historical process. But both sides missed its deeper irony, which consists in the fact that the communicative potential of reason first had to be released in the patterns of modern lifeworlds before the unfettered imperatives of the economic and administrative subsystems could react back on the vulnerable practice of everyday life and could thereby promote the cognitive-instrumental dimension to domination over the suppressed moments of practical reason. The communicative potential of reason has been simultaneously developed and distorted in the course of capitalist modernization.

606

The paradoxical contemporaneity and interdependence of the two processes can only be grasped if the false alternative set up by Max Weber, with his opposition between substantive and formal rationality, is overcome. Its underlying assumption is that the disenchantment of religious-metaphysical world views robs rationality, along with the contents of tradition, of all substantive connotations and thereby strips it of its power to have a structure-forming influence on the lifeworld beyond the purposive-rational organization of means. As opposed to this, I would like to insist that, despite its purely procedural character as disburdened of all religious and metaphysical mortgages, communicative reason is directly implicated in social life-processes insofar as acts of mutual understanding take on the role of a mechanism for coordinating action. The network of communicative actions is nourished by resources of the lifeworld and is at the same time the *medium* by which concrete forms of life are reproduced.

Hence, the theory of communicative action can reconstruct Hegel's concept of the ethical context of life (independently of premises of the philosophy of consciousness). It disenchants the unfathomable causality of fate, which is distinguished from the destining of Being by reason of its *inexorable immanence*. Unlike the "from-time-immemorial" character of the happening of Being or of power, the pseudo-natural dynamics of impaired communicative life-contexts retains something of the character of a destining for which one is *"at fault" oneself* – though one can speak of "fault" here only in an intersubjective sense, that is, in the sense of an involuntary product of an entanglement that, however things stand with individual accountability, communicative agents would have to ascribe to communal responsibility. It is not by chance that suicides set loose a type of shock among those close to them, which allows even the most hardhearted to discover something of the *unavoidable communality* of such a fate.

In the theory of communicative action, the feedback process by which lifeworld and everyday communicative practice are intertwined takes over the mediating role that Marx and Western Marxism had reserved to social practice. In this social practice, reason as historically situated, bodily incarnated, and confronted by nature was supposed to be mediated with its other. If communicative action is now going to take over the same mediating function, the theory of communicative action is going to be suspected of representing just another version of praxis philosophy. In fact, both are supposed to take care of the same task: to conceive of rational practice as reason concretized in history, society, body, and language.

We have traced the way praxis philosophy substituted labor for self-consciousness and then got caught in the fetters of the production paradigm. The praxis philosophy renewed by phenomenology and anthropology, which has at its disposal the tools of the Husserlian analysis of the lifeworld, has learned from the critique of Marxian productivism. It relativizes the status of labor and joins in the aporetic attempts to accommodate the externalization of subjective spirit, the temporalization, socialization, and embodiment of situated reason, within *other* subject-object relationships. Inasmuch as it makes use of phenomenological-anthropological tools of thought, praxis philosophy renounces originality precisely at the point where it cannot afford to: in specifying praxis as a rationally structured process of mediation. It is once again subjected to the dichotomizing basic concepts of the philosophy of the subject: *History* is projected and made by subjects who find themselves in turn already projected and made in the historical process (Sartre); *society* appears to be an objective network of relations that is either set, as a normative order, above the heads of subjects with their transcendentally prior mutual understandings (Alfred Schütz) or is generated by them, as instrumental orders, in the battle of reciprocal objectifications (Kojève); the subject either finds itself centered in its *body* (Merleau-Ponty) or is related eccentrically to itself, regarding its body as an object (Plessner).[xviii] Thought that is tied to the philosophy of the subject cannot bridge over these dichotomies but, as Foucault so acutely diagnosed, oscillates helplessly between one and the other pole.

Not even the linguistic turn of praxis philosophy leads to a paradigm change. Speaking subjects are either masters or shepherds of their linguistic systems. Either they make use of language in a way that is creative of meaning, to disclose their world innovatively, or they are always already moving around within a horizon of world-disclosure taken care of for them by language itself and constantly shifting behind their backs – language as the medium of creative practice (Castoriadis) or as differential event (Heidegger, Derrida).

Thanks to the approach of linguistic philosophy, Cornelius Castoriadis, with his theory of the imaginary institution, can boldly advance praxis philosophy.[xix] In order to give back again to the concept of social practice its revolutionary explosiveness and normative content, he conceives of action no longer expressivistically, but poetically-demiurgically, as the originless creation of absolutely new and unique patterns, whereby each of them discloses an incomparable horizon of meaning. The guarantee of the rational content of modernity – or self-consciousness, authentic self-realization, and self-determination in solidarity – is represented as an imaginary force creative of language. This, of course, comes uncomfortably close to a

---

[xviii] Alexander Kojève (1902–68), twentieth-century French Hegelian philosopher, and three phenomenologists: Alfred Schütz (1899–1959), Maurice Merlau-Ponty (1908–61), contemporary Helmuth Plessner.

[xix] Cornelius Castoriadis, contemporary Greek-born French political philosopher.

Being operating without reason. In the end, there is only a rhetorical difference between voluntaristic "institution" and fatalistic "dispensation."

According to Castoriadis, society is split (like transcendental subjectivity) into the generating and the generated, the instituting and the instituted, whereby the stream of the imaginary, as originative of meaning, flows into changing linguistic world views. This ontological creation of absolutely new, constantly different and unique totalities of meaning occurs like a dispensation of Being; one cannot see how this *demiurgic setting-in-action* of historical truths could be transposed into the *revolutionary project* proper to the practice of consciously acting, autonomous, self-realizing individuals. Autonomy and heteronomy are ultimately supposed to be assessed in terms of the authenticity of the self-transparency of a society that does not hide its imaginary origin beneath extrasocietal projections and knows itself explicitly as a self-instituting society. But who is the subject of this knowledge? Castoriadis acknowledges no reason for revolutionizing reified society except the existentialist resolve: "because we will it." Thus, he has to allow himself to be asked who this "we" of the radical willing might be, if indeed the socialized individuals are merely "instituted" by the "social imaginary." Castoriadis ends where Simmel began: with *Lebensphilo-sophie.*[xx]

This results from the concept of language Castoriadis borrows from hermeneutics as well as from structuralism. Castoriadis proceeds – as do Heidegger, Derrida, and Foucault, in their own ways – from the notion that an ontological difference exists between language and the things spoken about, between the constitutive understanding of the world and what is constituted in the world. This difference means that language discloses the horizon of meaning within which knowing and acting subjects interpret states of affairs, that is, encounter things and people and have experiences in dealing with them. The world-disclosing function of language is conceived on analogy with the generative accomplishments of transcendental consciousness, prescinding, naturally, from the sheerly formal and supra-temporal character of the latter. The linguistic world view is a concrete and historical a priori; it fixes interpretative perspectives that are substantive and variable and that cannot be gone behind. This constitutive world-understanding changes independently of what subjects experience concerning conditions in the world interpreted in the light of this preunderstanding, and independently of what they can *learn* from their practical dealings with anything in the world. No matter whether this metahistorical transformation of linguistic world views is conceived of as Being, différance,[xxi] power, or imagination, and whether it is endowed with connotations of a mystical

[xx] Georg Simmel (1858–1918), German sociologist.
[xxi] Derrida's term for the differing-deferring intrinsic to all signs.

experience of salvation, of aesthetic shock, of creaturely pain, or of creative intoxication: What all these concepts have in common is the peculiar uncoupling of the horizon-constituting productivity of language from the consequences of an intramundane practice that is wholly prejudiced by the linguistic system. Any interaction between world-disclosing language and learning processes in the world is excluded.

In this respect, praxis philosophy had distinguished itself sharply from every kind of linguistic historicism. It conceived of social production as the self-generative process of the species, and the transformation of external nature achieved through labor as an impulse to a learning self-transformation of our own nature. The world of ideas, in light of which socialized producers interpret a pregiven, historically formed nature, changes in turn as a function of the learning processes connected with their transformative activity. By no means does this *innerworldly praxis* owe its *world-building effects* to a mechanical dependence of the suprastructure upon the basis, but to two simple facts: The world of ideas is what first makes possible determinate interpretations of a nature that is then cooperatively worked upon; but it is affected in turn by the learning processes set in motion by social labor. Contrary to linguistic historicism, which hypostatizes the world-disclosing force of language, historical materialism takes into account (as do, later on, pragmatism and genetic structuralism) a dialectical relationship between the world-view structures that make intermundane practice possible by means of a prior understanding of meaning, on the one hand, and, on the other, learning processes deposited in the transformation of world-view structures.

This reciprocal causality goes back to an intrinisic connection between meaning and validity, which nevertheless does not eliminate the difference between the two. Meaning could not exhaust validity. Heidegger jumped to conclusions in identifying the disclosure of meaning-horizons with the truth of meaningful utterances; it is only the *conditions* for the validity of utterances that change with the horizon of meaning – the changed understanding of meaning has to prove itself in experience and in dealing with what can come up within its horizon. And yet praxis philosophy is unable to exploit the superiority it possesses in this respect, because, as we have seen, with its paradigm of production it screens out of the validity spectrum of reason every dimension except those of truth and efficiency. Accordingly, what is learned in innerworldly practice can only accumulate in the development of the forces of production. With this productivist conceptual strategy, the normative content of modernity can no longer be grasped; it can at most be tacitly used to circle about a purposive rationality that has grown into a totality in the exercise of an accusatory negative dialectics.

This unfortunate consequence may be what moved Castoriadis to entrust the rational content of socialism (that is, of a form of life that is supposed to make autonomy and self-realization in solidarity possible) to a demiurge creative of meaning, which brushes aside the difference between meaning and validity and no longer relies upon the profane verification of its creations. A totally different perspective results when we transfer the concept of praxis from labor to communicative action. Then we recognize the interdependences between world-disclosing systems of language and intramundane learning processes along the entire spectrum of validity: Learning processes are no longer channeled only into processes of social labor (and ultimately into cognitive-instrumental dealings with an objectified nature). As soon as we drop the paradigm of production, we can affirm the internal connection between meaning and validity for the whole reservoir of meaning – not just for the segment of meaning of linguistic expressions that play a role in assertoric and intentional sentences. In communicative action, which requires taking yes/no positions on claims of rightness and truthfulness no less than reactions to claims of truth and efficiency, the background knowledge of the lifeworld is submitted to an ongoing test across its entire breadth. To this extent, the concrete a priori of world-disclosing language systems is exposed – right down to their widely ramifying ontological presuppositions – to an indirect revision in the light of our dealings with the intramundane.

This does not mean that the internal connection between meaning and validity is to be undone now from the other side. The potency to create meaning, which in our day has largely retreated into aesthetic precincts, retains the contingency of genuinely innovative forces.

There is a more serious question: whether the concepts of communicative action and of the transcending force of universalistic validity claims do not reestablish an idealism that is incompatible with the naturalistic insights of historical materialism. Does not a lifeworld that is supposed to be reproduced only via the medium of action oriented to mutual understanding get cut off from its material life processes? Naturally, the lifeworld is materially reproduced by way of the results and consequences of the goal-directed actions with which its members intervene in the world. But these instrumental actions are interlaced with communicative ones insofar as they represent the execution of plans that are linked to the plans of other interaction participants by way of common definitions of situations and processes of mutual understanding. Along these paths, the solutions to problems in the sphere of social labor are also plugged into the medium of action oriented by mutual understanding. The theory of communicative action takes into account the fact that the symbolic reproduction of the lifeworld and its material reproduction are internally interdependent.

It is not so simple to counter the suspicion that with the concept of action

611

oriented to validity claims the idealism of a pure, nonsituated reason slips in again, and the dichotomies between the realms of the transcendental and the empirical are given new life in another form.

There is no pure reason that might don linguistic clothing only in the second place. Reason is by its very nature incarnated in contexts of communicative action and in structures of the lifeworld.[19] To the extent that the plans and actions of different actors are interconnected in historical time and across social space through the use of speech oriented toward mutual agreement, taking yes/no positions on criticizable validity claims, however implicitly, gains a key function in *everyday* practice. Agreement arrived at through communication, which is measured by the intersubjective recognition of validity claims, makes possible a networking of social interactions and lifeworld contexts. Of course, these validity claims have a Janus[xxii] face: As claims, they transcend any local context; at the same time, they have to be raised here and now and be de facto recognized if they are going to bear the agreement of interaction participants that is needed for effective cooperation. The transcendent moment of *universal* validity bursts every provinciality asunder; the obligatory moment of accepted validity claims renders them carriers of a *context-bound* everyday practice. Inasmuch as communicative agents reciprocally raise validity claims with their speech acts, they are relying on the potential of assailable grounds. Hence, a moment of *unconditionality* is built into *factual* processes of mutual understanding – the validity laid claim to is distinguished from the social currency of a de facto established practice and yet serves it as the foundation of an existing consensus. The validity claimed for propositions and norms transcends spaces and times, *"blots out" space and time*; but the claim is always raised *here and now*, in specific contexts, and is either accepted or rejected with factual consequences for action. Karl-Otto Apel speaks in a suggestive way about the entwinement of the real communication community with an ideal one.[20]

The communicative practice of everyday life is, as it were, reflected in itself. This "reflection" is no longer a matter of the cognitive subject relating to itself in an objectivating manner. The stratification of discourse and action built into communicative action takes the place of this prelinguistic and isolated reflection. For factually raised validity claims point directly or indirectly to arguments by which they can be worked out and in some cases resolved. This argumentative debate about hypothetical validity claims can be described as the reflective form of communicative action: a relation-to-self that does without the compulsion to objectification found in the basic concepts of the philosophy of the subject. That is to say, the "vis-à-vis" of proponents and opponents reproduces at a reflective level that

[xxii] A Roman god with two faces.

basic form of intersubjective relationship which always mediates the self-relation of the speaker through the performative relation to an addressee. The tense interconnection of the ideal and the real is also, and especially clearly, manifest in discourse itself. Once participants enter into argumentation, they cannot avoid supposing, in a reciprocal way, that the conditions for an ideal speech situation have been sufficiently met. And yet they realize that their discourse is never definitively "purified" of the motives and compulsions that have been filtered out. As little as we can do without the supposition of a purified discourse, we have equally to make do with "unpurified" discourse.

At the end of the fifth lecture, I indicated that the internal connection between contexts of justification and contexts of discovery, between validity and genesis, is never utterly severed. The task of justification, or, in other words, the critique of validity claims carried out from the perspective of a participant, cannot ultimately be separated from a genetic consideration that issues in an ideology critique – carried out from a third-person perspective – of the mixing of power claims and validity claims. Ever since Plato and Democritus,[xxiii] the history of philosophy has been dominated by two opposed impulses: One relentlessly elaborates the transcendent power of abstractive reason and the emancipatory unconditionality of the intelligible, whereas the other strives to unmask the imaginary purity of reason in a materialist fashion.

In contrast, dialectical thought has enlisted the subversive power of materialism to undercut these false alternatives. It does not respond to the banishment of everything empirical from the realm of ideas merely by scornfully reducing relationships of validity to the powers that triumph behind their back. Rather, the theory of communicative action regards the dialectic of knowing and not knowing as embedded within the dialectic of successful and unsuccessful mutual understanding.

Communicative reason makes itself felt in the binding force of intersubjective understanding and reciprocal recognition. At the same time, it circumscribes the universe of a common form of life. Within this universe, the irrational cannot be separated from the rational in the same way as, according to Parmenides, ignorance could be separated from the kind of knowledge that, as the absolutely affirmative, rules over the "nothing." Following Jacob Böhme and Isaac Luria, Schelling correctly insisted that mistakes, crimes, and deceptions are not simply without reason; they are forms of manifestation of the inversion of reason.[xxiv] The violation of claims to truth, correctness, and sincerity affects the whole permeated by the bond

---

[xxiii] Greek Atomist philosopher (*c.*460–*c.*370 BC).
[xxiv] Jacob Böhme (1575–1624) German mystic and philosopher; Isaac Luria (1534–72) cabalist (Jewish mystic).

of reason. There is no escape and no refuge for the few who are in the truth and are supposed to take their leave of the many who stay behind in the darkness of their blindness, as the day takes leave of the night. Any violation of the structures of rational life together, to which all lay claim, affects everyone equally. This is what the young Hegel meant by the ethical totality that is disrupted by the deed of the criminal and that can only be restored by insight into the indivisibility of suffering due to alienation. The same idea motivates Klaus Heinrich in his confrontation of Parmenides with Jonah.[xxv]

In the idea of the convenant made by Yahweh with the people of Israel, there is the germ of the dialectic of betrayal and avenging force: "Keeping the covenant with God is the symbol of fidelity; breaking this covenant is the model of betrayal. To keep faith with God is to keep faith with life-giving Being itself – in oneself and others. To deny it in any domain of being means breaking the covenant with God and betraying one's own foundation. . . . Thus, betrayal of another is simultaneously betrayal of oneself; and every protest against betrayal is not just protest in one's own name, but in the name of the other at the same time. . . . The idea that each being is potentially a 'covenant partner' in the fight against betrayal, including anyone who betrays himself and me, is the only counterbalance against the stoic resignation already formulated by Parmenides when he made a cut between those who know and the mass of the ignorant. The concept of 'enlightenment' familiar to us is unthinkable without the concept of a potentially universal confederation against betrayal."[21] Peirce and Mead[xxvi] were the first to raise this religious motif of a confederation to philosophical status in the form of a consensus theory of truth and a communication theory of society. The theory of communicative action joins itself with this pragmatist tradition; like Hegel in his early fragment on crime and punishment, it, too, lets itself be guided by an intuition that can be expressed in the concepts of the Old Testament as follows: In the restlessness of the real conditions of life, there broods an ambivalence that is due to the dialectic of betrayal and avenging force.[22]

In fact, we can by no means always, or even only often, fulfill those improbable pragmatic presuppositions from which we nevertheless set forth in day-to-day communicative practice – and, in the sense of transcendental necessity, from which we *have to* set forth. For this reason, sociocultural forms of life stand under the structural restrictions of a communicative reason *at once claimed and denied*.

The reason operating in communicative action not only stands under, so to speak, external, situational constraints; its own conditions of possibility

---

[xxv] Parmenides, the ancient Greek philosopher (b. 515 BC), and the Biblical Jonah, swallowed and regurgitated by a whale.

[xxvi] American philosopher George Herbert Mead (1863–1931).

necessitate its branching out into the dimensions of historical time, social space, and body-centered experiences. That is to say, the rational potential of speech is interwoven with the *resources* of any particular given lifeworld. To the extent that the lifeworld fulfills the resource function, it has the character of an intuitive, unshakeably certain, and holistic knowledge, which cannot be made problematic at will – and in this respect it does not represent "knowledge" in any strict sense of the word. This amalgam of background assumptions, solidarities, and skills bred through socialization constitutes a conservative counterweight against the risk of dissent inherent in processes of reaching understanding that work through validity claims.

As a resource from which interaction participants support utterances capable of reaching consensus, the lifeworld constitutes an equivalent for what the philosophy of the subject had ascribed to consciousness in general as synthetic accomplishments. Now, of course, the generative accomplishments are related not to the form but to the content of possible mutual understanding. To this extent, *concrete* forms of life replace transcendental consciousness in its function of creating unity. In culturally embodied self-understandings, intuitively present group solidarities, and the competences of socialized individuals that are brought into play as know-how, the reason expressed in communicative action is mediated with the traditions, social practices, and body-centered complexes of experience that coalesce into *particular* totalities. These particular forms of life, which only emerge in the plural, are certainly not connected with each other only through a web of family resemblances; they exhibit structures common to lifeworlds in general. But these universal structures are only stamped on particular life forms through the medium of action oriented to mutual understanding by which they have to be reproduced. This explains why the importance of these universal structures can increase in the course of historical processes of differentiation. This is also the key to the rationalization of the lifeworld and to the successive release of the rational potential contained in communicative action. This historical tendency can account for the normative content of a modernity threatened by self-destruction without drawing upon the constructions of the philosophy of history.

Notes

1 See the unique lecture delivered by Foucault in 1983 on Kant's "What Is Enlightenment?," in Paul Rabinow (ed.), *The Foucault Reader* (New York, 1984), pp. 32–50. I refer to this in my evocation in the *t a z* (2 July 1984).
2 Jürgen Habermas, "Remarks on the Concept of Communicative Action," in G. Seebass and R. Tuomela (eds), *Social Action* (Dordrecht, 1985), pp. 151–78.
3 Jürgen Habermas, "Interpretive Social Science and Hermeneuticism," in N.

Haan, R. Bellah, P. Rabinow, and W. Sullivan (eds), *Social Science as Moral Inquiry* (New York, 1983), pp. 251–70.

4 Jürgen Habermas, "A Postscript to *Knowledge and Human Interests*", *Philosophy of Social Science*, 3 (1973): 157–89, here pp. 161ff. Also H. Dahmer, *Libido und Gesellschaft* (Frankfurt, 1982), pp. 8ff.

5 Jürgen Habermas, "The Hermeneutic Claim to University," in J. Bleicher (ed.) *Contemporary Hermeneutics* (London and Boston, 1980), pp. 181–211.

6 Jürgen Habermas, *Theorie des kommunikativen Handelns*, vol. 2 (Frankfurt, 1981), pp. 589ff. English: *Theory of Communicative Action*, vol. 2: *System and Lifeworld: A Critique of Functionalist Reason* (Boston, 1987).

7 Cf. Richard J. Bernstein, *Beyond Objectivism and Relativism* (Philadelphia, 1983).

8 H. Böhme and G. Böhme, *Das Andere der Vernunft* (Frankfurt, 1983), p. 326.

9 See the excursus following leecture VII.

10 Böhme and Böhme, *Das Andere der Vernunft*, p. 11.

11 Ibid., p. 18.

12 Ibid., p. 19.

13 Whereas Schiller and Hegel want to see the moral idea of self-legislation realized in an aesthetically reconciled society or in the totality of the context of ethical life, the Böhmes can see only the work of disciplinary power in moral autonomy: "If one wanted to envision the inner judicial process conducted in the name of the moral law with regard to maxims, one would have to recur to the Protestant examination of conscience, which displaced the model of the witch trial into the interiority of humans; or better still, go forward into the cool, hygienic interrogation rooms and the silent, elegant computer arsenals of the police gone scientific, whose ideal is the categorical imperative – the uninterrupted apprehension and control of everything particular and resistant, right into the interiority of the human being." (Böhme and Böhme, *Das Andere der Vernunft*, p. 349).

14 Ibid., p. 13.

15 Ibid., p. 23.

16 Karl-Otto Apel, "Die Logosauszeichnung der menschlichen Sprache. Die philosophische Tragweite der Sprechakttheorie" (1984), manuscript.

17 Ernst Tugendhat, *Einführung in die sprachanalytische Philosophie* (Frankfurt, 1976).

18 Albrecht Wellmer has shown that the harmony of a work of art – aesthetic truth, as it is called – can by no means be reduced, without further ado, to authenticity or sincerity: see his "Truth, Semblance and Reconciliation," *Telos*, 62 (1984/85): 89–115.

19 J. H. Hamann, "Metakritik über den Purismus der Vernunft," in J. Simon (ed.) *Schriften zur Sprache* (Frankfurt, '1967), pp. 213ff.

20 Karl-Otto Apel, *Towards a Transformation of Philosophy* (London, 1980), pp. 225ff. See also my response to Mary Hesse in John Thompson and David Held (eds), *Habermas: Critical Debates* (Cambridge, MA, and London, 1982), pp. 276ff.

21 K. Heinrich, *Versuch über die Schwierigkeit nein zu sagen* (Frankfurt, 1964), p. 20; see also his *Parmenides und Jona* (Frankfurt, 1966).

22 H. Brunkhorst, "Kommunikative Vernunft und rächende Gewalt," *Sozialwissenschaftliche Literatur-Rundschau*, 8/9 (1983): 7–34.

chapter thirty-eight

"From Feminist Empiricism to Feminist Standpoint Epistemologies"

Sandra Harding

To those unfamiliar with the term, "feminist epistemology" may seem an odd combination of words, but it refers to a major movement in contemporary philosophy. If feminism is, in its most general sense, the examination of any phenomenon through the lens of gender and the historical meaning of gender, then traditional notions of knowledge and even scientific method can be critically analyzed with respect to their possible expression of and dependence on gender relations and stereotypes. Philosopher of science Sandra Harding (1935–) discusses the development of feminist epistemology and its attempt to explore the extent to which modern ideals of knowledge have embodied particularly male aspirations, and excluded possible forms of knowing that have traditionally been characterized as female.

THE FEMINIST STANDPOINT EPISTEMOLOGIES

The feminist standpoint epistemologies ground a distinctive feminist science in a theory of gendered activity and social experience. They simultaneously privilege women or feminists (the accounts vary) epistemically and yet also claim to overcome the dichotomizing that is characteristic of the Enlightenment/bourgeois world view and its science.[1] It is useful to think of the standpoint epistemologies, like the appeals to feminist empiricism, as

From Sandra Harding, "From Feminist Empiricism to Feminist Standpoint Epistemologies," chapter 6 of The Science Question in Feminism (Ithaca, NY: Cornell University Press, 1986), pp.141–61.

617

"successor science" projects: in significant ways, they aim to reconstruct the original goals of modern science. In contrast, feminist postmodernism more directly challenges those goals (though there are postmodernist strains even in these standpoint writings).

An observer of these arguments can pick out five different though related reasons that they offer to explain why inquiry from a feminist perspective can provide understandings of nature and social life that are not possible from the perspective of men's distinctive activity and experience. I shall identify each of these reasons in the writing of one theorist who has emphasized this particular aspect of the gendered division of activity, though most of these theorists recognize more than one. Whatever their differences, I think the accounts should be understood as fundamentally complementary, not competing.

The Unity of Hand, Brain and Heart in Craft Labor

Hilary Rose's "feminist epistemology for the natural sciences" is grounded in a post-Marxist analysis of the effects of gendered divisons of activity upon intellectual structures.[2] In two recent papers, she has developed the argument that it is in the thinking and practices of women scientists whose inquiry modes are still characteristically "craft labor," rather than the "industrialized labor" within which most scientific inquiry is done, that we can detect the outlines of a distinctively feminist theory of knowledge. Its distinctiveness is to be found in the way its concepts of the knower, the world to be known, and processes of coming to know reflect the unification of manual, mental, and emotional ("hand, brain, and heart") activity characteristic of women's work more generally. This epistemology not only stands in opposition to the Cartesian dualisms – intellect vs. body, and both vs. feeling and emotion – that underlie Enlightenment and even Marxist visions of science but also grounds the possibility of a "more complete materialism, a truer knowledge" than that provided by either paternal discourse (1984, 49).[i] The need for such a feminist science "is increasingly acute," for "bringing caring labor and the knowledge that stems from participation in it to the analysis becomes critical for a transformative program equally within science and within society" if we are to avoid the nuclear annihilation and deepening social misery increasingly possible otherwise (1983, 89).

Rose starts by analyzing the insights of post-Marxist thinking upon which feminists can build. Sohn-Rethel saw that it was the separation of manual from mental labor in capitalist production that resulted in the mystifying

---

[i] For textual references of this type, see References following the author's endnotes.

abstractions of bourgeois science.[3] But social relations include far more than the mere production of commodities where mental and manual labor are assigned to different classes of people. Like Marx, Sohn-Rethel failed to ask about the effect on science of assigning *caring* labor exclusively to women.[4] Rose argues that in this respect, post-Marxists such as Sohn-Rethel are indistinguishable from the sociobiological theorists to whom they are vehemently opposed; they tacitly endorse the "far-from-emancipatory program of sociobiology, which argues that woman's destiny is in her genes." Feminists must explain the relationship between women's unpaid and paid labor to show that women's caring skills have a social genesis, not a natural one, and that they "are extracted from them by men primarily within the home but also in the work place" (1983, 83–4).

Rose goes on to analyze the relationship of the conditions of women's activities within science with those in domestic life, and the possibilities created by these kinds of activities for women to occupy an advantaged standpoint as producers of less distorted and more comprehensive scientific claims. A feminist epistemology cannot originate in meditations upon what women do in laboratories, since the women there are forced to deny that they are women in order to survive, yet are still "by and large shut out of the production system of scientific knowledge, with its ideological power to define what is and what is not objective knowledge" (1983, 88). They are prohibited from becoming (masculine) scientific knowers and also from admitting to being what they are primarily perceived as being: women.[5]

In her earlier paper, Rose argues that a feminist epistemology must be grounded in the practices of the women's movement. In its consideration of such biological and medical issues as menstruation, abortion, and self-examination and self–health care, the women's movement fuses "subjective and objective knowledge in such a way as to make new knowledge." "Cartesian dualism, biological determinism, and social constructionism fade when faced with the necessity of integrating and interpreting the personal experience of [menstrual] bleeding, pain, and tension," Rose declares. "Working from the experience of the specific oppression of women fuses the personal, the social, and the biological." Thus a feminist epistemology for the natural sciences will emerge from the interplay between "new organizational forms" and new projects (1983, 88–9). The organizational forms of the women's movement, unlike those of capitalist production relations and its science, resist dividing mental, manual, and caring activity among different classes of persons. And its project is to provide the knowledge women need to understand and manage our own bodies: subject and object of inquiry are one. Belief emerging from this unified activity in the service of self-knowledge is more adequate than that emerging from activity that is divided and that is performed for the purposes of monopolizing profit and social control.

This first paper left a gap between the kind of knowledge/power relations possible in a science grounded in women's understandings of our own bodies and the kind needed if a feminist science is to develop sufficient muscle to replace the physics, chemistry, biology, and social sciences we have. In the later paper, Rose inches across this gap by expanding the domain in which she thinks we can identify the origins of a distinctive feminist epistemology. The origins of an epistemology which holds that appeals to the subjective are legitimate, that intellectual and emotional domains must be united, that the domination of reductionism and linearity must be replaced by the harmony of holism and complexity, can be detected in what Foucault would call "subjugated knowledges" – submerged understandings within the history of science (1984, 49).

Rose has in mind here the ecological concerns reported and elaborated by Carolyn Merchant and evident in Rachel Carson's work, and the calls for moving beyond reductionism toward a holistic "feminization of science" evident in writers such as David Bohm and Fritjof Capra.[6] She might also have cited here Joseph Needham's romantic idealization of Chinese science as more feminized than Western science.[7] And then we would have to think about the contradictions between China's history of a "feminized science" and the far from emancipatory history of Chinese misogyny. This raises the troublesome issue of the conflation of gender dichotomies as a metaphor for other dichotomies (gender symbolism) with explanations that treat social relations between the sexes as a causal influence on history – a point to be pursued later. Furthermore, this line of thought leads directly toward feminist distrust of men's conceptions of the androgyny men desire for themselves. When men want androgyny, they usually intend to appropriate selectively parts of "the feminine" for their projects, while leaving the lot of real women unchanged.[8]

Within recent scientific research by women in biology, psychology, and anthropology – areas where "craft" forms of scientific inquiry are still possible, in contrast to the "industrial" forms confronting women in masculine-dominated labs – Rose detects the most significant advances toward "a more complete materialism, a truer knowledge." In all of these areas, feminist thinking has produced a new comprehension of the relationships between organisms, and between organisms and their environment. The organism is conceptualized "not in terms of the Darwinian metaphor, as the passive object of selection by an indifferent environment, but as [an] active participant, a subject in the determination of its own future" (1984, 51). (Keller has argued that Barbara McClintock's work provides a paradigm of this kind of alternative to the "master theory" of Darwinian biology.[9])

620

Thus Rose proposes that the grounds for a distinctive feminist science and epistemology are to be found in the social practices and conceptual schemes of feminists (or women inquirers) in craft-organized areas of inquiry. There women's socially created conceptions of nature and social relations can produce new understandings that carry emancipatory possibilities for the species. These conceptions are not necessarily original to women scientists: hints of them can be detected in the "subjugated knowledges" in the history of science. However, we can here hazard an observation Rose does not make: where these notions neither originate in nor give expression to any distinctive social/political experience, they are fated to remain mere intellectual curiosities – like the ancient Greek ideas about atoms – awaiting their "social birth" within the scientific enterprise at the hands of a group which needs such conceptions in order to project onto nature its destiny within the social order. One cannot help noticing that the notion of organisms as active participants in the determination of their own futures "discovers" in "nature" the very relationship that feminist theory claims has been permitted only to (dominant group) men but *should* exist as well for women, who are also history-making social beings. Men have actively advanced their own futures within masculine domination; women, too, could actively participate in the design of their futures within a degendered social order.

Whether or not Rose would agree to this conclusion, she does argue that the origins of a feminist epistemology for a successor science are to be found in the conceptions of the knower, the processes of knowing, and the world to be known which are evident in this substantive scientific research. The substantive claims of this research are thus to be justified in terms of women's different activities and social experiences created in the gendered division of labor/activity. As I shall ask of each of these standpoint theorists, does this epistemology still retain too much of the Enlightenment vision?

Women's Subjugated Activity: Sensuous, Concrete, Relational

Like Rose, political theorist Nancy Hartsock locates the epistemological foundations for a feminist successor science in a post-Marxist theory of labor (activity) and its effects upon mental life. For Hartsock, too, Sohn-Rethel provides important clues. But Hartsock begins with Marx's metatheory, his "proposal that a correct vision of class society is available from only one of the two major class positions in capitalist society."[10] By starting from the lived realities of women's lives, we can identify the grounding for a theory of knowledge that should be the successor to both Enlightenment and Marxist epistemologies. For Hartsock as for Rose, it is in the gendered division of labor that one can discover both the reason for the greater

621

adequacy of feminist knowledge claims, and the root from which a full-fledged successor to Enlightenment science can grow. However, the feminist successor science will be anti-Cartesian, for it transcends and thus stands in opposition to the dichotomies of thought and practice created by divisions between mental and manual labor, though in a way different from that which Rose identifies.

Women's activity consists in "sensuous human activity, practice." Women's activity is institutionalized in two kinds of contributions – to "subsistence" and to child-rearing. In subsistence activities, contributions to producing the food, clothing, and shelter necessary for the survival of the species.

> the activity of a woman in the home as well as the work she does for wages keeps her continually in contact with a world of qualities and change. Her immersion in the world of use – in concrete, many-qualitied, changing material processes – is more complete than [a man's]. And if life itself consists of sensuous activity, the vantage point available to women on the basis of the contribution to subsistence represents an intensification and deepening of the materialist world view and consciousness available to the producers of commodities in capitalism, an intensification of class consciousness. (p. 292)

However, it is in examining the conditions of women's activities in child care that the inadequacy of the Marxist analysis appears most clearly. "Women also produce/reproduce men (and other women) on both a daily and a long-term basis. This aspect of women's 'production' exposes the deep inadequacies of the concept of production as a description of women's activity. One does not (cannot) produce another human being in anything like the way one produces an object such as a chair.... Helping another to develop, the gradual relinquishing of control, the experience of the human limits of one's action" are fundamental characteristics of the child care assigned exclusively to women. "The female experience in reproduction represents a unity with nature which goes beyond the proletarian experience of interchange with nature" (p. 293).

Furthermore, Hartsock draws on the feminist object-relations theory of Jane Flax and Nancy Chodorow to show that women are "made, not born" in such a way as to define and experience themselves concretely and relationally.[11] In contrast, newborn males are turned into men who define and experience themselves abstractly and as fundamentally isolated from other people and nature. Not-yet-gendered newborn males and females are shaped into the kinds of personalities who will want to perform characteristic masculine and feminine activities. The consequences that object-relations theorists describe are just what Hartsock finds when she examines the adult division of labor by gender: relational femininity vs. abstract masculinity. Both the epistemology and the society constructed by "men suffering from the effects of abstract masculinity" emphasize "the separation and opposition of social and natural worlds, of abstract and concrete, of permanence and change" – the same oppositions as those stressed in the Marxist analysis of bourgeois labor. Thus the true counter to the bourgeois subjugations and mystifications is not to be found in a science grounded in proletarian experience, for this is fundamentally still a form of men's experience; it is instead to be found in a science grounded in women's experience, for only there can these separations and oppositions find no home (pp. 294–8).

The conditions under which women contribute to social life must be generalized for all humans if an effective opposition to androcentric and bourgeois political life and science/epistemology is to be created. Politically, this will lead to a society no longer structured by masculinist oppositions in either their bourgeois or proletarian forms; epistemologically, it will lead to a science that will both direct and be directed by the political struggle for that society.

A feminist epistemological standpoint is an interested social location ("interested" in the sense of "engaged," not "biased"), the conditions for which bestow upon its occupants scientific and epistemic advantage. The subjugation of women's sensuous, concrete, relational activity permits women to grasp aspects of nature and social life that are not accessible to inquiries grounded in men's characteristic activities. The vision based on men's activities is both partial and perverse – "perverse" because it systematically reverses the proper order of things: it substitutes abstract for concrete reality; for example, it makes death-risking rather than the reproduction of our species form of life the paradigmatically human act. Even early feminists such as Simone de Beauvoir think within abstract masculinity: "It is not in giving life but in risking life that man is raised above the animal: that is why superiority has been accorded in humanity not to the sex that brings forth but to that which kills".[12]

Moreover, men's vision is not simply false, for the ruling group can make their false vision become apparently true: "Men's power to structure social relations in their own image means that women, too, must participate in social relations which manifest and express abstract masculinity" (p. 302). The array of legal and social restrictions on women's participation in public life makes women's characteristic activities appear to both men and women as merely natural, as merely continuous with the activities of female termites or apes (as the sociobiologists would have it), and thus as suitable objects of men's manipulations of whatever they perceive as purely natural. The restriction of formal and informal educational opportunities for women makes women appear incapable of understanding the world within which men move, and as appropriately forced to deal with that world in men's terms.

623

The vision available to women "must be struggled for and represents an achievement which requires both science to see beneath the surface of the social relations in which all are forced to participate, and the education which can only grow from struggle to change those relations" (p. 285). The adoption of this standpoint is fundamentally a moral and political act of commitment to understanding the world from the perspective of the socially subjugated. It constitutes not a switch of epistemological and political commitments from one gender to the other but a commitment to the transcendence of gender through its elimination. Such a commitment is social and political, not merely intellectual.

Hartsock is arguing that divisions of labor more intensive than those Marx identified create dominating political power and ally perverse knowledge claims with the perversity of dominating power. Therefore, a science generated out of a transcendence, a transformation, of these divisions and their corresponding dualisms will be a powerful force for the elimination of power. In an earlier paper, Hartsock argued that the concept of power central to the history of political theory is only one available concept. Against power as domination *over* others, feminist thinking and organizational practices express the possibility of power as the provision of energy *to* others as well as self, and of reciprocal empowerment.[13] I think this second notion of power and the kind of knowledge that could be allied with it can remove the apparent paradox from her adoption of both successor science and postmodern tendencies. One can insist on an epistemology-centered philosophy only if the "policing of thought" that epistemology entails is a reciprocal project – with the goal of eliminating the kind of dominating power that makes the policing of thought necessary.[14] That is, such an epistemology would be a transitional project, as we transform ourselves into a culture uncomfortable with domination and thereby into peoples whose thought does not need policing.

Hartsock's grounds for a feminist epistemology are both broader and narrower than Rose's. They are narrower in that it is feminist political struggle and theory ("science") – not simply characteristic women's activities – in which the tendencies toward a specifically feminist epistemology can be detected. Unmediated by feminist struggle and analysis, women's distinctive practices and thinking remain part of the world created by masculine-domination.[15] But her grounds are also broader, for any feminist inquiry that starts from the categories and valuations of women's subsistence and domestic labor and is *interested* (again in the sense of *engaged*) in the struggle for feminist goals provides the grounding for a distinctive epistemology of a successor to Enlightenment science. The women's health movement and the alternative understandings of the relationship between organism and environment that Rose points to would provide significant examples of such inquiries (insofar as they are motivated by the goals of feminist emancipation). But so would any of the natural or social science inquiries that begin by taking women's activities as fully social and try to explain nature and social life for feminist political purposes. There is still a significant gap in Hartsock's account between feminist activity and a science/epistemology robust and politically powerful enough to unseat the Enlightenment vision. But in both its broader and narrower aspects, Hartsock's account inches yet further across the gap by extending the foundation for the successor science to the full array of feminist political and scientific projects and, at least implicitly, to activities in which men as well as women feminists engage.

There is an another important difference in the groundings these two theorists identify for the successor epistemology. Hartsock does not directly focus on the "caring" labor of women, which Rose takes to be the distinctive human activity missing in the Marxist accounts. For Hartsock, the uniqueness of women's labor, in contrast to proletarian labor, is to be found in its more fundamental opposition to the mental/manual dualities that structure masculine/bourgeois thought and activity. For Hartsock, (men's) proletarian labor is transitional between bourgeois/masculine and women's labor, since women's labor is more fundamentally involved with the self-conscious, sensuous processing of our natural/social surroundings in daily life – is the distinctively human activity. For Rose, women's labor is different in kind from (masculine) proletarian/bourgeois labor.

The "Return of the Repressed" in Feminist Theory

Jane Flax, a political theorist and psychotherapist, explicitly describes the successor science and postmodern tendencies in feminist epistemology as conflicting. In the later of two papers I shall examine, she argues for the postmodern direction to replace the successor science tendency, yet in both papers the two tendencies are linked in a way that evidently appears noncontradictory to her.

In a paper written in 1980, though not published until 1983, Flax calls for a "successor science" project:

> The task of feminist epistemology is to uncover how patriarchy has permeated both our concept of knowledge and the concrete content of bodies of knowledge, even that claiming to be emancipatory. Without adequate knowledge of the world and our history within it (and this includes knowing how to know), we cannot develop a more adequate social practice. A feminist epistemology is thus both an aspect of feminist theory and a preparation for and a central element of a more adequate theory of human nature and politics.[16]

625

"Feminist philosophy thus represents the return of the repressed, of the exposure of the particular social roots of all apparently abstract and universal knowledge. This work could prepare the ground for a more adequate social theory in which philosophy and empirical knowledge are reunited and mutually enriched" (p. 249).

Flax argues that feminist philosophy should ask the question, "What forms of social relations exist such that certain questions and ways of answering them become constitutive of philosophy?" (p. 248). Here a feminist reading of psychoanalytic object-relations theory (see Chapter 5) becomes a useful philosophic tool; it directs our attention to the distinctively gendered senses of self, others, nature, and relations among the three that are characteristic in cultures where infant care is primarily the responsibility of women. For Flax, what is particularly interesting is the fit between masculine senses of self, others, and nature and the definition of what is problematic in philosophy. From this perspective, "apparently insoluble dilemmas within philosophy are not the product of the immanent structure of the human mind and/or nature but rather reflect distorted or frozen social relations" (p. 248). For men more than for women, the self remains frozen in a defensive infantile need to dominate and/or repress others in order to retain its individual identity. In cultures where primary child care is assigned exclusively to women, male infants will develop unresolvable dilemmas concerning the separation of the infantile self from its first "other" and the establishment of individual identity. These are the very same distinctively masculine dilemmas that preoccupy Western philosophers in whose work they appear as "the human dilemma."

Western philosophy problematizes the relationships between subject and object, mind and body, inner and outer, reason and sense; but these relationships would not need to be problematic for anyone were the core self not always defined exclusively against women.

> In philosophy, being (ontology) has been divorced from knowing (epistemology) and both have been separated from either ethics or politics. These divisions were blessed by Kant and transformed by him into a fundamental principle derived from the structure of mind itself. A consequence of this principle has been the enshrining within mainstream Anglo-American philosophy of a rigid distinction between fact and value which has had the effect of consigning the philosopher to silence on issues of utmost importance to human life. (p. 248)

Were women not exclusively the humans against whom infant males develop their senses of a separate and individuated self, "human knowledge" would not be so preoccupied with infantile separation and individuation dilemmas. "Analysis reveals an arrested stage of human development . . . behind most forms of knowledge and reason. Separation-individuation [of infants from their caretakers] cannot be completed and true reciprocity emerge if the 'other' must be dominated and/or repressed rather than incorporated into the self while simultaneously acknowledging difference" (p. 269). Human knowledge can come to reflect the more adult issues of maximizing reciprocity and appreciating difference only if the first "other" is "incorporated into the self" rather than dominated and/or repressed.

Flax's point is *not* that the Great Men in the history of philosophy would have better spent their time on psychoanalytic couches (had they been available) than in writing philosophy. Nor is it that philosophy is nothing but masculine rationalization of painful infantile experience. Rather, she argues that a feminist exposure of the "normal" relations between infantile gendering processes and adult masculine thought patterns "reveals fundamental limitations in the ability of [men's] philosophy to comprehend women's and children's experiences"; in particular, it reveals the tendency of philosophers to take their own experience as paradigmatically human rather than merely as typically masculine (p. 247). We can move toward a feminist epistemology through exposing the infantile social dilemmas repressed by adult men, the "resolutions" of which reappear in abstract and universalizing form as both the collective motive for and the subject matter of patriarchal epistemology. The feminine dimensions of experience tend to disappear in all thinking within patriarchies. But women's experience cannot, in itself, provide a sufficient ground for theory, for "as the other pole of the dualities it must be incorporated and transcended." Thus an adequate feminist philosophy requires "a revolutionary theory and practice . . . Nothing less than a new stage of human development is required in which reciprocity can emerge for the first time as the basis of social relations" (p. 270).

In this earlier paper, Flax is arguing that infantile dilemmas are more appropriately resolved, less problematic, for women than for men. This small gap between the genders prefigures a larger gap between the defensive gendered selves produced in patriarchal modes of child rearing and the reciprocal, degendered selves that *could* exist were men as well as women primary caretakers of infants, and women as well as men responsible for public life. The forms and processes of knowing as well as what is known will be different for reciprocal selves than for defensive selves. Truly human knowledge and ways of knowing toward which a feminist epistemology points the way, will be less distorted and more nearly adequate than the knowledge and ways of knowing we now have. And while the concepts of reciprocal knowing must be relational and contextual, and thus will no longer enshrine the dualities of Enlightenment epistemology, it is indeed a successor epistemology toward which feminism moves us all.[17]

627

Flax's argument in a paper written four years later contrasts sharply with the foregoing argument. Whereas the earlier paper claims that child-rearing practices leave distinctive marks on philosophers as culturally diverse as Plato, Locke, Hobbes, Kant, Rousseau, and contemporary Anglo-American thinkers, the later one is skeptical that there can be a *single* way that patriarchy has permeated thinking. She finds problematic the notion of "*a* feminist standpoint which is more true than previous (male) ones." She says, "Any feminist standpoint will necessarily be partial. Each person who tries to think from the standpoint of women may illuminate some aspects of the social totality which have been previously suppressed with the dominant view. But none of us can speak for 'woman' because no such person exists except within a specific set of (already gendered) relations – to 'man' and to many concrete and different women."

Here it is feminist theory's affinities with postmodern philosophy that Flax finds most distinctive:

> As a type of post modern philosophy, feminist theory shares with other such modes of thought an uncertainty about the appropriate grounding and methods for explaining and/or interpreting human experience. Contemporary feminists join other post modern philosophers in raising important metatheoretical questions concerning the possible nature and status of theorizing itself. . . . Consensus rules on categorization, appraisal, validity, etc. are lacking.[18]

This affinity is more fundamental, she argues, than feminist attempts at successor science projects: "Despite an understandable attraction to the (apparently) logical, orderly world of the Enlightenment, feminist theory more properly belongs in the terrain of post modern philosophy." And yet the substance of this later paper argues for a particular way of understanding gender that Flax thinks should replace the inadequate and confusing ways it is conceptualized in both traditional and feminist social theory. Gender should be understood as relational; gender relations are not determined by nature but are social relations of domination, and feminist theorists "need to recover and write the histories of women and our activities into the accounts and self-understanding of the whole" of social relations.

On the one hand, in effect Flax has located the feminist successor science tendencies as part of the projects of the defensive self which are most evident in men. She identifies postmodern skepticism about the Enlightenment dualities, which ensure the epistemological "policing of thought," as the entering wedge into projects for the reciprocal self. Overcoming the (distinctively masculine) Enlightenment dualities will be possible for our whole culture only after a "revolution in human development." On the other hand, does not Flax's own account of the distorted and frozen social relations characteristic of masculine-dominant societies suggest both that there is "objective basis for distinguishing between true and false beliefs" and that she is herself committed to this kind of epistemology? Even though any particular historical understanding available to feminists ("a feminist standpoint") is partial, may it not also be "more true than previous (male) ones"?

The Bifurcated Consciousness of Alienated Women Inquirers

Canadian sociologist of knowledge Dorothy Smith has explored in a series of papers what it would mean to construct a sociology that begins from the "standpoint of women." Through her stated concern is sociology, her arguments are generalizable to inquiry in all the social and natural sciences. In the most recent of these papers, she directly articulates the problem of how to fashion a successor science that will transcend the damaging subject-object, inner-outer, reason-emotion dualities of Enlightenment science. "Here, I am concerned with the problem of methods of thinking which will realize the project of a sociology for women; that is, a sociology which does not transform those it studies into objects but preserves in its analytic procedures the presence of the subject as actor and experiencer. Subject then is that knower whose grasp of the world may be enlarged by the work of the sociologist."[19] Smith thinks that the forms of alienation experienced by women inquirers make it possible to carry out what I have been calling successor science and postmodern projects simultaneously and without contradiction.

Like the other theorists, Smith's epistemology is grounded in a successor to the Marxist theory of labor. (It is perhaps inaccurate to conjoin Flax with the others in this respect, unless we focus on her discussion of the process through which the infant becomes a social person as the first human labor, which is divided, of course, by the gender of the "laboring" infant.) Smith eschews questions of the developmental origins of gender; of the origins in men's infantile experiences of the defensive abstractions of Western social theory, science, and epistemology; and thus of the reasons why men and women *want* to participate in characteristically masculine and feminine activity. That is, she does not discuss the issue of how initially androgynous infantile "animals" of our species interact with their social/physical environments to become the gendered humans we see around us. Like Rose, she turns to the structure of the workplace for women scientists (sociologists) to locate an enriched notion of the material conditions that make possible a distinctively feminist science.

Where Rose focuses on the unity of hand, brain, and heart common to women's characteristic activities, Smith looks at three other shared aspects

629

of women's work. In the first place, it relieves men of the need to take care of their bodies or of the local places where they exist, freeing them to immerse themselves in the world of abstract concepts. Second, the labor of women thereby "articulates," shapes, men's concepts into those of administrative forms of ruling. The more successfully women perform this concrete work (Hartsock's "world of sensuousness, of qualities and change"), the more invisible does their work become to men. Men who are relieved of the need to maintain their own bodies and the local places where they exist can now see as real only what corresponds to their abstracted mental world. Like Hegel's master, to whom the slave's labor appears merely as an extension of his own being and will, men see women's work not as real activity – self-chosen and consciously willed – but only as "natural" activity, as instinctual or emotional labors of love. Women are thus excluded from men's conceptions of culture and its conceptual schemes of "the social," "the historical," "the human." Finally, women's actual experience of their own labor is incomprehensible and inexpressible within the distorted abstractions of men's conceptual schemes. Women are alienated from their own experience, for men's conceptual schemes are also the ruling ones, which then define and categorize women's experience for women. (This is Hartsock's point about ideologies structuring social life for everyone.) For Smith, education for women, for which nineteenth-century feminists struggled, completed the "invasion of women's consciousness" by ruling-class male experts.[20]

These characteristics of women's activities are a resource that a distinctively feminist science can use. A "line of fault" develops for many women between our own experience of our activity and the categories available to us within which to express our experience: the categories of ruling and of science. The break is intensified for women inquirers. We are first of all women, who – even if single, childless, or with servants – maintain our own bodies and our places of local existence, and usually also the bodies and domestic places of children and men. But when entering the world of science, we are trained to describe and explain social experience within conceptual schemes that cannot recognize the character of this experience. Smith cites the example of time-budget studies, which regard housework as part leisure and part labor – a conceptualization based on men's experience of wage labor for others vs. self-directed activity. But for wives and mothers, housework is neither wage labor nor self-directed activity. An account of housework from "the standpoint of women" – our experience of our lives – rather than in the terms of masculine science would be a quite different account; the voice of the subject of inquiry and the voice of the inquirer would be culturally identifiable.[21] It would be an example of science *for* women rather than *about* women; it would seek to explain/interpret social relations rather than behavior (human "matter in motion"), and do so in a way that makes comprehensible to women the social relations within which their experience occurs.

Smith fuses here what have been incompatible tendencies toward interpretation, explanation, and critical theory in the philosophy of social science. None of these discourses locates "authoritative accounts" in those of the inquirer as an active agent in inquiry. Once Smith puts the authority of the inquirer on the same epistemological plane as the authority of the subjects of inquiry – the woman inquirer interpreting, explaining, critically examining women's condition is simultaneously explaining her own condition – then issues of absolutism vs. relativism can no longer be posed. Both absolutism and relativism assume separations between the inquirer and subject of inquiry that are not present when the two share a subjugated social location.[23]

I think Smith is arguing that this kind of science would be "objective," not because it would use the categories available from an "Archimedean," dispassionate, detached "third version" of the conflicting perspectives people have on social relations but because it would use the more complete and less distorting categories available from the standpoint of historically locatable subjugated experiences.[23] However, it is difficult to generalize from her explicit assumptions about intepreting/explaining women's world to a feminist science that takes as its project explaining the whole world. She often admonishes the reader that the experience of the subject of inquiry (the experience of the women whose lives the inquirer is explaining) is to be taken as the final authority. But many feminist inquirers take men's experience as well as women's to be inadequately interpreted, explained or criticized within the existing "corpus of knowledge": think of all the recent writing on men's war mentality; of object-relations theory's critical reinterpretation of the masculine experience of gendering; of Smith's own rethinking of men's experiences as sociologists. Yet she does not assign ruling-class men's experience the kind of authority she insists on for women's experience; through all four papers her argument shows why we should regard women's subjugated experience as starting and ending points for inquiry that are epistemologically preferable to men's experience. (Smith's argument here is similar to Hartsock's assertion of the epistemological preferability of the categories of women's activities, and to Flax's focus on feminism as the exposure of what men repress; all three return to Hegel's passage about the master and the slave to make their points.)

Interpreting Smith in this way leaves a few loose ends in her account, but it makes sense of the origins of the scientific authority she clearly intends to give to women as both subjects of inquiry and inquirers. For her, what feminism should distrust is not objectivity or epistemology's policing of thought per se but the particular distorted and ineffectual form of

631

objectivity and epistemology entrenched in Enlightenment science. Like Flax, Smith stresses that there will be many different feminist versions of "reality," for there are many different realities in which women live, but they should all be regarded as producing more complete, less distorting, and less perverse understandings than can a science in alliance with ruling-class masculine activity.

New Persons and the Hidden Hand of History

Finally, it is historical changes that make possible feminist theory and consequently a feminist science and epistemology, as I have argued elsewhere.[24] Here, too, we can learn from the Marxist analysis. Engels believed that "the great thinkers of the Eighteenth Century could, no more than their predecessors, go beyond the limits imposed upon them by their epoch."[25] He thought that only with the emergence in nineteenth-century industrializing societies of a "conflict between productive forces and modes of production" – a conflict that "exists, in fact, objectively, outside us, independently of the will and actions even of the men that have brought it on" – could the class structure of earlier societies be detected in its fullness for the first time. "Modern socialism is nothing but the reflex, in thought, of this conflict in fact; its ideal reflection in the minds, first, of the class directly suffering under it, the working class."[26]

Similarly, only now can we understand the feminisms of the eighteenth and nineteenth centuries as but "utopian" feminisms.[27] The men and women feminists of those cultures could recognize the misery of women's condition and the unnecessary character of that misery, but both their diagnoses of its causes and their prescriptions for women's emancipation show a failure to grasp the complex and not always obvious mechanisms by which masculine dominance is created and maintained. Liberal feminism, Marxist feminism and perhaps even the more doctrinaire strains of the radical and socialist feminisms of the mid-1970s do not have conceptual schemes rich or flexible enough to capture masculine domination's historical and cultural adaptability, nor its chameleonlike talents for growing within such other cultural hierarchies as classism and racism.[28] More complex and culture-sensitive (though not unproblematic) analyses had to await the emergence of historical changes in the relations between the genders. These changes have created a massive conflict between the culturally favored forms of producing persons (gendered, raced, classed persons) and the beliefs and actions of increasing numbers of women and some men who do not want to live out mutilated lives within the dangerous and oppressive politics these archaic forms of reproduction encourage.

If we cannot exactly describe this historical moment through an analogy to a "conflict between productive forces and modes of production" (and why should we have to?), we can nevertheless see clearly many aspects of the specific economic, political, and social shifts that have created this moment. There was the development and widespread distribution of cheap and efficient birth control, undertaken for capitalist and imperialist motives of controlling Third World and domestically colonized populations. There was the decline in the industrial sector combined with growth in the service sectors of the economy, which drew women into wage labor and deteriorated the centrality of industrialized "proletariat" labor. There were the emancipatory hopes created by the civil rights movement and the radicalism of the 1960s in both the United States and Europe. There was the rapid increase in divorce and in families headed by females – brought about in part by capitalism's seduction of men out of the family and into a "swinging singles" lifestyle, where they would consume more goods; in part by women's increased, though still severely limited, ability to survive economically outside of marriage; and no doubt in part by an availability of contraceptives that made what in olden days was called "philandering" less expensive. There was the increasing recognition of the feminization of poverty (probably also an actual increase in women's poverty), which combined with the increase in divorce and the drawing of women into wage labor to make women's life prospects look very different from those of their mothers and grandmothers: now women of every class could – and should – plan for lives after or instead of marriage. There was the escalation in international hostilities, revealing the clear overlap between masculine psychic needs for domination and nationalist domination rhetoric and politics. No doubt other significant social changes could be added to this list of preconditions for the emergence of feminism and its successor science and epistemology.

Thus, to paraphrase Engels, feminist theory is nothing but the reflex in thought of these conflicts in fact, their ideal reflection in the minds first of the class most directly suffering under them – women.[29] Feminist science and epistemology projects are not the products of observation, will power, and intellectual brilliance alone – the faculties that Enlightenment science and epistemology hold responsible for advances in knowledge. They are expressions of ways in which nature and social life can be understood by the new kinds of historical persons created by these social changes.[30] Persons whose activities are still characteristically "womanly," yet who also take on what have traditionally been masculine projects in public life, are one such important group of new persons. This "violation" of a traditional (at least, in our recent history) gendered division of labor both provides an epistemically advantaged standpoint for a successor science project and also resists the continuation of the distorting dualities of modernism. Why should we be loath to attribute a certain degree of, if not historical inevitability, at least historical possibility to the kinds of understandings arrived at in feminist science and epistemology?

633

I still think a historical account is an important component of the feminist standpoint epistemologies: it can identify the shifts in social life that make possible new modes of understanding. A standpoint epistemology without this recognition of the "role of history in science" (Kuhn's phrase) leaves mysterious the preconditions for its own production. However, I now think that the kind of account indicated above retains far too much of its Marxist legacy, and thereby also of Marxism's Enlightenment inheritance. It fails to grasp the historical changes that make possible the feminist postmodernist challenges to the Enlightenment vision as well as to Marxism.

Notes

1 The offensively dichotomized categories of labor vs. leisure, which appear in the parental Enlightenment/bourgeois and Marxist theories, are themselves the target of criticism in the standpoint epistemologies; it is a theory of human *activity* and social experience they are proposing.

2 Rose (1983; 1984). Subsequent page references to these papers appear in the text.

3 Sohn-Rethel (1978).

4 Hartsock (1983b; 1984) also raises this criticism about Sohn-Rethel.

5 Cf. the discussion of this dilemma in Stehelin (1979).

6 Merchant (1980); Rachel Carson, *Silent Spring* (New York: Fawcett, 1978, originally published in 1962); David Bohm, *Wholeness and the Implicate Order* (Boston: Routledge & Kegan Paul, 1980); Fritjof Capra, *The Tao of Physics* (New York: Random House, 1975).

7 Needham (1976).

8 See Bloch and Bloch (1980) on the deradicalization of the thought of Rousseau and other French thinkers that occurred once they recognized that the logic of their radical arguments was about to lead them directly to the conclusion that "the good" which should direct the social order was identical to what, in fact, women do.

9 Keller (1983).

10 Hartsock (1983b, 284). This paper also appears as ch. 10 in Hartsock (1984). Page numbers in the text refer to the 1983 version.

11 Flax (1983); Chodorow (1978).

12 Simone de Beauvoir (1953, 58), cited in Hartsock (1983, 301).

13 Hartsock (1974).

14 This critique of epistemology-centered philosophy and its policing of thought is central to the postmodernists. See, e.g. Rorty (1979) and Foucault (1980).

15 Rose would probably agree with this; many of her other writings would support such an argument. See, e.g. the papers in Rose and Rose (1976).

16 Flax (1983, 269). Subsequent page references appear in the text.

17 Although she stresses here women's less defensive "resolution" of infantile separation and individuation dilemmas, see Flax (1978) for a discussion of those unfortunate residues of the feminine infantile dilemma that create tensions within women and for feminist organizations.

18 Flax (1986, 37).

19 Smith (1981, 1). See the discussion of Smith's work in Westkott (1979).

20 Smith (1979, 143). We should note that Smith was writing on these topics earlier than the other theorists I have discussed, though her work did not become widely known in the United States until recently. The aspects of women's labor Smith identifies so clearly and so early also appear to be on the minds of the other theorists, as a perusal of their work will show.

21 Smith (1979, 154; 1981, 3).

22 Cf. Harding (1980).

23 Smith (1981, 6).

24 Harding (1983b). As I shall show, I now have postmodernist questions about my earlier defenses of the standpoint epistemologies.

25 Engels (1972, 606).

26 Engels (1972, 624).

27 O'Brien (1981) also makes this point.

28 For an analysis of these four main forms of feminism, see Jaggar (1983).

29 See Faderman (1981, 178–89) for a valuable analysis of the similar "causes" for the nineteenth-century women's movement in England and America.

30 Chapter 9 outlines the precedents for this kind of analysis in accounts of the breakdown of the medieval division of labor, which permitted the emergence of the new class of craftspeople who created experimental observation in the fifteenth century. See Zilsel (1942) and Van den Daele (1977).

References

Bloch, Maurice, and Jean Bloch. 1980. "Women and the Dialectics of Nature in Eighteenth Century French Thought." In *Nature, Culture and Gender*, ed. C. MacCormack and M. Strathern. Cambridge: Cambridge University Press.

Chodorow, Nancy. 1978. *The Reproduction of Mothering*. Berkeley: University of California Press.

de Beauvoir, Simone. 1953. *The Second Sex*, trans. H. M. Parshley. New York: Knopf.

Engels, F. 1972. "Socialism: Utopian and Scientific." In *The Marx and Engels Reader*, ed. R. Tucker. New York: Norton.

Faderman, Lillian. 1981. *Surpassing the Love of Men: Romantic Friendship and Love between Women from the Renaissance to the Present*. New York: Morrow.

Flax, Jane. 1978. "The Conflict between Nurturance and Autonomy in Mother–Daughter Relationships and within Feminism." *Feminist Studies*, 4 (no. 2).

——. 1983. "Political Philosophy and the Patriarchal Unconscious: A Psychoanalytic Perspective on Epistemology and Metaphysics." In *Discovering Reality:*

635

Feminist Perspectives on Epistemology, Metaphysics, Methodology and Philosophy of Science, ed. S. Harding and M. Hintikka. Dordrecht: Reidel.

——. 1986. "Gender as a Social Problem: In and For Feminist Theory." *American Studies/Amerika Studien,* journal of the German Association for American Studies.

Foucault, Michel. 1980. *A History of Sexuality.* Vol. 1: *An Introduction.* New York: Random House.

Harding, Sandra. 1980. "The Norms of Social Inquiry and Masculine Experience." In *PSA, 1980,* vol. 2, ed. P. D. Asquith and R. N. Giere, East Lansing, Mich.: Philosophy of Science Association.

——. 1983b. "Why Has the Sex-Gender System Become Visible Only Now?" In *Discovering Reality: Feminist Perspectives on Epistemology, Metaphysics, Methodology and Philosophy of Science,* ed. S. Harding and M. Hintikka. Dordrecht: Reidel.

Hartsock, Nancy. 1974. "Political Change: Two Perspectives on Power." *Quest: A Feminist Quarterly,* 1 (no. 1). Reprinted in *Building Feminist Theory: Essays from Quest,* ed. Charlotte Bunch. New York: Longman, 1981.

——. 1983b. "The Feminist Standpoint: Developing the Ground for a Specifically Feminist Historical Materialism." In *Discovering Reality: Feminist Perspectives on Epistemology, Metaphysics, Methodology and Philosophy of Science,* ed. S. Harding and M. Hintikka. Dordrecht: Reidel.

——. 1984. *Money, Sex and Power.* Boston: Northeastern University Press.

Jaggar, Alison. 1983. *Feminist Politics and Human Nature.* Totowa, NJ: Rowman & Allenheld.

Keller, Evelyn Fox. 1983. *A Feeling for the Organism.* San Francisco: Freeman.

Merchant, Carolyn. 1980. *The Death of Nature: Women, Ecology and the Scientific Revolution.* New York: Harper & Row.

Needham, Joseph. 1976. "History and Human Values: A Chinese Perspective for World Science and Technology." In *Ideology of/in the Natural Sciences,* ed. H. Rose and S. Rose. Cambridge, Mass.: Schenkman.

O'Brien, Mary. 1981. *The Politics of Reproduction.* New York: Routledge & Kegan Paul.

Rorty, Richard. 1979. *Philosophy and the Mirror of Nature.* Princeton, NJ: Princeton University Press.

Rose, Hilary. 1983. "Hand, Brain and Heart: A Feminist Epistemology for the Natural Sciences." *Signs: Journal of Women in Culture and Society,* 9 (no. 1).

——. 1984. "Is a Feminist Science Possible?" Paper presented to MIT Women's Studies Program, April 1984.

Rose, Hilary, and Steven Rose (eds). 1976. *Ideology of / in the Natural Sciences.* Cambridge, Mass.: Schenkman.

Smith, Dorothy. 1979. "A Sociology For Women." In *The Prism of Sex: Essays in the Sociology of Knowledge,* ed. J. Sherman and E. T. Beck. Madison: University of Wisconsin Press.

——. 1981. "The Experienced World as Problematic: A Feminist Method." Sorokin Lecture no. 12. Saskatoon: University of Saskatchewan.

Sohn-Rthel, Alfred. 1978. *Intellectual and Manual Labor*. London: Macmillan.

Stehelin, Liliane. 1976. "Sciences, Women and Ideology." In *Ideology of/in the Natural Sciences*, ed. Hilary Rose and Steven Rose. Cambridge, Mass.: Schenkman.

Van den Daele, W. 1977. "The Social Construction of Science." In *The Social Production of Scientific Knowledge*, ed. E. Mendelsohn, P. Weingart, R. Whitley. Dordrecht: Reidel.

Westkott, Marcia. 1979. "Feminist Criticism of the Social Sciences." *Harvard Educational Review*, 49.

Zilsel, Edgar, 1942. "The Sociological Roots of Science." *American Journal of Sociology*, 47.

chapter thirty-nine

"The Cartesian Masculinization of Thought"

Susan Bordo

Feminist philosopher of culture, Susan Bordo (1947–) combines a number of themes common among postmodernists, but is no postmodernist herself. She employs psychodynamic theory to connect the Cartesian and scientific impulses of modernity to the repression of external nature, inner nature, and women. Cartesian modernity is inherently bound to a "flight from the feminine" motivated by a fear of the uncertainty, revulsion, and mortality of the mundane bodily existence with which women have been identified by the same tradition. She thereby gives a feminist cast to the critique of modern foundationalism that had earlier been led by John Dewey, in his *The Quest for Certainty* (1929), and more recently by Richard Rorty, in his *Philosophy and the Mirror of Nature* (1979).

> [I]f a kind of Cartesian ideal were ever completely fulfilled, i.e., if the whole of nature were only what can be explained in terms of mathematical relationships – then we would look at the world with that fearful sense of alienation, with that utter loss of reality with which a future schizophrenic child looks at his mother. A machine cannot give birth.
>
> Karl Stern, *The Flight From Woman*

Philosophical Reconstruction, Anxiety and Flight

If the transition from Middle Ages to early modernity can be looked on as a kind of protracted birth, from which the human being emerges as a decisively separate entity, no longer continuous with the universe with which it had once shared a soul, so the possibility of objectivity,

---

Susan Bordo, "The Cartesian Masculinization of Thought," chapter 6 of *The Flight to Objectivity: Essays on Cartesianism and Culture* (Albany: State University of New York Press, 1987), pp. 97–118.

strikingly, is conceived by Descartes as a kind of *rebirth*, on one's own terms, this time.

We are all familiar with the dominant Cartesian themes of starting anew, alone, without influence from the past or other people, with the guidance of reason alone. The product of our original and actual birth, childhood, being ruled by the body, is the source of most obscurity and confusion in our thinking. As Descartes says in the *Discourse*,[i] "since we have all been children before being men . . . it is almost impossible that our judgements should be so excellent or solid as they would have been had we had complete use of our reason since our birth, and had we been guided by its means alone" (HR, I, 88). The specific origins of obscurity in our thinking are, as we have seen, the appetites, the influence of our teachers, and the "prejudices" of childhood. Those "prejudices" all have a common form: the inability, due to our infantile "immersion" in the body, to distinguish properly between subject and object. The purification of the relation between knower and known requires the repudiation of childhood, a theme which was not uncommon at the time. The ideology of childhood as a time of "innocence," and the child as an epistemological *tabula rasa*,[ii] had yet to become popular (Aries, 100–33). Rather, childhood was commonly associated, as Descartes associated it, with sensuality, animality, and the mystifications of the body.[1]

For Descartes, happily, the state of childhood *can* be revoked, through a deliberate and methodical reversal of all the prejudices acquired within it, and a beginning anew with reason as one's only parent. This is precisely what the *Meditations* attempts to do. The mind is emptied of all that it has been taught. The body of infancy, preoccupied with appetite and sense-experience, is transcended. The clear and distinct ideas are released from their obscuring material prison. The end-result is a philosophical reconstruction which secures all the boundaries which, in childhood (and at the start of the *Meditations*) are so fragile: between the "inner" and the "outer," between the subjective and the objective, between self and world.

It is crucial to recall here that what for Descartes is conceived as epistemological threat – "subjectivity," or the blurring of boundaries between self and world – was not conceived as such by the medievals. Rather, the medieval sense of relatedness to the world, as we know from its art, literature, and philosophy, had not depended on "objectivity" but on continuity between the human and physical realms, on the interpenetrations, through meanings, of self and world. But *locatedness* in space and

---

[i] *Discourse on Method.* "HR" refers to the Haldane and Ross edition of Descartes' work. For this and similar references see the author's References after the endnotes.
[ii] Blank slate.

time, by Descartes's era, had inexorably come to the forefront of human experience, and the continuities and interpenetrations which had once been a source of intellectual and spiritual satisfaction now presented themselves as "distortions" caused by personal attachment and "perspective." Objectivity, not meaning, became the issue, and "so long as the human being is embedded in nature and united with it, objectivity is impossible" (Stern, 76). By the time of Kant, this "condition" for knowledge – the separation of knower and known – is philosophically apprehended. Human intelligence, Kant discovers, is *founded* on the distinction between subject and object. The condition of *having* an objective world, on the Kantian view, is to grasp phenomena as unified and connected by the embrace of a discrete consciousness, capable of representing to itself its own distinctness from the world it grasps. But what Kant here "discovers" (and what came to be regarded as a given in modern science and philosophy) was a while in the making. For Descartes, the separation of subject and object is a *project*, not a "foundation" to be discovered.

The Cartesian reconstruction has two interrelated dimensions. On the one hand, a new model of knowledge is conceived, in which the purity of the intellect is guaranteed through its ability to transcend the body. On the other hand, the ontological blueprint of the order of things is refashioned. The spiritual and the corporeal are now two distinct substances which share no qualities (other than being created), permit of interaction but no merging, and are each defined precisely in opposition to the other. *Res cogitans* is "a thinking and unextended thing"; *res extensa* is "an extended and unthinking thing" (I, 190). This mutual exclusion of *res cogitans* and *res extensa* made possible the conceptualization of complete intellectual independence from the body, *res extensa* of the human being and chief impediment to human objectivity. The dictotomy between the spiritual and the corporeal also established the utter diremption of the natural world from the realm of the human.[2] It now became inappropriate to speak, as the medievals had done, in anthropocentric terms about nature, which for Descartes is pure *res extensa*, "totally devoid of mind and thought." More important, it means that the values and significances of things in relation to the human realm must be understood as purely a reflection of how *we* feel about them, having nothing to do with their "objective" qualities.

"Thus," says Whitehead, in sardonic criticism of the "characteristic scientific philosophy" of the seventeenth century, "the poets are entirely mistaken. They should address their lyrics to themselves, and should turn them into odes of self-congratulation . . . Nature is a dull affair, soundless, scentless, colourless; merely the hurrying of material, endlessly, meaninglessly" (1925, p. 54). For the model of knowledge which results, neither bodily response (the sensual or the emotional) nor associational thinking, exploring the various personal or spiritual meanings the object has for us, can tell us anything about the object "itself." *It* can only be grasped, as Gillispie puts it, "by measurement rather than sympathy" (p. 42). Thus, the specter of infantile subjectivism is overcome by the possibility of a cool, impersonal, distanced cognitive relation to the world. At the same time, the nightmare landscape of the infinite universe has become the well-lighted laboratory of modern science and philosophy.

The conversion of nightmare into positive vision is characteristic of Descartes. Within the narrative framework of the *Meditations*, "dreamers, demons, and madmen" are exorcised, the crazily fragmented "enchanted glass" of the mind (as Bacon called it) is transformed into the "mirror of nature," the true reflector of things. But such transformations, as Descartes's determinedly upbeat interpretation of his own famous nightmare suggests, may be grounded in *defense* – in the suppression of anxiety, uncertainty, and dread. Certainly, anxiety infuses the *Meditations*, as I have argued through my reading of the text. I have tried, too, to show that Cartesian anxiety was a *cultural* anxiety, arising from discoveries, inventions, and events which were major and disorienting.

That disorientation, I have suggested, is given psychocultural coherence via a "story" of *parturition* from the organic universe of the Middle Ages and Renaissance, out of which emerged the modern categories of "self," "locatedness," and "innerness." This parturition was initially experienced as *loss*, that is, as estrangement, and the opening up of a chasm between self and nature. Epistemologically, that estrangement expresses itself in a renewal of scepticism, and in an unprecedented anxiety over the possibility of reaching the world as "it" is. Spiritually, it expresses itself in anxiety over the *enclosedness* of the individual self, the isolating uniqueness of each individual allotment in time and space, and the arbitrary, incomprehensible nature of that allotment by an alien, indifferent universe. We may speak here, meaningfully, of a *cultural* "separation anxiety."

The particular genius of Descartes was to have philosophically transformed what was first experienced as estrangement and loss – the sundering of the organic ties between the person and world – into a requirement for the growth of human knowledge and progress. And at this point, we are in a better position to flesh out the mechanism of *defense* involved here. Cartesian objectivism and mechanism, I will propose, should be understood as a *reaction-formation* – a denial of the "separation anxiety" described above, facilitated by an aggressive intellectual *flight* from the female cosmos and "feminine" orientation towards the world. That orientation (described so far in this study in the gender-neutral terminology of "participating consciousness") had still played a formidable role in medieval and Renaissance thought and culture. In the seventeenth century, it was decisively purged from the dominant intellectual culture, through the Cartesian "rebirthing" and restructuring of knowledge and world as *masculine*.

I will begin by exploring the mechanist flight from the female cosmos (which Carolyn Merchant has called "The Death of Nature"). Then, I will focus on the specifically epistemological expression of the seventeenth-century flight from the feminine: "the Cartesian masculinization of thought." Both the mechanist reconstruction of the world and the objectivist reconstruction of knowledge will then be examined as embodying a common psychological structure: a fantasy of "re-birthing" self and world, brought into play by the disintegration of the organic, female cosmos of the Middle Ages and Renaissance. This philosophical fantasy will be situated within the general context of seventeenth-century attitudes toward female generativity, as chronicled by a number of feminist authors. Finally, the relevance of these ideas to current discussions about gender and rationality, and to current reassessments of Cartesianism, will be considered in a concluding section of this chapter.

The Death of Nature and the Masculinization of Thought

Discussion of "masculinity" and "femininity" is a new motif in this study. Yet gender has played an implicit role all along. For the medieval cosmos whose destruction gave birth to the modern sensibility was a *mother*-cosmos, and the soul which Descartes drained from the natural world was a *female* soul. Carolyn Merchant, whose ground-breaking interdisciplinary study, *The Death of Nature*, chronicles the changing imagery of nature in this period, describes the "organic cosmology" which mechanism overthrew:

> Minerals and metals ripened in the uterus of the Earth Mother, mines were compared to her vagina, and metallurgy was the human hastening of the living metal in the artificial womb of the furnace ... Miners offered propitiation to the deities of the soil, performed ceremonial sacrifices ... sexual abstinence, fasting, before violating the sacredness of the living earth by sinking a mine. (p. 4)

The notion of the natural world as *mothered* has sources, for the Western tradition, in both Plato and Aristotle. In Plato's *Timeaus*, the formless "receptacle" or "nurse" provides the substratum of all determinate materiality. (It is also referred to as "space" – *chora* – in the dialogue.) The "receptacle" is likened to a mother because of its receptivity to impression; the father is the "source or spring" – the eternal forms which "enter" and "stir and inform her." The child is the determinate nature which is formed through their union: the *body* of nature (51).

In this account, the earth is not a mother, but is itself a child of the union of "nurse" and forms. The notion that the earth *itself* mothers things, for example, metals and minerals, required the inspiration of the Aristotelian theory of animal reproduction. In that theory, the female provides not only matter as "substratum," but matter as sensible "stuff": the *catamenia*, or menstrual material, which is "worked upon" and shaped by the "effective and active" element, the semen of the male (729a–b). In the fifteenth and sixteenth centuries, this account of animal generation was "projected" onto the cosmos. A "stock description" of biological generation in nature was the marriage of heaven and earth, and the impregnation of the (female) earth by the dew and rain created by the movements of the (masculine) celestial heavens (Merchant, 16).

The female element here is *natura naturata*,[iii] of course – passive rather than creative nature. But passivity here connotes *receptivity* rather than inertness; only a living, breathing earth can be impregnated. And indeed, for Plato most explicitly, the world *has* a soul – a female soul – which permeates the corporeal body of the universe. In the seventeenth century, as Merchant argues, that female world-soul died – or more precisely, was *murdered* – by the mechanist re-visioning of nature.

This re-visioning of the universe as a *machine* – most often, a clockwork – was not the work of philosophers alone. Astronomy and anatomy had already changed the dominant picture of the movements of the heavens and the processes of the body by the time the *Meditations* were written. But it was philosophy, and Descartes in particular, that provided the cosmology that integrated these discoveries into a consistent and unified view of nature. By Descartes's brilliant stroke, nature became *defined* by its lack of affiliation with divinity, with spirit. All that which is God-like or spiritual – freedom, will, and sentience – belong entirely and exclusively to *res cogitans*. All else – the earth, the heavens, animals, the human body – is merely mechanically interacting matter.

The seventeenth century saw the death, too, of another sort of "feminine principle" – that cluster of epistemological values, often associated with feminine consciousness,[3] and which apparently played a large and re-spected role in hermetic philosophy and, it might be argued, in the prescientific orientation toward the world in general. If the key terms in the Cartesian hierarchy of epistemological values are clarity and distinctness – qualities which mark each object off from the other and from the knower – the key term in this alternative scheme of values might be designated (following Gillispie's contrast here) as *sympathy*. "Sympathetic" under-standing of the object is that which understands it through "union" with

---

[iii] Medieval philosophers distinguished nature as active, nature natur*ing* (*natura naturans*), from nature as acted upon, nature natur*ed* (*natura naturata*).

it (Stern, 42–3), or, as James Hillman describes it, though "merging with" or "marrying" it. To merge with or marry that which is to be known means, for Hillman, "letting interior movement replace clarity, interior closeness replace objectivity" (*The Myth of Analysis*, 293). It means granting personal or intuitive response a positive epistemological value, even (perhaps especially) when such response is contradictory or fragmented. "Sympathetic" thinking, Marcuse suggests, is the only mode which truly respects the object, that is, which allows the variety of its meanings to unfold without coercion or too-focused interrogation (p. 74).

Barfield's and Berman's discussions of medieval "participating consciousness," Bergson's notion of "intellectual sympathy," Jasper's "causality from within," all contain elements of what I have here called "sympathetic thinking." The deepest understanding of that which is to be known comes, each argues, not from analysis of parts but from "placing oneself within" the full being of an object, as Bergson puts it (at which point it ceases to be an "object" in the usual sense), and allowing *it* to speak.

An emphasis on the knower's *passivity* is shared by this ideal of knowledge and the Cartesian ideal. But whereas passivity for Descartes (and for Bacon) meant yielding to the authority of the object's "own" nature, for sympathetic thinking, the objective and subjective *merge*, participate in the creation of meaning. The most inspired and articulate contemporary advocates of what I am here calling "sympathetic thinking" are Carol Gilligan (1982) and Evelyn Fox Keller (1985), each of whom speaks forcefully to the need for integration of such thinking into our dominant conceptions of rationality. This does not mean a rejection, but a *re-visioning* of "objectivity." Keller's conception of "dynamic objectivity" is especially relevant here:

> Dynamic objectivity is . . . a pursuit of knowledge that makes use of subjective experience . . . in the interests of a more effective objectivity. Premised on continuity, it recognizes difference between self and other as an opportunity for a deeper and more articulated kinship. The struggle to disentangle self from other is itself a source of insight – potentially into the nature of both self and other. It is a principle means for divining what Poincaré calls "hidden harmonies and relations." To this end, the scientist employs a form of attention to the natural world that is like one's ideal attention to the human world: it is a form of love. (p. 117)

In contrast to the conception of "dynamic objectivity," Descartes' program for the purification of the understanding, as we have seen, has as its ideal the rendering *impossible* of any such continuity between subject and object. The scientific mind must be cleansed of all its "sympathies" toward the objects it tries to understand. It must cultivate absolute *detachment*.

Recognizing the centrality of such ideals to modern science has led writers like Sandra Harding to characterize modern science in terms of a "super-masculinization of rational thought."[4] Similarly, Karl Stern has said that "[what] we encounter in Cartesian rationalism is the pure masculinization of thought" (p. 104). The notion that modern science crystallizes masculinist modes of thinking is a theme, too, in the work of James Hillman; "The specific consciousness we call scientific, Western and modern," says Hillman, "is the long sharpened tool of the masculine mind that has discarded parts of its own substance, calling it 'Eve,' 'female,' and 'inferior' " (*The Myth of Analysis*, 250). Evelyn Fox Keller's *Reflections On Gender and Science* systematically explores various perspectives (including developmental perspectives) on the connection between masculinity and modern science.

It must be stressed that descriptions of modern science as a "masculinization of thought" refer to what these authors view as characteristic cognitive and theoretical biases of male-dominated science, *not* the fact of that male dominance itself, or science's attitudes toward women. Science has, of course, a long history of discrimination against women, insisting that women cannot measure up to the rigor, persistence, or clarity that science requires. It also has its share of explicitly misogynist doctrine, as do its ancient forefathers, Aristotle and Galen. But the most interesting contemporary discussions of the "masculinist" nature of modern science describe a different, though related, aspect of its "masculinism": a characteristic cognitive style, an epistemological stance which is required of men *and* women working in the sciences today. In the words of Evelyn Fox Keller:

> The scientific mind is set apart from what is to be known, i.e., from nature, and its autonomy is guaranteed . . . by setting apart its modes of knowing from those in which the dichotomy is threatened. In this process, the characterization of both the scientific mind and its modes of access to knowledge as masculine is indeed significant. Masculine here connotes, as it so often does, autonomy, separation, and distance . . . a radical rejection of any commingling of subject and object. (p. 79)

It is in this sense that the dominant scientific and philosophic culture of the seventeenth century indeed inaugurated "a truly masculine birth of time," as Francis Bacon had proclaimed it (Farrington). Similarly and strikingly, Henry Oldenberg, secretary of the Royal Society, asserted in 1664 that the business of that society was to raise "a masculine philosophy" (Easlea, 152). In her penetrating and imaginative study of sexual metaphors in the history of epistemology, Keller pays very serious attention to such historical associations of gender and "cognitive style," which we might have thought to belong to a peculiarly contemporary mentality, but which in fact crop up frequently in Royal Society debates. As Keller reads them, the controversies between Bacon and Paracelsus become an explicit contest between masculine and feminine principles: head versus heart, domination over versus merging with the object, purified versus erotic orientation toward knowledge, and so forth (43–65). Bacon's own deepest attitudes, Keller suggests, were more complicated and ambivalent than his oft-reproduced and notorious images of male seduction, penetration, and rape of nature may indicate. But what emerges with clarity, despite any subtleties in the attitudes of individual thinkers, is that the notion of science as "masculine" is hardly a twentieth-century invention or feminist fantasy. The founders of modern science consciously and explicitly proclaimed the "masculinity" of science as inaugurating a new era. And they associated that masculinity with a cleaner, purer, more objective and more disciplined epistemological relation to the world.

The emergence of such associations, in an era which lacked our heightened modern consciousness of gender as an issue, is remarkable. They suggest that the contemporary notion that thought *became* "super-masculinized" at a certain point in time is not merely, as some might argue, a new, fashionable way of labelling and condemning the seventeenth-century objectivist turn – a turn, many would say, which has already been adequately described, criticized, and laid to rest by Whitehead, Heidegger, and, more recently, Richard Rorty. Bacon's metaphor, rather, urges us in the direction of confronting a profound "flight from the feminine" at the heart of both Cartesian rationalism and Baconian empiricism. To appreciate the dimensions of that "flight," however, necessitates a return to the insights of developmental psychology.

The Cartesian "Rebirth" and the "Father of Oneself" Fantasy

> *Descartes envisages for himself a kind of rebirth. Intellectual salvation comes only to the twice-born.*
>
> Frankfurt, *Demons, Dreamers, and Madmen*

Psychoanalytic theory urges us to examine that which we actively repudiate for the shadow of a loss we mourn. Freud, in *Beyond the Pleasure Principle*, tells the story of an eighteen-month-old boy – an obedient, orderly little boy, as Freud describes him – who, although "greatly attached to his mother," never cried when she left him for a few hours.

This good little boy, however, had an occasional disturbing habit of taking any small objects he could get hold of and throwing them away from him into a corner, under the bed, and so on, so that hunting for his toys and picking them up was often quite a business. As he did this he gave vent to a loud, long-drawn-out 'o-o-o-o', accompanied by an expression of interest and satisfaction. His mother and the writer of the present account were agreed in thinking that this was not a mere interjection but represented the German word *'fort'* ('gone'). I eventually realized that it was a game and that the only use he made of any of his toys was to play 'gone' with them . . . [T]he complete game [was] disappearance and return . . . The interpretation . . . became obvious. It was related to the child's great cultural achievement – the instinctual renunciation (that is, the renunciation of instinctual satisfaction) which he had made in allowing his mother to go away without protesting. He compensated himself for this, as it were, by himself staging the disappearance and return of the objects within his reach . . . Throwing away the object so that it was 'gone' might satisfy an impulse of the child's, which was suppressed in his actual life, to revenge himself on his mother for going away from him. In that case it would have a defiant meaning: 'All right, then, go away! I don't need you. I'm sending you away myself'. (33–5)

The "fort-da"[iv] game and Freud's interpretation of it places the Cartesian facility for transforming anxiety into confidence, loss into mastery, in a striking new perspective. Within the context of the cultural separation anxiety described in this study, Descartes's masculine "rebirthing" of the world and self as decisively separate appears, not merely as the articulation of a positive new epistemological ideal, but as a reaction-formation to the loss of "being-one-with-the-world" brought about by the disintegration of the organic, centered, female cosmos of the Middle Ages and Renaissance. The Cartesian reconstruction of the world is a "fort-da" game – a defiant gesture of independence from the female cosmos, a gesture which is at the same time compensation for a profound loss.

Let us explore the interpretation proposed above in more detail, turning again to developmental theory for insight. The project of growing up is to one degree or another (depending on culture and child-raising practice) a project of *separation*, of learning to deal with the fact that mother and child are no longer one and that gratification is not always available. Social and personal strategies for the child's accomplishing this are varied; every culture no doubt has its own modes of facilitating the separation of mother and child, to the degree that such separation is required by the culture. Psychoanalytic theory has focused on *internal* mechanisms, describing the different responses – longing, mourning, denial – that the child may have to separation. The mechanism of *denial* is of particular interest for my

---

[iv] *Da* means "there," meaning the object is present, as in "Da!" ("There it is!").

purposes. Although the dream of total union can persist throughout life, another, contradictory project may be conceived, pychoanalytic thinkers have suggested, centered around the denial of any longing for the lost maternal union. Instead, the child seeks mastery over the frustrations of separation and lack of gratification through an assertion of self against the mother and all that she represents and a rejection of all dependency on her. In this way, the pain of separateness is assuaged, paradoxically, by an even more definitive separation – but one that is *chosen* this time and aggressively pursued. It is therefore experienced as autonomy rather than helplessness in the fact of the discontinuity between self and mother.

One mode of such self-assertion is through the fantasy of becoming the parent of oneself, of "rebirthing" the self, playing the role of active parental figure rather than passive, helpless child. Such a notion of "rebirthing" or "reparenting" the self figures in both Freudian and object-relations frameworks. Building on Winnicott's[v] concept of the "transitional object" (a blanket, toy, or stuffed animal which eases the child's accommodation to and ultimate mastery over the process of separation from the mother), Ross argues that such objects function, symbolically, as the child himself. In cuddling and scolding the object, the child is actually playing at self-parenting, at being his own baby. Such self-parenting allows the child to feel less precariously at the mercy of the mother, more in control of his or her own destiny (1977).

Working from a more Freudian framework, Norman O. Brown reinterprets the Oedipal desire to "sexually" possess the mother as a fantasy of "beoming the father of oneself" (rather than the helpless child of the mother) (p. 127). Sexual activity here (or rather, the fantasy of it) becomes a means of denying the actual passivity of having been born from that original state of union into "a body of limited powers, and at a time and place [one] never chose" (deBeauvoir, 146), at the mercy of the now-alien will of the mother. The mother is still "other," but she is an other whose power has been harnessed by the will of the child. The pain of separateness is thus compensated for by the peculiar advantages of separateness: the possibility of mastery and control over that person on whom one is dependent. Melanie Klein (writing in 1928, much earlier than Brown) emphasizes the aggressive, destructive, envious impulses which may be directed against parts of the mother's body – particularly against the breasts and reproductive organs – in the child's effort to achieve such control (pp. 98–111).

Certainly, the famous Baconian imagery of sexual assault and aggressive overpowering of a willful and unruly female nature (she must "be taken by the forelock" and "neither ought a man to make scruple of entering and

---

[v] D. W. Winnicott (1896–1971), British child psychiatrist.

penetrating these holes and corners," etc.[5] makes new psychocultural sense in the context of these ideas. More subtly, the Cartesian project of starting anew through the revocation of one's actual childhood (during which one was "immersed" in body and nature) and the (re)creation of a world in which absolute separateness (both epistemological and ontological) from body and nature are keys to control rather than sources of anxiety can now be seen as a "father of oneself" fantasy on a highly symbolic, but profound, plane.[6] The sundering of the organic ties between person and nature – originally experienced, as we have seen, as epistemological estrangement, as the opening up of a chasm between self and world – is reenacted, *this* time with the human being as the engineer and architect of the separation. Through the Cartesian "rebirth," a new "masculine" theory of knowledge is delivered, in which detachment from nature acquires a positive epistemological value. And a new *world* is reconstructed, one in which all generativity and creativity fall to God, the spiritual father, rather than to the female "flesh" of the world. With the same masterful stroke – the mutual opposition of the spiritual and the corporeal – the formerly female earth becomes inert matter and the objectivity of science is insured.

"She" becomes "it" – and "it" can be understood and controlled. Not through "sympathy," of course, but by virtue of the very *object*-ivity of the "it." At the same time, the "wound" of separateness is healed through the *denial* that there ever "was" any union: For the mechanists, unlike Donne,[vi] the female world-soul did not die; rather the world *is* dead. There is nothing to mourn, nothing to lament. Indeed, the "new" epistemological anxiety is evoked, not over loss, but by the "memory" or suggestion of *union*; "sympathetic," associational, or bodily response obscures objectivity, feeling for nature muddies the clear lake of the mind. The "otherness" of nature is now what allows it to be known.

The Seventeenth-century Flight from the Feminine

The philosophical "murder" of the living female earth, explored in the preceding section as a reaction-formation to the dissolution of the medieval self-world unity, must be placed in the context of other issues in the gender politics of the sixteenth and seventeenth centuries. Thanks to the historical research of such writers as Carolyn Merchant, Brian Easlea, Barbara Ehrenreich, Dierdre English, and Adrienne Rich, we have been enabled to recognize the years between 1550 and 1650 as a particularly gynophobic

[vi] English poet, John Donne (1572–1631), whose "Anatomy of the world" connects his wife's death to the world's demise.

649

century. What has been especially brought to light is what now appears as a virtual obsession with the untamed natural power of female generativity, and a dedication to bringing it under forceful cultural control.

Nightmare fantasies of female power over reproduction and birth run throughout the era. Kramer and Sprenger's *Malleus Maleficarum*, the official witch-hunter's handbook, accuses "witches" of every imaginable natural and supernatural crime involving conception and birth. The failure of crops and miscarriages were attributed to witches, and they are accused both of "inclining men to passion" and of causing impotence, of obstructing fertility in both men and women, of removing the penises of men, or procuring abortion, and of offering newborns to the devil (Lederer, 209).

Such fantasies were not limited to a fanatic fringe. Among the scientific set, we find the image of the witch, the willful, wanton virago, projected onto generative nature, whose scientific exploration, as Merchant points out, is metaphorically likened to a witch trial (169–170). The "secrets" of nature are imagined as deliberately and slyly "concealed" from the scientist (Easlea, 214). Matter, which in the *Timeaus*[vii] is passively receptive to the ordering and shaping masculine forms, now becomes, for Bacon, a "common harlot" with "an appetite and inclination to dissolve the world and fall back into the old chaos" and who must therefore be "restrained and kept in order" (Merchant, 171). The womb of nature, too (and this is striking, in connection with Melanie Klein), is no longer the beneficent mother but rather the *hoarder* of precious metals and minerals, which must be "searched" and "spied out" (Merchant, 169–70).

There were the witchhunts themselves, which, aided more politely by the gradual male takeover of birthing, and healing in general, virtually purged the healing arts of female midwives.[7] The resulting changes in obstetrics, which rendered women passive and dependent in the process of birth, came to identify birth, as Bacon identified nature itself, with the potentiality of disorder and the need for forceful male control.[8] So, too, in the seventeenth century, female sexuality was seen as voracious and insatiable, and a principal motivation behind witchcraft, which offered the capacious "mouth of the womb" the opportunity to copulate with the devil.[9]

The ideology of the voracious, insatiable female may not be unique to the sixteenth and seventeenth centuries. But it is not historically ubiquitous. By the second half of the nineteenth century, medical science had declared women to be naturally passive and "not much troubled by sexual feeling of any kind" (Vicinus, 82). Peter Gay suggests that this medical fantasy was a reaction-formation to that era's "pervasive sense of manhood in danger" (p. 93), brought about by its own particular social disruptions in gender relations and the family. I would suggest, along similar lines, that key

---

[vii] One of Plato's dialogues.

changes in the seventeenth-century scientific theory of reproduction functioned in much the same way, although in reaction to different threats and disruptions.

Generativity, not sexuality, is the focus of the seventeenth century's fantasies of female passivity. Mechanist reproductive theory ("happily," as Brian Easlea sarcastically puts it) made it "no longer necessary to refer to any women at all" in its "scientific" descriptions of conception and gestation (Easlea, 49). Denied even her limited, traditional Aristotelian role of supplying the (living) menstrual material (which, shaped by the individuating male "form" results in the fetus), the woman becomes instead the mere *container* for the temporary housing and incubation of already-formed human beings, originally placed in Adam's semen by God, and parcelled out, over the ages, to all his male descendants.[10] The specifics of mechanistic reproductive theory are a microcosmic recapitulation of the mechanistic vision itself, where God the father is the sole creative, formative principle in the cosmos. We know, from what now must be seen as almost paradigmatic examples of the power of belief over perception, that tiny horses and men were actually "seen" by mechanist scientists examining sperm under their microscopes.

All this is only to scratch the surface of a literature that has become quite extensive over the last decade. Even this brief survey, however, yields striking parallels. The mechanization of nature, we see, theoretically "quieted" the "common harlot" of matter (and sanctioned nature's exploitation) as effectively as Baconian experimental philosophy did so practically. Mechanistic reproductive theory successfully eliminated any active, generative role for the female in the processes of conception and gestation. And *actual* control over reproduction and birth was wrested away from women by the witch-hunters and the male medical establishment. Something, it seems, had come to be felt as all too powerful and in need of taming.

What can account for this upsurge of fear of female generativity? No doubt many factors – economic, political, and institutional – are crucial. But I would suggest that the themes of "parturition" and "separation anxiety" discussed in this study can provide an illuminative psychocultural framework within which to situate seventeenth-century gynophobia.

The culture in question, in the wake of the dissolution of the medieval intellectual and imaginative system, had lost a world in which the human being could feel nourished by the sense of oneness, of continuity between all things. The new, infinite universe was an indifferent home, an "alien will," and the sense of separateness from her was acute. Not only was she "other," but she seemed a perverse and uncontrollable other. During the years 1550–1650, a century that had brought the worst food crisis in history, violent wars, plague, and devastating poverty, the Baconian

651

imagery of nature as an unruly and malevolent virago was no paranoid fantasy. More important, the cruelty of the world could no longer be made palatable by the old medieval sense of organic justice – that is, justice on the level of the workings of a whole with which one's identity merged and which, while perhaps not fully comprehensible, was nonetheless to be trusted. Now there is no organic unity, but only "I" and "She" – an unpredictable and seemingly arbitrary "She," whose actions cannot be understood in any of the old "sympathetic" ways.

"She" is *Other*. And "otherness" itself becomes dreadful – particularly the otherness of the female, whose powers have always been mysterious to men, and evocative of the mystery of existence itself. Like the infinite universe, which threatens to swallow the individual "like a speck," the female, with her strange rhythms, long acknowledged to have their chief affinities with the rhythms of the natural (now alien) world, becomes a reminder of how much lies outside the grasp of man.

"The quintessential incarnation" of that which appears to man as "mysterious, powerful and not himself," as Dorothy Dinnerstein says, is "the woman's fertile body" (p. 125). Certainly, the mother's body holds these meanings for the infant, according to Klein. If Dorothy Dinnerstein is right, women (particularly the woman-as-mother, the original "representative" of the natural world, and virtually indistinguishable from it for the human infant) are always likely targets for all later adult rage against nature.[11] Supporting Dinnerstein's highly theoretical account are the anthropologist Peggy Reeves Sanday's cross-cultural findings that in periods of cultural disruption and environmental stress, male social dominance – particularly over female fertility – tends to be at its most extreme (172–84). In the seventeenth century, with the universe appearing to man more decisively "not-himself" than ever before, more capricious and more devastating in her capacity for disorder, both the mystery of the universe and the mystery of the female require a more definitive "solution" than had been demanded by the organic world view.[12]

The project that fell to both empirical science and "rationalism" was to tame the female universe. Empirical science did this through aggressive assault and violation of her "secrets." Rationalism, as we have seen, tamed the female universe through the philosophical neutralization of her vitality. The barrenness of matter correlatively insured the revitalization of human hope of conquering nature (through knowledge, in this case, rather than through force). The mystery of the female, however, could not be bent to man's control simply through philosophical means. More direct and concrete means of "neutralization" were required for that project. It is within this context that witch-hunting and the male medical takeover of the processes of reproduction and birth, whatever their social and political causes, can be seen to have a profound psychocultural dimension as well.

The Contemporary Revaluation of the Feminine

My next focus will be on the recent scholarly emergence and revaluation of epistemological and ethical perspectives "in a different voice." That voice, which classical as well as contemporary writers identify as feminine (as, e.g. in the work of Carol Gilligan, Sarah Ruddick, and Nancy Chodorow), claims a natural foundation for knowledge, not in detachment and distance, but in what I have called "sympathy": in closeness, connectedness, and empathy. It finds the failure of connection (rather than the blurring of boundaries) as the principal cause of breakdown in understanding.

In the seventeenth century, when Paracelsus articulated the alchemical conception of knowledge as a merger of mind and nature, the "female" nature of this ideal operated for him as a metaphor, as did Bacon's contrasting ideal of a virile, "masculine" science. In the second half of our own more sociologically oriented century, women themselves – not some abstract "feminine principle" – have been identified as cultural bearers of the alternative, "sympathetic" scheme of values. The research of Chodorow and Gilligan, in particular, has suggested that men and women (growing up within a particular cultural framework, it needs emphasizing) *do* appear to experience and conceptualize events differently, the key differences centering around different conceptions of the self/world, self/other relation.

> Girls emerge . . . with a basis for "empathy" built into their primary definition of self in a way that boys do not. Girls emerge with a stronger basis for experiencing another's needs or feelings as one's own (or thinking that one is so experiencing another's needs or feelings) . . . girls come to experience themselves as less differentiated than boys, more continuous with and related to the external object-world and as differently oriented to their inner object-world as well. (Chodorow, 167)

Carol Gilligan has described how these developmental differences result, in men and women, in differing valuations of attachment and autonomy, and correspondingly different conceptions of morality.

The association of cognitive style with gender is in itself nothing new. We find it in ancient mythology, in archetypal psychology, in philosophical and scientific writings, and in a host of enduring popular stereotypes about men and women (for example, that women are more "intuitive," men are more "logical," etc.) In the second half of the nineteenth century, the celebration of a distinctively female moral sensibility was widely held by both feminists and sexual conservatives. What *is* new in the recent feminist exploration of gender and cognitive style is a (characteristically modern) emphasis on gender as a social construction, rather than a biological or ontological given. If men and women think differently, it is argued, that is not because the sexes inevitably embody timeless "male" and "female" principles of existence, but because the sexes have been brought up differently, develop different social abilities, have occupied very different power positions in most cultures. Using a psychoanalytic framework, Nancy Chodorow explores the origins of these differences in the differing degrees of individuation from the mother demanded of boys and girls in infancy.[13]

An appreciation of the *historical* nature of the masculine model of knowledge to which the feminine "different voice" is often contrasted helps to underscore that the embodiment of these gender-related perspectives in actual men and women is a cultural, not a biological phenomenon. There have been cultures in which (using *our* terms now, not necessarily theirs) men thought more "like women," and there may be a time in the future when they do so again. In our own time, many women may be coming to think more and more "like men." The conclusion is not, however, that any association of gender and cognitive style is a reactionary mythology with no explanatory value. For the sexual division of labor within the family in the modern era has indeed fairly consistently reproduced significant cognitive and emotional differences along sexual lines. The central importance of Chodorow's work has been to show that boys have tended to grow up learning to experience the world like Cartesians, while girls do not, *because* of developmental asymmetries resulting from female-dominated infant care, rather than biology, anatomy, or "nature."[14]

It is of crucial importance, however, that feminist scholars like Chodorow more explicitly and emphatically underscore the fact that they are describing elements of a social construction, characteristic of certain (though not all) forms of gender organization, and *not* the reified dualities of an "eternal feminine" and "essential masculine" nature. A great deal of current division among feminists rests on lack of clarity and understanding regarding this distinction. This is unfortunate, because the sociological emphasis and understanding of gender as a social construction is one crucial difference between the contemporary feminist revaluation of the "feminine" and the nineteenth-century doctrine of female moral superiority. Too often, recently, the two have been conflated.

A still more central difference between nineteenth-century and twentieth-century feminism is the contemporary feminist emphasis on the *insufficiency* of any ethics or rationality – "feminine" or "masculine" – that operates solely in one mode without drawing on the resources and perspective of the other.[15] The nineteenth-century celebration of a distinctively feminine sensibility and morality functioned in the *service* of pure masculinized thought, by insisting that each "sphere" remain distinct and undiluted by the other. This was, of course, precisely what the seventeenth-century masculinization of thought had accomplished – the exclusion of "feminine" modes of knowing, not from culture in general, but from the scientific and philosophical arenas, whose objectivity and purity needed to be guaranteed. Romanticizing "the feminine" within its "own" sphere is no alternative to Cartesianism, because it suggests that the feminine has a "proper" (domestic) place. Only in establishing the scientific and philosophical legitimacy of alternative modes of knowing in the *public* arena (rather than glorifying them in their own special sphere of family relations) do we present a real alternative to Cartesianism.

Feminism and the "Recessive" Strain in Philosophy

The Cartesian ideals are under attack in philosophy today, and philosophers who subscribe to those ideals, whether in their analytic or phenomenological embodiment, are on the defensive. [Because philosophy has been so dominated by the Cartesian standpoint, the erosion of Cartesianism has been interpreted by some as signalling the "death of philosophy," and many of the current debates among philosophers are couched in those terms. If anything is dying, however, it is the intellectual rule of a particular model of knowledge and reality. Philosophers who grew up under that rule, and who were taught to identify philosophy *with* it, may experience the end of that rule as portending the "end of philosophy". But in fact, philosophy has always spoken in many voices (although they have seldom been heard by the Cartesian "cultural overseer"), some of which are being revived and renovated today.] More significantly, alternative voices from those groups which philosophy has traditionally excluded are now offering the discipline the very means of its revitalization: the truths and values which it has suppressed from its dominant models. Those truths and values have been living underground, throughout the Cartesian reign, and are now emerging to make a claim on the culture.

This emergence cannot be adequately understood unless seen against the backdrop of the last several decades of social and political life. Philosophers may think that the widespread self-critique in which philosophy is currently engaged began with the publication of Richard Rorty's *Philosophy and the Mirror of Nature*. But (as Rorty would probably be the first to acknowledge), the impact of that work had much to do with its timely crystallization of historicist currents that had been gathering momentum since the 1960s. Those currents were themselves activated by the various "liberation" movements of that decade. There is a certain similarity here with the Renaissance, in the cultural reawakening to the multiplicity of possible human perspectives, and to the role of culture in shaping those perspectives. But in our era, the reawakening has occurred in the context of a recognition not merely of the undiscovered "other," but of the *suppressed* other. Women, people of color, and various ethnic and national groups have forced the culture into a critical reexamination not only of diversity (as occurred for Renaissance culture), but of the forces that *mask* diversity. That which appears as "dominant," by virtue of that very fact, comes to be suspect: It has a secret story to tell, in the alternative perspectives to which it has denied legitimacy, and in the historical and political circumstances of its own dominance.

Fueled by the historicist tradition in epistemology, psychoanalytic thought, *and* the political movement for women's rights, representation, and participation in cultural life, feminist ethics and epistemology now appears as one of the most vital forces in the development of post-Cartesian focus and paradigm. The feminist exposure of the gender biases in our dominant Western conceptions of science and ethics – the revelation that the history of their development, the lenses through which they see the world, their methods and priorities have been decisively shaped by the fact that it has been men who have determined their course – has come as a startling recognition to many contemporary male philosophers.[16] Inspired by the work of Gilligan, Chodorow, Harding, and Keller, feminist theory has been systematically questioning the historical identification of rationality, intelligence, "good thinking," and so forth, with the masculine modes of detachment and clarity, offering alternative models of fresher, more humane, and more hopeful approaches to science and ethics.[17]

It is not only in explicitly feminist writing that these phenomena are occurring. Many of the "new paradigms" being proposed in the recent spate of literature on modernity and modern science are grounded in sympathetic, participatory alternatives to Cartesianism. (See Berman and Capra, in particular.) In philosophy, a whole slew of reconsiderations of traditional epistemological "problems" such as relativism, perspectivism, the role of emotions and body in knowledge, the possibility of ultimate foundations, and so on, has brought the feminine perspective in through the back door, as it were. Without explicit commitment to feminism *or* "the feminine," philosophers are nonetheless participating in a (long overdue) philosophical acknowledgement of the limitations of the masculine Cartesian model, and are recognizing how tightly it has held most modern philosophy in its grip.

This is not to say that detachment, clarity, and precision will cease to have enormous value in the process of understanding. Rather, our culture needs to reconceive the status of what Descartes assigned to the shadows. Such reevaluation has been a constant, although "recessive" strain in the history of philosophy since Descartes. Leibniz's declaration that each monad is its *own* "mirror" of the universe, Hume's insistence that "reason is and ought to be the slave of the passions," and, perhaps most importantly,

Kant's revelation that objectivity itself is the result of human structuring, opened various doors that in retrospect now appear as critical openings.

Hume, for example, may now be seen as having a rightful place – along with Nietzsche, Scheler, Peirce, Dewey, James, Whitehead, and, more recently, Robert Neville – in the critical protest against the Cartesian notion that reason can and should be a "pure" realm free from contamination by emotion, instinct, will, sentiment, and value. Within this protest, we see the development both of a "naturalist" *anthropology* of the Cartesian ideals of precision, certainty, and neutrality (Nietzsche, Scheler, Dewey, and James), and a complementary *metaphysics* (Peirce, Whitehead, and Neville) in which "vagueness" as well as specificity, tentativeness, and valuation are honored as essential to thought.

In emphasizing the active, constructive nature of cognition, Kant undermined the Cartesian notion that the mind reflects and the scientist "reads off" what is simply *there* in the world. The Kantian "knower" is transcendental, of course, and Kant's "constructionism" begins and ends, like most Enlightenment thought, with a vision of universal law – in this case, the basic, ahistorical requirements of "knowability," represented by the categories. But the "Copernican Revolution in Thought," in asserting the activity of the subject, opened the door, paradoxically, to a more historical and contextual understanding of knowing. The knower, not the known, now comes under scrutiny – and not, as Descartes scrutinized the knower, for those contaminating elements which must be purged from cognition, but for those "active and interpreting forces," as Nietzsche says, "through which alone seeing becomes seeing *something*." The postulation of an inner "eye" in which these forces "are supposed to be lacking . . . [is] an absurdity and a nonsense" (1969, 119).

The articulation of the historical, social and cultural determinants of what Nietzsche called "perspective" can be seen as one paradigm of modern thought. The main theoretical categories of that paradigm have been worked out by various disciplines: the "philosophical anthropology" of Max Scheler, Karl Mannheim's work on ideology, and, historically fontal, the dialectical materialism of Karl Marx. Marx, of course, was not primarily interested in epistemological questions. But he is nonetheless the single most important philosophical figure in the development of modern historicism, with his emphasis on the historical nature of all human activity and thought and our frequent "false consciousness" of this. It was Marx who turned the tables on the Enlightenment, encouraging suspicion of all ideas that claim to represent universal, fundamental, "inherent," or "natural" features of reality.

The Cartesian ideal of the detached, purely neutral observer is here viewed as a type of mystification, and the ideals of absolute objectivity and ultimate foundations seen as requiring historical examination. In the modern era, "universal" after "universal" has fallen, under the scrutiny of Marxists, anthropologists, critical theorists, feminists, philosophers of science, and deconstructionists. The various claims regarding human nature and human sexuality (the "naturalness" of competition, the "necessity" of sexual repression, the "biological" nature of gender differences) have been challenged. Rorty and Foucault, respectively, have argued that the "mind" and "sexuality" are historical "inventions." And Patrick Heelan has shown that our most basic perceptions of space have a cultural history.

None of this signals the end of philosophy. What it *has* meant, however, is that it is extremely difficult today for the Cartesian philosopher to sit comfortably on the throne of the cultural overseer, "neutrally" legislating "how rational agreement can be reached" and where others have gone astray. The ideal of absolute intellectual purity and the belief in a clear and distinct universe are passing, though not without protest, out of the discipline. It is too soon to tell what sort of impact feminist and other reconstructions will have on the future development of philosophy, not to mention on the general intellectual and political life of our culture. But what does seem clear is that coherent alternatives to Cartesianism are emerging out of Cartesianism's "shadow" itself. If a "flight from the feminine," as I have argued, motivated the birth of the Cartesian ideals, the contemporary revaluation of the feminine has much to contribute to the world that will replace them.[18]

Notes

1 Bossuet, too, believed that the sense-rule of childhood represents something "depraved in the common source of our birth" (Harth, 218). LaRochefoucault called childhood "a perpetual intoxication, a fever on the brain" (Harth, 219). In a popular treatise on education, written in 1646, Balthazar Gratien writes of "that insipidity of childhood which disgusts the sane mind; that coarseness of youth which finds pleasure in scarcely anything but material objects and which is only a very crude sketch of the man of thought ... Only time can cure a person of childhood and youth, which are truly ages of imperfection in every respect" (Ariès, 131–2).

2 Since the body is the *res extensa* of the human being, as mechanical in its operations as a machine (see II, 104; I, 116), this means that our purely bodily existence is not only less than "truly human," but is comparable to animal existence. Animals, as Descartes is notorious for maintaining, are mere automata (PL, 53–4, 121, 206–8, 243–5; HR, I, 117) ["PL" is Anthony Kenny's *Descartes: Philosophical Letters*], and had we not the evidence of the human being's extraordinary flexibility of response (as demonstrated by the adaptability of language and reason to particular circumstances)

we would have no reason to think otherwise of human beings either (HR, I, 116).

3   See Dinnerstein, Hillman, Brown, Marcuse, Stern, and Griffin, among many others.

4   As this book goes to press, Harding's eagerly-awaited *The Science Question in Feminism* (Cornell University Press) is just being released, too late for inclusion as one of the works surveyed in this essay. Harding's contribution to contemporary discussions of modern science, especially among philosophers, is very important.

5   See Keller, Merchant, and Easlea for excellent discussions of the Baconian imagery of nature.

6   These themes are symbolically represented, as I have argued elsewhere, in the structures of tragedy and comedy. There, we find all the elements of the "infant" drama: the pain of individuation, the dream of lost union, and (as in Descartes) the attempt to triumph over one's (unchosen) birth through the denial of its power over the "self-made" self. The meaning of the mother, and of the "feminine," in all this was not discovered by Freud either, as he recognized. Throughout tragedy and comedy, the woman (and most particularly, the mother) represents the historical roots of the self, the authority of the flesh, and the dangers (for tragedy) and joys (for comedy) of union with another. The desire for mastery through individuation, on the other hand, is "masculine" – and we may now recognize it as strikingly Cartesian, too: the project of the self-making self in willful repudiation of historical and familial ties, the limitations of the body, and the power of the flesh. In *Oedipus*, all these come together, which Freud, of course, saw. He emphasized, however, rather the wrong point. The spiritual center of the classic Oedipal story is not the desire to sleep with one's mother, but to become the father of oneself, to be the creator rather than the helpless pawn in the drama of one's own life. (See Bordo, "The Cultural Overseer and the Tragic Hero", *Soundings*, 1982.)

7   This is the social reality behind the witch-hunters' fantasies of female power. The fact is that a great many of the women accused of witchcraft *were* involved in conception and birth, as well as all other aspects of sickness and health. They, indeed, *did* have control (though not of the sort fantasized by Kramer and Sprenger), for healing had traditionally been the province of women, and, in the case of midwifery, remained overwhelmingly so until the eighteenth century (Rich, 121). These female lay-healers, according to Ehrenreich and English, were "singled out particularly" in the witch hunts (p. 36). Called "good witches," they were condemned even more strongly than the "bad." But "the greatest injuries to the Faith as regards the heresy of witches are done by mid-wives" (Kramer and Sprenger). Why? First, because they relieved women of the curse of Eve's original sin, through the use of ergot to dull the pain of childbirth (in 1591, Agnes Simpson was burned for just this crime) (Rich, 117). Second, because they were able to control miscarriage through the use of Belladonna (Ehrenreich and English, 37). It was not until the seventeenth century, however, that midwifery finally begins to give way to the male practice of "obstetrics," described by Suzanne Arms as the final stage in "the

659

gradual attempt by man to extricate the processes of birth from women and call it his own" (Rich, 90).

8   It was male practitioners who established the lying-down position for women in labor, rendering women passive and dependent in the process of birth (Rich, 137), and who, in the late sixteenth century, invented and promulgated the use of forceps in delivery. For Adrienne Rich, the "hands of iron" which replace the "hands of flesh" of the female midwives "symbolize the art of the obstetrician" (p. 133). They began to be used promiscuously, preparation for control over possible difficulty becoming the too-routine practice of such control (as has happened similarly today with the Caesarean section). Midwives campaigned against the overuse and abuse of the forceps (Rich, 137–41). They themselves, of course, could not use the forceps, which was a technology available only to the licensed physician, and there is no doubt an element of political battle at work here. But even the strongest feminists among the midwives argued for the intervention of the male physician when complications arose; it was chiefly against the premature use of forceps, to shorten delivery time, and against their clumsy use, by male surgeons inexperienced at deliveries, that the midwives railed. Male physicians, most notable among them being William Harvey, mounted, in return, a ferocious campaign against midwives (Merchant, 153–5).

9   The fact that there were more female than male witches was linked to the excessive carnality of the female. "All witchcraft comes from carnal lust, which is in women insatiable," say Kramer and Sprenger (Easlea, 80). This view of women was not idiosyncratic, as Easlea points out, citing Walter Charleton's *Ephesian Matron* (1659) and Burton's *Anatomy of Melancholy* (1621). "You are the true Hiena's," says Charleton,

> that allure us with the fairness of your skins; and when folly hath brought us within your reach, you leap upon us and devour us. You are the traitors to Wisdom; the impediment to Industry . . . the clogs to virtue, and goads to drive us all to Vice, Impiety, and Ruine. You are the Fools Paradise, the Wisemans Plague, and the grand Error of Nature. (Easlea, 242)

"Of women's unnatural, insatiable lust, what country, what village doth not complain" notes Burton (Easlea, 242). It is for the sake of fulfilling the insatiable "mouth of the womb," according to Sprenger and Kramer, that "they consort even with the devil" (Easlea, 8). The accusation of copulation with the devil was a common charge at witch trials, and the rampant eroticism of the witch a common theme of paintings on the subject (Merchant, 134).

10   This is the widely accepted "animalculist" version. In the much less influential "ovist" version, the animacules are placed in the woman's womb by God at the time of creation. In either version, the original source of the animalcules is God. The virtue of preformation and embôitement, for the mechanists, was its thoroughly mechanical solution to the vexing problem of generation: If the body is pure *res extensa*, and if *res extensa* is barren and nonsentient, how does a sentient human being develop out of it? The new reproductive theory

enabled the imaging of the sentient human being as being merely "housed" within matter, and not as developing out of it, its true father acknowledged as God.

11 Dorothy Dinnerstein discusses, at some length, what she takes to be the psychological sources of the dominant cultural equation of femaleness and the natural world. We first encounter the mother "before we are able to distinguish between a center of sentience and an impersonal force of nature" (p. 106). As we grow to learn the distinction, she claims, our associations to each remain contaminated by this ancient "confusion." The woman remains something less-than-human (in contrast to the father, whom we come to know from the start as a distinct center of independent subjectivity) and nature remains something more than an "impersonal" force. "She" is also a female force, of course, since it was from the mother that she was originally indistinguishable.

But women not only remain *associated* with nature. They also, claims Dinnerstein, become a natural target for all later rage *against* nature. "Like nature, which sends blizzards and locusts as well as sunshine and strawberries," the mother (and later, women in general) is perceived "as capricious, sometimes actively malevolent. Her body is the first important piece of the physical world that we encounter, and the events for which she seems responsible the first instances of fate. Hence mother nature, with her hurricane daughters . . . hence that fickle female, Lady Luck" (p. 95).

12 That which appears as mysterious and powerful may not always be regarded as dreadful or as requiring *taming*. The unpredictable caprice of fortune, for example, was believed to rule earthly life in the Middle Ages – but its vicissitudes were regarded in a spirit of acceptance (Lewis, 139–40). For Machiavelli, in contrast, "Fortune is a woman, and it is necessary if you wish to master her, to conquer her by force" (Merchant, 130). And, while the evidence for there having been true matriarchal cultures is debated, the existence of what Rich calls *gynocentric* cultures – cultures in which women were venerated, not feared, for their strength and power, especially in their maternal function – is unquestionable (Rich, 80–9; Sanday, 15–33, 113–28). Moreover, that which appears as mysterious and powerful may not always be experienced as decisively "notself." The Middle Ages, while hardly a gynocentric culture, *was* a culture in which the mystery and power of nature did not appear as the whim of an alien "other."

13 Knowledge "by sympathy," as Karl Stern says, has its "natural fundament" in the "primary bond with the mother" (p. 54). But mothers, according to Chodorow, treat their female children and male children differently. Identification and symbiosis with daughters tends to be stronger. Daughters, in response, tend to perceive *themselves* as more closely identified with the mother, less distinct from her, and more comfortable, in adult life, with experiences of "merger" with others. By contrast, boys are experienced by their mothers as a "male opposite," and are more likely to have had to "curtail their primary love and sense of empathic tie with their mother" (pp. 166–7). Moreover, for the boy, issues of differentiation from the mother become

intertwined with issues of gender identification. "Dependence on his mother, attachment to her, and identification with her represent that which is not masculine; a boy must reject dependence and deny attachment and identification" (p. 181). The result, according to Chodorow, is that "girls emerge . . . with a basis for 'empathy' built into their primary definition of self in a way that boys do not" (p. 167). The analysis is not only developmental, but institutional, for the proposed differences in male and female modes of knowing all hinge on the institution of female nurturing.

14 An examination of the relevance of this contemporary developmental explanation to the Cartesian era must fall to the sociologist and historian of the family. No doubt Ariès's profound thesis that childhood itself was not "discovered" until the sixteenth century has some relevance here, for until that time, as Ariès argues, very little in the way of nurturing of *either* sex went on. It is in the sixteenth and seventeenth centuries, therefore, that we might expect the developmental processes described by Chodorow to begin to have some striking application. My own study here is certainly suggestive of the fruitfulness of further investigation along these lines.

15 See, especially, the final chapter in Gilligan, in which it becomes clear that Gilligan is calling, not for a "feminization" of knowledge, from which more masculinist modes are excluded, but the recognition that each, cut off from the other, founders on its own particular reefs, just as it offers its own partial truths about human experience.

16 See, as a striking example, Ian Hacking's review of Keller's *Gender and Science*. Hacking is obviously unaware of the long feminist literature (including Keller's own earlier work) in which Keller's volume of essays is grounded, and apparently considers the notion that gender has influenced the construction of fact and theory to be an idea that has burst forth, for the first time, with the publication of this 1985 collection. He also is unwilling to accept Keller's own identification of herself as a radical feminist (apparently, for Hacking, the term cannot refer to anyone whose work he appreciates, and must always signal crude and negative thinking). He is genuinely taken, however, with the revolutionary import and the potential cultural value of work such as Keller's.

17 See Harding and Hintikka, *Discovering Reality*, and Alison Jaggar, *Feminist Politics and Human Nature*, chapter 11. French feminism has its own traditions of conceptual reconstruction; see Marks and Courtivron, *New French Feminisms*. Recently, conferences and seminars, explicitly organized around themes of "revisioning" or reconstructing ethics and epistemology, have begun to appear. To cite just two examples: Seminars entitled "Feminist Reconstructions of Self and Society" and "Feminist Ways of Knowing" were held in 1985 at Douglass College, Rutgers University; a conference entitled "Women and Moral Theory" was held in March, 1985 at the State University of New York at Stony Brook. Papers delivered at the Douglass seminar included topics such as the role of emotions in knowing, non-dualist perspectives on knowledge, the role of the body, and the role of "care" in morality. A collection of these papers – *Feminist Reconstructions of Being and Knowing* – is now in preparation (editors Alison Jaggar and Susan Bordo, Rutgers University Press). The Stony Brook

conference was devoted to an exploration of the work of Carol Gilligan and its intellectual implications. Several papers presented offered Gilligan-inspired reconstructions of ethical theory.

18 It seems clear that so long as masculine values continue to exert their grip on the public domain, there are severe constraints on the potential that women may bring, as they enter that domain, to transform it. Many radical feminists fault liberal feminism, which has prioritized equal opportunity without a corresponding emphasis on the need for cultural transformation, with contributing to more of a "masculinization" than "feminization" of contemporary culture. Women have been "allowed" in the public domain, but they have been required to adopt the values of that domain. On the other hand, unless the promotion of "feminine" values is consistently and explicitly wedded to a critique of the sexual division of labor, it may operate as a justification and romanticization of that division of labor, and a banner under which women can be encouraged to return to (or remain in) the private sphere where "their" virtues flourish. The critique of cultural values must always be joined to a recognition of the "material" inequalities and power imbalances that those values serve. But the cultural critique is essential. Without it, women surrender the power of our "critical alterity" (as Ynestra King calls it) to be instrumental in the realization of a different social and intellectual order.

References

Ariès, Philippe. *Centuries of Childhood: A Social History of Family Life.* New York: Vintage, 1962.

Berman, Morris. *The Re-enchantment of the World.* Ithaca; Cornell University Press, 1981.

Bordo, Susan. "The Cultural Overseer and the Tragic Hero: Comedic and Feminist Perspectives on the Hubris of Philosophy." *Soundings,* LXV, No. 2, Summer 1982, pp. 181–205.

Brown, Norman O. *Life Against Death.* New York: Random House, 1959.

Capra, Fritjof. *The Turning Point.* New York: Simon and Schuster, 1983.

Chodorow, Nancy. *The Reproduction of Mothering.* Berkeley: University of California Press, 1978.

—— "Family Structure and Feminine Personality." In *Woman, Culture and Society,* pp. 43–66. Ed. Michele Rosaldo and Louise Lamphere. Standford: Stanford University Press, 1974.

deBeauvoir, Simone. *The Second Sex.* New York: Alfred A. Knopf, 1957.

Descartes. *Philosophical Works.* vols I and II. Ed. Elizabeth Haldane and G. R. T. Ross. Cambridge: Cambridge University Press, 1969.

Dinnerstein, Dorothy. *The Mermaid and the Minotaur.* New York: Harper and Row, 1977.

Easlea, Brian. *Witch-hunting, Magic and the New Philosophy.* Atlantic Highlands, NJ: Humanities Press, 1980.

Ehrenreich, Barbara, and Dierdre English. *For Her Own Good*. New York: Anchor/Doubleday, 1979.

Farrington, Benjamin. *Temporis Partus Masculus: An Untranslated Writing of Francis Bacon. Centaurus I*, 1951.

Freud, Sigmund. *Beyond the Pleasure Principle*. New York: Bantam, 1959.

Gay, Peter. *The Bourgeois Experience*, vol. one, *Education of the Senses*. New York: Oxford University Press, 1984.

Gilligan, Carol. *In a Different Voice*. Cambridge: Harvard University Press, 1982.

Gillispie, Charles. *The Edge of Objectivity*. Princeton: Princeton University Press, 1960.

Hacking, Ian. "Liberating the Laboratory." *The New Republic*, July 15 and 22, 1985, pp. 47–50.

Harding, Sandra and Hintikka, Merril. *Discovering Reality: Feminist Perspectives on Epistemology, Science, and Philosophy of Science*. Dordrecht: Reidel, 1983.

Harth, Erica. "Classical Innateness." *Yale French Studies*, no. 49 (1973): 212–30.

Hillman, James. *The Myth of Analysis*. New York: Harper and Row, 1972.

Jaggar, Alison. *Feminist Politics and Human Nature*. New Jersey: Rowman and Allanheld, 1983.

Keller, Evelyn Fox. *Reflections on Gender and Science*. New Haven: Yale University Press, 1985.

Kenny, Anthony (ed.). *Descartes: Philosophical Letters*, trans. Anthony Kenny. Oxford: Clarendon, 1970.

Klein, Melanie. "Early Stages of the Oedipus Conflict." In *The World of the Child*. ed. Toby Talbot. New York: Jason Aronson, 1974, pp. 98–111.

Lederer, Wolfgang. *The Fear of Women*. New York: Harcourt Brace, 1968.

Lewis, C. S. *The Discarded Image*. Cambridge: Cambridge University Press, 1964.

Marcuse, Herbert. *Counter-Revolution and Revolt*. Boston: Beacon, 1972.

Merchant, Carolyn. *The Death of Nature*. San Francisco: Harper and Row, 1980.

Neville, Robert. *Reconstruction of Thinking*. Albany: State University of New York Press, 1981.

Plato *Timeaus*. Translated by Benjamin Jowett. Indianapolis: Bobbs-Merrill, 1949.

Rich, Adrienne. *Of Woman Born*. New York: Bantam, 1976.

Rorty, Richard. *Philosophy and the Mirror of Nature*. Princeton: Princeton University Press, 1979.

Ross, John. "Towards Fatherhood: The Epigenesis of Paternal Identity During a Boy's First Decade." *International Review of Psychoanalysis*, 4, 1977, pp. 327–47.

Sanday, Peggy Reeve. *Female Power and Male Dominance: On the Origins of Sexual Inequality*. Cambridge: Cambridge University Press, 1981.

Stern, Karl. *The Flight From Woman*. New York: Noonday, 1965.

Vicinus, Martha. *Suffer and Be Still*. Bloomington: Indiana University Press, 1972.

Whitehead, Alfred North. *Science and Modern World*. 1925; reprint edn, Toronto: Collier Macmillan, 1967.

chapter forty

The Reenchantment of Science
David Ray Griffin

Professor of philosophy of religion, David Griffin (1939–   ) proposes a positive, revisionary postmodernism. Inspired both by various developments in twentieth-century science (e.g. general relativity, quantum theory, the "Gaia hypothesis," and recognition of mind–body interactions in immunology), and by Alfred North Whitehead's philosophy of "organism," Griffin seeks to develop a postmodern cosmology. This cosmology denies certain characteristically modern philosophical and scientific notions, especially mechanism, atomism, determinism, and the Cartesian dualism of mind and body. Griffin argues that contemporary science itself, in discarding these modern notions for holistic and indeterminist alternatives, is becoming postmodern.

Modern Science and the Disenchantment of the World

In disenchanting nature, the modern science of nature led to its own disenchantment. This happened because the mechanistic, disenchanted philosophy of nature, which was originally part of a dualistic and theistic vision of reality as a whole, eventually led to the disenchantment of the whole world. This first section spells out this development.

What does the "disenchantment of nature" mean? Most fundamentally, it means the denial to nature of all subjectivity, all experience, all feeling. Because of this denial, nature is disqualified – it is denied all qualities that are not thinkable apart from experience.

These qualities are legion. Without experience, no aims or purposes can exist in natural entities, no creativity in the sense of self-determination or final causation. With no final causation toward some ideal possibility, no role exists for ideals, possibilities, norms, or values to play: causation is

David Ray Griffin, "Introduction: The Reenchantment of Science," in his edited volume, *The Reenchantment of Science* (Albany: State University of New York Press, 1988), sections 1 and 3, pp. 2–8 and 22–30.

665

strictly a matter of efficient causation from the past. With no self-determination aimed at the realization of ideals, no value can be achieved. With no experience, even unconscious feeling, there can be no value received: the causal interactions between natural things or events involve no sharing of values. Hence, no intrinsic value can exist within nature, no value of natural things for themselves. Also, unlike the way our experience is internally affected, even constituted in part, by its relations with its environment, material particles can have no internal relations. Along with no internalization of other natural things, no internalization of divinity can occur. Friedrich Schiller, who spoke of the disenchantment of nature a century before Weber, used the term *Entgotterung*, which literally means the dedivinization of nature. Deity, for the founders of the modern worldview, such as Descartes, Boyle, and Newton, was in no way immanent in the world; it was a being wholly external to the world who imposed motion and laws upon it from without. The laws of nature were, hence, not at all analogous to sociological laws which reflect the habits of the members of human society. A further and in fact central feature of the disenchantment of nature was the denial of action at a distance. Weber's term for disenchantment was *Entzauberung*, which literally means "taking the magic out." It was at the heart of the mechanistic vision to deny that natural things had any hidden ("occult") powers to attract other things (a denial that made the phenomena of magnetism and gravitation very difficult to explain).[1] In these ways, nature was bereft of all qualities with which the human spirit could feel a sense of kinship and of anything from which it could derive norms. Human life was rendered both alien and autonomous.

Whereas this disenchantment of nature was originally carried out (by Galileo, Descartes, Boyle, and Newton & Company) in the framework of a dualistic supernaturalism in which the soul and a personal deity were assigned explanatory functions and hence causal power, the successes of the objectifying, mechanistic, reductionistic approach in physics soon led to the conviction that it should be applied to all of reality. God was at first stripped of all causal power beyond that of the original creation of the world; later thinkers turned this deism into complete atheism. The human soul or mind was at first said to be "epiphenomenal," which meant that it was real but only as an effect, not as a cause; later thinkers, believing nature should have no idle wheels, denied that it was a distinct entity at all, declaring it to be simply one of the brain's emergent properties. In those ways, the "animistic" viewpoint, which attributes causality to personal forces, was completely rejected. All "downward causation" from personal to impersonal processes was eliminated; the reductionistic program of explaining everything in terms of elementary impersonal processes was fully accepted. The world as a whole was thus disenchanted. This disenchanted view means that experience plays no real role not only in "the natural world" but in the world as a whole. Hence, no role exists in the universe for purposes, values, ideals, possibilities, and qualities, and there is no freedom, creativity, temporality, or divinity. There are no norms, not even truth, and everything is ultimately meaningless.

The ironic conclusion is that modern science, in disenchanting nature, began a trajectory that ended by disenchanting science itself. If all human life is meaningless, then science, as one of its activities, must share in this meaninglessness. For some time, many held that science at least gives us the truth, even if a bleak one. Much recent thought, however, has concluded that science does not even give us that. The disenchantment is complete.

The main point to emphasize is that modern thinkers have assumed that this disenchantment of the world is *required by science itself*. A few examples: just as Darwin felt that any "caprice" in the world would make science impossible, so that both divine and free human activity had to be eliminated from our worldview,[2] so Michael Ghiselin, a contemporary Darwinian, says that to deny the ideal of predictive determinism by affirming teleological causation "is to opt out of science altogether."[3] Jacques Monod says:

> The cornerstone of the scientific method is the postulate that nature is objective. In other words, the *systematic* denial that 'true' knowledge can be got at by interpreting phenomena in terms of final causes – that is to say, of 'purpose' . . . [T]he postulate of objectivity is consubstantial with science. . . . There is no way to be rid of it, even tentatively or in a limited area, without departing from the domain of science itself.[4]

While recognizing that the objectivist view of the world outrages our values and forces us to live in an alien world, Monod nevertheless insists that we must adopt it, because all "animist" views, which make us feel at home in nature by attributing purpose to it, are "fundamentally *hostile* to science."[5]

"So-called purposive behavior," said behaviorist psychologist Clark Hull, is to be regarded as a secondary, epiphenomenal reality, derivative from "more elementary objective primary principles."[6] Likewise, B.F. Skinner argues that psychology must follow physics and biology in rejecting "personified causes," and that to be "natural" is to be completely determined by one's environment. From the viewpoint of "the science of behavior," says Skinner, the notion of the "autonomous," which "initiates, originates and creates," is the notion of the "miraculous." He adds: "A scientific analysis of behavior dispossesses autonomous man and turns the control he has been said to exert over to the environment."[7] Whereas this statement suggests that determinism is a *result* of the application of the scientific approach, Skinner had earlier revealed that it is a *presupposition*: "We cannot apply the methods of science to a subject matter which is assumed to move about capriciously. . . . The hypothesis that man is not free is essential to the application of scientific method to the study of human behavior."[8]

While Hull and Skinner come from a previous generation, and advocated a behaviorist psychology which is now widely rejected, William Uttal is a contemporary psychobiologist. He says that reductionism, according to which all the activities of the mind are reducible to the most elementary levels of organization of matter, is "the foundation upon which the entire science of psychobiology is built." To introduce any definition of consciousness that goes beyond the operations used in surgery and the behavioral laboratory would mean "a total collapse into prescientific modes of thought."[9]

The idea that science requires a reductionistic account, and rules out all downward causation from personal causes and all action at a distance, is illustrated by the treatment of apparent parapsychological phenomena by physicist John Taylor. After studying several people who he had come to believe had the psychokinetic power to bend metal without touching it, he published a book entitled *Superminds*, complete with supporting photographs.[10] However, after deciding later that no explanation was to be found for psychokinetic effects within the scientific worldview, he wrote a second book called *Science and the Supernatural* in which he declared that no such events can occur. Although he still believed that there was good evidence for psychokinetic events, and admitted that he could not explain how the particular events he had witnessed could have been faked, he concluded that all such reports must be due to hallucination, trickery, credulity, the fear of death, and the like. "Such an explanation is the only one which seems to fit in with a scientific view of the world."[11] The reasoning behind this conclusion was as follows: First, scientific explanation can only be in materialistic terms; if anything, such as the human mind, could not be explained in quantitative, materialistic terms, then the scientist would have to choose between silence and irrationality. Second, according to "the scientific viewpoint," all explanation must be in terms of the four forces of physics. Third, none of these forces can explain psychokinesis. Therefore, he says, we must believe that no genuine psychokinesis occurs. Taylor concludes by castigating himself and other scientists for having seriously investigated "phenomena which their scientific education should indicate are impossible."[12]

This idea that the very nature of science rules out the scientific study of anything not understandable in materialistic terms has in our century probably been more prevalent in fields other than physics. James Alcock, a social psychologist, says that a "spiritual science," which parapsychology is sometimes said to be, is a contradiction in terms. "How can a science of the spirit exist, given that science is by its very nature materialistic?"[13]

Besides ruling out purpose, freedom, personal causation, and any nonmaterialistic interactions from the scientific account of nature, the dominant viewpoint has even eliminated temporality. Ilya Prigogine regards the fact that modern science has been nontemporal as the root of the cleavage between the "two cultures" (C. P. Snow) of science and the humanities.[14] This elimination of temporality has been supported by many twentieth-century physicists, including Albert Einstein, who said: "For us believing physicists, the distinction between past, present and future is only an illusion, even if a stubborn one." [15] A contemporary physicist, P. C. W. Davies, spells out the implied dualism between objective nature and subjectivity:

> The notion that time flows in a one-way fashion is a property of our consciousness. It is a subjective phenomenon and is a property that simply cannot be demonstrated in the natural world. This is an incontrovertible lesson from modern science. . . . A flowing time belongs to our mind, not to nature.[16]

A well-read physician, citing several physicists who endorse this view, says that we must assimilate it, in spite of the fact that it is an affront to common sense, because "we cannot ignore what modern physical science has revealed to us about the nature of time."[17]

As stated earlier, the final disenchantment of modern science is its conclusion that its own discoveries prove the meaninglessness of the whole universe, which must include the scientists and their science. Near the end of his popular book, *The First Three Minutes*, physicist Steven Weinberg says, "The more the universe seems comprehensible, the more it also seems pointless."[18]

I momentarily interrupt the recital of evidence to respond to a counterargument that is probably growing in the mind of many readers. This is the argument that it is not the job of the scientist *qua* scientist to deal with the true nature of time and matter in themselves and with the question whether the universe is meaningful. These are the tasks, it could be argued, for metaphysicians and theologians, or for poets, whom Shelley called the "unacknowledged legislators of mankind." Hence, according to this argument, no need exists for a postmodern science; it is only necessary to point out the inherent limitations of science so that people will look elsewhere for answers to these larger questions. The problem with this solution is that the ideal of an "inherently limited science" does not work in practice. Science is inherently not only realistic, trying to describe the way things really are, but also imperialistic, bent on providing the only genuine description. The word *science*, after all, means *knowledge*; what is not vouchsafed by "science" is not considered knowledge in our culture. The cultural effect of modern science has been to make scientists the only "acknowledged legislators" of humankind, because its worldview has ruled out the possibility that metaphysics, theology, or poetry would have anything to add. Unless science itself is seen as giving a different answer, the disenchantment of the world will continue. With this brief apologia, I return to the topic.

Not only scientists themselves but also many philosophers have supported the view that science necessarily disenchants the world, proving that experience and those qualities that presuppose it are inoperative. D. M. Armstrong says that we have "general scientific grounds for thinking that man is nothing but a physical mechanism," that "mental states are, in fact, nothing but physical states of the central nervous system," so that we should be able to "give a complete account of man in purely physico-chemical terms."[19] In his 1956 preface to *The Modern Temper*, originally published in 1929, Joseph Wood Krutch summarized the book's thesis (with which he had later come to disagree):

> The universe revealed by science, especially the sciences of biology and psychology, is one in which the human spirit cannot find a comfortable home. That spirit breathes freely only in a universe where what philosophers call Value Judgements are of supreme importance. It needs to believe, for instance, that right and wrong are real, that Love is more than a biological function, that the human mind is capable of reason rather than merely of rationalization, and that it has the power to will and to choose instead of being compelled merely to react in the fashion predetermined by its conditioning. *Since science has proved that none of these beliefs is more than a delusion*, mankind will be compelled either to surrender what we call its humanity by adjusting to the real world or to live some kind of tragic existence in a universe alien to the deepest needs of its nature.[20]

Better known is the following purple passage from "A Free Man's Worship," in which Bertrand Russell summarizes "the world which Science presents for our belief":

> That Man is the product of causes which had no prevision of the end they were achieving; that his origin, his growth, his hopes and fears, his loves and beliefs, are but the outcome of accidental collocations of atoms; . . . that all the labours of the ages, all the devotion, all the inspiration, all the noonday brightness of human genius, are destined to extinction in the vast death of the solar system . . . – all these things, if not quite beyond dispute, are yet so nearly certain, that no philosophy which rejects them can hope to stand.[21]

The modern consensus then, as reflected in the preceding quotations, has been that science and disenchantment go hand in hand. On the one hand, it is assumed, science can only be applied to that which has already been disenchanted, which means deanimated.[22] To deanimate is to remove all anima or soul, in Plato's sense of a self-moving thing which determines itself, at least partly, in terms of its desire to realize particular values. On the other hand, it is assumed that the application of the scientific method to anything confirms the truth of the disenchanted view of it, that it can be adequately understood in purely impersonal terms, as embodying no creativity, no self-determination in terms of values or norms, and nothing that could be considered divine.

The only way to prevent the disenchantment of the universe as a whole, on this view, is to draw a line, usually between the human being as purposive agent and the rest of nature, above which the scientific method is said to be inapplicable. But any such essential dualism is undermined by several things: the fact that human behavior, including human experience, is subject to a great extent to causal analysis; the idea that we, like all other species, are products of the evolutionary process; the difficulty of understanding how a human mind, which operates in terms of reasons, purposes, or final causes, could interact with bodily parts operating strictly in terms of mechanistic causes; and the general pressure toward a unified approach to knowledge. Accordingly, the attempt to prevent total disenchantment by means of an essential dualism – between mind and matter, understanding and explanation, hermeneutics and science[23] – is difficult to maintain intellectually. Whereas all people live in terms of the conviction that they are more than behaviorism, sociobiology, and psychobiology allow, and may feel that the totally disenchanted approach to human beings is inappropriate, it has been extremely difficult to state these convictions and feelings in an intellectually defensible way. Besides thereby seeming to leave no alternative beyond antihumanitarianism or a humanitarianism based on an arbitrary choice, modern science also seems to alienate us from our bodies and from nature in general. Because it has disenchanted the world, many people have become disenchanted with science.

Others, however, have distinguished between *modern science*, which disenchants, and *science as such*, which may be open to reenchantment.

Postmodern Organicism and the Unity of Science

The postmodern organicism represented in this series has been inspired primarily by the scientist-turned-philosopher Alfred North Whitehead. . . .

This postmodern organicism can be considered a synthesis of the Aristotelian, Galilean (both forms), and Hermetic paradigms. Aristotelian organicism had a unified science by attributing purposive or final causation to everything, most notoriously saying that a falling stone seeks a state of rest. The Galilean paradigm, in its first form, distinguished absolutely between two types of primary beings: (1) those that exercised purposive or final causation; and (2) those that did not and could consequently be understood completely in terms of receiving and transmitting efficient causation. At first, limiting the beings in the first category to human minds was customary, but that limitation is neither necessary to the dualistic paradigm nor very credible. Many Galilean dualists have accordingly, as mentioned in the previous section, extended final causation further down the animal kingdom: those who are termed *vitalists* see it as arising with the first form of life. Wherever the line was drawn, the drawing of a line between two ontologically different types of primary beings split science into two parts. One science spoke only of efficient causes; the other science (psychology) spoke in terms of final causes or purposes. The second form of the Galilean paradigm tried to restore unity to science by abolishing an internalistic psychology of final causes. Psychology, under the name of *behaviorism*, was transformed into an attempt to describe and explain human and other animal behavior solely in terms of efficient causes and other externalistic terms. *Eliminative materialism*, mentioned earlier, is the extreme version of this way to achieve unity.

Postmodern organicism holds that all primary individuals are organisms who exercise at least some iota of purposive causation. But it does not hold that all visible objects, such as stones and planets, are primary individuals or even analogous to primary individuals. Rather, it distinguishes between two ways in which primary organisms can be organized: (1) as a compound individual,[24] in which an all-inclusive subject emerges; and (2) as a nonindividuated object, in which no unifying subjectivity is found. Animals belong to the first class; stones to the second. In other words, there is no ontological dualism, but there is an organizational duality which takes account of the important and obvious distinction that the dualists rightly refused to relinquish. Hence, there are (1) things whose behavior can only be understood in terms of both efficient causes and their own purposive response to these causes, and (2) things whose behavior can be understood, for most purposes, without any reference to purposive or final causation. In this sense, there is a duality within science.

However, the qualification *for most purposes* is important. Whereas the Galilean paradigm maintained that a nonteleological explanation of material things could be adequate for all purposes, including a complete understanding, at least in principle, the postmodern paradigm contends that any explanation devoid of purposive causation will necessarily abstract from concrete facts. *Fully* to understand even the interaction between two billiard balls requires reference to purposive reactions – not indeed of the balls as aggregates, but of their constituents. Because the study of nonindividual objects as well as that of primary individuals and compound individuals requires, at least ultimately, reference to final as well as efficient causes, there is a unity of science.

The relation between final and efficient causation in Whiteheadian postmodern organicism is different from their relation in any previous form of thought, even from other forms of panexperientialism (often called panpsychism), although it was anticipated in Buddhist thought. Other forms of thought that have attributed experience to all individuals, such as that of Gottfried Leibniz and Teilhard de Chardin, have assumed the ultimate constituents of the world to be enduring individuals. An individual was physical from without to others, but was conscious or mental from within, for itself. From without, it interacted with other enduring individuals in terms of efficient causation; from within, it lived in terms of purposes or final causation. Given this picture, relating efficient and final causation to each other was difficult. The common view has been that they do not relate, but simply run along parallel to each other. However, as discussed above in relation to materialistic identism, this parallelism raises serious problems. If experience or mentality makes no difference to an individual's interactions with its environment, how can we explain why the higher forms of experience have evolved? And without appeal to a supernatural coordinator, how can we explain the parallelism between inner and outer; e.g. why should my brain's signal to my hand to lift a glass follow right after my mental decision to have a drink, if my decision in no way *causes* the appropriate neurons in the brain to fire?

However, if the ultimate individuals of the world are momentary events, rather than enduring individuals, a positive relation can exist between efficient and final causation. Efficient causation still applies to the exterior of an individual and final causation to the interior. But because an enduring individual, such as a proton, neuron, or human psyche, is a temporal *society* of momentary events, exterior and interior oscillate and feed into each other rather than running parallel. Each momentary event in an enduring individual originates through the inrush of efficient causation from the past world, i.e. from previous events, including the previous events that were members of the same enduring individual. The momentary subject then makes a self-determining response to these causal influences; this is the moment of final causation, as the event aims at achieving a synthesis for itself and for influencing the future. This final causation is in no way unrelated to efficient causation; it is a purposive response to the efficient causes on the event. When this moment of subjective final causation is over, the event becomes an object which exerts efficient causation on future events. Exactly what efficient causation it exerts is a function both of the efficient causes upon it *and* of its own final causation. Hence, the efficient causes of the world do not run along as if there were no mentality with its final causation. An event does not necessarily simply transmit to others what it received; it may do this, but it also may deflect and transform the energy it receives to some degree or another, before passing it on. (*We* do this to the greatest degree when we return good for evil.)

To say that the categories of both final and efficient causation must be employed for the study of all actual beings does *not* imply that the two categories will be *equally* relevant for all beings. Indeed, as already indicated, an appeal to final causation is irrelevant for almost all purposes when studying nonindividuated objects, such as rocks, stars, and computers.[25] Even with regard to individuals, the importance of final or purposive causation will vary enormously. In primary individuals, such as photons and electrons (or quarks, if such there be), final causation is minimal. For the most part, the behavior of these individuals is understandable in terms of efficient causes alone. They mainly just conform to what they have received and pass it on to the future in a predictable way. But not completely: behind the epistemic "indeterminacy" of quantum physics lies a germ of ontic self-determinacy. The importance of self-determination or final causation increases in compound individuals, especially in those normally called *living*. It becomes increasingly important as the study focuses upon more complex, highly evolved animals; all the evidence suggests that final causation is the most important, on our planet, in determining the experience and behavior of human beings. The importance of efficient causes, i.e. of influence from the past, does not diminish as one moves toward the higher individuals; indeed, in a sense higher beings are influenced by *more* past events than are lower ones. But the totality of efficient causes from the past becomes less and less explanatory of experience and behavior, and the individual's own present self-determination in terms of desired ends becomes more explanatory.

From this perspective we can understand why a mechanistic, reductionistic approach has been so spectacularly successful in certain areas and so unsuccessful in others. The modern Galilean paradigm was based on the study of nonindividuated objects, such as stellar masses and steel balls, which exercise *no final causation*[i] either in determining their own behavior or that of their elementary parts. Absolute predictability and reduction is possible in principle. This paradigm was next applied to very low-grade individuals, in which the final causation is *negligible* for most purposes

---

[i] Aristotle's notion of the "final cause" of a being is its end, purpose, or goal (which need not be conscious or intentional).

except to the most refined observation. With this refinement, the absolute predictability of behavior broke down with the most elementary individuals; the ideal of predictability could be salvaged only by making it statistical and applying it to large numbers of individuals. With low-grade forms of life, and in particular with their inherited characteristics and certain abstract features of their behavior, Galilean science has still been very successful, but not completely. Certain features of even low-grade life seemed intractable to this approach, just those features which led to the rise of vitalism. This paradigm has been even less successful with rats than with bacteria. At this level, various problems are virtually ignored, because little chance of success is apparent, and scientists are interested in applying their method where the chances for success are most promising. Finally, the method has been less successful yet with humans than with rats. The record of success at this level is so miserable that many scientists and philosophers of science refuse to think of the so-called social or human sciences, such as psychology, sociology, economics, and political science, as sciences at all. This pattern of success and failure of the Galilean paradigm fits exactly what the postmodern paradigm predicts. As one leaves nonindividuated objects for individuals, and as one deals with increasingly higher individuals, final causation becomes increasingly important, and regularity and hence predictability become increasingly less possible. Hence, nothing but confusion and unrealistic expectations can result from continuing to regard physics as the paradigmatic science.[26]

This framework can explain why it has been even less possible to discover regularities and attain repeatability in parapsychology than in certain aspects of ordinary psychology. Although every event (by hypothesis) exerts influence directly upon remote as well as spatially and temporally contiguous events, its influence on contiguous events is much more powerful. Hence, the effects of the kind of influence that is exerted upon remote events indirectly *via* a chain of contiguous events will be much more regular and hence predictable than the effects of the kind of influence that is exerted on remote events directly, without the intervening chain. Accordingly, because sensory perception arises from a chain of contiguous events (photons and neuron firings in vision) connecting the remote object with the psyche, the sensory perception of external objects is much more regular and reliable, hence predictable, than any extrasensory perception of them. Likewise, because effects produced in the external world by the psyche by means of the body are mediated by a chain of contiguous causes, whose reliability, like that of the sensory system, has been perfected over billions of years of evolution, such effects are much more reliable than any psychokinetic effects produced by the direct influence of the psyche upon outer objects without the body's mediation. Additionally, although *unconscious* extrasensory perception and *subtle* and *diffused* psychokinetic action occur continually (by hypothesis), the power to produce *conscious* extrasensory perception and *conspicuous* psychokinetic effects *on specific objects* is – at least for the majority of human beings most of the time – evidently lodged in an unconscious level of experience, which by definition is not under conscious control. Given these assumptions, the fact that parapsychology has attained little repeatability with conspicuous psychokinetic effects and conscious extrasensory perception is what should be expected.[27] In this way, the element of truth in the Hermetic paradigm is coordinated with the elements of truth from the Aristotelian and Galilean paradigms.

What then is science – what constitutes its unity? The anarchistic or relativistic view that "anything goes," that there is no such thing as a scientific method, is surely too strong. But it serves a useful function, as indeed it was intended,[28] to shake us free from parochial limitations on what counts as science. A description of science for a postmodern world must be much looser than the modern descriptions (which were really *pre*scriptions).

Any activity properly called *science* and any conclusions properly called *scientific* must, first, be based on an overriding concern to discover truth.[29] Other concerns will of course play a role, but the concern for truth must be overriding, or the activity and its results would better called by another name, such as *ideology*, or *propaganda*, or *politics*.[30] Second, science involves demonstration. More particularly, it involves testing hypotheses through data or experiences that are in some sense repeatable and hence open to confirmation or refutation by peers. In sum, science involves the attempt to establish truth through demonstrations open to experiential replication. What is left out of this account of science are limitations (1) to any particular domain, (2) any particular type of repeatability and demonstration, or (3) any particular contingent beliefs.

(1) Science is not restricted to the domain of things assumed to be wholly physical, operating in terms of efficient causes alone, or even to the physical aspects of things, understood as the aspects knowable to sensory perception or instruments designed to magnify the senses.[31] As the impossibility of behaviorism in human and even animal psychology has shown, science must refer to experience and purposes to comprehend (and even to predict) animal behavior. Although we cannot *see* the purposes motivating our fellow humans or other animals, assuming that such purposes play a causal role is not unscientific, if this hypothesis can be publicly demonstrated to account for the observable behavior better than the opposite hypothesis. And, once it is explicitly recognized that science *can* deal with subjectivity, there is no reason in principle for it to limit itself to the objective or physical side of other things, if there is good reason to suspect that an experiencing side exercising final causation exists. At the very least, even if we cannot imagine very concretely what the experience of a

bacterium or a DNA molecule would be like, we need not try to account for its observable behavior on the metaphysical assumption that it has no experience and hence no purposes.

Just as the need for experiential replication by peers does not limit science to the physical or objective side of actual things, it does not even limit it to the realm of actuality. Mathematics deals with relationships among ideal entities, and is able to achieve great consensus; geometry was for Descartes of course the paradigmatic science. Therefore, the fact that logic, aesthetics, and ethics deal with ideal entities does not, in itself, exclude them from the realm of science.

Furthermore, the domain of scientific study should not be thought to be limited to regularities, or law-like behavior. There is no reason why the discussion of the origin of laws should not belong to science. If the laws of nature are reconceived as habits, the question of how the habits originated should not be declared off-limits.[32] In fact, we should follow Bohm in replacing the language of "laws" with the more inclusive notion of "orders," for the reasons Evelyn Fox Keller has suggested: the notion of "laws of nature" retains the connotation of theological imposition, which is no longer appropriate but continues to sanction unidirectional, hierarchical explanations; it makes the simplicity of classical physics the ideal, so that the study of more complex orders is regarded as "softer" and less fully scientific; and it implies that nature is dead and "obedient" rather than generative and resourceful.[33]

(2) While science requires repeatable experiential demonstration, it does not require one particular type of demonstration, such as the laboratory experiment. As Patrick Grim says:

> Field studies, expeditions, and the appearances of comets have played a major role in the history of science. Contemporary reliance on mathematics reflects a willingness to accept a priori deductive as well as inductive demonstration. And there are times when the course of science quite properly shifts on the basis of what appear to be almost purely philosophical arguments.[34]

In regard to Grim's last example, I have suggested above that the philosophical difficulties with both dualism and materialistic identism provide a good reason for the scientific community to reconsider the metaphysical-scientific hypothesis that the ultimate constituents of nature are entirely devoid of experience and purpose. More generally, the bias toward the laboratory experiment in the philosophy of science has philosophically reflected the materialistic, nonecological assumption that things are essentially independent of their environments, so that the scientist abstracts from nothing essential in (say) removing cells from the human body or animals from a jungle to study them in a laboratory; it reflects the reductionistic assumption

677

that all complex things are really no more self-determining than the elementary parts in isolation, so that they should be subject to the same kind of strong laboratory repeatability;[35] it reflects the assumption that the main purpose of science is to predict and control repeatable phenomena; and it reflects the assumption that the domain of science is limited to the actual, especially the physical. Recognizing the wide domain of science means recognizing the necessity and hence appropriateness of diverse types of demonstrations, and the artificiality of holding up one type as the ideal.

(3) Besides not being limited to one domain or one type of demonstration, the scientific pursuit of truth is not tied to any set of contingent beliefs, meaning beliefs that are not inevitably presupposed by human practice, including thought, itself. Science is, therefore, not limited to any particular type of explanation.[36] For example, science is not tied to the belief that the elementary units of nature are devoid of sentience, intrinsic value, and internal relations, that time does not exist for these units, that the laws of nature for these units are eternal, that all natural phenomena result from the (currently four) forces rooted in these elementary units, that according- ly all causation is upward and that freedom and purposive or teleological causation are illusory,[37] that ideal entities other than mathematical forms play no role in nature, that there is no influence at a distance,[38] that the universe as a whole is not an organism which influences its parts, or that the universe and its evolution have no inherent meaning.

However, the fact that science as such is not permanently wedded to these contingent beliefs that reigned during the modern period does not mean that there are *no* beliefs that science as such must presuppose. If beliefs exist that are presupposed by human practice, including human thought, as such, then scientific practice and thought must presuppose them. Any theories that verbally deny them should therefore be eschewed on this ground alone. Although any such beliefs would transcend perspec- tivalism, because they by hypothesis would be common to all people, regardless of their worldview, the questions of whether there are any such beliefs, and if so what they are, are matters not for pontification from some supposedly neutral point of view, because no human point of view is neutral, but for proposals to be subjected to ongoing public discussion among those with diverse worldviews.[39]

To illustrate the types of beliefs intended and to show that they are not limited to innocuous, noncontroversial issues, I propose five principles as candidates. The first three principles relate to the crucial issue of causality. First, every event is causally influenced by other events. This principle rules out, for example, the idea that the universe arose out of absolute nothing- ness or out of pure possibility.[40] Second, neither human experience nor anything analogous to it is wholly determined by external events; rather, every genuine individual is partially self-determining. Incidentally, these first two principles, taken together, provide the basis for a scientific understanding of the activity of scientists themselves in terms of a combination of external and internal causes, which is increasingly seen to be necessary.[41]

Third, every event that exerts causal influence upon another event precedes that event temporally. (Self-determination or self-causation does not fall under this principle, because in it the same event is both cause and effect.) This principle rules out the notion of particles "going backwards in time," the notion of "backward causation," and any notion of "precognition" interpreted to mean that an event affected the knower before it happened or to mean that temporal relations are ultimately unreal.[42]

The final two principles proffered deal with science's concern for truth. These are the traditional principles of correspondence and noncontradiction, which are recovered in a postmodern context.

The idea that truth is a correspondence between statements and objective reality has been subject to a great deal of criticism. Much of this criticism is based upon confusion, inasmuch as the critics, often while verbally rejecting positivism, still presuppose the positivistic equation of the meaning of a statement with the means of its verification. The correspondence notion of truth properly refers only to the *meaning* of "truth," which is not even identical with the question of knowledge, let alone with the question of the justification of knowledge-claims. Much of the rejection of the relevance of the correspondence notion of truth has conflated truth with knowledge and then assumed that there could be no knowledge, in the sense of justified true belief, in the absence of adequate evidence to defend the knowledge-claim.[43]

However, much of the criticism of the notion of truth as correspondence is valid, especially in relation to naïvely realistic ideas of a one-to-one correspondence between statements and objective facts. For one thing, our ideas about physical objects, insofar as they are based primarily upon visual and tactile perception, surely involve enormous simplifications, constructions, and distortions of the realities existing independently of our perception. For another, language is inherently vague and, in any case, cannot as such "correspond" in the sense of being similar to nonlinguistic entities. Language aside, the way in which an idea can correspond to a physical object is not self-evident, because an idea can only be similar to another idea. Even many conceptions of truth as the correspondence between one's ideas and the ideas in another mind are held in falsely naïve ways, insofar as it is assumed that achieving truth, in the sense of absolute correspondence, is possible. Many critics go on from these valid starting points to argue that the meaning of a statement is exhausted by its relation to other statements, so that language constitutes a closed system, or in some other way argue that our statements can in no meaningful sense correspond to

679

any nonlinguistic entities. Science, in this extreme view, is a linguistic system disconnected from any larger world.

Postmodern organicism rejects this view of language. While language as such does not correspond to anything other than language, it expresses and evokes modes of apprehending nonlinguistic reality that can more or less accurately correspond to features of that reality.[44] Hence, science can lead to ways of thinking about the world that can increasingly approximate to patterns and structures genuinely characteristic of nature.

The other traditional principle involved in science's concern for truth is the principle of noncontradiction. It says that if two statements contradict each other, both cannot be true. This principle has also been subject to much valid criticism. Certainly two statements that appear to contradict each other may not in reality when one or both are more deeply understood. This can be because language is vague and elusive, because various levels of meaning exist, and/or because seemingly contradictory assertions may apply to diverse features of the referent or to different stages of its development. There are yet other objections to simple-minded applications of the principle of noncontradiction. But after all necessary subtleties and qualifications have been added, the principle remains valid and is necessarily presupposed even in attempts to refute it. Accordingly, science must aim for coherence between all its propositions and between its propositions and all those that are inevitably presupposed in human practice and thought in general. (Obtaining such coherence is indeed the primary method of checking for correspondence.)

All of these principles are in harmony with postmodern organicism. Indeed, they are not epistemically neutral principles but ones that are, especially in regard to their exact formulation, suggested by postmodern organicism. However, the claim is made that they are, in fact, implicit in human practice, including human thought (although not, of course, in the content of all the theories produced by human thought). If this claim is sustained through widespread conversation, then this set of beliefs (along with any others that could prove their universality in the same way) should be considered to belong to science as such.[45]

Notes

1 Mary Hesse points out that the rejection of action-at-a-distance in favor of action-by-contact explanations was based on the replacement of all organismic and psychological explanations by mechanical ones (*Forces and Fields: The Concept of Action at a Distance in the History of Physics* [Totowa, NJ: Littlefield, Adams & Co, 1965], 98, 291). Richard Westfall makes clear how central was the change:

the mechanical philosophy also banished . . . attractions of any kind. No scorn was too great to heap upon such a notion. From one end of the century to another, the idea of attractions, the action of one body upon another with which it is not in contact, was anathema. . . . An attraction was an occult virtue, and 'occult virtue' was the mechanical philosophy's ultimate term of opprobrium.

Westfall reports that Christiaan Huygens wrote that he did not care whether Newton was a Cartesian "as long as he doesn't serve us up conjectures such as attractions"("The Influence of Alchemy on Newton," Marsha P. Hanen, Margaret J. Osler, and Robert G. Weyant (eds), *Science, Pseudo-Science and Society* [Waterloo, Ontario: Wilfrid Laurier University Press, 1980], 145–70, esp. 147, 150). Brian Easlea has provided convincing evidence that the desire to rule out the possibility of attraction at a distance was, in fact, the main motivation behind the mechanical philosophy and its denial of all hidden qualities within matter; see his *Witch Hunting, Magic and the New Philosophy: An Introduction to Debates of the Scientific Revolution 1450–1750* (Atlantic Highlands, NJ: Humanities Press, 1980), esp. 93–5, 108–15, 121, 132, 135.

2 Neal C. Gillespie, *Charles Darwin and the Problem of Creation* (Chicago: University of Chicago Press, 1979), 55–6, 120, 139–40.

3 Michael Ghiselin, *The Economy of Nature and the Evolution of Sex* (Berkeley: University of California Press, 1974), x, 13.

4 Jacques Monod, *Chance and Necessity: An Essay on the Natural Philosophy of Modern Biology* (New York: Vintage Books, 1972), 21.

5 Ibid., 172–3, 171.

6 Clark Hull, *Principles of Behavior: An Introduction to Behavior Theory* (New York: Appleton-Century, 1943), 29.

7 B. F. Skinner, *Beyond Freedom and Dignity* (New York: Vintage Books, 1972), 12, 191, 196.

8 B. F. Skinner, *Science and Human Behavior* (New York: Free Press, 1965), 6, 447.

9 William R. Uttal, *The Psychobiology of Mind* (Hillsdale, NJ: L. Erlbaum Associates, 1978), 9, 10, 27, 52–3.

10 John G. Taylor, *Superminds* (London: Macmillan, 1975).

11 John G. Taylor, *Science and the Supernatural* (London: Panther Books, 1981), 6, 69, 108, 164.

12 Ibid., 25–30, 83, 165–9. The issue here is not whether Taylor's original evidence was solid (which many parapsychologists doubt), but only that the modern worldview by itself led him to deny his own data.

13 James A. Alcock, "Parapsychology as a 'Spiritual' Science," Paul Kurtz (ed.), *A Skeptic's Handbook of Parapsychology* (Buffalo, NY: Prometheus Books, 1985), 537–65, esp. 562. Interestingly enough, Alcock makes his claim even though he realizes that a nonmaterialistic science is advocated by John Eccles, a Nobel prizewinner, and Karl Popper, the most influential philosopher of science of the twentieth century (558). Also, he repeats the conventional idea that "the path of science . . . [was] laid down upon the foundation of materialism," even though he had reviewed recent writings of Eugene Klaaren, Martin Rudwick,

and others who show that this was not true, especially for Isaac Newton (562, 555).

14 Ilya Prigogine and Isabelle Stengers, *Order Out of Chaos: Man's New Dialogue with Nature* (New York: Bantam Books, 1984), xxvii.

15 Einstein's statement, which occurred in a letter, is cited in Banesh Hoffman (with Helen Dukas), *Albert Einstein: Creator and Rebel* (New York: Viking Press, 1972), 258.

16 P. C. W. Davies, *The Physics of Time Asymmetry* (Berkeley: University of California Press, 1976), 151.

17 Larry Dossey, *Space, Time and Medicine* (Boulder, Co.: Shambhala, 1982), 152, 153. Many people, rightly assuming that linear time has been a central feature of modernity, especially in the notions of *progress* and *evolution*, have wrongly assumed that the assertion of the ultimate unreality of time, vouchsafed by physics, would be a postmodern idea, liberating us from one of the shackles of modernity. The truth is that Western (as well as most Eastern) thought has generally held temporality to be unreal for the ultimate form of being, be it Plato's ideas (in one side of his thought), Aristotle's unmoved mover, the God of classical theists such as Augustine, Maimonides, and Thomas Aquinas, or the ultimate particles of modern physics. Although temporality has been central for Western thought and experience, especially in the modern period, it has seldom, as Stephen Toulmin and June Goodfield have shown (*The Discovery of Time* [New York: Harper & Row, 1965]), been considered to be fundamental, in the sense of real for the most real type of existent. Twentieth-century physics, in speaking of the ultimate unreality of time (largely through the influence of the interpretation given to relativity theory by Einstein with his Spinozistic leanings), has thereby not introduced a new idea but simply revitalized an old one. For further discussion, see the introduction to David Ray Griffin (ed.), *Physics and the Ultimate Significance of Time: Bohm, Prigogine, and Process Philosophy* (Albany: State University of New York Press, 1986).

18 Steven Weinberg, *The First Three Minutes: A Modern View of the Origin of the Universe* (New York: Basic Books, 1977), 154.

19 D. M. Armstrong, "The Nature of Mind," C. V. Borst (ed.), *The Mind–Brain Identity Theory* (London: Macmillan, 1979), 75, 67.

20 Joseph Wood Krutch, *The Modern Temper: A Study and a Confession* (New York: Harcourt, Brace & World [A Harvest Book], 1956), xi; emphasis added. By 1956, Krutch had decided that, of the two options noted in that final sentence, "Social Engineering rather than Existentialist resignation [has become] the dominant religion of today" (xiii). Krutch himself had in the meantime come to reject the view, which he still regarded as "the most prevalent educated opinion," that "there is no escaping the scientific demonstration that religion, morality, and the human being's power to make free choices are merely figments of the imagination" (xii). He no longer believed that "the mechanistic, materialistic, and deterministic conclusions of science do have to be accepted as fact and hence as the premises upon which any philosophy of life or any estimate of man and his future must be based" (xiii). His reasons for this change of mind were set forth in *The Measure of Man: On Freedom, Human*

Values, Survival and the Modern Temper (Indianapolis, Ind.: Bobbs-Merrill, 1953), which is in harmony with the present volume, while not going as far and of course not having the advantage of the historical and scientific evidence that has appeared in the intervening decades.

21 Robert E. Egner and Lester E. Dennon (eds), *The Basic Writings of Bertrand Russell 1903–1959* (New York: Simon & Schuster, 1961), 67.

22 Krutch says of modern individuals: "It is easy for . . . all of us to believe that a man may be 'the product of' any one of a number of external 'forces'. . . . The one thing which we find it hard to believe is that what he might be 'the product of' is himself." And Krutch gives one of the reasons why: "The idea that [the realm of the subjective] might be autonomous and creative suggests the possibility that the methods which were working everywhere else might not work there. Concern with it was unscientific and therefore unintelligent" (*The Measure of Man*, 254, 117).

23 For a discussion and critique of Hans-Georg Gadamer's methodological dualism between hermeneutics and science, see Joel C. Weinsheimer, *Gadamer's Hermeneutics: A Reading of Truth and Method* (New Haven, Conn.: Yale University Press, 1985), 1–41; on Jürgen Habermas's views, see Richard J. Bernstein (ed.), *Habermas and Modernity* (Cambridge, Mass.: MIT Press, 1985), especially the essays by Martin Jay, Thomas McCarthy, and Albrecht Wellmer.

24 See Charles Hartshorne, "The Compound Individual," Otis H. Lee (ed.), *Philosophical Essays for Alfred North Whitehead* (New York: Longmans Green, 1936), 193–220.

25 Of course, to understand a computer one must take into account final causation in the sense of the purpose for which it was made. But throughout this discussion the subject is internal, immanent final causation, not external, imposed final causation.

26 Sandra Harding supports this change, pointing out that physics, among other restrictions, "looks at either simple systems or simple aspects of complex systems," so that it need not deal with the difficult question of intentional causality (*The Science Question in Feminism* [Ithaca, NY: Cornell University Press, 1986], 44, 46).

27 For a development of the ideas in these two sentences, see the writings of psychiatrist Jule Eisenbud, whom philosopher Stephen Braude has called "parapsychology's premier living theoretician." Many of Eisenbud's essays have been collected in *Parapsychology and the Unconscious* (Berkeley, Calif.: North Atlantic Books, 1983), the "Preface" of which contains the accolade by Braude (7). For the various ideas, see 21, 22, 40, 72, 125, 167, 173, 183. On the resultant unlikelihood of obtaining repetable experiments in the ordinary sense, see 156–61. These points are also supported in Braude's own *The Limits of Influence: Psychokinesis and the Philosophy of Science* (London: Routledge & Kegan Paul, 1986), esp. 7–10, 23, 70, 278.

28 [Contemporary philosopher of science Paul Feyerabend is famously regarded as an "anarchist" who denies that science is true. The author argues (in an earlier note) that Feyerabend merely offers his critique as a therapeutic

attempt to subvert the notion that modern science is the only method yielding truth.]

29 My discussion in this and the following paragraph is dependent upon Patrick Grim, *Philosophy of Science and the Occult* (Albany: State University of New York, 1982), 314–15; Ken Wilber, *Quantum Questions: Mystical Writings of the World's Great Physicists* (Boston: Shambala, 1984), 13–14; and Nicholas Rescher, "The Unpredictability of Future Science," Robert S. Cohen and Larry Lauden (eds), *Physics, Philosophy and Psychoanalysis: Essays in Honor of Adolf Grünbaum* (Dordrecht: D. Reidel, 1983), 153–68.

30 It is often said that power and knowledge (or truth) have been the twin aims of modern science (e.g. Evelyn Fox Keller, *Reflections on Gender and Science*, 71). Of these twin aims, traditional descriptions spoke mainly of the quest for truth, while recent appraisals, whether condemnatory or positivistic, have seen the drive for power as the central aim. My position is that, while much of modern science has sought those truths that would provide power over nature (and sometimes thereby over other humans), it is not the quest for power that makes modern science "science" but the quest for truth (in the way specified in the second criterion), regardless of how limited these truths are and of the ulterior purposes for which they are sought . . .

31 Nicholas Rescher, "The Unpredictability of Future Science," 165, says: "Domain limitations purport to put entire sectors of fact wholly outside the effective range of scientific explanation, maintaining that an entire range of phenomena in nature defies scientific rationalization." See also Ken Wilber, *Quantum Questions*, 14.

32 This is one topic on which I disagree with Rupert Sheldrake, who wishes to exclude the topic of the origin of laws from science, assigning it instead to theology or metaphysics; see the final chapter of his *A New Science of Life*.

33 Evelyn Fox Keller, *Reflections on Gender and Science* (New Haven, Conn.: Yale University Press, 1985), 131–6.

34 Patrick Grim, *Philosophy of Science and the Occult*, 315.

35 Jule Eisenbud (*Psi and Psychoanalysis* [New York: Grune & Stratton, 1970], 96) says that one particular kind of repeatability has given parts of physics such reliability that "few people (strangely) question its right to provide a model of 'reality'." But, as he says, this kind of repeatability is only one of many considerations in authentication, not relevant for many questions in geology, meteorology, astronomy, biology, and much of psychology. Both Kurtz and Alcock [see Paul Kurtz, *A Skeptic's Handbook of Parapsychology* (Buffalo, NY: Prometheus, 1985) and James Alcock's essay, "Parapsychology as a 'Spiritual' Science," in Kurtz, pp. 537–65.] have claimed that parapsychological experiments, to be acceptable, would have to exemplify "strong" repeatability, meaning that, in Alcock's words, "any competent researcher following the prescribed procedure can obtain the reported effect" (540). But if the kind of phenomenon with which parapsychology is concerned is held to be an inherently elusive, not consciously controllable one, as Eisenbud and Stephen Braude hold (see note 28 above), this requirement for strong replicability

amounts to a "Catch-22": parapsychologists could only prove that it exists by proving that it does not!

36   Nicholas Rescher ("The Unpredictability of Future Science," 163) says: "The contention that this or that explanatory resource is inherently unscientific should always be met with instant scorn. For the unscientific can only lie on the side of process and not that of product – on the side of *modes* of explanation and not its *mechanism*; of arguments rather than phenomena."

37   Rescher (ibid., 166) says that "there is no reason why, in human affairs any more than in quantum theory, the boundaries of science should be so drawn as to exclude the unpredictable." Long ago, William James said that "the spirit and principles of Science are mere affairs of method; there is nothing in them that need hinder Science from dealing successfully with a world in which personal forces are the starting points of new effects" ("Presidential Address," *Proceedings of the Society for Psychical Research*, 12 [1896–97], 2–10, esp. 10).

38   Rescher (ibid., 169) says:

> Not only can we never claim with confidence that the science of tomorrow will not resolve the issues that the science of today sees as intractable, but one can never be sure that the science of tomorrow will not endorse what the science of today rejects. This is why it is infinitely risky to speak of this or that explanatory resource (action at a distance, stochastic processes, mesmerism, etc.) as inherently unscientific. Even if X lies outside the range of science as we nowadays construe it, it by no means follows that X lies outside science as such.

39   If there are such common beliefs, their recognition by members of diverse linguistic communities is, while difficult, not impossible. Even though a given worldview will predispose its adherents to recognize some such beliefs while ignoring, distorting, or even verbally denying other such beliefs that are noticed by adherents of other worldviews, it is possible, when the search for truth through public demonstration is sincere, to recognize such beliefs through conversation and self- observation.

40   In spite of my agreement, expressed in prior notes, with Nicholas Rescher's formal ideas, I cannot accept his substantive idea that actualities could have emerged out of a realm of mere possibility. I do not see how we can abandon the notion that agency requires actuality, and hence the "hoary dogma," as Rescher calls it, that *ex nihilo nihil fit*. I have reviewed Rescher's *The Riddle of Existence: An Essay in Idealistic Metaphysics* (Lanham, Md.: University of America Press, 1985) in *Canadian Philosophical Reviews*, December, 1986, 531–2.

41   Sandra Harding points out that the one-sided attempts to explain science either from a purely externalist or a purely internalist approach lead to paradox. The externalist approach, which understands the development of science in terms of external causes alone, leads to a self-refuting relativism. "Why should changes in economic, technological, and political arrangements make the new ideas reflecting these arrangements better ideas? Why shouldn't we regard the externalist program itself as simply an epiphenomenon of

nineteenth- and twentieth-century social relations destined to be replaced as history moves along?" (*The Science Question in Feminism*, 215). The internalist or intentionalist approach praises natural science for showing that all natural and social phenomena are to be explained in externalistic terms, then supports the truth of this idea by "defending an intentionalist approach to explaining the development of science alone" (212). What we need is an approach that recognizes the two-way causal influences between ideas and social relations, and which thereby allows us both to understand how "social arrangements shape human consciousness" and "to retain the internalist assumption that not all beliefs are equally good" (209, 231, 214). . . .

42 I have dealt with these issues in "Introduction: Time and the Fallacy of Misplaced Concreteness" in *Physics and the Ultimate Significance of Time*; there is a brief discussion of apparent precognition on 30–1. See also Jule Eisenbud, *Parapsychology and the Unconscious*, 45. Although Stephen Braude has not changed his earlier opinion that arguments against the very intelligibility of backward causation are unconvincing, perhaps because he has not developed a general theory of causation (*The Limits of Influence*, 261), he has concluded that the idea is very problematic, and that ostensible precognition can be explained without resort to this idea (261–77).

43 Frederick Suppe has pointed out that most discussions of the idea of knowledge as "justified true belief" have assumed that "knowing that X is true" entails "knowing that one knows that X is true," i.e. having adequate evidence to defend the claim to know that it is true (*The Structure of Scientific Theories* [Urbana: University of Illinois, 1977], 717–28). This unjustified requirement, which leads to a vicious infinite regress, lies behind Hume's skeptical attacks on the possibility of knowledge and most recent rejections, by Kuhn, Feyerabend, and others, of the relevance of the correspondence notion of truth to scientific beliefs (718, 719, 723). Suppe argues rightly for "a separation of the role of evidence in the rational evaluation and defense of knowledge claims from the role evidence plays in obtaining knowledge" (725). With that separation, we can maintain the traditional definitions of knowledge as justified true belief and of truth as correspondence of belief to reality. None of this entails, I would insist perhaps more strongly than Suppe, that the modern scientific worldview is true, or that any of the current scientific theories gives us anything approaching the whole truth about their referents. Indeed, it is only if we hold to these traditional definitions of truth and knowledge that we have a rational standard in terms of which to criticize the dominant contemporary knowledge-claims.

44 The way in which panexperiential philosophy can make sense of a notion of correspondence is to be dealt with in essays in volume 4 of this series.

45 These principles, especially the latter four, have all, in fact, been denied by modern science-related thought. However, their explicit denial has been accompanied by implicit affirmation, producing massive incoherence. The reason for their explicit denial is *not* that they conflict with the implications of any other equally universal principles but that they conflict with the implications of contingent beliefs of modernity, which have been discussed above.

chapter forty-one

"Towards a Postmodern Pedagogy"

Henry A. Giroux

American educational theorist, Henry Giroux (1943–) proposes a "border peda-gogy" that rejects many of the traditional aims of education. Education for Giroux is intrinsically a political process aimed at producing a democratic egalitarian society. The primary contemporary obstacle to this end is the marginalization of social groups by racism and sexism. In response, border pedagogy aims to bring students to an experiential understanding of those deemed "other" by their official culture. In the piece that follows Giroux summarizes what are in effect the basic principles of a multicultural educational practise.

> As long as people are people, democracy in the full sense of the word will always be no more than an ideal. One may approach it as one would a horizon, in ways that may be better or worse, but it can never be fully attained. In this sense, you too, are merely approaching democracy. You have thousands of problems of all kinds, as other countries do. But you have one great advantage: You have been approaching democracy uninterruptedly for more than 200 years.
>
> Vaclav Havel, cited in *The New York Times*, March 18, 1990

> How on earth can these prestigious persons in Washington ramble on in their sub-intellectual way about the "end of history"? As I look forward into the twenty-first century I sometimes agonize about the times in which my grandchildren and their children will live. It is not so much the rise in population as the rise in universal material expectations of the globe's huge population that will be straining its resources to the very limits. North-

---

Henry A. Giroux, "Towards a Postmodern Pedagogy," section of the Introduction to *Postmodernism, Feminism, and Cultural Politics* (Albany: State University of New York Press, 1991), pp. 45–55.

687

South antagonisms will certainly sharpen, and religious and national fundamentalisms will become more intransigent. The struggle to bring consumer greed within moderate control, to find a level of low growth and satisfaction that is not at the expense of the disadvantaged and poor, to defend the environment and to prevent ecological disasters, to share more equitably the world's resources and to insure their renewal – all this is agenda enough for continuation of "history."

E. P. Thompson, *The Nation*, January 29, 1990

A striking character of the totalitarian system is its peculiar coupling of human demoralization and mass depoliticizing. Consequently, battling this system requires a conscious appeal to morality and an inevitable involvement in politics.

A. Michnik, *New York Times Magazine*, March 11, 1990.

All these quotes stress, implicitly or explicitly, the importance of politics and ethics to democracy. In the first quote, the newly elected president of Czechoslovakia, Vaclav Havel, addressing a joint session of Congress reminds the American people that democracy is an ideal that is filled with possibilities but always has to be seen as part of an ongoing struggle for freedom and human dignity. As a playwright and former political prisoner, Havel is a living embodiment of such a struggle. In the second quote, E. P. Thompson, the English peace activist and historian, reminds the American public that history has not ended but needs to be opened up in order to engage the many problems and possibilities that human beings will have to face in the twenty-first century. In the third quote, Adam Michnik, a founder of Poland's Workers' Defense Committee and an elected member of the Polish parliament, provides an ominous insight into one of the central features of totalitarianism, whether on the Right or the Left. He points to a society that fears democratic politics while simultaneously reproducing in people a sense of massive collective despair. None of these writers are from the United States and all of them are caught up in the struggle to recapture the Enlightenment model of freedom, agency, and democracy while simultaneously attempting to deal with the conditions of a postmodern world.

All of these statements serve to highlight the inability of the American public to grasp the full significance of the democraticization of Eastern Europe in terms of what it reveals about the nature of our own democracy. In Eastern Europe and elsewhere there is a strong call for the primacy of the political and the ethical as a foundation for democratic public life whereas in the United States there is an ongoing refusal of the discourse of politics and ethics. Elected politicians from both sides of the established parties in the Congress complain that American politics is about "trivializ-ation, atomization, and paralysis." Politicians as diverse as Lee Atwater, the Republican Party chairman, and Walter Mondale, former Vice President, agree that we have entered into a time in which much of the American public believes that "Bull permeates everything . . . [and that] we've got a kind of politics of irrelevance" (Oreskes, *The New York Times*, March 18, 1990, 16). At the same time, a number of polls indicate that while the youth of Poland, Czechoslovakia, and East Germany are extending the frontiers of democracy, American youth are both unconcerned and largely ill-prepared to struggle for and keep democracy alive in the twenty-first century.

Rather than being a model of democracy, the United States has become indifferent to the need to struggle for the conditions that make democracy a substantive rather than lifeless activity. At all levels of national and daily life, the breadth and depth of democratic relations are being rolled back. We have become a society that appears to demand less rather than more of democracy. In some quarters, democracy has actually become subvers-ive. What does this suggest for developing some guiding principles in order to rethink the purpose and meaning of education and critical pedagogy within the present crises? Since I outline the particulars of a postmodern critical pedagogy in the last chapter of this book, I want to conclude with some suggestive principles for a critical pedagogy that emerge out of my discussion of the most important aspects of modernism, postmodernism, and postmodern feminism.

1. Education must be understood as producing not only knowledge but also political subjects. Rather than rejecting the language of politics, critical pedagogy must link public education to the imperatives of a critical democracy (Dewey, 1916; Giroux, 1988a). Critical pedagogy needs to be informed by a public philosophy dedicated to returning schools to their primary task: places of critical education in the service of creating a public sphere of citizens who are able to exercise power over their own lives and especially over the conditions of knowledge production and acquisition. This is a critical pedagogy defined, in part, by the attempt to create the lived experience of empowerment for the vast majority. In other words, the language of critical pedagogy needs to construct schools as democratic public spheres. In part, this means educators need to develop a critical pedagogy in which the knowledge, habits, and skills of critical rather than simply good citizenship are taught and practiced. This means providing students with the opportunity to develop the critical capacity to challenge and transform existing social and political forms, rather than simply adapt to them. It also means providing students with the skills they will need to locate themselves in history, find their own voices, and provide the convictions and compassion necessary for exercising civic courage, taking

689

risks, and furthering the habits, customs, and social relations that are essential to democratic public forms. In effect, critical pedagogy needs to be grounded in a keen sense of the importance of constructing a political vision from which to develop an educational project as part of a wider discourse for revitalizing democratic public life. A critical pedagogy for democracy cannot be reduced, as some educators, politicians, and groups have argued, to forcing students to say the Pledge of Allegiance at the beginning of every school day or to speak and think only in the language of dominant English (Hirsch Jr, 1987). A critical pedagogy for democracy does not begin with test scores but with the questions: What kinds of citizens do we hope to produce through public education in a postmodern culture? What kind of society do we want to create in the context of the present shifting cultural and ethnic borders? How can we reconcile the notions of difference and equality with the imperatives of freedom and justice?

2. Ethics must be seen as a central concern of critical pedagogy. This suggests that educators attempt to understand more fully how different discourses offer students diverse ethical referents for structuring their relationship to the wider society. But it also suggests that educators go beyond the postmodern notion of understanding how student experiences are shaped within different ethical discourses. Educators must also come to view ethics and politics as a relationship between the self and the other. Ethics, in this case, is not a matter of individual choice or relativism but a social discourse grounded in struggles that refuse to accept needless human suffering and exploitation. Thus, ethics is taken up as a struggle against inequality and as a discourse for expanding basic human rights. This points to a notion of ethics attentive to both the issue of abstract rights and those contexts which produce particular stories, struggles, and histories. In pedagogical terms, an ethical discourse needs to be taken up with regards to the relations of power, subject positions, and social practices it activates (Simon, forthcoming). This is neither an ethics of essentialism nor relativism. It is an ethical discourse grounded in historical struggles and attentive to the construction of social relations free of injustice. The quality of ethical discourse, in this case, is not simply grounded in difference but in the issue of how justice arises out of concrete historical circumstances (Shapiro, 1990).

3. As Sharon Welch indicates[i] critical pedagogy needs to focus on the issue of difference in an ethically challenging and politically transformative way. There are at least two notions of difference at work here. First,

---

[i] Sharon Welch, "An Ethic of Solidarity and Difference," in Henry A. Giroux, *Posmodernism, Feminism and Cultural Politics: Redrawing Educational Boundaries* (Albany: State University of New York, 1991), pp. 83–99.

difference can be incorporated into a critical pedagogy as part of an attempt to understand how student identities and subjectivities are constructed in multiple and contradictory ways. In this case, identity is explored through its own historicity and complex subject positions. The category of student experience should not be limited pedagogically to students exercising self-reflection but opened up as a race, gender, and class specific construct to include the diverse ways in which their experiences and identities have been constituted in different historical and social formations. Second, critical pedagogy can focus on how differences between groups develop and are sustained around both enabling and disabling sets of relations. In this instance, difference becomes a marker for understanding how social groups are constituted in ways that are integral to the functioning of any democratic society. Difference in this context does not focus only on charting spatial, racial, ethnic, or cultural differences but also analyzes historical differences that manifest themselves in public struggles.

As part of a language of critique, teachers can make problematic how different subjectivities are positioned within a historically specific range of ideologies and social practices that inscribe students in modes of behavior that subjugate, infantilize, and corrupt. Similarly, such a language can analyze how differences within and between social groups are constructed and sustained both within and outside the schools in webs of domination, subordination, hierarchy, and exploitation. As part of a language of possibility, teachers can explore the opportunity to construct knowledge/power relations in which multiple narratives and social practices are constructed around a politics and pedagogy of difference that offers students the opportunity to read the world differently, resist the abuse of power and privilege, and construct alternative democratic communities. Difference in this case cannot be seen as simply a politics of assertion, of simply affirming one's voice or sense of the common good, it must be developed within practices in which differences can be affirmed and transformed in their articulation with categories central to public life: democracy, citizenship, public spheres. In both political and pedagogical terms, the category of difference must be central to the notion of democratic community.

4. Critical pedagogy needs a language that allows for competing solidarities and political vocabularies that do not reduce the issues of power, justice, struggle, and inequality to a single script, a master narrative that suppresses the contingent, historical, and the everyday as a serious object of study (Cherryholmes, 1988). This suggests that curriculum knowledge not be treated as a sacred text but developed as part of an ongoing engagement with a variety of narratives and traditions that can be re-read and re-formulated in politically different terms. At issue here is constructing a discourse of textual authority that is power-sensitive and developed as

691

part of a wider analysis of the struggle over culture fought out at the levels of curricula knowledge, pedagogy, and the exercise of institutional power (Aronowitz and Giroux, 1991). This is not merely an argument against a canon, but one that disavows the very category. Knowledge has to be constantly re-examined in terms of its limits and rejected as a body of information that only has to be passed down to students. As Ernesto Laclau (1988a) has pointed out, setting limits to the answers given by what can be judged as a valued tradition (a matter of argument also) is an important political act. What Laclau is suggesting is the possibility for students to creatively appropriate the past as part of a living dialogue, an affirmation of the multiplicity of narratives, and the need to judge them not as timeless or as monolithic discourses, but as social and historical inventions that can be refigured in the interests of creating more democratic forms of public life. This points to the possibility for creating pedagogical practices characterized by the open exchange of ideas, the proliferation of dialogue, and the material conditions for the expression of individual and social freedom.

5. Critical pedagogy needs to create new forms of knowledge through its emphasis on breaking down disciplinary boundaries and creating new spaces where knowledge can be produced. In this sense, critical pedagogy must be reclaimed as a cultural politics and a form of counter-memory. This is not merely an epistemological issue, but one of power, ethics, and politics. Critical pedagogy as a cultural politics points to the necessity of inserting the struggle over the production and creation of knowledge as part of a broader attempt to create a public sphere of citizens who are able to exercise power over their lives and the social and political forms through which society is governed. As a form of counter-memory, critical pedagogy starts with everyday and the particular as a basis for learning, it reclaims the historical and the popular as part of an ongoing effort to legitimate the voices of those who have been silenced, and to inform the voices of those who have been located within narratives that are monolithic and totalizing. At stake here is a pedagogy that provides the knowledge, skills, and habits for students and others to read history in ways that enable them to reclaim their identities in the interests of constructing forms of life that are more democratic and more just. This is a struggle that deepens the pedagogical meaning of the political and the political meaning of the pedagogical. In the first instance, it raises important questions about how students and others are constructed as agents within particular histories, cultures, and social relations. Against the monolith of culture, it posits the conflicting terrain of cultures shaped within asymmetrical relations of power, grounded in diverse historical struggles. Similarly, culture has to be understood as part of the discourse of power and inequality. As a pedagogical issue, the relationship between culture and power is evident in

questions such as "Whose cultures are appropriated as our own? How is marginality normalized?" (Popkewitz, 1988, 77). To insert the primacy of culture as a pedagogical and political issue is to make central how schools function in the shaping of particular identities, values, and histories by producing and legitimating specific cultural narratives and resources. In the second instance, asserting the pedagogical aspects of the political raises the issue of how difference and culture can be taken up as pedagogical practices and not merely as political categories. For example, how does difference matter as a pedagogical category if educators and cultural workers have to make knowledge meaningful before it can become critical and transformative? Or what does it mean to engage the tension between being theoretically correct and pedagogically wrong? These are concerns and tensions that make the relationship between the political and the pedagogical both mutually informing and problematic.

6. The Enlightenment notion of reason needs to be reformulated within a critical pedagogy. First, educators need to be skeptical regarding any notion of reason that purports to reveal the truth by denying its own historical construction and ideological principles. Reason is not innocent and any viable notion of critical pedagogy cannot exercise forms of authority that emulate totalizing forms of reason that appear to be beyond criticism and dialogue. This suggests that we reject claims to objectivity in favor of partial epistemologies that recognize the historical and socially constructed nature of their own knowledge claims and methodologies. In this way, curriculum can be viewed as a cultural script that introduces students to particular forms of reason which structure specific stories and ways of life. Reason in this sense implicates and is implicated in the intersection of power, knowledge, and politics. Second, it is not enough to reject an essentialist or universalist defense of reason. Instead, the limits of reason must be extended to recognizing other ways in which people learn or take up particular subject positions. In this case, educators need to understand more fully how people learn through concrete social relations, through the ways in which the body is positioned (Grumet, 1988), through the construction of habit and intuition, and through the production and investment of desire and affect. . . .

7. Critical pedagogy needs to regain a sense of alternatives by combining a language of critique and possibility. Postmodern feminism exemplifies this in both its critique of patriarchy and its search to construct new forms of identity and social relations. It is worth noting that teachers can take up this issue around a number of considerations. First, educators need to construct a language of critique that combines the issue of limits with the discourse of freedom and social responsibility. In other words, the question of freedom needs to be engaged dialectically not only as one of individual rights but also as part of the discourse of social responsibility. That is,

693

whereas freedom remains an essential category in establishing the conditions for ethical and political rights, it must also be seen as a force to be checked if it is expressed in modes of individual and collective behavior that threaten the ecosystem or produce forms of violence and oppression against individuals and social groups. Second, critical pedagogy needs to explore in programmatic terms a language of possibility that is capable of thinking risky thoughts, that engages a project of hope, and points to the horizon of the "not yet." A language of possibility does not have to dissolve into a reified form of utopianism; instead, it can be developed as a precondition for nourishing convictions that summon up the courage to imagine a different and more just world and to struggle for it. A language of moral and political possibility is more than an outmoded vestige of humanist discourse. It is central to responding not only with compassion to human beings who suffer and agonize but also with a politics and a set of pedagogical practices that can refigure and change existing narratives of domination into images and concrete instances of a future which is worth fighting for.

There is a certain cynicism that characterizes the language of the Left at the present moment. Central to this position is the refusal of all utopian images, all appeals to "a language of possibility." Such refusals are often made on the grounds that "utopian discourse" is a strategy employed by the Right and therefore is ideologically tainted. Or, the very notion of possibility is dismissed as an impractical and therefore useless category. In my mind, this represents less a serious critique than a refusal to move beyond the language of exhaustion and despair. Essential to developing a response to this position is a discriminating notion of possibility, one which makes a distinction between a discourse characterized as either "dystopian" or utopian. In the former, the appeal to the future is grounded in a form of nostalgic romanticism, with its call for a return to a past, which more often than not serves to legitimate relations of domination and oppression. Similarly, in Constance Penley's terms a "dystopian" discourse often "limits itself to solutions that are either individualist or bound to a romanticized notion of guerilla-like small-group resistance. The true atrophy of the utopian imagination is this: we can imagine the future but we *cannot* conceive the kind of collective political strategies necessary to change or ensure that future" (Penley, 1989, 122). In contrast to the language of dystopia, a utopian discourse rejects apocalyptic emptiness and nostalgic imperialism and sees history as open and society worth struggling for in the image of an alternative future. This is the language of the "not yet", one in which the imagination is redeemed and nourished in the effort to construct new relationships fashioned out of strategies of collective resistance based on a critical recognition of both what society is and what it might become. Paraphrasing Walter Benjamin, this is a discourse of imagination and hope that pushes history against the grain.[ii] Nancy Fraser (1989) illuminates this sentiment by emphasizing the importance of a language of possibility for the project of social change: "It allows for the possibility of a radical democratic politics in which immanent critique and transfigurative desire mingle with one another" (107).

8. Critical pedagogy needs to develop a theory of teachers as transformative intellectuals who occupy specifiable political and social locations. Rather than defining teacher work through the narrow language of professionalism, a critical pedagogy needs to ascertain more carefully what the role of teachers might be as cultural workers engaged in the production of ideologies and social practices. This is not a call for teachers to become wedded to some abstract ideal that removes them from everyday life, or one that intends for them to become prophets of perfection and certainty; on the contrary, it is a call for teachers to undertake social criticism not as outsiders but as public intellectuals who address the most social and political issues of their neighbourhood, nation, and the wider global world. As public and transformative intellectuals, teachers have an opportunity to make organic connections with the historical traditions that provide them and their students with a voice, history, and sense of belonging. It is a position marked by a moral courage and criticism that does not require educators to step back from society in the manner of the "objective" teacher, but to distance themselves from those power relations that subjugate, oppress, and diminish other human beings. Teachers need to take up criticism from within, to develop pedagogical practices that not only heighten the possibilities for critical consciousness but also for transformative action (Walzer, 1987). In this perspective, teachers would be involved in the invention of critical discourses and democratic social relations. Critical pedagogy would represent itself as the active construction rather than transmission of particular ways of life. More specifically, as transformative intellectuals, teachers can engage in the invention of languages so as to provide spaces for themselves and their students to rethink their experiences in terms that both name relations of oppression and offer ways in which to overcome them.

9. Central to the notion of critical pedagogy is a politics of voice that combines a postmodern notion of difference with a feminist emphasis on the primacy of the political. This suggests taking up the relationship between the personal and the political in a way that does not collapse the political into the personal but strengthens the relationship between the two so as to engage rather than withdraw from addressing those institutional forms and structures that contribute to racism, sexism, and class exploitation. This suggests some important pedagogical interventions. First the self

[ii] Walter Benjamin (1892–1940), Frankfurt School aesthetician.

must be seen as a primary site of politicization. That is, the issue of how the self is constructed in multiple and complex ways must be analyzed both as part of a language of affirmation and a broader understanding of how identities are inscribed in and between various social, cultural, and historical formations. To engage issues regarding the construction of the self is to address questions of history, culture, community, language, gender, race, and class. It is to raise questions regarding what pedagogical practices need to be employed that allow students to speak in dialogical contexts that affirm, interrogate, and extend their understandings of themselves and the global contexts in which they live. Such a position recognizes that students have several or multiple identities, but also asserts the importance of offering students a language that allows them to reconstruct their moral and political energies in the service of creating a more just and equitable social order, one that undermines relations of hierarchy and domination. Second, a politics of voice must offer pedagogical and political strategies that affirm the primacy of the social, intersubjective, and collective. To focus on voice is not meant to simply affirm the stories that students tell, it is not meant to simply glorify the possibility for narration. Such a position often degenerates into a form of narcissism, a carthartic experience that is reduced to naming anger without the benefit of theorizing in order to both understand its underlying causes and what it means to work collectively to transform the structures of domination responsible for oppressive social relations. Raising one's consciousness has increasingly become a pretext for legitimating hegemonic forms of separatism buttressed by self-serving appeals to the primacy of experience. What is often expressed in such appeals is an anti-intellectualism that retreats from any viable form of political engagement, especially one willing to address and transform diverse forms of oppression. The call to simply affirm one's voice has increasingly been reduced to a pedagogical process that is as reactionary as it is inward looking. A more radical notion of voice should begin with what Bell Hooks (1989) calls a critical attention to theorizing experience as part of a broader politics of engagement. In referring specifically to feminist pedagogy, she argues that the discourse of confession and memory can be used to "shift the focus away from mere naming of one's experience. . . . to talk about identity in relation to culture, history, politics"(110). For Hooks, the telling of tales of victimization, or the expression of one's voice is not enough; it is equally imperative that such experiences be the object of theoretical and critical analyses so that they can be connected rather than severed from broader notions of solidarity, struggle, and politics.

References

Aronowitz, S. and H. A. Giroux (1991). *Postmodern Education: Politics, Culture and Social Criticism*. Minneapolis: University of Minnesota Press.

Cherryholmes, C. (1988). *Power and Criticism: Poststructural Investigations in Education*. New York: Teachers College Press

Dewey, J. (1916). *Democracy and Education*. New York: Macmillan.

Fraser, N. (1989). *Unruly Practices*. Minneapolis: University of Minnesota Press.

Giroux, H. (1988a). *Schooling and the Struggle for Public Life*. Minneapolis: University of Minnesota Press.

Grumet, M. (1988). *Bitter Milk: Women and Teaching*. Massachusetts: University of Massachusetts Press.

Hooks, B. (1989). *Talking Back*. Boston: South End Press.

Hirsch Jr, E. D. (1987). *Cultural Literacy: What Every American Needs to Know*. Boston: Houghton Mifflin.

Laclau, E. (1988a). Politics and the limits of modernity. In A. Ross (ed.), *Universal Abandon? The Politics of Postmodernism*. Minneapolis: University of Minnesota Press, 63–82.

Michnik, A. (March 11, 1990). *Notes on the Revolution*. The New York Times Magazine.

Oreskes, M. (March 18, 1990). America's politics loses way as its vision changes world. *The New York Times*, vol. CXXXIX, No. 48, 178 (Sunday), 1, 16.

Penley, C. (1989). *The Future of an Illusion: Film, Feminism and Psychoanalysis*. Minneapolis: University of Minnesota

Popkewitz, T. (1988). Culture, pedagogy, and power: issues in the production of values and colonialization. *Journal of Education*, 170(2), 77–90.

Shapiro, S. (1990). *Between Capitalism and Democracy*. Westport: Bergin and Garvey Press.

Simon, R. (forthcoming). *Teaching against the Grain*. Westport: Bergin and Garvey.

Thompson, E. P. (January 29, 1990). History turns on a new hinge. *The Nation*, 117–22.

Walzer, M. (1987). *Interpretation and Criticism*. Cambridge: Harvard University Press.

chapter forty-two

"Modern China and the Postmodern West"

David Hall

American comparative philosopher David Hall (1937–) attempts in this 1989 essay to show that traditional Chinese philosophy contains resources that answer some of the problems represented by the debate over modernity and postmodernism. Indeed, Hall literally claims that classical, which is to say "premodern," Chinese thought is *postmodern*. In particular, he argues that the Derridean notion of difference (*différance*), of the primacy of what cannot be captured by truth-governed philosophical utterance, is central to both Taoism and Confucianism.

The metaphysical tradition of the West is implicitly or explicitly grounded in a "philosophy of presence" – that is, the desire to make present the presence of Being in beings. Jacques Derrida terms this disposition to make *being* present "logocentrism."[1] The logocentric bias of Western philosophy motivates thinkers to attempt to present the truth, being, essence, or logical structure of that about which they think and discourse. The senses of modernity sketched above all had at their heart the attempt to characterize the capital "T" Truth of things. The failure of that undertaking is the failure of the philosophy of presence – and the failure of modernity.

The postmodern enterprise aims at the development of a philosophy of *difference*. Our purported inability to think difference and otherness in their most general senses threatens the entire metaphysical project of Western thought.

The most general question of difference concerns the difference between the "whatness" and the "thatness" of a thing. "A rose is a *rose*. . . ." Yes. In addition, "a rose *is*. . . ." Asking *what* a being is is a cosmological question; considering *that* it is is an ontological appreciation. A rose as an

David Hall, "Modern China and the Postmodern West," in *Culture and Modernity: East-West Philosophic Perspectives*, ed. Eliot Deutsch (Honolulu: University of Hawaii Press, 1991), fourth through sixth sections pp. 57–67.

698

item related with the other items in its ecosystem in complex spatiotemporal and biochemical manners is a *cosmological* entity. *That* the rose is – its isness – indicates its *ontological* character.

Of course, the contrast of cosmological and ontological cannot be imagined without the cosmogonic tradition out of which it arises. For the ontological bias of Western philosophy derives from its attitude toward the chaos of beginnings.

The creation and maintenance of order from out of and over against the threat of chaos is the fundamental fact which establishes our sense of beginnings. Speculative philosophy, both as general ontology and as universal science, attempts to explain the fundamental fact of *order*. The ontologist asks the ontological question: "Why are there beings rather than no being?" Or "Why is there something rather than nothing at all?" Proponents of *scientia universalis*[i] ask the cosmological question: "What kinds of things are there?" The cosmogonic tradition in the Hellenic West has determined that metaphysical speculation must involve the search for beings or principles which, as transcendent sources of order, account for the order(s) experienced or observed.

As traditionally interpreted, both the cosmological and ontological questions presuppose an ordered ground. It is this, of course, which defines the logocentric motive of Western philosophy – the desire to illumine and articulate the order and structure in things.

All this may seem extremely abstract and quite irrelevant to any discussion of the modernization of China. But I think not. There is a most serious issue at stake here. If our most general understandings of our world involve us always in presuming a universal ground such as the essence or structure of beings, we can easily lose sight of the particularities of both our experience of things and of the things themselves. Capital "T" Truth and capital "B" Beauty and capital "G" Goodness become the subject matters of our discourse instead of the truth, beauty, and goodness concretely realized by the insistent particularities of our world. We then claim to know generalities, universalities, absolutes, and essences, but we lose sight of the brute facticities of our world.

Any serious claim to objective truth involves us in insisting that reality shine through our assertions. The very being of things is present in one's theory or ideology. Our age is altogether too suspicious of such claims. The pluralism of doctrines and theories within a single culture such as ours, as well as the pluralism of cultures, makes any claim to the truth of things an implicitly political act. Dogmatism, totalitarianism, and narrow intolerance are all directly connected with unjustified claims to final truth.

---

[i] Universal science.

The philosophy of presence is certainly not purposefully pernicious. Enlightenment rationality emerged from the idea that generic principles of logic and rationality may generate a common discourse for all cultures. Such rationalism was born from the need to connect diverse, pluralistic ideas, beliefs, and practices. Our reason was the gift of the ancient city-states, spread from Italy to the Peloponnesus, spun through the shuttles of Hebraic monotheism and Latin conceptions of *humanitas* and refined in the various furnaces of German, French, and English forms of colonialism.

The desire to see essential unity among cultures is a function of our missionizing activity expressed initially through Roman and Christian expansion, and now through our rational technologies motored by an incipient economic imperialism or, more politely put, an expanding market mentality. Proponents of Western values believe them to be exportable because they represent the grounds and consequences of a rational set of principles.

Our cultural values are housed in *doctrines* – propositions that may be entertained as beliefs. Philosophic and scientific principles are rational in form and are therefore open to public entertainment apart from specific cultural practices. Technology as a rational system carries with it the algorithms of its replication, requiring a minimum of human intervention.

In their attempts at modernization the Chinese are confronted with an uncomfortable dilemma. China must modernize, but the effects of a modernization understood in terms of liberal democracy, free enterprise, and rational technologies cannot but threaten its cultural integrity. China's ritual-based culture depends upon a commonality of traditions that liberal democracy renders quite fragile. The laws, rules, and values that define the Chinese sensibility are immanent within and relevant to the relatively specific character of the Chinese people. The paternalism of the Chinese form of government, its stress upon the solidarity of community over issues of abstract rights, its cultivation of and response to the psychological need for dependency are all delicate enough characteristics to be effaced by the impersonality of technology, the self-interest of free enterprise, and the individualizing ideals of democracy. Whatever benefits they might offer, each of these elements of modern culture leads to a bloating of the private sphere and threatens community.

Clearly, the problematic of distinctly modern Anglo-European philosophy is distinct from that of classical Chinese philosophy as regards the question of "difference." For a variety of reasons associated with the choices made at the origins of their cultural development, the Chinese find it easier to think difference, change, and becoming than do most of us. On the other hand, it has been easier in the modern West to think in terms of identity, being, and permanence.

I certainly have not failed to notice the dazzling incongruity that seems to lurk within my central claim. Could it really be the case that the country most identified with cultural continuity, inflexible tradition, and the most provincial intolerance toward other civilizations is expert in the philosophy of difference? My answer is – yes, certainly. Though I shall not discuss the background and significance of this question in any detail, I do hope to provide sufficient hints as to the plausibility of my affirmative response in the remarks which follow.

In defense of my somewhat exotic thesis I want to call attention to the evidence for thinking that Confucianism and philosophical Taoism share something like the problematic of postmodernism insofar as it is shaped by the desire to find a means of thinking difference. In its strongest and most paradoxical form my argument amounts to the claim that classical China is in a very real sense *postmodern*.

Two benefits may come from such an investigation as this. First, since it is rather obvious that the postmodern critique is neither an atavistic nor Luddite enterprise, one can hope that there may develop from out of the postmodern impulse alternative strategies for engaging and accommodating the practical consequences of the modern world. This means that China should be free to reflect upon the very difficult problems of modernization in terms of its own postmodern past.

A second benefit of the postmodern connection is that Anglo-European thinkers can discover in classical China supplemental resources for the development of a vision of cosmological difference and the language which articulates that vision. Certain of those resources may be found, as I now shall attempt to show, in the original Taoist and Confucian sensibilities.

Taoism and Cosmological Difference

I have argued elsewhere[2] that a philosophically coherent understanding of classical Taoism depends upon a recognition that neither of the two fundamental metaphysical contrasts of the Western tradition – that is, between "being" and "not being" and between "being" and "becoming" – is helpful in understanding the Taoist sensibility. In Taoism, the sole fact is that of process or becoming. Being and nonbeing are abstractions from that process.

The first words of the *Tao Te Ching* may be rendered in this way:

> The way *(tao)* that can be spoken of is not the constant way. The name that can be named is not the constant name. The nameless was the beginning of Heaven and earth.[3]

701

David Hall

Throughout the *Tao Te Ching*, *tao* is characterized as both nameless and nameable. *Tao* per se is the total process of becoming, becoming-itself. Nameless and nameable *tao* function analogously to "nonbeing" and "being," respectively. Thus being and nonbeing are abstractions from the generic process of becoming-itself. *Tao* is the *that which* – a name for *process*. That which *is* and that which *is not*[4] are the polar elements of becoming-itself.

The fundamental truth of the Taoist vision is contained in this but mildly ironic send-up of Parmenides' infamous maxim: Only becoming is; not-becoming is not. That is, there is only coming into being which illustrates some mixture of being and nonbeing. Neither being nor nonbeing abstracted from its polar relationship with its opposite can be finally real.

Each particular element in the totality has its own intrinsic excellence. The Chinese term is *te*. *Te* may be understood as the "particular focus" or "intrinsic excellence" of a thing. The *te* of an element serves as the means in accordance with which it construes the totality of things from its perspective and thus "names" and creates a world.

The concepts of *tao* and *te* may be interpreted together in a polar fashion. *Tao-te* is best understood in terms of the relationships of field *(tao)* and focus *(te)*. The model of a hologram is helpful, for as in a holographic display each element contains the whole in adumbrated forms, so in the Taoist sensibility each item of the totality focuses the totality in its entirety. The particular focus of an item establishes its world, its environment. In addition, the totality as sum of all possible orders is adumbrated by each item.

Taoism is radically perspectival. "If a man lie down in a damp place," says Chuang Tzu,[ii] "he contracts lumbago. But what of an eel?"[5] The eel will be at least as uncomfortable as the man – but for the opposite reason. The Taoist totality is horizontal. There are no hierarchies; no great chain of being or ladder of perfections exists in the Taoist cosmology. For the Taoist, the anthropocentrism implicit in almost every form of Anglo-European ethical system is only one of a myriad of possible centrisms.

A familiar tale from the *Chuang Tzu* is enlightening in this regard:[6]

> The emperor of the South Sea was called Shu, the emperor of the North Sea was called Hu, and the emperor of the central region was called Hun-tun (Chaos). Shu and Hu from time to time came together for a meeting in the territory of Hun-tun, and Hun-tun treated them very generously. Shu and Hu discussed how they could repay his kindness. "All men," they said, "have seven openings so they can see, hear, eat, and breathe. But Hun-tun alone doesn't have any. Let's try boring him some!" Every day they bored another hole, and on the seventh day Hun-tun died.

[ii] Chuang Tzu (369–286 BC) was the most important early interpreter of Taoism.

Taoism is not a vision grounded upon order, but upon chaos. It is a vision in which harmony has a special kind of meaning associated with the breechless, faceless, orifice-free Lord Hun-tun. Assuming that *tao* is becoming-itself, and therefore the sum of all orders, provides a helpful response to Benjamin Schwartz' provocative query concerning the meaning of "*tao*" in *The World of Thought in Ancient China.* "How may a word which refers to *order*," he asks, "come to have a mystical meaning?"[7] The mystical meaning of *tao* lies in the mystery of chaos as the sum of all orders.

Tao is not organic in the sense that a single pattern or *telos* could be said to characterize its processes. It is not *a* whole but many wholes. Its order is not rational or logical but aesthetic – that is there can be no transcendent pattern determining the existence or efficacy of the order. The order is a consequence of the particulars comprising the totality of existing things.

This interpretation of *tao* makes of it a totality not in the sense of a single-ordered cosmos, but rather in the sense of the sum of all possible cosmological orders. Any given order is an existing world that is construed from the perspective of a particular element of the totality. But as a single world it is an abstraction from the totality of possible orders. The *being* of this order is not ontological, but cosmological. Such an abstracted, selected order cannot serve as fundament or ground. In the Taoist sensibility *all differences are cosmological differences.*

Taoism is based upon the affirmation rather than the negation of chaos. In the Anglo-European tradition, chaos is emptiness, separation, or confusion, and is to be overcome. In Taoism it is to be left alone to thrive in its spontaneity, for "the myriad things manage and order themselves."[8] Any attempt to make present a ground – the being of beings – is rejected. Chuang Tzu insists that "each thing comes into being from its own inner reflection and none can tell how it comes to be so."[9]

Taoism provides a model for thinking difference as strictly *cosmological* difference. Cosmological difference can be thought to the extent that we give up the distinction between cosmological and ontological realms. For it is the putatively ontological dimension that ultimately conceals the differences among cosmological entities by implicit appeal to the unity of being shared by all beings.

Reason and rationality presuppose the ontological philosophy of presence. But it is a simple-enough feat to demonstrate that rational ordering is an anthropocentric notion. For the various psychological and physiological uniformities defining the human species determine in advance the sorts of ordering that will be anticipated as defining the natural world. The sorts of beings we presume ourselves to be define the sorts of orders we may recognize and deem important. Alternative orders are recognized only from our anthropocentric perspective, since to know an order we must discern its pattern regularities, appreciate its realized uniformities, and establish plausible grounds for casual sequences among the elements serving to instantiate those uniformities.

The aesthetic ordering of the Taoist presupposes an alternative method of knowing. Such knowledge has as its subject matter insistently unique particulars which cannot be discussed in terms of pattern concepts defining regularities or uniformities. They can only be considered in terms of the cosmological differences grounded in the particularity of each item.

Confucius and the Language of Deference

One of the difficulties in communicating a vision of cosmological difference is that we lack a language which can adequately accommodate such aesthetic understandings. There is, of course, just such a language in philosophical Taoism and I could quite appropriately attempt to articulate it in the following paragraphs. Instead, I want to shift to the Confucian context to adumbrate the view of language and communication underlying the *Analects*. I shall do this in order to demonstrate that, however great the differences between Taoism and Confucianism *within* Chinese culture, judged from the perspective of Western thought they belong to essentially the same family. This is so because both Taoism and Confucianism presuppose the priority of cosmological difference over ontological presence – or, put another way, the priority of an aesthetic over a rational mode of understanding and discourse.

In the West two sorts of language have dominated the tradition. The first, the language of ontological presence, is that against which the postmodern thinkers are in full-scale revolt. Besides the language of presence, however, our tradition also allows the employment of language in a mystical or mythopoetic way. In this usage, language advertises the absence of the referent. This is the language of the mystical *via negativa* or the language of the poet who holds metaphor to be constitutive of discourse rather than merely parasitical upon a literal ground. We may call such expression the language of "absence."

A language of presence is grounded upon the possibility of univocal or unambiguous propositional expressions. This possibility requires criteria for determining the literalness of a proposition. For this to be so, literal language must have precedence over figurative or metaphorical language. This means that in addition to richly vague sorts of language associated with images and metaphors, there must be concepts as candidates for univocal meaning.

Since Aristotle's still-dominating discussion of metaphor, literal language has most often been privileged over figurative. And though to say this seems truistic and almost trivial, it is certainly *not* the case that such a preference was somehow built into the origins of language.

In the West, metaphors are usually deemed parasitical upon literal significances. Thus rhetoric, insofar as it employs the trope, metaphor, is rigidly tied to logic as ground. This serves to discipline intellectual and aesthetic activity, precluding untrammeled flights of the imagination.

If we are to have a language that evokes difference, however, we must find a new sort of metaphor. In place of metaphors which extend the literal sense of a term, we shall have to employ "allusive metaphors."[10] Allusive metaphors are distinct from the expressive variety since they are not tied to a literal or objective signification. They are free-floating hints and suggestions. They *allude;* they do not *express.* Their referents are other allusive metaphors, other things that hint or suggest. All language, at its fundamental level, may be nothing more than an undulating sea of suggestiveness.

Saussurean linguistics[11] and some semiologists influenced by Peirce and Saussure, as well as the poststructuralists who would expunge from language such "myths" as "authorial intent," "textual coherence," or "univocity," all employ something like allusive interpretations. Language as a system of differences, as a structure or context within which meaning is indefinitely deferred, is nothing more than an allusive system.

The Saussurean interpretation certainly may be said to apply to Chinese language and literature. The importance of context to meaning in Chinese language argues for the play of differences establishing meaning. Of course, in China almost all that may be said with respect to allusive metaphor may be said using the word "image."

In Anglo-European culture, the word "image" is used with distinctive connotations in literary criticism, psychology, and philosophy. The best understanding in this context is that an image is a sensory (that is, visual, auditory, tactile, olfactory) presentation of a perceptual, imaginative, or recollected experience. The form of the perception, memory, or imagination may be distinct from the mode of its presentation. For example, the olfactory or visual experience of a rose may be imaged in the words of a poet.

In such a case, the image is constituted by the word-picture as experienced by the celebrant of the poem and may or may not re-present the private experience of the poet. The most productive manner of insuring some resonance between the expressor of the image and the subsequent experiences of it is to reference them within a community of interpretation. Only communally experienced images are efficacious in promoting interpersonal and social relationships.

This suggests a real difference between Anglo-European and Chinese culture. In China, tradition, as a communal resource for meaning, more

705

certainly disciplines the indefinite allusiveness of the language. In fact, it is tradition as the resource of meaning and value that serves to render plausible what seemed originally so paradoxical – namely, that Chinese culture has an appreciation of difference, which, historically, Western culture has never displayed.

Allusiveness requires vague[12] boundaries of self and world. The most desirable circumstance is one in which images, as richly vague complexes capable of a variety of evocations, are communally fixed and ritually protected as images. This is the aim of the classical Chinese, though it is obvious that Confucian orthodoxy was often guilty of providing a too narrowly fixed meaning for the relevant images. In any case, there is nothing behind the language in the form of a structure or logos to which appeal may be made to establish the presence of objective truth. Meanings derive from the allusive play of differences among the words and images of the language.

The images associated with the hexagrams of the *I Ching* are good examples of such communally fixed and ritualistically protected images. The images of the "creative" and the "receptive" associated with the first two hexagrams are housed in the communal memory and practices associated with the institutions, ritual practices, music, and literature which contextualize the book of oracles as a classic of Chinese culture. The concrete experiences of the individual consulting the *I Ching* resonate with the repository of significances in the larger communal context.

One of the signal consequences of a logocentric language is that there must be real independence of a proposition from the state of affairs it characterizes. This entails dualistic relations of propositions and states of affairs. Without such independence, in the senses of dualism and transcendence, nothing like logical truth may be formulated.

The presence of transcendent beings and principles in the formation of Western culture is uncontroversial. The dualism entailed by this transcendence, though often discomfiting to the theologically doctrinaire, is also a well-accepted characteristic of the rational interests of Anglo-European societies. Neither dualism nor transcendence is present in the original Confucian or Taoist sensibilities.

For a proposition to have a univocal sense, terms must be strictly delimitable. A polar sensibility precludes such delimitation in any but the grossest terms. Thus, the classical Chinese understanding of *yin* and *yang* as complementary concepts cannot coherently lead to dualistic translations or interpretations. *Yin* is becoming-*yang*; *yang* is becoming-*yin*. The locution "as different as night and day" would then have to mean "as different as night-becoming-day from day-becoming-night."

In a polar sensibility, terms are clustered with opposing or complementary alter-terms. Classical Chinese may be uncongenial to the development

706

of univocal propositions for this reason. Without such propositions, seman-tic notions of truth are ultimately untenable. And without a capital "T" Truth lurking behind our acts of communication, notions such as "logocen-trism" and "presence" cannot serve as standards for philosophical dis-course.

The Confucian doctrine of the rectification of names well illustrates the way language is used concretely, evocatively, and allusively. This doctrine, central to Confucianism, is often outrageously misunderstood as a concern for univocity, for getting the definitions of terms straight and proper. Such an interpretation parodies the intent of Confucius' doctrine.

> Tzu-lu asked Confucius, "If the Lord of Wei were waiting for you to bring order to his state, to what would you give first priority?" Confucius replied, "without question, it would be to order names properly."[13]

The motive for the ordering of names is functional and pragmatic, rather than logical or strictly semantic. That is to say, the activity of matching name with role – calling a father a father when he is in fact a father – establishes coherence between roles already spelled out by ritual practices (li) and the actions of individuals – husbands, fathers, ministers, sons – whose ostensive identity as functionaries within the society may be in question.

It is quite interesting to see how closely related are the treatments of language in the sayings of Confucius and in the thought of a certain French thinker writing twenty-four hundred years later. I refer, of course, to Jacques Derrida. Derrida's well-rehearsed notion of *différance* tells the story.[14] The neologism *différance*, is meant to suggest that the differences investigated with respect to language have both an active and a passive dimension.

Meaning is always deferred. It cannot be present in language as *structure*, when that is the focus – for that omits the meanings associated with the use of the language. But focusing upon language as *event*, language as constituted by speech acts, does not solve the problem because, once more, the supplemental character of language – this time its structure – has been shifted to an inaccessible background.

To resonate most productively with Confucius, however, Derrida would have to accept an emendation to his notion of *différance* which would enrich the meaning of the deferring function. If one introduces the homonymic "defer," meaning "to yield," then the resultant notion of difference, as connoting both active and passive senses of differing and of deferring, well suits Confucius' rich use of language.

Confucius' language of difference is grounded in the sense of deference – a listening, a yielding to the appropriate models of the received tradi-

707

tions and to the behaviors of those who resonate with those models. In the *Great Preface* to the *Book of Songs*, traditionally attributed to Confucius, we read:[15]

> Poetry is the consequence of dispositions and is articulated in language as song. One's feelings stir within his breast and take the form of words. When words are inadequate, they are voiced as sighs. When sighs are inadequate, they are chanted. When chants are inadequate, unconsciously, the hands and feet begin to dance them. One's feelings are expressed in sounds, and when sounds are refined, they are called musical notes.

Confucius understands language after the analogy with music. Names are like notes. Harmony is a function of the particularity of names and notes and of their mutual resonances. Neither in Chinese music nor in Chinese language is there the stress upon syntax that one finds in the rationalistic languages of the West.

Confucian language is the bearer of tradition, and tradition, made available through ritualistic evocation, is the primary context of linguistic behavior. The sage appeals to present praxis and to the repository of significances realized in the traditional past in such a manner as to set up deferential relationships between himself, his communicants, and the authoritative texts invoked.

It is important to recognize that Confucius never tied the significances of language to the norms of present praxis. He insisted upon deferential access to the appropriate traditional models. If such models are not coopted by an authoritarian government or a rigid bureaucratic elite, as has been the case in the tawdrier periods of Chinese history, there is a rich and varied resource for the criticism of present praxis in spite of the fact that the language as a system lacks any transcendent reference.

The language of presence re-presents an otherwise absent object. The language of absence uses indirect discourse to advertise the existence of a nonpresentable subject. In either case there is a referent, real or putative, beyond the act of referencing. But the language of deference is based upon the recognition of mutual resonances among instances of communicative activity. There is no referencing beyond the act of communication as it resonates with the entertained meanings of the models from the tradition.

Notes

1 Derrida's most sustained attempt at charting the "logocentric" bias of Western metaphysics is to be found in *Dissemination*, trans. by Barbara Johnson (Chicago: University of Chicago Press, 1981).

2 See my "Process and Anarchy – A Taoist Vision of Creativity," *Philosophy East & West*, 28, no. 3 (July 1978): 271–85. See also the chapter "The Way Beyond Ways," in my *The Uncertain Phoenix* (New York: Fordham University Press, 1982).

3 See D. C. Lau, trans., *The Tao Te Ching* (New York: Penguin Books, 1963), p. 57.

4 In his "Being in Western Philosophy Compared with *Shan/Fei* and *Yu/Wu* in Chinese Philosophy," in *Studies in Chinese Philosophy and Philosophical Literature* (Singapore: Institute of East Asian Philosophies, 1986), pp. 322–59, A. C. Graham has indicated that the sense of *wu* ("have not," "there is not") contrasts with locutions entailed by the ontological sense of "Nothing" in that "Nothing" entails the sense of "no entity" while *wu* indicates merely the absence of concrete things.

    This point, which concerns the concrete mode of the contrast between "being" and "not-being" is, I believe, at least obliquely relevant to my argument that Taoism is strictly concerned with cosmological differences and not at all with the contrast between the cosmological and ontological characters of things.

5 See Burton Watson, trans., *The Complete Works of Chuang Tzu* (New York: Columbia University Press, 1968), p. 56.

6 Ibid., p. 97.

7 *The World of Thought in Ancient China* (Cambridge, Massachusetts: Harvard University Press, 1985), p. 194.

8 See *Wang Pi's Commentary on the Lao tzu*, trans. by Arrienne Rump in collaboration with Wing-tsit Chan, Society of Asian and Comparative Philosophy monograph, no. 6 (Honolulu: University of Hawaii Press, 1979), p. 17.

9 See *Chuang Tzu*, chapter 8. The translation, admittedly a controversial rendering of an obscure segment of the text, is cited from Chang Chung-Yuan, *Creativity and Taoism* (New York: Harper & Row, 1963), p. 66.

10 See my *Eros and Irony* (Albany: SUNY Press, 1983), pp. 46–7, 180–2 and Roger T. Ames' and my *Thinking Through Confucius* (Albany: SUNY Press, 1987), pp. 192–8 for the characterization of "allusive metaphor" and "allusive analogy," respectively.

11 See Ferdinand Saussure's *A Course in General Linguistics* (London: Peter Owen, 1960).

12 The word "vague" is used in the systematic sense given it by Charles Peirce. The term means "open to rich and varied articulation." For a discussion of "vagueness" as a theoretical concept see Robert Neville's *Reconstruction of Thinking* (Albany: SUNY Press, 1981), pp. 39–42.

13 *Analects* 13/3; Roger T. Ames' translation.

14 See Derrida's *Writing and Difference*, trans. by Alan Bass (Chicago: University of Chicago Press, 1978), passim.
15 *Chih-ching*, Harvard-Yenching Institute Sinological Index Series, Supp. 9 (Peking: Harvard-Yenching Institute, 1934); Roger T. Ames' translation.

Select Bibliography

It is both impossible and inadvisable to attempt a comprehensive bibliography of works that deal with postmodernism and its relation to modernism and/or modernity. The topic's interdisciplinary nature would make for an immense list of marginally related works (unless only those that prominently use the terms "postmodern," "modernity," etc., are included, but that would exclude many relevant texts). Too many different kinds of phenomena and too many disciplines are involved in the subject. The following bibliography aims merely to aid those readers who seek some additional reading. It includes only works that I consider especially interesting or useful for students, and, with rare exceptions, only works available in English. It is organized into four parts: the first contains general introductions to or commentaries on postmodernism; the second, works of interest for tracing the history of the concept of the "postmodern" and the related term "post-industrial"; the third, some important works on modernity and/or modernism; and the fourth, the titles selected in this volume with other relevant works by their authors. For the sake of simplicity there is no redundancy among the four parts; works relevant to multiple sections appear only once. Consequently, interested readers ought to peruse all four.

1 Works on Postmodernism

Best, Stephen and Douglas Kellner. *Postmodern Theory: Critical Interrogations*. New York: Guilford, 1991.

Descombes, Vincent. *Modern French Philosophy*, trans. L. Schott-Fox and J.M. Harding. New York: Cambridge University Press, 1980.

Dews, Peter. *Logics of Disintegration: Post-Structuralist Thought and the Claims of Critical Theory*. New York: Verso, 1987.

Foster, Hal. *The Anti-Aesthetic: Essays on Postmodern Culture*. Port Townsend, Wash.: Bay Press, 1983.

Harvey, David. *The Condition of Postmodernity: An Enquiry into the Origins of Cultural Change*. Oxford and New York: Blackwell, 1989.

Jencks, Charles. *The Post-Modern Reader*. London: Academy Editions, 1992.

Klotz, Heinrich. *The History of Postmodern Architecture*, trans Radka Donnell. Cambridge: MIT Press, 1988.

Select Bibliography

Macksey, Richard and Eugenio Donato. *The Structuralist Controversy: The Languages of Criticism and the Sciences of Man*. Baltimore: Johns Hopkins University Press, 1972.

Portoghesi, Paolo. *Postmodern, The Architecture of Postindustrial Society*, trans. Ellen Shapiro. New York: Rizzoli, 1983.

Rose, Margaret. *The Post-Modern and the Post-Industrial: A Critical Analysis*. Cambridge: Cambridge University Press, 1991.

Rosenau, Pauline Marie. *Post-Modernism and the Social Sciences: Insights, Inroads, and Intrusions*. Princeton, NJ: Princeton University Press, 1992.

2 Works of Historical Interest

Bell, Bernard Iddings. *Religion For Living: A Book for Postmodernists*. London: The Religious Book Club, 1939.

Bell, Daniel. *The Cultural Contradictions of Capitalism*. New York: Basic Books, 1976.

De Onis, Federico. *Antologia de la Poesia española e hispanoamericana: 1882–1932*. Madrid: 1934.

Etzioni, Amitai. *The Active Society: A Theory of Societal and Political Processes*. New York: Free Press, 1968.

Fiedler, Leslie. "The New Mutants," in *The Collected Essays of Leslie Fiedler*, vol. II. New York: Stein and Day, 1971, pp. 379–99.

Hassan, Ihab. *The Dismemberment of Orpheus: Toward a Postmodern Literature*. Madison: University of Wisconsin Press, 1971.

Hebdige, Dick. *Hiding in the Light: on Images and Things*. New York: Routledge, 1988.

Howe, Irving. *The Decline of the New*. New York: Harcourt, Brace and World, 1970, pp. 190–207.

Hudnut, Joseph. "The Post-Modern House." *Architectural Record*, 97, May 1945, pp. 70–5.

Jacobs, Jane. *The Death and Life of Great American Cities*. New York: Random House, 1961.

Jencks, Charles. "The Rise of Post-Modern Architecture." *Architectural Association Quarterly*, Summer, 1976, 7:4, pp. 7–14.

Levin, Harry. "What was Modernism?" in *Refractions: Essays in Comparative Literature*. New York: Oxford University Press, 1966, pp. 271–95.

McLuhan, Marshall. *Understanding Media: the Extensions of Man*. New York: McGraw-Hill, 1964.

Mills, C. Wright. *The Sociological Imagination*. New York: Oxford University Press, 1959.

Pannwitz, Rudolf. *Die Krisis der Europaeischen Kultur*. Nürnberg: Hans Carl, 1917.

Penty, Arthur J. and Ananda K. Coomaraswamy. *Essays in Post-Industrialism: A Symposium of Prophecy Concerning the Future of Society*. London: 1914.

Reisman, David. "Leisure and Work in Post-Industrial Society," in *Mass Leisure*, ed. E. Larrabee and R. Meyershon. Glencoe, Ill.: Free Press, 1958, pp. 363–85.

Touraine, Alaine. *The Post-Industrial Society*, trans. Leonard F. X. Mayhew. New York: Random House, 1971; original, 1969.

Toynbee, Arnold J. *A Study of History*. London: Oxford University Press, 1939 and 1954, vols V and VIII.

3 Works on Modernity and Modernism

Berger, Peter, Brigitte Berger, and Hansfried Kellner. *The Homeless Mind: Modernization and Consciousness*. New York: Vintage, 1974.

Bernstein, Richard. *Habermas and Modernity*. Cambridge: MIT Press, 1985.

Berman, Marshall. *All That Is Solid Melts Into Air: The Experience of Modernity*. New York: Viking Penguin, 1988.

Blumenberg, Hans. *The Legitimacy of the Modern Age*, trans. Robert Wallace. Cambridge: MIT Press, 1983.

Cahoone, Lawrence. *The Dilemma of Modernity: Philosophy, Culture, and Anti-Culture*. Albany: State University of New York Press, 1988.

Durkheim, Emile. *The Division of Labour in Society*. New York: Free Press, 1964.

Frisby, David. *Fragments of Modernity: Theories of Modernity in the work of Simmel, Kracauer, and Benjamin*. Cambridge: MIT Press, 1986.

Gehlen, Arnold. *Man in the Age of Technology*, trans. Patricia Lipscomb. New York: Columbia, 1980.

Giddens, Anthony. *The Consequences of Modernity*. Stanford: Stanford University Press, 1990.

Hughes, Robert. *The Shock of the New*. New York: Knopf, 1981.

Levy Jr, Marion. *Modernization: Latecomers and Survivors*. New York: Basic Books, 1972.

—— *Modernization and the Structure of Societies*, vols 1 and 2. Princeton, NJ: Princeton University Press, 1966.

Mumford, Lewis. *The Myth of the Machine: The Pentagon of Power*. New York: Harcourt, Brace, Jovanovich, 1970.

Parsons, Talcott. *Societies: Evolutionary and Comparative Perspectives*. Englewood Cliffs, NJ: Prentice-Hall, 1966.

—— *Structure and Process in Modern Societies*. Glencoe, Ill.: Free Press, 1960.

Pippin, Robert. *Modernism as a Philosophical Problem: On the Dissatisfactions of European High Culture*. Cambridge: Basil Blackwell, 1991.

Rosenberg, Harold. *The Tradition of the New*. New York: Horizon, 1959.

Rorty, Richard. *Philosophy and the Mirror of Nature*. Princeton, NJ: Princeton University Press, 1979.

Rosen, Stanley. *The Ancients and the Moderns: Rethinking Modernity*. New Haven: Yale University, 1989.

Sennett, Richard. *The Fall of Public Man: On the Social Psychology of Capitalism*. New York: Vintage, 1974.

Taylor, Charles. *Sources of the Self: the Making of the Modern Identity*. Cambridge: Harvard University Press, 1989.

Tönnies, Ferdinand. *Community and Society*, trans. and ed. Charles Loomis. East Lansing, Mich.: Michigan State University Press, 1957.

Toulmin, Stephen. *Cosmopolis: the hidden agenda of Modernity*. New York: Free Press, 1990.

Sandel, Michael. *Liberalism and its Critics*. New York: New York University Press, 1984.

Simmel, Georg. *The Philosophy of Money*, trans. Tom Bottomore and David Frisby. Boston: Routledge & Kegan Paul, 1978.

Spengler, Oswald. *The Decline of the West*, trans. Charles Atkinson. New York: Knopf, 1932. [abridged edn: ed. Helmut Werner, trans. Charles Atkinson. New York: Modern Library, 1965.]

Strauss, Leo. *Natural Right and History*. Chicago: University of Chicago Press, 1953.

4 Writers Selected in this Volume

Baudelaire, Charles. "The Painter of Modern Life," trans. Jonathan Mayne, in *The Painter of Modern Life and Other Essays*. London: Phaidon, 1964.

Baudrillard, Jean. *Symbolic Exchange and Death*, trans. Iain H. Grant. London: Sage, 1993.

—— *Selected Writings*, ed. Mark Poster. Stanford: Stanford University Press, 1988.

Bell, Daniel. *The Coming of Post-Industrial Society*. New York: Basic Books, 1976; original, 1973.

—— *The End of Ideology*. Glencoe, Ill.: Free Press, 1960.

Bordo, Susan. *The Flight to Objectivity: Essays on Cartesianism and Culture*. Albany: State University of New York Press, 1987.

—— "Feminism, Postmodernism, and Gender-Scepticism," in *Feminism/Postmodernism*, ed. Linda Nicholson. New York: Routledge, 1990, pp. 133–56.

Burke, Edmund. *Reflections on the Revolution in France*. ed. J.G.A. Pocock. Indianapolis: Hackett, 1987.

Condorcet, Marie Jean Antoine Nicolas Caritat, marquis de. *Sketch for an Historical Picture of the Progress of the Human Mind*, trans. June Barraclough. New York: Hyperion, rpt of 1955 Noonday Press edn.

de Saussure, Ferdinand. *Course in General Linguistics*, trans. Wade Baskin. New York: McGraw-Hill, 1966.

Deleuze, Gilles and Félix Guattari. *Anti-Oedipus: Capitalism and Schizophrenia*, trans. Helen Lane, Mark Seem, and Robert Hurley. New York: Viking Penguin, 1977.

—— *A Thousand Plateaus: Capitalism and Schizophrenia*, trans. Brian Massumi. Minneapolis: University of Minnesota Press, 1987.

Derrida, Jacques. *Of Grammatology*, trans. Gayatri Chakravorty Spivak. Baltimore: Johns Hopkins University Press, 1974.

—— *A Derrida Reader: Between the Blinds*, ed. Peggy Kamuf. New York: Columbia University Press, 1991.

Descartes, René. *Meditations on First Philosophy*, trans. Elizabeth Haldane and G.R.T. Ross, in *The Philosophical Works of Descartes*, vol. I. Cambridge: Cambridge University Press, 1975.

Foucault, Michel. *The Foucault Reader*, ed. Paul Rabinow. New York: Pantheon, 1984.

—— "Nietzsche, Genealogy, History," trans. Donald Bouchard and Sherry Simon, in *Language, Counter-Memory, Practise: Selected Essays and Interviews*, ed. Donald Bouchard. Ithaca, NY: Cornell University Press, 1977, pp. 139–64.

—— "Truth and Power," trans. Colin Gordon, in *Power/Knowledge: Selected Interviews and Other Writings 1972–77*, ed. Colin Gordon. New York: Pantheon, 1972, pp. 131–3.

Freud, Sigmund. *Civilization and its Discontents*, trans. James Strachey. New York: Norton, 1961.

Giroux, Henry A. *Postmodernism, Feminism, and Cultural Politics: Redrawing Educational Boundaries*. Albany: State University of New York Press, 1991.

Griffin, David Ray. *The Reenchantment of Science*. Albany: State University of New York Press, 1988.

Habermas, Jürgen. "Modernity versus Postmodernity." *New German Critique*, no. 22, 1981, pp. 3–14.

—— *The Philosophical Discourse of Modernity*, trans. Frederick Lawrence. Cambridge: MIT Press, 1987.

—— *Theory of Communicative Action*, 2 vols, trans. Thomas McCarthy. Boston: Beacon, 1984, 1987.

Hall, David. "Modern China and the Postmodern West," in *Culture and Modernity: East-West Philosophic Perspectives*, ed. Eliot Deutsch. Honolulu: University of Hawaii Press, 1991, pp. 57–67.

Harding, Sandra. *The Science Question in Feminism*. Ithaca, NY: Cornell University Press, 1986.

Hassan, Ihab. *Paracriticisms: Seven Speculations of the Times*. Urbana: University of Illinois Press, 1975.

—— *The Postmodern Turn: Essays in Postmodern Theory and Culture*. Columbus: Ohio State University Press, 1987.

Hegel, Georg Wilhelm Friedrich. *Phenomenology of Spirit*, trans. A.V. Miller. Oxford: Oxford University Press, 1977.

—— *The Philosophy of History*, trans. J. Sibree. New York: Dover, 1956.

Heidegger, Martin. "Letter on Humanism," in *Martin Heidegger: Basic Writings*, ed. David Farrell Krell, trans. Frank A. Capuzzi, with J. Glenn Gray and David Farrell Krell. New York: Harper and Row, 1977, pp. 193–242.

—— "The Question Concerning Technology," in *Martin Heidegger: Basic Writings*, pp. 287–317.

—— "The End of Philosophy and the Task of Thinking," in *Martin Heidegger: Basic Writings*, pp. 373–92.

Horkheimer, Max and Theodor Adorno. *Dialectic of Enlightenment*, trans. John Cumming. New York: Seabury, 1972.

Husserl, Edmund. *The Crisis of European Sciences and Transcendental Phenomenology*, trans. David Carr. Evanston: Northwestern University Press, 1970.

Irigaray, Luce. "The Sex Which is Not One," trans. Claudia Reeder, in *New French Feminisms*, ed. Elaine Marks and Isabelle de Courtivron. New York: Schoken, 1981.

—— *The Sex Which is Not One*, trans. Catherine Porter with Carolyn Burke. Ithaca, NY: Cornell University Press, 1985.

715

—— *Speculum of the Other Woman*, trans. Gillian Gill. Ithaca, NY: Cornell University Press, 1985.

Jameson, Fredric. *Postmodernism, Or, The Cultural Logic of Late Capitalism*. Durham: Duke University Press, 1991.

Jencks, Charles. *The Language of Post-Modern Architecture*. New York: Rizzoli, 1984.

—— *What Is Post-Modernism?* London: Academy Editions, 1986.

Kant, Immanuel. "An Answer to the Question: What is Enlightenment?" in *Kant's Political Writings*, trans. H.B. Nisbet, ed. Hans Reiss. Cambridge: Cambridge University Press, 1970, pp. 54–60.

Kuhn, Thomas. *The Structure of Scientific Revolutions*. Chicago: University of Chicago Press, 1962.

Le Corbusier (né Charles-Edouard Jeanneret). *Towards a New Architecture*, trans. Frederick Etchells. New York: Dover, 1986.

Lyotard, Jean-François. *The Postmodern Condition: A Report on Knowledge*, trans. Geoff Bennington and Brian Massumi. Minneapolis: Minnesota University Press, 1984.

—— *Toward the Postmodern*, ed. Robert Harvey and Mark Roberts. Atlantic Highlands. NJ: Humanities, 1993.

MacIntyre, Alasdair. *After Virtue*. Notre Dame, Ind.: University of Notre Dame Press, 1984.

—— *Three Rival Versions of Moral Enquiry: Encyclopedia, Genealogy, and Tradition*. Notre Dame, Ind.: University of Notre Dame Press, 1990.

—— *Whose Justice? Which Rationality?* Notre Dame, Ind.: University of Notre Dame Press, 1988.

Marinetti, Filippo Tommaso. "The Founding and Manifesto of Futurism," trans. R.W. Flint and Arthur W. Coppotelli, in *Marinetti: Selected Writings*, ed. R.W. Flint. New York: Farrar, Straus, Giroux, 1972.

Marx, Karl and Friedrich Engels. *Manifesto of the Communist Party*, trans. Samuel Moore, in Robert Tucker, *The Marx–Engels Reader*. New York: Norton, 1978.

Nietzsche, Friedrich. *The Gay Science*, trans. with commentary by Walter Kaufmann. New York: Random House, 1974.

—— *Beyond Good and Evil*, trans. with commentary by Walter Kaufmann. New York: Random House, 1966.

—— *The Genealogy of Morals*, trans. Walter Kaufmann and R.J. Hollingdale. New York: Random House, 1967.

—— *The Will to Power*, ed. Walter Kaufmann, trans. Walter Kaufmann and R.J. Hollingdale. New York: Random House, 1967.

Ortega y Gasset, Jose. *The Revolt of the Masses*, trans. Anthony Kerrigan, ed. Kenneth Moore, Notre Dame, Ind.: University of Notre Dame Press, 1985.

Peirce, Charles S. "How to Make Our Ideas Clear." *Collected Papers of Charles Sanders Peirce*, vol. V, ed. Charles Hartshorne and Paul Weiss. Cambridge: Harvard University Press, 1965.

Rorty, Richard. *Consequences of Pragmatism: Essays, 1972–1980*. Minneapolis: University of Minnesota Press, 1982.

—— *Contingency, Irony, and Solidarity*. New York: Cambridge University Press, 1989.

—— *Essays on Heidegger and Others*. Cambridge: Cambridge University Press, 1991.

—— "Solidarity or Objectivity?" in *Objectivity, Relativism, and Truth*. Cambridge: Cambridge University Press, 1991, pp. 21–34.

Rousseau, Jean-Jacques. *Discourse on the Sciences and the Arts*, in *The Basic Political Writings of Jean-Jacques Rousseau*, trans. Donald Cress. Indianapolis: Hackett, 1987.

—— *Discourse on the Foundations and Origin of Inequality Among Men*, in *The Basic Political Writings of Jean-Jacques Rousseau*.

Sartre, Jean-Paul. "Existentialism," trans. Bernard Frechtman, in *Existentialism and Human Emotions*. New York: Citadel, 1985.

Taylor, Mark. C. *Erring: A Postmodern A/theology*. Chicago: University of Chicago Press, 1984.

Venturi, Robert. *Complexity and Contradiction in Architecture*. New York: Museum of Modern Art, 1966.

—— with Denise Scott Brown and Steven Izenour. *Learning from Las Vegas*. Cambridge: MIT Press, 1972.

Weber, Max. *The Protestant Ethic and the Spirit of Capitalism*, trans. Talcott Parsons. New York: Scribner, 1958.

—— "Science as a Vocation," in *From Max Weber: Essays in Sociology*, trans. and ed. H.H. Gerth and C. Wright Mills. New York: Oxford University Press, 1946.

Wittgenstein, Ludwig. "Lecture on Ethics." *The Philosophical Review*, 74, no. 1, January 1965, pp. 3–12.

—— *Tractatus Logico-Philosophicus*, trans. D.F. Pears and B.F. McGuinness. London: Routledge and Kegan Paul, 1961.

Index

Index

Index

723

Index

Index

Index

730